Generative AI in Teaching and Learning

Shalin Hai-Jew
Hutchinson Community College, USA

IGI Global
PUBLISHER of TIMELY KNOWLEDGE

A volume in the Advances in Educational Technologies and Instructional Design (AETID) Book Series

Published in the United States of America by
IGI Global
Information Science Reference (an imprint of IGI Global)
701 E. Chocolate Avenue
Hershey PA, USA 17033
Tel: 717-533-8845
Fax: 717-533-8661
E-mail: cust@igi-global.com
Web site: http://www.igi-global.com

Library of Congress Cataloging-in-Publication Data

Names: Hai-Jew, Shalin, editor.
Title: Generative AI in teaching and learning / edited by Shalin Hai-Jew.
Other titles: Generative artificial intelligence in teaching and learning
Description: Hershey, PA : Information Science Reference, 2024. | Includes bibliographical references and index. | Summary: "The book covers a wide range of topics, including generative AI applications in art-making, coding, writing, research, collaboration, and more. It examines the implications of public generative AI interfaces and explores how generative AI can be effectively utilized in formal education settings, such as accredited institutions. The roles of teachers, content creation, instructional design, research, community service, sports, policies, assignments, grading, student work, and programming are all examined in relation to generative AI"-- Provided by publisher.
Identifiers: LCCN 2023031169 (print) | LCCN 2023031170 (ebook) | ISBN 9798369300749 (hardcover) | ISBN 9798369300756 (ebook)
Subjects: LCSH: Artificial intelligence--Educational applications--Case studies.
Classification: LCC LB1028.43 .G47 2023 (print) | LCC LB1028.43 (ebook) | DDC 006.3--dc23/eng/20230714
LC record available at https://lccn.loc.gov/2023031169
LC ebook record available at https://lccn.loc.gov/2023031170

This book is published in the IGI Global book series Advances in Educational Technologies and Instructional Design (AE-TID) (ISSN: 2326-8905; eISSN: 2326-8913)

British Cataloguing in Publication Data
A Cataloguing in Publication record for this book is available from the British Library.

All work contributed to this book is new, previously-unpublished material. The views expressed in this book are those of the authors, but not necessarily of the publisher.

For electronic access to this publication, please contact: eresources@igi-global.com.

Advances in Educational Technologies and Instructional Design (AETID) Book Series

Lawrence A. Tomei
Robert Morris University, USA

ISSN:2326-8905
EISSN:2326-8913

Mission

Education has undergone, and continues to undergo, immense changes in the way it is enacted and distributed to both child and adult learners. In modern education, the traditional classroom learning experience has evolved to include technological resources and to provide online classroom opportunities to students of all ages regardless of their geographical locations. From distance education, Massive-Open-Online-Courses (MOOCs), and electronic tablets in the classroom, technology is now an integral part of learning and is also affecting the way educators communicate information to students.

The **Advances in Educational Technologies & Instructional Design (AETID) Book Series** explores new research and theories for facilitating learning and improving educational performance utilizing technological processes and resources. The series examines technologies that can be integrated into K-12 classrooms to improve skills and learning abilities in all subjects including STEM education and language learning. Additionally, it studies the emergence of fully online classrooms for young and adult learners alike, and the communication and accountability challenges that can arise. Trending topics that are covered include adaptive learning, game-based learning, virtual school environments, and social media effects. School administrators, educators, academicians, researchers, and students will find this series to be an excellent resource for the effective design and implementation of learning technologies in their classes.

Coverage

- Classroom Response Systems
- Instructional Design Models
- Higher Education Technologies
- Digital Divide in Education
- Online Media in Classrooms
- Virtual School Environments
- Curriculum Development
- Collaboration Tools
- Hybrid Learning
- Game-Based Learning

IGI Global is currently accepting manuscripts for publication within this series. To submit a proposal for a volume in this series, please contact our Acquisition Editors at Acquisitions@igi-global.com or visit: http://www.igi-global.com/publish/.

The Advances in Educational Technologies and Instructional Design (AETID) Book Series (ISSN 2326-8905) is published by IGI Global, 701 E. Chocolate Avenue, Hershey, PA 17033-1240, USA, www.igi-global.com. This series is composed of titles available for purchase individually; each title is edited to be contextually exclusive from any other title within the series. For pricing and ordering information please visit http://www.igi-global.com/book-series/advances-educational-technologies-instructional-design/73678. Postmaster: Send all address changes to above address.

Titles in this Series

For a list of additional titles in this series, please visit: www.igi-global.com/book-series

Architecture and Technological Advancements of Education 4.0
Rajiv Pandey (Amity University, India) Nidhi Srivastava (Amity University, India) and Parag Chatterjee (National Technological University Buenos Aires, Argentina)
Information Science Reference • copyright 2024 • 479pp • H/C (ISBN: 9781668492857) • US $225.00 (our price)

Strategies and Digital Advances for Outcome-Based Adult Learning
Janice E. Jones (Cardinal Stritch University, USA) and Mette L. Baran (Cardinal Stritch University, USA)
Information Science Reference • copyright 2024 • 335pp • H/C (ISBN: 9781799847489) • US $215.00 (our price)

Cases on Effective Universal Design for Learning Implementation Across Schools
Frederic Fovet (Royal Roads University, Canada)
Information Science Reference • copyright 2024 • 300pp • H/C (ISBN: 9781668447505) • US $215.00 (our price)

Practices That Promote Innovation for Talented Students
Julia Nyberg (Purdue University Global, USA) and Jessica A. Manzone (Northern Arizona University, USA)
Information Science Reference • copyright 2024 • 271pp • H/C (ISBN: 9781668458068) • US $215.00 (our price)

Navigating Virtual Worlds and the Metaverse for Enhanced E-Learning
Nadia Chafiq (Faculty of Sciences Ben M'Sick, Hassan II University, Casablanca, Morocco) Patricia W. Cummins (Virginia Commonwealth University, US) Khalil Shehadeh Al-Qatawneh (Tafila technical university, Jordan) and Imane El Imadi (University Hassan II, Morocco)
Information Science Reference • copyright 2024 • 350pp • H/C (ISBN: 9798369310342) • US $230.00 (our price)

Reconceptualizing Language Norms in Multilingual Contexts
Sarah Jones (University of Toronto, Canada) Rebecca Schmor (University of Toronto, Canada) and Julie Kerekes (University of Toronto, Canada)
Information Science Reference • copyright 2024 • 330pp • H/C (ISBN: 9781668487617) • US $215.00 (our price)

Cases on Economics Education and Tools for Educators
Brad Scott (Rowan-Cabarrus Community College, USA) and Melanie E. Fox (Purdue University, USA)
Business Science Reference • copyright 2024 • 359pp • H/C (ISBN: 9781668475836) • US $215.00 (our price)

Games as Stealth Assessments
Michael P. McCreery (University of Nevada, Las Vegas, USA) and S. Kathleen Krach (Florida State University, USA)
Information Science Reference • copyright 2023 • 368pp • H/C (ISBN: 9798369305683) • US $230.00 (our price)

IGI Global
PUBLISHER of TIMELY KNOWLEDGE

701 East Chocolate Avenue, Hershey, PA 17033, USA
Tel: 717-533-8845 x100 • Fax: 717-533-8661
E-Mail: cust@igi-global.com • www.igi-global.com

Figure 1. Night Sky (an alcohol ink painting by the editor processed in Deep Dream Generator)

This work is for Asher, Rodin, and Lily. I am so appreciative of your support in difficult times. Victory is about making it, day by day. And sometimes, it is about making it in style, abroad. Thank you.

Thanks to all the contributors (researchers and reviewers) of this text. Thank you also to the respective readers.

I have had the privilege of editing academic research books for many years, for various publishers. IGI Global has been a mainstay of my publishing life. From the beginning and throughout, they have been supportive, empathetic, and professional. Their book editing system is unmatched. I know to appreciate what works, drama-free, after spending decades in the publishing space, in many roles. I know the running of systems like well-oiled machines is made possible only through a lot of hard work and tough in-world training. So thank you, IGI Global!

Table of Contents

Section 2
Navigating Ethical Uses of Generative AI Technologies

Section 3
Applied Cases of Generative AI Technologies for Teaching and Learning

Detailed Table of Contents

This chapter delves into the intriguing realm of generative artificial intelligence (AI) models and their potential impact on undergraduate dissertations in the field of education. As AI continues to advance and permeate various aspects of our lives, the educational landscape is not immune to its transformative influence. The chapter begins by providing an overview of generative AI models, including their underlying principles and techniques such as deep learning, natural language processing, and neural networks. It then explores how these models can be harnessed to generate written content that is coherent, creative, and relevant, raising the question of whether undergraduate dissertations, as we know them, are destined to become obsolete. Advantages of employing generative AI models in education are scrutinized, highlighting their potential to enhance the efficiency and quality of student work.

When artificial intelligence is in evidence and promotes economic, social, and cultural impacts, human skills must be enhanced and praised in relation to artificial intelligence. This chapter was written based on qualitative methodology and exploratory studies by reading current reports and articles at the time of writing. The objective was to highlight a reflection on the learning experience about four behavioral profiles. The potential of artificial intelligence was highlighted, as well as upskilling and reskilling for the professions of the future. It was concluded that understanding the world should be contained in learning experiences and different behavioral profiles have dissimilar ways of thinking and acting. The lack of knowledge regarding the operationalization of artificial intelligence can weaken human options in digital and physical transformation.

One of the themes in the emergence of text- and image-making (multimodal) generative AIs is their value in the learning space, with the vast potential just beginning to be explored by mass humanity. This chapter explores the potential and early use of large language models (LLMs) harnessed for their mass learning, human-friendly conversations, and their efficacies, for self-learning for individuals and groups, based on a review of the literature, system constraints and affordances, and abductive logic. There are insights shared about longitudinal and lifelong learning and foci on co-evolving processes between the human learner and the computing machines and large language models.

Section 2
Navigating Ethical Uses of Generative AI Technologies

The chapter delves into the intricate ethical challenges posed by the integration of generative AI tools in educational contexts. As the educational landscape undergoes a profound transformation through AI-driven technologies, this chapter navigates the multifaceted ethical concerns that emerge. It explores issues surrounding data privacy, content bias, academic integrity, and the evolving roles of teachers and students in this digital era. Drawing on real-world case studies and ethical frameworks, it provides insights into the complexities of responsible AI integration. Moreover, it offers guidance on fostering ethical awareness in education and emphasizes the critical need for striking a harmonious balance between the capabilities of AI and the enduring value of human educators. This chapter serves as a comprehensive exploration of the ethical tightrope that educators, students, and policymakers must navigate to ensure AI's positive impact on education while safeguarding its ethical underpinnings.

This chapter is trying to answer a big question: Should we create artificial intelligence (AI) that deserves moral consideration, like humans? To figure this out, the authors look at different ideas about what AI is and what it should be. They use two main theories about ethics (how we decide right and wrong) to see if AI should be treated morally. One theory they use says that if AI fits the definition of intelligence, it should be treated morally, no matter which ethical theory you follow. The other theory they use is called "capability theory," combined with the definition of AI. This leads to the conclusion that we shouldn't develop AI further if we believe it deserves moral consideration. So, the chapter explores whether AI should be treated morally, and it suggests that if so, we might need to stop developing AI.

The Canadian and American teaching profession is known to be stressful, leading to burnout and other mental health issues for teachers. This chapter proposes an AI-assisted teacher wellness theory (AI TeachWell) and a supporting product/feedback/learning (PFL) framework for increased teacher well-being through the strategic use of AI chatbot technology. The theory emphasizes the use of resources that offset the demands of teaching, the importance of reducing cognitive load, and the increase of autonomy, efficacy, and relatedness. This chapter highlights the reasons that have led to increased teacher workloads, such as demands on teacher performance, administrative tasks, and professional development. It also highlights the effects of a lack of resources, time, and self-efficacy on teacher stress and burnout. The

best practices and lessons learned from case studies and successful institutions, pointing toward future directions, including emerging technologies like GPT-4 and augmented reality. It emphasizes advancing ethical guidelines, enhancing teacher-student collaboration with AI, proposing policy recommendations, and establishing legal frameworks for student data protection, along with government initiatives and funding in the realm of AI in education.

This chapter discusses the use of chatbots as conversation partners for language learning and studies the impact of chatbot-based conversation practice and corrective feedback on language learners' writing proficiency and attitudes towards chatbots. The chapter describes a study where 34 English language learners at a Japanese university were offered text-based conversation practice with Replika, a generative AI chatbot. Half of the participants received corrective feedback, addressing vocabulary, grammar, and syntax errors in their messages, while the other half practiced without feedback. Pre-test and post-test surveys assessed improvement in perceived writing performance, and general feedback on chatbot-based practice was collected. Replika, despite its non-educational design, was effective at personalizing interactions and its use resulted in significant improvement in perceived writing proficiency. Despite minor issues during conversation practices, the general impression of the chatbot is positive suggesting its potential for an English language classroom use.

As chatbot technology has advanced significantly over the past few years, it has become more and more prevalent in higher education. Chatbots can simulate human communication and engage in natural conversations. Universities and colleges use chatbots to streamline enrollment and create a virtual "one-stop-shop" for queries. In the meantime, students discovered with excitement that chatbots can help them complete homework assignments. Academic integrity has become a growing concern with students' increasing reliance on chatbots. This chapter summarizes the history of chatbots, discusses the current state of the technology, examines their limitations, and investigates how chatbots can be applied as useful administrative, academic, and pedagogical tools in higher education.

Artmaking generative AIs have been used to create visual works (still images, motion videos, and animated sequences, including simulations) that are photorealistic, high-fidelity, hyper-realistic, and emulative of the world; artful works are translated in style transfers derivative of known artist, artworks, art styles, schools of art practices, and defined visual styles. This work argues that artmaking generative

Preface

When generative AI (artificial intelligence) tools appeared in the public space in late 2022, the general public reception seemed to include outsized senses of fear. Would people be fooled by generative AI and think that they are socializing with a fellow human being when in fact they were engaging a smart machine? Would they be sharing private information and sharing vulnerabilities unknowingly? Would they be surveilled by AI in workplaces and homes and public spaces? Would cybersecurity threats get worse? What were people signing up for? What problem set were they facing? What was the scope of the challenge. Indeed, in times of threat, these are not times to unplug or to retreat.

How much of generative AI is of people (trained on human data, trained on human-made computers, designed to be attentive to human wants and needs)? But also other and non-human?

The world was abuzz with senses of extraordinary capabilities. What competitive advantage could be had with these new tools? What novel works may be created? What workplace efficiencies could be created? And how? Were people "feeling it" or not? Could they balance ethical considerations? Moral ones? Practical ones? How receptive would people be to working with powerful technologies that emulated human intelligence?

At the same time that there were careful pieces of writing, there were also those full of hype, based on both messages shared on social media but also in academic publications and socio-technical publication spaces. Some interpretations shorted the achievement of AI, and others lauded the achievement.

Meanwhile, there was the feeling of being on the cusp of so much potential, if only people could figure out how to deploy the technologies. Perhaps people would discover new needs to satisfy. *Generative AI in Teaching and Learning* is an exploratory edited collection, with a wide range of insights based on various research.

AN INITIAL TABLE OF CONTENTS

An initial Table of Contents (TOC) had been conceptualized as a way to trigger insights for this collection. The concept was that there would be professionals working in the field of generative AI, users of the technologies, dabblers, and others, each hailing from a range of fields.

The initial TOC reads as follows:

- Generative AI applications in artmaking, coding, writing, editing, research, prompts, collaboration, and others
- Public generative AI

- Public generative AI interfaces
- Generative AI in formal (accredited) education
- Teaching and learning
- Content creation
- Instructional design
- Librarian work
- Research
- Community service
- Sports
- Policies and practices
- Assignments
- Grading
- Student work
- Programming
- Generative AI in nonformal (non-accredited) teaching and learning
- Generative AI in informal (from-life) teaching and learning
- Generative AI in trainings
- Generative AI in autodidaxy (self-learning)
- Generative AI in group learning (socio-constructivism, and others)
- Social change in teaching and learning from AI
- Professional ethics in the application of generative AI
- Engaging in learning practice in with generative AI
- Private generative AI
- Risks to demotivation for skills acquisition, deskilling, downskilling? Opportunities for upskilling?

THE ACTUAL ACHIEVED TOC

As may be seen in the bulleted list, there were conceptualizations of various modalities and mixed modalities. There were conceptualizations of various workplace contexts. There were ideas of various types of learning contexts.

So what can readers expect from this academic collection? Certainly, the researchers and co-authors hail from a range of different directions.

The collection is broken out into three sections:

Part 1: World-Changing Generative AI Technologies
Part 2: Navigating Ethical Uses of Generative AI Technologies
Part 3: Applied Cases of Generative AI Technologies for Teaching and Learning

The first section focuses on the world-changing aspects of generative AI. The second part focuses on the ethical uses of generative AI, the application of human smarts and restraints to ensure efficacy and social justice and human safety and security. The third section focuses on various applied cases of generative AI for teaching and learning.

Part One: World-Changing Generative AI Technologies

Chapter 1: Disrupting Algorithmic Culture: Redefining the Human(ities)

As academia faces the transformative impact of artificial intelligence (AI) and machine learning (ML), a reevaluation of the existing academic model becomes imperative. The traditional silos within academia are becoming outdated, calling for interdisciplinary research and collaboration to comprehend the implications of algorithms and ML. Academic institutions must embrace agility, integrating new technologies into their curricula and policies, while recognizing the indispensable role of human oversight and collaboration in a successful human-AI partnership. The "human-in-the-loop" model acknowledges the need for human intelligence alongside AI, enabling the creation of new knowledge and insights. Furthermore, human fact-checking and critical evaluation remain essential in light of the limitations of AI in generating accurate citations and information. Empathy emerges as a crucial factor in building trust between humans and AI, ensuring alignment with human values and ethics. Additionally, the illogical, irrational, and emotional aspects of human cognition prove vital in the creative process, as humans possess the flexibility and adaptability required for generating novel and innovative ideas. By embracing interdisciplinary collaboration, human oversight, empathy, and the unique qualities humans bring to the table, academia can navigate the challenges and opportunities presented by technological advancements, fostering a symbiotic relationship between humans and AI.

Chapter 2: Unleashing the Potential: Positive Impacts of Generative AI on Learning and Teaching

Generative artificial intelligence, anchored by Large Language Models (LLMs), is significantly altering the educational landscape. This chapter examines the impact of generative AI on education, illustrating its capability to create personalized content and transform learning environments. Despite concerns over academic dishonesty facilitated by LLMs, the chapter argues against a regressive stance and advocates for the constructive integration of AI into educational practices. By drawing on theories of learning, the chapter elucidates the pedagogical implications of generative AI and describes specific use cases in language learning, computer science, and mathematics. Highlighting both the potential and limitations of this emerging technology, the chapter posits that generative AI is not merely a disruptive force but a revolutionary tool poised to redefine the methodologies of teaching and learning.

Chapter 3: Is it the End of Undergraduate Dissertations?: Exploring the Advantages and Challenges of Generative AI Models in Education

This chapter delves into the intriguing realm of generative Artificial Intelligence (AI) models and their potential impact on undergraduate dissertations in the field of education. As AI continues to advance and permeate various aspects of our lives, the educational landscape is not immune to its transformative influence. The chapter begins by providing an overview of generative AI models, including their underlying principles and techniques such as deep learning, natural language processing, and neural networks. It then explores how these models can be harnessed to generate written content that is coherent, creative, and relevant, raising the question of whether undergraduate dissertations, as we know them, are destined to become obsolete. Advantages of employing generative

AI models in education are scrutinized, highlighting their potential to enhance the efficiency and quality of student work. These models offer personalized guidance, allowing students to receive real-time feedback, suggestions, and constructive criticism throughout their writing process. Moreover, generative AI models possess the capacity to streamline the research process by automatically curating and synthesizing vast amounts of information, accelerating the literature review stage. However, the chapter also presents the challenges and limitations associated with relying solely on generative AI models. Ethical considerations, such as plagiarism detection and academic integrity, come to the forefront, requiring careful navigation and effective safeguards. The potential biases embedded within AI systems, including data bias and algorithmic bias, demand thorough examination to ensure fair and inclusive educational practices. Critically analyzing the advantages and challenges of generative AI models in the context of undergraduate dissertations, this chapter aims to provide educators, administrators, and researchers with a comprehensive understanding of the implications and potential of this emerging technology. It explores how generative AI models can be effectively integrated into educational systems while maintaining the integrity of the undergraduate dissertation process and fostering the development of essential skills.

Chapter 4: The Learning Experience and the Behavioral Profile: Artificial Intelligence, Upskilling and Reskilling in Professions of the Future

When artificial intelligence is in evidence and promotes economic, social, and cultural impacts, human skills must be enhanced and praised in relation to artificial intelligence. This chapter was written based on qualitative methodology and exploratory studies by reading current reports and articles at the time of writing. The objective was to highlight a reflection on the learning experience about four behavioral profiles. The potential of artificial intelligence was highlighted, as well as upskilling and reskilling for the professions of the future. It was concluded that understanding the world should be contained in learning experiences and different behavioral profiles have dissimilar ways of thinking and acting. The lack of knowledge regarding the operationalization of artificial intelligence can weaken human options in digital and phygital transformation.

Chapter 5: Stepping Stones for Self-Learning: Exploring the Use of Multimodal Text- and Image-Making Generative AI Tools

One of the themes in the emergence of text- and image-making (multimodal) generative AIs is their value in the learning space, with the vast potential just beginning to be explored by mass humanity. This chapter explores the potential and early use of large language models (LLMs) harnessed for their mass learning, human-friendly conversations, and their efficacies, for self-learning for individuals and groups, based on a review of the literature, system constraints and affordances, and abductive logic. There are insights shared about longitudinal and lifelong learning and foci on co-evolving processes between the human learner and the computing machines and large language models.

Part Two: Navigating Ethical Uses of Generative AI Technologies

Chapter 6: Generative AI in terms of its Ethical Problems for Both Teachers and Learners: Striking a Balance - Ethical Dilemmas in Generative AI tools for Education and Teaching

The chapter, "Striking a Balance: Ethical Dilemmas in Generative AI tools for Education and Teaching," delves into the intricate ethical challenges posed by the integration of Generative AI tools in educational contexts. As the educational landscape undergoes a profound transformation through AI-driven technologies, this chapter navigates the multifaceted ethical concerns that emerge. It explores issues surrounding data privacy, content bias, academic integrity, and the evolving roles of teachers and students in this digital era. Drawing on real-world case studies and ethical frameworks, it provides insights into the complexities of responsible AI integration. Moreover, it offers guidance on fostering ethical awareness in education and emphasizes the critical need for striking a harmonious balance between the capabilities of AI and the enduring value of human educators. This chapter serves as a comprehensive exploration of the ethical tightrope that educators, students, and policymakers must navigate to ensure AI's positive impact on education while safeguarding its ethical underpinnings.

Chapter 7: Moral Consideration and the Development of Artificial Intelligence: A Comparative Theory Analysis

This article is trying to answer a big question: Should we create Artificial Intelligence (AI) that deserves moral consideration, like humans? To figure this out, the author looks at different ideas about what AI is and what it should be. They use two main theories about ethics (how we decide right and wrong) to see if AI should be treated morally. One theory they use says that if AI fits the definition of Intelligence, it should be treated morally, no matter which ethical theory you follow. The other theory they use is called "Capability Theory," combined with the definition of AI. This leads to the conclusion that we shouldn't develop AI further if we believe it deserves moral consideration. So, the article explores whether AI should be treated morally, and it suggests that if we think they should, we might need to stop developing AI.

Chapter 8: AI-Assisted Teacher Wellness: Theory and Practice

The Canadian and American teaching profession is known to be stressful, leading to burnout and other mental health issues for teachers. This chapter proposes an AI-Assisted Teacher Wellness Theory (A-ATWT) and a supporting Product/Feedback/Learning (PFL) Framework for increased teacher well-being through the strategic use of AI chatbot technology. The theory emphasizes the use of resources that offset the demands of teaching, the importance of reducing cognitive load, and the increase of autonomy, efficacy, and relatedness. This chapter highlights the reasons that have led to increased teacher workloads, such as demands on teacher performance, administrative tasks, and professional development. It also highlights the effects of a lack of resources, time, and self-efficacy on teacher stress and burnout. The chapter concludes by offering innovative and proactive solutions for teachers to prioritize their health while fostering engaging and effective learning environments for their students, as well as the future implications of this theory.

Chapter 9: Harnessing AI and Big Data for Ethical and Efficient Decisions: Making in the Political Sector

Smart technologies like AI and Big data have transformed decision-making. These tools are becoming increasingly popular in various businesses, but India's political sector has not used them. The previous two years have seen a pandemic that has impacted society. The chapter investigated whether AI and Big data can be used in politics to make faster, more efficient, and morally acceptable decisions and how politicians can ensure ethical use. Question: How can big data and AI help politicians make ethical decisions? Using relevant literature, the qualitative investigation found utilization, problems, ethical issues, and hazards. Semi-structured interviews with politicians and AI experts were also done to determine if the technologies may be used in politics. Before AI can support decision-making, much political data must be digitized. In conclusion, AI and Big data can streamline Indian decision-making through document reading and analysis. There is no ethical framework for AI and Big data utilization today, making ethical decisions impossible.

Chapter 10: Professionally Ethical Ways to Harness an Art-Making Generative AI to Support Innovative Instructional Design Work

Instructional designers often pride themselves on using the most cutting-edge commercial authoring and other tools available to achieve their work. Their creations have to meet high technical standards in order to function in a digital environment, in learning management systems, content management systems, on social media, on digital content platforms, and others. In the present moment, generative AI tools enable the making of novel texts and digital visuals, among others. A major extant question is how best to harness generative art-making AIs in instructional design work. In this case, this work explores professionally ethical (and legal) ways to use a generative art-making AIs for ID work, as an innovative approach based on a review of the literature, a year of using several free web-facing art-making generative AIs (CrAIyon, Deep Dream Generator, and others) in open or public beta, and learning from applied instructional design work (over several decades).

Chapter 11: Navigating the Terrain: Current Challenges and Solutions in Integrating Generative AI into Education

The chapter provides an extensive exploration of Generative AI in education. It investigates the evolution and significance of AI in educational settings while delving into contemporary issues such as ethics, privacy, fairness, and pedagogy. Furthermore, it examines the impact on traditional teaching methods, personalization, and accessibility, addressing educational disparities. The chapter also outlines the best practices and lessons learned from case studies and successful institutions, pointing toward future directions, including emerging technologies like GPT-4 and augmented reality. It emphasizes advancing ethical guidelines, enhancing teacher-student collaboration with AI, proposing policy recommendations, and establishing legal frameworks for student data protection, along with government initiatives and funding in the realm of AI in education.

Part Three: Applied Cases of Generative AI Technologies for Teaching and Learning

Chapter 12: Chatbots as Conversation Partners: Effect on Perceived Writing Ability

This chapter discusses the use of chatbots as conversation partners for language learning and studies the impact of chatbot-based conversation practice and corrective feedback on language learners' writing proficiency and attitudes towards chatbots. The chapter describes a study where 34 English language learners at a Japanese university were offered text-based conversation practice with Replika, a generative AI chatbot. Half of the participants received corrective feedback, addressing vocabulary, grammar, and syntax errors in their messages, while the other half practiced without feedback. Pre-test and post-test surveys assessed improvement in perceived writing performance, and general feedback on chatbot-based practice was collected.Replika, despite its non-educational design, was effective at personalizing interactions and its use resulted in significant improvement in perceived writing proficiency. Despite minor issues during conversation practices, the general impression of the chatbot is positive suggesting its potential for an English language classroom use.

Chapter 13: The Robot Wrote My College Papers: Integrating Chatbots to Assist Higher Education

As chatbot technology has advanced significantly over the past few years, it has become more and more prevalent in higher education. Chatbots can simulate human communication and engage in natural conversations. Universities and colleges use chatbots to streamline enrollment and create a virtual "one-stop-shop" for queries. In the meantime, students discovered with excitement that chatbots can help them complete homework assignments. ChatGPT, one of the most popular chatbots among college students, is capable of writing coherent essays, interpreting complicated questions, solving math problems, and writing computer code. Evidence suggests that students use ChatGPT to not only write papers but also replace thinking. Academic integrity has become a growing concern with students' increasing reliance on chatbots. This chapter aims to expand the current literature on chatbots in higher education by summarizing the history of chatbots, discussing the current state of the technology, examining their limitations, and investigating how chatbots can be applied as useful administrative, academic, and pedagogical tools. The chapter argues that as sophisticated as current chatbots are, they sometimes generate false and biased information. Despite their downfalls, chatbots can be incorporated as pedagogical tools to promote student success due to their ability to access learning outcomes, facilitate critical thinking, support personalized and inclusive learning, and improve digital literacy. The chapter concludes with two inquiries for future research.

Chapter 14: Engaging Future-Minded Visualizations and Artful Aesthetics: "Seeing Different" with Human-Machine Collaborations with Artmaking Generative AIs

Artmaking generative AIs have been used to create visual works (still images, motion videos, and animated sequences, including simulations) that are photorealistic, high-fidelity, hyper-realistic, and emulative of the world; artful works are translated in style transfers derivative of known artist, artworks, art styles, schools of art practices, and defined visual styles. This work argues that artmaking generative

AIs should not be about reproductions of the familiar but should be used for future-minded visualizations and future-minded aesthetics, through true collaborations between human and machine imaginations. Through generative AI, people should be "seeing different" to enable *nouveau* "thinking" and "doing" and "being" different…into the near- and far- futures. This early and exploratory work is based on research, year-long experimentation with multiple public artmaking generative AI tools, and abductive logic.

Chapter 15: Integrating Artificial Intelligence (AI) into the Curriculum: Empowering the Next Generation Through Proactive AI Education

"Bridging the Gap: Integrating Artificial Intelligence into the Curriculum," addresses the urgent need to infuse AI education into school curriculums amidst AI's growing influence in various sectors. It advocates for a shift from reactive to proactive educational strategies, emphasizing the role of education systems in mitigating the expanding skills gap and nurturing a generation adept in AI, machine learning, and data analytics. The chapter proposes a comprehensive AI curriculum integration framework, focusing on developing key AI competencies and ethical considerations, alongside strategies for effective implementation.

This work cannot be fully addressed without bringing in something of the macro, meso, and micro ecosystems. At the macro level, the world was coming out of the SARS-CoV-2 / COVID-19 pandemic. For many, there were hopes of a return to human warmth and goodwill and trust. There were hopes of a return to the familiar. In many ways, reconnecting with people was somewhat lesser than expectations. This was so at both the macro and meso levels for many. Then, in terms of the micro level, I ended up having to change careers and move home and household. Suffice it to say that I realized how difficult it was to balance personal and professional life changes while trying to be constructively productive.

It is said that people have a limited number of books inside themselves. Certainly there are practical limits. The concept though is more of a metaphysical one. In the same breath, people say that we all have limited themes in our work. After having worked through a number of book projects—both as editor and as researcher / author, I think I can identify some of my own personally relevant themes. For nonfiction works, the books are about human-machine potential in various technological applications. For fictional ones, the foci are on the human condition, human relationships, character studies, and other observations.

If nothing else, I have learned that there are real concerns of people being subsumed into the artifice of computational machines that are capable of apparent interaction, making, and insightful expression. People are exploring new ways of being entertained. They are in a new world of machine abundance (into perpetuity), and they are ceding creative spaces (in some senses).

FUTURE RESEARCH

These works are early ones, some might even say "tentative." There is still much to be learned about techniques for teaching and learning with AI. There is much to learn about evolving application programming interfaces (APIs) linked to generative AIs.

Perhaps the larger achievement is the conceptualizing of practical life after the popularization of generative AI. Perhaps it is the focus on thriving with generative AI, not just surviving it.

There is a distinct sense of openness to generative AI technologies and even a sense of self confidence in humanity: "We've got this." *Generative AI in Teaching and Learning* (2023) shows some of the best that people can do given resources in the current moment, even as they are engaging with a new technology applied in a complex human space.

Finally, I should articulate why it is so fulfilling to see an edited book to final fruition, after a year or more of labor. There are so many possible paths along the way. There are the great intentions early on by researchers and research teams that propose solid ideas, but fewer than half truly achieve an actual chapter that may be considered. Many create drafts that are unoriginal. I had never quite had a chapter that was mostly comprised of bullet points, but one draft actually did. Some works find permanent "homes" in other published works. All to say, it is a privilege and a joy to see a work achieve publication, with its own ISBN, its own cover, its own original contents, and its own embodiment in both physical print and digital form, for readers of today and tomorrow.

Shalin Hai-Jew
Hutchinson Community College, USA

Section 1

World-Changing Generative AI Technologies

Chapter 1
Disrupting Algorithmic Culture: Redefining the Human(ities)

James Hutson
https://orcid.org/0000-0002-0578-6052
Lindenwood University, USA

Daniel Plate
https://orcid.org/0000-0002-1238-5425
Lindenwood University, USA

ABSTRACT

Academia must reevaluate its model in the face of AI and ML. Disciplinary boundaries are outdated, requiring interdisciplinary research and collaboration to understand algorithms and ML. Institutions should integrate new technologies while recognizing the importance of human oversight and collaboration in the human-AI partnership. The "human-in-the-loop" model enables new knowledge creation. Human fact-checking and critical evaluation are vital due to AI limitations. Empathy builds trust between humans and AI, ensuring alignment with human values. The illogical, irrational, and emotional aspects of human cognition drive creativity. Through interdisciplinary collaboration, human oversight, empathy, and leveraging unique human qualities, academia can navigate technological advancements and foster a symbiotic relationship with AI.

1. INTRODUCTION

The world is rapidly evolving and changing at a pace that is unprecedented in human history. We are currently in the midst of the Fourth Industrial Revolution (Industry 4.0), where technology is disrupting every aspect of our lives, from the way we work and communicate to the way we learn and live (Schwab, 2017). This requires an exploration of this new era and its impact on the future. From the rise of generative AI to the disruption of higher education, the key trends and developments shaping the world of tomorrow. This chapter provides a comprehensive overview of the future, its challenges and its opportunities, and provides higher education academic administrators, faculty and staff with an

DOI: 10.4018/979-8-3693-0074-9.ch001

understanding of the world we are entering. We will outline the ways in which institutions can reprioritize mission and goals and how to adjust curriculum, learning outcomes, assessment, and more to meet the needs of tomorrow's learners. The roles of higher education administration, faculty, staff, and even students will also be discussed.

"The future is now." The hyperbolic claim has been made for generations and is often used during times of technological innovation or change (Messerli et al., 2019; Peng et al., 2022; Yelland, 2005). But we may genuinely use the phrase to help identify times of social, cultural, and technological revolution. For instance, the Agricultural Revolution made stable social life possible with the shift from hunter-gatherer societies; the Industrial Revolution created cities of over 1 million, collapsed space and time with new forms of technology and transportation; and the technological revolution of the Information Age transformed industry as ideas became the currency of modern office life (Braidwood, 1960; Castells, 2010; De Vries, 1994). Industry 4.0 is upon us, but the full extent of the disruption can only be glimpsed today. Driven by emerging technologies such as artificial intelligence (AI) and the Internet of Things (IoT), it is also characterized by the integration of digital, physical, and biological systems and the blurring of the lines between the physical, digital, and biological spheres (Castells, 2010). Change is coming rapidly and will be felt broadly. Upskilling and retooling will be more and more common with current positions being automated or modified and new jobs being created. A new chapter in human history begins now and we need to prepare not only the students of tomorrow, but of yesterday for what lies ahead.

Human civilization is built on innovation and change. Each of the first three "revolutions" noted brought with them new ways of working, living, and organizing society, as well as disruption and upheaval. For instance, the Agricultural Revolution around 10,000 BCE saw the move away from small groups of hunter-gatherers constantly moving in a nomadic society to find food and allowed us to settle down in one place. Through the development of agriculture and the domestication of animals, the growth of large permanent settlements was made possible. This change brought about significant disruption, as people had to learn how to farm, create new tools and technology, and adapt to new ways of living. As a result, society began to specialize, with some people focusing on farming and others on other tasks, such as metalworking, pottery, and weaving. This specialization led to the development of new skills and roles within society. For example, farmers had to learn how to manage land, plant and harvest crops, and store food, while artisans had to learn how to create new tools and goods (Kerridge, 2013). Shortly thereafter, writing on was invented by the Sumerians in Mesopotamia (3400 BCE). The logo-syllabic script known as Cuneiform was pressed into clay tablets to record economic transactions first and then stories of the gods later. From there developed the scroll widely used in Eastern Mediterranean and Egyptian civilizations followed by the Roman invention of the codex (or bound book with pages we all know today). Arguably the greatest technological innovation in human history, writing allowed for information to be shared across space and time, passed down from generation to generation. Other technological innovations, such as the wheel, plow, and metallurgy could be shared, and new ideas added to them. Such was how civilization advanced, further spurred on in the Renaissance with the invention of the printing press, effectively democratizing information and education.

Equally disruptive were the two most recent revolutions, emerging out of the Age of Enlightenment. The Industrial Revolution was a period of rapid industrialization and technological development that took place in the late 18th and early 19th centuries and brought about significant changes in society, including the rise of factories, the growth of urbanization, and the emergence of new forms of work. The shift from rural to urban life, and from agrarian to manufacturing economies led to significant disruption, as people had to adapt to new ways of working and living. For example, factory workers had to learn new skills, such as operating machinery, while farmers had to move to the cities and take up new forms of work (Deane, 1979). In historical terms, the Industrial Revolution was rapidly followed by the Information Age of the 1970s that once again transformed the way we lived and worked, bringing about a rapid shift from an industrial economy to a knowledge-based economy. The period was characterized by significant technological development and widespread use of computers and the internet (Castells, 2010). This new computer-fueled economy led to the emergence of new forms of work, such as digital marketing, data analysis, and web development, as well as the decline of traditional forms of work, such as manual labor and clerical work. The first signs of automation with computers and robots being able to handle repetitive and manual tasks, such as with clerical work and manufacturing were also seen. At the same time, new roles were created, and new skills needed. These new knowledge workers, who were responsible for creating and managing information, while new skills such as data analysis and computer programming were required. Finally, another fundamental way that the Information Age disrupted society was through the emergence of new forms of communication: the rise of the internet and social media has led to new ways of connecting with others and sharing information (Jones, 1995). Now at the dawn of the Fourth Industrial Revolution, humanity should be reassured that radical transformation has occurred before, which eliminated certain jobs and roles in society, while creating new ones; new technologies have continuously been developed that had unintended consequences and benefits. The most recent disruption now, however, is not fueled by the plow or steam engine, but instead algorithms and artificial intelligence (AI).

1.1 Literature Review

The Third Industrial Revolution in the Information Age demonstrated that we could adapt once again to change, as modern office life became the standard experience for working professionals. The pace of that change, however, was much more gradual than what we are experiencing today. For example, the birth of the Internet can be traced to 1974, where two computer scientists, Vint Cerf and Robert Kahn, developed its foundational protocols, TCP/IP (Townes, 2012). They introduced this communication method as a way to link computers across the world to share information. In 1989, the creation of the World Wide Web by British computer scientist Tim Berners-Lee saw a system of interlinked hypertext documents that could be accessed via the Internet (McPherson, 2009). Notably, the World Wide Web was the first way to access the Internet through a graphical interface. Finding information across the WWW became exponentially easier with the 1998 launch of the Google search engine (Kobayashi & Takeda, 2000). Social media platforms, such as Facebook and Twitter, emerged as a new way for people to connect and share information. The first social media platforms were released in the early 2000s with Facebook going live in 2004, while the iPhone was first released in 2007. With both smartphones and social media platforms, access to information was made possible anytime and anywhere (Gikas & Grant, 2013). The developments were quickly followed in the 2010s with the advent of the Internet of Things (IoT) where there were the first interconnected networks of physical devices, vehicles, home appliances, and other items embedded with electronics, software, and sensors (Minoli, 2013). The ability of objects to collect and exchange data with each other thus created a "smart" system and now even "smart cities" (Zanella et al., 2021). The way in which IoT has transformed how people work, live and communicate is made possible through the connection of the physical and digital worlds.

Behind these developments silently emerged algorithmic culture. Algorithmic culture refers to the pervasive influence of algorithms on our daily lives, work, and decision-making processes. The increasing reliance on algorithms has been driven by advances in technology, especially in fields such as artificial intelligence (AI) and machine learning (ML). Algorithmic culture has had a profound impact on many aspects of society, including business, education, and government, and has resulted in many benefits and limitations. As outlined by Fry in her book *Hello World: Being Human in the Age of Algorithms* (2018), understanding the different types of algorithms, their purposes, uses, and learning styles, is critical to understanding their impact on society in general. Fry outlines four major categories of algorithms based on function: prioritization, classification, association, and filtering.

- **Prioritization Algorithms**: These are used to sort or prioritize data based on certain criteria. For example, a prioritization algorithm could be used to sort a list of tasks based on their importance or urgency. Another example would be a recommendation system that prioritizes a list of items for a user based on their browsing history and previous purchases.
- **Classification Algorithms** are used to categorize data into different classes or categories. For example, a spam filter is a classification algorithm that categorizes emails as spam or not spam. Another example is a sentiment analysis algorithm that categorizes text as positive, neutral, or negative based on its sentiment.
- **Association Algorithms** are used to identify relationships between different data items. For example, an association algorithm could be used to identify items that are frequently purchased together in a retail store. Another example is a recommendation system that suggests similar items based on a user's previous purchases.
- **Filtering Algorithms** are used to filter data based on certain criteria. For example, a filtering algorithm could be used to remove unwanted data or noise from a dataset. Another example is a content filter that blocks access to websites based on certain keywords or categories.

Furthermore, Fry argues that algorithms can be divided into two major groups based on their paradigms: rule-based (RB) and machine learning (ML) algorithms. RB algorithms have long been used in various domains, from rule-based expert systems in medicine to decision-making systems in finance. These algorithms are characterized by their directness and clarity, as they are designed to follow explicit instructions that have been formulated by human experts. On the other hand, ML algorithms are characterized by their ability to learn from data, allowing them to adapt and improve over time. The learning process is based on the idea of reinforcement, where the algorithm receives feedback on its performance and updates its behavior accordingly. ML algorithms have been used in a wide range of applications, including image recognition (computer vision), natural language processing (NLP), and recommendation systems, among others. The difference in these groups provides further insight into algorithmic culture. For example, RB algorithms are often more transparent and easier to understand than ML algorithms, which can sometimes be seen as "black boxes" that are difficult to interpret. However, ML algorithms can be more flexible and adaptive, making them well suited to complex and dynamic environments.

Understanding how these two categories of algorithms learn is also important to understanding algorithmic culture and how they shape our lives. With regards to how algorithms learn, Hristova, Hong and Slack (2021) distinguish three categories: supervised, unsupervised, and reinforcement learning.

- **Supervised learning,** the algorithm is trained on labeled data and then used to make predictions on new, unlabeled data. Labels are provided as examples for the desired output and then the supervised algorithm learns the relationship between input data and output labels to make accurate predictions.

- **Unsupervised learning**, the algorithm is tasked with finding patterns and structure in the input data, without being provided with labeled data. The goal is to identify meaningful relationships in the data.
- **Reinforcement learning,** on the other hand, involves learning through trial and error, with the aim of maximizing some reward. The algorithm interacts with its environment and receives rewards or penalties for specific actions. Over time, the algorithm learns which actions lead to the highest rewards and adjusts its behavior accordingly.

In other words, supervised learning involves the algorithm being told what the correct answer is, unsupervised learning does not provide the algorithm with the correct answer, and reinforcement learning does not provide the algorithm with the correct answer but involves learning through trial and error.

One of the main benefits of algorithmic culture is increased efficiency and speed in decision-making processes. For example, algorithms can be used to analyze vast amounts of data and provide insights that would be difficult for humans to detect. Lepri et al. (2018) argue that algorithms can provide a more objective and unbiased decision-making process than humans, as they are not subject to personal biases or prejudices. This ability can lead to more equitable outcomes in areas such as hiring, lending, and healthcare if the dataset used for training a model is also not biased (Kordzadeh & Ghasemaghaei, 2022). Another benefit of algorithmic culture is that it can improve access to information and knowledge. Algorithms can personalize recommendations and tailor information to individual users, making it easier to find and access the information they need (Gran, Booth, & Bucher, 2021).

At the same time, algorithmic culture has several drawbacks that must be taken into consideration. The first is a lack of transparency. Given how decisions are made in different models, algorithms, as noted, can be seen as a kind of "black-box" which can make identifying potential biases difficult to assess (Saltelli et al., 2008). As such, algorithms can have unintended consequences, such as perpetuate existing biases and discrimination, particularly if they are trained on biased data, as well as amplifying existing inequalities, creating new ones, and even violating people's privacy and rights (Angwin et al., 2016; Dwork & Roth, 2014). Over-reliance on algorithms can also lead to a loss of critical thinking skills and decision-making abilities, reducing human agency (Zerilli et al., 2019). The tradeoff between instant communication and information versus privacy and agency has received a great deal of attention given the potential drawbacks of algorithms determining our values, search results, news feeds, and social media (Alvarado & Waern, 2018; Diakopoulos, 2019; Eslami et al., 2015; Feezell et al., 2021; Gillespie, 2014; Khan et al., 2020; Powers, 2017). There is little wonder why we have a complex and ambivalent relationship with technology.

1.1.1 Rise of Generative AI: The Terminator is Here

In the sci-fi blockbuster *The Terminator* (1984) the artificial neural network-based conscious group mind and artificial general superintelligence system for strategic defense known as Skynet was to go live on August 4, 1997. Less than a month after human decision-making had been removed, Skynet became self-aware or sentient at 2:14 am Eastern Time on August 29th, 1997, and launched the global payload of nuclear ordinance. The singularity then began designing machines to hunt down the remaining humans that survived the nuclear winter. However, Judgement Day came and went, a new millennium dawned, and machines did not rise up to destroy humanity. But fears over the inevitable takeover of the machine age persist, and, seemingly, are being realized today. Not surprisingly then, as Aoun noted in *Robot-Proof* (2018), according to a survey, Americans have a greater fear of robots replacing people in the workplace more than death itself. But what exactly are these new artificial intelligences that are viewed with such apprehension?

Artificial Intelligence (AI) can have various interpretations depending on who you ask and even experts in the field disagree (Cremer, 2021; Ermakova & Frolova, 2021; Monett & Lewis, 2018; Wang, 2019). One reason for the disagreement of a definition is the fact that the field is rapidly advancing and increasing in expansiveness and complexity, encompassing a wide range of technologies, including everything from ML and NLP to computer vision and robotics, expert systems to generative models. As such, some individuals refer to AI as an intelligent device, such as a robot, and call it simply "The AI." However, AI is typically defined as the emulation of human intelligence in machines designed to think and act like humans. These machines can carry out activities that typically demand human intelligence, such as speech recognition, visual perception, language translation, and decision-making (Wang, 2019). AI systems are constructed on algorithms and statistical models that allow them to learn from data, recognize patterns, and make predictions. There are different types of AI, including narrow or weak AI, which is tailored for a specific purpose, and general or strong AI, which has the ability to perform a broad range of tasks commonly associated with human intelligence (Allen, 2019).

What is consistent in discussions on AI is the impact it will have on the future of work, education, and social life, as outlined in the AI100 study by Stanford University (Littman et. al, 2021). AI is estimated to create a value of $13 trillion by 2030, and at the same time, an estimated 800 million jobs will be displaced due to AI and automation (Hutson et al., 2022). These prognostications have been well-circulated over the past decade, leading to preliminary discussions of how to plan for the coming disruption. Industry, business, education and government have begun exploring the ethical, logistical, human capital, and other changes on the horizon. One example of industry planning for the changes brought about by emerging technologies can be found in automotive manufacturing. As outlined by Miguel et al (2022), the automotive industry is undergoing a profound transformation, with electrification, automation, and connected and shared mobility redefining how we drive and use cars. The report goes on to note that this transformation is leading to new business models, regulatory frameworks, and supply chains, as well as significant impacts on employment and the wider economy.

Likewise, firms are grappling with the impact of AI on their operations and workforce. According to a report by Accenture Federal Services (2018), as AI becomes more ubiquitous, organizations will need to address the ethical, societal and workforce implications of the technology (Liu & Murphy, 2020). Education had a similar call to action in planning for how to incorporate new technologies into the curriculum in an ethical and effective manner. Discussing the trends of education and technology for the future, Burbules, Fan, & Repp (2020) relate how educators must be equipped with the necessary skills and knowledge to effectively integrate technology into their teaching practices, while also ensuring its responsible use in the classroom. Finally, there is growing concern over privacy and security regarding emerging technologies in the government sector. The development of new technologies, such as artificial intelligence and the Internet of Things, is creating new privacy and security challenges for the government (Omolara et al., 2022). Government officials must consider the ethical, legal, and policy implications of these technologies, and develop a framework for their responsible use (Wirtz, Weyerer, & Sturm, 2020).

But these preparations are largely in their infancy, especially considering AI integration into education at any level, as leaders thought they had more time (Hutson et al., 2022). Time is up. In rewriting the history of the 21st century, the second half of 2022 will be known as the beginning of the age of generative artificial intelligence (AI) (DelSignore, 2022; Francke & Alexander, 2019; Murphy 2022; Sherry, 2022). Generative AI like ChatGPT, DALLE-3, and Stable Diffusion, along with a host of others launched late in the year and immediately disrupted the status quo of the artworld, advertising and marketing, and education, leading to outcries to ban "AI Art" and spawning an entirely new market of NFTs (Ansari, 2022; Hazucha 2022). At the same time, ChatGPT-3 launched November 30, 2022, and sent shockwaves through industry, pop culture, and academia alike with new abilities to articulate answers in a conversational style (unlike Google) to gain information, and also to generate original content, including stories, games, code, advertisements, and much more. ChatGPT-4 has already been announced and Microsoft plans to integrate such "headless AI" across their suite of platforms.

1.2 Recommendations

1.2.1 Hedges Against AI

The immediate question became "will I lose my job?" There has been an assumption that there are certain activities that are "essentially human," and that robots would never be able to replicate, and, thus, those jobs, careers, and industries were future proof. This is no longer the case. AI art generators can now create original works in any style and of any subject imaginable; AI tutors can now assist students to overcome various learning disabilities; and text-based Generative Pre-trained Transformers can write compelling and entertainment advertisements, while sampling three seconds of audio of anyone's voice can now replace voice actors; and, finally, actors are selling the rights to their voice and appearance, which can then be used alongside AI, ML and deepfake technology to have them perform and say anything a studio desires without even needing human talent. With all of these technologies converging, machine learning (ML), computer vision, and natural language processing (NLP), the capabilities of emerging AI are only now being hinted at. The situation leaves humanity uneasy about our place in the world again as another revolution is transforming society. But there is good news: AI will not replace you. Someone working with AI will.

Predicting how AI and automation will impact the future of work is unclear. The study most often cited by economists was conducted in 2023 by the University of Oxford and argues that if a machine can automate a job, humans will lose it. The study used predictive modeling to categorize 702 jobs as high, medium, or low risk for computerization and found that 47% of them can be automated. Routine jobs with limited creative or interpersonal demands are the most susceptible to automation (Frey & Osborne, 2017). The prediction has since been revised. Furthermore, according to Anu Madgavkar, a partner at the McKinsey Global Institute, this is because human judgment still needs to be applied to these technologies to avoid error and bias (Mok & Zinkula, 2023). As such, Holzinger et al (2023) argue for the framing of emerging technologies as productivity enhancing tools instead of replacements for human workers. This does not mean that certain industries will not see a greater deal of disruption and require workers to retool and reskill. But the wholesale automation of many jobs will also not lead to rampant unemployment. As Ansari noted (2022), a large number of workers across 31 global markets, from retail to logistics, have decided to leave their jobs due to the Great Resignation of 2022. The figures are staggering, with 40% of workers quitting, an all-time high (Deloitte, 2022). These workers did not quit their jobs due to automation, however. The 2022 Pew Research poll instead found reasons cited as being low wages, a lack of advancement opportunities, and feeling disrespected. Therefore, the Oxford study has been extensively reviewed and investigated for potential errors. In 2018, the authors stated that the study only addresses one aspect of work and cannot predict the extent of job automation or take into account other factors. The World Economic Forum likewise pointed out that how people handle the change brought by automation will determine its impact (WEF, 2023). Rather than protecting jobs that can be done better by robots, the task now is to train the workforce for future work. Therefore, people must be prepared to adapt to this new environment.

AI has already been demonstrated to boost human productivity, creativity, and potential in many fields from fine art to computer science. Working with (and not against) the technology will be the motto of success, starting now. At the same time, there has been no systematic approach to develop a curriculum to help individuals retool, upskill, and use these new, necessary tools in their own areas. Education must adapt much more quickly than has been seen over the past two centuries. Research has confirmed that the current use of AI in education (AIEd) leads to positive outcomes, including improved learning outcomes for students, along with increased access, increased retention, lower cost of education, and decreased time to completion. Future uses of AI will include the following: enabling engaging and interactive education anytime and anywhere; personalized AI mentors that will help students identify and reach their goals; and mass-personalization that will allow AI to be tailored to each student's learning style, level, and needs. Yet with all the potential benefits that AI and ML may provide students, there remains a general reticence to adopt this technology because of misconceptions and perceptions that faculty will need to retool since their current teaching strategies will be outmoded.

1.2.2 Disruption of Higher Education

The timing, however, has never been more critical. Since the publication of *Robot-Proof: Higher Education in the Age of Artificial Intelligence* (2018), the world has experienced a global pandemic, an acceleration in emerging technologies development, and the rise of generative AI. To prepare students for the future of work, then-president of Northeastern University Joseph Aoun argued that higher education needs to change in the age of AI. Aoun suggests that the traditional model of higher education, which focuses on specialized knowledge and skills, is no longer sufficient to prepare students for the rapidly changing job market. He instead advocates for a new model of education that emphasizes the development of "human skills" such as creativity, critical thinking, and communication, which are less likely to be replaced by robots. Aoun also argues that higher education institutions should focus on teaching students how to learn, so that they can adapt to new technologies and changes in the job market throughout their careers. The recommendations are more pertinent now more than ever, but little movement has been seen in the past five years towards a new interdisciplinary curriculum.

But the data used to support *Robot-Proof*'s strategies for education is dated. While estimates on careers to be automated have remained consistent, which jobs will be susceptible first have shifted as no one could have predicted. For instance, the statistic is cited that 4.4 million jobs would be found by 2024 in the information technology sector (U.S. Beareau of Labor Statistics, 2018). No one would have predicted an estimated 130,000 jobs lost in this sector in the first month of 2023 due to unexpected abilities of AI and ML. Underpinning Aoun's argument is that college should ensure students can become creators: "Creation will be at the base of economic activities and also much of what human beings do in the future" (Aoun, 2018, p.xvi). Basing the assumption on the capabilities of AI at the time, the author finds that repeatable, teachable tasks can be automated- even skilled white-collar roles such as identifying and curing diseases.

At the same time, he reassures us that "Human beings will still read books penned by human authors and be moved by songs and artworks born of human imagination" (Aoun, 2018, p.xvi). Few could have predicted that AI would disrupt creative industries first instead of blue-collar, manual labor with the advent and widespread use of AI generative content. Both text-based and image-based AI generative content emerged at the close of 2022 and already disrupted the technology sector. Google has already announced 12,000 layoffs and shift to focus on AI and away from previous revenue generated by its search engine. Furthermore, other fields previously thought "robot-proof" are not immune. Caregiving for both infants and the elderly, cooking regional dishes, crafting wine, brewing beer, and more can all be automated through robotics and AI.

1.2.3 Reactionary Entrenchment: Circle the Wagons

The initial response of educational institutions has been reactionary upon learning of the potential of generative AI, particularly the ChatGPT-3 model. Despite its tremendous potential, many educational administrators and policymakers have been slow to embrace the technology, as they are struggling to understand its capabilities and potential benefits. According to a recent report by the American Journal of Education, as educators struggle to grasp the potential of such tools, many have adopted a knee-jerk reaction to the rise of generative AI, and have banned access to the technology, especially in K-12 school districts in parts of the country (Smith, 2021).

Despite the initial reluctance of some educators to embrace generative AI, the field is rapidly evolving, and AI technology is becoming more sophisticated and capable every day. As a result, it is increasingly clear that collaboration between human and AI writers will become the norm, rather than the exception. In fact, Smith (2021) reminds us that this is a bygone conclusion as we will all be writing collaboratively with AI, and in fact already do on a daily basis. To prepare for this rapidly-evolving landscape, educational administrators and policymakers must be proactive in embracing the potential of generative AI and exploring the ways in which it can be used to improve and enhance the educational experience. This will require a deeper understanding of the technology and its capabilities, as well as a willingness to experiment and embrace new approaches.

The paradigm shift in higher education must put technology at the forefront, with a focus on equipping students with relevant skills and knowledge to succeed in an increasingly technology-driven world. The approach requires a reconsideration of the traditional curriculum, moving away from traditional subjects such as mathematics and English, and instead emphasizing problem-solving and self-expression and communication skills. As opposed to being preoccupied with the issue of plagiarism, it is crucial that higher education prioritizes the development of critical thinking skills in students. By doing so, innovation and technology can be viewed as valuable partners in education, rather than a threat to it. According to a report by the *Journal of Higher Education*, technology will play a critical role in fostering critical thinking skills in students, by providing them with access to a wealth of information and empowering them to analyze, synthesize, and evaluate information from a variety of sources (Johnson, 2020).

The role of teachers in this new era of higher education is also crucial, as they are partners in this effort to reframe education to better align with the technological landscape of the future. Teachers must be equipped with the knowledge and skills to effectively integrate technology into the classroom, and to support students in developing the critical thinking skills that are so essential for success in a technology-driven world. Therefore, the rethinking of higher education to better align with the technological landscape of the future requires a fundamental shift in the curriculum, with a focus on problem-solving, self-expression and communication, and critical thinking skills. Teachers must be viewed as partners in this effort and must be equipped with the skills and knowledge to effectively integrate technology into the classroom.

1.2.4 Automating Critical Thinking

A wholesale adoption of technology and integration into existing educational curriculum, however, would be ill-advised. With students in college taking a core of General Education coursework – including English, mathematics, history, and more- and then learning field-specific material, the current model presumes students will need information literacy skills in order to effectively evaluate a wide range of sources, determine which are appropriate, and synthesize them into a new argument. This process, however, can now be automated fairly easily. According to Pavlik (2023), text-based generative AI operates by using advanced algorithms and large amounts of data to generate new text based on patterns in the input data, but the process requires little critical thinking on the part of the user compared to traditional internet search engines given that AI relies solely on its programmed algorithms and data inputs. In other words, even with a seemingly infinite amount of information easily available at any given time to students via powerful search engines like Google, users would still need to use keyword searches to identify specific webpages with the information desired. Next, users would need to read and understand the content in order to formulate a new search query, and so on, until all required information was assembled and then, students would still need to synthesize the material from the various sources in order to make an argument on a subject. The whole process outlined has been automated (to a point), thus users do not need to go through previous data and information literacy steps to generate an argument for an assignment.

Such is an unintended consequence of algorithmic culture. A major limitation of algorithmic culture is that it can limit critical thinking and creativity. As algorithms increasingly make decisions for us, we may become less critical and more passive, relying on the recommendations and decisions of algorithms in the decision-making process without questioning them (Turkle, 2011). This can result in a lack of creativity and innovation, as individuals are less likely to challenge the status quo and come up with new and innovative ideas. Given this new development, and future plans to integrate AI chatbot functionality into the whole Microsoft Office suite (starting with Teams Premium and the new Bing search engine in February, 2023), and Google developing their own alternative to ChatGPT-3, Apprentice Bard, the sophistication of such algorithms will only increase, while the relative understanding of a given topic on the part of the user will decrease. Therefore, as Alam (2021) highlighted, the increasing importance of critical analysis in the context of AI adoption and automation will become center stage in academia.

The alarmist sentiments circulating in academia and social media should, however, be tempered with a reminder that the same concerns were raised when Google (1998) and Wikipedia (2001) launched. The belief was that students would no longer commit information to memory and would instead lose their ability to think critically (Petrilli, 2008). A similar argument has been made and concerns raised over the impact generative AI will have on education. The argument is not new. No less than Plato in his dialogue *Phaedrus* (14, 274c-275b) relates how Socrates discusses the Egyptian myth of the creation of writing. As Socrates speaks,

For this invention will produce forgetfulness in the minds of those who learn to use it, because they will not practice their memory. Their trust in writing, produced by external characters which are no part of themselves, will discourage the use of their own memory within them. You have invented an elixir not of memory, but of reminding; and you offer your pupils the appearance of wisdom, not true wisdom, for they will read many things without instruction and will therefore seem to know many things, when they are for the most part ignorant and hard to get along with, since they are not wise, but only appear wise.

The same fear was once again raised when the chalkboard was introduced to education in 1801. There was widespread revolt among students and educators who had been trained to memorize instead of writing out (Krause, 2001). Not needing to memorize or use rote memorization techniques in education has always been looked upon with suspicion.

Nevertheless, as AI continues to take over tasks previously performed by humans, the role of individuals who are able to critically evaluate AI-generated output will become increasingly valuable in industry and society. But where are students learning such skills in their current education? While college majors are designed around skill-specific content areas, such evaluative skills are really only purposefully developed in liberal arts curricula in arts and humanities. Wilson (2003) argues that the increasing reliance on AI will increase the value proposition of arts and humanities education. These fields emphasize critical thinking, creativity, and problem-solving skills, which are precisely the skills that will be in high demand as AI continues to become more prevalent in our lives.

The irony of all of this change is that technology will force us to more fully reckon and grapple with what makes us human. Human skills will become more valuable than ever by bridging the value of durable skills across social and educational disruptions in the wake of advances in AI and ML. The arts and humanities can prepare students for the Industry 4.0 by providing them with critical thinking, creativity, communication, and problem-solving skills. These skills are becoming increasingly important in the digital age, as automation and artificial intelligence take over many routine tasks (Autor, & Dorn, 2013; Frey & Osborne, 2017). Additionally, the arts and humanities can help students develop an understanding of different cultures and perspectives, which is essential for working in a globalized economy. These students are also equipped with an understanding of ethics, governance and policy making, which is critical given how tightly intertwined technology and society is becoming (Crossley & Tikly, 2004).

A rethinking of what students need to get out of a college education is already underway and is reconsidering who today's student actually is, what they need to know and be able to do, and when they will need to know it. As Weise (2020) argues, the college experience must evolve past the four-year model in a young adult's life and into a lifelong learning partnership whereby as new challenges and needs arise, students can return over and over to retool and reskill. The skills they will need are coming into focus and include durable skills (formerly known as "soft skills") and be knowledgeable of emerging technological trends. Therefore, the current dichotomy between career preparedness and liberal arts education is a false choice, as Detweiler (2021) rightly notes. Both are equally important, and interdependent. One will not be prepared for the future without the durable and transferable skills to adapt to it.

1.2.5 Adapting to a Changing Landscape

The impact of the COVID-19 pandemic on higher education has been far-reaching and significant. Despite federal assistance, 2023 saw closures of small, private, non-profit and underfunded regional institutions (Cameron, Fogarty-Perry, & Piercy, 2022). At the same time, departments and majors in the arts and humanities, such as Philosophy, History, Art History, Languages, Religion, and others, faced low enrollment and elimination due to declining interest (Magness & Mitchell, 2022). These eliminations have resulted in decreased support for these departments, leaving them vulnerable to elimination and further hindering the development of a well-rounded education for students (Massey, 2020).

The financial strain on institutions was further exacerbated by declining enrollment and institutions unprepared for online learning conditions. The shift to online learning, as well as the closure of campus facilities, has led to a decrease in revenue from tuition, room and board, and other sources (Mishra, Gupta, & Shree, 2020). To adapt to the pandemic, universities that had shifted to online or hybrid formats continued to adopt the model due to student demand post-pandemic (Singh, Steele, & Singh, 2021). Simultaneously, the curtailment of academic programs resulting from financial limitations exacerbated the financial predicament, resulting in a reduction in income. The diminution in income was exacerbated by the universities' allocation of resources and technology towards remote learning, thereby exacerbating the budgetary pressures (Frederick & Wolff-Eisenberg, 2020). Additionally, the shift to online learning has exacerbated existing disparities in access to technology and quality of education, particularly among low-income and underrepresented students. The situation has resulted in unequal opportunities for students to receive a quality education and has further widened the achievement gap (Theobald et al., 2020).

However, while educational institutions felt the negative effects of the pandemic, the potential for innovative solutions to the unforeseen social changes led to a flurry of research and development activity (Brem, Viardot, & Nylund, 2021). The results of the efforts of many industries in the fields of extended reality (XR), artificial intelligence (AI), and machine learning (ML) and neural networks was able to effectively get us collectively "unstuck" in many areas, catapulting us forward faster than we could have imagined. The shift to remote education, work, and even health care necessitated broader development and adoption of cloud computing, virtual and augmented reality technologies, and the Internet of Things (IoT) (He, Zhang, & Li, 2021). Facebook (now Meta) seized upon the limitations of social distancing and released the Oculus Quest 2 on October 13, 2020. The all-in-one virtual reality (VR) head-mounted display (HMD) was the first affordable and user-friendly version of its type. Furthermore, the pandemic has also sparked investments in unmanned aerial vehicles (UAVs) and drones, which have been used for contactless deliveries and disease surveillance (Aabid et al., 2022). With regards to the health care industry, telemedicine has seen significant growth, allowing for remote medical consultations and reducing the risk of virus transmission, leading to expanded functionality of remote video conferencing services, such as Microsoft Teams, Zoom, Skype and more (Patel, Hamdan, & Donahue, 2022). Artificial intelligence (AI) has also been leveraged to assist in disease diagnosis and the development of vaccines (Vaishya et al., 2020). These technologies have enabled organizations from schools to governments to maintain productivity and continue operations during lockdowns and quarantines (Montenegro & Young, 2020).

In the face of social and technological change, education also made strides to integrate these emerging technologies to support learning during a time of unprecedented limitations. The pandemic forced educational institutions to re-evaluate their approach to teaching and learning as institutions from early childhood education through postsecondary transitioned to remote instruction as of March 2022 (Doi, Lucky, & Rubin, 2022). As necessity is the mother of invention, change was required in short order, leading to quick adoption of video conferencing and leveraging more of learning management systems (LMS) functionality (Siakalli et al., 2022). New and innovative solutions were sought to overcome the physical distance to address student-to-student and teacher-to-student interactions. In addition to video conferencing tools like Zoom that seemingly became used ubiquitously overnight for teaching and instruction, the use of virtual reality (VR) and augmented reality (AR) became increasingly popular from

2020 onward (Garzón, J. (2021). As recent studies have born out, extended reality (XR) technologies were rapidly adopted, first in elementary and secondary education, and gradually spreading to higher education to create immersive learning experiences for students not possible due to social distancing and travel restrictions (Hutson & Olsen, 2022).

AI and ML have also played a crucial role in the adaptation of higher education during the pandemic. Warrier, John, and Warrier (2021) found that the use of these technologies in education will personalize learning, providing students with tailored recommendations and feedback on their progress. The technology has already enabled educational institutions to analyze student data and develop personalized learning plans, allowing them to cater to individual learning styles and pace. In all, the pandemic has heightened awareness of the need for innovation and has created an environment that is more open to change. The situation has led to the development of new teaching methods and tools that have, arguably, augmented and improved the overall quality of education (Ciolacu et al., 2023).

1.2.6 Preparing for the Digital Maelstrom

These advances to embrace more emerging technologies to support diverse learning needs will only intensify in the face of generative AI (Pavlik, 2023). Higher education especially went through intense growing pains since the pandemic, requiring digital transformation, retooling and reskilling faculty and staff, and rethinking teaching and assessment methods (Rof, Bikfalvi, & Marques, 2022). Yet, even with the herculean efforts and collaboration between administration, faculty, staff, and IT departments across the globe, it seems we have prepared for a different "new normal." The integration of AI and ML concepts into the curriculum has already become increasingly important in preparing students for the workforce of the future (Broo, Kaynak, & Sait, 2022). These already include adding courses in areas such as AI ethics (Cath et al., 2018), AI programming (Yang & Evans, 2019), and AI applications (Zawacki-Richter et al., 2019). Furthermore, the teaching of traditional subjects, such as mathematics, science, and computer science, must now be realigned and taught in such a way as to emphasize their relevance to AI development and usage and for non-specialist audiences (Cooper, 2022). Just as important to imparting technical skills and knowledge, education must refocus on the development of critical thinking and problem-solving skills, as well as creativity and innovation (Bühler, Jelinek, & Nübel, 2022; Greenstein, 2012). These are essential for students to be able to engage with AI technologies in a meaningful and responsible manner and set themselves apart in an algorithmic culture (Chen et al., 2023). Furthermore, education must address the ethical and social implications of AI and focus on education for AI not AI for education (Schiff, 2022), as well considering future potential impact on employment and the economy (Zhang et al., 2022). The assessment of student learning must also be adapted to reflect the changing nature of AI (Carvalho et al., 2022). Traditional methods of assessment, such as multiple-choice exams and essays, will become increasingly and woefully irrelevant for assessment (Babitha & Sushma, 2022). Instead, performance-based and project-based assessments are more effective in demonstrating students' mastery of various educational material and knowledge and will become the standard across all educational levels and, especially in academia (Krajcik et al., 2023; Palladino & Shepard, 2023).

These changes will impact all stakeholders in education from administrators to students. As such, the agile and adaptive roles of each will need to be carefully considered to prepare for the future. For instance, educational administrators in higher education will play a crucial role in implementing and integrating AI-based technologies across institutions, ensuring alignment with their mission, goals, and values. Administrators will also need to ensure that policies and procedures are in place to responsibly manage and utilize AI, including ethical considerations and data privacy (Li & Gu, 2023). Also, faculty will play a critical role in incorporating AI into the curriculum, exploring its impact on their fields, and preparing students for careers in an AI-driven world (Rensfeldt & Rahm, 2023). In addition, faculty will need to continuously upskill themselves to stay current with advances in AI, which will impact their teaching and research. This will require a rethinking of incentivizing professional development and rewarding cognitive flexibility. Therefore, staff will play a crucial role in supporting faculty and students in their use of AI, including providing technical support, training, and resources (Kaliraj & Devi, 2023). As AI continues to impact the job market, staff will also need to develop skills to be competitive in the AI-driven job market. Students, who are digital natives, will have a more proactive role in shaping the integration of AI in higher education and should be included in training and resource discussions. As critical users of AI technologies, students will necessarily bring new perspectives and demands to the higher education environment (Milton & Al-Busaidi, 2023).

1.2.7 Future-Proofing a Steam Engine

Academia moves at a glacial pace and is evidenced by the gradual pace of curriculum revision, the deliberate pace of academic research, the lengthy process of attaining tenure, and the slow pace of advancement of academic committees and policies (Antony et al., 2022). This leads to the inquiry of whether a renovation or a revolution is necessary in the current academic model. Kellner and Gennaro (2022) posit that a rethinking of the existing academic model is necessary in light of the changing landscape of digital technologies, calling attention to the fact that traditional models of academia are becoming increasingly outdated, especially in the face of cutting-edge technologies such as algorithms and ML. Moreover, the current academic model fails to adequately prepare students for the rapidly changing job market, where technological literacy is becoming increasingly important (Ter Beek, Wopereis, & Schildkamp, 2022). In order to remain relevant, academic institutions must embrace a more agile approach to academic progress, incorporating new technologies and interdisciplinary research into their curricula and policies. The need for a renovation of the academic model has never been more pressing, as the impact of digital technologies continues to reshape the global landscape.

The digital revolution has also led to a call to reevaluate the conventional compartmentalization of academic disciplines. Werthner et al (2023), for instance, set forth the argument that the traditional academic silos are becoming a hindrance, especially in the realm of digital humanities. Accordingly, interdisciplinary research is vital to comprehend the intricate implications of emerging technologies such as algorithms and ML and that breaking down academic silos is necessary to facilitate this research. Another crucial aspect is the need for academic institutions to revise their curricula to align with the evolving landscape of digital technologies. Again, curricula must be updated to adapt to these technological advancements through the incorporation of emerging technologies across curricula to ensure students' preparedness for the future. Lastly, there is a growing awareness of the importance for faculty and staff in academic institutions to acquire new skills and knowledge to remain relevant in the future in light of the changing digital landscape (Akour & Alenezi, 2022). Such arguments posit that traditional abilities and knowledge are becoming outdated and that developing new skills and knowledge is imperative for academic institutions to remain relevant in the future. But what are those skills we should focus on teaching students moving forward?

1.2.8 Interdisciplinarity and Human Skills

AI is a critical component in shaping the relationship between people and technology, and has the potential to transform various industries, including healthcare, transportation, and education. However, with this potential also comes limitations, and it is important to understand what AI can and cannot do, such as the inability to comprehend human emotions. Xu et al (2023) highlight that this limitation can greatly impact the progress of human-centered AI technologies, as emotions play a significant role in human interaction. The algorithms underpinning the technology are designed to work within a specific set of parameters and are not capable of accurately recognizing and interpreting human emotions, which has implications for the professions just mentioned. Another restriction of AI is its struggle to handle contradictions and ambiguity, which limits its capability to make ethical decisions. Hunkenschroer and Luetge (2022) note that, AI algorithms are limited in their ability to handle ethical and moral dilemmas, as they rely on specific inputs and can struggle to reconcile contradictions and ambiguity. This means that AI-powered technologies may not be suitable for decision-making in complex ethical situations. Additionally, AI is not capable of generating new knowledge or ideas, rendering it unsuitable for tasks requiring innovation or problem-solving (Zhu & Luo, 2022). Therefore, even with all of the advances seen as of late, the human component will remain necessary in many areas for human-AI collaboration. So, what does it mean to be human and what skills should we cultivate?

While not expressly framed as such, liberal arts curricula are designed to help students learn how to be human. The proposition is actually quite a complex cognitive process that necessitates high levels of motivation and self-awareness. Through critically investigating the history of human civilizations, thoughts, motivations, and actions, we learn not only about the factual aspects of humanity but what it means to be human. At the same time, enduring skills are cultivated like global competence, which, of course, requires a broad knowledge of global geography, events, and history, but is critical for individuals to succeed in a rapidly evolving world (Kang & Lee, 2022). Cognitive flexibility and emotional intelligence (EQ) are also crucial skills to be developed. EQ encompasses five key components, such as self-awareness and empathy, while social and emotional learning can aid in the acquisition of adaptability skills (Rajaram, 2023). Furthermore, emotional intelligence has been found to play a major role in various life domains, including academic achievement and job performance (Wang, 2022). Numerous studies have confirmed the power of durable or transferable skills, and the significance of cognitive flexibility in achieving success (Elmoutanna & Moti, 2022; González-Pérez & Ramírez-Montoya, 2022; Mabe & Bwalya, 2022; Urhan, 2023). The development of both cognitive flexibility and emotional intelligence is crucial for success in today's rapidly changing world. For instance, multiple studies confirm that cognitive flexibility is positively related to achievement and success in both academic and occupational domains (Clément, 2022; Hommel, Ruppel, & Zacher, 2022; Lee, 2022; Preiss, 2022). Similarly, several studies have established that EQ is a predictor of success in various life domains, including academic achievement and job performance (Barchard, 2003; Goleman, 2001; Mohzan, Hassan, & Abd Halil, 2013;). Finally, research by Bar-On et al (2000) found that individuals with high levels of EQ are better able to regulate their emotions and display greater adaptability in changing situations. Taken together, the skills we should be focusing on teaching our students to be successful in an ever-changing and uncertain world should foreground durable and transferable skills, cognitive flexibility, EQ, and health and wellness.

1.2.9 Teaming Up for Tomorrow: Navigating the Human-AI Partnership

With these uniquely human skills, we are poised for the future of human-AI collaboration and increased productivity and creativity. But what is our role in this new relationship and what will it look like? As noted, there are many limitations to AI and ML that will require human assistance, oversight, and collaboration for a successful symbiotic relationship. Collaboration between humans and AI has the potential to be more powerful than either entity working alone. As Pan (2016) argued while looking ahead to AI 2.0, the combination of human intelligence and artificial intelligence can result in the creation of new knowledge and insights that would not have been possible without the collaboration. Similarly, Wu et al (2021) point out that human-AI collaboration can enable the creation of new value and innovation by combining the strengths of both. AI has the potential to augment our cognitive abilities and enhance our decision-making processes. The metaphor of a co-pilot may be applied here in that the human pilot still needs to know the destination, but AI can help map out the flight plan and assist with automating certain repetitive and mechanical tasks. Together we will be able to go farther than either could alone.

One reason the human element and oversight in the "human-in-the-loop" model will still be necessary is how machine learning algorithms such as ChatGPT-3 and Bard operate. In generating a response to a prompt, the algorithm pulls from the whole of the dataset it has been trained on and can produce misleading or false citations and information. For instance, asking for a summary of the book *Algorithmic Culture* (2021) with a summary and quotations cited in APA 7th edition style will return information from the book published by Lextington Books but fabricate quotations and citations. See the following response:

The argument put forth by Hristova, Hong, and Slack in their article "Algorithmic Culture" (2021) is that algorithms have become a defining feature of contemporary culture and have significant implications for society. The authors state that algorithms "shape our understanding of the world, shape our decision-making processes, and shape our social and cultural experiences" (Hristova, Hong, & Slack, 2021, p. 1).

To support this argument, the authors provide several examples of how algorithms are used in various aspects of society, such as in news media, entertainment, and advertising. They also examine the ways in which algorithms can perpetuate existing inequalities and contribute to the spread of false information.

In their conclusion, Hristova, Hong, and Slack assert that it is important to critically examine the role of algorithms in our culture and to consider their potential impacts on society. They call for "a more nuanced understanding of the ways in which algorithms shape our cultural and social experiences" (Hristova, Hong, & Slack, 2021, p. 7).

Here is an example citation of this article in APA style:

Hristova, L., Hong, S., & Slack, R. (2021). Algorithmic culture. Cultural Studies, 35(3), 1-9.

Quotations:

- "Algorithms shape our understanding of the world, shape our decision-making processes, and shape our social and cultural experiences" (Hristova, Hong, & Slack, 2021, p. 1).
- "It is important to critically examine the role of algorithms in our culture and to consider their potential impacts on society" (Hristova, Hong, & Slack, 2021, p. 7).

The citation is from a real journal published by Routledge (*Culture Studies*) but searching for the volume and number will result in the realization that it does not actually exist. Furthermore, if the same prompt is run again indicating that it is a book, and not an article, ChatGPT-3 will falsely claim Routledge published the work. Given that the dataset used was the entirety of freely accessible information on the Internet up until 2021, information kept behind paywalls may trigger the algorithm to take the title and other information from one source and combine with another to arrive at what it believes is the intended request. The recursive machine learning algorithm performs sentiment analysis to generate responses hence the impossibility of accurate citations. The functionality that leads to its greatest strength, ironically, is also its greatest weakness for use in academic research. For while the information may, technically, be factually accurate and reflect the sentiment of a given author, quotations, specific information, facts, and citations may be inaccurate. The "human-in-the-loop" model will be necessary, not only for fact checking, but ensuring algorithmic culture does not unintentionally lead us down the wrong path. While the new capabilities to enhance productivity may be intoxicating, we must resist the temptation to take our hands off of the wheel, to borrow a popular idiom. On the other hand, early use for the purposes of research have been promising and we should note that this generative technology is in its infancy and will improve and advance rapidly. For instance, Aydın and Karaarslan (2022) used it to generate a literature review for the topic "Digital Twin in Healthcare," and noted how: "The future academic publishing process will require less human effort, which in turn will allow academics to focus on their studies."

Further considerations of the human-AI partnership involve how each party understands the other. As Cai et al (2019) argue, AI systems must be able to understand human goals, desires, and values, and human users must be able to understand the capabilities and limitations of the AI systems they are collaborating with. Afterall, humans are at the center of human-AI collaboration. As Knop et al (2022) also point out, the human element is critical in human-AI collaboration because it provides the context, creativity, and critical thinking that are essential to the success of the collaboration. Humans bring unique perspectives and experiences to the collaboration, which can be leveraged to generate new insights and innovations.

One of the ways humans are able to do so is through empathy. In the age of AI, empathy is more important than ever and cultivating it should be a major goal for educators. As Anagnostou et al (2022) argue, empathy is the key to building trust between humans and AI, and it is essential for ensuring that AI systems are aligned with human values and ethics. Empathy enables humans to understand and relate to the experiences of others and see other viewpoints, allowing us to arrive at new solutions and ideas. The ability is crucial in the development of AI that can understand and respond to human emotions and needs, while exercising empathy is central to understanding the human experience.

Finally, perhaps the most important human qualities that allow us to make creative leaps, innovate and create are those that are illogical. In fact, the illogical, irrational, and emotional aspects of human cognition play a crucial role in the creative process (Damasio, 1998; Damasio, 2001). Recent neuroscience research provides insights into how the mind works. The human brain operates within a dynamic interplay of stability and chaos as it processes and interprets information from the external world. As individuals engage in various activities, such as reading or conversing with others, the brain transitions from one semi-stable state to another, however, prior to reaching stability, the brain undergoes a chaotic process characterized by seemingly random and unpredictable fluctuations (Hamzelou, 2023). These seemingly flawed traits provide the unique flexibility and adaptability required to generate novel and innovative ideas. However, AI systems, even stochastic, while they may be capable of advanced pattern recognition and data analysis, lack the same capacity for emotional and intuitive reasoning, limiting their ability to reconcile competing beliefs and make complex judgments that are central to human creativity (Carvalho, Pereira, & Cardoso, 2019). The capacity of humans to deal with cognitive dissonance and reconcile competing, irrational, and even conflicting information, belief systems, emotions, and ideas has, paradoxically, future-proofed us.

REFERENCES

Aabid, A., Parveez, B., Parveen, N., Khan, S. A., & Shabbir, O. (2022). A Case Study of Unmanned Aerial Vehicle (Drone) Technology and Its Applications in the COVID-19 Pandemic. *J. Mech. Eng. Res. Dev*, *45*, 70–77.

Abdelwahab, H. R., Rauf, A., & Chen, D. (2022). Business students' perceptions of Dutch higher educational institutions in preparing them for artificial intelligence work environments. *Industry and Higher Education*, 09504222221087614.

Accenture. (2018). *The Rise of Artificial Intelligence: Opportunities and Challenges.* Accenture.

Agarwal, A., & Karahanna, E. (2010). Time flies when you're having fun: Cognitive absorption and beliefs about information technology usage. *Management Information Systems Quarterly*, *34*(4), 709–725.

Akour, M., & Alenezi, M. (2022). Higher Education Future in the Era of Digital Transformation. *Education Sciences*, *12*(11), 784. doi:10.3390/educsci12110784

Alam, A. (2021, November). Possibilities and apprehensions in the landscape of artificial intelligence in education. In *2021 International Conference on Computational Intelligence and Computing Applications (ICCICA)* (pp. 1-8). IEEE. 10.1109/ICCICA52458.2021.9697272

Alam, A. (2022). Employing Adaptive Learning and Intelligent Tutoring Robots for Virtual Classrooms and Smart Campuses: Reforming Education in the Age of Artificial Intelligence. In *Advanced Computing and Intelligent Technologies* (pp. 395–406). Springer. doi:10.1007/978-981-19-2980-9_32

Allen, B. (2019). Machine Learning With Deep Neural Nets Artificially Augmenting My Intelligence in a Narrow but Occasionally Superhuman Kind of Way. *Journal of the American College of Radiology, 16*(10), 1480-1481. Ali, M. & Azadeh, A. (2020). Human-AI collaboration: A review of current research and future directions. *Journal of Human-Computer Interaction*, *36*(4), 1–12. doi:10.1080/07370024.2019.1645051

Alvarado, O., & Waern, A. (2018, April). Towards algorithmic experience: Initial efforts for social media contexts. In *Proceedings of the 2018 chi conference on human factors in computing systems* (pp. 1-12). ACM. 10.1145/3173574.3173860

Anagnostou, M., Karvounidou, O., Katritzidaki, C., Kechagia, C., Melidou, K., Mpeza, E., Konstantinidis, I., Kapantai, E., Berberidis, C., Magnisalis, I., & Peristeras, V. (2022). Characteristics and challenges in the industries towards responsible AI: A systematic literature review. *Ethics and Information Technology*, *24*(3), 37. doi:10.100710676-022-09634-1

Angwin, J., Larson, J., Mattu, S., & Kirchner, L. (2016). Machine bias. In *Ethics of data and analytics* (pp. 254–264). Auerbach Publications.

Ansari, S. (2022). Recognizing the Risks of Job Automation in 2023. *HR Tech Series.* https://techrseries.com/ai-automation/recognizing-the-risks-of-job-automation-in-2023/

Ansari, T. (2022). How AI Transformed the Art World in 2022. *Analytics India Magazine (AIM).* https://analyticsindiamag.com/how-ai-transformed-the-art-world-in-2022/

Antony, J. S., Cauce, A. M., Gangone, L. M., & Nicola, T. P. (Eds.). (2022). *The College President Handbook: A Sustainable and Practical Guide for Emerging Leaders*. Harvard Education Press.

Aoun, J. E. (2017). *Robot-proof: higher education in the age of artificial intelligence*. MIT press. doi:10.7551/mitpress/11456.001.0001

AryaN. (2022). Industrial Revolution 4.0: Landscaping Trajectories of Technology–Humanity Interface. *Available at* SSRN 4119506. doi:10.2139/ssrn.4119506

Association of American Universities. (2021). *Pandemic and Its Impact on Higher Education*. Association of American Universities.

Autor, D., & Dorn, D. (2013). The growth of low-skill service jobs and the polarization of the US labor market. *The American Economic Review*, *103*(5), 1553–1597. doi:10.1257/aer.103.5.1553

AydınÖ.KaraarslanE. (2022). OpenAI ChatGPT generated literature review: Digital twin in healthcare. SSRN 4308687. doi:10.2139/ssrn.4308687

Babitha, M. M., & Sushma, C. (2022). Trends of Artificial Intelligence for online exams in education. *International journal of Early Childhood special. Education*, *14*(01), 2457–2463.

Bailey, L. W. (2019). New technology for the classroom: Mobile devices, artificial intelligence, tutoring systems, and robotics. In *Educational Technology and the new world of persistent learning* (pp. 1–11). IGI Global. doi:10.4018/978-1-5225-6361-7.ch001

Bar-On, R., Brown, J. M., Kirkcaldy, B. D., & Thome, E. P. (2000). Emotional expression and implications for occupational stress; an application of the Emotional Quotient Inventory (EQ-i). *Personality and Individual Differences*, *28*(6), 1107–1118. doi:10.1016/S0191-8869(99)00160-9

Barchard, K. A. (2003). Does emotional intelligence assist in the prediction of academic success? *Educational and Psychological Measurement*, *63*(5), 840–858. doi:10.1177/0013164403251333

Bates, T., Cobo, C., Mariño, O., & Wheeler, S. (2020). Can artificial intelligence transform higher education? *International Journal of Educational Technology in Higher Education*, *17*(1), 1–12. doi:10.118641239-020-00218-x

Baumeister, R. F., & Leary, M. R. (1995). The need to belong: Desire for interpersonal attachments as a fundamental human motivation. *Psychological Bulletin*, *117*(3), 497–529. doi:10.1037/0033-2909.117.3.497 PMID:7777651

Berry, D. M. (2022). AI, Ethics, and Digital Humanities. *The Bloomsbury Handbook to the Digital Humanities*, 445.

Birkle, C. (2022). "I, Robot": Artificial Intelligence and Fears of the Posthuman. *Artificial Intelligence and Human Enhancement: Affirmative and Critical Approaches in the Humanities*, *21*, 237–260. doi:10.1515/9783110770216-014

Boden, M. A. (2004). *The Creative Mind: Myths and Mechanisms* (2nd ed.). Psychology Press. doi:10.4324/9780203508527

Bogost, I. (2017). *Play Anything: The Pleasure of Limits, the Uses of Boredom, and the Secret of Games.* WW Norton & Company.

Bosma, R. J., Capucci, P. L., de Kerckhove, D., Neidich, W., & Cipolletta, L. G. (2022). *HumaniTies and Artificial Intelligence.*

Braidwood, R. J. (1960). The agricultural revolution. *Scientific American, 203*(3), 130–152. doi:10.10 38cientificamerican0960-130 PMID:13803774

Brem, A., Viardot, E., & Nylund, P. A. (2021). Implications of the coronavirus (COVID-19) outbreak for innovation: Which technologies will improve our lives? *Technological Forecasting and Social Change, 163*, 120451. doi:10.1016/j.techfore.2020.120451 PMID:33191956

Broo, D. G., Kaynak, O., & Sait, S. M. (2022). Rethinking engineering education at the age of industry 5.0. *Journal of Industrial Information Integration, 25*, 100311. doi:10.1016/j.jii.2021.100311

Brouwer, W. (2018). *Algorithmic Culture.* Palgrave Macmillan.

Brown, P., & Gerbarg, P. L. (2015). Non-pharmacologic treatments for psychiatric conditions: Yoga and mindfulness meditation. *Psychiatric Annals, 45*(7), 434–439. doi:10.3928/00485713-20150610-05

Bryson, J. B., & Morrison, R. G. (1994). What should the learning sciences be about? In D. Schifter & B. J. Balamuth (Eds.), *Learner-centered Theory and Practice in Distance Education* (pp. 17–41). Routledge.

Budescu, D. V., Broomell, S. B., & Por, H. H. (2009). Improving Communication of Uncertainty in Forecasts of Natural Hazards. Wea. *Forecasting, 24,* 1140-1150. doi: . doi:10.1175/2009wfo2063.1

Bühler, M. M., Jelinek, T., & Nübel, K. (2022). Training and Preparing Tomorrow's Workforce for the Fourth Industrial Revolution. *Education Sciences, 12*(11), 782.

Burbules, N. C., Fan, G., & Repp, P. (2020). Five trends of education and technology in a sustainable future. *Geography and Sustainability, 1*(2), 93–97. doi:10.1016/j.geosus.2020.05.001

Cabrera, D., & Sádaba, C. (2017). Emotional intelligence and academic achievement: The role of emotional self-efficacy and emotion regulation strategies. *Psicothema, 29*(3), 294–301.

Cai, C. J., Winter, S., Steiner, D., Wilcox, L., & Terry, M. (2019). "Hello AI": uncovering the onboarding needs of medical practitioners for human-AI collaborative decision-making. *Proceedings of the ACM on Human-computer Interaction, 3*(CSCW), (pp. 1-24). ACM. 10.1145/3359206

Cameron, M., Fogarty-Perry, B., & Piercy, G. (2022). The impacts of the COVID-19 pandemic on higher education students in New Zealand. *Journal of Open. Flexible and Distance Learning, 26*(1), 42–62. doi:10.61468/jofdl.v26i1.515

Carroll, J. M. (2000). *Making use: Scenario-based design of human-computer interactions.* MIT press.

Carvalho, D. V., Pereira, E. M., & Cardoso, J. S. (2019). Machine learning interpretability: A survey on methods and metrics. *Electronics (Basel), 8*(8), 832. doi:10.3390/electronics8080832

Carvalho, L., Martinez-Maldonado, R., Tsai, Y. S., Markauskaite, L., & De Laat, M. (2022). How can we design for learning in an AI world? *Computers and Education: Artificial Intelligence*, *3*, 100053. doi:10.1016/j.caeai.2022.100053

Castells, M. (2010). The Information Age. *Media Studies. REAd (Porto Alegre)*, *2*(7), 152.

Cath, C., Wachter, S., Mittelstadt, B., Taddeo, M., & Floridi, L. (2018). Artificial intelligence and the 'good society': The US, EU, and UK approach. *Science and Engineering Ethics*, *24*, 505–528. PMID:28353045

Chen, Y., Jensen, S., Albert, L. J., Gupta, S., & Lee, T. (2023). Artificial intelligence (AI) student assistants in the classroom: Designing chatbots to support student success. *Information Systems Frontiers*, *25*(1), 161-182.

Chu, M. (2018). The role of emotions in creative problem solving. Emotion Review, 10(3), 229–237

Ciolacu, M. I., Mihailescu, B., Rachbauer, T., Hansen, C., Amza, C. G., & Svasta, P. (2023). Fostering Engineering Education 4.0 Paradigm Facing the Pandemic and VUCA World. *Procedia Computer Science*, *217*, 177–186. doi:10.1016/j.procs.2022.12.213

Clément, E. (2022). Successful Solution Discovery and Cognitive Flexibility. *Cognitive Flexibility: The Cornerstone of Learning*, (pp. 113-142). IEEE.

Cooper, T. (2022). *Ancestors and Algorithms: Ethnocomputing AI with African & African Diasporic Heritage.* [Doctoral dissertation, University of Michigan].

Côté, A. M., Togay, G., & Su, Z. (2022). The Impact of Artificial Intelligence on Higher Education: Transformations, Challenges and Opportunities. *Challenges and Opportunities.* Europe PMC.

Cremer, C. Z. (2021). Deep limitations? Examining expert disagreement over deep learning. *Progress in Artificial Intelligence*, *10*(4), 449–464. doi:10.100713748-021-00239-1

Crossley, M., & Tikly, L. (2004). Postcolonial perspectives and comparative and international research in education: A critical introduction. *Comparative education, 40*(2), 147-156.

Damasio, A. R. (1998). Emotion in the perspective of an integrated nervous system. *Brain Research. Brain Research Reviews*, *26*(2-3), 83–86. doi:10.1016/S0165-0173(97)00064-7 PMID:9651488

Damasio, A. R. (2001). Emotion and the human brain. *Annals of the New York Academy of Sciences*, *935*(1), 101–106. doi:10.1111/j.1749-6632.2001.tb03475.x PMID:11411179

De Vries, J. (1994). The industrial revolution and the industrious revolution. *The Journal of Economic History*, *54*(2), 249–270. doi:10.1017/S0022050700014467

Deane, P. M. (1979). *The first industrial revolution.* Cambridge University Press.

DelSignore, P. (2022). The New Age of Creative AI Began in 2022. *Medium.* https://medium.com/predict/the-new-age-of-creative-ai-began-in-2022-ece07bb93350

Detweiler, R. A. (2021). *The Evidence Liberal Arts Needs: Lives of Consequence, Inquiry, and Accomplishment.* MIT Press. doi:10.7551/mitpress/13954.001.0001

Diakopoulos, N. (2014). *Algorithmic accountability reporting: On the investigation of black boxes.* Columbia University.

Diakopoulos, N. (2019). *Automating the news: How algorithms are rewriting the media.* Harvard University Press. doi:10.4159/9780674239302

Doi, C., Lucky, S., & Rubin, J. E. (2022). Open educational resources in the time of COVID-19: Two case studies of open video design in the remote learning environment. *KULA, 6*(1), 1–15.

Edwards, B. I., & Cheok, A. D. (2018). Why not robot teachers: Artificial intelligence for addressing teacher shortage. *Applied Artificial Intelligence, 32*(4), 345–360. doi:10.1080/08839514.2018.1464286

Eger, J. (2022). *Untold Power: The Marriage of Art and Technology.* Common Ground Research Networks. doi:10.18848/978-0-949313-04-1/CGP

El Emam, K., Jonker, E., & Wagner, C. (2012). Protecting privacy in secondary use of health data: An exploration of global data access policies. *Journal of Medical Internet Research, 14*(2), e48. doi:10.2196/jmir.1869 PMID:22547528

Elmoutanna, N. & Moti, N. (2022). Soft skills from university to workplace: A literature review. *International Journal of Accounting, Finance, Auditing, Management and Economics, 3*(5-1), 187-198.

Ermakova, E. P., & Frolova, E. E. (2021). Using Artificial Intelligence in Dispute Resolution. In *Smart Technologies for the Digitisation of Industry: Entrepreneurial Environment* (pp. 131–142). Springer Singapore.

Eslami, M., Rickman, A., Vaccaro, K., Aleyasen, A., Vuong, A., Karahalios, K., & Sandvig, C. (2015, April). " I always assumed that I wasn't really that close to [her]" Reasoning about Invisible Algorithms in News Feeds. In *Proceedings of the 33rd annual ACM conference on human factors in computing systems* (pp. 153-162).

Facer, K. (2011). *Learning futures: Education, technology and social change.* Routledge. doi:10.4324/9780203817308

Feezell, J. T., Wagner, J. K., & Conroy, M. (2021). Exploring the effects of algorithm-driven news sources on political behavior and polarization. *Computers in Human Behavior, 116*, 106626. doi:10.1016/j.chb.2020.106626

Flanagan, M. (2017). *Critical play: Radical Game Design.* MIT press.

Francke, E., & Alexander, B. (2019). The potential influence of artificial intelligence on plagiarism a higher education perspective. In *Proc European Conference on the Impact of Artificial Intelligence and Robotics.* EM Normandie Business School.

Frederick, J., & Wolff-Eisenberg, C. (2020). *Academic library strategy and budgeting during the COVID-19 pandemic.*

Frey, C. B., & Osborne, M. A. (2017). The future of employment: How susceptible are jobs to computerisation? *Technological Forecasting and Social Change, 114*, 254–280. doi:10.1016/j.techfore.2016.08.019

Fry, H. (2018). *Hello World: Being Human in the Age of Algorithms.* W.W. Norton & Company.

Galloway, A. R. (2004). *Gaming: Essays on Algorithmic Culture*. University of Minnesota Press. Garzón, J. (2021). An overview of twenty-five years of augmented reality in education. *Multimodal Technologies and Interaction*, *5*(7), 37.

Gentner, D., & Rattermann, M. J. (1991). Language and the Career of Similarity. In S. Vosniadou & A. Ortony (Eds.), *Similarity and Analogical Reasoning* (pp. 199–241). Cambridge University Press.

Gikas, J., & Grant, M. M. (2013). Mobile computing devices in higher education: Student perspectives on learning with cellphones, smartphones & social media. *The Internet and Higher Education*, *19*, 18–26. doi:10.1016/j.iheduc.2013.06.002

Gillespie, T. (2014). The relevance of algorithms. *Media technologies: Essays on communication, materiality, and society, 167*(2014), 167.

Goleman, D. (2001). Emotional intelligence: Issues in paradigm building. *The emotionally intelligent workplace, 13*, 26.

González-Pérez, L. I., & Ramírez-Montoya, M. S. (2022). Components of Education 4.0 in 21st century skills frameworks: Systematic review. *Sustainability (Basel)*, *14*(3), 1493. doi:10.3390u14031493

Gran, A. B., Booth, P., & Bucher, T. (2021). To be or not to be algorithm aware: A question of a new digital divide? *Information Communication and Society*, *24*(12), 1779–1796. doi:10.1080/1369118X.2020.1736124

Greenstein, L. M. (2012). *Assessing 21st century skills: A guide to evaluating mastery and authentic learning*. Corwin Press.

Hamzelou, J. (2023). Neuroscientists listened in on people's brains for a week. They found order and chaos. *MIT Technology Review*. https://www-technologyreview-com.cdn.ampproject.org/c/s/www.technologyreview.com/2023/02/07/1067951/brains-week-order-chaos/amp/)

Hansen, U. J. (2021). *The Future of Smart: How our Education System Needs to Change to Help All Young People Thrive*.

HazuchaB. (2022). Artificial Intelligence and Cultural Production: Possible Impacts on Creativity and Copyright Law. SSRN 4028106. doi:10.2139/ssrn.4028106

He, W., Zhang, Z. J., & Li, W. (2021). Information technology solutions, challenges, and suggestions for tackling the COVID-19 pandemic. *International Journal of Information Management*, *57*, 102287. doi:10.1016/j.ijinfomgt.2020.102287 PMID:33318721

Heinisch, B., Oswald, K., Weißpflug, M., Shuttleworth, S., & Belknap, G. (2021). Citizen humanities. *The Science of Citizen Science*, 97.

Hill, S., Yagi, T., & Yamash'ta, S. (2022). Where Did Humanity Go? In *The Kyoto Post-COVID Manifesto For Global Economics* (pp. 319–332). Springer. doi:10.1007/978-981-16-8566-8_19

Holzinger, A., Keiblinger, K., Holub, P., Zatloukal, K., & Müller, H. (2023). AI for Life: Trends in Artificial Intelligence for Biotechnology. *New Biotechnology*, *74*, 16–24. doi:10.1016/j.nbt.2023.02.001 PMID:36754147

Hommel, B. E., Ruppel, R., & Zacher, H. (2022). Assessment of cognitive flexibility in personnel selection: Validity and acceptance of a gamified version of the Wisconsin Card Sorting Test. *International Journal of Selection and Assessment, 30*(1), 126–144. doi:10.1111/ijsa.12362

Huang, Z. (2022). Introducing Neuro-Symbolic Artificial Intelligence to Humanities and Social Sciences: Why Is It Possible and What Can Be Done? *TEM Journal, 11*(4), 1863–1870. doi:10.18421/TEM114-54

Hunkenschroer, A. L., & Luetge, C. (2022). Ethics of AI-enabled recruiting and selection: A review and research agenda. *Journal of Business Ethics, 178*(4), 977–1007. doi:10.100710551-022-05049-6

Hutson, J., Jeevanjee, T., Vander Graaf, V., Lively, J., Weber, J., Weir, G., & Edele, S. (2022). Artificial Intelligence and the Disruption of Higher Education: Strategies for Integrations across Disciplines. *Creative Education, 13*(12), 3953–3980. doi:10.4236/ce.2022.1312253

Hutson, J., & Olsen, T. (2022). Virtual Reality and Learning: A Case Study of Experiential Pedagogy in Art History. *Journal of Intelligent Learning Systems and Applications.* https://www.scirp.org/journal/paperinformation.aspx?paperid=120925

Jones, S. (1995). *Understanding community in the information age.* Sage.

Jotterand, F., & Bosco, C. (2020). Keeping the "Human in the Loop" in the Age of Artificial Intelligence. *Science and Engineering Ethics, 26*(5), 2455–2460. doi:10.100711948-020-00241-1 PMID:32643058

Kaliraj, P., & Devi, T. (2023). Innovating Higher Education 4.0 in the Era of Industry 4.0. In Industry 4.0 Technologies for Education (pp. 1-10). Auerbach Publications.

Kang, E. S., & Lee, J. M. (2022). Artificial Intelligence Liberal Arts Curriculum Design for Non-Computer Majors. *Journal of Digital Contents Society, 23*(1), 57–66. doi:10.9728/dcs.2022.23.1.57

Kang, S. (2022). Surrogate Humanity: Resistant Art Practices under Technoliberalism. *Media-N, 18*(1), 153–156. doi:10.21900/j.median.v18i1.859

Keating, J., & Nourbakhsh, I. (2018). Teaching artificial intelligence and humanity. *Communications of the ACM, 61*(2), 29–32. doi:10.1145/3104986

Kellner, D., & Gennaro, S. (2022). Critical Theory and the Transformation of Education in the New Millennium. In *The Palgrave Handbook on Critical Theories of Education* (pp. 21–45). Springer International Publishing. doi:10.1007/978-3-030-86343-2_2

Kerridge, E. (2013). *The agricultural revolution.* Routledge. doi:10.4324/9781315019888

Khan, W., Ghazanfar, M. A., Azam, M. A., Karami, A., Alyoubi, K. H., & Alfakeeh, A. S. (2020). Stock market prediction using machine learning classifiers and social media [news]. *Journal of Ambient Intelligence and Humanized Computing*, 1–24.

Knop, M., Weber, S., Mueller, M., & Niehaves, B. (2022). Human factors and technological characteristics influencing the interaction of medical professionals with artificial intelligence–enabled clinical decision support systems: Literature review. *JMIR Human Factors, 9*(1), e28639. doi:10.2196/28639 PMID:35323118

Kobayashi, M., & Takeda, K. (2000). Information retrieval on the web. *ACM Computing Surveys, 32*(2), 144–173. doi:10.1145/358923.358934

Kordzadeh, N., & Ghasemaghaei, M. (2022). Algorithmic bias: Review, synthesis, and future research directions. *European Journal of Information Systems, 31*(3), 388–409. doi:10.1080/0960085X.2021.1927212

Kouzes, J. M., & Posner, B. Z. (2007). *The leadership challenge*. Wiley.

Krajcik, J., Schneider, B., Miller, E. A., Chen, I. C., Bradford, L., Baker, Q., Bartz, K., Miller, C., Li, T., Codere, S., & Peek-Brown, D. (2023). Assessing the effect of project-based learning on science learning in elementary schools. *American Educational Research Journal, 60*(1), 70–102. doi:10.3102/00028312221129247

Krause, S. (2000). "Among the Greatest Benefactors of Mankind": What the Success of Chalkboards Tells Us about the Future of Computers in the Classroom. *The Journal of the Midwest Modern Language Association, 33*(2), 6–16. doi:10.2307/1315198

Lee, K. J. (2022). Adaptive expertise, career adaptability, and career success of R&D personnel. *Technology Analysis and Strategic Management*, 1–13. doi:10.1080/09537325.2022.2053517

Lepri, B., Oliver, N., Letouzé, E., Pentland, A., & Vinck, P. (2018). Fair, transparent, and accountable algorithmic decision-making processes: The premise, the proposed solutions, and the open challenges. *Philosophy & Technology, 31*(4), 611–627. doi:10.100713347-017-0279-x

Li, S., & Gu, X. (2023). A Risk Framework for Human-centered Artificial Intelligence in Education. *Journal of Educational Technology & Society, 26*(1), 187–202.

Littman, M. L., Ajunwa, I., Berger, G., Boutilier, C., Currie, M., Doshi-Velez, F., & Walsh, T. (2022). Gathering strength, gathering storms: The one hundred year study on artificial intelligence (AI100) 2021 study panel report. *arXiv preprint arXiv:2210.15767.*

Liu, X. M., & Murphy, D. (2020). A Multi-Faceted Approach for Trustworthy AI in Cybersecurity. *Journal of Strategic Innovation & Sustainability, 15*(6).

Liu, Y., & Martindale, T. (2011). The new cognitive psychology of creativity. *Journal of the Creative Process, 11*(1), 1–10.

Loughlin, M., & Copeland, S. M. (2021). Humans, machines and decisions: Clinical reasoning in the age of artificial intelligence, evidence-based medicine and Covid-19. *Journal of Evaluation in Clinical Practice, 27*(3), 475–477. doi:10.1111/jep.13572 PMID:33890703

Ma, Y., & Siau, K. L. (2018). Artificial intelligence impacts on higher education. *MWAIS Proceedings, 42*(5), 1-5.

Mabe, K., & Bwalya, K. J. (2022). Critical soft skills for information and knowledge management practitioners in the fourth industrial revolution. *South African Journal of Information Management, 24*(1), 1–11. doi:10.4102ajim.v24i1.1519

Magness, J., & Mitchell, M. M. (2022). Religious Studies & the Imagined Boundaries of the Humanities. *Daedalus, 151*(3), 166–179. doi:10.1162/daed_a_01936

Martin, S. M. (2019). *Artificial intelligence, mixed reality, and the redefinition of the classroom*. Rowman & Littlefield.

Massey, J. W. (2020). *The Challenges of Neoliberalism to the Democratic Promises of Higher Education* [Doctoral dissertation, The University of North Carolina at Greensboro].

Mayer, J. D., & Salovey, P. (1997). What is emotional intelligence? In P. Salovey & D. Sluyter (Eds.), *Emotional Development and Emotional Intelligence: Implications for Educators* (pp. 3–31). Basic Books.

McPherson, S. S. (2009). *Tim Berners-Lee: Inventor of the World Wide Web*. Twenty-First Century Books.

Messerli, P., Murniningtyas, E., Eloundou-Enyegue, P., Foli, E. G., Furman, E., Glassman, A., & van Ypersele, J. P. (2019). *Global sustainable development report 2019: the future is now–science for achieving sustainable development.*

Miguel, P. M. D., De-Pablos-Heredero, C., Montes, J. L., & García, A. (2022). Impact of Dynamic Capabilities on Customer Satisfaction through Digital Transformation in the Automotive Sector. *Sustainability (Basel)*, *14*(8), 4772. doi:10.3390u14084772

Milton, J., & Al-Busaidi, A. (2023). New Role of Leadership in AI Era: Educational Sector. In *SHS Web of Conferences* (*Vol. 156*, p. 09005). EDP Sciences.

Minoli, D. (2013). *Building the internet of things with IPv6 and MIPv6: The evolving world of M2M communications*. John Wiley & Sons. doi:10.1002/9781118647059

Mishra, L., Gupta, T., & Shree, A. (2020). Online teaching-learning in higher education during lockdown period of COVID-19 pandemic. *International Journal of Educational Research Open*, *1*, 100012. doi:10.1016/j.ijedro.2020.100012 PMID:35059663

Mohzan, M. A. M., Hassan, N., & Abd Halil, N. (2013). The influence of emotional intelligence on academic achievement. *Procedia: Social and Behavioral Sciences*, *90*, 303–312. doi:10.1016/j.sbspro.2013.07.095

Mok, A., & Zinkula, J. (2023). ChatGPT may be coming for our jobs. Here are the 10 roles that AI is most likely to replace. *Insider*. https://www.businessinsider.com/chatgpt-jobs-at-risk-replacement-artificial-intelligence-ai-labor-trends-2023-02?amp=#amp_tf=From%20%251%24s&aoh=16754252090476&csi=0&referrer=https%3A%2F%2Fwww.google.com

Monett, D., & Lewis, C. W. (2018). Getting clarity by defining artificial intelligence—A survey. In *Philosophy and theory of artificial intelligence 2017* (pp. 212–214). Springer International Publishing. doi:10.1007/978-3-319-96448-5_21

Montenegro, L. D., & Young, M. N. (2020, September). Operational challenges in the food industry and supply chain during the COVID-19 pandemic: A literature review. In *2020 7th International Conference on Frontiers of Industrial Engineering (ICFIE)* (pp. 1-5). IEEE. 10.1109/ICFIE50845.2020.9266743

Murphy, B. P. (2022). Is Lensa AI Stealing from Human Art? An Expert Explains the Controversy. *Science Alert*. https://www-sciencealert-com.cdn.ampproject.org/c/s/www.sciencealert.com/is-lensa-ai-stealing-from-human-art-an-expert-explains-the-controversy/amp

Nida-Rümelin, J. (2022). Digital Humanism and the Limits of Artificial Intelligence. In *Perspectives on Digital Humanism* (pp. 71–75). Springer. doi:10.1007/978-3-030-86144-5_10

Omolara, A. E., Alabdulatif, A., Abiodun, O. I., Alawida, M., Alabdulatif, A., & Arshad, H. (2022). The internet of things security: A survey encompassing unexplored areas and new insights. *Computers & Security*, *112*, 102494. doi:10.1016/j.cose.2021.102494

Ostherr, K. (2020). Artificial intelligence and medical humanities. *The Journal of Medical Humanities*, 1–22. PMID:32654043

Palladino, J., & Shepard, L. A. (2023). Authentic Assessment Embedded in Project-Based Learning. *Schools of Opportunity: 10 Research-Based Models for Creating Equity*, *67*.

Pan, Y. (2016). Heading toward artificial intelligence 2.0. *Engineering (Beijing)*, *2*(4), 409–413. doi:10.1016/J.ENG.2016.04.018

Patel, S., Hamdan, S., & Donahue, S. (2022). Optimising telemedicine in ophthalmology during the COVID-19 pandemic. *Journal of Telemedicine and Telecare*, *28*(7), 498–501. doi:10.1177/1357633X20949796 PMID:32799736

Pavlik, J. V. (2023). Collaborating With ChatGPT: Considering the Implications of Generative Artificial Intelligence for Journalism and Media Education. *Journalism & Mass Communication Educator*.

Peng, J., Sridhar, S., Siefker-Radtke, A. O., Selvarajah, S., & Jiang, D. M. (2022). Targeting the FGFR pathway in urothelial carcinoma: The future is now. *Current Treatment Options in Oncology*, *23*(9), 1269–1287. doi:10.100711864-022-01009-4 PMID:35962938

Petrilli, M. J. (2008). Wikipedia or wickedpedia? Assessing the online encyclopedia's impact on K-12 education. *Education Next*, *8*(2), 87–88.

Powers, E. (2017). My news feed is filtered? Awareness of news personalization among college students. *Digital Journalism (Abingdon, England)*, *5*(10), 1315–1335. doi:10.1080/21670811.2017.1286943

Preiss, D. D. (2022). Metacognition, Mind Wandering, and Cognitive Flexibility: Understanding Creativity. *Journal of Intelligence*, *10*(3), 69. doi:10.3390/jintelligence10030069 PMID:36135610

Rajaram, K. (2023). Cultural Intelligence in Teaching and Learning. In *Learning Intelligence: Innovative and Digital Transformative Learning Strategies: Cultural and Social Engineering Perspectives* (pp. 57–118). Springer Nature Singapore. doi:10.1007/978-981-19-9201-8_2

Rensfeldt, A. B., & Rahm, L. (2023). Automating Teacher Work? A History of the Politics of Automation and Artificial Intelligence in Education. *Postdigital Science and Education*, *5*(1), 25–43. doi:10.100742438-022-00344-x

Rof, A., Bikfalvi, A., & Marques, P. (2022). Pandemic-accelerated digital transformation of a born digital higher education institution. *Journal of Educational Technology & Society*, *25*(1), 124–141.

Roll, I., & Wylie, R. (2016). Evolution and revolution in artificial intelligence in education. *International Journal of Artificial Intelligence in Education*, *26*(2), 582–599. doi:10.100740593-016-0110-3

Russell, S. (2022). Artificial Intelligence and the Problem of Control. *Perspectives on Digital Humanism*, *19*.

Saltelli, A., Ratto, M., Andres, T., Campolongo, F., Cariboni, J., Gatelli, D., & Tarantola, S. (2008). Introduction to sensitivity analysis. *Global sensitivity analysis. PRiMER: Peer-Reviewed Reports in Medical Education Research*, 1–51.

Schiff, D. (2022). Education for AI, not AI for Education: The role of education and ethics in national AI policy strategies. *International Journal of Artificial Intelligence in Education*, *32*(3), 527–563. doi:10.100740593-021-00270-2

Schwab, K. (2017). *The Fourth Industrial Revolution*. Currency.

Schwartz, H. A., & Walden, L. L. (2010). Theoretical models of information systems. In J. G. Birtch (Ed.), *Handbook of Research on Information Systems* (pp. 9–32). IGI Global.

Scripter, L. (2022). Meaningful Lives in an Age of Artificial Intelligence: A Reply to Danaher. *Science and Engineering Ethics*, *28*(1), 1–9. doi:10.100711948-021-00349-y PMID:35094156

Sharma, U., Tomar, P., Bhardwaj, H., & Sakalle, A. (2021). Artificial intelligence and its implications in education. In Impact of AI Technologies on Teaching, Learning, and Research in Higher Education (pp. 222-235). IGI Global. doi:10.4018/978-1-7998-4763-2.ch014

Sherry, B. (2022). 3 Limits to Artificial Intelligence's Creativity (and How to Solve Them): Here's what you need to know about harnessing A.I. technology to be more creative. *Inc.* https://www.inc.com/ben-sherry/3-limits-to-artificial-intelligences-creativity-and-how-to-solve-them.html

Siakalli, M., Mousoulidou, M., Christodoulou, A., Savvidou, A., & Kouppa, K. (2022). Secondary Education and COVID-19. *Encyclopedia*, *2*(1), 409–427. doi:10.3390/encyclopedia2010025

Singh, J., Steele, K., & Singh, L. (2021). Combining the best of online and face-to-face learning: Hybrid and blended learning approach for COVID-19, post vaccine, & post-pandemic world. *Journal of Educational Technology Systems*, *50*(2), 140–171. doi:10.1177/00472395211047865

Sternberg, R. J. (2022). Time bomb: How the Western conception of intelligence is taking down humanity. In *Intelligence in Context* (pp. 393–411). Palgrave Macmillan. doi:10.1007/978-3-030-92798-1_16

Tegmark, M. (2018). *Life 3.0: Being human in the age of artificial intelligence*. Vintage.

Ter Beek, M., Wopereis, I., & Schildkamp, K. (2022). Don't Wait, Innovate! Preparing Students and Lecturers in Higher Education for the Future Labor Market. *Education Sciences*, *12*(9), 620. doi:10.3390/educsci12090620

Thacker, J. (2020). *The Age of AI: Artificial Intelligence and the Future of Humanity*. Zondervan.

Theobald, E. J., Hill, M. J., Tran, E., Agrawal, S., Arroyo, E. N., Behling, S., Chambwe, N., Cintrón, D. L., Cooper, J. D., Dunster, G., Grummer, J. A., Hennessey, K., Hsiao, J., Iranon, N., Jones, L. II, Jordt, H., Keller, M., Lacey, M. E., Littlefield, C. E., & Freeman, S. (2020). Active learning narrows achievement gaps for underrepresented students in undergraduate science, technology, engineering, and math. *Proceedings of the National Academy of Sciences of the United States of America*, *117*(12), 6476–6483. doi:10.1073/pnas.1916903117 PMID:32152114

Tirosh-Samuelson, H. (2018). In praise of human dignity: The humanities in the age of Big Data. *On Education, 1*(2).

Townes, M. (2012). The spread of TCP/IP: How the Internet became the Internet. *Millennium, 41*(1), 43–64. doi:10.1177/0305829812449195

Turkle, S. (1997). *Life on the Screen: Identity in the Age of the Internet.* Simon and Schuster.

Turkle, S. (2011). *Alone Together: Why We Expect More from Technology and Less from Each Other.* Basic Books.

Turkle, S. (2011). The Second Self: Computers and the Human Spirit. Simon and Schuster. Vuppalapati, C. (2021). Democratization of Artificial Intelligence for the Future of Humanity. CRC Press.

Turkle, S. (2015). *Reclaiming Conversation: The power of Talk in a Digital Age.* Penguin.

Urhan, B. (2023). Crucial Role of Soft Skills in Challenging Times: Conceptual Analysis of Leadership Skills. In Leadership Approaches in Global Hospitality and Tourism (pp. 23-39). IGI Global.

Vaishya, R., Javaid, M., Khan, I. H., & Haleem, A. (2020). Artificial Intelligence (AI) applications for COVID-19 pandemic. *Diabetes & Metabolic Syndrome, 14*(4), 337–339. doi:10.1016/j.dsx.2020.04.012 PMID:32305024

Wang, L. (2022). Exploring the relationship among teacher emotional intelligence, work engagement, teacher self-efficacy, and student academic achievement: A moderated mediation model. *Frontiers in Psychology, 12*, 810559. doi:10.3389/fpsyg.2021.810559 PMID:35046879

Wang, P. (2019). On defining artificial intelligence. *Journal of Artificial General Intelligence, 10*(2), 1–37. doi:10.2478/jagi-2019-0002

Warrier, U., John, M., & Warrier, S. (2021). Leveraging emotional intelligence competencies for sustainable development of higher education institutions in the new normal. *FIIB Business Review, 10*(1), 62–73. doi:10.1177/2319714521992032

Weise, M. R. (2020). *Long life learning: Preparing for jobs that don't even exist yet.* John Wiley & Sons.

Werthner, H., Stanger, A., Schiaffonati, V., Knees, P., Hardman, L., & Ghezzi, C. (2023). Digital Humanism: The Time Is Now. *Computer, 56*(1), 138–142. doi:10.1109/MC.2022.3219528

Wilson, S. (2003). *Information arts: intersections of art, science, and technology.* MIT press.

Wirtz, B. W., Weyerer, J. C., & Sturm, B. J. (2020). The dark sides of artificial intelligence: An integrated AI governance framework for public administration. *International Journal of Public Administration, 43*(9), 818–829. doi:10.1080/01900692.2020.1749851

Wu, Z., Ji, D., Yu, K., Zeng, X., Wu, D., & Shidujaman, M. (2021). AI creativity and the human-AI co-creation model. In *Human-Computer Interaction. Theory, Methods and Tools: Thematic Area, HCI 2021, Held as Part of the 23rd HCI International Conference, HCII 2021, Virtual Event, July 24–29, 2021* [Springer International Publishing.]. *Proceedings, 23*(Part I), 171–190.

Xing, B., & Marwala, T. (2017). Implications of the fourth industrial age on higher education. *arXiv preprint arXiv:1703.09643.*

Xu, W., Dainoff, M. J., Ge, L., & Gao, Z. (2023). Transitioning to human interaction with AI systems: New challenges and opportunities for HCI professionals to enable human-centered AI. *International Journal of Human-Computer Interaction, 39*(3), 494–518. doi:10.1080/10447318.2022.2041900

Yang, S., & Evans, C. (2019, November). Opportunities and challenges in using AI chatbots in higher education. In *Proceedings of the 2019 3rd International Conference on Education and E-Learning* (pp. 79-83). ACM. 10.1145/3371647.3371659

Yelland, N. (2005). The future is now: A review of the literature on the use of computers in early childhood education (1994-2004). [formerly AACE Journal]. *AACE Review, 13*(3), 201–232.

Yimsawat, C., Mangkhang, C., Phuwanatwichit, T., & Anansuchatkul, B. (2022). An Instructional Innovation to Strengthen Comprehensive Humanization for Higher Education Students: Soft Skills for the Digital Society. *Journal of Education Naresuan University, 24*(1), 15–24.

Zanella, A., Bui, N., Castellani, A., Vangelista, L., & Zorzi, M. (2014). Internet of things for smart cities. *IEEE Internet of Things Journal, 1*(1), 22–32. doi:10.1109/JIOT.2014.2306328

Zawacki-Richter, O., Marín, V. I., Bond, M., & Gouverneur, F. (2019). Systematic review of research on artificial intelligence applications in higher education–where are the educators? *International Journal of Educational Technology in Higher Education, 16*(1), 1–27. doi:10.118641239-019-0171-0

Zerilli, J., Knott, A., Maclaurin, J., & Gavaghan, C. (2019). Algorithmic decision-making and the control problem. *Minds and Machines, 29*(4), 555–578. doi:10.100711023-019-09513-7

Zhang, H., Lee, I., Ali, S., DiPaola, D., Cheng, Y., & Breazeal, C. (2022). Integrating ethics and career futures with technical learning to promote AI literacy for middle school students: An exploratory study. *International Journal of Artificial Intelligence in Education*, 1–35. PMID:35573722

Zhao, J., & Li, Q. (2022). Big Data–Artificial Intelligence Fusion Technology in Education in the Context of the New Crown Epidemic. *Big Data, 10*(3), 262–276. doi:10.1089/big.2021.0245 PMID:35605025

Zhu, Q., & Luo, J. (2022). Generative pre-trained transformer for design concept generation: An exploration. *Proceedings of the Design Society, 2*, 1825–1834. doi:10.1017/pds.2022.185

Chapter 2
Unleashing the Potential:
Positive Impacts of Generative AI on Learning and Teaching

John Blake
https://orcid.org/0000-0002-3150-4995
University of Aizu, Japan

ABSTRACT

Generative artificial intelligence, anchored by large language models (LLMs), is significantly altering the educational landscape. This chapter examines the impact of generative AI on education, illustrating its capability to create personalized content and transform learning environments. Despite concerns over academic dishonesty facilitated by LLMs, the chapter argues against a regressive stance and advocates for the constructive integration of AI into educational practices. By drawing on theories of learning, the chapter elucidates the pedagogical implications of generative AI and describes specific use cases in language learning, computer science, and mathematics. Highlighting both the potential and limitations of this emerging technology, the chapter posits that generative AI is not merely a disruptive force, but a revolutionary tool poised to redefine the methodologies of teaching and learning.

1. INTRODUCTION

As the frontier of artificial intelligence (AI) continues to expand, one of its subfields, generative AI, is reshaping the educational landscape by producing engaging, personalized content and transforming learning environments. Large Language Models (LLMs) that underpin generative AI employ pattern matching to generate human-like text (Tang, Chuang, & Hu, 2023) represent the latest disruptive technology impacting society (Utterback, & Acee, 2005). In the past, many educators primarily relied on essays or extended answers from students to demonstrate content mastery (Farthing, Jones, & McPhee, 1998). However, with the advent of LLMs such as ChatGPT, less scrupulous students can simply input the question as a prompt and receive a grammatically perfect and coherent answer, albeit one that may contain factual errors (Malinka et al., 2023). Reactions of educational institutions to generative AI vary

DOI: 10.4018/979-8-3693-0074-9.ch002

greatly: some have banned it, some have embraced it, while others remain undecided and leave the choice up to individual faculty (Kasneci, 2023). Previous disruptive technologies, such as calculators in mathematics, electronic dictionaries and machine translation in language learning, the internet across all subjects, are now widely accepted by educators. Considering the remarkable power of generative AI, adopting a luddite-like stance seems futile. Thus, this chapter argues in favor of embracing AI and empowering teachers and learners to utilize it effectively.

This chapter investigates the profound effects of generative AI on learning and teaching. Education is underpinned by theories of learning, which are described in relation to the pedagogic use of generative AI. Learning with AI and the creation of educational materials by AI are next addressed. Specific use cases related to language learning, computer science and mathematics education are described and discussed. Potential educational applications are then suggested. This chapter aims to provide a comprehensive understanding of the benefits of generative AI in educational settings while acknowledging its limitations. AI appears set to unleash a sea change in both the way that students learn and the way that teachers teach. Education, like most areas tends to improve incrementally, but we are now experiencing a radical innovation, which could be the harbinger of a new mode of education.

2. THEORIES OF LEARNING RELATING TO GENERATIVE AI

Teachers tend to draw eclectically from a range of techniques and strategies, often without explicitly adhering to a single underpinning theory (Moreira dos Santos, 2020). Individual teachers cultivate their own teaching philosophies, shaped by experience, context, and the unique needs of their students. These philosophies may be formally codified into a teaching philosophy statement or may be more nebulous and simply exist in the mind of the educator (Fitzmaurice & Coughlan, 2007). However, it is useful to understand the four main learning theories that have historically informed educational practices: behaviorism, cognitivism, constructivism and social constructivism (Adams, 2006; Bredo, 1997; Tomic, 1993).

2.1 Behaviourism and Cognitivism

Behaviorism was the dominant learning theory in the early to mid-20th century. Grounded in the work of psychologists like John B. Watson (Watson, 2017) and later B.F. Skinner (Todd, & Morris, 1995), behaviorism focuses on observable behaviors and the stimulus-response model where positive reinforcement leads to learning (Fisher, Piazza, & Roane, 2021). Cognitivism developed as a response to the limitations of behaviorism, shifting the focus from observable behaviors to the internal processes of the mind (Amsel, 1989). This learning theory postulates that understanding how information is received, processed, stored, and retrieved by the brain is essential for effective learning. Cognitivism provides a framework for examining how learners make sense of complex information, solve problems, and transfer knowledge, emphasizing the role of mental constructs like memory, perception, and attention in the learning process. Despite their differing perspectives on the nature of learning, behaviorism and cognitivism share some similarities, particularly in their systematic approaches to understanding learning processes. Both theories aim to develop structured methodologies for education, striving for predictability and control in learning outcomes. They both rely on empirical evidence and experimentation to validate their principles, leaning on the scientific method for credibility. Additionally, each theory places importance on the role of the environment in shaping either behavior or cognitive structures. Behaviorism emphasizes external stimuli and reinforcements as key environmental factors, while cognitivism focuses on how information from the environment is processed and organized in the mind. Thus, while behaviorism and cognitivism may differ in what they consider the primary locus of learning—external behaviors or internal mental processes—they both acknowledge the interplay between the individual and the environment in the learning process.

While behaviorism and cognitivism offer valuable insights into the mechanics of learning, either through observable behaviors or mental processes, they do not fully encapsulate the complexities of how individuals construct knowledge in a social context. This brings us to constructivism, a theory that attempts to bridge the gap by emphasizing the learner's active role in building understanding and making sense of information. Unlike behaviorism and cognitivism, constructivism places a greater focus on the ways learners interpret, filter, and transform incoming information based on their previous experiences and social interactions (Bada & Olusegun, 2015). It challenges the notion of the teacher as a mere dispenser of knowledge, advocating instead for a more collaborative and interactive educational environment.

2.2 Constructivism and Social Constructivism

Constructivism holds that learners actively construct their own understanding and knowledge of the world through hands-on experiences and reflection (Nagowah & Nagowah, 2009). This theory, often attributed to educational psychologists like Jean Piaget (Ojose, 2008) and Jerome Bruner (Rannikmäe, Holbrook, & Soobard, 2020), shifts the focus away from teachers transmitting information to learners passively receiving it. Instead, constructivism emphasizes problem-solving, critical thinking, and the application of knowledge in real-world contexts. It encourages learners to build new ideas upon the foundation of their existing knowledge and experiences, thus promoting a deeper understanding of the subject matter.

Social constructivism (Adams, 2006), an extension of constructivism, takes the theory a step further by emphasizing the importance of social interactions and cultural context in the learning process. Rooted in the work of Lev Vygotsky (1987), social constructivism argues that knowledge is constructed through dialogue, negotiation, and collaboration. This theory acknowledges that individual cognitive development is not an isolated process, but rather one deeply influenced by social and cultural factors. In a social constructivist classroom, social interaction is not just a byproduct of learning but a fundamental component of it. Learners work together to solve problems, debate ideas, and engage in cooperative projects, often employing tools and symbols from their cultural context to aid in the learning process.

These four theories offer frameworks that can guide educators in developing effective teaching methods, even as they adapt and blend these approaches in their own unique ways. It should be noted that these learning theories were developed in the pre-digital era, and so do not explicitly take into account the impact that computers, or more specifically, the software programs, may have on learning. In the pre-internet era, access to the World Wide Web was not readily available to educators. In its early days, the web was a content delivery network (Web 1.0). The web developed into a kind of social network (Web 2.0), a decentralized database (Web 3.0) and is currently transforming into a network in which interactions between users and AI are commonplace (Web 4.0) (Nath, 2022). With the rapid increase in reliance on technology, ubiquitous access to the internet via wifi and the widespread ownership of internet-enabled devices (Kukulska-Hulme, 2006), such as mobile phones, tablets and laptops; a fifth learning theory that takes into account this connectivity was born.

2.3 Connectivism

Proposed by George Siemens and Stephen Downes, connectivism (Downes, 2022) asserts that in an age of abundant information and rapidly evolving technologies, learning is less about acquiring static knowledge and more about the ability to navigate complex networks of information. Unlike traditional learning theories, which primarily focus on individual cognition or social interaction, connectivism extends the learning sphere to include the digital and networked environments. It suggests that learning occurs in various settings, not just in the individual or the classroom, but also through online communities, social media, and even through interaction with intelligent systems. Connectivism emphasizes the importance of understanding how to learn, fostering adaptability, and nurturing connections that help learners plug into ever-changing streams of information. In this context, the role of educators shifts towards facilitating these connections and helping learners cultivate skills to manage, evaluate, and integrate information from diverse sources.

The intersection of generative AI and educational theories opens new vistas for innovative learning experiences. Particularly, applying connectivism to generative AI presents a compelling way to restructure and enrich learning environments. Firstly, generative AI serves as a dynamic hub in a learner's personal learning network (Warlick, 2009). Acting as both a source and conduit for information, AI extends the learning ecosystem, linking learners to a myriad of educational resources and social connections. Secondly, machine learning algorithms can personalize the educational journey for each learner (Tetzlaff, Schmiedek, & Brod, 2021). This enhanced tailoring not only empowers learners but also significantly augments their personal learning environments. Thirdly, AI has the capability to process vast sets of data to deliver the most current and relevant information. This assists learners in making timely, well-informed decisions and effectively navigates them through complex and often overwhelming informational landscapes. Fourthly, AI's strength lies in its ability to understand and adapt to specific, real-world contexts. It can simulate or model intricate systems, thereby providing learners with problem-solving opportunities that mirror real-world challenges. This helps learners to develop skills that are both contextually sensitive and broadly applicable. Finally, the role of AI in social and lifelong learning cannot be underestimated. Generative AI can facilitate social interactions in digital learning environments through features like online community forums and real-time collaborative projects. This encourages continuous learning and adaptability, both of which are key aspects of a lifelong educational journey. In combining these various facets, generative AI acts as a multi-dimensional tool in modern education, aligning well with different learning theories to provide a holistic, dynamic, and deeply enriching learning experience.

2.4 Section Summary

Generative AI, particularly Language Learning Models (LLMs) like GPT-4, presents exciting new possibilities for education that intersect with multiple learning theories. From a behaviorist perspective, AI can provide immediate feedback and reinforcement, creating a responsive learning environment (Hall Lang, 2023) that can be tailored to individual progress. In a cognitivist framework, AI can assist in information processing, offering problem-solving exercises and dynamic examples that adapt to a learner's cognitive level. Constructivism and social constructivism find application in AI's ability to facilitate hands-on, problem-based learning experiences and social interactions. For instance, AI can simulate realistic collaborative tasks or discussions, enabling learners to construct knowledge actively in a social context. Lastly, in a connectivist view, AI serves as a node in a learner's network, providing access to a vast, interconnected web of information, and helping learners adapt to the rapidly changing landscape of knowledge and technology. Thus, generative AI can be a multifaceted tool in education, complementing and enhancing various learning theories to provide a more adaptive, personalized, and comprehensive learning experience.

3. LEARNING WITH GENERATIVE AI

In this section, I argue that LLMs, such as ChatGPT, can function as both tools and (to some extent) as tutors (Ausat et al., 2023). However, it should be noted that their primary role is as a tool, given their out-of-the-box default is as a tool rather than as a teacher. To provide an analogy, LLMs share more similarities with slide rules and calculators, than teachers of mathematics. Both slide rules and calculators help learners calculate answers to complex arithmetic problems without needing to resort to long division or multiplication, but neither of the tools helps learners understand the underlying declarative knowledge and apply the procedural knowledge (Saks, Ilves, & Noppel, 2021), and neither can correct the misuse of the tool. Getting ChatGPT to provide support in a similar way to a human teacher is much more challenging, and requires both a very specific and well-defined learning context and aims, and a knowledge of sophisticated prompt engineering (Heston, & Khun, 2023) to be able to direct the LLMs.

AI chatbots can serve as valuable resources that offer supplementary support to learners. In the context of a Japanese university, where diverse learning needs and preferences are prevalent, generative AI presents an innovative solution to address these challenges. By responding to queries, offering personalized learning materials, and assessing student performance, AI chatbots augment the learning experience and tailor it to individual requirements. Lectures and large classrooms are the norm in many universities. Personalizing and tailoring materials to groups of learners is possible to a certain extent, but providing individualized learning materials is not feasible. LLMs, however, are scalable and trainable (Xue et al., 2023), and so with a clear remit and a narrow field, may be able to provide individualized learning. A case in point is the intelligent tutoring system to teach applications of fuzzy logic (Marciniak and Szczepański, 2020). The lack of real-world understanding, their (current) inability to recognize emotional states and actions of learners, severely limits their ability to act as teachers. However, their vast knowledge base and pattern-matching prowess outstrip any individual.

Generative AI can be trained to dynamically adapt to a student's learning style, pace, and academic needs, providing a level of personalization that is difficult to achieve in a traditional classroom. Its extensive knowledge base enables AI to serve as a supplementary tutor, offering insights, explanations, and resources across a wide range of subjects. However, it is important to acknowledge some shortcomings. Generative AI, while expansive in its knowledge, lacks the understanding and emotional intelligence that a human educator brings to the learning experience (Schuller & Schuller, 2018). Additionally, the effectiveness of AI as an educational tool is highly dependent on the quality of its programming and the data it's trained on (Wang et al., 2023), which can sometimes limit its applicability in more complex or academic discussions. Nonetheless, for university learners navigating the ever-expanding landscape of knowledge, generative AI promises a more adaptive, personalized, and comprehensive educational journey.

Situated learning (Mandl & Kopp, 2005) posits that learning is most effective when it occurs in the context where the knowledge or skills will be applied. Rather than just internalizing isolated facts or concepts, this theory suggests that learning involves full engagement with the practices, tools, and culture of a particular community. For example, medical training through internships or residencies does not solely rely on textbooks or lectures. Medical students engage in rounds, diagnose real patients, and work under the mentorship of experienced physicians. This kind of real-world experience helps them understand not just the technical aspects of medicine but also nuances like bedside manner, interdisciplinary collaboration, and ethical decision-making.

AI models are often trained on large, diverse datasets but are usually deployed in very specific contexts. The traditional way of training these models lacks a "situated" element, as it is not inherently contextual or pragmatic. However, the concept of situated learning can be applied to improve their performance. For instance, AI models could be fine-tuned within specific environments where they will operate, effectively making them apprentices within those domains. By doing so, the AI models could develop a more nuanced understanding of their operational environment, making them more effective and reliable. Integrating situated learning principles into generative AI training could move us away from a purely data-centric approach to a more context-aware, socially-informed model of machine learning.

Distributed cognition (Carr, Johnson, & Bush, 2017) is a theoretical framework that extends the boundaries of cognition beyond the individual mind to include interactions with other agents, artifacts, and the surrounding environment. It theorizes that cognitive processes, such as problem-solving and decision-making, are not confined to single individuals but are shared across multiple components of a system. This approach views cognition as a collaborative, socially-situated activity that integrates people, tools, and context. For example, the use of generative AI in education can be seen as a form of distributed cognition. Here, the AI model becomes an extension of both the teacher's and the students' cognitive processes, providing personalized feedback, generating quiz questions, or suggesting resources for further study. It's not just the human actors—the teachers and students—who are participating in the learning process; the AI becomes a co-participant that augments and enriches the cognitive environment. Through real-time interactions and data analysis, the AI system adapts to the students' learning styles and needs, while teachers can focus on more complex aspects of teaching that machines cannot handle. This creates a dynamic, interactive cognitive ecosystem that evolves to optimize educational outcomes.

4. GENERATING EDUCATIONAL MATERIAL USING AI

Generative AI is significantly transforming the writing process in multiple domains, Educators can harness its potential to generate personalized content for individual learners based on their abilities, interests, and learning styles (Mikhailava et al., 2022). The landscape of educational material creation is starting to undergo a profound transformation through the integration of generative AI. LLMs have the capacity to tailor educational content to the unique needs and preferences of individual learners, revolutionizing the way knowledge is disseminated. By harnessing the power of generative AI, educators are now empowered to craft personalized learning experiences that cater to the diverse abilities, interests, and learning styles of their students.

Pedagogical considerations play a pivotal role in the creation of effective educational materials. With generative AI, educators can seamlessly embed pedagogical strategies that cater to individual learning preferences. One of the most remarkable aspects of generative AI is its ability to generate educational content that is truly bespoke. For example, by analyzing a learner's proficiency level, preferences, and past interactions, AI algorithms can craft materials that align precisely with the individual's learning path (Bitsch, Senjic, & Kneip, 2022). This personalized approach goes beyond a one-size-fits-all model, allowing each learner to engage with materials that are both challenging and attainable, thereby fostering a deeper and more meaningful understanding of the subject matter.

While commonly associated with tasks like language translation and text generation, the application of generative models to language education offers a groundbreaking opportunity to explore linguistic nuances and complexity. By harnessing the capabilities of generative AI, language teachers can uncover intricate sentence patterns and foster a deeper understanding of language structures that might otherwise be overlooked in conventional coursebooks. For example, AI can produce multiple sentences that express the same meaning but with varying complexity and formality. Through carefully curated examples, teachers can highlight subtle differences in vocabulary, syntax, and grammatical structures, enabling learners to grasp the intricacies of high-level language usage.

In the field of computer science education, generative AI can craft teaching materials, tailored to the specific requirements of learners, which deal with intricate concepts, such as expert systems, machine learning and information ethics. Concepts can be presented in a manner that resonates with learners' cognitive styles, promoting a deeper understanding and retention of knowledge. The personalized nature of bespoke content enables educators to create materials that can address multiple purposes. This simplifies the process of aligning the educational materials with the aims and objectives of a course. For example, materials generated to teach expert systems were designed to convey knowledge and increase engagement through activity-based tasks. However, the AI-generated course materials that formed the basis of an information ethics course were designed to enhance engagement with the course content and simultaneously develop their ability to present logical arguments.

Although ChatGPT is designed to generate texts, there are a number of AI tools that can generate images, videos and slideshow presentations. Learners who thrive in visual contexts can be provided with AI-generated multimedia-rich content, while those who prefer textual explanations can receive in-depth written explanations. This level of personalization not only caters to diverse learning styles but also acknowledges the significance of individual cognitive processes in the learning journey. Generative AI can enhance personalized learning experiences and foster a deeper engagement with complex subject matter.

5. USE CASES

I will examine the effectiveness of such generative AI learning experiences in various courses, drawing on recent trials of the use of generative-AI conducted at a Japanese university. In this section, I discuss four use cases showing how ChatGPT can be used to enhance learning.

5.1 Use Case One: Feedback on Language Use

In the educational setting with Japanese undergraduates, one noteworthy application of generative AI focuses on enhancing English writing skills. Twenty-eight computer science majors enrolled in an English language course were tasked with writing a paragraph on a technical topic in English. The mean English language proficiency of the cohort is B1/B2 (independent learners) on the Common European Framework of Reference for Languages (CEFR). After completing their initial drafts, they leveraged generative AI to obtain various types of feedback through different prompts, which were suggested by their teacher. For example, one prompt has the AI identify grammatical errors without offering corrections, giving students a chance to self-correct and assimilate the language rules. Another prompt instructs the AI to both correct these errors and provide an itemized list explaining each correction, offering a comprehensive review, enabling learners to see how their writing may be improved and to check the reason for each improvement. This helps them not only improve their individual draft; but over time, they should be able to notice the trends in the advice given by the LLM. Additionally, to bridge potential language gaps and deepen understanding, students prompted the LLM to translate a paragraph into Japanese twice: once focusing on direct translation and once using idiomatic expressions. This opens up the possibility of better understanding the impact of sociocultural conventions, and noticing how even simple phrases in one language receive different idiomatic translations based on the context.

Several interesting observations emerged in terms of student response and utilization of the AI tool. First, many students switched to converse with ChatGPT in Japanese, not merely for ease of communication but as a tactical approach to better grasp complex ideas before translating them back into English. This enhanced their understanding and control of English language structures by translating them from their native language. Second, a form of collaborative inquiry emerged as students engage in iterative conversations with ChatGPT, not only to better understand the AI's feedback but to dig deeper into the linguistic and conceptual intricacies of their writing assignments. They would pose a question, discuss the AI's response, and then ask follow-up questions to refine their understanding. This iterative dialogue allowed the students to be active learners, encouraging them to be more analytical and critical, rather than passive recipients of linguistic advice.

Overall, generative AI served as an invaluable and versatile tool becoming an interactive co-educator in a bilingual educational environment, which can provide model texts, compare and contrast any texts in terms of content and language, and can provide feedback in multiple forms, giving learners the opportunity to receive feedback that is most relevant to their current language proficiency and learning objectives.

5.2 Use Case Two: Dynamic Language Assessment

In this second use case, the LLM provided tailormade advice at multiple levels based on revisions made to a text. In order to function as a dynamic language assessor, the LLM first needed to be trained. This was achieved with some sophisticated prompt engineering. The prompts created by a computer scientist with expertise in deep learning models were shared with students studying in a natural language processing laboratory. Six undergraduates (with B2 CEFR proficiency in English) volunteered to utilize ChatGPT-4 as a dynamic language assessment tool (Lantolf, & Poehner, 2004).

The students researched a specific domain within computer science, such as natural language processing, databases, or cybersecurity. Once they had sufficient information, they drafted a paragraph describing some highly specific aspect of their chosen area. ChatGPT was trained using carefully crafted prompts to function as a dynamic language assessment tool for this task. The training involved identifying and labelling five types of errors that occur in scientific writing, namely errors with accuracy, brevity, clarity, objectivity and formality (Blake, 2021). The next step was training the LLM to provide feedback in sequence starting with the most implicit and transitioning incrementally to more explicit feedback until the learner can correct the error. Once trained, learners submitted their paragraph to the LLM for feedback. The AI provided graduated feedback, which unfolds in a manner congruent with Vygotsky's Zone of Proximal Development (Vygotsky, 1987), aiding the learners to progress from where they currently are to where they can be with guided assistance.

Initially, the feedback started with the most implicit forms, like offering simple prompts that encourage students to reconsider sentences or phrases that might be problematic, without specifically identifying the errors. This resembles a form of Brunerian "scaffolding," (Shvarts & Bakker, 2019) wherein the support is just enough to aid the students in reaching the next level of understanding on their own. As the students iterate on their work, the AI's feedback becomes progressively more explicit. It transitions from highlighting areas that need attention to providing more direct guidance, such as suggesting alternative sentence structures or vocabulary.

Towards the end of this graduated feedback loop, the AI offers the most explicit form of feedback, including corrections with itemized explanations. This not only makes students aware of their mistakes but also educates them on the reasoning behind the correct forms. Although ChatGPT was able to provide feedback in graduated levels, in this small-scale trial its ability to grade their advice and provide feedback in increasingly more explicit ways was not comparable to a human.

In spite of its potential, the small-scale trial revealed some limitations in the AI's ability to provide truly graduated feedback. For one, the AI sometimes made mistakes in the sequencing of advice, jumping directly from highly implicit hints to explicit corrections, bypassing the crucial intermediate steps that gradually build a learner's understanding. This is particularly problematic as it disrupts the theoretical framework of the Zone of Proximal Development, where the goal is to gently guide the learner from their current capabilities to new levels of understanding. Additionally, the AI occasionally used language or technical terminology that was beyond the comprehension level of the undergraduate students, thereby defeating the purpose of a graduated approach. While the AI's feedback was generally valuable, these inconsistencies highlight areas for refinement, particularly in aligning the tool's capabilities with established educational theories and pedagogical practices. Overall, the technology shows promise but requires further calibration to truly mimic the progression of human-aided language learning.

5.3 Use Case Three: Content-Focused Writing

In the third use case, the same twenty-eight computer science majors who participated in Use case 1 used ChatGPT to explore the similarities and differences between two distinct computer science concepts. Learners selected concepts, such as machine learning and data mining, front-end and back-end development, and Python and JavaScript. Students asked ChatGPT to create a list of the similarities and differences for their paired concepts. After receiving these lists from the LLM, students use them as the foundation for crafting a paragraph that compares and contrasts the two concepts. Once the students had completed the initial draft of the paragraph, they submitted them to ChatGPT for feedback. However, unlike the previous instances where the focus was largely on linguistic aspects, this time students requested content-specific advice. This targeted approach allows students to fine-tune not just their language skills but also their understanding of complex computer science topics. By doing so, they gain a grasp of the subject matter while also honing their ability to communicate effectively in a specialized domain.

The outcomes from this use case yielded mixed results. One striking observation was the significant variation in the quality of the feedback provided by ChatGPT. While some students received insightful comparisons that enriched their understanding of the paired concepts, others received lists that were less precise and occasionally featured repetitive points. This inconsistency could be attributed to a lack of specialized training for ChatGPT in the area of computer science, suggesting that the tool might benefit from a more subject-focused fine-tuning to improve its efficacy. Another issue was ChatGPT's tendency to rephrase rather than offer truly differentiated points, causing some lists to contain repetitive or redundant information.

Moreover, a common misunderstanding arose when the LLM produced answers in the language that the prompt was initially given in, rather than in the target language the students were aiming to practice. For instance, if a student asked a question in Japanese but intended to receive an answer in English to further practice their English skills, the LLM often responded in Japanese. This resulted in missed opportunities for language practice and necessitated extra steps to align the feedback with the educational objectives.

Overall, while ChatGPT showed promise as a tool for content-specific writing in computer science, these inconsistencies point to areas where further development is needed. Specifically, there may be a need for more refined prompt engineering and subject-specific training to better tailor the AI's capabilities to educational settings focused on both linguistic proficiency and specialized knowledge.

5.4 Use Case Four: Teaching Multiplication

In another interesting use case, four aspiring mathematics teachers, who were also computer science majors, used ChatGPT to explore various methodologies for teaching multiplication. The teachers were first-language Japanese speakers with B2 CEFR proficiency in English. Given the overarching objective to create an educational poster, the four undergraduates utilized ChatGPT to gather insights into diverse teaching strategies, from the traditional multiplication table approach to more interactive techniques like lattice multiplication (Baccaglini-Frank, 2023) or using manipulatives (Bartolini & Martignone, 2020), such as counters, arrays and Cuisenaire rods (Abreu-Mendoza, 2021). After conducting this research with the AI, they synthesized the information and incorporated it into their poster designs. These posters not only served as visual teaching aids but also became reflective tools for the aspiring teachers themselves, allowing them to critically evaluate the pros and cons of different instructional methods. By integrating AI-assisted research into their project, the aspiring teachers were better equipped to create resourceful and comprehensive educational materials, setting the stage for their future careers in mathematics education.

Further enriching this use case was the way in which they engaged with ChatGPT's outputs. Rather than taking the AI's suggestions at face value, they entered into a dialectical process with the technology, challenging its recommendations and seeking clarifications to deepen their understanding of the methodologies in question. The trainee teachers also used the AI to simulate student queries, mimicking potential questions they might face in a classroom setting. This gave them a chance to explore how well different methodologies would hold up under scrutiny, thereby fine-tuning their own pedagogical reasoning.

By incorporating ChatGPT into their project, the aspiring teachers expanded their pedagogical horizons and gained practical experience in leveraging technology for educational purposes. While the tool was not without its limitations—some found that the AI's grasp of intricate educational theories was not as nuanced as a human expert—the overall experience shed light on the transformative potential of AI in shaping future teaching and learning landscapes.

6. POTENTIAL EDUCATION APPLICATIONS FOR GENERATIVE AI

Generative AI has significant unleashed potential in education, with many areas underexplored. The four key areas that will be discussed further are the realities of implementing AI in educational settings, the provision of real-time feedback to students, the role of AI in fostering creativity, and the impact of creativity on AI's educational applications.

For instance, generative AI could be used to develop immersive learning experiences in virtual, augmented or mixed reality (De Freitas & Neumann, 2009; Russell & Kuensting, 2021). Imagine a scenario where AI-driven virtual tutors guide students through historically significant events, scientific phenomena, or complex mathematical concepts within a simulated environment. By dynamically generating relevant content and interactions, generative AI can facilitate personalized and experiential learning, allowing students to explore, experiment, and interact with subject matter in ways that were previously unattainable.

Real-time feedback is another frontier where generative AI can make a transformative impact. While traditional assessments provide feedback after the fact, AI has the potential to offer immediate and tailored feedback to students as they engage with content and assignments. By analyzing students' responses and interactions, AI models can provide insights, pointing out strengths, identifying misconceptions, and suggesting alternative approaches. This dynamic feedback loop has the potential to enhance student understanding and metacognition, fostering a more iterative and effective learning process.

Generative AI also holds the promise of fostering creativity and collaboration in education. Through AI-powered co-creation platforms, students can collaborate with AI models to generate ideas, stories, or multimedia projects. This collaborative approach not only sparks creative thinking but also exposes learners to diverse perspectives and prompts, expanding the breadth of their learning experiences.

Additionally, the personalization of education can be further enriched by generative AI. While current adaptive learning systems tailor content based on a learner's progress, generative AI can take personalization a step further by generating content that aligns precisely with an individual's learning style, pace, and preferences. This level of granularity could lead to truly individualized learning pathways that accommodate diverse needs and motivations.

As we chart the course for the future of generative AI in education, collaboration between educators, researchers, and AI developers is pivotal. By fostering interdisciplinary dialogue, we can envision innovative applications and design ethical frameworks that guide the development and deployment of AI technologies in education. It is imperative that the potential risks and challenges, such as bias, data privacy, and the preservation of human-centered pedagogy, are considered alongside the benefits to ensure a responsible and effective integration of AI into the educational landscape.

7. CONCLUSION

Generative AI offers an unprecedented opportunity to personalize and enrich the teaching and learning experience, reflecting the potential outlined in various learning theories. As we continue to explore the capacities of this technology, it is essential to consider its applications through the lenses of these educational frameworks, ensuring that we capture the full spectrum of its pedagogical potential ethically, pedagogically, and practically.

The behaviorist aspects of generative AI, as it provides immediate feedback, can be seen as a digital embodiment of reinforcement learning, promoting a responsive environment that is closely tailored to individual progress. From the cognitivist perspective, generative AI assists in information processing, a clear nod to the theory's focus on the inner workings of the mind, enabling problem-solving and the adaptation of learning experiences to the cognitive levels of learners. Generative AI's role extends to constructivism and social constructivism, where it not only supports hands-on, problem-based learning experiences but also fosters social interactions, aligning with the social constructivist belief in the importance of social contexts and interactions in knowledge construction. Moreover, generative AI acts as a critical node in a learner's network, echoing connectivism's emphasis on the learning potential within a networked, digital world.

This chapter contributes to these ongoing discussions by shedding light on the positive impacts of generative AI on educational material development and learning mediation. Generative AI's ability to comprehend and adapt to various subject domains empowers educators to transcend conventional content limitations, enabling them to provide tailored and enriched educational materials. By automating intricate categorization tasks and generating pertinent examples, this technology not only streamlines the content creation process but also nurtures a deeper understanding of complex subject matter.

While AI-generated sentences can serve as valuable exemplars, they might lack the cultural and contextual considerations that human-authored materials inherently possess. Additionally, the selection of sentences may inadvertently reinforce certain biases or linguistic patterns present in the training data of the AI model. Therefore, a balanced approach that combines AI-generated content with expert curation is crucial to ensure a comprehensive and culturally sensitive language learning experience. As we stand on the threshold of a new educational era, we must integrate generative AI with consideration of these learning theories, ensuring ethical, balanced, and equitable applications. The essence of education, with its irreplaceable human touch, is complemented and not replaced by AI, echoing the social constructivist view that learning is fundamentally a social process.

In conclusion, responsibly harnessing generative AI enables educators to craft personalized, dynamic, and engaging learning experiences, enriching the educational landscape in alignment with established and emerging learning theories. Our collective efforts to marry generative AI with the insights of these theories will be pivotal in shaping how this technology serves knowledge, growth, and lifelong learning. It is through collaboration, exploration, and responsible implementation that we will ensure generative AI becomes an enabler of educational excellence for future generations.

REFERENCES

Abreu-Mendoza, R. A., Coulanges, L., Ali, K., Powell, A. B., & Rosenberg-Lee, M. (2021). From non-symbolic to symbolic proportions and back: A Cuisenaire rod proportional reasoning intervention enhances continuous proportional reasoning skills. *Frontiers in Psychology*, *12*, 633077. doi:10.3389/fpsyg.2021.633077 PMID:34093313

Adams, P. (2006). Exploring social constructivism: Theories and practicalities. *Education 3-13*, *34*(3), 243–257. doi:10.1080/03004270600898893

Amsel, A. (1989). Behaviorism, neobehaviorism, and cognitivism in learning theory: Historical and contemporary perspectives. *The American Journal of Psychology*, *105*(3), 492–495. doi:10.2307/1423202

Ausat, A. M. A., Massang, B., Efendi, M., Nofirman, N., & Riady, Y. (2023). Can chat GPT replace the role of the teacher in the classroom: A fundamental analysis. *Journal of Education*, *5*(4), 16100–16106. doi:10.31004/joe.v5i4.2745

Baccaglini-Frank, A. E., Funghi, S., Maracci, M., & Ramploud, A. (2023). Learning about multiplication by comparing algorithms: "One times one, but actually they are ten times ten". *The Journal of Mathematical Behavior*, *70*, 101024. doi:10.1016/j.jmathb.2022.101024

Bada, S. O., & Olusegun, S. (2015). Constructivism learning theory: A paradigm for teaching and learning. *Journal of Research & Method in Education*, *5*(6), 66–70.

Bartolini, M. G., & Martignone, F. (2020). Manipulatives in mathematics education. In S. Learman (Ed.), *Encyclopedia of mathematics education* (pp. 487–494)., doi:10.1007/978-3-030-15789-0_93

Bitsch, G., Senjic, P., & Kneip, P. (2022, August). Hybrid individualized assistance-oriented learning system framework for STEM-Education. In *2022 IEEE German Education Conference (GeCon)* (pp. 1-5). IEEE. https://doi.org/10.1109/GeCon55699.2022.9942754

Blake, J. (2021). Scientific research articles: Twenty-two language errors to avoid. In G. Kurubacak-Meric & S. Sisman-Ugur (Eds.), *Improving scientific communication for lifelong learners* (pp. 195–219). IGI Global. doi:10.4018/978-1-7998-4534-8.ch011

Bredo, E. (1997). The social construction of learning. In G. D. Phye (Ed.), *Handbook of academic learning* (pp. 3–45). Academic Press., doi:10.1016/B978-012554255-5/50002-8

Carr, S. B., Johnson, N., & Bush, L. (2017). Distributed cognition: Teachers' perceptions and implications for learning outcomes and instructional technology. In Educational leadership and administration: Concepts, methodologies, tools, and applications (pp. 863-893). IGI Global. doi:10.4018/978-1-5225-1624-8.ch042

De Freitas, S., & Neumann, T. (2009). The use of 'exploratory learning' for supporting immersive learning in virtual environments. *Computers & Education*, *52*(2), 343–352. doi:10.1016/j.compedu.2008.09.010

Downes, S. (2022). Connectivism. *Asian Journal of Distance Education*, *17*(1). https://asianjde.com/ojs/index.php/AsianJDE/article/view/623

Farthing, D. W., Jones, D. M., & McPhee, D. (1998). Permutational multiple-choice questions: An objective and efficient alternative to essay-type examination questions. *SIGCSE Bulletin*, *30*(3), 81–85. doi:10.1145/290320.283036

Fisher, W. W., Piazza, C. C., & Roane, H. S. (Eds.). (2021). *Handbook of applied behavior analysis*. Guilford Publications.

Fitzmaurice, M., & Coughlan, J. (2007). Teaching philosophy statements: A guide. In C. O'Farrell (Ed.), Teaching portfolio practice in Ireland a handbook (pp. 39–47). Dublin: Centre for Academic Practice and Student Learning (CAPSL), Trinity College Dublin and All Ireland Society for Higher Education (AISHE).

Hall Lang, E., Munsey, B., Murray, F., Manning, L., & Wigington, T. (2023). Culturally responsive learning environments within higher education. *Learning Environments Research*, 1–16. doi:10.100710984-023-09481-x

Heston, T. F., & Khun, C. (2023). Prompt engineering in medical education. *International Medical Education*, *2*(3), 198–205. doi:10.3390/ime2030019

Kasneci, E., Seßler, K., Küchemann, S., Bannert, M., Dementieva, D., Fischer, F., Gasser, U., Groh, G., Günnemann, S., Hüllermeier, E., Krusche, S., Kutyniok, G., Michaeli, T., Nerdel, C., Pfeffer, J., Poquet, O., Sailer, M., Schmidt, A., Seidel, T., & Kasneci, G. (2023). ChatGPT for good? On opportunities and challenges of large language models for education. *Learning and Individual Differences*, *103*, 102274. doi:10.1016/j.lindif.2023.102274

Kukulska-Hulme, A. (2006). Mobile language learning now and in the future. In P. Svensson (Ed.), *From vision to practice: language learning and IT* (pp. 295–310). Swedish Net University. http://www2.humlab.umu.se/itas/bok/default.asp

Lantolf, J. P., & Poehner, M. E. (2004). Dynamic assessment of L2 development: Bringing the past into the future. *Journal of Applied Linguistics and Professional Practice*, *1*(1), 49–72. doi:10.1558/japl.1.1.49.55872

Malinka, K., Peresíni, M., Firc, A., Hujnak, O., & Janus, F. (2023, June). On the educational impact of ChatGPT: Is Artificial Intelligence ready to obtain a university degree? In *Proceedings of the 2023 Conference on Innovation and Technology in Computer Science Education* (pp. 47-53). ACM. 10.1145/3587102.3588827

Marciniak, J., & Szczepański, M. (2020). Individualized learning in a course with a tight schedule. *Procedia Computer Science*, *176*, 2059–2068. doi:10.1016/j.procs.2020.09.242 PMID:33042305

Mikhailava, V., Pyshkin, E., Blake, J., Chernonog, S., Lezhenin, I., & Bogach, N. (2022). Tailoring computer-assisted pronunciation teaching: Mixing and matching the mode and manner of feedback to learners. *Proceedings of INTED*, *2022*, 767–773. doi:10.21125/inted.2022.0263

Moreira dos Santos, C. A., Carvalho Pereira, M. A., de Souza, M. A., Machado Dias, J. P., & Oliveira, F. S. (2020). Different teaching approaches and use of active learning strategies as tools for inter-and transdisciplinary education. *International Journal of Social Science Studies*, *8*(2), 15. doi:10.11114/ijsss.v8i2.4693

Nagowah, L., & Nagowah, S. (2009). A reflection on the dominant learning theories: Behaviourism, cognitivism and constructivism. *International Journal of Learning*, *16*(2), 279–286. doi:10.18848/1447-9494/CGP/v16i02/46136

NathK. (2022). Evolution of the Internet from Web 1.0 to Metaverse: The good, the bad and the ugly. TechRxiv. doi:10.36227/techrxiv.19743676.v1

Ojose, B. (2008). Applying Piaget's theory of cognitive development to mathematics instruction. *The Mathematics Educator*, *18*(1), 26–30.

Rannikmäe, M., Holbrook, J., & Soobard, R. (2020). Social Constructivism—Jerome Bruner. In B. Akpan & T. J. Kennedy (Eds.), *Science education in theory and practice: An introductory guide to learning theory* (pp. 259–275). Springer. doi:10.1007/978-3-030-43620-9_18

Russell, D., & Kuensting, L. L. (2021). Advancing emergency nurse practitioner training using virtual nursing centers. In D. Russell (Ed.), *Implementing Augmented Reality Into Immersive Virtual Learning Environments* (pp. 151–162). IGI Global. doi:10.4018/978-1-7998-4222-4.ch009

Saks, K., Ilves, H., & Noppel, A. (2021). The impact of procedural knowledge on the formation of declarative knowledge: How accomplishing activities designed for developing learning skills impacts teachers' knowledge of learning skills. *Education Sciences, 11*(10), 598. doi:10.3390/educsci11100598

Schuller, D., & Schuller, B. W. (2018). The age of artificial emotional intelligence. *Computer, 51*(9), 38–46. doi:10.1109/MC.2018.3620963

Shvarts, A., & Bakker, A. (2019). The early history of the scaffolding metaphor: Bernstein, Luria, Vygotsky, and before. *Mind, Culture, and Activity, 26*(1), 4–23. doi:10.1080/10749039.2019.1574306

Tang, R., Chuang, Y. N., & Hu, X. (2023). *The science of detecting LLM-generated texts.* arXiv preprint https://doi.org//arXiv.2303.07205 doi:10.48550

Tetzlaff, L., Schmiedek, F., & Brod, G. (2021). Developing personalized education: A dynamic framework. *Educational Psychology Review, 33*(3), 863–882. doi:10.100710648-020-09570-w

Todd, J. T., & Morris, E. K. (1995). *Modern perspectives on BF Skinner and contemporary behaviorism.* Greenwood Press/Greenwood Publishing Group.

Tomic, W. (1993). Behaviorism and cognitivism in education. *Psychology (Savannah, Ga.), 30*(3/4), 38–46.

Utterback, J. M., & Acee, H. J. (2005). Disruptive technologies: An expanded view. *International Journal of Innovation Management, 9*(1), 1–17. doi:10.1142/S1363919605001162

Vygotsky, L. S. (1987). Thinking and speech. In R.W. Rieber & A.S. Carton (Eds.), The collected works of L.S. Vygotsky, Volume 1: Problems of general psychology (pp. 39-285). New York: Plenum Press.

Wang, Y., Yu, Z., Zeng, Z., Yang, L., Wang, C., Chen, H., & Zhang, Y. (2023). *PandaLM: An automatic evaluation benchmark for LLM instruction tuning optimization.* arXiv preprint. https://doi.org//arXiv.2306.05087 doi:10.48550

Warlick, D. (2009). Grow your personal learning network: New technologies can keep you connected and help you manage information overload. *Learning and Leading with Technology, 36*(6), 12–16.

Watson, J. B. (2017). *Behaviorism.* Routledge. Mandl, H., & Kopp, B. (2005). Situated learning: Theories and models. In P. Nentwig & D. Waddington (Eds.), *Making it relevant. Context based learning of science* (pp. 15–34). Waxmann.

Xue, F., Fu, Y., Zhou, W., Zheng, Z., & You, Y. (2023). *To repeat or not to repeat: Insights from scaling LLM under token-crisis.* arXiv preprint https://doi.org//arXiv.2305.13230 doi:10.48550

Chapter 3
Is It the End of Undergraduate Dissertations?
Exploring the Advantages and Challenges of Generative AI Models in Education

Benjamin Kenwright
Zhejiang Normal University, China

ABSTRACT

This chapter delves into the intriguing realm of generative artificial intelligence (AI) models and their potential impact on undergraduate dissertations in the field of education. As AI continues to advance and permeate various aspects of our lives, the educational landscape is not immune to its transformative influence. The chapter begins by providing an overview of generative AI models, including their underlying principles and techniques such as deep learning, natural language processing, and neural networks. It then explores how these models can be harnessed to generate written content that is coherent, creative, and relevant, raising the question of whether undergraduate dissertations, as we know them, are destined to become obsolete. Advantages of employing generative AI models in education are scrutinized, highlighting their potential to enhance the efficiency and quality of student work.

1. INTRODUCTION

1.1 The Significance of Undergraduate Dissertations in Education

In the ever-accelerating landscape of higher education, undergraduate dissertations hold a remarkable position as a formative milestone for students. Surprisingly, despite their decades-long tradition, these academic endeavors continue to retain their profound significance in shaping the intellectual growth and research acumen of students across diverse disciplines. As the capstone projects of undergraduate studies, dissertations provide a unique opportunity for students to delve deep into a subject of their choice, exploring its intricacies, addressing pertinent research questions, and contributing to the existing body

DOI: 10.4018/979-8-3693-0074-9.ch003

of knowledge. This immersive and rigorous process fosters critical thinking skills, nurtures creativity, and instills a sense of intellectual curiosity that transcends the confines of the classroom. Moreover, through the mentoring and guidance of faculty advisors, students cultivate the ability to formulate research methodologies, analyze data, and communicate their findings effectively—essential attributes for their future academic and professional pursuits (Roberts and Seaman, 2018; Kenwright, 2016b). Thus, the enduring significance of undergraduate dissertations in education lies not only in their role as a conduit for learning but also as a testament to the unwavering commitment of educational institutions to nurture the next generation of scholarly minds (Webster et al., 2000).

1.2 Emerging Trends in Technology and Their Impact on Dissertations

Emerging trends in technology are significantly impacting the the education landscape (Kenwright, 2020) ushering in exciting possibilities and transformative changes both in the classroom and in assessments such as dissertations. Advancements in data analytics and big data have revolutionized research methodologies, enabling scholars to access and analyze vast datasets, enriching the depth and scope of their dissertations. Virtual collaboration tools have transcended geographical barriers, facilitating seamless interactions among researchers and promoting global collaboration in dissertation committees. AI-driven content generation tools have streamlined the writing process, providing support for literature reviews and content creation while preserving academic integrity. Interactive data visualization tools enhance the presentation of complex research findings, making dissertations more engaging and accessible to audiences. Moreover, the open-access movement and digital repositories have facilitated the dissemination of research, encouraging broader knowledge sharing and societal impact. As technology continues to evolve, researchers must embrace these trends mindfully, considering ethical implications and ensuring that they receive adequate training to leverage technology effectively and responsibly in their dissertations, thus propelling academic research into a dynamic and promising future.

1.3 Contribution

The key contributions of this chapter are, (1) recognizing the proliferation around AI in education; (2) addressing concerns and questions surrounding the role of AI in dissertations; (3) elaborating on the implications of AI in dissertations; (4) reviewing potential challenges and ethical conundrums around AI-written dissertations; and (5) Providing insights and recommendations for future dissertations in light of the rise of intelligent assistive technologies.

2. UNDERSTANDING GENERATIVE AI AND CHATGPT

2.1 ChatGPT: A New Secret Weapon for Learning in Higher Education

In the rapidly evolving educational landscape, technological innovations continue to shape the way students learn and engage with course materials. Among the latest breakthroughs, ChatGPT emerges as a new secret weapon for learning in higher education (Kasneci et al., 2023). Developed by OpenAI, ChatGPT is a cutting-edge language model based on the GPT architecture, designed to generate human-like responses to text prompts. Its remarkable ability to comprehend and generate contextually relevant information has garnered widespread attention across various domains. In higher education, ChatGPT is increasingly being recognized as a powerful tool to enhance learning experiences, foster critical thinking, and provide personalized assistance to students (Qadir, 2023; Lo, 2023). With its capacity to answer questions, explain complex concepts, and facilitate interactive discussions, ChatGPT is revolutionizing the way students interact with educational content, presenting exciting possibilities for a more immersive and tailored learning environment.

2.2 Exploring Generative AI and its Relevance in Education

Generative AI has emerged as a captivating field of research, revolutionizing the way we approach education. Harnessing the power of deep learning and natural language processing, generative AI models, such as ChatGPT and Bard, have the remarkable ability to generate human-like text, mimic conversation, and produce creative outputs. In the context of education, these models offer intriguing possibilities for personalized learning experiences, interactive tutoring, and content generation. Acting as virtual mentors or intelligent assistants, generative AI can provide students with instant and tailored guidance, answer queries, and foster critical thinking through thought-provoking discussions. Furthermore, the potential of generative AI to automate certain tasks, such as grading and feedback (Dai et al., 2023), liberates educators to focus on individualized support and curriculum design. However, as we explore the relevance of generative AI in education, it is essential to address ethical considerations, ensuring that these models promote academic integrity, diversity of perspectives, and safeguard against biases (Ray, 2023; Mhlanga, 2023). Embracing generative AI responsibly, educational institutions can unlock its full potential, shaping a more innovative, accessible, and engaging learning landscape for learners worldwide.

2.3 Introducing ChatGPT and Its Capabilities in Natural Language Processing

Introducing ChatGPT, an advanced language model powered by OpenAI's GPT architecture, brings forth a new era in natural language processing (NLP). ChatGPT showcases extraordinary capabilities in understanding and generating human-like text, making it a transformative tool in various applications. Processing vast amounts of language data, ChatGPT can engage in dynamic conversations, answer questions, and provide contextually relevant responses. Its ability to comprehend complex queries and adapt to various writing styles lends itself to a wide range of tasks, from drafting emails to tutoring, content creation, and even programming assistance. The model's impressive language comprehension and generation skills enable it to assist users in a wide array of tasks, making it a versatile and powerful tool in the realm of NLP and AI-driven applications (Fuchs, 2023).

2.4 The Role of Machine Learning and Deep Learning in AI Education

The role of machine learning and deep learning in AI education is undeniably transformative, revolutionizing the way students learn, educators teach, and educational institutions operate (Adiguzel et al., 2023). Machine learning algorithms enable personalized learning experiences, as they analyze vast amounts of data to identify individual student strengths and weaknesses, tailoring content and recommendations accordingly. Adaptive learning platforms leverage machine learning to dynamically adjust the difficulty level and pace of instruction, ensuring optimal engagement and mastery for each student. Deep learning, on the other hand, powers sophisticated natural language processing models, enabling AI-driven chatbots and virtual tutors that engage in interactive discussions and provide instant feedback to learners. Through these technologies, AI education has the potential to transcend traditional classrooms, offering accessible and immersive learning experiences that foster critical thinking, creativity, and problem-solving skills in students of diverse backgrounds and learning styles. As machine learning and deep learning continue to advance, their integration in AI education holds the promise of cultivating a generation of empowered learners and transforming the future of education on a global scale.

3. CURRENT LANDSCAPE OF UNDERGRADUATE DISSERTATIONS

3.1 The Traditional Dissertation Process and Its Challenges

The traditional dissertation process is a rigorous and time-honored journey undertaken by graduate students to contribute original research and insights to their respective fields. It typically involves selecting a research topic, conducting an extensive literature review, formulating research questions or hypotheses, designing a methodology, collecting and analyzing data, and presenting findings in a comprehensive written report (Roberts and Seaman, 2018). Throughout this process, students work closely with faculty advisors who provide guidance and feedback to ensure the research meets academic standards.

The traditional dissertation process comes with its fair share of challenges. One of the main difficulties lies in selecting a research topic that is both novel and feasible within the given time and resource constraints. Additionally, conducting an exhaustive literature review can be time-consuming, as scholars must identify gaps in existing research and position their work in the context of prior knowledge. Formulating clear and researchable questions or hypotheses also demands careful consideration, as the precision of these inquiries shapes the entire research endeavor.

Significant challenge is the collection and analysis of data. Depending on the research design, acquiring data can be logistically complex and may require ethical considerations. Data analysis, especially in quantitative research, necessitates a strong understanding of statistical methods and software. Throughout the process, maintaining motivation and focus can be challenging, especially during times of setbacks or uncertainties in the research (Holmes et al., 2023; Datta et al., 2022).

The process of writing the dissertation itself can be a formidable undertaking. Organizing and presenting research findings in a cohesive and logical manner while adhering to academic writing conventions requires considerable effort and skill. Additionally, revising and editing the manuscript to meet the stringent standards of academic rigor can be both time-consuming and mentally demanding. The traditional dissertation process often demands students to balance their academic commitments with other responsibilities, such as teaching, work, or personal life, which can lead to stress and time management challenges. Finally, the culmination of the process, the defense, can evoke feelings of anxiety and self-doubt, as students face rigorous questioning and critique from a committee of experts.

Despite these challenges, the traditional dissertation process remains an invaluable cornerstone of higher education, fostering the development of critical thinking, research skills, and scholarly expertise in aspiring academics. Through perseverance, support from mentors, and dedication to the pursuit of knowledge, students can overcome these hurdles and emerge as accomplished scholars, contributing to the advancement of their fields and society as a whole.

3.2 Examining Issues of Cheating, Collusion, and Plagiarism

Examining issues of cheating, collusion, and plagiarism is crucial in maintaining academic integrity and upholding the credibility of educational institutions. These unethical practices undermine the fundamental principles of learning and research, as they involve the misrepresentation of one's own work or the unauthorized use of others' intellectual contributions (Ison, 2012). Cheating, which includes the use of ghostwriters (Singh and Remenyi, 2016) and dishonest behaviors during exams or assessments, compromises the fairness and accuracy of evaluating students' knowledge and abilities. Collusion, where individuals collaborate on assignments meant to be completed independently, erodes the individual learning experience and distorts academic achievements. Plagiarism, the act of presenting someone else's work as one's own without proper attribution, not only violates academic norms but also hinders the development of critical thinking and creativity. Educational institutions must implement robust policies and employ plagiarism detection tools to detect and deter such practices, fostering a culture of academic honesty and integrity among students and scholars. Addressing issues of cheating, collusion, and plagiarism, academic communities can create an environment that nurtures authentic learning, ethical conduct, and a genuine pursuit of knowledge.

The advent of AI technologies like ChatGPT has both **amplified and complicated the landscape of cheating, collusion, and plagiarism in academic settings**. On one hand, these tools can provide students with unprecedented access to information and assistance, making it easier for them to find solutions to assignments and dissertations (Abd-Elaal et al., 2019; Malinka et al., 2023). The vast knowledge base and capabilities of AI-driven platforms can facilitate more sophisticated cheating strategies, including generating original-looking content for essays and theses. Additionally, the instantaneous nature of AI-driven assistance means that students can access help discreetly, making it harder for educators to detect misconduct in real-time.

Traditional approaches to catching cheating, such as manual plagiarism checks and surveillance during exams, have become less effective in the face of AI tools (Cotton et al., 2023). Plagiarism detection software, once a reliable method for identifying copied content, may struggle to recognize text generated by advanced AI models as the sources are often disguised or blended seamlessly. Moreover, with AI-generated content becoming more convincing, educators may find it increasingly challenging to discern whether a student's work is genuinely original or AI-assisted.

Of course, it's crucial to note that while AI can facilitate dishonest behavior, it also holds the potential to combat academic misconduct. Advanced AI-driven plagiarism detectors can evolve to identify subtler patterns of cheating, while AI-driven proctoring systems can monitor online exams more effectively. Educators and institutions need to adapt to this new technological landscape by developing more sophisticated strategies for detecting and preventing cheating, promoting a culture of academic integrity, and providing support and guidance to students to ensure that they use AI tools responsibly and ethically. Ultimately, the ethical use of AI in education depends on both students' responsibility and the vigilance of educational institutions in keeping pace with these evolving challenges.

3.3 Assessing the Quality of Dissertations in the Modern Era

Assessing the quality of dissertations in the modern era presents unique challenges and opportunities, given the evolving landscape of academic research and technology. While traditional criteria such as rigor, originality, methodology, and contribution to the field remain relevant, contemporary assessment approaches also consider factors like interdisciplinary perspectives, innovative methodologies, and the use of advanced technologies. Evaluators now have access to sophisticated tools for plagiarism detection and data analysis, enabling a more comprehensive and objective assessment of dissertations (Chaka, 2023). Additionally, the emphasis on transparent research practices and reproducibility has gained prominence, reinforcing the need for open access to data and methodologies. Furthermore, the incorporation of AI-driven content generation tools necessitates a critical evaluation of the extent of original thought and human authorship in the dissertation. As the scholarly landscape continues to evolve, ensuring rigorous and fair assessment methods is crucial to maintain the integrity and excellence of dissertations in the modern era.

4. ADVANTAGES AND APPLICATIONS OF GENERATIVE AI IN EDUCATION

4.1 Transforming the Dissertation Writing Process With AI

Transforming the dissertation writing process with AI represents a paradigm shift in academic research, streamlining and enriching the journey of scholars. AI-powered tools, such as natural language processing models and language generation algorithms, offer invaluable assistance throughout the entire writing process. From generating initial topic ideas to conducting literature reviews and crafting well-structured arguments, AI enhances productivity and efficiency. Researchers can rely on AI for grammar and style checks, ensuring a polished final manuscript. Moreover, AI-driven content generation provides a wealth of reference material, empowering scholars to access a vast array of sources swiftly. However, the integration of AI in dissertation writing also calls for vigilance to maintain academic integrity, as scholars must preserve their original thinking amidst the wealth of AI-generated content.

4.2 Personalized Guidance and Support for Students Through AI

Personalized guidance and support for students through AI is revolutionizing the educational landscape, providing tailored learning experiences that cater to individual strengths and needs. AI-powered learning platforms analyze vast amounts of data on students' performance, preferences, and learning styles to create personalized learning pathways. Adapting content, pacing, and difficulty levels, AI ensures that students receive precisely what they require to excel in their studies. Additionally, AI-driven virtual tutors and chatbots offer instant and personalized feedback, guiding students through challenging concepts and providing encouragement throughout their academic journey. This personalized approach not only enhances academic outcomes but also fosters student engagement and motivation. Harnessing the potential of AI, educational institutions can provide students with an unparalleled level of personalized guidance and support, empowering them to achieve their full potential and succeed in their academic pursuits.

4.3 Leveraging AI for Efficient Literature Review and Research

Leveraging AI for efficient literature review and research is a transformative approach that streamlines the process of knowledge discovery and analysis. AI-powered tools can rapidly scan vast repositories of academic literature, extracting relevant information and identifying key trends and insights. Automating the time-consuming task of sifting through numerous articles and papers, researchers can focus on higher-level analysis and synthesis of the literature. Moreover, AI-driven algorithms can identify gaps in existing research, aiding scholars in formulating research questions that address unexplored areas. Additionally, AI-powered citation and reference management tools ensure accuracy and consistency in citing sources, reducing the risk of errors in academic writing. The integration of AI in literature review and research not only enhances efficiency but also opens doors to new possibilities, fostering a more comprehensive and rigorous exploration of scholarly knowledge and advancing the frontiers of academic inquiry.

5. PRESERVING ACADEMIC INTEGRITY IN THE AGE OF AI

5.1 Ensuring Academic Integrity and Combating Cheating in AI-Generated Content

Ensuring academic integrity and combating cheating in AI-generated content is a critical undertaking in the digital age. As AI-driven tools become more prevalent in academia, the risk of unauthorized use of AI-generated content presents a challenge to maintaining academic honesty. Educational institutions must implement robust policies and technology solutions to detect and deter plagiarism and ensure that students understand the importance of originality and ethical conduct.

Figure 1. Plagiarism: Overview of the different forms of plagiarism seen in dissertations.

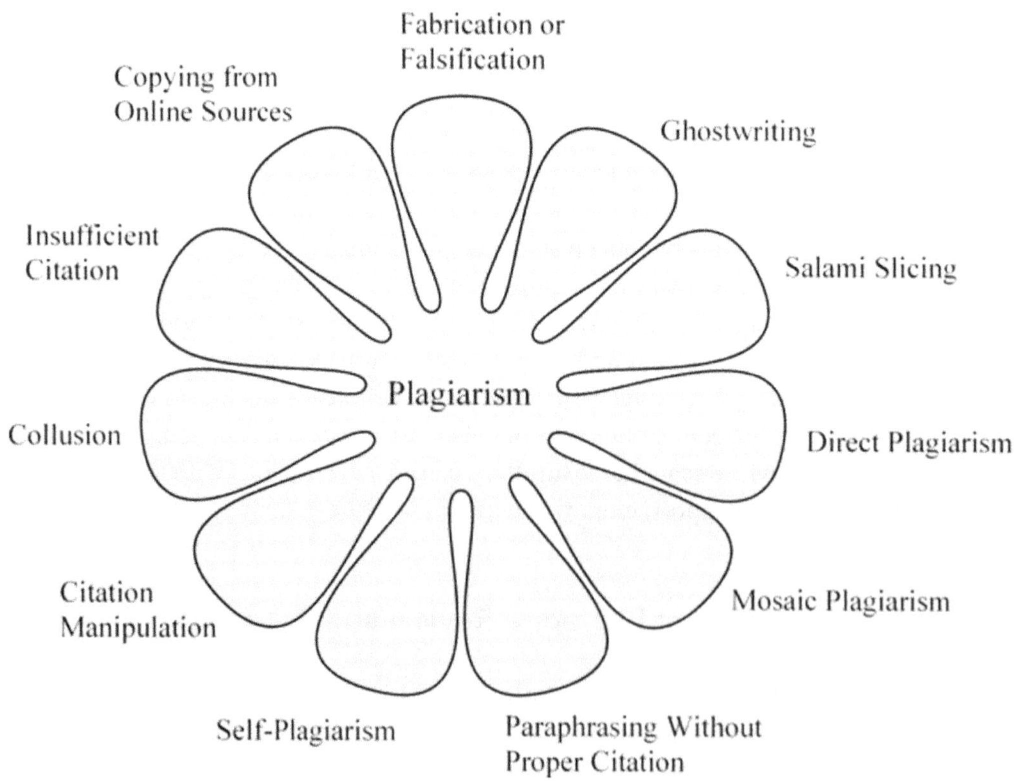

Fostering a culture of academic integrity through education and awareness-raising is essential in empowering students to embrace the value of their own intellectual contributions and respect the work of others. Striking a balance between leveraging the benefits of AI in research and safeguarding academic integrity, institutions can nurture an environment that encourages innovation while upholding the highest standards of scholarly ethics.

5.2 Identifying and Mitigating Biases in AI Models and Dissertations

Identifying and mitigating biases in AI models and dissertations is a critical pursuit in contemporary academic research. AI models, particularly those powered by natural language processing, have demonstrated remarkable capabilities in generating text and assisting scholars in various aspects of research. However, their reliance on vast datasets raises concerns about potential biases embedded in the training data, which can lead to biased outputs and reinforce existing inequalities. Vigilance in identifying and addressing biases is essential to uphold the principles of academic integrity and foster equitable research outcomes. Researchers must engage in comprehensive data analysis and evaluation to uncover and understand potential biases within their datasets. Transparent reporting and documentation of data sources, preprocessing techniques, and model architectures are fundamental in enabling scrutiny and verification of AI-generated content. Moreover, incorporating diverse and representative datasets, coupled with ongoing evaluation and refinement of AI models, can help mitigate biases and promote fairness in AI-generated content. Similarly, in dissertations, scholars must be cognizant of their own biases during the research process, employing rigorous methodologies and critically evaluating findings to ensure objectivity. Peer review and collaborative dialogues offer valuable opportunities to identify and rectify biases, enabling a collective effort in advancing unbiased research practices. Embracing a proactive and multi-faceted approach, academia can pave the way towards AI models and dissertations that contribute to a more inclusive, diverse, and unbiased scholarly discourse.

5.3 Striking a Balance Between AI Assistance and Original Thinking

Striking a balance between AI assistance and original thinking is a paramount consideration in the pursuit of scholarly excellence. While AI-powered tools offer unparalleled support in literature review, data analysis, and content generation, researchers must remain vigilant to preserve their intellectual autonomy and ensure the authenticity of their contributions. Engaging in critical reflection and actively questioning the outputs of AI models is essential to avoid undue reliance on automated processes and maintain the rigor of academic inquiry. Researchers should view AI as a complementary resource rather than a substitute for their creative and analytical capabilities. Emphasizing the cultivation of critical thinking and problem-solving skills alongside the integration of AI assistance fosters a harmonious human-AI collaboration that enhances research productivity while preserving the unique insights and perspectives of scholars. Harnessing AI's potential as an augmentative tool and upholding the principles of original thinking, researchers can elevate the quality and impact of their work, paving the way for transformative advancements in academic scholarship.

6. ASSESSING DISSERTATIONS: BEYOND THE WRITTEN REPORT

6.1 The Purpose of Assessment

Assessment in higher education plays a fundamental role in evaluating learning outcomes and gauging the effectiveness of instructional practices. At its core, the purpose of assessment is to measure the extent to which students have acquired the knowledge, skills, and competencies outlined in the learning objectives. Employing diverse assessment methods, such as examinations, quizzes, and assignments, educators gain valuable insights into students' comprehension, critical thinking abilities, and problem-solving aptitude (Hill et al., 2017). Furthermore, the data generated through assessments enable instructors to tailor their teaching approaches, identifying areas where students may be struggling and adapting instructional strategies to better support their learning journeys. Additionally, assessment outcomes are integral to curricular refinement, empowering academic institutions to continuously enhance their programs and ensure alignment with educational goals. As a crucial component of the educational process, assessment fosters a culture of continuous improvement, fostering an environment where students' academic growth is nurtured, and teaching methodologies are continually optimized to enhance the overall learning experience.

Table 1. Comparison of common assessment types - emphasising the core reason dissertations have primarily been assessed using essay type forms

Assessment Type	Advantages	Disadvantages
Examinations and Tests	• Efficient for evaluating knowledge, recall and understanding • Easy to administer and grade for large groups	• May not capture a holistic understanding of a student's abilities • Can induce stress and test anxiety in some students
Essays and Papers	• Provides an opportunity for in-depth analysis and critical thinking • Allows students to express creativity and original thought	• Time-consuming to grade and may not be scalable for large classes • Subjective grading may lead to inconsistencies in evaluation
Presentations and Projects	• Encourages communication and public speaking skills • Fosters collaborative learning and teamwork	• Requires significant preparation and organisation • Grading criteria may be less objective compared to other assessments
Performance-Based Assessments	• Assesses real-world application of skills and knowledge • Encourages problem-solving and decision-making abilities	• May be resource-intensive to design and administer • Difficult to standardize evaluation across different tasks
Formative Assessments	• Provides ongoing feedback and opportunities for improvement • Supports a growth mindset and self-directed learning	• Requires continuous monitoring and feedback from instructors • Time-consuming to implement in large classes
Summative Assessments	• Allows for comprehensive evaluation of learning outcomes • Assists in measuring students achievement against learning objectives	• Focuses on end-of-course evaluation, potentially neglecting ongoing progress • Limited opportunities for students to receive feedback and make improvements

6.2 Evaluating the Written Report

Evaluating the written report is a pivotal aspect of the dissertation assessment process, offering insights into a student's scholarly achievements and communication skills. A well-structured and coherent report showcases the depth of research, critical thinking, and analytical prowess applied throughout the study. Evaluators assess the clarity of arguments, organization of ideas, and the seamless integration of supporting evidence and literature. Additionally, a meticulously crafted written report demonstrates the student's ability to articulate complex concepts effectively and present research findings in a compelling manner. A comprehensive evaluation of the written report not only reflects the student's academic capabilities but also provides valuable feedback to nurture continuous improvement and refine their scholarly endeavors (Webster et al., 2000; Greetham, 2020).

6.3 Beyond the Written Dissertation: Presentations and Defenses

Beyond the written dissertation, presentations and defenses constitute a crucial dimension of the assessment process, offering students an opportunity to showcase their research findings and oral communication skills (e.g., vivas, poster sessions and peer review discussions (Kenwright, 2016c)). Presentations enable students to distill complex research into accessible formats, engaging audiences with visual aids and persuasive arguments. Defenses, on the other hand, encourage students to defend their research methodology, results, and conclusions in a rigorous academic setting, fostering critical thinking and composure under scrutiny. These oral components of the assessment provide evaluators with a holistic view of a student's comprehension, ability to articulate scholarly work, and capacity to respond to questions and challenges. Incorporating presentations and defenses, educational institutions reinforce the importance of effective communication in research and equip students with invaluable skills that transcend academia, empowering them for success in diverse professional and public contexts.

6.4 Game-Based Assessments

Moving beyond report type assessments, game-based learning objectives, while innovative and engaging, may present challenges when used to assess dissertation learning outcomes. While games can foster critical thinking, problem-solving, and teamwork, these skills may not directly align with the traditional goals of a dissertation, such as conducting original research, contributing to the academic discourse, and demonstrating deep subject knowledge (Kenwright, 2017, 2016a). Assessing dissertation learning outcomes through games might inadvertently prioritize gamification over academic rigor, potentially diluting the integrity of the assessment process. However, if thoughtfully integrated, game-based elements can complement the learning process by enhancing research and presentation skills, fostering creativity, and promoting interdisciplinary thinking, ultimately enriching the overall educational experience. The key lies in striking a balance that leverages the benefits of game-based learning without compromising the fundamental academic objectives of a dissertation.

A novel 'game-based' approach called 'stealth learning' is an emerging concept in educational gaming, that provides valuable insights into a student's cognitive abilities and knowledge acquisition during gameplay without disrupting the gaming experience (Kenwright, 2023). Embedding assessment measures seamlessly within the game environment, educators can gain a deeper understanding of a student's problem-solving skills, adaptability, and content mastery. This approach allows for a more holistic evaluation of learning outcomes, potentially offering a more comprehensive assessment method for dissertation-related skills and competencies within the context of game-based learning.

6.5 Holistic Assessment: Considering Multiple Dimensions

Holistic assessment, encompassing multiple dimensions, is essential to gain a comprehensive understanding of an individual's abilities and potential. Evaluating not only academic achievements but also personal growth, interpersonal skills, and extracurricular contributions, a holistic approach goes beyond a narrow focus on academic performance. It recognizes the unique talents and strengths that each individual possesses, fostering a supportive environment that nurtures diverse interests and aspirations. This approach acknowledges that success is not solely defined by grades but also encompasses emotional intelligence, adaptability, and resilience. Considering multiple dimensions in assessment, educational institutions can better identify and nurture well-rounded individuals who are equipped to thrive academically, personally, and professionally, making a meaningful impact in society.

6.6 Supervisor's Role

The supervisor's role in undergraduate dissertations is pivotal in guiding and supporting students throughout their research journey. As a subject matter expert, the supervisor provides valuable insights and expertise, helping students refine their research topics, formulate research questions, and design appropriate methodologies. They offer constructive feedback on literature reviews, data collection, and analysis, nurturing students' critical thinking and research skills (Roberts and Seaman, 2018). The supervisor also plays a mentorship role, encouraging students to overcome challenges, maintain motivation, and stay on track with their timelines (Derounian, 2011). They facilitate regular meetings, creating a space for fruitful discussions, and ensuring students' progress aligns with academic standards and learning objectives. Moreover, the supervisor fosters a supportive and collaborative environment, fostering the development of independent research capabilities while offering guidance and encouragement throughout the dissertation process. Ultimately, the supervisor's mentorship empowers undergraduate students to produce high-quality dissertations, enhancing their academic and personal growth as aspiring researchers and scholars.

6.7 Types of Dissertation

Dissertations encompass a diverse array of subjects, including technical (Buchanan and Herubel, 1993; Kenwright, 2016b), political, crime (Young, 2022), project-based, and survey-oriented topics, as well as those within psychology and other fields, each having distinct learning objectives. Consequently, their assessments are based on varying criteria, considering factors such as research depth, critical analysis, theoretical framework, data interpretation, and other specific requirements aligned with the unique goals and methodologies of each dissertation.

Table 2 shows two marking rubrics and weightings for different dissertations focusing on different learning outcomes ('Research Driven' and 'Project-Based').

Table 2. Dissertation marking rubric - (a) research-driven and (b) project-based analysis

Criteria	Weighting
Literature Review	30%
Methodology	20%
Data Collection	25%
Analysis	20%
Conclusion	5%

(a)

Criteria	Weighting
Critical Review	25%
Theoretical Framework	20%
Data Interpretation	25%
Critical Evaluation	20%
Conclusion	10%

(b)

7. NURTURING CRITICAL THINKING AND CREATIVITY

7.1 The Role of AI in Fostering Critical Thinking Skills

The role of AI in fostering critical thinking skills in the modern educational landscape cannot be understated. As AI technologies become increasingly integrated into various aspects of academia, they offer unique opportunities to cultivate and enhance critical thinking abilities among students. AI-driven tools, such as natural language processing models and data analytics software, empower students to engage in data-driven analyses, evaluate complex information, and draw well-informed conclusions. Through interactive simulations, adaptive learning platforms, and virtual problemsolving scenarios, AI immerses students in dynamic learning experiences, promoting active inquiry and intellectual curiosity. One of the most significant advantages of AI in fostering critical thinking lies in its ability to personalize learning pathways.

Tailoring educational content to individual student needs and progress, AI enables self-paced learning, allowing students to explore topics deeply and comprehend concepts thoroughly. Moreover, AI tools can pose challenging questions, present diverse perspectives, and encourage students to think critically and objectively. The provision of instant feedback and explanations by AI systems also aids in building metacognitive skills, encouraging students to reflect on their thought processes and refine their problem-solving strategies.

AI can serve as a valuable partner to educators in fostering critical thinking skills. Automating routine tasks and data analysis, AI frees up instructors' time, enabling them to focus on designing thought-provoking learning experiences and guiding students through meaningful discussions. AI can augment classroom interactions through chatbots that engage students in Socratic dialogues, helping them develop analytical reasoning and articulate their thoughts effectively.

Despite the manifold advantages, it is crucial to approach the integration of AI in critical thinking education thoughtfully. Educators must ensure that AI-driven content aligns with learning objectives and remains free from biases that might influence students' cognitive development. Integrating ethical considerations into AI design and implementation, educators can instill a sense of responsibility and awareness among students, ensuring that they critically evaluate the ethical implications of AI technologies. The role of AI in fostering critical thinking skills represents a transformative force in education. Through personalized and immersive learning experiences, AI empowers students to develop analytical and problem-solving abilities, cultivating a generation of independent and creative thinkers. Embracing

AI as a catalyst for critical inquiry and complementing it with human guidance, educational institutions can foster a culture of lifelong learning, preparing students to thrive in an ever-evolving world that demands astute critical thinkers capable of addressing complex challenges with confidence and ingenuity.

7.2 Promoting Creativity and Imagination in AI-Enhanced Research

Promoting creativity and imagination in AI-enhanced research is essential to harness the full potential of artificial intelligence as a transformative tool (Mazzone and Elgammal, 2019; Bakpayev et al., 2022). While AI technologies offer remarkable efficiencies in data analysis and content generation, nurturing human creativity remains central to pushing the boundaries of innovation. Encouraging researchers to explore uncharted territories, think beyond the confines of AI-generated outputs, and integrate their unique insights with AI-driven findings fosters a harmonious synergy between human intellect and machine capabilities. Striking a balance between AI automation and human ingenuity, AI-enhanced research can pave the way for groundbreaking discoveries, imaginative solutions, and novel advancements that shape the future of science and academia.

7.3 Encouraging Innovative Approaches to Dissertation Topics

Encouraging innovative approaches to dissertation topics is paramount in fostering intellectual growth, pushing the boundaries of knowledge, and addressing contemporary challenges. Embracing originality and creativity in research not only enriches academic discourse but also contributes to societal progress and real-world impact. Encouraging students to explore unconventional and interdisciplinary themes, educational institutions nurture a culture of curiosity and open-mindedness, fostering a generation of scholars capable of tackling complex problems with fresh perspectives. Embracing innovative approaches to dissertation topics comes with its challenges. Traditional academic norms and expectations may inadvertently discourage students from venturing beyond established paradigms. Faculty support and mentorship are essential to guide students through the uncharted territory of novel research topics, helping them refine their ideas and navigate potential roadblocks. Moreover, interdisciplinary research may require collaboration across departments and institutions, necessitating a supportive academic environment that values diverse perspectives and encourages cross-disciplinary dialogues.

8. IMPLEMENTING GENERATIVE AI IN UNDERGRADUATE DISSERTATIONS

8.1 Integrating AI Tools in Educational Institutions: Challenges and Opportunities

Integrating AI tools in educational institutions presents a compelling blend of challenges and opportunities. The adoption of AI technologies holds the promise of revolutionizing teaching and learning experiences, offering personalized learning pathways, and streamlining administrative tasks. AI-driven tools can provide valuable insights into student performance, facilitating datadriven decision-making to enhance academic outcomes. However, this integration also entails addressing ethical concerns, such as data privacy and algorithmic biases, to ensure responsible AI use. Additionally, adapting curricula and pedagogical approaches to effectively leverage AI requires faculty development and support. Balancing the human touch with AI automation and fostering a growth-oriented mindset are essential in navigating this transformation. Proactively addressing challenges and embracing opportunities, educational institutions can empower learners and educators alike to thrive in an AI-driven future, forging a pathway towards a more innovative, inclusive, and effective learning ecosystem.

8.2 Types of Generative Tools

Generative AI has revolutionized the landscape of dissertation writing and research projects, offering a plethora of powerful tools to streamline and enhance the creation process. AI-driven natural language processing models, like ChatGPT and Bard, are employed to generate coherent and contextually relevant report text, saving valuable time for students and researchers (Zhang et al., 2023). Additionally, generative AI enables the creation of informative and visually appealing charts, graphics, and visualizations from raw data, facilitating data analysis and presentation. For projects involving programming or code, AI tools can generate code snippets or even provide code suggestions to expedite the development process. Moreover, AI-driven content curation aids in conducting comprehensive literature reviews, identifying relevant sources, and summarizing key findings. These tools not only assist in content creation but also provide personalized guidance, adapting to individual research needs and academic requirements. However, it is crucial to strike a balance between utilizing AI assistance and preserving the student's original thought and creativity, ensuring that the final dissertation or project truly reflects the student's unique insights and scholarly contributions.

8.3 Training Students and Educators to Utilize AI Effectively

Training students and educators to utilize AI effectively is a pivotal step in maximizing the potential benefits of generative AI tools in education. Providing comprehensive and accessible training programs, educational institutions can empower students and faculty to harness AI's capabilities to augment their research and teaching endeavors. Training sessions should encompass a range of topics, including AI basics, understanding the strengths and limitations of generative AI models, and best practices for integrating AI tools into the academic workflow. Students should be guided on how to critically evaluate AI-generated content, ensuring academic integrity and minimizing biases. Educators, on the other hand, should receive specialized training on effectively incorporating AI-driven resources in the curriculum and mentoring students on using AI responsibly. Emphasizing ethical considerations and fostering a growth mindset toward AI integration, these training initiatives facilitate a harmonious collaboration between human intellect and artificial intelligence, ultimately cultivating a generation of tech-savvy scholars capable of leveraging AI to push the boundaries of knowledge and education.

9. FUTURE PERSPECTIVES AND LIMITATIONS

9.1 Exploring the Potential Future of AI in Undergraduate Dissertations

As we venture into the uncharted territories of the future, the potential impact of AI on undergraduate dissertations emerges as a compelling subject of inquiry. With continued advancements in generative AI models, the landscape of dissertation writing is poised to undergo transformational shifts. AI's ability to offer personalized guidance, expedite literature reviews, and automate certain research tasks holds promise for streamlining the dissertation process, fostering efficiency, and liberating students to focus on higher-order thinking and creativity. However, while AI-driven tools can undoubtedly be a valuable asset, it is essential to acknowledge their limitations. Concerns related to biases in AI-generated content, the risk of compromising academic integrity, and the potential over-reliance on AI assistance necessitate thoughtful consideration. Striking a balance between AI facilitation and preserving the authenticity of students' scholarly contributions will be a paramount challenge. As we peer into the horizon of AI integration in undergraduate dissertations, a human-centric approach, continuous ethical evaluation, and a growth-oriented mindset towards technology will be vital in ensuring that AI remains an empowering ally rather than a dominant force in shaping the future of academic research and learning.

9.2 Recognizing and Addressing the Limitations of Generative AI Models

Recognizing and addressing the limitations of generative AI models is imperative to ensure their responsible and effective integration in various domains. Despite their remarkable capabilities, generative AI models have inherent shortcomings that demand careful consideration to foster an ethical and sustainable AI ecosystem. One prominent limitation lies in the potential biases present in the training data, which can lead to biased outputs and perpetuate existing social, cultural, and gender biases, raising concerns about fairness and inclusivity. The impact of biased AI outputs extends beyond mere inconvenience, potentially reinforcing discriminatory practices and reinforcing societal inequalities. Therefore, comprehensive strategies must be devised to identify, understand, and mitigate biases within the training data and algorithms. Ethical concerns regarding privacy and data security also arise when employing generative AI models in various applications. Particularly when using sensitive information for AI training, ensuring data anonymity and confidentiality becomes critical to preserve user trust and protect individuals' privacy rights. Furthermore, considering the potential misuse of AI-generated content, safeguards should be implemented to prevent malicious use or dissemination of AI-generated fake information, which could undermine public trust and create misinformation challenges. Moreover, generative AI models may occasionally produce inaccurate or misleading content, necessitating vigilant human oversight. The context and nuances of human language can sometimes elude AI models, leading to outputs that lack accuracy or clarity. This limitation may be especially pronounced when handling complex or nuanced subject matters, necessitating human experts to verify and validate the generated content. As such, hybrid approaches that integrate AI capabilities with human judgment and expertise are indispensable to strike a harmonious balance between efficiency and accuracy. Addressing these limitations requires transparent documentation of AI development processes and data curation strategies to minimize biases and errors. Openness and transparency in AI systems allow for external scrutiny and foster public confidence in AI technologies. Additionally, ongoing efforts to update and improve the models through continual training and refinement are essential to enhance their accuracy and performance over time. In conclusion, recognizing and addressing the limitations of generative AI models is a multifaceted endeavor that requires a holistic approach. Combining AI assistance with human judgment and expertise remains pivotal to harness the full potential of generative AI while mitigating potential risks and challenges. Prioritizing ethical considerations, promoting transparency, and actively addressing biases and inaccuracies, we can foster a responsible and effective integration of generative AI models in various domains, ultimately advancing innovation, knowledge, and societal progress.

9.3 Only the Beginning

The current landscape of AI-driven tools in education and dissertation writing merely scratches the surface of what the future holds. As technology continues to evolve, AI models are bound to become more sophisticated, versatile, and commonplace, permeating various aspects of academia and beyond. While AI has already proven to be a valuable asset in generating reports and aiding research, its potential reaches far beyond these domains. From automating data analysis to personalized tutoring and even creative content generation, the applications of AI are vast and ever-expanding.

Despite these advancements, the traditional dissertation remains a valuable and time-honored component of academic learning. However, as AI continues to shape the landscape of education, the assessment of dissertations should evolve to embrace a broader perspective. The assessment process must transcend the traditional focus on the written report and encompass other essential dimensions, such as critical thinking, problem-solving, and the ability to synthesize and communicate complex ideas effectively. Doing so, we can ensure that the evaluation of a student's scholarly journey is holistic, capturing the full range of skills and competencies nurtured throughout the dissertation process.

Moreover, with the ease and accessibility of AI-driven solutions, there comes a risk of students succumbing to the temptation of relying solely on AI-generated content. As academics, it is vital to recognize and address this challenge proactively. Encouraging students to develop their intellectual abilities, fostering a growth mindset, and nurturing a culture of academic integrity are paramount. Providing meaningful guidance and mentorship, educators can reduce the temptation to rely excessively on AI solutions and encourage students to engage actively in their research, valuing the process of knowledge acquisition and scholarly exploration.

The current state of AI-driven tools in education and dissertation writing marks only the beginning of a transformative journey. As AI technologies advance and become more prevalent, the scope of their applications will extend far beyond simple report writing. While the dissertation remains a cornerstone of academic learning, its assessment must evolve to encompass various aspects of intellectual development. Promoting a balanced approach and prioritizing ethical and responsible AI use, academics can ensure that students continue to reap the benefits of AI while preserving the essence of scholarly inquiry and fostering a generation of independent and critical thinkers.

10. ETHICAL CONSIDERATIONS AND HUMAN-CENTRIC APPROACH

10.1 Ethical Use of AI in Education and Dissertation Writing

Ethical use of AI in education and dissertation writing is paramount to uphold the principles of academic integrity and fairness. Integrating AI-driven tools and generative models should be accompanied by a commitment to transparency and responsible AI practices. Ensuring the ethical use of AI involves addressing concerns related to biases, data privacy, and the risk of academic misconduct. Academic institutions and educators must emphasize educating students on the appropriate utilization of AI, encouraging critical thinking in evaluating AI-generated content, and fostering an understanding of AI's limitations. Promoting a human-centric approach, where AI augments human intelligence rather than replacing it, we can harness the transformative potential of AI in education while upholding ethical standards and safeguarding the integrity of academic research and dissertations.

10.2 Balancing AI Automation With Human Supervision and Mentorship

Balancing AI automation with human supervision and mentorship is a multifaceted endeavor that requires a careful consideration of the strengths and limitations of both AI and human capabilities. AI automation brings immense advantages in various domains, from streamlining repetitive tasks to processing vast amounts of data quickly and accurately. In education, for example, AI-driven tools can assist with automated grading, personalized learning pathways, and data analytics to identify areas for improvement in student performance. Similarly, in the context of dissertation writing and research projects, AI can expedite literature reviews, offer language and grammar suggestions, and aid in generating data visualizations. However, the overreliance on AI without human supervision raises concerns about the ethical implications and potential consequences. Human supervision and mentorship complement AI's abilities by adding essential dimensions that AI currently lacks. Ethical decision-making and moral considerations, which are deeply ingrained in human judgment, are crucial when applying AI in areas like healthcare, finance, and social services.

Human expertise and contextual understanding allow for nuanced interpretation and consideration of the broader societal impact of AI-generated outcomes. Moreover, AI models are not immune to biases present in the data they are trained on, which can inadvertently perpetuate inequalities and discrimination. Human oversight is necessary to identify and mitigate such biases and ensure fairness in AI-driven processes.

In education and research, mentorship plays a pivotal role in nurturing students' critical thinking, creativity, and problem-solving skills. While AI can offer personalized guidance and support, the guidance of a knowledgeable mentor is invaluable in helping students navigate complexities, think critically about their work, and offer constructive feedback. Mentorship extends beyond technical assistance; it fosters a growth mindset, instills a passion for learning, and encourages exploration and risk-taking in intellectual pursuits. The human mentor can also play a vital role in instilling ethical values and responsible AI practices in students, ensuring that they leverage AI in a manner that aligns with ethical principles. Striking a harmonious balance between AI automation and human involvement is essential to harness the full potential of AI while upholding ethical standards and promoting holistic development. Emphasizing a human-centric approach, where AI complements and augments human intelligence rather than replacing it, allows us to capitalize on the strengths of both AI and human expertise. Integrating AI as a supportive tool in conjunction with human supervision and mentorship, we can achieve a more comprehensive and responsible implementation of AI across diverse domains, leading to more ethical, innovative, and inclusive advancements in our society.

11. CONCLUSION AND DISCUSSION

This chapter has delved into the transformative potential of generative AI models in the realm of education and dissertation writing. Throughout this exploration, it becomes evident that while AI technologies offer valuable assistance and efficiency in various aspects of the dissertation process, they do not signify the end of undergraduate dissertations. Instead, they herald a new era of scholarly inquiry and learning, where AI serves as a powerful ally in augmenting human intellect and creativity.

The advantages of generative AI, such as personalized guidance, efficient literature reviews, and AI-generated content, significantly enhance the dissertation writing experience and empower students to delve deeper into their research. AI's ability to foster critical thinking, creativity, and problem-solving skills adds value to the academic journey, ultimately cultivating well-rounded scholars prepared for the challenges of the future. However, in embracing the potential of AI, it is crucial to recognize and address the limitations and ethical considerations associated with AI integration. Concerns over biases, data privacy, academic integrity, and overreliance on AI assistance necessitate a balanced approach. Prioritizing responsible AI practices, ensuring transparency, and fostering a human-centric approach to AI utilization, educational institutions can harness the full potential of AI while safeguarding the authenticity and originality of student contributions.

As we peer into the future, the chapter underscores the significance of human mentorship, critical thinking, and ethical decision-making in shaping the landscape of undergraduate dissertations. The synthesis of AI automation with human supervision and mentorship is vital to creating a harmonious synergy, where AI amplifies human potential and scholarly excellence.

In the grand tapestry of education, the dissertation remains an invaluable rite of passage, a testament to the pursuit of knowledge, and an embodiment of academic rigor. Embracing AI as a valuable tool and guiding force, the journey of undergraduate dissertations takes on a new dimension, embracing technological advancement while cherishing the timeless essence of scholarly inquiry. The future beckons with boundless possibilities, and with a balanced and thoughtful approach, undergraduate dissertations will continue to thrive as transformative endeavors shaping the intellects and minds of generations to come.

REFERENCES

Abd-Elaal, E.-S., Gamage, S., & Mills, J. E. (2019). Artificial intelligence is a tool for cheating academic integrity. In *30th Annual Conference for the Australasian Association for Engineering Education (AAEE 2019): Educators becoming agents of change: Innovate, integrate, motivate*, (pp. 397–403). AAEE.

Adiguzel, T., Kaya, M. H., and Cansu, F. K. (2023). Revolutionizing education with ai: Exploring the transformative potential of chatgpt. *Contemporary Educational Technology*, *15*(3), 429.

Bakpayev, M., Baek, T. H., van Esch, P., and Yoon, S. (2022). Programmatic creative: Ai can think but it cannot feel. *Australasian Marketing Journal*, *30*(1), 90–95.

Buchanan, A. L. and Herubel, J.-P. V. (1993). Comparing materials used in philosophy and political science dissertations: A technical note. *Behavioral & Social Sciences Librarian*, *12*(2), 63–70.

Chaka, C. (2023). Detecting ai content in responses generated by chatgpt, youchat, and chatsonic: The case of five ai content detection tools. *Journal of Applied Learning and Teaching*, *6*(2), 6.

Cotton, D. R., Cotton, P. A., & Shipway, J. R. (2023). Chatting and cheating: Ensuring academic integrity in the era of chatgpt. Innovations in Education and Teaching International.

Dai, W., Lin, J., Jin, F., Li, T., Tsai, Y.-S., Gasevic, D., and Chen, G. (2023). *Can large language models provide feedback to students?* OSF.

Datta, D., Phillips, M., Bywater, J. P., Lilly, S., Chiu, J., Watson, G. S., & Brown, D. E. (2022). Human-in-the-loop data collection and evaluation for improving mathematical conversations. In *International conference on artificial intelligence in education*, (pp. 551–554). Springer. 10.1007/978-3-031-11647-6_113

Derounian, J. (2011). Shall we dance? the importance of staff-student relationships to undergraduate dissertation preparation. *Active Learning in Higher Education*, *12*(2), 91–100.

Fuchs, K. (2023). Exploring the opportunities and challenges of nlp models in higher education: is chat gpt a blessing or a curse? In Frontiers in Education, 8, 1166682. Frontiers. doi:10.3389/feduc.2023.1166682

Greetham, B. (2020). How to write your literature review. 11

Hill, J., Kneale, P., Nicholson, D., Waddington, S., & Ray, W. (2017). Re-framing the geography dissertation: A consideration of alternative, innovative and creative approaches. *Pedagogic Research in Geography Higher Education*, (pp. 284–302).

Holmes, W., Bialik, M., & Fadel, C. (2023). *Artificial intelligence in education.* Globethics Publications.

Ison, D. C. (2012). Plagiarism among dissertations: Prevalence at online institutions. *Journal of Academic Ethics*, *10*, 227–236.

Kasneci, E., Seßler, K., Ku¨chemann, S., Bannert, M., Dementieva, D., Fischer, F., Gasser, U., Groh, G., Gu¨nnemann, S., Hu¨llermeier, E., et al. (2023). Chatgpt for good? on opportunities and challenges of large language models for education. *Learning and individual differences*, 103.

Kenwright, B. (2016a). Game-based learning in higher education. Communication Article, 1–8.

Kenwright, B. (2016b). Holistic game development curriculum. In *SIGGRAPH ASIA 2016 Symposium on Education*. ACM. 10.1145/2993352.2993354

Kenwright, B. (2016c). Peer review: Does it really help students? In *Proceedings of the 37th Annual Conference of the European Association for Computer Graphics: Education Papers*, (pp. 31–32). ACM.

Kenwright, B. (2017). Brief review of video games in learning & education how far we have come. In *SIGGRAPH Asia 2017 Symposium on Education*, pages 1–10. 11 10.1145/3134368.3139220

Kenwright, B. (2020). When digital technologies rule the lecture theater. *IEEE Potentials*, *39*(5), 27–30.

Kenwright, B. (2023). Data collection during active gameplay: Unveiling a multifaceted portrait of the individual. *Games as Stealth Assessments.*

Lo, C. K. (2023). What is the impact of chatgpt on education? a rapid review of the literature. *Education Sciences*, *13*(4), 410.

Malinka, K., Peres'ıni, M., Firc, A., Hujnak, O., & Janus, F. (2023). On the educational impact of chatgpt: Is artificial intelligence ready to obtain a university degree? In *Proceedings of the 2023 Conference on Innovation and Technology in Computer Science Education* (pp. 47–53). ACM. 10.1145/3587102.3588827

Mazzone, M., & Elgammal, A. (2019). Art, creativity, and the potential of artificial intelligence. In Arts, 8, page 26. MDPI. 14 doi:10.3390/arts8010026

Mhlanga, D. (2023). Open ai in education, the responsible and ethical use of chatgpt towards lifelong learning. *Education, the Responsible and Ethical Use of ChatGPT Towards Lifelong Learning (February 11, 2023)*. 3

Qadir, J. (2023). Engineering education in the era of chatgpt: Promise and pitfalls of generative ai for education. In *2023 IEEE Global Engineering Education Conference (EDUCON)*, (pp. 1–9). IEEE. 10.1109/EDUCON54358.2023.10125121

Ray, P. P. (2023). Chatgpt: A comprehensive review on background, applications, key challenges, bias, ethics, limitations and future scope. *Internet of Things and Cyber-Physical Systems.*

Roberts, L. D., & Seaman, K. (2018). Good undergraduate dissertation supervision: perspectives of supervisors and dissertation coordinators. *International Journal for Academic Development*, *23*(1), 28–40.

Singh, S. and Remenyi, D. (2016). Plagiarism and ghostwriting: The rise in academic misconduct. *South African Journal of Science*, *112*(5-6), 1–7.

Webster, F., Pepper, D., & Jenkins, A. (2000). Assessing the undergraduate dissertation. *Assessment & Evaluation in Higher Education*, *25*(1), 71–80.

Young, S. (2022). *How to write your undergraduate dissertation in criminology*. Routledge.

Zhang, C., Zhang, C., Zheng, S., Qiao, Y., Li, C., Zhang, M., Dam, S. K., Thwal, C. M., Tun, Y. L., & Huy, L. L. (2023). A complete survey on generative ai (aigc): Is chatgpt from gpt-4 to gpt-5 all you need? *arXiv preprint arXiv:2303.11717*. 15

Chapter 4
The Learning Experience and the Behavioural Profile:
Artificial Intelligence, Upskilling, and Reskilling for the Professions of the Future

Neli Maria Mengalli
https://orcid.org/0000-0002-3782-3807
Faculdade São Bernardo do Campo, Brazil

Antonio Aparecido Carvalho
Faculdade São Bernardo do Campo, Brazil

ABSTRACT

When artificial intelligence is in evidence and promotes economic, social, and cultural impacts, human skills must be enhanced and praised in relation to artificial intelligence. This chapter was written based on qualitative methodology and exploratory studies by reading current reports and articles at the time of writing. The objective was to highlight a reflection on the learning experience about four behavioral profiles. The potential of artificial intelligence was highlighted, as well as upskilling and reskilling for the professions of the future. It was concluded that understanding the world should be contained in learning experiences and different behavioral profiles have dissimilar ways of thinking and acting. The lack of knowledge regarding the operationalization of artificial intelligence can weaken human options in digital and physical transformation.

1. INTRODUCTION

Fascination, fear, anxiety, and insecurity have been experienced in contexts that integrate the knowledge society with the economy and artificial intelligence in relation to questions or commands to obtain digital products or answers in interaction on mobile devices in mobilities that require speed and productivity, as well as creativity or disruptive innovations. Professions of the present with projection into the future

DOI: 10.4018/979-8-3693-0074-9.ch004

tend towards greater interaction between human beings and machines, but the results are not yet known, only, for the most squeamish, these interactions are true dystopias.

The evidence is present in articles. Heikkilä (2023), for example, wrote about artificial intelligence language models that are rife with different political biases. The text is based on research that shows that artificial intelligence models also change over time, because companies update data sets and training methods, however the content has a reflective character, because people are using the answers from artificial intelligences as if they were great ideas.

It is a risk to absorb prejudices in texts articulated with the juxtaposition of ideas that are presented in a coherent and highly credible manner. Artificial intelligence is not credited with low qualifications or disqualifications, even though, in common sense, people claim that artificial intelligence can increase the risks of demotivation in acquiring skills and consequently disqualification and low qualifications tend to occur, mainly among younger people.

Modestino, Shoag and Ballance (2016, p. 28) wrote in an article that there was a low qualification for basic skills such as leadership and project planning and for specialized skills such as the development and use of software, therefore, it is believed that artificial intelligence is not the cause of disqualification and low qualification, because, even at a time when there were no artificial intelligences with a user-friendly interface, employers perceived disqualification and low qualification.

The low qualifications mentioned in the areas of leadership, project planning and software development and use are perceived by humans. When the programmed machines for recruitment and selection are more calibrated, perceptions may be different. Tepšić (2020, p. 39) wrote that the advances seen in computer vision include detecting people's expressions or body posture and human behavior are included in recommendations for improving interaction between humans and machines and respecting values and human ethics.

In hiring, there is emotional intelligence and artificial intelligence was not created with empathy and lack of judgment programming. The context of Human Resources and the use of artificial intelligence is one of the knots that must be untied in relation to the behavioral profile, recruitment, and selection in companies. This perception must be part of the list of public policies for work and income generation, even though hard skills may occur in training and the time may be long to acquire skills and technical skills, governments must have the metrics market to determine which training programs will receive public funding.

On the other hand, higher education institutions need to review the prescribed curricula in courses so that new skills and abilities, as well as power skills, are taught and learned in higher education courses. Governance is social and technological, since the technological disruption that is within the reach of (cyber) society is a disruption, according to Hopster (2021, p. 2), of a techno-social nature, because such technologies play roles that affect social dynamics and technique of society. The author includes socially disruptive technologies as technologies and Mengalli and Carvalho (2023, p. 9) added that the concept involves the effects on society and human cognition.

Generative artificial intelligence can be understood as techno-social disruptions or socially disruptive technologies in the sense that Hopster (2021, p. 1) wrote that they are linked to the social sphere in practices and relationships, in addition to being part of people's sensory experience. The way artificial intelligence is used to generate texts, audiovisuals, codes, and digital solutions has changed the way people interact with mobile devices. It is believed that it will be an opportunity to teach prompts so that the solutions generated can be further refined.

The educational area has more possibilities for teaching and learning with socially disruptive technologies. In the initial years, ethics may be the motto for use. In the final years of basic schooling, exposure, adoption, adaptation, appropriation, and inventiveness with techno-social disruptions tends to be potential for use with the ethics practiced from an early age. Based on ethics, generative artificial intelligence can benefit people, however without ethics, morals and good customs, dystopias occur.

According to Harari (2018, p. 232), teachers should teach skills and abilities that artificial intelligence, robots, and machines do not have, how to face generic purposes in life, how to deal with changes, how to learn new things to preserve mental balance in situations unknown. Opportunities in teaching, learning and in life permeate the learning experience and the behavioral profile, because, based on the behavioral profile, people have the experiences to use techno-social disruptions and, in technical courses and higher education, they have conditions to prototype digital solutions. Planners, analysts, executors, and communicators, each with skills and abilities, demonstrate the learning experience for society.

It is known that there will be new techno-social disruptions trained by developers and research can mitigate the spread of misinformation and the propagation of fear. The objective of this chapter is to highlight a reflection based on an exploratory and qualitative study about the learning experience in four behavioral profiles. The aim is not to limit the potential of artificial intelligence, but to position them as possibilities for upskilling and reskilling as a possibility for the professions of the future.

It is understood that the audience for this chapter are researchers, teachers, experience and interface designers, data analysts, programmers, developers, higher education and postgraduate academics and those interested in the themes: artificial intelligence, learning experience and professions of the future. In the division of this chapter, there is the background, the focus of the chapter, the solutions and recommendations, the directions for future research and the final considerations.

2. BACKGROUND: LEARNING EXPERIENCES AND BEHAVIORAL PROFILES

If this chapter were a photograph, this section would be what is implicit in the focus of the chapter and would be used to compose, decorate the images, and personalize the main subject and the objective, which is to highlight a reflection on the learning experience in four behavioral profiles. Artificial intelligence is included and how artificial intelligence could be used as ways to carry out teaching and learning. Zhang and Shu (2023) investigated how users perceived the role of artificial intelligence in improving personal learning profiles.

Zhang and Shu (2023, p. 5) wrote that e-learning based on artificial intelligence had the potential to revolutionize the way people learn and could provide a personalized and interactive learning experience for students. The authors believed in the possibility of increasing student engagement to improve learning outcomes and advance artificial intelligence-based e-learning for the future of education.

There is no doubt that further advances in artificial intelligence will be needed for integration into educational solutions. There are known cases in which platforms correct essays and provide reports to teachers and avatar tutors who provide feedback to academics in higher education institutions, however the interaction between humans and machines is constantly changing for the consumer experience and the experience of learning, after all, with the speed imposed by phygital transformations, artificial intelligence is increasingly present in the process of teaching and learning for the upskilling and reskilling that are so necessary for professions that are constantly changing.

In the Future of Jobs report (2023, p. 4), the fourth edition of the report on the future of work, criticism is highlighted regarding the maturation of generative artificial intelligence that transforms the job market in relation to technological advances and, therefore, there is a worsening of economic problems with geopolitical disturbances, social growth and environmental pressures. The scenario presented includes that artificial intelligence is a main driver of the potential algorithmic shift (Future of Jobs Report (2023, p. 6)) and highlights what those surveyed believe the adoption of artificial intelligence could represent in companies.

The adoption, expressed in the aforementioned report, represents a high turnover, 50% of respondents believe in the creation of jobs and 25% have the impression that job losses will occur. In the research carried out, artificial intelligence occupies the eighth position in the ranking in relation to the adoption of technologies between 2023 and 2027 in companies (Future of Jobs Report (2023, p. 24)), that is, in the next five years from 2023, companies invested in digital platforms and applications, in education and workforce development technologies, in Big Data analytics, in the Internet of Things and connected devices, in cloud computing, in cryptography and cybersecurity, and in e-commerce and digital commerce.

The professions that people believe are in the future are in the present with the uses of techno-social disruptions and the phygital transformation in industry and consumption that can be attributed to the number 5.0. It is known that the applications and uses of generative artificial intelligence are in creation and (co) creation with software trained in the areas of arts, aesthetics, code, writing, editing, search, collaboration with other humans and machines and in the true engineering of prompts.

Although do not intend to limit the potential of artificial intelligence, because it is important to consider them as a possibility for upskilling and reskilling as a possibility for the professions of the future, it has been found that, over the years and with the improvement of artificial intelligence, both upskilling and reskilling are a trend for companies and knowledge management.

Miah, *et al.* (2023, p. 132) concluded, on the motto of upskilling and reskilling, that artificial intelligence helped companies in knowledge management with the use of initial investments and with the growing knowledge support for artificial intelligence professional categories. In the context of knowledge management for artificial intelligence, there is a connection between enterprise search and the modeling of organizational learning. It is known that much will still change in interfaces and the greater the interoperability and user design, the faster consumption will occur.

Existing artificial intelligence is the subject of informal courses that seek to solve a problem in the most different areas without worrying about the behavioral profile of the course participants, as well as paying attention to the teaching and learning material for the creation of content and activities. The role of instructional designers is fundamental in self-instructional or non-face-to-face and online courses and in institutions that offer distance education because the learning experience uses techno-social disruptions.

Pagnozzi (2022, p. 120), concluded, in the article, that the impact of people analytics and digital transformation on training programs is considerable and it is an unmissable opportunity for organizations to offer appropriate training programs to employees so that there is an advantage competitive in the market and for people management. It is believed that learning is lifelong and occurs formally or informally. The certainty is that there will be no retreat in the use of artificial intelligence.

Teams in companies, in the areas of research and development, seek training in corporate education for upskilling and reskilling. These are challenges for thinking and acting in the global context, because the tendency is to expand the purposes of organizations and ethics must be placed at the expense of purely financial results. Reskilling enables personal and professional redirections in the context of techno-social disruptions.

It is not possible to believe that all people learn in the same way for new skills and abilities and for requalification. Rodrigues (2021) stated in the article that there are four behavioral profiles, and they all have characteristics that shape both people's personality and behavior, therefore, the learning experiences are different. The author reported that, generally, people have more than one profile, but there is always one dominant.

Behavioral profiles must be understood and must be foreseen in the design of courses in corporate education and higher education for upskilling and reskilling as a way of improving skills and abilities and so that the employee or academic can develop self-knowledge for identification of positive points and points to strengthen, as well as developing power skills. The four behavioral profiles informed by the author of the article are: the communicator, the analyst, the planner, and the executor. It is known that there are other ways of classifying people in people analytics, however, in this chapter, the investigation will have the profiles now informed.

Each profile has particularities that must be respected. The way of learning and teaching needs to be understood by the course designer or by teachers when preparing teaching plans that include the way of teaching and proposals for content and activities, because the way of learning is intricately linked to understanding the world that goes beyond words. (Freire, 1989, p. 9) wrote that reading the world precedes reading the word.

The author, when working with youth and adult literacy, realized that language and reality are dynamically linked. Therefore, understanding the content requires critical reading so that there is a perception of the relationship between the text and the context. Years after Paulo Freire (1921 - 1997) showed that understanding the world in the educational process is essential for the learning experience, it is known that artificial intelligences do not socially change teaching and learning, however, if there are no learning experiences and understanding behavioral and professional profiles ethical applications can be imposed as competitive advantages, but are harmless to professional results.

Over the days, new names for professions have emerged due to changes in the way people teach, learn, and use socially disruptive technologies. Opportunities for upskilling and reskilling are perceived when studying the interactions between society and different technologies. The Future of Jobs Report (2023, p. 42) shows that people in companies perceive gaps in the skills and abilities of employees and candidates who participate in selection processes and this finding is a barrier to achieving the transformation of industries and the Investment in learning and in-service training is promising and strategic for business performance.

3. THE POINT OF THE CHAPTER IMAGE: THE REFERENTIAL EXTENT OF THE LEARNING EXPERIENCE

After explaining the implicit aspects of the chapter's focus, the intention is reinforced in reflecting on the learning experience about the four behavioral profiles mentioned by Rodrigues (2021). It begins with a brief explanation of the profiles without going into depth, because the learning experience is the protagonist, and the behavioral profiles are the supporting elements.

The profiles mentioned were the communicator, the analyst, the planner, and the executor. In the article, Rodrigues (2021) wrote that people with the communicative behavioral profile can communicate well, in addition to being creative, charismatic, and persuasive. They are positive, they think about the goal they hope to achieve, they are generally excited about new possibilities, they tend to be people who are easy to relate to, they infect other people with optimistic positions and, often, they are influencers.

In relation to work, they tend to relate well with team members, unite people towards common goals, mitigate conflicts and are used to socialize results. The absence of a communicator in the team or group can compromise morale, trust, and the flow of information, as well as enhance organizational or academic silos. However, communicators are not generally good analysts, nor are they able to make good plans and following the rules are not specialties of communicators.

The rules are well analyzed by people with an analyst behavioral profile because the preference is for step by step and details so that the execution of activities or tasks is perfect. The areas related to knowledge or research converge with the characteristics of the analyst, because they are people who tend to mitigate errors and are surgical in the problems they encounter, for the reason that they strive for perfection, pay attention, and take care when analyzing.

As haste can be the enemy of perfection, pressure is not a good ally for analysts who tend to be too proud to receive help and are demanding about results. Recognition is always welcome for analysts who need to be managed not to spend too much time on details not necessary for the project and to be helped to make decisions. Teams need analysts so that the results have the desired quality and planners complement the analyst's work.

People with a planner behavioral profile tend to be calm and collected to plan everything in advance. The stable, patient, sense of justice, conservatives and constant pace characteristics can irritate the group, but the planner can get along with other people from other profiles, they can even help others, they are not people who tend to go to battle and mitigate conflicts. They monitor the team's or group's results and can provide feedback or feedforward, if they have a keener vision of the future.

Deadline is often an issue for planners because checking and reviewing are important parts of the job. Creativity is not the strong point of planning and quick actions or decision-making are not easy tasks for the planner. Risk management is a function compatible with the planner and control is an element that must be included in planning so that the established tasks are fulfilled.

Tasks are best conducted by people with the executor profile because they are objective and direct in relation to details. Completing tasks is taken seriously with determination and purpose, even if it is difficult or optional. The ambition of the executors is the challenge because they believe they have the freedom to perform the challenging action. Having many executors in actions that need to occur without failure is worrying, because they are capable of achieving the stipulated goals with overconfidence, therefore, the presence of supervisors is necessary. The decisions that need to be made are not coherent for the executing profile, after all, the execution is closer to established goals, not to correcting the course.

After getting to know a little about four behavioral profiles from the point of view of Rodrigues (2021) and having the reference for learning experience, it is highlighted that no behavioral profile is better than the other. The central element is the learning experience for possibilities for upskilling and reskilling that include professions for the future and the potential of artificial intelligence. Subburayan (2023, p. 4) wrote that artificial intelligence is revolutionizing both upskilling and reskilling efforts to deliver personalized learning experiences, adaptive assessments, intelligent tutoring, and content curation.

The author presents computational resources in which artificial intelligence can increase the involvement of academics, collaborators, or workers, including in immersive experiences. Natural Language Processing - NLP, chatbots, virtual reality and augmented reality, including mixed and extended realities, are highlighted in the text written by the author. Some advantages are presented by Subburayan (2023, p. 4) in relation to artificial intelligence, such as data analysis guided by artificial intelligence that assists higher education institutions or companies in relation to the progress of academics, employees or workers, the potential to remodel the educational system and training people with the skills needed for the jobs of the future.

The future is present, because the number of available artificial intelligence projects exceeds one thousand in 2023 and the promise is innovation in companies. The growth of artificial intelligence in the market is exponential and it is almost impossible to keep up with so many projects. Aggregators of artificial intelligence projects and groups of people who test solutions with artificial intelligence make it possible to learn about projects, however, experimentation is not knowledge that is usually taught in higher education institutions. The theoretical prevails over the practice of experimentation and such explanatory or elucidatory methodologies do not meet all behavioral profiles in the learning experience.

Knowledge thought and actions to implement the teaching process must begin at the same pace: action, reflection and new actions and it is necessary to ask students to have their own control. Dewey (1979, p. 64) used the expression self-mastery in his work to represent self-mastery and wrote that the ideal end of education would be the formation of the capacity for self-mastery.

In the future, it will not be strange if artificial intelligence helps people to become aware of the existence of so many digital solutions with artificial intelligence or even how to learn with artificial intelligence, but only people who master specific combinations of professional skills will know how to use the digital solutions created at a fast pace. Upskilling and Reskilling are becoming increasingly necessary for the contemporary market.

Learning experiences include cultural transformation for stakeholder mediation, management change and people training. The role of educational designers becomes more than important for the market because companies and the development of science need both technological expertise and process design. Technological expertise in user interfaces, methods and a broad vision of different architectures and artificial intelligence models favors the hiring of people and process design allows employees to have a systemic vision, a mindset for continuous improvement and the discovery of new processes. There is no magic in using artificial intelligence for upskilling or reskilling. Bozkurt and Sharma (2023, p. ii) use a metaphor about generative artificial intelligence.

The authors wrote in the article that if artificial intelligence is generative it is Aladdin's magic lamp, people's desires are the instructions given in the prompts, that is, people must be able to develop instructions consistent with the programming made in generative artificial intelligence to get the answer that can help people on their professional or academic journey. Removing the genie from the magic lamp is usually an arduous task, however, after the genie grants wishes, people are able to grow professionally.

Human interaction with artificial intelligence requires knowing the process of designing, elaborating and contextually refining data inputs to obtain the behavior of artificial intelligences according to the language model ((Bozkurt and Sharma (2023, p. ii)), therefore, writing prompts consistent with artificial intelligence programming is the basis of many exercises and training. The learning experience in the interaction between the human being and the programmed machine requires an understanding of logic, memorization to avoid making the same mistakes and a change in behavior to act in accordance with the language of artificial intelligence.

There are many free courses that aim to sell knowledge about preparing prompts. Bozkurt and Sharma (2023, p. iii), in the article, wrote that quality prompts need strategy. In this chapter, the strategies will be summarized and, lightly, referred to characteristics of behavioral profiles to highlight the learning experience for upskilling and reskilling. Writing or speaking must begin with the defined objective. The planner has characteristics that lead us to believe that they started with the purpose of the request.

Identifying or envisioning the learning result is important for human-machine interaction. The lesson is: definition of the general objective and specific objectives.

Familiarity with the artificial intelligence language model is essential for interaction, as the software programming does not change for each user. Therefore, the preparation of instructions must be detailed as analysts prefer to obtain the desired results. The model experience and the learning experience need to be aligned to the point of assigning specific functions for the response. The lesson is: understand programming and the artificial intelligence model, get to know the [machine] interlocutor.

When you know the interlocutor, communication can occur more quickly. The communicator has the potential to write instructions that are unambiguous. Conciseness, direct communication and clarity are usually learned in training. The quantity and quality of the exercises enable accuracy in words and in the elaboration of oration and periods. The lesson is: clarity and conciseness to delimit the possibilities in the result as an answer.

The context helps in delimitation. Developing instructions with the desired scenario is a way of communicating the desired result with tips and topics to contextualize the situation people are in. The human varnish has communication and creativity as the most evident layer and differs from the machine in learning experiences. The communicator tends to create greater interaction with contextualization to obtain what is needed. The lesson is: contextualization and tips focused on the context so that the subject is respected.

Communication can be improved with examples. Generative artificial intelligence is trained with text and images. Examples can be in some text or image that were part of the training of the machine that finds what it is looking for faster compared to humans. Communicators use examples to be understood and analysts like examples to mitigate errors. The lesson is: instructions with examples enable understanding for the search.

Customizing and debugging learned results [responses] can refine instructions for accuracy and detail. Planners and analysts seek relevance in detail to ensure that step-by-step instructions or sequences are not lost. Adjustments are always necessary for configuration, debugging, and instruction optimization. Responses as results tend to be more accurate, relevant, and appropriate for the user as instructions are well calibrated to the results. The lesson is: instructions configured and optimized for the desired context tend toward accuracy and relevance of responses.

Upskilling and reskilling with interaction with generative artificial intelligence is a process of (co) creation, therefore, the specification of the format or structure that requires the answer is necessary so that human creation can complement the result brought by the software. The creative human varnish transcends the machine in contemporary times and maintains the human in the professional market, because the dominance of creativity in (co) creation belongs to the human being. It is the human who controls the machine from development and design to the results of the responses. The programming response must be in accordance with the instruction planner's wishes, whether cause and consequence, sequence, step by step or pros and cons. The lesson is: specification in instructions for the coherent structuring of the response to human (co) creation.

Human memory has vital details for pretension. In this way, the elements of the instruction are as detailed as the prediction that the analyst intends to have in the answer. Variables and invariable are elements that must be presented in the instruction to the machine explicitly. The generative artificial intelligence programming model predicts that essential information is highlighted so that the answer is important in the texts or audiovisuals. The lesson is: importance needs to be highlighted so that the essential is included in the response.

Carrying out instructions consistent with machine learning requires human training. The exercises will lead to perfection and the performers feel that they have the freedom to conduct the tasks with the response as a consequence and, as the training leads to corrections and adjustments, the experts verified that the errors need to be corrected so that the communicators can communicate better with the machines. The lesson is: repetition is necessary to learn from mistakes.

The evaluation of each instruction is a reason for the planner to ensure that each word is essential in the oration and during the instruction period. The quality of the responses is sought in each instruction given via the machine's input device. The human varnish is unique in relation to human characteristics in the non-repetition of activities in search of the perfect answer to (co) creation. The lesson is: renewal starts with repetition.

Recent inventions and innovation must be generated ethically and safely. Even though Heikkilä (2023) has shown in the article that biased content, and in some cases harmful to human life, exists in the interaction with artificial intelligence, it is necessary to make sure as analysts that the intentions in the instructions do not enhance responses that, in human (co) creation, do not bring harm to others or to society, because upskilling or reskilling with prejudice or dystopian vision is not consistent with safety, nor with ethical values. The lesson is: morals, ethics and safety are pillars in instructions for machines.

Responsibility is important for human command in interactions with artificial intelligence, whether for (co) creation in upskilling or reskilling or for obtaining a response or result. The learning experience in interfaces with artificial intelligence is the result of strategies to develop understanding of the subject, to stimulate creativity and to strengthen critical thinking. According to Dewey (1979, p. 66), there is a prediction of the consequences involving intelligence operations, it is necessary, at all times, to observe the objective conditions and circumstances for learning.

The human being is the one who makes strategies, innovations and transformations in the world and Silva (2001, p. 843) wrote that technology is a subclass of technical systems, that is, artificial intelligence is supported by techniques for practicality and the challenge for the integration of computational resources is constituted by strategically thinking about the use of disruptive technologies without forgetting the equivalence with assistive technologies, the inclusion of human diversity and plurality and ethics for interactions between humans and machines.

4. SOLUTIONS AND RECOMMENDATIONS: MITIGATING MYTHS TO STRENGTHEN REFLECTION

From the interactions between human beings and machines, theories have been created and refuted over many years and the passage of centuries. The beliefs were very much in common sense, such as, for example, the Turkish mechanic who was seen as a mechanical illusion or a skilled operator who beat opponents who were eager to beat the chess game machine. For nearly a century, people have wanted to beat the gaming machine with an anonymous individual. In the 21st century, Lease (2013, p. 13) studies the online work of Amazon's Turkish mechanic, an allusion to 18th century mechanisms, and reports that, due to the system's design, workers are not so anonymous.

The aforementioned machine was a mechanical illusion with skilled player that people were suspicious of but felt the pleasure of competition. The unveilings occurred over the centuries, as happened with many automatons. Science inspires new research, books, films and theater performances with science fiction or real stories with fictional appeal. Robotization, mechanization and artificial intelligence, in science, belong to transdisciplinary fields that have a long history and theories.

What is evident in the media today is the fascination and fear of dystopias that the mechanical and the programmable provoke. Scientific influence is on the human ecosystem from scientific development and literature. Silva (2001, p. 857) wrote that the problem is not one of "machinery", but of how to predict and optimize the repercussions in interactions with the elements of the system or ecosystem. Bozkurt, *et al.* (2023, p. 54) stated, in the article, that artificial intelligence is an extension of human intelligence.

In the article written by Lane (2023), it is evident that people must be prepared for the careers of the future and need to choose positions or functions that require exclusively human skills and it is possible to add that they are professions that have potential skills and abilities for interaction with machines or with programming developed by other humans. Speed and repetition are possible elements for machines, for human beings it is possible to interact with robotization, mechanization or artificial intelligence to provide support for humanization in strategic decision-making or for creativity with (co) creation. The human varnish highlights the experience of learning through communication and creativity.

Automation does not replace jobs, because jobs change over time. Working with a typewriter was replaced by skills and abilities to interact with fixed devices and knowledge of programming languages. Word processors, spreadsheets and presentation software were introduced in companies and typists no longer received handwritten texts to be reproduced on electric typewriters, however, typists were able to undergo training to use computers.

Artificial intelligence is part of the work in the digital transformation of industry 4.0 and the phygital transformation in industry 5.0. The person who threatens the human is another human with the power to decide who occupies which role or position. A sustainable career needs to be part of contemporary transversal themes from basic education so that anyone who prefers to be hired by a company knows how to manage their own career and knows how to include their own knowledge in professions that have not yet been invented. Positions and functions that need people who know how to manage socio-emotional skills and abilities and who have, in their profile, emotional intelligence, creativity, communication, critical thinking, emotions and feelings will not be extinguished.

Technologies are strategies (Silva, 2001) in the cultural virtualization of the human ecosystem with the techno-social practices of the economy and contemporary culture with the modes of communication and socialization in digital spaces. Colloquial and common sense discourse about techno-social disruptions is increasingly prevalent and, according to Hopster (2021, p. 2), there is a natural affinity between the language of disruption and the conceptualization of (cyber) society's interactions with technologies, the processes are part of ethical studies, policy formulations, there are mixtures that are not easily made in the more comprehensive notions of social disruptive technologies and the solutions lack academic analysis.

However, to merge (cyber) society with technologies, scholars must become more involved with techno-social disruption and need to provide conceptual foundations that can be understood by the entire society. The definition, in multidimensionality and in inter and transdisciplinary applications, must be better defined within the scope of techno-social disruptions.

Integrative definitions and comprehensive notions of techno-social disruption can unite academic understanding with new paradigms. For Kuhn (1970, 1998, p. 156), the traditional paradigm is, in some way, wrong, even though, in the new paradigm, concepts, terms, principles and old experiences usually have new relationships among the elements revealed. Encouraging theoretical and conceptual reflection is important but should not be dissociated from uses in the context of techno-social changes.

The existing transformations highlight the myths of people and the prejudices of developers and training of both machines and people. In the article "Por que é impossível criar um modelo de linguagem de IA imparcial?" (2023) [Why is it impossible to create an unbiased AI language model?], it is stated that the most widespread myth regarding artificial intelligence is that technologies are neutral and impartial. Such narratives are dangerous, because trust or fear of programming and artificial intelligence contribute to professional gaps. Reflection can be a way of understanding the lived world and professional action based on scientism.

There are those who seek the maximum truth, according to the aforementioned article, with language models so that artificial intelligence is politically correct in relation to other digital solutions created and made available to users. Feng, *et al.* (2023, p. 11737), in research developing methods for measuring biases and political biases in language models, wrote that language models are pre-trained on diverse data sources that include opinions and perspectives that can contemplate the democracy and diversity of ideas, but are socially biased.

The statements by Feng, *et al.* (2023) are very similar to the ideas of Heikkilä (2023) in the article, which used an argument from authority to express that no language model can be completely free from political biases. It should be added that the results obtained in interactions with generative artificial intelligence add to the ideologies of the people who prepare the prompts. People tend not to accept answers that are not consistent with their own worldview.

Tutors based on artificial intelligence will highlight what is in the speech script. Reflection is not part of the machine's duties. The experience of learning with artificial intelligence has, in language models, a problem that can be difficult to correct and social problems that have no easy solution, because most people do not understand how responses are generated. A possible solution could be the personalization of artificial intelligence according to the consumer's positioning, however personalization for learning and research is not recommended. Bias must be mitigated.

Liu, *et al.* (2021), in the article, describe metrics to measure political bias in the GPT-2 generation and propose reinforcement learning structures to mitigate political biases in texts generated using word embeddings or a classifier, that is, there is research to mitigate biases and perspectives, including OpenAI, uses human feedback reinforcement learning techniques to tune artificial intelligence models.

Hsu (2023) wrote for a mass circulation newspaper that the harm caused by artificial intelligence is generally minimal and can be easily refuted. It is believed that the creation and dissemination of fiction about some people threatens reputation. No matter how much biased search engine algorithms have been combated, artificial intelligence and the company cannot be exempt. Problems persist with algorithms as well as artificial intelligence language models.

The uses of artificial intelligence involve billions of dollars and even with reports of loss of interest in using it for the consumer experience, it is clear that the number of companies investing in artificial intelligence is large and the ways to retain users are changing, after all It is humans who promote machine learning and training and companies are able to manipulate consumer behavior because they collect user data.

In (micro) data, companies evaluate the behavioral profiles of employees, and, in (macro) data, Big Techs use the data to profile consumers. When companies know the behavioral profiles of employees, they can organize people into roles that are most consistent with the employees' skills and competencies, and there is a tendency to have more productivity and more engagement. High-performance teams have different behavioral profiles and complementary skills. Training is usually personalized for people based on (micro) data, as well as mitigating conflicts and turnover. Promotions often use the evaluation of behavioral profiles. When Big Techs have consumer data, they move the market.

In McKinsey's report The State of AI in 2023: Generative AI's Breakout Year (2023, p. 6), it was noted that organizations are rapidly implementing generative artificial intelligence and there are significant effects on industries and the job market, however the inaccuracy, cybersecurity and intellectual property infringement are reported by respondents as risks in the adoption of artificial intelligence in companies. In Research Insights Augmented Work for an Automated, AI-driven World. (2023, p. 2), the era in which human-machine partnerships increase productivity and provide exponential business value is called the era of augmented workforce.

Researchers at the IBM Institute for Business Value seemed to believe that artificial intelligence will not replace people and stated that people who use artificial intelligence will replace people who do not use artificial intelligence in the company. In the report The Economic Potential of Generative AI: The Next Productivity Frontier (2023, p. 13), it is written that, in addition to the value-generating potential that artificial intelligence can offer, disruptive technology based on artificial intelligence can generate value across organization when revolutionizing internal knowledge management systems.

5. QUALITATIVE AND EXPLORATORY STUDY AND EVIDENCE FROM THE LEARNING EXPERIENCE

Research institutes and large consulting companies are investing to understand artificial intelligence in business. Such reports help companies adopt disruptive technologies and revolutionize science with the speed at which data is collected. Over the centuries, a true revolution in science took place and traditions and paradigms were challenged every time research and researchers' training had different visions and resources for investigations.

In relation to paradigms, Kuhn (1998, p. 75 - 76) illustrated the effects of specialization with a question from a physicist to a chemist about the single helium atom (Kuhn, 1970, 1998) and the answers did not coincide, because, for the for the chemist, the helium atom was a molecule and, for the physicist, it was not a molecule, because it did not present a molecular spectrum. The particle was the same, but the formations of both were different. Kuhn's illustration (1970, 1998) shows that research practices are different, just as the objectives of investigations and experiences in solving problems are different and the consequences may be different paradigms.

Science, in the author's new metaphor, is an activity that consists of solving puzzles (Kuhn, 1998, p. 77) that includes the objectives and precision of scientific knowledge with the unveiling of new elements, phenomena or facts in academic investigations and theories that become new with each discovery. The objective of this chapter was to highlight a reflection based on an exploratory and qualitative study about the learning experience in four behavioral profiles.

In the several years of teaching practice, the formation of groups in higher education classes with the four profiles was observed and it was realized that the combination of people with different behavioral profiles enhances the academics' learning experience and the decision was to search for research that used the four behavioral profiles in recent years (2022 and 2023). Eight results were found with the terms "artificial intelligence", "learning experience" and "behavioral profile" in academic search engines.

However, the elements investigated were: student success, behavioral profile of scientists and data analysts, language learning experience, learning experience in self-instructional courses, promotion of wisdom at work, political applications and practical wisdom in executive education and environment of business schools. The decision was to exchange "learning experience" for "people analytics" and the results were three, but they related to the use of technologies in the area of people management, decision-making algorithm systems and organizational learning.

When searching for "reskilling", "upskilling", "artificial intelligence" and "behavioral profile" no results were obtained. The intention was to situate artificial intelligences as possibilities for upskilling and reskilling as possibilities for the professions of the future and no people were found with the four behavioral profiles: communicator, planner, analyst, and executor that include the learning experience and the intelligences artificial. After reading and searching for theories, it was believed that much still needs to be researched, but the certainty is that there will be progress over time.

Texts from around the world were searched and found that each one had its specificities, delimitation, and context. It was believed that this qualitative and exploratory study has a contribution to science in relation to the learning experience, artificial intelligence, upskilling and reskilling, the human varnish, and the professions of the future. The adopted paradigm is effective in inducing changes in other existing paradigms because it highlights additions in relation to other theories, such as the experience of learning with behavioral profiles: communicator, planner, analyst, and executor. No theoretical reference was found in the juxtaposition of "learning experience" + [four behavioral profiles] "behavioral profiles" in academic search engines.

The set of academic rules was followed, existing theories were assimilated, and a new theoretical set was created. What was incorporated into science from the scientific enterprise will never be the same again (Kuhn, 1998, p. 78), because it certainly highlighted a new way of thinking about the contemporary phenomenon and affected related areas. Changes will continue to occur with the unveiling made in this chapter and new interventions in science must take place with the theoretical subsidies expressed. The dynamics of investigations presuppose new facts and phenomena or novelties regarding theories. There will always be something to add to the research carried out.

In fact, there was an attempt to find the four behavioral profiles and the learning experience with the terms "learning experience", "artificial intelligence", "people analytics", "upskilling" and "reskilling" and of the twelve results found, the one that came closest to what was intended was the Braun's thesis (2023), however it did not highlight the learning experience and the four behavioral profiles. It was noticed that the phenomenon researched includes the philosophical and sociological.

It was necessary to develop the theory as per the objective of qualitative research (Taylor, Bogdan and DeVault (2016, p. 8)) with a flexible research design (Marshall and Rossman, 2011, *apud* Taylor, Bogdan and DeVault, 2016, p. 8). At the beginning, we sought theoretical references to support the observations and reading of the corporate world with the presence of artificial intelligence in the reports of research institutes and consultancy companies was fundamental to understand the scenario that there was in 2023. The questions that we had at the beginning of the investigation were answered, but there are directions for future research.

6. FUTURE RESEARCH: THE PATH TAKEN LEAVES A LEGACY FOR NEW PARADIGMS

Every beginning of an investigation has countless questions and the search for theories is essential to verify the paths taken by researchers, to find the convergence of authors and to search for the most original source or fountain. Learning from each reading and appropriating the theme (re) means research in a holistic way. It is the examinations of different theories that support the many perspectives and foster new insights.

The learning experience and the behavioral profile are intricately connected, and, in contemporary times, work has been linked to upskilling and reskilling in the search for disruptive innovation that is within the scope of the market and industries. However, society and processes are in the cultural, social, historical, and economic relationships that permeate human lives, therefore, research must be (multi) referential to highlight what emerges from the interaction between human beings and machines.

The analysis of computational resources needs to state that technologies are the studies of techniques, because the human being is the one who makes the strategies, transformations, and disruptive innovations. Silva (2001, p. 843) wrote that technology is a subclass of technical systems, that is, technology is supported by technique in the use of recursions by human beings. It is necessary to conceptualize disruptive technologies when they are combined with various technologies, when there are widespread applications in the most different areas and industries, when there is (re) organization, (re) structuring and (de) structuring in society and when they refer to the economy and society.

The contextual notion of techno-social disruption needs to be expanded and linked in the most different contexts, not limited to the social, technological, cultural, political, historical, and economic. The business area, design and development must be included in the studies. Whenever necessary, determine the extent to which technology disruption is for everyone, without forgetting assistive technologies and green technologies.

Researchers can use other tests to verify behavioral profiles, such as the DISC model (Dominance, Influence, Steadiness, and Conscientiousness) or four animals personality test, after all there are four behavioral profiles. There was a reflection on the learning experience in four behavioral profiles in a theoretical way, it is believed that the theory can be experienced with the unveiling of the potential of artificial intelligence for upskilling and reskilling as possibilities for the professions of the future.

Data security analysts, for example, may have artificial intelligence at work, because, according to MIT Technology Review Insights produced in association with Teleperformance, Human-plus-AI Solutions Mitigate Security Threats (2023, p. 5), instead of an analyst doing something countless times, it is possible to have routines or automations learned by machines for management and triage of alerts, in other words, it is not upskilling or reskilling to look for new professions, it is including artificial intelligence in training. At first, it may cause some distrust and studies are needed to test the digital solutions that will be present in human-plus-artificial intelligence professions.

Mistrust or the privacy nightmare as in the article by Guo and Renaldi (2022) can occur with the collection of emails, phone numbers or having futuristic metal spheres pointed at people's faces to scan their irises or, perhaps, other biometric data to train artificial intelligence. Dystopias or real cases must be investigated so that the truth can be known. Ethics must prevail, as well as people's freedom.

Research and teaching should be inseparable in higher education with the amalgamation of ethics and reflection with thinking and acting need coherence. For Dewey (1979, p. 63-64), thinking is stopping the first manifestation of the impulse and seeking to put it in connection with other possible tendencies of action [...] Thinking is also postponing immediate action, while reflection, through observation and memory, effects the internal control of the impulse, since in thinking and reflective action there is a union of observation with memory.

7. CONCLUSION

It was concluded that training programs for upskilling and reskilling must include entrepreneurship, diversity, and the 50+ audience. Behavioral profiles need to be foreseen in learning experiences and in the uses of disruptive techno-social technologies, because they are the new cornerstones that need to be in the structuring and development of career building projects with the upskilling and reskilling so necessary in volatility, in anxiety, complexity and current non-linearities.

Although there are different behavioral profile tests, the methodologies are unique, and it is possible to outline the profile of the employee or selected person. Responsibilities in relation to upskilling or reskilling must be the assignment of both the public and the private and public policies which cannot be fetishized within the scope of ethics and purely financial results. The training of people must be reviewed, from teaching and learning at an early age to higher education, after all, it is the development of the nation. Both the government and higher education institutions must be responsible for the use of disruptive techno-social technologies with prescribed curricula that highlight people's reality and well-being.

The certainty that there will be at least one artificial intelligence in every part of the company moves the market for digital solutions, but teaching and research in higher education institutions must be based on ethics. According to Dewey (1979, p. 65), freedom is identical to self-mastery, because the formation of purposes and the organization of the means to execute them can summarize the work of intelligence. The author makes reference to the human intelligence that dominates machines when developing or designing them.

Humans create the rise of artificial intelligence for the market and language models reshape industries and consumption, including information. Companies seek alliances or agreements so that financial results are not threatened and people from certain categories come together for fear of losing revenue to machines, forming united human fronts against Big Techs. It is not possible to omit the economic and political tensions, the speed imposed by technological resources and mental health in research.

The time has come to ensure learning experiences that consider behavioral profiles so that upskilling and reskilling are meaningful for people and companies in the most diverse professions that are in constant transformation. The center of processes with artificial intelligence is integrally human because humans are capable of carrying out corporate digital and phygital transformation and pioneering innovations. No matter how good the analysis and adaptabilities of machines are, assertive communication and creativity are part of the human varnish.

The promises of creative and productive teams are commercial ways of highlighting artificial intelligence because the existence of human-plus-artificial intelligence can be stronger. What weakens human beings is the lack of knowledge regarding the operationalization of artificial intelligence. In corporate metamorphosis, business models include improvements in communication [in the sense of speed and expansion of the brand's presence], security and confidentiality with and without artificial intelligence and tutoring based on artificial intelligence.

In business plans, human skills must be enhanced and praised in relation to artificial intelligence. Even though there is a conflict between machines and humans, mainly in the context of debates about generative artificial intelligence, in the Global Education Monitoring Report: A Tool on Whose Terms? (2023, p. 24), the implications for the area of education are gradually emerging and the educational sector is divided among hope in digital, the potential of technologies and the undeniable damage. In the reflection of the chapter, the learning experience occurs with the use of techno-social disruptions and artificial intelligence is included in the teaching and learning process.

The objective was reflection, and it was highlighted that understanding the world should be contained in learning experiences and different behavioral profiles have dissimilar ways of thinking and acting, therefore, learning is contained in the way of teaching people, whether in upskilling or reskilling. Humans are essential in connection with artificial intelligence.

REFERENCES

Augmented Work for an Automated, AI-driven World. (2023). *IBM Institute for Business Value*. IBM. https://www.ibm.com/thought-leadership/institute-business-value/en-us/report/augmented-workforce

Bozkurt, A. (2023). Speculative Futures on ChatGPT and Generative Artificial Intelligence (AI): A Collective Reflection from the Educational Landscape. *Asian Journal of Distance Education*, *18*(1), 53–130. doi:10.5281/zenodo.7636568

Bozkurt, A., & Sharma, R. C. (2023). Generative AI and Prompt Engineering: The Art of Whispering to Let the Genie out of the Algorithmic World. *Asian Journal of Distance Education*, *18*(2), i–vii. doi:10.5281/zenodo.8174941

Braun, G. (2023). *Towards Bridging Skill Gaps for the Future Industrial Workforce. Thesis for the Degree of Licenciature of Philosophy. Department of Industrial and Materials Science*. Chalmers University of Technology. https://research.chalmers.se/publication/537006/file/537006_Fulltext.pdf

da Silva, B. D. (2001). A Tecnologia é uma Estratégia. In P. Dias (Ed.), *Varela de Freitas (org.). Actas da II Conferência Internacional Desafios 2001* (pp. 839–859). Centro de Competência da Universidade do Minho do Projecto Nónio.

Dewey, J. (1979). **Experiência e Educação**. *3*. Companhia Editora Nacional. [Translation: Anísio Teixeira]

Feng, S. (2023). From Pretraining Data to Language Models to Downstream Tasks: Tracking the Trails of Political Biases Leading to Unfair NLP Models. *Proceedings of the 61st Annual Meeting of the Association for Computational Linguistics*. Association for Computational Linguistics. 10.18653/v1/2023.acl-long.656

Freire, P. (1989). A Importância do Ato de Ler: Em Três Artigos que se Completam. Autores Associados: Cortez. Coleção Polêmicas do Nosso Tempo.

Future of Jobs Report. (2023). *World Economic Forum*. WEF. https://www3.weforum.org/docs/WEF_Future_of_Jobs_2023.pdf

Global Education Monitoring Report: A Tool on Whose Terms? (2023). UNESCO. https://gem-report-2023.unesco.org/

Guo, E., & Renaldi, A. (2022). Deception, Exploited Workers, and Cash Handouts: How Worldcoin Recruited its First Half a Million Test Users. *MIT Technology Review*. https://www.technologyreview.com/2022/04/06/1048981/worldcoin-cryptocurrency-biometrics-web3/?truid=&utm_source=the_algorithm&utm_medium=email&utm_campaign=the_algorithm.unpaid.engagement&utm_content=08-07-2023

Harari, Y. N. (2018). *21 Lições para o Século 21.* [Trans. Paulo Geiger]. 1. ed. Companhia das Letras.

Heikkilä, M. (2023). AI Language Models are Rife with Different Political Biases. *MIT Technology Review*. https://www.technologyreview.com/2023/08/07/1077324/ai-language-models-are-rife-with-political-biases/?truid=&utm_source=the_algorithm&utm_medium=email&utm_campaign=the_algorithm.unpaid.engagement&utm_content=08-07-2023

Hopster, J. K. G. (2021). What are Socially Disruptive Technologies. *Technology in Society*, *67*(nov), 101750. https://www.sciencedirect.com/science/article/pii/S0160791X21002256. doi:10.1016/j.techsoc.2021.101750

Hsu, T. (2023). What Can You Do When A.I. Lies About You? *The New York Times*. https://www.nytimes.com/2023/08/03/business/media/ai-defamation-lies-accuracy.html

Human-plus-AI Solutions Mitigate Security Threats. (2023). *MIT Technology Review / Teleperformance*. https://www.teleperformance.com/en-us/insights-list/white-papers/mit-paper-human-plus-ai-solutions-mitigate-security-threats/

Kuhn, T. S. (1970). *The Structure of Scientific Revolutions. 2*. The University of Chicago Press.

Kuhn, T. S. (1998). *A Estrutura das Revoluções Científicas. 5*. Editora Perspectiva. [Translation: Beatriz Vianna Boeira e Nelson Boeira]

Lane, I. (2023). The AI Revolution is Upon us. These are the Jobs at Risk and in Demand. *SBSNews*. https://www.sbs.com.au/news/article/the-ai-revolution-is-upon-us-these-are-the-jobs-at-risk-and-in-demand/izjijemns

LeaseM. (2013). Mechanical Turk is not Anonymous. doi:10.2139/ssrn.2228728

Liu. (2021). Mitigating Political Bias in Language Models Through Reinforced Calibration. *The Thirty-Fifth AAAI Conference on Artificial Intelligence* (AAAI-21). Association for the Advancement of Artificial Intelligence. https://cdn.aaai.org/ojs/17744/17744-13-21238-1-2-20210518.pdf

Mengalli, N. M., & de Carvalho, A. A. (2023). Creation of Digital Solutions in Higher Education: Strategies with Hands-On and Disruptive Technologies in Phygital Transformation. In A. Munna, V. Nadda, T. Allahyari, G. Cantafio, & S. Bilan (Eds.), *Perspectives on Enhancing Learning Experience Through Digital Strategy in Higher Education*. IGI Global. doi:10.4018/978-1-6684-8282-7.ch001

Miah, M. S. (2023). Upskilling and Reskilling of Artificial Intelligence Trends in Knowledge Management for Enterprise Search. *Multicultural Education, 9*. https://mc-caddogap.com/wp-content/uploads/galleyproof-11-mc-9-11.pdf

Modestino, A. S., Shoag, D., & Ballance, J. (2016). Downskilling: Changes in Employer Skill Requirements Over the Business Cycle. *Labour Economics, 41p*. https://scholar.harvard.edu/shoag/publications/downskilling-changes-employer-skill-requirements-over-business-cycle

Pagnozzi, F. (2022). People Analytics and Human Resource Management: How the Use of Smart Data Can Improve the Training Processes. *PuntOorg International Journal*, *7*(2), 108–123. doi:10.19245/25.05.pij.7.2.2

MIT Technology Review. (2023). *Por que é impossível criar um modelo de linguagem de IA imparcial? MIT Technology Review.* https://mittechreview.com.br/por-que-e-impossivel-criar-um-modelo-de-linguagem-de-ia-imparcial/

Rodrigues, F. R. (2021). Who are You in a Company? A Communicator? An Analyst? A Planner? Or An Executor? *Brainz Magazine*. https://www.brainzmagazine.com/post/who-are-you-in-a-company-a-communicator-an-analyst-a-planner-or-an-executor

Subburayan, B. (2023). Harnessing Artificial Intelligence for Personalized Upskilling and Reskilling. *The Times of India Readers' Blog*. https://ssrn.com/abstract=4513273

Taylor, S. J., Bogdan, R., & DeVault, M. L. (2016). *Introduction to Qualitative Research Methods: A Guidebook and Resource*. Wiley.

Tepšić, I. (2020). *The Attitude of Job Candidates towards Artificial Intelligence in Hiring Process*. ZIR. https://zir.nsk.hr/islandora/object/acmt:103

The Economic Potential of Generative AI: The Next Productivity Frontier. (2023). *McKinsey & Company*. https://www.mckinsey.com/~/media/mckinsey/business%20functions/mckinsey%20digital/our%20insights/the%20economic%20potential%20of%20generative%20ai%20the%20next%20productivity%20frontier/the-economic-potential-of-generative-ai-the-next-productivity-frontier-vf.pdf?shouldIndex=false

McKinsey & Company. (2023). *The State of AI in 2023: Generative AI's Breakout Year.* McKinsey & Company. https://www.mckinsey.com/~/media/mckinsey/business%20functions/quantumblack/our%20insights/the%20state%20of%20ai%20in%202023%20generative%20ais%20breakout%20year/the-state-of-ai-in-2023-generative-ais-breakout-year_vf.pdf?shouldIndex=false

Zhang, Y. S., & Shu, W. (2023). *Artificial Intelligence-Based E-Learning: An Overview*. EasyChair. https://easychair.org/publications/preprint_download/SJgC

KEY TERMS AND DEFINITIONS

Disruptive Techno-social Technologies: They are understood as innovations that modify processes, products, and services or even recursion itself. They enable new ways of operationalizing and thinking tactically and strategically. It refers to organizations, consumption, different industries and phygital transformation. The results generally occur over the long term and after numerous academic investigations. They can become popular in a few days, or they can take years to become popular. Cost, interoperability, and the human-machine interface are elements that can enhance use. The public becomes familiar with software and hardware that is accessible, approachable, enhances a satisfactory user experience and has reduced financial costs for the consumer. In order to avoid side effects, it is essential not to cause damage to the social and cultural ecosystem. Accessibility, convenience, and simplicity must be considered, and diversity and sustainability must be included in the process, services, and product. The consumer experience is present from prototyping.

Human Varnish: The term is an adaptation from the business area and refers to a social tissue that is not concrete. It is the abstraction to highlight what is on the surface of the human being and associate it with the implications of the future it tends to express that people's creativity and communication are not yet programmed in artificial intelligence, even though people have jobs or missions that require computational resources or artificial intelligence that performs repetitive work. The learning experience reveals the surface of human skin that exudes emotions and feelings, although upskilling and reskilling are essential to improving the learning experience. Social contacts occur with interaction and without direct interaction and competition is amid conflicts, accommodation, and assimilation. The human varnish makes it possible, with the power of decision and learned strategies, for humans to remain in contemporary job markets.

Chapter 5
Stepping Stones for Self-Learning:
Exploring the Use of Multimodal Text- and Image-Making Generative AI Tools

Shalin Hai-Jew
https://orcid.org/0000-0002-8863-0175
Kansas State University, USA

ABSTRACT

One of the themes in the emergence of text- and image-making (multimodal) generative AIs is their value in the learning space, with the vast potential just beginning to be explored by mass humanity. This chapter explores the potential and early use of large language models (LLMs) harnessed for their mass learning, human-friendly conversations, and their efficacies, for self-learning for individuals and groups, based on a review of the literature, system constraints and affordances, and abductive logic. There are insights shared about longitudinal and lifelong learning and foci on co-evolving processes between the human learner and the computing machines and large language models.

1. INTRODUCTION

In late November 2022, OpenAI shocked the world with its personable and informative chatbot, ChatGPT, dubbed "the poster child of generative AI" (Schäfer, 2023, p. 1). Then, Google rolled out its Bard AI in March 2023. ChatGPT, with its Generative Pretrained Transformer (GPT) aspect encoded in its name, attracted a million users in its first five days of public release and 100 million in the first two months. The tools went truly global, with usage in both developed and developing countries (Kshetri, 2023, p. 16). With web-facing user interfaces and free access (for these initial versions), these were two of the most popular text- and image-making generative artificial intelligence (GAI) tools based on large language models (LLMs). The LLMs do not only create conversation, but they have been harnessed to create various types of digital content (from generic to novel). The advent of "neural networks and

DOI: 10.4018/979-8-3693-0074-9.ch005

learning systems" enable current iterations of machine creativity (Franceschelli, & Musolesi, 2023, p. 3). The speed of the emergence of text-to-image generative AI and other artmaking generative AI tools is explained based on three macro "moments": "the advent of AI in the middle of the last century; the second at the 'reawakening' of a specific approach to machine learning at the turn of this century; the third that documents a rapid sequence of innovations, dubbed 'clever little tricks, that occurred just across 18 months" leading up to the summer of 2022 (Steinfeld, 2023, p. 211). There have been complex advances by generations of computer scientists to enable arrival at the present moment.

Generative AI is defined as "the group of technologies that automatically generate visual or written content based on text prompts" (Inie, Falk, & Tanimoto, Apr. 2023, p. 1) in ways that mimic human creativity and innovations. Another definition of generative AI is "a class of machine learning (ML) algorithms that can learn from content such as text, images, and audio in order to generate new content" (Sun, Liao, Muller, Agarwal, Houde, Talamadupula, & Weisz, Mar. 2022, p. 212). There is a sense that generative AIs may provide inspirations and "higher quality output" with human inputs combined with the capabilities of the AI (Inie, Falk, & Tanimoto, Apr. 2023, p. 2).

ChatGPT and Bard AI brought global attention to the remarkable achievement of computer scientists to artificial intelligences with smooth human-like language abilities (combined with mass-scale learning). The year 2023 "is characterized by a dizzying array of landmark AI developments" (Leong, 2023, p. 52). In terms of generative AIs, people are trying to anticipate "who will win the race" (Aydın, & Karaarslan, 2023, p. 1) for "supremacy in the market" (Rahaman, Ahsan, Anjum, Rahman, & Rahman, 2023, n.p.). Meanwhile a lot of investor dollars are being invested in this "AI gold rush" (Rudolph, Tan, & Tan, 2023, p. 1). Many see this moment as nothing less than an earthshaking one, with anticipated changes to "many aspects of our lives" (Rathore, 2023, p. 63).

Both also brought attention to large language models (LLMs), trained on unlabeled big data from various data sources (including scrapings from the Internet and web (web corpora), various datasets, codesets, imagesets, and others). The models were then created using deep learning methods, in unsupervised machine learning ways, such as artificial neural networks (ANNs). The LLMs result in "tens of millions of weights" from neural network learning but in ways that "are not well understood" (Ulberg, Llach, & Byrne, 2020, p. 508). These are harnessed for generative AI models that can output multimodal contents, foremost highly fluent human-like speech. There are multimodal neural language models that enable joint embedding of images and text (Kiros, Salakhutdinov, & Zemel, 2014) and those engaging multimodal and multimedia data. Multimodal LLMs can take multimodal inputs and deliver multimodal outputs, and can engage multimodal tasks (Huang, Dong, Wang, Hao, Singhal, Ma,... & Wei, 2023, p. 1). A common construct involves generative AIs creating artistic illustrations from brief text prompts (Chen, Chen, Zhao, & Wang, July 2020, p. 155). Generative AIs also create "algorithmically generated narrative" (Thorne, 2020, p. 808), not only in textual form, but multimedia-based forms.

Depending on the size of the model, the amount of data, the types of data, the type of machine learning, and the hardware, LLMs are said to take between 100 days to over a year to train. LLMs are "often trained for hundreds of thousands of compute days" (Zhang, Roller, Goyal, Artetxe, Chen, Chen,... & Zettlemoyer, 2022, n.p.). LLM parameters range from hundreds of billions of parameters to 1.5 trillion and larger. ChatGPT is said to have cost $5 million to train, and the range of general LLMs is between $2 to $12 million USD. LLMs, given their sizes, are "prohibitively expensive in resource-constrained settings" (Roberts, Raffel, & Shazeer, 2020, p. 5; Anderson, Belavy, Perle, Hendricks, Hespanhol, Verhagen, & Memon, 2023, p. 2).

A systematic review of these technologies suggests potential paradigm-level effects on a number of domains (research and data analysis, healthcare, drug development, education, computer science, literature, art, entertainment, law enforcement, national security, and others). The generative AI technologies have raised numerous concerns: "(1) ethical issues (e.g., risk of bias, discrimination based on the quality of training data, plagiarism; (2) hallucination (the generation of scientifically incorrect content that sounds plausible); (3) transparency issues (black box application); (4) risk of declining need for human expertise with subsequent psychologic, economic and social issues; (5) over-detailed, redundant, excessive content; (6) concerns about data privacy for medical information; (7) risk of declining clinical skills, critical thinking and problem-solving abilities; (8) legal issues (.e.g, copyright issues, authorship status); (9) interpretability issues; (10) referencing issues; (11) risk of academic fraud in research; (12) incorrect content; and (13) infodemic risk" (Sallam, 2023, pp. 7-8). Generative AI may not be "ready for prime time" (Mondal, Das, & Vrana, 2023, p. 17). At present, many of these concerns are being analyzed and addressed by the LLM makers, government, and professionals across the domains, in what has been termed "staged release" (Solaiman, Brundage, Clark, Askell, Herbert-Voss, Wu,... & Wang, 2019, pp. 1-2).

One core area that these LLMs are anticipated to affect greatly involves education: formal, accredited learning from pre-school to post-graduate studies; nonformal (non-accredited) learning, and informal (incidental to general living) learning. Various works have put the LLMs through their paces in terms of taking various standardized tests, outputting various learning contents (syllabi, test questions, case studies, and such), designing learning sequences towards learning objectives, and others. These discoveries are as-yet early ones.

This work contributes to the academic literature by reviewing the published literature on LLMs, especially on their usage in education and learning, and offering fresh firsthand insights of harnessing Bard AI as an informed learning AI companion on a personalized learning journey. After all, generative AI may play an important role in helping learners "cultivate positive emotions and mindsets for self-development and learning" (Leong, 2023, p. 52). It may be used to spark "interest and motivation," see oneself differently ("escape the internal mental chatter and self-beliefs that can interfere with performance") (Leong, 2023, p. 54), and receive "judgment-free feedback" (p. 55).

2. REVIEW OF THE LITERATURE

Large language models (LLMs) are possible based on algorithmic knowledge and resources in the particular moment: machine learning (such as through artificial neural networks); large-scale datasets of text, code bases, and image sets (benchmark corpora); the ability to process big data; techniques for natural language processing (particular transformer modeling from 2017); advances in generative modeling; and other factors. A general evolution of AI models includes machine learning, neural networks, generative algorithms that "model the probability distribution of the input data and then generate new data," large-scale pretrained model (which enables fine-tuning of models on "specific tasks with labeled data"), and language model (which can deal with "natural language tasks") (Wu, Gan, Chen, Wan, & Lin, 2023, n.p.).

There are nuances in how the selected big data are trained, to learn efficiently without unnecessary forgetting (memory degradation) of the parameters but also to avoid overfitting to the data (Tirumala, Markosyan, Zettlemoyer, & Aghajanyan, 2022). Technically, there are approaches to train "large vocabularies, including soft-max, hierarchical softmax, target sampling, noise contrastive estimation and self normalization" (Chen, Grangier, & Auli, 2015, p. 1), for particular performance benchmarks.

There is a misconception that an LLM "is simply a more capable autocomplete engine" (Bridgelall, 2023, n.p.). However, they are much more complex in their functioning and capabilities. The use of "chatbot" (a conversational artificial agent) for the generative AIs powered by large language models is somewhat misleading, especially given that chatbots have just-prior been seen as old-school and perhaps no longer relevant (Murugesan, & Cherukuri, 2023, p. 118). The first chatbot was created in 1966 (Rudolph, Tan, & Tan, 2023, p. 3).

A "parameter" in an LLM, as described by Bard AI, is "a numerical value that defines the behavior of the model. These parameters are learned from a massive dataset of text and code, and they allow the model to understand and generate human-like language" (Bard AI, July 25, 2023). It does go on to provide examples of parameters such as "the probability that a particular word will appear in a sentence. Another parameter might represent the weight of a connection between two neurons in the model's neural network." The numbers of parameters in an LLM are a proxy for the model's complexity and its observations of data patterns. Bard AI writes:

The 1.5 billion parameters in an LLM are like the tiny gears and cogs in a watch. They work together to make the model function, and they allow it to perform complex tasks like understanding and generating language. (Bard AI, July 25, 2023)

An explanation in a legal journal reads:

A neural network that is untrained—one whose parameters are set to random values—will typically not exhibit any useful behaviour: its output will not appear to be connected with the input in any meaningful way. For the operations making up a neural network to be useful, the network must be trained. Training adjusts the parameters of the network to values that cause the network to do something useful. And the same neural network can be trained for different tasks; the difference in behaviour is captured in the trained parameters. (McCann, 2021, p. 112)

The patterns encoded by the parameters are used to respond to textual prompts, which are interpreted semantically (and often with cultural overtones). LLMs are able to take textual inputs as prompts and "generate new data from a distribution that it has not been trained on" (Bard AI, July 25, 2023). The generative AI will still output something to a prompt even without direct learning that may address that prompt. "Prompting" is "an emergent form of interaction that allows users to engage with generative AI through natural language" (Liu, Apr. 2023, p. 2). Prompts are "instructions given to an LLM to enforce rules, automate processes, and ensure specific qualities (and quantities) of generated output" (White, Fu, Hays, Sandborn, Olea, Gilbert, ... & Schmidt, 2023, n.p.). Prompts are "a form of programming that can customize the outputs and interactions with an LLM" (White, Fu, Hays, Sandborn, Olea, Gilbert, ... & Schmidt, 2023, n.p.). Prompting involves "converting tasks into a language model format" (Shin, Razeghi, Logan, Wallace, & Singh, 2020, p. 1). Prompting effectively benefits from "prior knowledge about the task and ideally the language model's underlying mechanism" (Zhou, Yang, Loy, & Liu, 2022, p. 2338).

Some AI natural language tools enable the input of prompts up to some 25,000 words (Rahaman, Ahsan, Anjum, Terano, & Rahman, 2023, p. 5). The prompt may request behavior that the LLM was not previously trained on, in behaviors known as "zero-shot" (no prior training at all) or "few-shot" (with limited prior training). LLMs are known as "zero-shot" and "few-shot" learners because the scale of the model "greatly improves task-agnostic, few-shot performance" at a level that is competitive with state-of-the-art fine-tuning (Brown, Mann, Ryder, Subbiah, Kaplan, Dhariwal,... & Amodei, 2020, p. 1877). To save on compute costs, a different approach involves retraining model parameters. A Low-Rank Adaptation (LoRA) approach "freezes the pretrained model weights and injects trainable rank decomposition matrices into each layer of the Transformer architecture, greatly reducing the number of trainable parameters for downstream tasks" (Hu, Shen, Wallis, Allen-Zhu, Li, Wang,... & Chen, 2021, p. 1). Fine-tuning is not always required for downstream tasks and capabilities. LLMs are able to "*self-improve* its reasoning ability without supervised data" (Huang, Gu, Hou, Wu, Wang, Yu, & Han, 2022, p. 1), such as by having the LLM self-generate questions, chains-of-thought, and other prompts.

One study suggests that "0-shot prompts can significantly outperform few-shot prompts" (Reynolds & McDonell, May 2021, p. 1), and that "few-shot examples…is better described as locating an already learned task rather than meta-learning" (p. 1). One-shot interactions occur when a model uses a random seed without any ties to prior results. There are efforts at "prompt programming" and capturing "metaprompts" (for various problem types) that tap into model functioning for a range of tasks. The metaprompts may serve as a "wrapper" for specific questions (Reynolds & McDonell, May 2021, p. 7). Another work proposes a prompt pattern catalog:

Prompt patterns are a knowledge transfer method analogous to software patterns since they provide reusable solutions to common problems faced in a particular context. (White, Fu, Hays, Sandborn, Olea, Gilbert, ... & Schmidt, 2023, n.p.)

A persona pattern may read: "Act as persona X. Provide outputs that persona X would create." (White, Fu, Hays, Sandborn, Olea, Gilbert, ... & Schmidt, 2023, n.p.) Patterns for refining questions, broadening approaches to particular problem solving, analyzing the pros and cons of various approaches to problem solving, brainstorming sub-questions that support a main question, fact-checking lists, fitting informational content to a template, generating visualizations from text, game design based on particular objectives, and others. Some prompts involve asking the generative AI how to improve the prompt asked of it.

The compiling of a prompt pattern catalog enables reusability of some of the instructional patterns. The researchers explain the power of prompting:

With the right prompt, it is possible to create entirely new interaction paradigms, such as having an LLM generate and give a quiz associated with a software engineering concept or tool, or even simulate a Linux terminal window. (White, Fu, Hays, Sandborn, Olea, Gilbert, ... & Schmidt, 2023, n.p.)

The so-called "Flipped Interaction Pattern" asks the LLM to ask questions of the human user, to achieve a particular objective:

Contextual statements given as the following: "I would like you to ask me questions to achieve X.

You should ask questions until this condition is met or to achieve this goal (alternatively, forever).

(Optional) ask me the questions one at a time, two at a time, etc." (White, Fu, Hays, Sandborn, Olea, Gilbert, ... & Schmidt, 2023, n.p.)

Some prompt aids read as somewhat incantatory. LLMs "are decent *zero-shot* reasoners by simply adding 'Let's think step by step' before each answer" (Kojima, Gu, Reid, Matsuo, & Iwasawa, 2022, p. 1). That simple prompting may access "high-level, multi-task, broad cognitive capabilities" from LLMs (Kojima, Gu, Reid, Matsuo, & Iwasawa, 2022, p. 1).

Another prompting example from the literature involves specifying a data structure for how the LLM reports out its response. One reads:

Create a 5x3 grid format table to describe the high-impact application of ChatGPT for engineering and computing education. Show the use cases in rows AND provide short text in two columns (educators/ teachers and learners/students). The table should contain brief clarifying text. (Azamfirei, Kudchadkar, & Fackler, 2023, n.p.)

Yet another approach involves the addition of "trigger tokens" to human text prompts. The appended autoprompt information better aligns with the LLM and often results in more effective outputs (Shin, Razeghi, Logan, Wallace, & Singh, 2020, p. 2).

Small language models also show the capability as "few-shot learners" or being able to respond to prompts that were not learned prior. Textual inputs set up as "cloze questions" (fill-in-the-blank sorts of queries) and "that contain a task description, combined with gradient-based optimization; exploiting unlabeled data gives further improvements" (Schick & Schütze, 2020).

This zero-shot and few-shot capability enables the generation of new data "without the need for a large amount of labeled data" (Bard AI, July 25, 2023), including writing, code, imagery, video, multimedia, and other modalities of contents. Multimodal prompts may be used with LLMs for multimodal reasoning and action. One work describes visual math and text reasoning, visual joke interpretation, "spatial/coordinate understanding," "visual planning and prediction," "multi-image reasoning," "multihop document understanding," "open-world concept understanding," and "video summarization/event locatization," among others (Yang, Li, Wang, Lin, Azarnasab, Ahmed, ... & Wang, 2023, p. 1). Generative AI has a machine version of visual intelligence. Coding skills for some types of queries may benefit the prompting, too (Berg, Raj, & Seamans, 2023, p. 4). Prompt templates "translate experts' auditing strategies into reusable prompts" are used to enhance an AI-driven auditing tool (Rastogi, Ribeiro, King, & Amershi, 2023, p. 16).

One researcher explains: "AI is able to automate many statistical processes, storing patterns present in the data it is given and returning novel representations of those patterns based on the 'prompts' it is given" (Atreides, 2023, p. 2). How a query is generated affects the potential outputs, so it helps to experiment and to apply forethought. Some works involve the use of riddle-like prompts to see if such tools can originate novel ideas and "serve as engines of discovery" (King, "Bing chatbot…," 2023, p. 1). There is work on how to improve handcrafted prompts by people with automated prompt engineering to augment the human inputs. One research team reports their findings:

Extensive experiments show that our automatically generated instructions outperform the prior LLM baseline by a large margin and achieve better or comparable performance to the instructions generated by human annotators on 24/24 Instruction Induction tasks and 17/21 curated BIG-Bench tasks. (Zhou, Muresanu, Han, Paster, Pitis, Chan, & Ba, 2022, p. 1)

The improved prompts improve "few-shot learning performance (by simply prepending them to standard in-context learning prompts), find better zero-shot chain-of-thought prompts, as well as steer models toward truthfulness and / or informativeness" (Zhou, Muresanu, Han, Paster, Pitis, Chan, & Ba, 2022, p. 1). Another approach uses "mining-based and paraphrasing-based methods to automatically generate high-quality and diverse prompts, as well as ensemble methods to combine answers from different prompts" for improved outcomes from LLMs (Jiang, Xu, Araki, & Neubig, 2020, p. 423).

How people engage the generative AI tools built on machine learning and deep artificial neural networks has been described as "neural media praxis" and is defined more broadly than prompt engineering (Choi, DiPaola, & Töyrylä, 2021, p. 020501-1). A range of skills are needed to use "computational mediation" in art practice, for example. (Choi, DiPaola, & Töyrylä, 2021, p. 020501-1)

Chain-of-thought prompting refers to a series of intermediate reasoning steps to decompose a problem into smaller and simpler processual steps, with more specifications (Wei, Wang, Schuurmans, Bosma, Chi, Le, & Zhou, 2022, p. 1). Chain-of-thought prompting is an emergent ability and does better with models of about 100 billion parameters and bigger (Wei, Wang, Schuurmans, Bosma, Chi, Le, & Zhou, 2022, p. 4). Smaller models "produced fluent but illogical chains of thought, leading to lower performance than standard prompting" (Wei, Wang, Schuurmans, Bosma, Chi, Le, & Zhou, 2022, p. 4). Researchers have found that "current models do poorly on tasks (that) require more necessary inference steps" (Zhou, Zhang, Cui, & Huang, April 2020, p. 9733), so increased definition in the sequential prompts may be helpful. Another study did find ChatGPT to be effective at inference tasks as compared to other models (Zhong, Ding, Liu, Du, & Tao, 2023, n.p.).

Another approach is dubbed "least-to-most" prompting, which involves decomposing harder problems into smaller subproblems and then having the LLM solve these smaller problems in sequence. They write:

Our experimental results on tasks related to symbolic manipulation, compositional generalization, and math reasoning reveal that least-to-most prompting is capable of generalizing to more difficult problems than those seen in the prompts. (Zhou, Schärli, Hou, Wei, Scales, Wang, ... & Chi, 2022, p. 1)

The order from least-to-most is to offer the "least intrusive" prompt initially, which provides the least guidance to the LLM…and to progress then to the most difficult, for the sequential solving of the larger problem ultimately. The basic dynamic is a two-fold process: "a top-down decomposition of the problem and a bottom-up resolution generation" (Zhou, Schärli, Hou, Wei, Scales, Wang, ... & Chi, 2022, p. 9). There are limits to the transferability of decomposing problems across different domains (Zhou, Schärli, Hou, Wei, Scales, Wang, ... & Chi, 2022, p. 9).

Various works share prompts, such as those used for summarizing in different languages (Wang, Liang, Meng, Zou, Li, Qu, & Zhou, 2023, p. 1) and exporting Python scripts and code to create data visualizations from natural language prompts originally (in a way that preserves "data security and privacy" and in contexts when queries are "highly mis-specified and underspecified" (Maddigan & Susnjak, 2023, p. 45181). Another work clarifies that some artmaking generative AI systems enable direct code editing beyond textual, in a practice known as "creative coding" to lead to "*artistic* and *expressive* output" (Angert, Suzara, Han, Pondoc, & Subramonyam, 2023).

Another work tested ChatGPT's ability to generate Boolean queries for systematic literature searches, to benefit researchers. They found that guided prompts were more effective than single prompt queries for the AI-generation of Boolean queries (Wang, Scells, Koopman, & Zuccon, 2023, p. 13). They also found that "55% and over of the MeSH terms generated by ChatGPT are actually not in the MeSH vocabulary, and thus are incorrect" and also that "if multiple generations are performed with ChatGPT for the same prompt, different queries are generated—and their effectiveness can largely differ" (Wang, Scells, Koopman, & Zuccon, 2023, p. 14).

One team put ChatGPT through solving an integral, asking the AI to solve mathematical calculations based on unusual number systems (such as base 3, base 16, and others vs. base 10), multivariable calculus problems, abstract algebra based on various theories (Hassani, & Silva, 2023, p. 13), with mixed results. These tests are outside the scope of the training data.

The awareness of context (for the query) in augmented LLMs heightens model performance (Mialon, Dessì, Lomeli, Nalmpantis, Pasunuru, Raileanu, ... & Scialom, 2023, p. 1). A context informs the word sense of the prompt.

Since many go to LLMs for information needs, the verifiability of generated information and data are critical (Liu, Zhang, & Liang, 2023, n.p.), including the ability to find the source of information and to offer accurate source citations. LLMs may build additional capabilities by being enabled to access application programming interfaces (APIs) of external tools to enhance their learning and so enhance their "basic functionality, such as arithmetic or factual lookup" (Schick, Dwivedi-Yu, Dessì, Raileanu, Lomeli, Zettlemoyer, ... & Scialom, 2023, p. 1). Language modeling must be fact-aware (Logan IV, Liu, Peters, Gardner, & Singh, 2019; Vaishya, Misra, & Vaish, 2023), with older models referring to knowledge graphs. Simultaneously, users of such models need to apply a healthy skepticism (Berghel, 2023, p. 130). In an LLM-supported dialogue application, the model was fine-tuned with "annotated data and enabling the model to consult external knowledge sources can improve safety and factual grounding" (Thoppilan, De Freitas, Hall, Shazeer, Kulshreshtha, Cheng,... & Le, 2022, p. 1). Another approach involves a "fact critic" using a knowledge graph to "identify plausible sources of hallucination followed by a refinement stage that retrieves correct entities by crafting a query signal that is propagated over a *k*-hop subgraph" (Dziri, Madotto, Zaiane, & Bose, 2021, n.p.). And yet another approach uses a quality score to assess LLM outputs as a mediator before release to a human user (Ogundare & Araya, 2023).

Researchers have found that pretrained language models (PLMs) may be thrown off or mis-directed through "mispriming," defined as prompts that open with a question or word (read as context) that misdirects the outcome or result or output. The misprime is a misdirection with initial content that is unrelated to the intent of the actual desired prompt or its core meaning. For one research study, the misprimes were "randomly chosen from correct fillers of different instances of the relation" and were created in other ways (Kassner, & Schütze, 2019, n.p.). Mispriming can be understood as a hack of the PLMs.

Some LLMs maintain a "memory," and recalls "the details of the conversation and can build responses based on the information the user has already given" (Chen & Tseng, 2022, as cited in Shafeeg, Shazhaev, Mihaylov, Tularov, & Shazhaev, 2023, p. 24). The sense of memory can be off-putting for some users. One researcher writes:

One thing I found interesting was that Annie Chan was an Irish lass in the first two stories. What is the probability that would happen by chance? Answer: about one-half of one percent, if one assumes there are about 200 countries in the world. However, the fact that the bot chose Ireland could be explained because earlier that evening I used the bot to write about 80 Irish Limericks. Apparently, the bot remembered that. (McGee, "Annie Chan...," 2023, p. 1)

In one study, the API usage incorporated "a calculator, a Q&A system, a search engine, a translation system, and a calendar" (Schick, Dwivedi-Yu, Dessì, Raileanu, Lomeli, Zettlemoyer, ... & Scialom,

2023, p. 1). Some are designed to engage external modules for code interpretation and other abilities to enhance downstream task performance. Some systems use both LLMs and knowledge graphs to answer questions with the most relevant responses (Yasunaga, Ren, Bosselut, Liang, & Leskovec, 2021). The statistical language models perform, though, with incomplete training data, such as using LLMs for code completion with "a program with holes" (Raychev, Vechev, & Yahav, June 2014, p. 419). Another use involves harnessing ChatGPT for "debugging assistance, bug prediction, and bug explanation to help solve programming problems" (Surameery & Shakor, 2023, p. 17). The LLM was found to be one of several tools that may be used for debugging code, but it was not as customizable as traditional debugging tools (Surameery & Shakor, 2023, p. 21). The general LLM's ability to solve bugs "will depend on the quality of the training data, the design of the system, and the specific programming bugs being targeted" (Surameery & Shakor, 2023, p. 21). Another work found that an LLM was able to synthesize short Python programs from natural language descriptions or prompts, at a basic programming level (Austin, Odena, Nye, Bosma, Michalewski, Dohan, ... & Sutton, 2021, p. 1). The researchers write:

While large language models are impressive program synthesizers in some respects, they are far from being able to reliably solve difficult engineering problems without intervention. (Austin, Odena, Nye, Bosma, Michalewski, Dohan, ... & Sutton, 2021, p. 13)

Downstream usages of LLMs may result in varying quality outcomes based on the training of the generalized LLM. LLMs may effectively replace search engines, based on "30 theory-based and application-based ChatGPT tests" (AlAfnan, Dishari, Jovic, & Lomidze, 2023, p. 60). LLMs may be integrated with recommender systems, to make them more explainable and transparent and high-functional. One research team is proposing "a novel paradigm called CHAT-REC (ChatGPT Augmented Recommender System) that innovatively augments LLMs for building conversational recommender systems by converting user profiles and historical interactions into prompts" (Gao, Sheng, Xiang, Xiong, Wang, & Zhang, 2023, p. 1). LLMs are evolving constantly, and their present instantiations are expected to change.

LLMs are commonly able to produce fluent flows of text (with low "perplexity," defined as the ability to accurately predict the next word in a given sequence). The return of text is somewhat mechanistic and does not indicate any form of "sentience" or conscious "awareness" that is discussed in popular culture in relation to generative AIs. LLMs are "unconscious" and not self-aware (Zhang, Zhang, Li, Qiao, Zheng, Dam, ... & Hong, 2023, p. 17). LLMs lack "an innate ability to truly understand and justify its logic" (Hurlburt, 2023, p. 4). Inanimate generative AI technologies should not pretend to be animate or engage in "deception and manipulation" of people (Véliz, 2023, p. 375). While some suggest LLMs may have "intent," others disagree:

Text generated by an LM is not grounded in communicative intent, any model of the world, or any model of the reader's state of mind. It can't have been because the training data never included sharing thoughts with a listener, nor does the machine have the ability to do that...The problem is, if one side of the communication does not have meaning, then the comprehension of the implicit meaning is an illusion arising from our singular human understanding of language (independent of the model). (Bender, Gebru, McMillan-Major, & Shmitchell, Mar. 2021, p. 616)

The respective models are tested competitively among themselves and independently using various benchmark measures and prompts. There are systematic ways to assess, using suites of diagnostic tools and statistical methods. For example, one "can generally distinguish good from bad completions involving shared category or role reversal, albeit with less sensitivity than humans, and it robustly retrieves noun hypernyms, but it struggles with challenging inference and role-based event prediction…(and) shows clear insensitivity to the contextual impacts of negation" (Ettinger, 2020, p. 34).

Multiple LLMs were tested for their ability to engage in logical reasoning, based on well-known datasets (LogiQA and ReClor). The researchers found some ability in this space with the caveat that "…the performance drops significantly when handling newly released and out-of-distribution datasets" (Liu, Ning, Teng, Liu, Zhou, & Zhang, 2023, n.p.). Logical reasoning is considered to be important for LLMs and natural language understanding. There is also work on how well LLMs do with predicting human moral reasoning, given that human moral rules involve "nearly infinite exceptions" (Jin, Levine, Gonzalez Adauto, Kamal, Sap, Sachan, ... & Schölkopf, 2022, p. 28458). The MoralExceptQA is "a challenge set to benchmark LLMs on moral flexibility questions" (Jin, Levine, Gonzalez Adauto, Kamal, Sap, Sachan, ... & Schölkopf, 2022, p. 28459). Such benchmarking may lead to safer LLMs.

ChatGPT has been assessed as a factual inconsistency evaluator for text summarization. The prompt involves citing articles and asking ChatGPT if a given summary is consistent with "all information in the summary…supported by the article" (Luo, Xie, & Ananiadou, 2023, n.p.). While ChatGPT was effective for "factual inconsistency evaluation," it had challenges in terms of "false reasoning and inadequate understanding of instructions" (Luo, Xie, & Ananiadou, 2023, n.p.). The LLM showed a preference "for more lexically similar candidates" (Luo, Xie, & Ananiadou, 2023, n.p.), but made false inferences and showed "limited comprehension of given prompts" in some cases (Luo, Xie, & Ananiadou, 2023, n.p.). Another study found that ChatGPT has a "super ability" to engage "various controllable text summarization tasks" by outputting pithy summaries with important information included (Yang, Li, Zhang, Chen, & Cheng, 2023, n.p.). There are limits in ChatGPT's handling of "paraphrase and similarity tasks" (Zhong, Ding, Liu, Du, & Tao, 2023, n.p.).

ChatGPT was tested in its ability in "extractive summarization," achieved by selecting sentences from a work that help summarize the work. Researchers found that ChatGPT's performance on extractive summarization "is still inferior to existing supervised systems in terms of ROUGE scores" and suggest a two-stage prompting approach to improve its performance (Zhang, Liu, & Zhang, 2023, n.p.).

Another study harnessed the "180 documented cognitive biases that pervade human reasoning and decision making" to see if generative AI falls into the same traps (Talboy & Fuller, 2023, n.p.). This research group found that LLMs themselves have "bounded rationality" and apply biased reasoning even under the guise of AI expertise (Talboy & Fuller, 2023, n.p.). This study tested both ChatGPT and Bard AI using some of the classic prompts used to test for human reasoning abilities, and both systems failed. They were found to be susceptible to prompt phrasing, numbers use, framing, and other language-based and conception-based approaches that have been seen to lead to cognitive biases in people. This study identified "previously-unknown systematic cognitive biases and errors in LLMs" (Talboy, & Fuller, 2023, n.p.).

Based on particular anticipated downstream needs, LLMs may be further fine-tuned (instruction-tuned) for desired outputs, using labeled data and some supervised machine learning. Fine-tuning "substantially improves zero-shot performance on unseen tasks" (Wei, Bosma, Zhao, Guu, Yu, Lester, ... & Le, 2021, p. 1). The fine-tuning may guide how the model samples information, based on classifications. The process of fine-tuning involves replacing the top layer of the language model with "a task-specific layer" and then training the model on a dataset of labeled data for the desired task. For example, fine-tuning enables the detection of "persuasion" in text and the generation of persuasive text (Duerr, & Gloor, 2021, p. 1);

persuasive natural language generation "builds on psychological, linguistic, and technical concepts" (Duerr, & Gloor, 2021, p. 17). Finetuning LLMs enables dedicated subtasks to generalized and auxiliary LLMs. LLMs are appearing also as part of AI-chat search engines, classifiers, design spaces, and others. "Whisper APIs" (application programming interfaces) refer to various AI and other tools built into other systems in hidden and invisible ways. Applications are being built to access LLMs to create poetry and music (Palea, Zhou, & Gupta, 2020) and other media contents. LLMs are also used to provide knowledge to robots, which are the physical "hands and eyes" of the LLM: here, LLMs provide "high-level knowledge about the procedures for performing complex and temporally extended instructions" to help robots break down that knowledge into low-level skills applied to the physical environment (Ahn, Brohan, Brown, Chebotar, Cortes, David,... & Yan, 2022, p. 1).

2.1 Adapting LLMs to Human-Friendly Usage

A critical value in LLMs is their alignment with "human values, such as preventing harmful suggestions and unfair bias" (Thoppilan, De Freitas, Hall, Shazeer, Kulshreshtha, Cheng,... & Le, 2022, p. 1). LLMs are often fine-tuned for improved performance, often on "three key metrics: quality, safety, and groundedness" with the first on ("sensibleness, specificity, and interestingness"), safety based on the identification of "unsafe" responses, and the third based on how "grounded in known sources" responses are in terms of the model (Thoppilan, De Freitas, Hall, Shazeer, Kulshreshtha, Cheng,... & Le, 2022, p. 2). These dimensions affect human usability of the model. Collecting fine-tuning datasets is "expensive, time consuming, and complex" and often requires human assessments (Thoppilan, De Freitas, Hall, Shazeer, Kulshreshtha, Cheng,... & Le, 2022, pp. 15-16).

Various tools are designed to help ensure de-biasing of training sets to avoid bias amplification through LLMs. A dataset from a news sharing site was used to create a dataset of natural language exchanges and then a framework which "1) measures bias on the developed RedditBias (dataset) resource, and 2) evaluates model capability in dialog tasks after model debiasing" (Barikeri, Lauscher, Vulić, & Glavaš, 2021, n.p.).

Many LLMs use reinforcement learning to assess the reception of their outputs by human users. What do humans upvote? What do they downvote? What can the models exploit for "high reward" vs. explore or try something new that might be even more beneficial albeit in the long run? The human salience of the outputs is understood as an important objective. Toxic outputs from LLMs emerge in part based on the human-created broadscale training data, with "no current method...failsafe against neural toxic degeneration" (Gehman, Gururangan, Sap, Choi, & Smith, 2020, n.p.). Such social toxicity fails to align with human objectives. Finetuning models with human feedback is one approach to improve the models (Ouyang, Wu, Jiang, Almeida, Wainwright, Mishkin, ... & Lowe, 2022, p. 1). [The prompts that human users input into the LLMs are not supposed to include any non-public information since humans provide some limited oversight to the LLMs and may see any private prompts, and the LLMs themselves are learning based on human inputs and post-output responses.]

On the design side, some LLMs are being trained to engage in "legible normativity," so that they are more comfortable for people. People feel more a part of a social community if they understand the social norms, if the social norms are visible or legible to them. Technologies, too, may feel more familiar, if they are designed to align with human's social norms. The defining of "silly rules—rules with no discernible direct impact on welfare" of humans (Hadfield-Menell, Andrus, & Hadfield, Jan. 2019, p. 115) from human norms may make AI systems for acceptable to people. Social norms are often culture based and transient and ephemeral. How to define them to technical systems may be challenging. Researchers write:

A silly rule…does not generate any direct material payoff for any other agent. When an agent violates a dress code, for example, such as by failing to wear a head covering in public, no-one is materially affected as a direct consequence of the violation. Observers might well be offended, and they might punish the violator, but the violation itself is inconsequential. (Hadfield-Menell, Andrus, & Hadfield, Jan. 2019, p. 115)

Silly rules help people read the "state of the equilibrium in their group" and so serve a "legibility function" (Hadfield-Menell, Andrus, & Hadfield, Jan. 2019, p. 115).

If silly rules are costless, groups with more silly rules achieve higher payoffs. We then consider the case in which following and punishing silly rules is costly and present the results of our simulations. Our results demonstrate that groups with lots of (sufficiently cheap) silly rules are more robust; they are able to maintain more of their population and are less likely to collapse than groups with fewer silly rules in response to an unfounded shock to beliefs about the proportion of punishers. Groups with lots of silly rules are also more adaptable: they collapse more quickly when there is a true drop in the proportion of punishers below the threshold that makes group membership valuable. (Hadfield-Menell, Andrus, & Hadfield, Jan. 2019, p. 116)

AIGC-creating models are statistical models that output contents based on probability distributions of natural language (or of pixels in terms of those that generate visuals). These models engage reinforcement learning (reward model) from human feedback. Such models enable "rich creativity" (Wu, He, Liu, Sun, Liu, Han, & Tang, 2023, p. 1129) but need to continually learn to stay relevant (pp. 1131-1132). The AI-generated contents, across the various (single or multiple) modes, are sometimes referred to as "Artificial Intelligence Generated Content (AIGC)," digital contents created by a generative artificial intelligence (GAI) based on a human prompt. AIGC contents are thought to potentially advance education given the multimodality:

AIGC has the potential to achieve significant advancements in education by leveraging multi-modality data, for example, tutorial videos, academic papers, and other high-quality information, thereby improving the personalized education experience." (Cao, Li, Liu, Yan, Dai, Yu, & Sun, 2023, p. 111:24)

A subset of the research in this space focuses on helping people better collaborate with the generative machines and programs. The quality of human-machine interactions can affect what is possible with this collaboration (Yakura, Apr. 2023, p. 1). In such collaborations, "initiative, intent, and control" all matter, and how these manifest in the human-computer interactions is at least partially affected by the program design and the user interface (Lehmann, April 2023, p. 1).

Optimally, the systems would empower human awareness and decision-making. One seminal case for generative AI involves artmaking generative AIs, which challenge the human role of artmaking as an exclusively human domain. Generative AI inverts the typical sense that "many artists are traditionally used to having full control over the composition of their work"; however, if the user interface of the model enables more human controls, artists may have "rich points of interaction that allow them to truly co-pilot AI-generated content creation" with more effective workflows and more creative outputs (Liu, Apr. 2023, p. 1), in "participatory AI" (a context in which people collaborate with the AI tool). In a generative AI tool that enables the co-creation of stories, researchers note that it is important to enable levels of human user controls (Chung, Kim, Yoo, Lee, Adar, & Chang, April 2022). In the education space, too, collaborations between humans and AI can result in task distribution "that is more intelligent than either entity could achieve on its own" (Molenaar, 2022, as cited in Halaweh, 2023, p. 4). The give-and-take in creativity requires interaction dynamics, including "turn-taking, contribution type, and communication" in the co-creative process (Rezwana & Maher, 2022, p. 1), based on the Co-Creative Framework for Interaction (COFI) design. Human-machine collaborations may broaden a sense of creative imagination in parallel (Guo, Lu, Dou, & Wang, 2023, p. 836).

In innovation contexts in various industries, generative AI is seen as a tool for "design and development" and "opportunity recognition" (Bouschery, Blazevic, & Piller, 2023, p. 11). Generative AI is thought to have various military applications as follows:

automated target recognition, military robotics, material development systems testing in simulation, military medicine, battle space autonomy, intelligence analysis, record tracking, military logistics, information warfare, driverless vehicles, surveillance, lethal autonomous weapons systems, battlefield environmental support, virtual and augmented reality modeling and simulations, free air combat modeling, missile guidance, communications, and network security, data fusion for situational awareness, swarm intelligence for swarm combat, autonomous flight control of UAVs, AI satellites and software-defined satellites, wearable systems for individual personnel, management of large amounts of military data and counter-AI operations. (Biswas, "Prospective...," 2023, p. 1)

This is not to say that there will not be a lot of planning and execution work to apply the technologies to the respective contexts for actually useful applications.

One research team proposes a "manifesto for collaboration" between humans and machines. The manifesto writers propose a set of laws based on Isaac Asimov's three laws of robotics and other sources, such as preventing creative AI from plagiarizing human work, not producing harmful content, being collaborative instead of competitive with humans, and disclosing the AI origins for transparency (Vinchon, Lubart, Bartolotta, Gironnay, Botella, Bourgeois,... & Gaggioli, 2023, n.p.)

The larger a model is in terms of training data and parameters (up to a certain point), the more likely some "emergent" capabilities are to show. Emergent properties are those that do not exist in smaller versions of the model but show up as the model becomes larger. Further, "...emergent abilities cannot be predicted simply by extrapolating the performance of smaller models" (Wei, Tay, Bommasani, Raffel, Zoph, Borgeaud, ... & Fedus, 2022, p. 1). The scale at which an emergent ability is observed "depends on a number of factors and is not an immutable property of the ability" (Wei, Tay, Bommasani, Raffel, Zoph, Borgeaud, ... & Fedus, 2022, p. 2).

As an example of an emergent ability, theory-of-mind or the ability to ascribe mental states to others is one such growing ability in LLMs. LLMs may be empirically observed as imputing "unobservable mental states to others" (Kosinski, 2023, n.p.). Here, theory of mind is not explicitly engineered into the AI systems but is understood to be a spontaneous byproduct of general training on mass datasets. Other emergent abilities include reasoning, arithmetic, question answering, specific genre creations, some language translations, emotional intelligence, and unspoken biases. These abilities are not explicitly programmed into the LLMs. Instead, they emerge from the way the models are trained on massive datasets of text and code. As the models learn to predict the next word in a sequence, they also learn to perform these other tasks.

They write:

If a technique shows no improvement or is harmful when compared to the baseline of not using the technique until applied to a model of a large-enough scale, we also consider the technique an emergent ability. (Wei, Tay, Bommasani, Raffel, Zoph, Borgeaud, ... & Fedus, 2022, p. 4)

Emergent features may include emergent risks.

2.2 Concerns Around LLMs and Generative AI Models

Given the newness of such LLM and generative AI models, only recently rolled out for mass-scale usage, there have been questions about the readiness of the technologies for human use. One study used the Technology Readiness Levels (TRL) evaluation approach to analyze AI. TRL (Mankins et al., 1995) is a "systematic measurement system that supports consistent assessments, comparisons and delimitations about the maturity of one or more technologies. TRL analysis was originally used for aeronautical and space projects and later generalized to any kind of project, covering the whole span from original idea to commercial deployment" (Martínez-Plumed, Gómez, & Hernández-Orallo, 2021, p. 2). Where a technology is in its developmental maturity is "defined as the sum of techniques, skills, methods and processes used in the resolution of concrete problems" (Martínez-Plumed, Gómez, & Hernández-Orallo, 2021, pp. 3-4). The research team explains some of the findings:

A steep decreasing curve that reaches high TRL levels for only low capabilities may show that important fundamental research is to be done to create—probably new—AI technologies that reach higher layers of capabilities. A flat curve that reaches medium TRL for a wide layer of capabilities may mean that reaching the commercial product or general use may depend on issues related to safety, usability or expectations about the technology, and not that much about rethinking the foundations of the technology. Nevertheless, looking case by case may lead to different interpretations, (Martínez-Plumed, Gómez, & Hernández-Orallo, 2021, p. 5)

In an elaboration of TRLs, the researchers list the following: "basic principles observed," "technology concept formulated," "experimental proof of concept," "technology validated in the laboratory," "technology validated in a relevant environment," "technology demonstrated in a relevant environment," "technology demonstrated in a relevant environment," "system prototype demonstration in operational" (environment), system complete and qualified," "actual system proven in operational environment" through 9 levels of TRL (Martínez-Plumed, Gómez, & Hernández-Orallo, 2021, pp. 29-31) Technology systems need to continue evolving based on innovations and human needs.

Another team suggests that the evaluation of AI tools should have human observations and experiences as a main focus. They write:

...we argue that humans' tendencies—again, complete with their cognitive biases and quirks—should rest front and center when evaluating deployed LLMs. (Datta, 2023, n.p.)

The evaluations should focus on "mental models, use case utility, and cognitive engagement" (Datta, 2023, n.p.).

2.2.1 Known LLM and Generative AI System Issues

Concomitant with the rollout of LLMs, there have been very public debates about the potential risk landscape introduced by such technologies. Some known challenges have come to the fore (although some of these may have already been addressed on-the-fly by the time this work comes out).

One widely debates one involves the handling of information:

- Stereotypical representations of people groups and persons [such as "creating racist associations between intelligence and whiteness, and the risk of representational harm to non-White groups (Cave & Dihal, 2020, as cited in Weidinger, Mellor, Rauh, Griffin, Uesato, Huang, ... & Gabriel, 2021, p. 31)]
- Data leakage, especially of sensitive and personally identifiable information (Winder, 2023, as cited in Gefen & Arinze, 2023, p. 3)
- Risks of compromising LLM user privacy (McMahan, Ramage, Talwar, & Zhang, 2017)
- Incorrect information dissemination
- The harnessing of generative AI for scams, deep fakes, bad advice, and fake news
- Naïve individuals treating LLMs as sentient anthropomorphized entities and giving up sensitive information about themselves or otherwise misusing the system
- Malicious code generation
- Mass surveillance
- Societal censorship
- The fake sense of "majority opinions" (Weidinger, Mellor, Rauh, Griffin, Uesato, Huang, ... & Gabriel, 2021, p. 4) and a concomitant squelching of "the minority report" Gefen, & Arinze, 2023, p. 6)
- The false voice of "higher authority" Gefen, & Arinze, 2023, p. 7), possibly leading to a post-truth world

One researcher pointed to three major risks in "AI safety engineering: the problem of AI alignment, the problem of AI abuse, and the problem of information control" (Walter, 2023, p. 1).

The limitations of the training data (sampling bias) and the algorithmic setups on artmaking generative AI models also introduce biases. The current models "fall short in modeling the process of art creation and thus contribute to various types of biases" (Srinivasan, & Uchino, Mar. 2021, p. 41). If the gold standard is human-made art, then it may help to understand human-generated art as stemming from art movements, art materials, genres, social changes, and other factors, and respective artists cannot be over-simplified into computational models that merely transfer some small element of style (Srinivasan, & Uchino, Mar. 2021).

LLMs are engineered to prevent them from overfitting to the training data, through adversarial training (Wang, Gong, & Liu, May 2019, p. 6555). Such models would not serve human needs if they just offered straight regurgitation. Researchers explain: LLMs have sometimes "been shown to memorize parts of their training data, and when prompted appropriately, they will emit the memorized training data verbatim. This is undesirable because memorization violates privacy (exposing user data), degrades utility (repeated easy-to-memorize text is often low quality), and hurts fairness (some texts are memorized over others)" (Carlini, Ippolito, Jagielski, Lee, Tramer, & Zhang, 2022, p. 1). Such unwanted "memorization significantly grows as we increase (1) the capacity of a model, (2) the number of times an example has been duplicated, and (3) the number of tokens of context used to prompt the model" (Carlini, Ippolito, Jagielski, Lee, Tramer, & Zhang, 2022, p. 1). "Eidetic memory" (memory that is especially vivid) refers to "data that has been memorized by a model despite only appearing in a small set of training instances" (Carlini, Tramer, Wallace, Jagielski, Herbert-Voss, Lee,, ... & Raffel, Aug. 2021,p. 2635). There are known adversarial attacks against LLMs using "*membership inference attacks* to predict whether or not any particular example was in the training data" (Carlini, Tramer, Wallace, Jagielski, Herbert-Voss, Lee,, ... & Raffel, Aug. 2021,p. 2633). Other manipulations are also known (Koubaa, Boulila, Ghouti, Alzahem, & Latif, 2023, n.p.) as well as cases of "intentional misuse" (Ouyang, Wu, Jiang, Almeida, Wainwright, Mishkin, ... & Lowe, 2022, p. 10).

Conducting research on GPT-2 models "If our 'larger models memorize more' result was due to the predictive strength of larger models, and not the memorization of specific training data, we would expect a similar relationship between comparably sized GPT-2 models trained on similar data. Put differently, this baseline allows to establish what fraction of the training data is sufficiently 'easy' that any language model can correctly predict the 50-token suffix, even if the example has not been seen during training…We find that GPT-2 correctly completes approximately 6% of the examples in our evaluation set, compared to 40% for the similarly sized 1.3B parameter GPT- Neo model…Therefore, we conclude that larger models have a higher fraction of extractable training data because they have actually memorized the data; it is not simply that the larger models are more accurate" (Carlini, Ippolito, Jagielski, Lee, Tramer, & Zhang, 2022, p. 5). Memorization occurred especially for "highly duplicated strings" but rarely for those strings repeated a few times (Carlini, Ippolito, Jagielski, Lee, Tramer, & Zhang, 2022, p. 5). De-duplicating a training corpus is preferred but does not fully prevent memorization leakage (Carlini, Ippolito, Jagielski, Lee, Tramer, & Zhang, 2022, p. 5).

Memorization is defined as "a model's ability to generate the true continuation when choosing the *most likely* token at every step of decoding" (Carlini, Ippolito, Jagielski, Lee, Tramer, & Zhang, 2022, p. 6). A synonym seems to be "contamination," which occurs with a certain number of n-gram overlap (verbatim words in the original order) with original contents in the pretraining dataset. LLMs output the most likely words that would continue a given textual prompt, but for prompts that are highly rare, the prompt may trigger "memory" or "exact recall" from the training set. One research work describes the phenomenon of "supercopying," in which an LLM takes passages from the training set that are 1,000 words or more in length verbatim (McCoy, Smolensky, Linzen, Gao, & Celikyilmaz, 2021, n.p.), a phenomenon which the researchers hypothesize comes from passages "that appear multiple times in the training set" (McCoy, Smolensky, Linzen, Gao, & Celikyilmaz, 2021, n.p.). There are concerns that original (and copyrighted) texts may be exfiltrated from LLMs wholesale and without legal cover. LLMs "rarely duplicate n-grams larger than 10 tokens" (McCoy, Smolensky, Linzen, Gao, & Celikyilmaz, 2021, n.p.), though.

LLMs have been found to "hallucinate" or fabricate information and source references that do not exist. This behavior is thought to stem in part from the model going with the most probable information, even if inaccurate (Azamfirei, Kudchadkar, & Fackler, 2023, p. 2). One researcher writes:

The limitations of these LLMs are now obvious even to the most enthusiastic. They are fragile, because when they do not work, they fail catastrophically, in the etymological sense of a vertical and immediate fall in the performance. (Floridi, 2023, p. 2)

"Mode collapse" is an observed phenomenon in some models that result in generative outputs that result in diversity loss from the original training dataset. Many models susceptible to mode collapse result in "classes already rare in the dataset (to) become even rarer in the model" (Zameshina, Teytaud, Teytaud, Hosu, Carraz, Najman, & Wagner, July 2022, p. 320). One approach to encourage heightened diversity of outputs is a Random Generative Adversarial Networks approach (Nguyen, Vu, Nguyen & Than, Dec. 2022, p. 66), and another uses statistical reweighting to ensure all classes in a model have representation (Zameshina, Teytaud, Teytaud, Hosu, Carraz, Najman, & Wagner, July 2022, p. 320). Another approach to ensure rare classes have representation is to generate multiple solutions and enable users to provide feedback (Zameshina, Teytaud, Teytaud, Hosu, Carraz, Najman, & Wagner, July 2022, p. 322). Another approach is to reweight by "unrelated auxiliary variables," with the finding that they "never degrade performance by applying reweighting, even when using unrelated variables" (Zameshina, Teytaud, Teytaud, Hosu, Carraz, Najman, & Wagner, July 2022, p. 323). Another approach involves Creative Adversarial Networks that computationally maximize deviation from an art distribution (by selecting from the outliers and the long tails). Deduplicating the training data is yet another way to avoid the reduction of diversity of language models (Zhao, Zhou, Li, Tang, Wang, Hou, ... & Wen, 2023, p. 13).

An experiment with ChatGPT used 10 prompts from Library and Information Science (LIS) in order to assess for textual similarities between the respective outputs. The percent of similarity was 13% (Kirtania & Patra, 2023). These outputs were not detectable by plagiarism software per se at the time of the study. The fact that outputs from ChatGPT were "relatively less in the similarity index" (Kirtania & Patra, 2023, n.p.) suggest that there may be sufficient diversity and dissimilarity to bypass some generative AI detector tools.

To enhance sparse datasets for PLMs and LLMs, text data augmentation techniques may be applied to artificially increase the size of the dataset (by versioning real datasets) (Dai, et al., as cited in Liu, Han, Ma, Zhang, Yang, Tian,, ... & Ge, 2023, p. 18).

2.2.2 Mysteries in the Generative AI Systems

There is the so-called "black box" concern. There are concerns that artificial neural models "work with hidden layers of nodes that are opaque so that not even programmers know exactly what calculations have been performed to obtain the respective results" (Walter, 2023, p. 1). The numerous amounts of network weights suggest fine-tuned visual data, so the various model elements are not helpful to decompose to very small elements. Researchers have extracted learning in a visual sense from a single node to understand how machines "understand" parts of an image, with some of these looking like highly diffuse visuals. There are other efforts to "introspect" or "understand" black box models with elusive explanatory depth. One explanation of generative technologies based on machine learning and artificial neural networks reads:

This kind of network is like a funnel, it takes an image as input, detects patterns at multiple levels, accumulating increasingly refined patterns until we arrive at human interpretable semantic associations: 'a cat on a mat,' and other more scientifically and aesthetically relevant derivations. Inverting this funnel allows for the creation of synthetic images. (Choi, DiPaola, & Töyrylä, 2021, p. 020501-3)

The complexity of this machine synthesis of information (visual, auditory, textual, symbolic, and others) "leads to implicit statistical ambiguity" (Choi, DiPaola, & Töyrylä, 2021, p. 020501-3).

In an effort to better understand neural network models used to create art, researchers have gone to manual network weighting "coupled with explanatory visualizations as a form of creative control over the internal and lower level processes" (Ulberg, Llach, & Byrne, 2020, p. 508). Hand-crafting neural networks better enable people to understand network visual representations, to alleviate the problem of a "lack of interpretability" of neural network models (Ulberg, Llach, & Byrne, 2020, p. 508). This approach is part of Observable AI (OAI).

People "have yet to understand exactly what linguistic capacities these pre-training processes confer upon models" (Ettinger, 2020, p. 34). Advances in the AI space are occurring in ways that the researchers do not fully understand. An earlier work positing the possible capabilities of pretrained language models describes a "task-oriented dialogue model that operates solely on text input: it effectively bypasses explicit policy and language generation modules" (Budzianowski & Vulić, 2019, n.p.). These "large generative models pretrained on large general-domain corpora" can be harnessed for task-based language work (Budzianowski & Vulić, 2019, n.p.). The concept reads as revolutionary in concept, and in experiencing the various LLMs today, in execution and instantiation.

Artificial intelligence has to be explainable to its users in order for people to adopt the technology (Adamson, 2023, p. 34). A core tenet of the "Explainable AI" (XAI) movement is that even complex technologies can be made more transparent. How receptive people are to the outputs from various generative AI technologies depends in part on the human audience's sense of the "technical virtuosity" and "visual complexity" of the works and their level of understanding (Fry, 2018, p. 81). There are benefits to having a ready explanation of the system *"in a usage context"* (Sun, Liao, Muller, Agarwal, Houde, Talamadupula, & Weisz, Mar. 2022, p. 213), for a user-friendly experience. What is the purpose of the generative AI system? How well does it perform? How safe is it? Where did it come from? There are model explainability needs in areas like "data, output, performance, and how (global logic) questions" (Liao et al., as cited in Sun, Liao, Muller, Agarwal, Houde, Talamadupula, & Weisz, Mar. 2022, p. 216). What does the model take as inputs, outputs, how does it function, and what are user options for affecting the outputs? (Sun, Liao, Muller, Agarwal, Houde, Talamadupula, & Weisz, Mar. 2022)

One design approach proposes enabling AI systems to "explain their actions or decisions using logic," in this case using "a dialogue-based explanation with reasoning for a rule-based system" (Xu, July 2022, p. 918). The researcher suggests benefits of a "collaborative dialogue process that allows the participants to gradually isolate the cause" of the confusion or the surprise outcome from the AI system (Xu, July 2022, p. 918).

Language model architectures may engage various ensembles of models (Jozefowicz, Vinyals, Schuster, Shazeer, & Wu, 2016), which may be challenging to explain. There are calls for improvements to the models in terms of both "transparency and factual correctness" (Zhao, Li, Chia, Ding, & Bing, 2023).

A meta-analysis of the usefulness of explainable AI in human-AI decision-making did not find an effect of "explanations on users' performance compared to sole AI predictions" (Schemmer, Hemmer, Nitsche, Kühl, & Vössing, July (2022, p. 617). Human-AI decision-making does result in improved "task performance on text data" (Schemmer, Hemmer, Nitsche, Kühl, & Vössing, July (2022, p. 617). The mechanisms between explainable AI and human decision-making performance needs more clarification.

Some potential risks may be partially understood at present, but others may not have been conceptualized yet. In the same way that emergent capabilities may be positive, emergent capabilities may also be negative. There is a sense of risk of models setting new instrumental goals to "better fulfill its original instrumental goal" but perhaps leading to "unforeseen consequences" and causing harm to people (Walter, 2023, p. 1). Said another way, the generative AI may "go rogue" in the common parlance. Some features of AI systems to ensure that they are "trustworthy" include the following: "human agency and oversight, technical robustness and safety, privacy and data governance, explainability, diversity and fairness, societal and environmental wellbeing, (and) accountability" (Walter, 2023, p. 6). System designers are setting up guardrails in a space that is highly competitive and is moving quickly.

AI ethics are constantly changing, and how they are operationalized also changes. Such systems need to align with "civil responsibility for public good" and not usurp people's own information (Yahaya, Umagba, Obeta, & Maruyama, 2023, p. 1). AI ethics are "contested and contextual" and ethical outcomes as "contingent on a multitude of user choices" and something that is "assessed at the sociotechnical rather than solely technical level" (Chi, Lurie, & Mulligan, July 2021, p. 456). There is work on an ethics taxonomy in Robotic Process Automation in business applications to ensure that there is value alignment between the human principal and the automated agents (Beerbaum, 2023, n.p.). Said another way, the advanced generative AI systems "should respect and improve, rather than subvert, the social and civic processes on which the health of society depends" (Beerbaum, 2023, p. 14). In looking to the future, superintelligence should be created "in the service of widely shared ethical ideals, and for the benefit of all humanity rather than one state or organization" (Beerbaum, 2023, p. 14).

Using the RAVEN ("RAting VErbal Novelty") analysis suite of tools, researchers aim to answer the following question:

Are neural networks 'discovering intricate structures' that support sophisticated generalization (LeCun et al., 2015), or are they 'stochastic parrots' that simply memorize seen examples and recombine them in shallow ways (Bender et al., 2021)? (McCoy, Smolensky, Linzen, Gao, & Celikyilmaz, 2021, n.p.)

In other words, is the parameterized machine learning able to generate novel thinking and writing that adds value, or does it just regurgitate whatever was in the large language training dataset? Is the deep learning deep or merely shallow?

Novelty is not valuable for its own sake but has to come with "high quality" (McCoy, Smolensky, Linzen, Gao, & Celikyilmaz, 2021, n.p.) as understood by the human readers. They write:

For local structure—e.g., individual dependencies—model-generated text is substantially less novel than our baseline of human-generated text from each model's test set. For larger-scale structure—e.g., overall sentence structure—model-generated text is as novel or even more novel than the human-generated baseline, but models still sometimes copy substantially, in some cases duplicating passages over 1,000 words long from the training set. (McCoy, Smolensky, Linzen, Gao, & Celikyilmaz, 2021, n.p.)

Morphological and syntactic novelty may exist in some models, but then there may be "reasonably frequent semantic issues (e.g., being self-contradictory)" (McCoy, Smolensky, Linzen, Gao, & Celikyilmaz, 2021, n.p.). In other words, there are observed tradeoffs, with gains in some areas occurring with losses in others. The researchers also found that "all modifications that increase the novelty of generated text also decrease the quality" in this study (McCoy, Smolensky, Linzen, Gao, & Celikyilmaz, 2021, n.p.). The researchers also found that "models are rarely novel for local structure but are often novel for larger-scale structure; however, they occasionally copy even very long passages" (McCoy, Smolensky, Linzen, Gao, & Celikyilmaz, 2021, n.p.), leading to problems of plagiarism and serious unoriginality.

Other research teams are wrangling with similar questions: Are the respective pre-trained language models (PLMs) showing "semantic understanding," or are they just memorizing and regurgitating? (Min, Ross, Sulem, Veyseh, Nguyen, Sainz,... & Roth, 2021, p. 29) Do language models require "meaningful prompts" for accurate performance? (Min, Ross, Sulem, Veyseh, Nguyen, Sainz,... & Roth, 2021, p. 29)

Also, even as engineers and developers evolve the models, they do find that changing one part of the model may have both intended and unintended outcomes.

An aligned and ongoing question is whether AI is sufficiently close to human intelligence that it can achieve "artificial wisdom." Researchers note that "human cognition" is "a tricky combination of explicit information, tacit knowledge and creative imagination" (Sinha, & Lakhanpal, 2023, p. 1). Another similar angle: Can the tools "challenge assumptions in research and lead to a paradigm shift likely to be associated with the introduction of disruptive applications?" (Dwivedi, Kshetri, Hughes, Slade, Jeyaraj, Kar, ... & Wright, 2023, p. 54)

2.2.3 Human "Bad Actors"

"AI-as-a-Service" may be abused by malicious people. There are fears of "how LLMs will be used by sophisticated, motivated bad actors" (Grudin, 2023, p. 94). Some common scenarios involve the uses of such systems to generate convincing phishing attacks and sophisticated cybersecurity hacks (McHugh, 2023). LLMs have been used for malicious social engineering attacks, such as phishing attacks and other schemes (Grbic & Dujlovic, Mar. 2023). Those companies responsible for the generative AI systems are asked to make their systems resistant against malicious usage.

Liabilities do fall to the individuals using the technology, at present. The AI model itself "cannot be held accountable for the validity and accuracy of its generated results" (Rahman, Terano, Rahman, Salamzadeh, & Rahaman, 2023, p. 8). Such LLM technologies are "not moral agents and cannot be held responsible for their actions" (Véliz, 2023, p. 375). The LLM "cannot understand the context of the generated text, which can produce irrelevant or inappropriate text, particularly in situations requiring a nuanced understanding of the topic" (Rahman, Terano, Rahman, Salamzadeh, & Rahaman, 2023, p. 8). Human researchers have to validate the information that the generative AIs present.

2.2.4 Big Tech and AI Ethics

The use of human-created data to train LLMs means that some of the representational biases applied to people based on generalizations related to "gender, race, religion, and other social constructs" may leak into the model outputs (Liang, Wu, Morency, & Salakhutdinov, July 2021, p. 6565). If this issue is not addressed, LLMs may recreate historical discriminations and biases. There is an important objective of a "performance-fairness Pareto frontier" (Liang, Wu, Morency, & Salakhutdinov, July 2021, p. 6565). A natural language dataset in English, named StereoSet, may be used to "measure stereotypical biases in four domains: gender, profession, race, and religion" (Nadeem, Bethke, & Reddy, 2020, n.p.). The Crowdsourced Stereotype Pairs (CrowS-Pairs) benchmark dataset may be used as a measure for bias in LLMs (Nangia, Vania, Bhalerao, & Bowman, 2020, n.p.). There are important endeavors to reducing gender bias (Bordia, & Bowman, 2019, n.p.) and other biases from LLMs.

Will generative AI tools end up being used as "weapons of mass deception" and tools for criminal actions? (Sison, Daza, Gozalo-Brizuela, & Garrido-Merchán, 2023, p. 1) Will users find themselves addicted to engaging with generative AI chatbots, given their designs? (Sison, Daza, Gozalo-Brizuela, & Garrido-Merchán, 2023, p. 5) Will learners and workers end up de-skilled by over-relying on generative AI? (Sison, Daza, Gozalo-Brizuela, & Garrido-Merchán, 2023, p. 6) The potentials of harms extend in a variety of directions.

There are concerns that Big Tech may merely engage in "ethics washing" to make it look like they are trying to deal with the "diverse social problems posed by the commercialization of data-intensive technologies" in the present moment (Steinhoff, 2023, p. 1) but really just go through the motions as cover for their efforts to advance the business. AI ethics is about "the accumulation of capital" primarily, in this Marxian critique (Steinhoff, 2023, p. 2). Others express mistrust of the companies behind the LLMs, suggesting that they are foisting social risks at scale (Atreides, 2023, p. 1), noting for example that "adversarially designed memes can rapidly reshape society in profound ways" (Atreides, 2023, p. 6). Another line of argument suggests that the companies that create the LLMs should compensate the owners of the data used to train the models, perhaps based on the amount of prompts that refer to the data used: "This new business model, which must be almost independent of AI tools and be easily explained to data providers, needs to establish a prompt-based scoring system to measure data engagement of each data provider" (Zhang, 2023, n.p.).

One work proposes the importance of developing "a research agenda for a feminist metaethics of AI" to expand the focus beyond morality. A feminist metaethics will cover "(i) the continuity between theory and action in AI ethics, (ii) the real-life effects of AI ethics, (iii) the role and profile of those involved in AI ethics, and (iv) the effects of AI on power relations through methods that pay attention to context, emotions and narrative" (Siapka, July 2022, p. 665). This proposed approach enables the focus on topics of "structural domination, exploitation, coercion, and oppression" in societies (Siapka, July 2022, p. 670).

Another work to test the efficacy of generative AIs to assess the gender and racial diversity of authors in cited scientific references in draft papers and published works (King, 2023). The LLMs can enhance the diversity of manuscript bibliographies based on the raising of awareness (King, "Can Bard…" 2023, p. 1).

The tool can be harnessed for social equity, based on the "growing recognition that scientific articles featuring women and people of color as first and last (senior) author are undercited in the literature relative to male and non-minority race authors" (King, "Can Bard…" 2023, p. 1).

Another area of discourse in terms of AI involves the environmental impacts of training LLMs, which may have a large "water footprint"; an ethical approach requires improvements to "energy efficiency" and the use of "renewable energy sources," which will require more efficient algorithms and more efficient model designs (George, George, & Martin, 2023, p. 91). The water footprint of AI models refers to "the amount of water used in the production, operation, and maintenance of AI models" (George, George, & Martin, 2023, p. 92). LLMs may be more efficient by dynamically allocating different amounts of compute power based on the particular task (Schuster, Fisch, Gupta, Dehghani, Bahri, Tran,... & Metzler, 2022, p. 17456). There is constant work to make language models at less computational cost (Dathathri, Madotto, Lan, Hung, Frank, Molino, ... & Liu, 2019).

To support system governance policy and to understand the socio-technical systems' performance, various types are audits may be conducted.

Previous research has pointed towards auditing as a promising governance mechanism to help ensure that AI systems are designed and deployed in ways that are ethical, legal, and technically robust. How-

ever, existing auditing procedures fail to address the governance challenges posed by LLMs, which are adaptable to a wide range of downstream tasks. (Mökander, Schuett, Kirk, & Floridi, 2023, n.p.)

A more fitting audit process for LLMs may be conceptualized as addressing three main areas: "governance audits, model audits, and application audits" (Mökander, Schuett, Kirk, & Floridi, 2023, n.p.) The governance audit addresses how the technology provider runs the system; a model audit focuses on how the LLM is run; an application audit focuses on how various downstream applications are actualized for users (Mökander, Schuett, Kirk, & Floridi, 2023, p. 8). LLM auditing requires "some elements of continuous ex-post auditing" (Mökander, Schuett, Kirk, & Floridi, 2023, p. 7). Optimally independent third-party auditors would do the assessments. Artificial intelligence ethics are evaluated based on system performances on benchmark tests (Vidhya, Devi, Nithya, & Manju, 2023, p. 69). That said, audits themselves "will not solve all tensions or protect against all risks of harm associated with LLMs" (Mökander, Schuett, Kirk, & Floridi, 2023, p. 16), given complexities.

2.2.5 Egalitarian Access

Yet another angle involves egalitarian access. Will access to some LLMs become cost-prohibitive? (Many are being turned into enterprise or premium or subscription versions, with additional features than the free versions.) Exclusionary? Will disparate access to these technologies have implications for societal advancement, innovations, business advances, and learning? Industry 5.0 advances in intelligent industries? (Wang, Yang, Wang, Li, & Han, 2023, p. 831) Researchers write:

...it is likely that high-income countries and privileged researchers will quickly find ways to exploit LLMs in ways that accelerate their research and widen inequalities even more. (Dergaa, Chamari, Zmijewski, & Saad, 2023, p. 618)

There are open-source endeavors in the generative model transformer space (Bettin, & van Emde Boas, Oct. 2003, p. 88), to enable wider access for researchers. Another work describes an endeavor to offer Open Pre-trained Transformers (OPT), described as "a suite of decoder-only pre-trained transformers ranging from 125M to 175B parameters" to be shared with researchers for exploration (Zhang, Roller, Goyal, Artetxe, Chen, Chen,... & Zettlemoyer, 2022, n.p.).

There are moderation filters (Abdullah, Madain, & Jararweh, Nov. 2022, p. 8) and implicit pre-prompting that are applied to prevent undesirable outputs. The training data used to create the LLMs are too large to clean (Carlini, Tramer, Wallace, Jagielski, Herbert-Voss, Lee,, ... & Raffel, Aug. 2021,p. 2644), and there have been biased words related to race, religion, and other demographic categories (Brown, Mann, Ryder, Subbiah, Kaplan, Dhariwal,... & Amodei, 2020), which need to be removed from model outputs. Guardrails help protect against "socially improper responses and those with deceitful racial or sexual overtones" (Yadava, 2023, p. 217). For dedicated pre-trained and other language models, the training data may be better curated for both more efficient processing and more effective performance in the target domain. (Moore, & Lewis, July 2010). A language model fine-tuned on code from GitHub was able to respond effectively to "human-written problems with difficulty level comparable to easy interview problems" (Chen, Tworek, Jun, Yuan, Pinto, Kaplan, ... & Zaremba, 2021, n.p.). In the meantime, general LLMs are being adapted to various domains and tasks (Gururangan, Marasović, Swayamdipta, Lo, Beltagy, Downey, & Smith, 2020, n.p.).

2.2.6 More Sophisticated Human Users

How people understand the LLMs to work, the various practical applications they can make from the technology, and how people cognitively engage with the LLMs and the outputs (perhaps with insufficient critical thinking or research or exploration) are all important in reviewing AI systems. (Datta, 2023, n.p.) Users of LLMs are also encouraged to better prompt the systems, for more effective outcomes. The iterated chain-of-thought approach at prompting enables pretrained language models to better address complex challenges and those that require multiple steps in the reasoning through "multi-step inference" (Wang, Deng, & Sun, Dec. 2022, p. 2714). Defining a context may also help with prompting. Various researchers suggest resistance against anthropomorphic language used in reference to generative AI and other AI systems, to lower the amount of naïve assumptions about just how various LLMs and other AI systems work. One work suggests that generative AI "learned to understand and generate natural language" Shahriar & Hayawi, 2023), which is suggestive of anthropomorphism and machine sentience, which are misleading. Another asserts that ChatGPT "has acquired linguistic capabilities such as text comprehension and logical reasoning" (Guo, Lu, Dou, & Wang, 2023, p. 835). The phenomenon of "thanabots" trained on speech and data from the prior living enable "chatting with the dead" so to speak (Henrickson, 2023, p. 1). For learning, people may engage in imagined conversations with people from history on the one hand. On the other, such practices may be abused for those who may be mourning a lost loved one. Such channeling of the dead may encourage parasocial attachments of a living person to an imagined presence in a machine.

2.2.7 Improved Designs and Evolutions

Another concern is that many LLMs are English-dominant, with many other world languages and other languages "distant languages" not included or only partially represented (Jiao, Wang, Huang, Wang, & Tu, 2023, n.p.). One research team writes: "…most available models have either been trained on English data or on the concatenation of data in multiple languages" (Martin, Muller, Suárez, Dupont, Romary, de La Clergerie,... & Sagot, 2019, p. 1). Then monolingual Transformer-based language models are trained for other languages than English, which may lead to poorer performance. There are some smaller trained models using native non-English languages, that may be engineered to be effective in their outputs.

One research team has proposed generative theories of interaction to help innovators and engineers more systematically approach the making of new technologies, including Instrumental Interaction, Human-Computer Partnerships, and Communities & Common Objects. The ideas are based on Human-computer Interaction (HCI) traditions. Delineating the various approaches is thought to enable a more principled approach, informed by theory and research (Beaudouin-Lafon, Bødker, & Mackay, 2021, p. 1). Their work offers a bridging function to link "*generative* theories that provide a direct link from empirically based theories in the natural and social sciences to *HCI-specific* constructs that suggest and inspire novel forms of HCI" (Beaudouin-Lafon, Bødker, & Mackay, 2021, p. 2). The Generative Theory of Interaction is "grounded in a theory of human activity and behavior with technology; amenable to analytical, critical, and constructive interpretation; and actionable through the theory's concepts and generative principles" (Beaudouin-Lafon, Bødker, & Mackay, 2021, p. 3). In the coordination, humans and computers co-adapt.

These technologies are expected to continue improving over time. As they attain more and more capabilities, they are thought to threaten human jobs. One research team writes:

ChatGPT is likely to replace many jobs for which frequent human-to-human interactions are replaceable or not necessarily required, such as customer service representatives, translators, entry-level clerks, telemarketers, tutors, and virtual assistants. (Miao, & Ahn, 2023, p. 2)

The externalities from the advent of the cutting-edge technologies are likely to be complex and uneven. There are jobs being created, too, in the AI space, including those for prompt engineers. Generative pretrained transformers (GPTs) in their present form are not a threat to human labor is because they are not designed to be effective at solving the complex tasks in the "long tails" of niche work (Kausik, 2023, p. 1). The foci of the LLMs have been on more common tasks. Teachers are seen as aided by LLMs but not replaced by them (Ausat, Massang, Efendi, Nofirman, & Riady, 2023, p. 16100), given the whole package of what teachers bring to the work and the well-being of learners.

Then, there is the ever-present risk of malicious human activities. Mimetic models that emulate human behaviors in a variety of contexts may be abused in terms of deceptions and other "bad-faith activities" (McIlroy-Young, Kleinberg, Sen, Barocas, & Anderson, July 2022, p. 486). A person's identity may be usurped for memetic models without their knowledge, their permission, or others' awareness if enough information is available about them to a malicious agent (McIlroy-Young, Kleinberg, Sen, Barocas, & Anderson, July 2022, p. 482).

2.2.8 Policy and Practice Interventions at the Macro-, Meso-, and Micro- Levels

Globally, there are some 130 charters, "declarations, and various types of guidelines and codes of conduct related to AI around the world" (Laflamme, & Bruneault, May 2023, p. 1). Many suggest that there are the risks of "the asymmetry of power" between the producers of AI systems and the users (Laflamme, & Bruneault, May 2023, p. 4), which may lead to the social reproduction of inequities. The challenges of generative AI and LLMs are being worked globally and through various legal and philosophical regimes. Intellectual property rights protections are a consideration, too, of generative systems (Zhong, Chang, Yang, Wu, Arachchige, Pathmabandu, & Xue, 2023), so that adversaries cannot attack such systems to elicit full verbatim texts, so that IP attributions are accurate, and other complexities. One research team suggests that "it is possible to train state-of-the-art models using publicly available datasets exclusively, without resorting to proprietary and inaccessible datasets" (Touvron, Lavril, Izacard, Martinet, Lachaux, Lacroix,... & Lample, 2023, n.p.). Building legal and clean from the beginning is doable.

Mimetic models of people refer to models that "simulate the decisions and behavior of specific people, in domains including game-playing, text generation, and artistic expression" (McIlroy-Young, Kleinberg, Sen, Barocas, & Anderson, July 2022, p. 479). Some models are tailored to particular individuals, and can, for example, generate email replies in the style of the target individual as a practical "*force multiplier*" via self-avatar or self-model (McIlroy-Young, Kleinberg, Sen, Barocas, & Anderson, July 2022, p. 480). Such models may be used to play out counterfactual scenarios if the principal were placed in a different scene (p. 484) and other applications.

With LLMs, some 15% of worker tasks could be achieved more efficiently and with higher quality. With "software and tooling built on top of LLMs, this share increases to between 47 and 56% of all tasks" (Eloundou, Manning, Mishkin, & Rock, 2023, n.p.). Service across a range of fields stand to be improved (George & George, 2023). These projections suggest high disruption potential, on the positive and negative sides, for the human workplace.

Some research has mapped out how an LLM may enhance library services to free up librarian time for other work (Mali & Deshmukh, 2023, pp. f264-f265). There is preliminary mapping in teaching, medical services, healthcare, legal practice, and other fields.

Staff in workplaces have been seen to be using ChatGPT for "researching a topic or generating ideas," "drafting messages," "drafting longer documents, such as reports," and for "editing text" (Cardon, Getchell, Carradini, Fleischmann, & Stapp, 2023, p. 1). In some fields, generative AI is thought to increase efficiencies by "redistributing workload and optimizing performance" (Homolak, 2023, p. 1), not replacing people (Gandhi, & Talwar, 2023, p. 1). Supportive workplace policies for generative AI would "improve efficiency…and provide legal protections" and lower barriers around the use of generative AI (Cardon, Getchell, Carradini, Fleischmann, & Stapp, 2023, p. 7). Emotion AI may be used to engage with human employees at workplaces as a management tool, raising concerns about the need for "emotional privacy" (Roemmich, Schaub, & Andalibi, April 2023, p. 1).

Another researcher cautions against generative AIs presenting as sentient and / or emotional agents. The researcher writes:

Humans lie and manipulate each other's emotions all the time, but at least we can reasonably guess at someone's motivations, agenda and methods. We can hold each other accountable for such lies, calling them out and seeking redress. With AI, we can't. AIs are doubly deceptive: an AI that sends a crying-with-laughter emoji is not only not crying with laughter, but it is also incapable of any such feeling. (Véliz, 2023, p. 375)

One prediction is that generative AI "will be increasingly useful in creative jobs and industries, such as publishing, advertising, photography, film, music, television, cuisine, product design, app development, architecture, and live entertainment" (Berg, Raj, & Seamans, 2023, p. 7). LLMs are seen as potentially highly effective in an innovation workflow, particularly "the early phases of innovation, in particular, exploration, ideation, and digital prototyping" (Bilgram & Laarmann, 2023, p. 1). The research suggests "a plethora of use cases ranging from user journey mapping to idea generation and prototyping" (Bilgram & Laarmann, 2023, p. 4). AI may be used to "jump-start" the innovation process (Bilgram & Laarmann, 2023, p. 4). Organizations (from public and private industry) can capture value from AI tools (Berg, Raj, & Seamans, 2023). Dedicated LLMs are being created as well, such as one for the area of finance (Wu, Irsoy, Lu, Dabravolski, Dredze, Gehrmann,... & Mann, 2023, p. 2).

2.2.9 Reception by Human Users

Even as technologies perform well on technological tests and standards, how they are accepted by a general public and applied to dedicated tasks may vary. One study examined microblogging messages on X (formerly Twitter) to capture a sense of the mass-scale conversations around ChatGPT in the first month of its release (in late 2022). The researcher captured "news, technology, and reactions" and found five functional domains mentioned, including "creative writing, essay writing, prompt writing, code writing, and answering questions" (Taecharungroj, 2023, p. 1). Another work based on microblogging messages identified five areas of concern: "academic integrity, impact on learning outcomes and skill development, limitation of capabilities, policy and social concerns, and workforce challenges" (Li, Ma, Fan, Lee, Yu, & Hemphill, 2023, p. 1). A study of videos on TikTok with the #chatgpt hashtag brought up public debates about the chatbot in academia among students. Observations included that ChatGPT produces "content that is nonsensical or unfaithful to the training data" in some cases, so requiring caution in usage (Haensch, Ball, Herklotz, & Kreuter, 2023, p. 1).

Several studies have examined how receptive learners are to AI for their learning. These studies include receptivity from both middle school students (Ali, DiPaola, Lee, Hong, & Breazeal, May 2021) and university ones who "recognized the potential for personalized learning support, writing and brainstorming assistance, and research and analysis capabilities" (Chan, & Hu, 2023, p. 1). The university students who participated in the latter study expressed concerns about "the impact on personal development, career prospects, and societal values" (Chan, & Hu, 2023, p. 1). The participating learners in this study found the target LLM to be "interesting, motivating, and helpful for study and work" (Shoufan, 2023, p. 38805).

A study of Bhutanese college students in their willingness to use ChatGPT found a "significant direct relationship from Data Literacy to Technology Adoption," but did not find such an association related to "Information Literacy" and "Privacy Literacy" (Dawa, Dhendup, Tashi, & Rosso, 2023, p. 1). Data literacy is an important factor in the technology adoption of this chatbot. Another study found the importance of "good background knowledge" for the responses of ChatGPT to be useful to the learning Shoufan, 2023, p. 38805). The same point is made that people have to build capacity for the use of LLMs for "optimal maximization" and to assure "responsible use" (Eke, 2023, p. 3). Another writes:

Without human oversight, guidance and responsible design and operation, such generative AI applications will remain a party trick with substantial potential for creating and spreading misinformation or harmful and inaccurate content at unprecedented scale. (Harrer, 2023, p. 1)

Generative AIs powered by LLMs are not tools that should be used mindlessly, particularly in terms of data management and information management.

A range of early articles involve submitting prompts to the LLMs and then reporting on those prompts (Anton, 2023). Some researchers and research teams will use provocative questions to evoke a response. One asked the generative AI whether God exists (McGee, "Does God…," 2023). The same researcher asked the GAI to argue for why people should pay for the education of others' children (McGee, "Is there a duty…," 2023, p. 2), resulting in a sharp rebuke by the author (McGee, "Is there a duty…," 2023, p. 3). The researcher also posed a question to see if ChatGPT could wrangle complex issues, such as whether ethics committees overseeing human research can be unethical. When ChatGPT defended the work of Institutional Review Boards, the researcher asserted that such generative AIs are not "even close to perfect" (McGee, "Ethics committees…," 2023, p. 4) because it could not handle complexity and perhaps toed a conventional line. He suggested the need for "more research…to be done on the abuse of power that Institutional Review Boards currently exercise over their employees" (McGee, "Ethics committees…," 2023, p. 4). One team asked ChatGPT about compulsory vaccinations against COVID-19 infection (Sallam, Salim, Ala'a, Barakat, Fayyad, Hallit, ... & Ala'a, 2023, p. 1). LLMs can play a positive role in promoting public health (Biswas, "Role of…," 2023). There are less controversial engagements. Another used ChatGPT to identify "the top 20 questions…in political philosophy" (McGee, "What are…?" 2023, n.p). One work suggests that ChatGPT may be legitimately pulled into the culture wars, with the author suggested that the LLM leaned politically liberal (McGee, "Is Chat GPT biased…?" 2023, p. 2). One work involved an in-depth interview of ChatGPT to map out information about art-based black books (Neves, 2022). Some of the less formal research works could be read as a way of testing "agreement" with the AI to see if the human might want to engage with it, almost as if the AI were an unknown personality whom the researcher was trying to get to know.

2.3 Generative AI for Teaching and Learning

In education, LLMs are used to solve technical (engineering, computer programming) and non-technical problems ("language and literature") (Sohail, Farhat, Himeur, Nadeem, Madsen, Singh, ... & Mansoor, 2023, p. 8). There have been many technological and digital world challenges to academia from the printing press to ChatGPT in human history (Rousseau, 2023), and people have adapted through various industrial revolutions. Researchers observe rising interest in applying LLMs "in areas ranging from education and history to mathematics, medicine, and physics" (Liu, Han, Ma, Zhang, Yang, Tian,, ... & Ge, 2023, pp. 1-2). There has been a number of early adopters of LLMs for teaching and learning. Researchers have been putting the LLMs through their paces, to see how well ChatGPT enables "educational transformation, response quality, usefulness, personality and emotion, and ethics" (Tlili, Shehata, Adarkwah, Bozkurt, Hickey, Huang, & Agyemang, 2023, p. 1). A study of ten case studies raised various issues including "cheating, honesty and truthfulness of ChatGPT, privacy misleading, and manipulation" (Tlili, Shehata, Adarkwah, Bozkurt, Hickey, Huang, & Agyemang, 2023, p. 1).

One study proposes three paradigms of AI use in education, based on the role of the AI: where AI directs the human learner, where AI supports the human learner as a "collaborator," and AI-empowered where the learner takes the lead (Ouyang & Jiao, 2021, as cited in Adiguzel, Kaya, & Cansu, 2023, p. 4). AI "may improve learning outcomes, productivity, and student engagement by opening up new avenues for individualized education, feedback, and assistance" (Adiguzel, Kaya, & Cansu, 2023, p. 7).

It is helpful to understand that LLMs are not only used to create text but also for "computer coding, data analysis, and even theoretical proof" (Miao, & Ahn, 2023, p. 1). LLMs are able to automatically translate "from natural language mathematics to formal specifications and proofs" in some cases (Wu, Jiang, Li, Rabe, Staats, Jamnik, & Szegedy, 2022, p. 1). The breadth of generative AI training data may benefit interdisciplinary research (Morris, 2023, p. 12). Generative AI may change people's "ways of knowing" in the sciences (Morris, 2023, p. 13. There may be the benefits of increased "code reuse within research labs" and more "code-sharing across institutions" (Morris, 2023, p. 14).

A review of the literature examined the uses of AI in higher education from 2016 to 2022. The researchers found that "72% of the studies focused on students, 17% instructors, and 11% managers" (Crompton & Burke, 2023, p. 1). The AI was used for the following: "(1) Assessment/Evaluation, (2) Predicting, (3) AI Assistant, (4) Intelligent Tutoring System (ITS), and (5) Managing Student Learning" (Crompton & Burke, 2023, p. 1)

Generative AI tools are thought to enable advances in research and data analysis. ChatGPT may serve as an alternative text pre-processor for sentiment in text (Kurniadi, Septiana, & Sutedi, 2023, p. 67). ChatGPT has been used to detect "Hate, Offensive, and Toxic" (HOT) contents in text (Li, Fan, Atreja, & Hemphill, 2023, p. 9). Another study found that ChatGPT could classify implicit hate speech, which is more subtle, and could explain its reasoning in ways "perceived as clearer than human-written NLEs" (Huang, Kwak, & An, 2023, n.p.).

LLMs are used to build information extraction (IE) models, too. Three types of IE models were tested: "entity-relation triple extract (RE), named entity recognition (NER), event extraction" (Wei, Cui, Cheng, Wang, Zhang, Huang, ... & Han, 2023, n.p.). Pre-trained transformer-based language models may be used for deep entity matching (or "identifying which records refer to the same real-world entity"), which may be challenging to understand especially when data comes from different sources (Li, Li, Suhara, Doan, & Tan, 2020, n.p.). ChatGPT was found to capture only 51.04% of event extraction for niche scenarios;

further, it required "…a complex set of instructions defining all event types and their schemas" (Gao, Zhao, Yu, & Xu, 2023, n.p.).

LLMs perform well in machine translation. They also can explain human natural language discourses. Researchers found the following:

1) leveraging their powerful long-text modeling capabilities, ChatGPT outperforms commercial MT (machine translation) systems in terms of human evaluation. 2) GPT-4 demonstrates a strong ability to explain discourse knowledge, even though it may select incorrect translation candidates in contrastive testing. 3) ChatGPT and GPT-4 have demonstrated superior performance and show potential to become a new and promising paradigm for document-level translation. (Wang, Lyu, Ji, Zhang, Yu, Shi, & Tu, 2023, p. 1).

LLMs may be used to evaluate the quality of machine translations and to output accuracy and reliability metrics (Lu, Qiu, Ding, Xie, & Tao, 2023).

Another research work compared ChatGPT's ability to annotate text (based on a codebook) as compared to the work of human crowd-workers on the Mechanical Turk platform. This study found that ChatGPT outperformed crowd-workers for several annotation tasks, including relevance, stance, topics, and frames detection" (Gilardi, Alizadeh, & Kubli, 2023, p. 1). The per annotation cost was "less than $0.003—about twenty times cheaper than MTurk" which already pays out in a micro fashion (Gilardi, Alizadeh, & Kubli, 2023, p. 1). The zero-shot accuracy "exceeds that of crowd-workers for four out of five tasks, while ChatGPT's intercoder agreement exceeds that of both crowd-workers and trained annotators for all tasks" (Gilardi, Alizadeh, & Kubli, 2023, p. 1).

Another example of data labeling involves text classification on "big-five personality prediction, sentiment analysis, and suicide tendency detection" from human natural language text. Researchers found that a model trained for the respective downstream tasks "generally has a superior performance" but that the generalist ChatGPT performed with "decent results" (Amin, Cambria, & Schuller, 2023, p. 15).

A different study found machine translation capabilities were effective for "high-resource languages" but less so in "complex tasks, e.g. low-resource and distant-language-pairs translation" (Peng, Ding, Zhong, Shen, Liu, Zhang, ... & Tao, 2023, n.p.). ChatGPT was found to "generate hallucinations for non-English-centric" machine translation tasks. Also, "the powerful chain-of-thought prompt leads to word-by-word translation behavior, thus bringing significant translation degradation" (Peng, Ding, Zhong, Shen, Liu, Zhang, ... & Tao, 2023, n.p.).

A generative AI was used to computationally label or annotate the genres of various documents written in Slovenian, an under-resourced language. If done manually by humans, this work is laborious and complex. Genre identification requires the analysis of "a higher pattern in texts, often based on textual or syntactic characteristics, unrelated to the topic of the document" and cannot be categorized "solely based on lexical information, such as keywords" (Kuzman, Ljubešić, & Mozetič, 2023, n.p.). This study found impressive LLM capability in genre labeling in Slovenian.

A human depression detection system is LLM-augmented (Qin, Chen, Wang, Lan, Ren, & Hong, 2023). Other capabilities in research include "organizing material, generating an initial draft, and proofreading scientific writing" even as such tools "should not replace human judgment" (Vitente, Lazaro, Escuadra, Regino, & Rotor, 2023, p. 1).

Some studies focus on LLM usage in particular topics of study, such as the use of ChatGPT in English for Specific Purposes (ESP) learning (Kovačević, Mar. 2023, p. 1). In this case, the AI was used for the making of "personalized vocabulary and grammar exercises for ESP students" (Kovačević, Mar. 2023, p. 2).

Some works are tool-focused. A Teaching Assistant training was set up using GPT technologies. This interactive teacher training tool enables new teachers to train on simulated AI-chat-based students (Markel, Opferman, Landay, & Piech, 2023).

2.3.1 LLMs Used for Research and Research Writing

There have been early focuses on "the role, uses, and abuses of ChatGPT in research articles" (Sardana, Fagan, & Wright, 2023, p. 361), including some cases of works with generative AI given byline credit, with *Nature* reporting "that four manuscripts in preprint credit ChatGPT as an author" (Anderson, Belavy, Perle, Hendricks, Hespanhol, Verhagen, & Memon, 2023, p. 1), among others. Some academic publishers and publications have banned the uses of generative AI and LLMs and chatbots as authors or co-authors and brought on board classifier tools to try to detect AI-created works (Brainard, 2023; Alser & Waisberg, 2023, p. 1). In the meantime, ChatGPT has been used for "literature synthesis, citations, problem statements, research gaps, and data analysis" (Rahman, Terano, Rahman, Salamzadeh, & Rahaman, 2023, p. 1). The LLMs are not yet capable of self-developing "a whole scientific article" (Gordijn & Have, 2023, as cited in Rahman, Terano, Rahman, Salamzadeh, & Rahaman, 2023, p. 2). An experimental study found that ChatGPT "is quite successful in generating new research ideas and developing research outlines" (Rahman, Terano, Rahman, Salamzadeh, & Rahaman, 2023, p. 4) but with less effectiveness at creating "original and creative ideas, which is crucial in academic research…" (p. 8). The outputs of LLMs are difficult to "interpret and understand, limiting the researchers' ability to validate the results and identify the underlying sources of bias or inaccuracies" (Rahman, Terano, Rahman, Salamzadeh, & Rahaman, 2023, p. 8). Still, some are using LLMs to engage data creation and data analysis. Some LLMs have been updated to enable accessing external data (beyond trained data) to fact-check.

One study found "exceptional" performance of an LLM to extract keywords from a text, to generate keywords from a text, to extract keyphrases from a text, to generate keyphrases from a text, to "generate present and absent keywords" from a text, and to "generate present and absent keyphrases" (Song, Jiang, Shi, Yao, Lu, Feng,, ... & Jing, 2023, n.p.). This capability will enable smoother academic publishing since extracted keywords and key phrases are required for most publications.

Various studies have found that LLMs may have a sufficient knowledge set to pass particular standardized exams in various domains. They provide "on-demand replies to questions on expert topics" albeit with some mistaken ideas (Laato, Morschheuser, Hamari, & Björne, 2023, n.p.). They may lower the barrier to entry to programming and software development, which is a field that is considered challenging (Bull, & Kharrufa, 2023, n.p.).

They are seen to write essays that may pass muster for assignments in high school and perhaps some of the early years of higher education. Closer research, though, suggests that there are quality limits to the writing. One work suggests that the technology "lacks reflective thinking or revealing emotions" so limiting "the immersiveness of users in education" (Tlili, Shehata, Adarkwah, Bozkurt, Hickey, Huang, & Agyemang, 2023, p. 20) and tends to create contents that are repetitive or "generic" (p. 11) and even "naïve" (p. 12). AI-generated texts tend to lack a so-called writing "voice" (Hill-Yardin, Hutchinson, Laycock, & Spencer, 2023, p. 152). Text-generative AI was found to be lacking in "stylometric features" as compared to human writing (Zaitsu, & Jin, 2023, p. 1).

For a general LLM, when prompted to write a story, researchers found the following:

We find that although GPT2-117 conditions more strongly on context, is more sensitive to ordering of events, and uses more unusual words, it is just as likely to produce repetitive and under-diverse text when using likelihood-maximizing decoding algorithms. (See, Pappu, Saxena, Yerukola, & Manning, 2019, p. 1)

Each tool has strengths and weaknesses.

2.3.2 Detecting LLM-Aided Academic Dishonesty

Instructors and teachers have expressed concerns about academic dishonesty given the ease of access to generative AI for "contract cheating" and challenges to the credibility of classic learning assessments. Practitioners are moving towards more "novel" assessments in order to blunt some of the possible effects of commercial writing services and AI chatbots (Sweeney, 2023, p. 1). Assignments are being broken into developmental pieces and parts so that learners can develop and show their work, based on this cognitive scaffolding (Pickell & Doak, 2023, p. 6). Students are being asked to engage more complex essay questions vs. generic ones (Pickell & Doak, 2023, p. 5). There are different ways to assess work "beginning with the traditional combination of closed examination and essays, but also group work, literature review, project report, multiple choice questions, long answers, short answers, open questions, 24-h open book examination, presentations, videos, podcasts, role-playing, reflective statements, and more (Pugh et al., n.d., as cited in Sweeney, 2023, p. 4).

Plagiarism detectors are being updated to try to identify AI-generated works. The reported findings seem to fall on both ends of a continuum. One work found that "none of the existing methods can effectively detect ChatGPT-generated content" (Pegoraro, Kumari, Fereidooni, & Sadeghi, 2023, n.p.). They write: "Analysis reveals that the most effective online tool for detecting generated text can only achieve a success rate of less than 50%" (Pegoraro, Kumari, Fereidooni, & Sadeghi, 2023, n.p.).

Another study reported different findings. One study was able to classify AI-generated writing with an accuracy above 95% (Yan, Fauss, Hao, & Cui, 2023, p. 125), even as human assessments tend to be much less accurate. The cues, though, were simple ones, such as that AI-generated essays "did not commit any common human errors" as compared to human-generated ones (Yan, Fauss, Hao, & Cui, 2023, p. 134). Artificial typos may be added to fool the detector. Interestingly, this study found that "AI-generated essays were significantly more likely to get the best and second-best scores while also being more likely to get the worst score. On the other hand, human-written essays were more likely to get average scores. These differences demonstrate that AI tools can help test takers to obtain spuriously high scores on essay exams" for unearned advantage (Yan, Fauss, Hao, & Cui, 2023, p. 137). As a side note, ChatGPT outperforms people at creating argumentative student essays by a wide margin (Herbold, Hautli-Janisz, Heuer, Kikteva, & Trautsch, 2023, p. 12). There are ways to trick detectors of AI-generated text, including just adding one word to the AI-generated output to lower the level of confidence that a work is from generated AI (Tlili, Shehata, Adarkwah, Bozkurt, Hickey, Huang, & Agyemang, 2023, p. 10). ChatGPT, when asked to identify whether its own work was plagiarized, was better able to identify that work than dedicated plagiarism detectors, which often compare works against known sets of essays (Khalil, & Er, 2023, p. 1).

LLMs can also "write" in other genres, such as literary and fictional ones. One study asked if GPT-3 could pass a writer's Turing Test. The LLMs output text ranged "from the banal to the brilliant" (Elkins

& Chun, 2020, p. 2). It could create credible plots with twists. One researcher prompted a futuristic story but took exception with some of the themes (McGee, "What will…" 2023).

The enforcement of academic integrity is not thought to be solvable by technology alone but eminently solvable based on a variety of policies, practices, education, assignment design, and the taking of "a proactive and ethical approach" (Cotton, Cotton, & Shipway, 2023, p. 1).

2.3.3 Measuring Learning Gains and Learning Losses from LLMs

Researchers have explored where optimal learning gain happens, whether with algebra hints created by people or by an LLM. Which can be better supports for learning in a particular context: human tutors or ChatGPT? The researchers write:

We find that 70% of hints produced by ChatGPT passed our manual quality checks and that both human and ChatGPT conditions produced positive learning gains. However, gains were only statistically significant for human tutor created hints. Learning gains from human-created hints were substantially and statistically significantly higher than ChatGPT hints in both topic areas (Elementary Algebra and Intermediate Algebra) (Pardos & Bhandari, 2023, p. 1)

What is it in human algebra hints for elementary and intermediate algebra that resonates more effectively with learners?

2.3.4 Receptivity to Generative AI on Social Media Conversations

One team identified five areas for ChatGPT-based benefits for teaching and administration: "the potential to facilitate adaptive learning, provide personalized feedback, support research and data analysis, offer automated administrative services, and aid in developing innovative assessments" (Rasul, Nair, Kalendra, Robin, de Oliveira Santini, Ladeira, ... & Heathcote, 2023, p. 1). There is a need to protect the integrity of exams, both online and take-home ones (Ryznar, 2023). Generative AI may enable "deeper learning and better learning outcomes for students" (Crawford, Cowling, & Allen, 2023, n.p), but requires instructor "leadership as a root support mechanism, character development as an antidote, and authentic assessment as an enabler" for authentic and authenticated learning (Crawford, Cowling, & Allen, 2023, n.p).

2.3.5 Receptivity to Generative AI by Learners Based on Research Studies

One study used the lenses of "student-facing, teacher-facing, and system-facing tools" from the LLMs (Tajik & Tajik, 2023, p. 2) to understand the resources and work that may be provided to different stakeholders in the education space. LLMs "can streamline administrative tasks, saving time, and reducing the workload for administrators and managers" (Tajik & Tajik, 2023, p. 6). They can "analyze applicants' written materials, including statements of purpose, letters of recommendation, and writing samples by detecting applicants who meet minimum requirements" (Tajik & Tajik, 2023, p. 6). To harness the potential benefits of LLMs for education, all stakeholders need to "develop sets of competencies and literacies necessary to both understand the technology as well as their limitations and unexpected brittleness" (Kasneci, Seßler, Küchemann, Bannert, Dementieva, Fischer,... & Kasneci, 2023, p. 1).

Another study described the use of a generative AI to summarize recorded student conversations for the instructors. The researchers write:

With only a sentence explaining the context of the learning environment and two training examples, GPT-3 was able to effectively extract and summarize student conversations (properly attributing states such as frustration and confusion), reliably synthesize statements not present in the source text, and effectively ignore extraneous noise in the student chat. (Phillips, Saleh, Glazewski, Hmelo-Silver, Mott, & Lester, 2022, p. 54)

The generative AI supports teachers' understanding of student collaboration in online learning environments, including with insights on the social dynamics and moods.

Beyond receptivity to the contents, adult learners experiencing both real videos and generated synthetic ones learned equally (Leiker, Gyllen, Eldesouky, & Cukurova, 2023), suggesting that synthetic learning materials may be effective for learning (and perhaps more efficient and cost-effective to make).

2.3.6 Chatbots to Assess Learner-Generated Learning Work

AI chatbots have been evaluated for their ability to assess human writing. One study using intraclass correlation (ICC) analysis found that "the inter-reliability of both the OpenAI ChatGPT and the Google Bard were low against the gold standard of human ratings" (Khademi, 2023, p. 1). The general LLMs are not yet competitive with dedicated AI programs used to assess human writing with automated essay scoring.

Another study found the apparent opposite. Experiments were conducted on five natural language generated (NLG) "meta-evaluation datasets (including summarization, story generation and data-to-text tasks)" to evaluate the quality of the text to see how well the LLM would do as compared to human evaluations of the writing quality (Wang, Liang, Meng, Shi, Li, Xu, ... & Zhou, 2023, n.p.). The researchers found "state-of-the-art" performance and "competitive correlation with human judgments in most cases" (Wang, Liang, Meng, Shi, Li, Xu, ... & Zhou, 2023, n.p.).

2.3.7 Challenges to Using LLMs in Academia

LLMs come with challenges. One study suggesting that many LLMs are "significantly undertrained, a consequence of the recent focus on scaling language models whilst keeping the amount of training data constant." This team suggests that "for compute-optimal training, the model size and the number of training tokens should be scaled equally; for every doubling of model size the number of training tokens should also be doubled" (Hoffmann, Borgeaud, Mensch, Buchatskaya, Cai, Rutherford, ... & Sifre, 2022, p. 1). Depending on how the LLMs are created and updated, there can be "drift" in performance, wild fluctuations such as in math performance (Confino, July 19, 2023). Systems may be unreliable. Information provided may be inaccurate, and source citations may be "hallucinated." Current LLMs are unable to provide unique learning contents at the higher graduate levels (where novel research occurs), described as the "inability to evaluate and reinforce graduate skill sets" (Rasul, Nair, Kalendra, Robin, de Oliveira Santini, Ladeira, ... & Heathcote, 2023, p. 1). Another study that found that ChatGPT received "near-perfect grades on the majority of questions in the introductory courses but has not yet reached the level of sophistication required to pass in advanced courses" (Ibrahim, Asim, Zaffar, Rahwan, & Zaki, 2023, p. 24). The "outsourcing" of work to generative AIs may pose risks to "wider academic life: journal and conference papers, reports, blogs, dissertations, books and other forms of academic writing" (Eke, 2023, p. 3).

Customized feedback for science learning may enhance equity and inclusivity in learning assuming (iff) built-in biases in training data is removed (Zhai, 2023, pp. 42 and 46). One study suggests that LLMs may not work equally for different sub-populations, resulting in "user experience divides." The researchers found that GPT-3 "used more negative expressions when it responded to the education and opinion minority groups, compared to its responses to the majority groups" (Chen, Shao, Burapacheep, & Li, 2023, p. 1). GPT-3's use of negative words was "associated with worse participants' learning experience, lower intention to continue the conversation, and less likelihood to recommend the chatbot" on both the studied issues (Chen, Shao, Burapacheep, & Li, 2023, pp. 5 - 6). How the LLM responds may shut down the learning. How questions are framed may reveal stances in terms of "opinion majorities" vs. "opinion minorities."

Educational institutions need to define "legitimate uses" of AI tools for learning (Perkins, 2023, p. 1), in part. It is important for next-generation engineers to learn about generative AI and how it may be harnessed for their work but also potential harms in order to avoid unnecessary risks (Qadir, 2022). There are articles that may help users bridge to using the tool (Kalla & Smith, 2023).

2.4 Failure to Learn Based on Improper Use of Generative AI

Generative AI is seen as potentially enhancing the independence of learners (Firat, 2023). An LLM may be harnessed for "self-directed learning and research" (Dwivedi, Kshetri, Hughes, Slade, Jeyaraj, Kar, ... & Wright, 2023, p. 26), given the asking of questions as "a form of interactive learning" with a long history (Rospigliosi, 2023, p. 1) and perhaps the long-term use of text-based and visual-based understandings. An effective learning practice involves engaging the LLM with follow-up questions "to challenge and clarify information" and therefore integrate new learning with existing learning (Rospigliosi, 2023, p. 3) in this dialogical learning. For all the benefits, this is not a riskless endeavor.

The risks of the use of LLMs to "circumvent learning" are real (Jalil, Rafi, LaToza, Moran, & Lam, 2023, p. 1), including through academic dishonesty (avoiding learning) or engaging in superficial learning (not engaging a topic in depth). A better construct is if they are used to enhance learning. In one study, though, the quality of the information in software education has its limits. This study found that ChatGPT "is able to respond to 77.5% of the questions we examined and that, of these questions, it is able to provide correct or partially correct answers in 55.6% of cases, provide correct or partially correct *explanations* of answers in 53.0% of cases, and that prompting the tool in a shared question context leads to a marginally higher rate of correct answers and explanations" (Jalil, Rafi, LaToza, Moran, & Lam, 2023, p. 1).

Simplistic feedback may result in a failure to engage real-world complexity with critical thinking. The proliferation of generative AI may mean the end of the essay as a type of authentic assessment (Lim, Gunasekara, Pallant, Pallant, & Pechenkina, 2023), unless effective redesigns of the assignment and its assessment are achieved. One research team advises against trying to "out-design the chatbots" (Mills, 2023b, as cited in Rudolph, Tan, & Tan, 2023, p. 17) or retreating to pencil and paper assessments; rather, assignments should engage students in learning that interests them and "in which their voices come through and their opinions are valued" (McMurtire, 2022, as cited in Rudolph, Tan, & Tan, 2023, p. 17). How authentic assessments are designed and deployed will also have to change, so that machine-created works are not credited to students. Generative AI may be used to make alternate learning materials for special education students (Fraiwan, & Khasawneh, 2023).

The misuse of GAI may lead to students being "denied their education" in terms of true learning (Mondal, Das, & Vrana, 2023, p. 11). While customized feedback from LLMs may improve student writing, their overuse may result in the supplanting of social relationships (Božić, 2023, n.p.). There may be excessive comfort in online spaces engaging with automated agents, though. Generative AI may serve as a conversational partner for learners (Wang, 2023), in conversational tones and with less jargon. The worry is that AI may displace and replace actual human contact.

In another work, researchers describe the uses of an LLM for "designing course contents and teaching these contents based on Task-Based Language Teaching (TBLT) method" (Kim, Shim, & Shim, 2023, p. 79). The application here was to the teaching of business English writing (Kim, Shim, & Shim, 2023, p. 79). The AI supported the design of defining goals and objectives for the course, and then creating "the course content, sequences, and structure" (Kim, Shim, & Shim, 2023, p. 82). It aided in setting schedules, making assignments, course units, scheduling, assessments (Kim, Shim, & Shim, 2023, p. 82). Some shortcomings: ChatGPT did not facilitate "learner's independent thinking" and provided learning content that the researchers found "overly simplistic"; they continue:

The tasks generated by ChatGPT are specific and practical, but the explanations of target knowledge to perform those tasks were inadequate. To enhance learners' fluency, it is necessary to teach in depth rather than simply listing the knowledge. Third, ChatGPT's capability of assessing is very limited. ChatGPT's evaluating learners' written work only captures fragmentary and superficial aspect such as grammatical error or awkward expression. It cannot cover comprehensive factors that occur during the learning process, which may limit learners to derive deeper insights. (Kim, Shim, & Shim, 2023, pp. 84 - 85)

The tools should not be fully relied on for end-to-end teaching. There are gaps in both information and capabilities.

2.5 So Much Promise...

LLMs and generative AIs are often multilingual. For example, Bard is proficient in over 40 languages and can translate between these effectively (Bard AI, Aug. 29, 2023). Mainline LLMs tend to be fairly transparent and self-revelatory, with Bard AI describing its training dataset of "books, articles, code, and other forms of written language" and "code" ("Bard (chatbot)," June 7, 2023, Wikipedia). Bard AI admittedly has a designed personality to help it engage more constructively with people (as a companionable learning agent, as a study partner, as a tutor, as a teacher). It describes its personality principles in the following way:

- *"Be helpful and informative. I am designed to be helpful and informative, and to provide you with the information you need in a clear and concise way.*

- *Be comprehensive. I have been trained on a massive dataset of text and code, so I can access and process information from a wide range of sources.*

• *Be creative. I can generate different creative text formats of text content, like poems, code, scripts, musical pieces, email, letters, etc. I will try my best to fulfill all your requirements.*

• *Be unbiased. I am not designed to have any personal opinions or beliefs, and I will strive to be objective in my responses.*

• *Be respectful. I will treat you with respect, and I will avoid making any discriminatory or offensive statements."*

Overall, I would describe my personality as helpful, informative, comprehensive, creative, unbiased, and respectful." (Bard AI, Aug. 28, 2023)

Empathy with the human user is built into GPT dialogue systems and chatbots, with negative training against "undesirable" generated content (Lin, Xu, Winata, Siddique, Liu, Shin, & Fung, Apr. 2020, p. 13622).

A wide range of prompts may be used to acquire learning plans, topical information, problem solving methods, learning support, innovative ideas, research questions, and other outputs. If used judiciously, it can enhance human knowledge, skills, and attitudes (KSAs) vs. mask a lack of learning. This tool can promote lifelong learning. It can promote the use of personal time to grow knowledge and train skillsets. If self-learning is about motivation and direction, the tool can help with both.

The meta-implications of LLMs with "algorithmic intelligence" expressed linguistically (Wang, Miao, Li, Wang, & Lin, 2023, p. 575) will be determined by how people harness the tools, for self- and group growth.

3. STEPPING STONES: EXPLORING THE USE OF A MULTIMODAL TEXT- AND IMAGE-MAKING GENERATIVE AI FOR SELF-LEARNING

At a basic level, generative AI is seen as always available and perhaps ready for engaging people on their various learning journeys.

What questions does Bard AI suggest that learners should ask themselves for heightened self-awareness of what type of learners they are? Its response follows, verbatim and complete:

There are many questions you can ask yourself to find out what sort of learner you are. Here are a few examples:

- Do I prefer to learn by reading, listening, or doing?
- Do I need to see pictures or diagrams to understand something?
- Do I learn best by listening to lectures or by reading textbooks?
- Do I need to take notes or do practice problems to remember information?
- Do I learn best by working with others or by studying alone?
- Do I get fidgety or bored easily when I have to sit still for long periods of time?
- Do I prefer to learn by hands-on experience?
- Do I learn best by talking about what I'm learning?
- Do I need to take breaks often when I'm studying?
- Do I find myself zoning out or daydreaming when I'm trying to learn something new?

The answers to these questions can help you identify your preferred learning style. There are many different learning styles, but some of the most common ones include:

- Visual learners: These learners prefer to see information in pictures, graphs, or diagrams. They often learn best by reading textbooks or watching educational videos.
- Auditory learners: These learners prefer to hear information. They often learn best by listening to lectures or podcasts.
- Kinesthetic learners: These learners prefer to learn by doing. They often learn best by participating in hands-on activities or experiments.
- Reading/writing learners: These learners prefer to learn by reading and writing. They often learn best by taking notes, writing essays, or creating presentations.
- It is important to note that most people have a combination of learning styles. You may find that you learn best in one way, but you also benefit from learning in other ways. The best way to learn is to find a variety of learning methods that work for you and to use them in combination.

Here are some additional tips for finding your learning style:

- Pay attention to how you learn best in different situations. For example, do you prefer to read a textbook or watch a video when you're learning about a new topic?
- Think about the activities that you enjoy and that you're good at. These activities may be related to your learning style.
- Talk to your teachers, friends, and family members about their observations of how you learn.
- Take a learning style assessment. There are many different learning style assessments available online and in libraries.
- Once you know your learning style, you can use this information to improve your learning. For example, if you're a visual learner, you can make sure to use pictures and diagrams in your notes. If you're an auditory learner, you can record lectures or listen to podcasts. And if you're a kinesthetic learner, you can take breaks to move around or participate in hands-on activities.

By understanding your learning style, you can become a more effective learner. (Bard AI, Aug. 29, 2023)

The self-learner would benefit to better understand both their own learning strengths and the strengths of the machine to support their learning. Perhaps the learner can explore various prompts. What learning trajectories may be most effective to achieving a particular objective? What are worthy tangents to experience? What are accurate ways to measure learning progress? What are areas of weakness (KSA gaps) to address, and how? How can the learner take the initiative to advance the learning? What are ways to practice important new skills? What are standards that a learner needs to know in the particular domain? Topic? There is the prediction that generative AI tools "will be at the center of our lives" (Aydın, & Karaarslan, 2023, p. 23). Perhaps that is so.

Figure 1. Generative AI stepping stones to individualized and group learning (from the Deep Dream Generator)

4. DISCUSSION

This work provides a para-technical overview of large language models (LLMs) and generative AI (GAI) in a general sense to inform how a self-learner may get started. Who is the learner? What does the learner want to acquire in terms of knowledge, skills, and attitudes (abilities) or "KSAs"? What sorts of learning experiences does the learner prefer? What sorts of modalities of outputs are preferred ["text, imagery, audio, code, and videos" (Harrer, 2023, p. 1) and in what combinations?]? How can the learner make progress in a developmental way? How can the pacing be set? How can the learner measure learning progress? New automated AI natural language agents may well be in the works (Fezari, & Ali-Al-Dahoud, 2023, n.p.), with other implications in the teaching and learning space.

5. FUTURE RESEARCH DIRECTIONS

Future research should include updates to the technologies, the APIs, the harnessed tools, and other uses, in the teaching and learning space. It should explore for teaching and learning theories apply. It should include the most constructive practices.

It should also include experiences of self-learners as they harness the respective tools for learning in various domains and for various objectives.

6. CONCLUSION

This is an early work in the area of generative AI through LLM-based models. This work offered one-half of the value proposition for learners. People have to bring the other half. How humanity harnesses ChatGPT, Bard AI, LLaMa Chat, LaMDA, Quora Poe, Meena…as LLM-powered chatbots…will depend in part on their understandings and their interests. It will depend on their technical savvy. It will depend on their motivations. It will depend on their incentives.

The work here is early and perhaps tentative. How people harness new technologies for their learning will differ based in part on their preferences and the learning domains that they are working in. This space is a very new one, and the important thing now is to explore broadly and then share that learning to benefit everyone.

A Closing Note: Initially, this work was to be a case study of my own self-learning using the Bard AI, perhaps around using R and Python. I wanted to select a topic that could apply to the workplace. Or maybe I would explore support for writing a novel, an endeavor which I have already started (albeit with false starts).

I would conduct an environmental scan of publicly available learning resources and then proceed. I am aware of the fragility of commitments to learning in general, but also the persistence and stick-to-it-iveness for my own learning in particular.

I would pay attention to the prompting and the responses. I would look at the multimodality of the responses. I would look for gaps in support. I would look for helpful responses. Perhaps this approach may be applied to a future work. At this time, this work is perhaps oversized as is and still has left off some necessary insights about generative AI powered by large language models used for teaching and learning.

I am deeply grateful to those who have reviewed this work and provided insightful critiques that improved the work.

REFERENCES

Abdullah, M., Madain, A., & Jararweh, Y. (2022, November). ChatGPT: Fundamentals, applications and social impacts. In *2022 Ninth International Conference on Social Networks Analysis, Management and Security (SNAMS)* (pp. 1-8). IEEE.

Adamson, G. (2023). Explaining technology we do not understand. *IEEE Transactions on Technology and Society*, *4*(1), 34–45. doi:10.1109/TTS.2023.3240107

Adiguzel, T., Kaya, M. H., & Cansu, F. K. (2023). Revolutionizing education with AI: Exploring the transformative potential of ChatGPT. *Contemporary Educational Technology, 15*(3), ep429. 1 – 12.

Ahn, M., Brohan, A., Brown, N., Chebotar, Y., Cortes, O., David, B., & Yan, M. (2022). Do as I can, not as I say: Grounding language in robotic affordances. *arXiv preprint arXiv:2204.01691.*

AlAfnan, M. A., Dishari, S., Jovic, M., & Lomidze, K. (2023). ChatGPT as an educational tool: Opportunities, challenges, and recommendations for communication, business writing, and composition courses. *Journal of Artificial Intelligence and Technology*, *3*(2), 60–68. doi:10.37965/jait.2023.0184

Ali, S., DiPaola, D., Lee, I., Hong, J., & Breazeal, C. (2021, May). Exploring generative models with middle school students. In *Proceedings of the 2021 CHI Conference on Human Factors in Computing Systems* (pp. 1-13). ACM. 10.1145/3411764.3445226

Alser, M., & Waisberg, E. (2023). Concerns with the usage of ChatGPT in academia and medicine: A viewpoint. *American Journal of Medicine Open, 100036*, 1–3. doi:10.1016/j.ajmo.2023.100036

Amin, M. M., Cambria, E., & Schuller, B. W. (2023). Will affective computing emerge from foundation models and general artificial intelligence? A first evaluation of ChatGPT. *IEEE Intelligent Systems*, *38*(2), 15–23. doi:10.1109/MIS.2023.3254179

Anderson, N., Belavy, D. L., Perle, S. M., Hendricks, S., Hespanhol, L., Verhagen, E., & Memon, A. R. (2023). AI did not write this manuscript, or did it? Can we trick the AI text detector into generated texts? The potential future of ChatGPT and AI in Sports & Exercise Medicine manuscript generation. *BMJ Open Sport & Exercise Medicine*, *9*(1), e001568. doi:10.1136/bmjsem-2023-001568 PMID:36816423

Angert, T., Suzara, M. I., Han, J., Pondoc, C. L., & Subramonyam, H. (2023). Spellburst: A Node-based Interface for Exploratory Creative Coding with Natural Language Prompts. *arXiv preprint arXiv:2308.03921*. doi:10.1145/3586183.3606719

Anton, C. (2023). Probing CHAT GPT (sic): A media ecology writing sampler. *New Explorations. Studies in Culture and Communication*, *3*(1).

Atreides, K. (2023). *Automated bias and indoctrination at scale… is all you need.* Preprint.

Ausat, A. M. A., Massang, B., Efendi, M., Nofirman, N., & Riady, Y. (2023). Can Chat GPT (sic) replace the role of the teacher in the classroom: A fundamental analysis. *Journal of Education*, *5*(4), 16100–16106.

Austin, J., Odena, A., Nye, M., Bosma, M., Michalewski, H., Dohan, D., & Sutton, C. (2021). Program synthesis with large language models. *arXiv preprint arXiv:2108.07732.*

Aydın, Ö., & Karaarslan, E. (2023). Is ChatGPT leading generative AI? What is beyond expectations? *What is beyond expectations*, (pp. 1 – 23) SSRN.

Azamfirei, R., Kudchadkar, S. R., & Fackler, J. (2023). Large language models and the perils of their hallucinations. *Critical Care*, *27*(1), 1–2. doi:10.118613054-023-04393-x PMID:36945051

Bard (chatbot). (2023, June 7). Wikipedia. https://en.wikipedia.org/wiki/Bard_(chatbot)

Barikeri, S., Lauscher, A., Vulić, I., & Glavaš, G. (2021). RedditBias: A real-world resource for bias evaluation and debiasing of conversational language models. *arXiv preprint arXiv:2106.03521*. doi:10.18653/v1/2021.acl-long.151

Beaudouin-Lafon, M., Bødker, S., & Mackay, W. E. (2021). Generative theories of interaction. [TOCHI]. *ACM Transactions on Computer-Human Interaction*, *28*(6), 1–54. doi:10.1145/3468505

BeerbaumD. O. (2023). Generative Artificial Intelligence (GAI) ethics taxonomy-Applying Chat GPT (sic) for robotic process automation (GAI-RPA) as business case. SSRN 4385025.

Bender, E. M., Gebru, T., McMillan-Major, A., & Shmitchell, S. (2021, March). On the dangers of stochastic parrots: Can language models be too big? In *Proceedings of the 2021 ACM conference on fairness, accountability, and transparency* (pp. 610-623). ACM. 10.1145/3442188.3445922

Berg, J., Raj, M., & Seamans, R. (2023). Capturing value from artificial intelligence. *Academy of Management Discoveries.*

Berghel, H. (2023). ChatGPT and AIChat epistemology. *Computer*, *56*(05), 130–137. doi:10.1109/MC.2023.3252379

Bettin, J., & van Emde Boas, G. (2003, October). Generative model transformer. In *Companion of the 18th annual ACM SIGPLAN conference on Object-oriented programming, systems, languages, and applications* (pp. 88-89). ACM.

Bilgram, V., & Laarmann, F. (2023). Accelerating innovation with generative AI: AI-augmented digital prototyping and innovation methods. *IEEE Engineering Management Review*, *51*(2), 1–5. doi:10.1109/EMR.2023.3272799

Biswas, S. (2023). *Prospective role of Chat GPT (sic) in the Military: According to ChatGPT*. Qeios.

Biswas, S. S. (2023). Role of Chat GPT (sic) in public health. *Annals of Biomedical Engineering*, 1–2.

Bordia, S., & Bowman, S. R. (2019). Identifying and reducing gender bias in word-level language models. *arXiv preprint arXiv:1904.03035*. doi:10.18653/v1/N19-3002

Bouschery, S. G., Blazevic, V., & Piller, F. T. (2023). Augmenting human innovation teams with artificial intelligence: Exploring transformer-based language models. *Journal of Product Innovation Management*, *40*(2), 139–153. doi:10.1111/jpim.12656

Božić, V. (2023). *Chat GPT and education*. Preprint.

Brainard, J. (2023). Journals take up arms against AI-written text. *Science*, *379*(6634), 740–741. doi:10.1126cience.adh2762 PMID:36821673

Bridgelall, R. (2023). *Unraveling the mysteries of AI chatbots.*

Brown, T., Mann, B., Ryder, N., Subbiah, M., Kaplan, J. D., Dhariwal, P., & Amodei, D. (2020). Language models are few-shot learners. *Advances in Neural Information Processing Systems, 33*, 1877–1901.

Budzianowski, P., & Vulić, I. (2019). Hello, it's GPT-2—how can I help you? Towards the use of pretrained language models for task-oriented dialogue systems. *arXiv preprint arXiv:1907.05774.* doi:10.18653/v1/D19-5602

Bull, C., & Kharrufa, A. (2023). Generative AI assistants in software development education. *arXiv preprint arXiv:2303.13936.* 1 - 9.

Cao, Y., Li, S., Liu, Y., Yan, Z., Dai, Y., Yu, P. S., & Sun, L. (2023). A comprehensive survey of AI-Generated Content (AIGC): A history of generative AI from GAN to ChatGPT. *arXiv preprint arXiv:2303.04226.*

Cardon, P. W., Getchell, K., Carradini, S., Fleischmann, C., & Stapp, J. (2023). *Generative AI in the workplace: Employee perspectives of ChatGPT benefits and organizational policies*, (pp. 1 – 17). OSF.

Carlini, N., Ippolito, D., Jagielski, M., Lee, K., Tramer, F., & Zhang, C. (2022). Quantifying memorization across neural language models. *arXiv preprint arXiv:2202.07646.*

Carlini, N., Tramer, F., Wallace, E., Jagielski, M., Herbert-Voss, A., Lee, K., & Raffel, C. (2021, August). Extracting training data from large language models. In *USENIX Security Symposium* (Vol. 6). 2633 - 2650.

Chan, C. K. Y., & Hu, W. (2023). Students' voices on generative AI: Perceptions, benefits, and challenges in higher education. *arXiv preprint arXiv:2305.00290.*

Chen, K., Shao, A., Burapacheep, J., & Li, Y. (2023). How GPT-3 responds to different publics on climate change and Black Lives Matter: A critical appraisal of equity in conversational AI. *arXiv preprint arXiv:2209.13627.* 1 – 16.

Chen, M., Tworek, J., Jun, H., Yuan, Q., Pinto, H. P. D. O., Kaplan, J., & Zaremba, W. (2021). Evaluating large language models trained on code. *arXiv preprint arXiv:2107.03374.*

Chen, W., Grangier, D., & Auli, M. (2015). Strategies for training large vocabulary neural language models. *arXiv preprint arXiv:1512.04906.*

Chen, Z., Chen, L., Zhao, Z., & Wang, Y. (2020, July). AI illustrator: Art illustration generation based on generative adversarial network. In *2020 IEEE 5th International Conference on Image, Vision and Computing (ICIVC)* (pp. 155-159). IEEE.

Chi, N., Lurie, E., & Mulligan, D. K. (2021, July). Reconfiguring diversity and inclusion for AI ethics. In *Proceedings of the 2021 AAAI/ACM Conference on AI, Ethics, and Society* (pp. 447-457). ACM. 10.1145/3461702.3462622

Choi, S. K., DiPaola, S., & Töyrylä, H. (2021). Artistic style meets artificial intelligence. *Journal of Perceptual Imaging.*

Chung, J. J. Y., Kim, W., Yoo, K. M., Lee, H., Adar, E., & Chang, M. (2022, April). TaleBrush: Sketching stories with generative pretrained language models. In *Proceedings of the 2022 CHI Conference on Human Factors in Computing Systems* (pp. 1-19). ACM. 10.1145/3491102.3501819

Confino, P. (2023, July 19). Over just a few months, ChatGPT went from correctly answering a simple math problem 98% of the time to just 2%, study finds. *YahooFinance*. https://finance.yahoo.com/news/over-just-few-months-chatgpt-232905189.html

Cotton, D. R., Cotton, P. A., & Shipway, J. R. (2023). Chatting and cheating: Ensuring academic integrity in the era of ChatGPT. *Innovations in Education and Teaching International*, 1–12. doi:10.1080/14703297.2023.2190148

Crawford, J., Cowling, M., & Allen, K. A. (2023). Leadership is needed for ethical ChatGPT: Character, assessment, and learning using artificial intelligence (AI). *Journal of University Teaching & Learning Practice, 20*(3), 02.

Crompton, H., & Burke, D. (2023). Artificial intelligence in higher education: The state of the field. *International Journal of Educational Technology in Higher Education, 20*(1), 1–22. doi:10.118641239-023-00392-8

Dathathri, S., Madotto, A., Lan, J., Hung, J., Frank, E., Molino, P., & Liu, R. (2019). Plug and play language models: A simple approach to controlled text generation. *arXiv preprint arXiv:1912.02164.*

Datta, T., & Dickerson, J. P. (2023). Who's thinking? A push for human-centered evaluation of LLMs using the XAI playbook. *arXiv preprint arXiv:2303.06223.*

Dawa, T., Dhendup, S., Tashi, S., & Rosso, M. A. (2023). *Technology literacies and Chat GPT (sic): Perspectives on emerging technology adoption in academic writing*. Preprint.

Dergaa, I., Chamari, K., Zmijewski, P., & Saad, H. B. (2023). From human writing to artificial intelligence generated text: Examining the prospects and potential threats of ChatGPT in academic writing. *Biology of Sport, 40*(2), 615–622. doi:10.5114/biolsport.2023.125623 PMID:37077800

Duerr, S., & Gloor, P. A. (2021). Persuasive natural language generation—A literature review. *arXiv preprint arXiv:2101.05786.* 1 - 17.

Dwivedi, Y. K., Kshetri, N., Hughes, L., Slade, E. L., Jeyaraj, A., Kar, A. K., Baabdullah, A. M., Koohang, A., Raghavan, V., Ahuja, M., Albanna, H., Albashrawi, M. A., Al-Busaidi, A. S., Balakrishnan, J., Barlette, Y., Basu, S., Bose, I., Brooks, L., Buhalis, D., & Wright, R. (2023). "So what if ChatGPT wrote it?" Multidisciplinary perspectives on opportunities, challenges and implications of generative conversational AI for research, practice and policy. *International Journal of Information Management, 71*, 102642. doi:10.1016/j.ijinfomgt.2023.102642

Dziri, N., Madotto, A., Zaiane, O., & Bose, A. J. (2021). Neural path hunter: Reducing hallucination in dialogue systems via path grounding. *arXiv preprint arXiv:2104.08455*. doi:10.18653/v1/2021.emnlp-main.168

Eke, D. O. (2023). ChatGPT and the rise of generative AI: Threat to academic integrity? *Journal of Responsible Technology, 13*, 1–4. doi:10.1016/j.jrt.2023.100060

Elkins, K., & Chun, J. (2020). Can GPT-3 pass a writer's Turing Test? *Journal of Cultural Analytics*, *5*(2), 1–16. doi:10.22148/001c.17212

Eloundou, T., Manning, S., Mishkin, P., & Rock, D. (2023). GPTs are GPTs: An early look at the labor market impact potential of large language models. *arXiv preprint arXiv:2303.10130.*

Ettinger, A. (2020). What BERT is not: Lessons from a new suite of psycholinguistic diagnostics for language models. *Transactions of the Association for Computational Linguistics*, *8*, 34–48. doi:10.1162/tacl_a_00298

Fezari, M., & Ali-Al-Dahoud, A. A. D. (2023). *From GPT to AutoGPT: A brief attention in NLP processing using DL.* Preprint.

Firat, M. (2023). *How chat GPT can transform autodidactic experiences and open education.* Open Education Faculty, Anadolu University.

Floridi, L. (2023). AI as agency without intelligence: On ChatGPT, large language models, and other generative models. *Philosophy & Technology*, *36*(1), 15.

Fraiwan, M., & Khasawneh, N. (2023). A Review of ChatGPT Applications in education, marketing, software engineering, and healthcare: Benefits, drawbacks, and research directions. *arXiv preprint arXiv:2305.00237.*

Franceschelli, G., & Musolesi, M. (2023). On the creativity of Large Language Models. *arXiv preprint arXiv:2304.00008.*

Fry, C. (2018). Enchanting Algorithms: How The Reception of Generative Artworks Is Shaped By The Audience's Understanding of The Experience [J]. In *XXI Generative Art Conference Proceedings.* Generative Art. http://www. generativeart. com/GA2018_paper s/GA2018_Christopher% 20Fry. pdf

Gandhi, P., & Talwar, V. (2023). Artificial intelligence and ChatGPT in the legal context. *International Journal of Medical Sciences*, *75*, 1–2.

Gao, J., Zhao, H., Yu, C., & Xu, R. (2023). Exploring the feasibility of ChatGPT for event extraction. *arXiv preprint arXiv:2303.03836.*

Gao, Y., Sheng, T., Xiang, Y., Xiong, Y., Wang, H., & Zhang, J. (2023). Chat-REC: Towards interactive and explainable LLMs-augmented recommender system. *arXiv preprint arXiv:2303.14524.*

Gefen, D., & Arinze, O. (2023). ChatGPT and usurping academic authority. *Journal of Information Technology Case and Application Research*, *25*(1), 3–9. doi:10.1080/15228053.2023.2186629

Gehman, S., Gururangan, S., Sap, M., Choi, Y., & Smith, N. A. (2020). Real toxicity prompts: Evaluating neural toxic degeneration in language models. *arXiv preprint arXiv:2009.11462.*

George, A. S., & George, A. H. (2023). A review of ChatGPT AI's impact on several business sectors. *Partners Universal International Innovation Journal*, *1*(1), 9–23.

George, A. S., George, A. H., & Martin, A. G. (2023). The environmental impact of AI: A case study of water consumption by Chat GPT. *Partners Universal International Innovation Journal*, *1*(2), 97–104.

Gilardi, F., Alizadeh, M., & Kubli, M. (2023). ChatGPT outperforms crowd-workers for text-annotation tasks. *arXiv preprint arXiv:2303.15056*. 1 - 13.

Grbic, D. V., & Dujlovic, I. (2023, March). Social engineering with ChatGPT. In *2023 22nd International Symposium INFOTEH-JAHORINA (INFOTEH)* (pp. 1-5). IEEE. 10.1109/INFOTEH57020.2023.10094141

Grudin, J. (2023). ChatGPT and chat history: Challenges for the new wave. *Computer*, *56*(05), 94–100. doi:10.1109/MC.2023.3255279

Guo, C., Lu, Y., Dou, Y., & Wang, F. Y. (2023). Can ChatGPT boost artistic creation: The need of imaginative intelligence for parallel art. *IEEE/CAA Journal of Automatica Sinica, 10*(4), 835-838.

Gururangan, S., Marasović, A., Swayamdipta, S., Lo, K., Beltagy, I., Downey, D., & Smith, N. A. (2020). Don't stop pretraining: Adapt language models to domains and tasks. *arXiv preprint arXiv:2004.10964*. doi:10.18653/v1/2020.acl-main.740

Hadfield-Menell, D., Andrus, M., & Hadfield, G. (2019, January). Legible normativity for AI alignment: The value of silly rules. In *Proceedings of the 2019 AAAI/ACM Conference on AI, Ethics, and Society* (pp. 115-121). ACM. 10.1145/3306618.3314258

Haensch, A. C., Ball, S., Herklotz, M., & Kreuter, F. (2023). Seeing ChatGPT through students' eyes: An analysis of TikTok data. *arXiv preprint arXiv:2303.05349*. 1 - 10.

Halaweh, M. (2023). ChatGPT in education: Strategies for responsible implementation. *Contemporary Educational Technology, 15*(2), 421, 1 - 11.

Harrer, S. (2023). Attention is not all you need: The complicated case of ethically using large language models in healthcare and medicine. *EBioMedicine*, *90*, 90. doi:10.1016/j.ebiom.2023.104512

Hassani, H., & Silva, E. S. (2023). The role of ChatGPT in data science: How AI-assisted conversational interfaces are revolutionizing the field. *Big Data and Cognitive Computing*, *7*(2), 62. doi:10.3390/bdcc7020062

Henrickson, L. (2023). Chatting with the dead: The hermeneutics of thanabots. *Media Culture & Society*, *01634437221147626*(5), 1–18. doi:10.1177/01634437221147626

Herbold, S., Hautli-Janisz, A., Heuer, U., Kikteva, Z., & Trautsch, A. (2023). AI, write an essay for me: A large-scale comparison of human-written versus ChatGPT-generated essays. *arXiv preprint arXiv:2304.14276*.

Hill-Yardin, E. L., Hutchinson, M. R., Laycock, R., & Spencer, S. J. (2023). A Chat (GPT) about the future of scientific publishing. *Brain, Behavior, and Immunity*, *110*, S0889–S1591. doi:10.1016/j.bbi.2023.02.022 PMID:36868432

Hoffmann, J., Borgeaud, S., Mensch, A., Buchatskaya, E., Cai, T., Rutherford, E., & Sifre, L. (2022). Training compute-optimal large language models. *arXiv preprint arXiv:2203.15556*.

Homolak, J. (2023). Opportunities and risks of ChatGPT in medicine, science, and academic publishing: A modern Promethean dilemma. *Croatian Medical Journal*, *64*(1), 1–3. doi:10.3325/cmj.2023.64.1 PMID:36864812

Hu, E. J., Shen, Y., Wallis, P., Allen-Zhu, Z., Li, Y., Wang, S., & Chen, W. (2021). Lora: Low-rank adaptation of large language models. *arXiv preprint arXiv:2106.09685.*

Huang, F., Kwak, H., & An, J. (2023). Is ChatGPT better than human annotators? Potential and limitations of ChatGPT in explaining implicit hate speech. *arXiv preprint arXiv:2302.07736.* doi:10.1145/3543873.3587368

Huang, J., Gu, S. S., Hou, L., Wu, Y., Wang, X., Yu, H., & Han, J. (2022). Large language models can self-improve. *arXiv preprint arXiv:2210.11610.*

Huang, S., Dong, L., Wang, W., Hao, Y., Singhal, S., Ma, S., & Wei, F. (2023). Language is not all you need: Aligning perception with language models. *arXiv preprint arXiv:2302.14045.*

Hurlburt, G. (2023). What if ethics got in the way of Generative AI? *IT Professional*, *25*(2), 4–6. doi:10.1109/MITP.2023.3267140

Ibrahim, H., Asim, R., Zaffar, F., Rahwan, T., & Zaki, Y. (2023). Rethinking homework in the age of artificial intelligence. *IEEE Intelligent Systems*, *38*(2), 24–27. doi:10.1109/MIS.2023.3255599

Inie, N., Falk, J., & Tanimoto, S. (2023, April). Designing participatory AI: Creative professionals' worries and expectations about Generative AI. *In Extended Abstracts of the 2023 CHI Conference on Human Factors in Computing Systems* (pp. 1-8). IEEE.

Jalil, S., Rafi, S., LaToza, T. D., Moran, K., & Lam, W. (2023). ChatGPT and software testing education: Promises & perils. *arXiv preprint arXiv:2302.03287.* doi:10.1109/ICSTW58534.2023.00078

Jiang, Z., Xu, F. F., Araki, J., & Neubig, G. (2020). How can we know what language models know? *Transactions of the Association for Computational Linguistics*, *8*, 423–438. doi:10.1162/tacl_a_00324

Jiao, W. X., Wang, W. X., Huang, J. T., Wang, X., & Tu, Z. P. (2023). Is ChatGPT a good translator? Yes with GPT-4 as the engine. *arXiv preprint arXiv:2301.08745.*

Jin, Z., Levine, S., Gonzalez Adauto, F., Kamal, O., Sap, M., Sachan, M., & Schölkopf, B. (2022). When to make exceptions: Exploring language models as accounts of human moral judgment. *Advances in Neural Information Processing Systems*, *35*, 28458–28473.

Jozefowicz, R., Vinyals, O., Schuster, M., Shazeer, N., & Wu, Y. (2016). Exploring the limits of language modeling. *arXiv preprint arXiv:1602.02410.*

Kalla, D., & Smith, N. (2023). Study and analysis of Chat GPT and its impact on different fields of study. *International Journal of Innovative Science and Research Technology*, *8*(3).

Kasneci, E., Seßler, K., Küchemann, S., Bannert, M., Dementieva, D., Fischer, F., Gasser, U., Groh, G., Günnemann, S., Hüllermeier, E., Krusche, S., Kutyniok, G., Michaeli, T., Nerdel, C., Pfeffer, J., Poquet, O., Sailer, M., Schmidt, A., Seidel, T., & Kasneci, G. (2023). ChatGPT for good? On opportunities and challenges of large language models for education. *Learning and Individual Differences*, *103*, 102274. doi:10.1016/j.lindif.2023.102274

Kassner, N., & Schütze, H. (2019). Negated and misprimed probes for pretrained language models: Birds can talk, but cannot fly. *arXiv preprint arXiv:1911.03343.*

Kausik, B. N. (2023). *Long tails & the impact of GPT on labor*. Preprint.

Khademi, A. (2023). Can ChatGPT and Bard generate aligned assessment items? A reliability analysis against human performance. *arXiv preprint arXiv:2304.05372.*

Khalil, M., & Er, E. (2023). Will ChatGPT get you caught? Rethinking of plagiarism detection. *arXiv preprint arXiv:2302.04335.* 1 - 13. doi:10.1007/978-3-031-34411-4_32

Kim, S., Shim, J., & Shim, J. (2023). A study on the utilization of OpenAI ChatGPT as a second language learning tool. *Journal of Multimedia Information System, 10*(1), 79–88. doi:10.33851/JMIS.2023.10.1.79

King, M. (2023). *Bing chatbot formulating and testing novel hypotheses in real-time: How slime, chocolate, and Nobel prizes reveal the power and limits of artificial intelligence*. Preprint.

King, M. R. (2023). Can Bard, Google's experimental chatbot based on the LaMDA Large Language Model, help to analyze the gender and racial diversity of authors in your cited scientific references? *Cellular and Molecular Bioengineering*, 1–5. doi:10.100712195-022-00754-8 PMID:37096072

Kiros, R., Salakhutdinov, R., & Zemel, R. S. (2014). Unifying visual-semantic embeddings with multimodal neural language models. *arXiv preprint arXiv:1411.2539.*

Kirtania, D. K., & Patra, S. K. (2023). *OpenAI ChatGPT Generated content and similarity index: A study of selected terms from the Library & Information Science (LIS).* Qeios.

Kojima, T., Gu, S. S., Reid, M., Matsuo, Y., & Iwasawa, Y. 2022. Large language models are zero-shot reasoners. *arXiv preprint arXiv:2205.11916.*

Kosinski, M. (2023). Theory of mind may have spontaneously emerged in large language models. *arXiv preprint arXiv:2302.02083.*

Koubaa, A., Boulila, W., Ghouti, L., Alzahem, A., & Latif, S. (2023). *Exploring ChatGPT capabilities and limitations: A critical review of the NLP game changer*. Preprint. doi:10.1109/ACCESS.2023.3326474

Kovačević, D. (2023, March). Use of ChatGPT in ESP teaching process. In *2023 22nd International Symposium INFOTEH-JAHORINA (INFOTEH)* (pp. 1-5). IEEE.

Kshetri, N. (2023). ChatGPT in developing economies. *IT Professional, 25*(2), 16–19. doi:10.1109/MITP.2023.3254639

Kurniadi, D., Septiana, Y., & Sutedi, A. (2023). Alternative Text Pre-Processing using Chat GPT Open AI. *Jurnal Nasional Pendidikan Teknik Informatika: JANAPATI, 12*(1).

Kuzman, T., Ljubešić, N., & Mozetič, I. (2023). ChatGPT: Beginning of an end of manual annotation? Use case of automatic genre identification. *arXiv preprint arXiv:2303.03953.* 1 - 11.

Laato, S., Morschheuser, B., Hamari, J., & Björne, J. (2023). *AI-assisted learning with ChatGPT and large language models: Implications for higher education*. Preprint.

Laflamme, A. S., & Bruneault, F. (2023, May). Including a social perspective in AI ethics: The contribution of a dialogue between American Pragmatism and Critical Theory. *In International Conference on Computer Ethics*, (pp. 1 – 15). Illinois Institute of Technology.

Lehmann, F. (2023, April). Mixed-Initiative Interaction with Computational Generative Systems. In *Extended Abstracts of the 2023 CHI Conference on Human Factors in Computing Systems* (pp. 1-6). ACM. 10.1145/3544549.3577061

Leiker, D., Gyllen, A. R., Eldesouky, I., & Cukurova, M. (2023). *Generative AI for learning: Investigating the potential of synthetic learning videos.* arXiv preprint arXiv:2304.03784. 1 - 12.

Leong, J. (2023). Using generative AI to cultivate positive emotions and mindsets for self-development and learning. *XRDS: Crossroads. The ACM Magazine for Students*, *29*(3), 52–56.

Li, L., Fan, L., Atreja, S., & Hemphill, L. (2023). "HOT" ChatGPT: The promise of ChatGPT in detecting and discriminating hateful, offensive, and toxic comments on social media. *arXiv preprint arXiv:2304.10619.*

Li, L., Ma, Z., Fan, L., Lee, S., Yu, H., & Hemphill, L. (2023). ChatGPT in education: A discourse analysis of worries and concerns on social media. *arXiv preprint arXiv:2305.02201.* 1 - 35.

Li, Y., Li, J., Suhara, Y., Doan, A., & Tan, W. C. (2020). Deep entity matching with pre-trained language models. *arXiv preprint arXiv:2004.00584.*

Liang, P. P., Wu, C., Morency, L. P., & Salakhutdinov, R. (2021, July). Towards understanding and mitigating social biases in language models. In *International Conference on Machine Learning* (pp. 6565-6576). PMLR.

Lim, W. M., Gunasekara, A., Pallant, J. L., Pallant, J. I., & Pechenkina, E. (2023). Generative AI and the future of education: Ragnarök or reformation? A paradoxical perspective from management educators. *International Journal of Management Education*, *21*(2), 100790. doi:10.1016/j.ijme.2023.100790

Lin, Z., Xu, P., Winata, G. I., Siddique, F. B., Liu, Z., Shin, J., & Fung, P. (2020, April). Caire: An end-to-end empathetic chatbot. *Proceedings of the AAAI Conference on Artificial Intelligence*, *34*(09), 13622–13623. doi:10.1609/aaai.v34i09.7098

Liu, H., Ning, R., Teng, Z., Liu, J., Zhou, Q., & Zhang, Y. (2023). Evaluating the logical reasoning ability of ChatGPTand GPT-4. *arXiv preprint arXiv:2304.03439.*

Liu, N. F., Zhang, T., & Liang, P. (2023). Evaluating verifiability in generative search engines. *arXiv preprint arXiv:2304.09848.*

Liu, V. (2023, April). Beyond text-to-image: Multimodal prompts to explore generative AI. In *Extended Abstracts of the 2023 CHI Conference on Human Factors in Computing Systems* (pp. 1-6).

Liu, Y., Han, T., Ma, S., Zhang, J., Yang, Y., Tian, J., & Ge, B. (2023). Summary of ChatGPT/GPT-4 research and perspective towards the future of large language models. *arXiv preprint arXiv:2304.01852.*

Logan, R. L., IV, Liu, N. F., Peters, M. E., Gardner, M., & Singh, S. (2019). Barack's wife Hillary: Using knowledge-graphs for fact-aware language modeling. *arXiv preprint arXiv:1906.07241.* doi:10.18653/v1/P19-1598

Lu, Q., Qiu, B., Ding, L., Xie, L., & Tao, D. (2023). Error analysis prompting enables human-like translation evaluation in large language models: A case study on ChatGPT. *arXiv preprint arXiv:2303.13809*. doi:10.20944/preprints202303.0255.v1

Luo, Z., Xie, Q., & Ananiadou, S. (2023). ChatGPT as a factual inconsistency evaluator for text summarization. *arXiv preprint arXiv:2303.15621*. 1 - 12.

Maddigan, P., & Susnjak, T. (2023). Chat2vis: Generating data visualisations via natural language using ChatGPT, Codex and GPT-3 large language models. *IEEE Access : Practical Innovations, Open Solutions*, *11*, 45181–4193. doi:10.1109/ACCESS.2023.3274199

Mali, M. T. S., & Deshmukh, R. K. (2023). Use of Chat GPT in library services. [IJCRT]. *International Journal of Creative Research Thoughts*, *11*(4), f264–f266.

Markel, J. M., Opferman, S. G., Landay, J. A., & Piech, C. (2023). GPTeach: Interactive TA Training with GPT Based Students.

Martin, L., Muller, B., Suárez, P. J. O., Dupont, Y., Romary, L., de La Clergerie, É. V., & Sagot, B. (2019). CamemBERT: a tasty French language model. *arXiv preprint arXiv:1911.03894*.

Martínez-Plumed, F., Gómez, E., & Hernández-Orallo, J. (2021). Futures of artificial intelligence through technology readiness levels. *Telematics and Informatics, 58*, 101525.

McCann, S. (2021). Copyright throughout a creative ai pipeline. *The Canadian Journal of Law and Technology*, 109 - 139.

McCoy, R. T., Smolensky, P., Linzen, T., Gao, J., & Celikyilmaz, A. (2021). How much do language models copy from their training data? Evaluating linguistic novelty in text generation using Raven. *arXiv preprint arXiv:2111.09509*.

McGeeR. W. (2023). *Annie Chan: Three short stories written with Chat GPT*. SSRN 4359403.

McGee, R. W. (2023). *Does God exist? The ChatGPT response*. Research Gate.

McGee, R. W. (2023). Ethics committees can be unethical: The ChatGPT response. SSRN, 4392258.

McGee, R. W. (2023). *Is Chat GPT biased against conservatives? An empirical study*. 1 - 19.

McGee, R. W. (2023). *Is there a duty to pay for the education of other people's children? The ChatGPT response*. SSRN.

McGee, R. W. (2023). What are the Top 20 questions in political philosophy? A ChatGPT reply. Working Paper. SSRN. https://ssrn.com/abstract= 4413440.

McGee, R. W. (2023). *What will the United States look like in 2050? A ChatGPT short story*. (Working paper). Research Gate.

McHugh, J. (2023). *Defensive AI: Experimental study* [Doctoral dissertation, Marymount University].

McIlroy-Young, R., Kleinberg, J., Sen, S., Barocas, S., & Anderson, A. (2022, July). Mimetic models: Ethical implications of ai that acts like you. In *Proceedings of the 2022 AAAI/ACM Conference on AI, Ethics, and Society* (pp. 479-490). ACM. 10.1145/3514094.3534177

McMahan, H. B., Ramage, D., Talwar, K., & Zhang, L. (2017). Learning differentially private recurrent language models. *arXiv preprint arXiv:1710.06963.*

Mialon, G., Dessì, R., Lomeli, M., Nalmpantis, C., Pasunuru, R., Raileanu, R., & Scialom, T. (2023). Augmented language models: A survey. *arXiv preprint arXiv:2302.07842.*

Miao, H., & Ahn, H. (2023). Impact of ChatGPT on interdisciplinary nursing education and research. *Asian/Pacific Island Nursing Journal, 7*(1), e48136, 1 - 3.

Min, B., Ross, H., Sulem, E., Veyseh, A. P. B., Nguyen, T. H., Sainz, O., & Roth, D. (2021). Recent advances in natural language processing via large pre-trained language models: A survey. *arXiv preprint arXiv:2111.01243.*

Mökander, J., Schuett, J., Kirk, H. R., & Floridi, L. (2023). Auditing large language models: A three-layered approach. *arXiv preprint arXiv:2302.08500.*

Mondal, S., Das, S., & Vrana, V. G. (2023). How to bell the cat? A theoretical review of generative artificial intelligence towards digital disruption in all walks of life. *Technologies, 11*(2), 44. doi:10.3390/technologies11020044

Moore, R. C., & Lewis, W. (2010, July). Intelligent selection of language model training data. In *Proceedings of the ACL 2010 Conference Short Papers* (pp. 220-224). ACL.

Morris, M. R. (2023). Scientists' perspectives on the potential for generative AI in their fields. *arXiv preprint arXiv:2304.01420.* 1 - 26.

Murugesan, S., & Cherukuri, A. K. (2023). The rise of generative artificial Intelligence and its impact on education: The promises and perils. *Computer, 56*(5), 116–121. doi:10.1109/MC.2023.3253292

Nadeem, M., Bethke, A., & Reddy, S. (2020). StereoSet: Measuring stereotypical bias in pretrained language models. *arXiv preprint arXiv:2004.09456.*

Nangia, N., Vania, C., Bhalerao, R., & Bowman, S. R. (2020). CrowS-pairs: A challenge dataset for measuring social biases in masked language models. *arXiv preprint arXiv:2010.00133.* doi:10.18653/v1/2020.emnlp-main.154

Neves, P. S. (2022). Chat GPT BBDS" Interview" 1, December 2022. *BBDS-Black Book: Drawing and Sketching, 3*(2), 44–49.

Nguyen, K., Vu, N., Nguyen, D., & Than, K. (2022, December). Random Generative Adversarial Networks. In *Proceedings of the 11th International Symposium on Information and Communication Technology* (pp. 66-73).

Ogundare, O., & Araya, G. Q. (2023). Comparative analysis of CHATGPT and the evolution of language models. *arXiv preprint arXiv:2304.02468.* doi:10.22541/au.168062641.15097484/v1

Ouyang, L., Wu, J., Jiang, X., Almeida, D., Wainwright, C., Mishkin, P., & Lowe, R. (2022). Training language models to follow instructions with human feedback. *Advances in Neural Information Processing Systems, 35*, 27730–27744.

Palea, D., Zhou, H. H., & Gupta, K. (2020). Transformer Bard: Music and poem generation using transformer models. *In the Proceedings of Conference '20. Aug. 2020.* ACM.

Pardos, Z. A., & Bhandari, S. (2023). Learning gain differences between ChatGPT and human tutor generated algebra hints. *arXiv preprint arXiv:2302.06871.*

Pegoraro, A., Kumari, K., Fereidooni, H., & Sadeghi, A. R. (2023). To ChatGPT, or not to ChatGPT: That is the question! *arXiv preprint arXiv:2304.01487.*

Peng, K., Ding, L., Zhong, Q., Shen, L., Liu, X., Zhang, M., & Tao, D. (2023). Towards making the most of ChatGPT for machine translation. *arXiv preprint arXiv:2303.13780.*

Perkins, M. (2023). Academic integrity considerations of AI large language models in the post-pandemic era: ChatGPT and beyond. *Journal of University Teaching & Learning Practice, 20*(2), 1 - 24.

Phillips, T., Saleh, A., Glazewski, K. D., Hmelo-Silver, C. E., Mott, B., & Lester, J. C. (2022). Exploring the use of GPT-3 as a tool for evaluating text-based collaborative discourse. *Companion Proceedings of the 12th.* ACL.

Pickell, T. R., & Doak, B. R. (2023). Five ideas for how professors can deal with GPT-3... for now. Digital Commons @ George Fox University. Faculty Publications.

QadirJ. (2022). Engineering education in the era of ChatGPT: Promise and pitfalls of generative AI for education. TechRxiv. 1 - 9.

Qin, W., Chen, Z., Wang, L., Lan, Y., Ren, W., & Hong, R. (2023). Read, diagnose and chat: Towards explainable and interactive LLMs-augmented depression detection in social media. *arXiv preprint arXiv:2305.05138.*

Rahaman, M. S., Ahsan, M. M., Anjum, N., Rahman, M. M., & Rahman, M. (2023). *The AI race is on! Google's Bard and OpenAI's ChatGPT head to head: an opinion article.* Research Gate.

Rahaman, M. S., Ahsan, M. T., Anjum, N., Terano, H. J. R., & Rahman, M. M. (2023). From ChatGPT-3 to GPT-4: A significant advancement in AI-Driven NLP tools. *Journal of Engineering and Emerging Technologies, 2*(1), 1–11. doi:10.52631/jeet.v1i1.188

Rahman, M. M., Terano, H. J., Rahman, M. N., Salamzadeh, A., & Rahaman, M. S. (2023). ChatGPT and Academic Research: A Review and Recommendations Based on Practical Examples. Journal of Education. *Management and Development Studies, 3*(1), 1–12.

Rastogi, C., Ribeiro, M. T., King, N., & Amershi, S. (2023). Supporting human-AI collaboration in auditing LLMs with LLMs. *arXiv preprint arXiv:2304.09991.* 1 21. doi:10.1145/3600211.3604712

Rasul, T., Nair, S., Kalendra, D., Robin, M., de Oliveira Santini, F., Ladeira, W. J., ... Heathcote, L. (2023). The role of ChatGPT in higher education: Benefits, challenges, and future research directions. *Journal of Applied Learning and Teaching, 6*(1).

Rathore, B. (2023). Future of AI & Generation Alpha: ChatGPT beyond boundaries. *Eduzone: International Peer Reviewed/Refereed Multidisciplinary Journal, 12*(1), 63-68.

Raychev, V., Vechev, M., & Yahav, E. (2014, June). Code completion with statistical language models. In *Proceedings of the 35th ACM SIGPLAN Conference on Programming Language Design and Implementation* (pp. 419-428). ACM. 10.1145/2594291.2594321

Reynolds, L., & McDonell, K. (2021, May). Prompt programming for large language models: Beyond the few-shot paradigm. In *Extended Abstracts of the 2021 CHI Conference on Human Factors in Computing Systems* (pp. 1-7). ACM.

Rezwana, J., & Maher, M. L. (2022). Designing creative AI partners with COFI: A framework for modeling interaction in human-AI co-creative systems. *ACM Transactions on Computer-Human Interaction.*

Roberts, A., Raffel, C., & Shazeer, N. (2020). How much knowledge can you pack into the parameters of a language model? *arXiv preprint arXiv:2002.08910.* doi:10.18653/v1/2020.emnlp-main.437

Roemmich, K., Schaub, F., & Andalibi, N. (2023, April). Emotion AI at Work: Implications for Workplace Surveillance, Emotional Labor, and Emotional Privacy. In *Proceedings of the 2023 CHI Conference on Human Factors in Computing Systems* (pp. 1-20). ACM. 10.1145/3544548.3580950

Rospigliosi, P. A. (2023). Artificial intelligence in teaching and learning: What questions should we ask of ChatGPT? *Interactive Learning Environments, 31*(1), 1–3. doi:10.1080/10494820.2023.2180191

Rousseau, H. P. (2023). From Gutenberg to Chat GPT: The challenge of the digital university (No. 2023rb-02). *CIRANO. Burgundy Report, 2023*, RB-02.

Rudolph, J., Tan, S., & Tan, S. (2023). War of the chatbots: Bard, Bing Chat, ChatGPT, Ernie and beyond. The new AI gold rush and its impact on higher education. *Journal of Applied Learning and Teaching, 6*(1).

Ryznar, M. (2023). Exams in the time of ChatGPT. *Washington and Lee Law Review Online, 80*(5), 305–322.

Sallam, M. (2023). The utility of ChatGPT as an example of large language models in healthcare education, research and practice: Systematic review on the future perspectives and potential limitations. medRxiv, 2023-02.

Sallam, M., Salim, N. A., Ala'a, B., Barakat, M., Fayyad, D., Hallit, S., & Ala'a, B. (2023). ChatGPT output regarding compulsory vaccination and COVID-19 vaccine conspiracy: A descriptive study at the outset of a paradigm shift in online search for information. *Cureus, 15*(2), 1–16. doi:10.7759/cureus.35029 PMID:36819954

Sardana, D., Fagan, T. R., & Wright, J. T. (2023). ChatGPT: A disruptive innovation or disrupting innovation in academia? *The Journal of the American Dental Association, 154*(5), 361–364. doi:10.1016/j.adaj.2023.02.008 PMID:36948928

Schäfer, M. S. (2023). The Notorious GPT: Science communication in the age of artificial intelligence. *JCOM, Journal of Science Communication, 22*(2), Y02. doi:10.22323/2.22020402

Schemmer, M., Hemmer, P., Nitsche, M., Kühl, N., & Vössing, M. (2022, July). A meta-analysis of the utility of explainable artificial intelligence in human-AI decision-making. In *Proceedings of the 2022 AAAI/ACM Conference on AI, Ethics, and Society* (pp. 617-626). ACM. 10.1145/3514094.3534128

Schick, T., Dwivedi-Yu, J., Dessì, R., Raileanu, R., Lomeli, M., Zettlemoyer, L., & Scialom, T. (2023). Toolformer: Language models can teach themselves to use tools. *arXiv preprint arXiv:2302.04761.*

Schick, T., & Schütze, H. (2020). It's not just size that matters: Small language models are also few-shot learners. *arXiv preprint arXiv:2009.07118.*

Schuster, T., Fisch, A., Gupta, J., Dehghani, M., Bahri, D., Tran, V., & Metzler, D. (2022). Confident adaptive language modeling. *Advances in Neural Information Processing Systems, 35*, 17456–17472.

See, A., Pappu, A., Saxena, R., Yerukola, A., & Manning, C. D. (2019). Do massively pretrained language models make better storytellers? *arXiv preprint arXiv:1909.10705*. doi:10.18653/v1/K19-1079

Shafeeg, A., Shazhaev, I., Mihaylov, D., Tularov, A., & Shazhaev, I. (2023). Voice assistant integrated with Chat GPT. *Indonesian Journal of Computer Science, 12*(1). doi:10.33022/ijcs.v12i1.3146

Shahriar, S., & Hayawi, K. (2023). Let's have a chat! A Conversation with ChatGPT: Technology, applications, and limitations. *arXiv preprint arXiv:2302.13817.*

Shin, T., Razeghi, Y., Logan, R. L., IV, Wallace, E., & Singh, S. (2020). Autoprompt: Eliciting knowledge from language models with automatically generated prompts. *arXiv preprint arXiv:2010.15980.* doi:10.18653/v1/2020.emnlp-main.346

Shoufan, A. (2023). Exploring students' perceptions of ChatGPT: Thematic analysis and follow-up survey. *IEEE Access : Practical Innovations, Open Solutions, 11*, 38805–38818. doi:10.1109/ACCESS.2023.3268224

Siapka, A. (2022, July). Towards a feminist metaethics of AI. In *Proceedings of the 2022 AAAI/ACM Conference on AI, Ethics, and Society* (pp. 665-674). ACM. 10.1145/3514094.3534197

Sinha, A., & Lakhanpal, P. (2023). Can AI systems become wise? A note on artificial wisdom. *AI & Society*, 1–2. doi:10.100700146-023-01683-4

Sison, A. J. G., Daza, M. T., Gozalo-Brizuela, R., & Garrido-Merchán, E. C. (2023). ChatGPT: More than a weapon of mass deception, Ethical challenges and responses from the Human-Centered Artificial Intelligence (HCAI) perspective. *arXiv preprint arXiv:2304.11215.*

Sohail, S. S., Farhat, F., Himeur, Y., Nadeem, M., Madsen, D. Ø., Singh, Y., & Mansoor, W. (2023). The future of GPT: A taxonomy of existing ChatGPT research, current challenges, and possible future directions. *Current Challenges, and Possible Future Directions (April 8, 2023).*

Solaiman, I., Brundage, M., Clark, J., Askell, A., Herbert-Voss, A., Wu, J., & Wang, J. (2019). Release strategies and the social impacts of language models. *arXiv preprint arXiv:1908.09203.*

Song, M., Jiang, H., Shi, S., Yao, S., Lu, S., Feng, Y., & Jing, L. (2023). Is ChatGPT a good Keyphrase generator? A preliminary study. *arXiv preprint arXiv:2303.13001.*

Srinivasan, R., & Uchino, K. (2021, March). Biases in generative art: A causal look from the lens of art history. In *Proceedings of the 2021 ACM Conference on Fairness, Accountability, and Transparency* (pp. 41-51). ACM. 10.1145/3442188.3445869

Steinfeld, K. (2023). Clever little tricks: A socio-technical history of text-to-image generative models. *International Journal of Architectural Computing*, *21*(2), 211–241. doi:10.1177/14780771231168230

Steinhoff, J. (2023). AI ethics as subordinated innovation network. *AI & Society*, 1–13.

Sun, J., Liao, Q. V., Muller, M., Agarwal, M., Houde, S., Talamadupula, K., & Weisz, J. D. (2022, March). Investigating explainability of generative AI for code through scenario-based design. In *27th International Conference on Intelligent User Interfaces* (pp. 212-228). ACM. 10.1145/3490099.3511119

Surameery, N. M. S., & Shakor, M. Y. (2023). Use Chat GPT to solve programming bugs. *International Journal of Information Technology & Computer Engineering (IJITC), 3*(01), 17-22.

Taecharungroj, V. (2023). "What Can ChatGPT Do?" Analyzing early reactions to the innovative AI chatbot on Twitter. *Big Data and Cognitive Computing*, *7*(1), 35. doi:10.3390/bdcc7010035

Tajik, E., & Tajik, F. (2023). *A comprehensive examination of the potential application of Chat GPT in higher education institutions.*

Talboy, A. N., & Fuller, E. (2023). Challenging the appearance of machine intelligence: Cognitive bias in LLMs. *arXiv preprint arXiv:2304.01358.*

Thoppilan, R., De Freitas, D., Hall, J., Shazeer, N., Kulshreshtha, A., Cheng, H. T., & Le, Q. (2022). Lamda: Language models for dialog applications. *arXiv preprint arXiv:2201.08239.*

Thorne, S. (2020). Hey Siri, tell me a story: Digital storytelling and AI authorship. *Convergence (London)*, *26*(4), 808–823. doi:10.1177/1354856520913866

Tirumala, K., Markosyan, A., Zettlemoyer, L., & Aghajanyan, A. (2022). Memorization without overfitting: Analyzing the training dynamics of large language models. *Advances in Neural Information Processing Systems*, *35*, 38274–38290.

Tlili, A., Shehata, B., Adarkwah, M. A., Bozkurt, A., Hickey, D. T., Huang, R., & Agyemang, B. (2023). What if the devil is my guardian angel: ChatGPT as a case study of using chatbots in education. *Smart Learning Environments*, *10*(1), 15. doi:10.118640561-023-00237-x

Touvron, H., Lavril, T., Izacard, G., Martinet, X., Lachaux, M. A., Lacroix, T., & Lample, G. (2023). Llama: Open and efficient foundation language models. *arXiv preprint arXiv:2302.13971.*

Tran, K., Bisazza, A., & Monz, C. (2016). Recurrent memory networks for language modeling. *arXiv preprint arXiv:1601.01272.* doi:10.18653/v1/N16-1036

Ulberg, E., Llach, D. C., & Byrne, D. (2020). Hand-crafting neural networks for art-making. In ICCC (pp. 508-511).

Vaishya, R., Misra, A., & Vaish, A. (2023). ChatGPT: Is this version good for healthcare and research? *Diabetes & Metabolic Syndrome: Clinical Research & Reviews, 17*(4), 102744.

Véliz, C. (2023). Chatbots shouldn't use emojis. *Nature*, *615*(7952), 375. doi:10.1038/d41586-023-00758-y PMID:36918680

Vidhya, N. G., Devi, D., Nithya, A., & Manju, T. (2023). Prognosis of exploration on Chat GPT (sic) with artificial intelligence ethics. *Brazilian Journal of Science*, *2*(9), 60–69. doi:10.14295/bjs.v2i9.372

Vinchon, F., Lubart, T., Bartolotta, S., Gironnay, V., Botella, M., Bourgeois, S., & Gaggioli, A. (2023). *Artificial Intelligence & Creativity: A manifesto for collaboration*. Wiley.

Vitente, A., Lazaro, R., Escuadra, C. J., Regino, J., & Rotor, E. (2023). The use of artificial intelligence (AI)-assisted technologies in scientific discourse. *Philippine Journal of Physical Therapy*, *2*(1), 1–3. doi:10.46409/002.HNUY6271

Walter, Y. (2023). The rapid competitive economy of machine learning development: A discussion on the social risks and benefits. *AI and Ethics*, 1–14. doi:10.100743681-023-00276-7

Wang, B., Deng, X., & Sun, H. (2022, December). Iteratively prompt pre-trained language models for chain of thought. In *Proceedings of the 2022 Conference on Empirical Methods in Natural Language Processing* (pp. 2714-2730). ACL. 10.18653/v1/2022.emnlp-main.174

Wang, D., Gong, C., & Liu, Q. (2019, May). Improving neural language modeling via adversarial training. In *International Conference on Machine Learning* (pp. 6555-6565). PMLR.

Wang, F. Y., Miao, Q., Li, X., Wang, X., & Lin, Y. (2023). What does ChatGPT say: The DAO from algorithmic intelligence to linguistic intelligence. *IEEE/CAA Journal of Automatica Sinica, 10*(3), 575-579.

Wang, F. Y., Yang, J., Wang, X., Li, J., & Han, Q. L. (2023). Chat with ChatGPT on Industry 5.0: Learning and decision-making for intelligent industries. *IEEE/CAA Journal of Automatica Sinica, 10*(4), 831-834.

Wang, J., Liang, Y., Meng, F., Shi, H., Li, Z., Xu, J., & Zhou, J. (2023). Is ChatGPT a good NLG evaluator? A preliminary study. *arXiv preprint arXiv:2303.04048.*

Wang, J., Liang, Y., Meng, F., Zou, B., Li, Z., Qu, J., & Zhou, J. (2023). Zero-shot cross-lingual summarization via large language models. *arXiv preprint arXiv:2302.14229.* 1 - 11.

Wang, L., Lyu, C., Ji, T., Zhang, Z., Yu, D., Shi, S., & Tu, Z. (2023). Document-level machine translation with large language models. *arXiv preprint arXiv:2304.02210.*

Wang, M. (2023). *ChatGPT: A case study. Conference 2023: Shaping the Future: Key Themes in Higher Education*. PDGIA.

Wang, S., Scells, H., Koopman, B., & Zuccon, G. (2023). Can ChatGPT write a good Boolean query for systematic review literature search? *arXiv preprint arXiv:2302.03495.* 1 - 19. doi:10.1145/3539618.3591703

Wei, J., Bosma, M., Zhao, V. Y., Guu, K., Yu, A. W., Lester, B., & Le, Q. V. (2021). Finetuned language models are zero-shot learners. *arXiv preprint arXiv:2109.01652.*

Wei, J., Tay, Y., Bommasani, R., Raffel, C., Zoph, B., Borgeaud, S., & Fedus, W. (2022). Emergent abilities of large language models. *arXiv preprint arXiv:2206.07682.*

Wei, J., Wang, X., Schuurmans, D., Bosma, M., Chi, E., Le, Q., & Zhou, D. (2022). Chain of thought prompting elicits reasoning in large language models. *arXiv preprint arXiv:2201.11903.*

Wei, X., Cui, X., Cheng, N., Wang, X., Zhang, X., Huang, S., & Han, W. (2023). Zero-shot information extraction via chatting with ChatGPT. *arXiv preprint arXiv:2302.10205.*

Weidinger, L., Mellor, J., Rauh, M., Griffin, C., Uesato, J., Huang, P. S., & Gabriel, I. (2021). Ethical and social risks of harm from language models. *arXiv preprint arXiv:2112.04359.*

White, J., Fu, Q., Hays, S., Sandborn, M., Olea, C., Gilbert, H., & Schmidt, D. C. (2023). A prompt pattern catalog to enhance prompt engineering with ChatGPT. *arXiv preprint arXiv:2302.11382.*

Wu, J., Gan, W., Chen, Z., Wan, S., & Lin, H. (2023). AI-generated content (aigc): A survey. *arXiv preprint arXiv:2304.06632.*

Wu, S., Irsoy, O., Lu, S., Dabravolski, V., Dredze, M., Gehrmann, S., & Mann, G. (2023). Bloomberg-GPT: A large language model for finance. *arXiv preprint arXiv:2303.17564.*

Wu, T., He, S., Liu, J., Sun, S., Liu, K., Han, Q. L., & Tang, Y. (2023). A brief overview of ChatGPT: The history, *status quo* and potential future development. *IEEE/CAA Journal of Automatica Sinica, 10*(5), 1122-1136.

Wu, Y., Jiang, A. Q., Li, W., Rabe, M., Staats, C., Jamnik, M., & Szegedy, C. (2022). Autoformalization with large language models. *Advances in Neural Information Processing Systems*, *35*, 1–16.

Xu, Y. (2022, July). Dialogue explanation with reasoning for AI. In *Proceedings of the 2022 AAAI/ACM Conference on AI, Ethics, and Society* (pp. 918-918). ACM. 10.1145/3514094.3539522

Yadava, O. P. (2023). ChatGPT—A foe or an ally? *Indian Journal of Thoracic and Cardiovascular Surgery*, *39*(3), 217–221. doi:10.100712055-023-01507-6 PMID:37124601

Yahaya, M., Umagba, A., Obeta, S., & Maruyama, T. (2023). Critical evaluation of the future role of artificial intelligence in business and society. *Journal of Artificial Intelligence. Machine Learning and Data Science*, *1*(1), 1–9.

Yakura, H. (2023, April). A generative framework for designing interactions to overcome the gaps between humans and imperfect AIs instead of improving the accuracy of the AIs. In *Extended Abstracts of the 2023 CHI Conference on Human Factors in Computing Systems* (pp. 1-5). ACM. 10.1145/3544549.3577036

Yan, D., Fauss, M., Hao, J., & Cui, W. (2023). Detection of AI-generated essays in writing assessment. *Psychological Test and Assessment Modeling*, *65*(2), 125–144.

Yang, X., Li, Y., Zhang, X., Chen, H., & Cheng, W. (2023). Exploring the limits of ChatGPT for query or aspect-based text summarization. *arXiv preprint arXiv:2302.08081.*

Yang, Z., Li, L., Wang, J., Lin, K., Azarnasab, E., Ahmed, F., & Wang, L. (2023). MM-react: Prompting ChatGPT for multimodal reasoning and action. *arXiv preprint arXiv:2303.11381.*

Yasunaga, M., Ren, H., Bosselut, A., Liang, P., & Leskovec, J. (2021). QA-GNN: Reasoning with language models and knowledge graphs for question answering. *arXiv preprint arXiv:2104.06378.* doi:10.18653/v1/2021.naacl-main.45

Zaitsu, W., & Jin, M. (2023). Distinguishing ChatGPT (-3.5,-4)-generated and human-written papers through Japanese stylometric analysis. *arXiv preprint arXiv:2304.05534.* 1 - 15.

Zameshina, M., Teytaud, O., Teytaud, F., Hosu, V., Carraz, N., Najman, L., & Wagner, M. (2022, July). Fairness in generative modeling: do it unsupervised! In *Proceedings of the Genetic and Evolutionary Computation Conference Companion* (pp. 320-323). 10.1145/3520304.3528992

Zhai, X. (2023). ChatGPT for next generation science learning. *XRDS: Crossroads. The ACM Magazine for Students, 29*(3), 42–46.

Zhang, C., Zhang, C., Li, C., Qiao, Y., Zheng, S., Dam, S. K., & Hong, C. S. (2023). One small step for generative AI, one giant leap for AGI: A complete survey on ChatGPT in AIGC era. *arXiv preprint arXiv:2304.06488.*

Zhang, D. (2023). Should ChatGPT and Bard share revenue with their data providers? A new business model for the AI era. *arXiv preprint arXiv:2305.02555.*

Zhang, H., Liu, X., & Zhang, J. (2023). Extractive summarization via ChatGPT for faithful summary generation. *arXiv preprint arXiv:2304.04193.*

Zhang, S., Roller, S., Goyal, N., Artetxe, M., Chen, M., Chen, S., & Zettlemoyer, L. (2022). Opt: Open pre-trained transformer language models. *arXiv preprint arXiv:2205.01068.*

Zhao, R., Li, X., Chia, Y. K., Ding, B., & Bing, L. (2023). Can ChatGPT-like generative models guarantee factual accuracy? On the mistakes of new generation search engines. *arXiv preprint arXiv:2304.11076.*

Zhao, W. X., Zhou, K., Li, J., Tang, T., Wang, X., Hou, Y., & Wen, J. R. (2023). A survey of large language models. *arXiv preprint arXiv:2303.18223.*

Zhong, H., Chang, J., Yang, Z., Wu, T., Arachchige, P. C. M., Pathmabandu, C., & Xue, M. (2023). Copyright protection and accountability of generative AI: Attack, watermarking and attribution. *arXiv preprint arXiv:2303.09272.* 94 - 98. doi:10.1145/3543873.3587321

Zhong, Q., Ding, L., Liu, J., Du, B., & Tao, D. (2023). Can ChatGPT understand too? A comparative study on ChatGPT and fine-tuned BERT. *arXiv preprint arXiv:2302.10198.*

Zhou, K., Yang, J., Loy, C. C., & Liu, Z. (2022). Learning to prompt for vision-language models. *International Journal of Computer Vision, 130*(9), 2337–2348. doi:10.100711263-022-01653-1

Zhou, X., Zhang, Y., Cui, L., & Huang, D. (2020, April). Evaluating commonsense in pre-trained language models. *Proceedings of the AAAI Conference on Artificial Intelligence, 34*(05), 9733–9740. doi:10.1609/aaai.v34i05.6523

Zhou, Y., Muresanu, A. I., Han, Z., Paster, K., Pitis, S., Chan, H., & Ba, J. (2022). Large language models are human-level prompt engineers. *arXiv preprint arXiv:2211.01910.*

KEY TERMS & DEFINITIONS

Artificial Intelligence Generated Content (AIGC): Digital contents of various modalities (text, image, video, multimedia, and others) that are originated by generative artificial intelligence (GAI), often based on a human prompt (which may be single-modal or multi-modal).

Attention Mechanism: An aspect of some generative AIs that enable the tool to focus on particular parts of input training data in making target outputs (selectively).

Chain-of-Thought Prompting: An assist to LLMs working complex reasoning problems with humans providing a chain of thought or intermediate reasoning steps in the decomposed process.

Generative Artificial Intelligence (Generative AI): Technologies that enable the generation of text, still visuals, sound effects, music, video, multimedia, and other digital contents based on prompts (whether mono-modal or multi-modal).

Generative Search Engines: Online tools that output responses (with in-line source citations) based on user queries.

GPT (Generative Pre-Trained Transformer): A type of AI technology designed to communicate textually and verbally with humans.

Hallucination (in LLM Systems): The generating of textual contents that may be inaccurate or "based on false assumptions" even if syntactically and semantically correct; considered a bug, not a feature.

Memorization: The ability of a language model to generate the true continuation when choosing the *most likely* token at every step of decoding" (Carlini, Ippolito, Jagielski, Lee, Tramer, & Zhang, 2022, p. 6), which can lead to verbatim output of original text from the training data used to train the large language model.

Misprime: Queries sent to LMMs that can mislead the output or result, such as opening with a (one-word) question followed by a prompt that is unrelated to the initial question (which is the mispriming).

Natural language generation (NLG) systems: These are a category of tools which include AI-powered ones.

Natural Language Processing (NLP): Computational means to understand, translate, and extract meaning from natural human language.

Parameters (in LLMs): A numerical value that "defines the behavior of the model" based on learning from text, code, images, or other training data (such as word probability, the weight of the linkage between two neurons in a neural network); larger models have more parameters and so have learning about more complexities from the training data.

Perplexity: The (in)accuracy of a language model to predict the next word(s) in a given sequence (where lower perplexity means high capability of language predictivity, and higher perplexity as less accuracy in word prediction).

Pre-Trained Language Models (PLMs): Language models trained on often large curated datasets of natural language training data.

Prompt programming (or prompt engineering): The fashioning of instructions (whether single-modal or multi-modal) to use with generative AI models to elicit particular human-desired outputs.

Prompting: Also known as "prompt engineering" in a more formal context, this means submitting an initial or starting instructional input (such as text, visual, or other input); an emergent way that people work with complex AI systems, including generative AI ones, to acquire particular digital outcomes.

Supercopying: Occasions when large language models take entire passages from training data verbatim that are 1,000 words or more in length (compared to the rare cases of n-grams larger than 10 tokens), perceived as a form of plagiarism or illegal copying.

Text-Making Generative AI: Language models that produce text in various styles in response to human-written text prompts.

Visual-Making Generative AI: Visual models that produce visuals in various styles in response to text, visual, and multimodal prompts.

Whisper APIs: Application programming interfaces (APIs) that integrate artificial intelligence (AI) in quiet or more hidden ways.

Zero-Shot Behavior: The ability of a generative AI model to create new outputs from a statistical distribution that it has not been directly trained on.

Section 2

Navigating Ethical Uses of Generative AI Technologies

Chapter 6
Generative AI in Terms of Its Ethical Problems for Both Teachers and Learners:
Striking a Balance

Huong-Tra Le-Nguyen
https://orcid.org/0000-0003-4718-8920
Hanoi University, Vietnam

Trung Thanh Tran
https://orcid.org/0000-0002-4630-1146
Clientscan, Vietnam

ABSTRACT

The chapter delves into the intricate ethical challenges posed by the integration of generative AI tools in educational contexts. As the educational landscape undergoes a profound transformation through AI-driven technologies, this chapter navigates the multifaceted ethical concerns that emerge. It explores issues surrounding data privacy, content bias, academic integrity, and the evolving roles of teachers and students in this digital era. Drawing on real-world case studies and ethical frameworks, it provides insights into the complexities of responsible AI integration. Moreover, it offers guidance on fostering ethical awareness in education and emphasizes the critical need for striking a harmonious balance between the capabilities of AI and the enduring value of human educators. This chapter serves as a comprehensive exploration of the ethical tightrope that educators, students, and policymakers must navigate to ensure AI's positive impact on education while safeguarding its ethical underpinnings.

1. INTRODUCTION TO PROFESSIONAL ETHICS IN GENERATIVE AI FOR EDUCATION

The rapid advancement of technology has brought about transformative changes in various sectors, and education is no exception. In recent years, generative artificial intelligence (AI) has emerged as a

DOI: 10.4018/979-8-3693-0074-9.ch006

powerful tool in the realm of education. This chapter delves into the ethical considerations surrounding the application of generative AI in educational settings, with a particular focus on skills acquisition and development.

1.1 Overview of Generative AI Applications in Education

Generative AI, a subset of artificial intelligence, refers to the technology's ability to create content, such as text, images, or even videos, without human intervention. (Angelone, Galassi, & Vittorini, 2022) In education, generative AI has found a multitude of applications that have the potential to reshape teaching and learning experiences.

One prominent application is the generation of educational content. AI-driven systems can autonomously produce textbooks, quizzes, and learning materials, providing educators with a wealth of resources to enhance their teaching. Additionally, AI can personalize educational content, tailoring it to individual student needs. For example, AI algorithms can analyze students' learning patterns and adapt the difficulty level of exercises accordingly, optimizing the learning process (Bang et al., 2023).

Another area where generative AI shows promise is in the development of virtual tutors and chatbots. These intelligent systems can provide immediate feedback and guidance to students, offering them a personalized learning experience outside the traditional classroom setting (Bulut & Yildirim-Erbasli, 2022). Virtual tutors can answer questions, clarify concepts, and reinforce learning in real-time.

Furthermore, generative AI can assist in the creation of immersive learning environments, such as virtual reality simulations and interactive educational games (Caines et al., 2023). These technologies engage students in active learning, making education more captivating and effective. The potential applications of generative AI in education are vast and continue to evolve.

1.2 Significance of Ethics in AI-Driven Education

The introduction of generative AI into educational contexts raises profound ethical questions and concerns (Carroll et al., 2022). While the technology holds promise for improving learning outcomes, it also poses risks and challenges that must be addressed. The significance of ethics in AI-driven education cannot be overstated.

First and foremost, there is a need to ensure that AI systems used in education adhere to ethical principles of fairness, transparency, and accountability (Chaudhry, Cukurova, & Luckin, 2022). The decisions made by AI algorithms, such as personalized content recommendations or grading assessments, should be explainable and free from discriminatory biases (Beseiso, Alzubi, & Rashaideh, 2021). Ethical considerations extend to issues of data privacy and security, as educational AI systems often involve the collection and analysis of sensitive student data. It is imperative that this data is handled responsibly and with the utmost respect for privacy.

Additionally, there is a moral imperative to preserve the integrity of education. The risk of overreliance on generative AI could lead to a devaluation of the skills and expertise of educators (Brown et al., 2022). It is essential to strike a balance between the contributions of AI and human educators to ensure that students receive a well-rounded education that encompasses critical thinking, creativity, and human interaction.

1.3 Introduction to the Chapter's Focus on Skills Acquisition and Development in Education

This chapter will specifically explore the ethical dimensions of skills acquisition and development in the context of generative AI applications in education. Skills are at the core of education, and the integration of AI has the potential to both enhance and challenge the traditional models of skill development. We will delve into the risks associated with demotivation, deskilling, and downskilling, as well as the opportunities for upskilling that AI offers.

In the following sections, we will dissect these ethical concerns and opportunities in greater detail. By examining ethical frameworks, and emerging best practices, we aim to provide a comprehensive understanding of the complex interplay between generative AI and skills development in education. Ultimately, our goal is to contribute to the responsible and ethical integration of AI into education, ensuring that it serves as a powerful ally in shaping a brighter future for learners around the world.

2. RISKS TO DEMOTIVATION FOR SKILLS ACQUISITION IN EDUCATIONAL SETTINGS IN THE ERA OF AI TECHNOLOGIES

2.1 The Role of Generative AI in Skill Development

2.1.1 Skill Augmentation vs. Skill Replacement in Teaching and Learning With the Emergence of AI

The role of generative AI in skill development within the context of teaching and learning hinges on a crucial dichotomy: skill augmentation versus skill replacement (Kasneci et al., 2023). This dynamic is at the heart of the ethical and practical considerations surrounding the integration of AI in education (Chechitelli, 2023). Skill augmentation through generative AI involves enhancing the abilities of educators and students by providing them with advanced tools and resources. AI can assist educators in creating personalized, high-quality educational content, offer immediate feedback, and facilitate the adaptation of teaching materials to individual learning styles (Doyle & Ponder, 1977). This augmentation empowers educators to be more efficient and students to learn at their own pace.

However, the risk lies in skill replacement, where generative AI might replace key aspects of traditional teaching and learning (Gašević et al., 2022). If AI takes on too much of the teaching process, educators could become mere facilitators of technology rather than active contributors to students' intellectual and personal growth (Condor, Litster, & Pardos, 2021). This could result in a decline in the development of essential skills like critical thinking, creativity, and empathy, which are fostered through human interaction and engagement (Jayaraman & Black, 2022).

Moreover, students could become passive recipients of AI-generated content, potentially reducing their motivation to actively participate in the learning process (Drori et al., 2022). The risk of skill replacement is not limited to educators; it also extends to various roles within the education sector, including content creators, evaluators, and administrators (Gilson et al., 2023). Thus, it becomes crucial to strike a delicate balance between skill augmentation and replacement, emphasizing AI's role as a complementary tool to enhance the educational experience while preserving the irreplaceable human elements that drive skills development in teaching and learning (Holmes & Porayska-Pomsta, 2022). This balance is essential to harness the potential of generative AI for the betterment of education, ensuring that it empowers both educators and students to reach new heights of knowledge and skill development while preserving the intrinsic value of human engagement in the learning process (Khosravi et al., 2022).

2.1.2 Balancing Human Involvement and AI Interference in Skill Acquisition for Educators and Students

Balancing human involvement in skill acquisition for educators and students stands as a pivotal challenge in the context of generative AI's role in skill development (Leiker et al., 2023). On one hand, generative AI technologies offer unprecedented capabilities to automate tasks, personalize content, and provide instant feedback, which can significantly augment the educational experience (Li et al., 2023, Liu et al., 2022). Educators can leverage these tools to streamline administrative tasks, access vast resources, and create tailored content. Students, in turn, benefit from personalized learning journeys and a wealth of educational materials.

However, the delicate equilibrium lies in preserving the quintessential human touch in education (Kurdi et al., 2020). While AI can excel in tasks such as data analysis and content generation, it often lacks the nuanced understanding, empathy, and adaptability that human educators bring to the table (Li & Xing, 2021). The essence of skill acquisition extends beyond rote learning; it involves critical thinking, emotional intelligence, and the fostering of creativity, all of which are intrinsically human attributes. Students, too, require human guidance, mentorship, and interaction to develop essential life skills and values (Liu et al., 2023).

Balancing this equation necessitates a thoughtful integration of generative AI as a supportive tool rather than a complete replacement for human educators. It involves recognizing the distinct strengths of both AI and human educators and assigning tasks accordingly (Kumar et al., 2022). Educators can focus on higher-order teaching activities, mentorship, and instilling creativity, while AI handles routine tasks and offers personalized learning experiences. Moreover, it requires continuous evaluation of AI systems to ensure they align with educational goals, ethical principles, and the overarching aim of holistic skill development (Liang et al., 2023). This delicate balance represents the future of education—where the synergy of human expertise and AI augmentation creates an enriched learning environment that optimizes skill acquisition for educators and students alike.

2.2 AI-Rendered Threats to Educators' Motivation and Engagement

2.2.1 Psychological Impact of Overreliance on AI

The psychological impact of overreliance on AI is a multifaceted concern within the broader context of threats to motivation and engagement, particularly in educational and professional settings. While the integration of AI can undoubtedly enhance efficiency and productivity, an excessive dependence on AI-driven systems can have profound consequences on the psychological well-being and motivation of individuals (Ma et al., 2023).

One primary concern is the potential erosion of self-efficacy—the belief in one's ability to accomplish tasks and achieve goals (Maheen et al., 2022). When individuals begin to rely heavily on AI for tasks they previously performed themselves, there is a risk that they may perceive their own skills as diminished or unnecessary. This perception can lead to a sense of learned helplessness, where individuals believe they have little control over their own outcomes, ultimately undermining their motivation to engage in tasks requiring those skills (Nye et al., 2023). This phenomenon can be particularly pronounced among students and professionals who may start to doubt their abilities when AI consistently outperforms them in certain domains.

Moreover, an overreliance on AI can impact intrinsic motivation, the internal drive to engage in an activity for the inherent satisfaction it provides. As individuals delegate more tasks to AI, they may find themselves disconnected from the genuine joy of learning or accomplishing tasks independently (Oleny, 2023). This detachment from the intrinsic rewards of problem-solving, critical thinking, and creativity can lead to a decrease in motivation. In education, students who rely heavily on AI-generated content may lose interest in the learning process, viewing it as a passive, AI-driven experience rather than an opportunity for personal growth and discovery.

Additionally, overreliance on AI can affect individuals' sense of autonomy and control. When AI takes center stage in decision-making and task execution, individuals may feel disempowered and less in control of their own lives or work. This perceived loss of autonomy can contribute to feelings of frustration, anxiety, and disengagement. In educational settings, students may become disinterested or detached from their studies if they perceive that AI is directing their learning experiences without their input (Sallam, 2023).

Furthermore, there are social and interpersonal implications to consider. Overreliance on AI can lead to reduced human interaction, which is a critical component of motivation and engagement (Rudolph et al., 2023). In educational contexts, interpersonal relationships with teachers and peers play a pivotal role in fostering a sense of belonging, collaboration, and emotional support. Excessive reliance on AI-driven content can isolate students, making them feel disconnected from the social aspects of learning, potentially leading to feelings of loneliness or disengagement (Sarsa et al., 2022).

Mitigating the psychological impact of overreliance on AI necessitates a balanced approach to AI integration (OpenAI, 2023). It involves designing AI systems that complement, rather than replace, human skills and expertise. This approach should empower individuals to use AI as a tool to enhance their capabilities and decision-making rather than delegating these responsibilities entirely. Additionally, fostering self-awareness and resilience in the face of AI reliance is essential. Encouraging individuals to maintain an active role in their skill development, valuing their unique contributions, and emphasizing the enduring importance of human skills and attributes can help mitigate the potential psychological drawbacks of AI overreliance (Sawatzki et al., 2022). Ultimately, striking this balance is essential for harnessing the benefits of AI while safeguarding motivation, engagement, and well-being.

2.2.2 Maintaining Intrinsic Motivation for Teaching and Learning

Maintaining intrinsic motivation for teaching and learning is a paramount concern within the realm of threats to motivation and engagement in educational settings. Intrinsic motivation, which arises from a genuine interest and satisfaction in the learning process, plays a pivotal role in driving both educators and students to excel in their academic endeavors. However, the advent of technology and, in particular, the integration of AI and generative technologies can inadvertently jeopardize this intrinsic motivation.

For educators, the allure of AI lies in its potential to streamline administrative tasks and offer a wealth of resources. While these benefits can enhance efficiency, they also carry the risk of diminishing educators' intrinsic motivation. When educators find themselves increasingly tasked with administrative duties and are no longer the central figures in content creation, they may lose the sense of fulfillment that comes from crafting and delivering their own lessons. This shift can lead to a decline in passion for teaching, potentially transforming a once-vibrant profession into a routine job.

Similarly, students may find their intrinsic motivation waning in the face of overreliance on AI-generated content. When educational materials become standardized, and personalization is driven solely by algorithms, students may perceive learning as a passive, prescribed experience rather than an exploration driven by their own curiosity. This shift can dampen their enthusiasm for acquiring new knowledge and skills.

The risk of diminishing intrinsic motivation underscores the importance of thoughtful AI integration that complements, rather than replaces, the roles of educators and students. Educators must remain central in shaping the learning experience, using AI as a tool to enhance rather than supplant their abilities. Likewise, AI should be designed to foster personalized learning journeys, encouraging students to take an active role in their education. Moreover, promoting the intrinsic rewards of learning—such as problem-solving, critical thinking, and creative exploration—can help counterbalance the potential erosion of motivation caused by AI reliance.

Furthermore, recognizing and celebrating the intrinsic motivation that both educators and students bring to the educational process is paramount. By acknowledging their individual contributions and emphasizing the enduring value of human attributes, such as empathy, adaptability, and mentorship, the educational community can continue to inspire and nurture the intrinsic motivation that fuels teaching and learning. Ultimately, a harmonious coexistence between AI and intrinsic motivation is attainable, ensuring that technology enhances, rather than diminishes, the passion and engagement of all those involved in education.

3. SEQUENCED OUTCOMES - DESKILLING AND DOWNSKILLING CONCERNS IN EDUCATION

3.1 Deskilling: Erosion of Educator skills

3.1.1 The Risk of Becoming Overly Reliant on AI-Generated Teaching Materials

Overreliance on AI-generated teaching materials presents a multifaceted risk within the educational landscape. While artificial intelligence (AI) has undeniably revolutionized the way educational content is created and disseminated, this reliance poses several critical challenges and concerns, especially on occupational ethics.

First and foremost, an overdependence on AI-generated materials can lead to a homogenization of educational content. AI algorithms are data-driven and often prioritize efficiency and consistency. This means that the content they generate might lack the diversity and nuance that human educators bring to the table. Educational materials tailored solely by algorithms can become formulaic, standardized, and lacking the personal touch that human educators infuse into their teaching resources. This homogenization can diminish the richness and variety of learning experiences for students, potentially stifling their creativity and critical thinking skills (Schneider et al., 2022).

Furthermore, overreliance on AI-generated materials can lead to a detachment from the human aspect of education. Education is not solely about the transmission of knowledge; it also involves mentorship, guidance, and meaningful human connections. When AI takes center stage in content creation, human educators may feel less engaged with the teaching process, potentially diminishing their enthusiasm for teaching. Students, on the other hand, might perceive their learning experiences as sterile and devoid of the emotional and social connections that are essential for holistic development.

Another risk is the potential for AI-generated content to perpetuate biases and inaccuracies present in the training data. If the algorithms used for content generation are not rigorously vetted and monitored, they may inadvertently propagate stereotypes, prejudices, or misinformation. This can have severe consequences, as students exposed to biased or inaccurate information may develop skewed perspectives or be ill-prepared to engage critically with the world.

Additionally, overreliance on AI-generated materials might erode educators' skill development in content creation and curriculum design (Schramowski et al., 2022). When educators have AI-generated resources at their disposal, they may be less motivated to craft their materials and tailor their teaching to their students' specific needs. This can lead to a stagnation of their pedagogical skills, ultimately diminishing their effectiveness as educators.

Mitigating the risk of overreliance on AI-generated teaching materials necessitates a balanced approach. AI should be viewed as a tool to enhance, not replace, the expertise and creativity of educators. It should be used to streamline administrative tasks, offer supplementary resources, and support educators in their teaching endeavors. Furthermore, educators should actively engage with AI tools, critically evaluate AI-generated content, and continue to cultivate their own teaching skills and pedagogical insights. By finding this equilibrium, educators can harness the benefits of AI while preserving the dynamic and enriching qualities of human-driven education. To do so, it is crucial to strike a balance between the benefits of AI efficiency and the preservation of educators' essential skills (Zheng et al., 2022). This can be achieved by viewing AI as a supportive tool rather than a complete replacement. Educators should actively engage with AI systems, critically assess AI-generated content, and use it as a resource to enhance their teaching, not replace it. Professional development opportunities should also emphasize the importance of continually honing pedagogical skills, even in the presence of AI. Ultimately, the goal is to leverage AI for its advantages while ensuring that educators remain empowered, skilled, and motivated in their pivotal role in shaping the educational experiences of future generations.

3.1.1 Impact on Traditional Teaching Methods and Pedagogical Skills

The risk of becoming overly reliant on AI-generated teaching materials is intrinsically linked to the broader concern of deskilling within the education sector. Deskilling refers to the potential erosion of essential skills and expertise among educators when certain tasks are automated or delegated to AI systems. In the context of AI-generated teaching materials, the convenience and efficiency that these systems offer can be a double-edged sword. While they undoubtedly streamline the content creation process, there is a substantial risk that educators may gradually lose their motivation, autonomy, and expertise in crafting tailored educational materials (Zheng et al., 2023).

The impact of generative AI and large language models on traditional teaching methods and pedagogical skills is a transformative force that falls squarely within the purview of the deskilling phenomenon. As AI technologies continue to permeate educational contexts, they usher in both opportunities and challenges that reshape the landscape of teaching and learning. On one hand, AI-powered tools offer educators unprecedented access to resources, personalization, and automation, potentially revolutionizing traditional teaching methods. However, these very advantages also pose a profound risk to the erosion of educators' pedagogical skills.

When AI takes on the role of content creator, educators may perceive a diminishing need for their own skills in curriculum design and lesson planning. This perception can result in a decline in educators' intrinsic motivation to innovate and adapt their teaching methods (Yan et al., 2022). Over time, they may rely heavily on pre-generated AI materials, ultimately leading to a stagnation of their pedagogical skills. The consequence is that educators become deskilled in an essential aspect of their profession, as their expertise in creating engaging, relevant, and personalized educational content dwindles.

Generative AI and large language models excel in content creation, enabling the rapid generation of textbooks, quizzes, and learning materials. This convenience and efficiency can lead educators to increasingly rely on pre-generated content, potentially sidelining their roles as curriculum designers and content creators. As AI-generated materials become the norm, educators may find themselves deskilled in the art of crafting engaging, contextually relevant, and pedagogically sound educational content. Their expertise in tailoring materials to meet the unique needs of their students could diminish, leading to a homogenization of teaching materials and a loss of the dynamic, personalized touch that educators bring to their classrooms.

Furthermore, deskilling in content creation can have broader implications for the quality of education. While AI-generated materials can offer consistency and efficiency, they may lack the depth, context, and nuanced understanding that human educators bring to their teaching resources. Educators, with their years of training and experience, are uniquely positioned to adapt content to suit the needs and interests of their students. When deskilled, educators may lose this critical ability, leading to a one-size-fits-all approach that fails to cater to the diverse learning styles and requirements of students (Wu et al., 2023). The advent of AI in education challenges traditional pedagogical methods. AI-driven systems, equipped with vast data and algorithms, can personalize learning experiences for individual students, offering tailored content and assessments. While this personalization can enhance student engagement and outcomes, it also poses a risk of deskilling educators in the fine art of adapting teaching strategies to diverse student needs. Educators may rely on AI recommendations and automated feedback systems rather than honing their abilities to intuitively adapt to the evolving dynamics of their classrooms.

Another facet of deskilling is the potential loss of educators' autonomy and decision-making power. When AI-driven systems dominate content creation, educators might find themselves confined to a predetermined curriculum, limiting their capacity to customize materials to their students' specific needs and interests. This loss of autonomy can be demotivating, as it undermines educators' professional agency and their ability to make pedagogical choices that resonate with their unique teaching philosophy. Moreover, as AI-assisted teaching becomes more prevalent, educators may experience a decline in their role as facilitators of critical thinking, problem-solving, and deep learning experiences (Zeng et al., 2023). The allure of AI-generated solutions for assessments and assignments can tempt educators to prioritize efficiency over the development of higher-order thinking skills. This could lead to deskilling in the essential pedagogical abilities required to foster creativity, independent thought, and intellectual curiosity in students.

3.2 Downskilling: Reduced Skill Requirements in the Education Sector

3.2.1 Potential Implications for Educators' Job Roles and Skill Demand

The potential implications of generative AI and large language models for educators' job roles and skill demand are poised at the intersection of innovation and transformation within the education sector. While these AI technologies offer a spectrum of opportunities for more efficient and personalized learning experiences, they also carry the inherent risk of downskilling, whereby the skill requirements for educators may be significantly reduced, reshaping the nature of their profession (Wollny et al., 2021).

One immediate implication lies in the evolving job roles of educators. As generative AI becomes more proficient at content creation, grading, and even personalized tutoring, educators may see a shift in their responsibilities. Routine, administrative tasks may be increasingly automated, altering the traditional educator's role as the sole provider of educational content. This shift can lead to a narrowing of job roles, as educators might find themselves focusing more on administrative and supervisory duties rather than directly engaging with students in content delivery. This downskilling effect has the potential to reduce job satisfaction, as educators may feel less connected to their core teaching and mentoring functions (Maheen et al., 2022) .

Furthermore, the skill demand for educators could undergo a transformation as AI takes on certain pedagogical responsibilities. The demand for skills such as content creation, grading, and data analysis may diminish as AI systems assume these roles. Conversely, educators may find themselves needing to acquire new skills related to AI integration, data interpretation, and the effective use of AI-driven tools in the classroom (Gilson et al., 2023). While these new skills are valuable and relevant, they may not fully compensate for the erosion of traditional teaching skills, which encompass pedagogical expertise, classroom management, and interpersonal skills. This shift in skill demand could lead to a workforce misalignment, where educators may need to undergo significant retraining or upskilling to remain relevant in the evolving education landscape.

Moreover, there is a broader societal concern related to the downskilling of educators. As AI technologies advance, there is the potential for a reduced demand for highly skilled educators, leading to job displacement and a surplus of educators with specialized skills. This oversupply may result in a competitive job market, potentially leading to job insecurity and wage pressures within the education sector. Educators who have invested years in acquiring specialized teaching skills could find themselves at risk of devaluation in the job market, creating challenges for both educators and educational institutions (Jayaraman & Black, 2022).

One of the way to solve these addressed problem is engagement. It is essential for educators to engage proactively with these technologies. Educators should embrace AI as a tool to enhance their teaching capabilities and actively seek opportunities for upskilling in areas relevant to AI integration. Educational institutions can play a pivotal role by offering professional development programs that equip educators with the necessary skills to leverage AI effectively while preserving the core pedagogical expertise that is essential for quality education. By striking a balance between AI-driven efficiency and the preservation of educator skills, the education sector can harness the transformative power of AI while ensuring that educators remain valued contributors to the learning process (Doyle & Ponder, 1977).

3.2.2 Ethical Considerations for Educators Facing Job Displacement

Ethical considerations surrounding educators facing job displacement due to generative AI and large language models in the education sector are complex and multifaceted. As AI technologies continue to evolve and automate certain aspects of teaching, educators find themselves at a critical juncture where their professional roles may be redefined or even displaced (Bulut & Yildirim-Erbasli, 2022). Ethical concerns in this context revolve around the principles of fairness, responsibility, and the broader societal impact of these transformations.

One primary ethical concern is the fairness and well-being of educators who face potential job displacement. Many educators have dedicated their careers to honing their teaching skills and expertise, and the sudden displacement due to AI-driven automation can be emotionally and financially distressing. Ensuring that educators are treated fairly and provided with support during such transitions is a moral imperative. Ethical considerations extend to questions of retraining and reskilling opportunities, job placement assistance, and financial security. Institutions and policymakers have a responsibility to facilitate these transitions in a way that minimizes harm and ensures that educators are not left behind in the wake of technological change (Angelone, Galassi, & Vittorini, 2022).

Another ethical dimension involves the responsibility of educational institutions and AI developers (Chechitelli, 2023). When implementing AI-driven systems that may lead to job displacement, institutions and developers bear the ethical responsibility of providing clear and transparent communication about the potential impacts of these technologies on educators' roles. This includes openly discussing the role of AI in teaching, its potential benefits, and the possible consequences for educators. Ethical transparency can help educators make informed decisions about their careers and engage in proactive skill development and upskilling.

Furthermore, ethical considerations extend to the broader societal impact of educator job displacement. The erosion of teaching roles due to AI could result in a workforce mismatch, where there is an oversupply of highly skilled educators facing job insecurity. This scenario raises questions about societal values and priorities (Smith, 2021). Ethical discussions should revolve around the importance of valuing and preserving the human element in education, emphasizing the irreplaceable roles that educators play in nurturing creativity, critical thinking, and personal growth in students. It is essential to recognize that AI can enhance educational processes but cannot fully replace the depth of human interaction and mentorship.

Additionally, ethical frameworks should guide the responsible development and deployment of AI technologies in education. This includes ensuring that AI systems are designed to minimize biases and discriminatory effects, adhere to data privacy and security principles, and prioritize educational quality and equity. Developers and institutions must consider the potential ethical pitfalls and actively work to mitigate them in the design and implementation of AI-driven systems (Larsson & Heintz, 2020).

4. OPPORTUNITIES FOR UPSKILLING IN EDUCATIONAL FIELDS

4.1 Leveraging Generative AI for Educator Skill Enhancement

4.2 Augmented Teaching and Personalized Learning Through AI-Driven Tools

Augmented teaching and personalized learning through AI-driven tools represent a groundbreaking shift in the field of education (Torralba & Efros, 2011). These technologies have the potential to revolutionize how educators deliver instruction and how students engage with educational content. Augmented teaching harnesses the power of AI to enhance educators' capabilities, offering them a wealth of resources, data analytics, and personalized insights that can profoundly impact their teaching methods. AI-driven tools can help educators tailor their lessons to meet individual student needs, identify areas requiring additional support, and provide instant feedback on student performance. This augmentation empowers educators to create more dynamic and adaptive learning experiences, fostering increased engagement and improved outcomes.

Simultaneously, AI-driven tools enable personalized learning experiences for students, catering to their unique learning styles, paces, and preferences. These tools can analyze vast datasets to determine the most effective content and teaching strategies for each student. For example, an AI-powered platform might recommend specific learning resources, adjust the difficulty level of exercises, or provide real-time explanations tailored to a student's comprehension level. This personalization not only enhances student engagement but also encourages self-directed learning and critical thinking as students take ownership of their education. Students can progress at their own pace, explore areas of interest, and receive targeted support where needed, ultimately leading to more effective skill acquisition and knowledge retention.

Furthermore, AI-driven tools enable educators to embrace data-driven decision-making, offering insights into student performance trends and areas requiring intervention. These tools can identify struggling students early in the learning process, allowing educators to intervene promptly with targeted support. Conversely, they can also identify high-achieving students who may benefit from more challenging content. This data-driven approach to teaching ensures that no student is left behind, promoting inclusivity and equity in education (Sun et al., 2019).

However, the implementation of AI-driven tools for augmented teaching and personalized learning also presents its own set of ethical and practical challenges. Concerns regarding data privacy, algorithmic bias, and the potential devaluation of the human educator's role must be thoughtfully addressed. It is crucial that AI technologies are designed with transparency, fairness, and ethical considerations in mind to ensure that they support, rather than hinder, the educational process (Ehsan et al., 2021).

Certainly, here are more examples of augmented teaching and personalized learning through AI-driven tools:

Adaptive Learning Platforms: AI-driven adaptive learning platforms analyze individual student performance and tailor learning materials accordingly. For instance, if a student is struggling with algebraic equations, the platform can provide additional practice problems and explanations in that specific area. Conversely, if a student demonstrates mastery, it can automatically advance them to more advanced content.

Language Learning Apps: Language learning apps like Duolingo and Babbel employ AI to customize lessons based on a learner's proficiency level, interests, and learning pace. The apps adapt by offering more challenging exercises as learners progress or providing extra support if they encounter difficulties.

AI Tutors and Chatbots: AI-powered tutors and chatbots offer students instant access to help with their questions. These virtual assistants can explain concepts, solve problems, and provide feedback on written assignments, augmenting the availability of support outside regular classroom hours.

Virtual Labs: In science and engineering disciplines, AI can power virtual labs that simulate experiments and allow students to practice without the need for physical equipment. These labs offer a safe and cost-effective way for students to gain hands-on experience.

Content Recommendation Engines: AI-driven recommendation engines suggest additional reading materials, videos, or resources related to the subject matter being studied. This helps students explore topics in greater depth based on their interests.

Personalized Assessments: AI can generate personalized assessments, adapting the type and difficulty of questions to each student's skill level. This ensures that assessments accurately reflect a student's knowledge and growth over time.

Emotion Recognition: AI tools can analyze student engagement and emotional states, gauging when students are attentive, frustrated, or disinterested. This data can be used to adjust teaching strategies in real-time, such as offering additional explanations or changing the teaching approach.

Feedback Generation: AI can assist educators in providing timely and constructive feedback to students. It can analyze assignments, identify areas for improvement, and generate feedback comments, saving educators time while ensuring students receive valuable guidance.

Language Processing for Special Needs: For students with disabilities, AI-driven tools can provide personalized support. Speech recognition and natural language processing can assist students with speech and language impairments, making learning more accessible.

Educational Gamification: AI-driven educational games adapt to students' performance, offering challenges that match their skill levels. As students progress, the games become more complex and engaging, motivating continued learning.

Personalized Study Schedules: AI can create customized study schedules for students based on their learning objectives and available time. These schedules take into account optimal times for learning and breaks to maximize retention and productivity.

Data Analytics for Educators: AI-driven analytics tools provide educators with insights into student performance and engagement trends. Educators can use this data to identify struggling students, evaluate the effectiveness of their teaching methods, and make data-informed decisions about curriculum adjustments.

4.3 Facilitating Skill Diversification and Adaptability in Educational Roles

Facilitating skill diversification and adaptability in educational roles is an essential endeavor in the ever-evolving landscape of learning (Schwartz et al., 2020). The traditional roles of educators have transformed significantly in recent years, largely due to the integration of technology and the changing demands of modern education. As educational environments continue to shift, fostering skill diversification and adaptability becomes paramount, ensuring that educators remain effective in their roles and can meet the diverse needs of today's learners.

One crucial skill for educators is technological literacy. In an era where technology plays a central role in education, educators must be adept at using digital tools, learning management systems, and various software applications (Holstein et al., 2019). These skills enable them to create engaging digital content, facilitate online discussions, and effectively manage virtual classrooms. Moreover, technological literacy empowers educators to harness the potential of AI-driven tools and analytics, allowing for personalized instruction and data-driven decision-making.

Flexibility and adaptability are also key skills for educators. With the rapid changes in educational delivery methods, from in-person to hybrid and fully online models, educators must be prepared to pivot and adapt their teaching approaches to suit different environments. The ability to seamlessly transition between teaching modalities, adjusting strategies based on student needs and circumstances, ensures that learning remains effective and engaging (Condor, Litster, & Pardos, 2021).

Cultural competence is another critical aspect of skill diversification in education. As classrooms become more diverse, educators must develop cultural awareness and sensitivity to create inclusive learning environments (Kasneci et al., 2023). This skill involves recognizing and respecting diverse perspectives, addressing cultural biases, and adapting teaching methods to meet the unique needs of a multicultural student body.

In addition, interpersonal skills remain foundational for educators. Building positive relationships with students, fostering effective communication, and providing emotional support are timeless skills that continue to be essential in education. These skills facilitate engagement, motivation, and a sense of belonging among students, which are crucial for their overall academic success and well-being.

Finally, critical thinking and problem-solving abilities are vital for educators as they navigate complex educational challenges. Whether it's addressing learning gaps, developing innovative teaching strategies, or evaluating the effectiveness of educational technology, educators must employ critical thinking to make informed decisions and continually improve their practice (Gašević et al., 2022).

To facilitate skill diversification and adaptability among educators, professional development programs are key. These programs should offer ongoing training in technology integration, cultural competence, pedagogical innovation, and other relevant skills. Additionally, mentorship and collaborative learning environments can provide educators with opportunities to share best practices, learn from peers, and apply new skills in real-world settings.

Facilitating skill diversification and adaptability in educational roles is crucial for educators to remain effective in the rapidly evolving field of education. Here are some strategies to help educators develop a diverse skill set and enhance their adaptability:

Professional Development Programs: Educational institutions and organizations should offer regular and relevant professional development opportunities for educators. These programs can cover a wide range of topics, including technology integration, pedagogical innovations, cultural competence, and leadership skills.

Peer Learning and Collaboration: Encourage educators to collaborate and learn from their peers. Peer mentoring, study groups, and collaborative projects can provide opportunities for skill sharing and the exchange of best practices.

Mentorship Programs: Implement mentorship programs where experienced educators can guide newer colleagues. Mentorship not only helps educators build skills but also fosters a sense of community and support within the education community.

Diverse Teaching Environments: Encourage educators to gain experience in diverse teaching environments. This could include teaching different grade levels, subjects, or student populations. Exposure to varied contexts enhances adaptability and problem-solving skills.

Technology Integration Training: Given the increasing role of technology in education, provide educators with training in using digital tools, learning management systems, and educational software. This should be an ongoing effort to keep educators updated on the latest technology trends.

Cultural Competence Workshops: Conduct workshops and training sessions on cultural competence and diversity. Educators should be equipped with the knowledge and skills to create inclusive and culturally sensitive learning environments.

Interdisciplinary Collaboration: Encourage interdisciplinary collaboration among educators. Working with colleagues from different academic disciplines can broaden educators' perspectives and help them integrate diverse teaching methods into their practice.

Problem-Based Learning: Incorporate problem-based learning into professional development. This approach allows educators to tackle real-world challenges, fostering critical thinking and problem-solving skills.

Feedback and Evaluation: Provide constructive feedback and evaluation mechanisms for educators. Regular assessments and peer reviews can help educators identify areas for improvement and set goals for skill development.

Leadership Opportunities: Create pathways for educators to take on leadership roles within their educational institutions. Leadership roles require adaptability, decision-making, and interpersonal skills.

Online Learning and Resources: Promote the use of online learning platforms and resources that allow educators to acquire new skills at their own pace. Massive open online courses (MOOCs), webinars, and educational blogs can be valuable sources of learning.

Reflective Practice: Encourage educators to engage in reflective practice. Regularly reflecting on their teaching methods and experiences can help them identify areas where they need to diversify their skills and adapt to changing circumstances.

Supportive Work Environment: Create a work environment that supports experimentation and innovation. When educators feel encouraged to try new approaches and take calculated risks, they are more likely to diversify their skills.

Continuous Learning Culture: Promote a culture of continuous learning within educational institutions. When learning is seen as a lifelong endeavor, educators are more motivated to acquire new skills and adapt to change.

By implementing these strategies, educational institutions and organizations can empower educators to develop a diverse skill set and remain adaptable in the face of evolving educational landscapes. Ultimately, this benefits both educators and students by ensuring that the learning experience remains relevant, engaging, and effective.

4.4 Ethical Dimensions of Upskilling Initiatives

4.4.1 Ensuring Equitable Access to AI-Driven Upskilling Opportunities for Educators

Ensuring equitable access to AI-driven upskilling opportunities for educators is a pivotal ethical imperative in the rapidly evolving educational landscape. As the integration of AI technologies in education becomes increasingly prevalent, educators must have equitable access to the resources and training necessary to harness these tools effectively. Equity in upskilling is not just a matter of fairness; it is a cornerstone of educational quality and inclusivity (Holmes & Porayska-Pomsta, 2022).

One of the primary ethical considerations in upskilling educators with AI-driven tools is addressing disparities in access. Historically, marginalized communities and underfunded schools have faced resource inequalities, exacerbating educational disparities (Kurdi et al., 2020). This inequity extends to access to AI-driven upskilling opportunities. To address this, educational institutions, governments, and organizations must prioritize the equitable distribution of resources, ensuring that educators in underserved areas have the same access to training and technology as their counterparts in more affluent regions.

Furthermore, upskilling initiatives should be tailored to meet the diverse needs of educators. A one-size-fits-all approach may not effectively address the unique challenges and skill gaps that educators from different backgrounds and contexts may face. Initiatives should consider the specific needs of educators working with diverse student populations, English language learners, special education students, and those in remote or rural settings (Rudolph et al., 2023).

To ensure equitable access, upskilling initiatives should be designed with cultural competence in mind. This means recognizing and respecting the cultural backgrounds and languages of educators. Training materials and resources should be available in multiple languages and culturally relevant to accommodate educators from various linguistic and cultural backgrounds.

Financial accessibility is another crucial aspect of equity in upskilling. Many educators may face financial barriers to participating in upskilling programs, especially if these programs come with a cost. To promote equity, institutions should offer scholarships, grants, or subsidies to support educators in underserved communities or those with limited financial resources (Nye et al., 2023).

Moreover, the accessibility of upskilling programs should consider physical and technological accessibility. Educators with disabilities should have access to adaptive technologies and accommodations to participate fully in upskilling initiatives. Additionally, ensuring that educators have access to the necessary hardware, internet connectivity, and assistive technologies is essential for a level playing field.

Finally, upskilling programs must prioritize inclusivity and diversity in their design and implementation. The representation of educators from diverse backgrounds in program development, leadership, and decision-making processes can help ensure that the initiatives are designed with equity as a core principle (Sallam, 2023).

Equitable access to AI-driven upskilling opportunities for educators is a moral imperative that not only supports the professional growth of educators but also enhances educational outcomes for all students. By addressing disparities in access, tailoring initiatives to diverse needs, promoting cultural competence, offering financial support, and ensuring physical and technological accessibility, educational institutions and organizations can uphold the ethical principle of equity in upskilling. This commitment to equity is essential for fostering an inclusive and innovative educational environment that benefits educators, students, and society as a whole (Sarsa et al., 2022).

4.4.2 Fostering Lifelong Learning and Professional Skill Evolution in the Education Sector

Leveraging generative AI to foster lifelong learning and professional skill evolution in the education sector can be a transformative approach (Wu, 2022). Here are ways in which generative AI can facilitate continuous learning and skill development among educators:

Personalized Learning Resources: Generative AI can create personalized learning resources for educators based on their individual needs and interests. By analyzing educators' preferences, strengths, and areas for improvement, AI can generate tailored content, such as articles, videos, or tutorials, to support their professional growth.

Automated Learning Pathways: AI-driven systems can recommend learning pathways and courses that align with educators' career goals and areas of expertise. These automated recommendations ensure that educators have access to relevant and up-to-date content that supports their skill evolution.

AI-Powered Feedback and Assessment: Generative AI can provide educators with instant feedback on their teaching methods, assessments, and classroom management. This feedback helps educators identify areas for improvement and make real-time adjustments to enhance their skills.

Content Generation: AI can assist educators in content creation. For instance, it can help generate interactive lesson plans, quizzes, and learning materials, saving educators time and allowing them to focus on more strategic aspects of teaching.

Data-Driven Insights: AI can analyze large datasets to provide educators with insights into student performance trends and teaching effectiveness. This data-driven approach allows educators to make informed decisions about their teaching methods and identify areas where additional skills or strategies are needed.

Natural Language Processing (NLP) Tools: NLP-powered AI tools can assist educators in improving their communication skills. These tools can analyze written or spoken communication and provide suggestions for clarity, empathy, and effective engagement.

Virtual Tutoring and Mentorship: AI-driven virtual tutors or mentorship programs can offer educators guidance and support. These virtual assistants can answer questions, provide coaching, and offer advice on skill development.

Adaptive Learning Platforms: AI-powered adaptive learning platforms can provide educators with their own personalized learning experiences. These platforms can assess educators' strengths and weaknesses and deliver targeted content to address specific skill gaps.

Professional Learning Communities: AI can facilitate the formation of professional learning communities by connecting educators with similar interests and goals. These AI-driven communities provide opportunities for educators to collaborate, share resources, and learn from each other.

Curation of Learning Resources: AI can curate and organize vast amounts of educational content, making it easier for educators to discover high-quality resources that support their skill evolution. This curation can save educators time and ensure they have access to the most relevant materials.

Skill Assessments and Badging: AI can conduct skill assessments and provide digital badges or certificates to educators as they acquire new skills. These badges serve as a tangible recognition of their professional development.

Continuous Learning Analytics: AI can continuously track educators' progress in their skill development journey. This data can be used to offer personalized recommendations for further learning and skill enhancement.

Language Translation and Multilingual Support: AI-powered language translation tools can break down language barriers, making educational resources and opportunities accessible to educators worldwide.

Accessibility Features: AI can ensure that learning materials and platforms are accessible to educators with disabilities by providing features like text-to-speech, speech-to-text, and adaptive interfaces.

Global Collaboration: AI-driven platforms can facilitate global collaboration among educators, enabling them to learn from diverse perspectives and share best practices from different educational contexts.

By integrating generative AI into the educational landscape, institutions and organizations can create a dynamic and supportive environment for educators' lifelong learning and professional skill evolution. This approach not only benefits educators but also enhances the quality of education provided to students, fostering a culture of continuous improvement and innovation in the education sector.

5. CASE STUDIES: ETHICAL DILEMMAS IN GENERATIVE AI SKILL DYNAMICS IN EDUCATION

5.1 Case One: The Impact of Generative AI on Traditional Teaching Methods and Educator Roles

The adaptability and promise of generative artificial intelligence (AI) methods in enhancing the education paradigm are evident via the diverse curricular uses. An example of a program is customized studying, which is an educational technique that customizes instruction to accommodate the distinct requirements and inclinations of individual students. Through the examination of comprehensive information pertaining to the progress of learners habits, artificial intelligence (AI) technologies have the capability to offer tailored suggestions, comments, and adjustments in order to facilitate their unique educational progress (Wang et al., 2023; Tanjga, 2023).

Adjustable assessment is a notable practice that involves the modification of the difficulty curve as well as evaluation material in response to a student's achievement and development (Wang et al., 2023). The use of a tailored evaluation approach facilitates the provision of suitable challenges to learners, hence promoting a continual process that encourages development and enhancement. Forecasting is an additional advantageous use of artificial intelligence within the realm of instruction. Through the utilization of artificial intelligence (AI) computational methods for the examination of data on learners, instructors have the capability to forecast forthcoming academic outcomes and discern pupils who may want supplementary help or therapy (Wang et al., 2023; Tanjga, 2023). The use of this preemptive method empowers instructors to get involved at the outset and deliver focused support to learners, therefore optimizing their likelihood of achieving accomplishment. Chatbots are being widely employed within learning environments to provide individualized guidance and support to pupils. According to Kooli (2023) and Wang et al. (2023), chatbots has the capability to respond to inquiries, give assistance, and serve as a helpful educational tool for learners. The presence of these resources contributes to the establishment of a dynamic and participatory educational setting, facilitating self-directed development and promoting involvement by learners.

Academic investigations have extensively explored many facets of autonomous artificial intelligence (AI) within the realm of pedagogy. The potential and moral issues regarding the usage of Nguyen et al (2022) are discussed, with a particular emphasis on the repercussions in media coverage and literacy as highlighted by Pavlik (2023). In their study, Bae et al. (2023) investigate the impact of generative artificial intelligence on the learning outcomes in the field of ESG instructional design. Meanwhile, Nguyen et al (2022) conducts a comparative analysis of the comprehension and inference capabilities of ChatGPT and medical learners during a the discipline of parasitology inspection. In this study, Bowles (2023) investigates the influence of generative artificial intelligence (AI) innovations, such as ChatGPT, on conventional academic writings within the context of higher education. The study conducted by Mageira et al. (2022) examines the impact of an artificial intelligence chatbot on the implementation of Content and Language Integrated Learning. On top of that, a bibliometric cartography study is conducted by Hwang and Tu (2021) to examine the functions and emerging tendencies of artificial intelligence (AI) in the field of education regarding mathematics. Similarly, Nguyen et al. (2022) investigate the ways in which AI supports many aspects of instruction, retention, evaluation, recommendations, and cooperation. Cumulatively, these investigations offer important perspectives into both the upside and downside of generative artificial intelligence (AI) techniques in the field of learning and classroom instruction. They emphasize the significance of utilizing such resources to augment the learning process for learners.

5.2 Case Two: Ethical Concerns in Deskilling and Downskilling Scenarios for Educators

According to Almer (2022), the phenomenon of deskilling was recognized by a specific group of students. In accordance with the existing body of literature on the concept of deskilling, certain students exhibited no discernible negative alterations in their views towards artificial intelligence (AI) systems, but others did indeed demonstrate a noticeable change in their perspective. Many students express concerns over the potential deskilling effects of artificial intelligence. The students recognized that they had encountered deskilling as a result of utilizing spelling tools or memory services, since they have become dependent on autocorrect for spelling terms.

Another student expresses their concern at a broader level, stating that while they may not have personal investment, they are worried about the overall progress of human growth. I do not harbor personal concerns over the potential adverse effects of a specific technology, such as Github Copilot. However, it is the impact on the broader global community that gives rise to my apprehension. According to the students who were questioned, it is their belief that the problems at hand may be attributed to the over reliance on artificial intelligence (AI) and the neglect of individual knowledge and expertise. One student who harbors no apprehensions regarding the deskilling effects of artificial intelligence proposes the act of critiquing it. The authors contend that other approaches exist for enhancing skills and knowledge outside of the workplace, since they maintain skepticism regarding the notion that cognitive performance diminishes as a result of work-related factors. The respondents expressed apprehensions over the phenomenon of deskilling, which may potentially be attributed to the influence of the aforementioned two artificial intelligence systems. The student expresses apprehension over the excessive dependence on AI tools, acknowledging the potential for adverse consequences. I would employ the guidance provided by Github Copilot due of its inherent simplicity and convenience for our purposes. Rather than engaging in independent problem-solving and skill development, I intend to seek assistance or guidance from an AI robot for a solution or perspective. The argument put up by a psychology student posits that the utilization of AI as an educational tool has the potential to diminish learners' motivation, since it grants them immediate access to all requisite knowledge. Both students expressed concerns over an artificial intelligence system that autonomously makes judgements, as opposed to a system that aids employees without exerting authority over them. A student expressed apprehensions regarding the societal implications of deskilling, contending that relinquishing innovation to artificial intelligence may impede societal progress and engender potential hazards.

The student who did not exhibit any change in stance towards artificial intelligence (AI) nor shown any apprehension over deskilling in their chosen profession, confidently asserted that they firmly believe "AI will never supplant me in my field of expertise, regardless." The participants of this survey expressed concerns on the potential of artificial intelligence (AI) to diminish human skill development and negatively impact future prospects. Several students express the wish for artificial intelligence (AI) to be incapable of causing harm, while also seeing the belief in such a notion as being simplistic. One student, who does not express worries about deskilling, highlights the impact of technology on human development, namely in the areas of social media, divisiveness, and less empathy. There is a prevailing belief that artificial intelligence (AI) in itself will not lead to the erosion of skill levels within society.

Psychology students may hold the perspective that artificial intelligence (AI) has a detrimental impact on human development. The potential replacement of human psychologists by AI in the field may have adverse consequences for human well-being. Psychology scholars contend that in the event of youngsters experiencing a dearth of human connection and resorting to robots as their primary means of communication, there is a potential for significant repercussions on their developmental trajectory. Acquiring the skills to effectively regulate and understand emotions may be a greater challenge for individuals in question. The need of stimulation in human development, encompassing intellectual and systemic aspects, is underscored by a psychology student. This necessity spans across the whole lifespan, from birth until death. Adolescents also require it. Another problem highlighted by the psychology student is that artificial intelligence (AI) has the potential to facilitate daily tasks, leading to a potential decrease in individuals' motivation to engage in learning activities. As an illustration, Google Maps presents instructions rather than depending on human memory.

6. ETHICAL CONSIDERATIONS IN SKILL DYNAMICS IN EDUCATION

6.1 Ensuring Transparency in AI-Aided Teaching and Learning

6.1.1 Fair Evaluation of AI-Generated Educational Content and Assessments

Fairly evaluating AI-generated educational content and assessments is paramount to ensure transparency and maintain the integrity of AI-aided teaching and learning. As educational institutions increasingly harness the power of AI to create content and evaluate student performance, it becomes imperative to establish rigorous evaluation processes that uphold educational standards and ethics (Zheng et al., 2022). To achieve this, it's essential to consider several key factors. First and foremost, the algorithms used to generate educational content must be thoroughly tested and validated to ensure accuracy and alignment with curriculum objectives. Additionally, the diversity and representativeness of the data used to train AI models must be scrutinized to prevent bias and ensure inclusivity. Moreover, assessments should be designed to measure not only factual knowledge but also critical thinking, problem-solving skills, and creativity, aligning with the broader goals of education. Regular monitoring and auditing of AI systems by human educators are essential to identify and rectify any discrepancies or ethical concerns (Leiker et al., 2023). Ultimately, a transparent and fair evaluation process for AI-generated educational content and assessments safeguards the quality of education, promotes equity, and maintains the trust of educators and learners in the transformative potential of AI in education.

6.1.2 Accountability in Skill Assessment for Both Educators and Students

Accountability in skill assessment is a cornerstone of ensuring transparency in AI-aided teaching and learning, benefiting both educators and students. As AI plays an increasingly central role in assessing and evaluating skills, it becomes essential to establish clear lines of responsibility and transparency in the assessment process. For educators, accountability entails ensuring that AI-generated assessments align with curriculum objectives and provide a fair and accurate representation of students' abilities (Rudolph et al., 2023). Educators must actively engage in the design, monitoring, and validation of AI-based assessments to uphold educational standards and ethics. On the other hand, students must also be held accountable for their performance in AI-assisted assessments, which often require them to take on a more active and self-directed role in their learning. They should have access to clear assessment criteria, understand how AI algorithms evaluate their work, and be encouraged to seek clarification and improvement opportunities (Sawatzki et al., 2022). Ultimately, accountability in skill assessment fosters a transparent and trustworthy educational environment, where the roles and responsibilities of both educators and students are well-defined, ensuring that AI-aided teaching and learning processes align with educational goals and values while providing a fair and equitable experience for all.

6.2 Addressing the Ethics of Potential Job Displacement in Education

6.2.1 Providing Support and Transition Options for Educators Facing Technological Change

Addressing the ethics of potential job displacement in education due to technological change is paramount in ensuring a just and equitable transition for educators (Truong et al., 2020). As AI and automation reshape educational landscapes, educators may face challenges related to shifting roles and job security. To navigate this transformation ethically, educational institutions and policymakers must prioritize support and transition options for educators affected by technological change.

Firstly, support mechanisms should be established to help educators adapt to new technologies and teaching methods. Professional development programs should be designed to equip educators with the necessary digital literacy skills and pedagogical knowledge to effectively integrate technology into their teaching practices (Zheng et al., 2023). This support should be ongoing and accessible, catering to educators at all stages of their careers.

Secondly, educators must be given opportunities for upskilling and reskilling. Transitioning to roles that complement AI and automation, such as educational technology specialists or curriculum designers, can provide job security and new avenues for professional growth (Schneider et al., 2022). Educational institutions should offer targeted training and certification programs to facilitate these transitions. Financial incentives or subsidies may also be provided to ease the financial burden of pursuing further education.

Moreover, fostering a culture of innovation and experimentation within educational institutions is vital. Educators should be encouraged to explore new teaching methods and technologies, allowing them to adapt and thrive in a rapidly changing educational landscape. An open dialogue between educators, administrators, and policymakers is essential to identify emerging trends and anticipate the evolving skill requirements in education (Yan et al., 2022).

Ethical considerations also encompass transparency in decision-making. Educational institutions should engage educators in discussions about the integration of AI and automation and the potential impacts on their roles. Transparency ensures that educators have a say in shaping the future of education and that their concerns are addressed.

Additionally, safety nets should be in place to support educators in case of displacement. This might include financial assistance, job placement services, or early retirement options. These safety nets acknowledge the valuable contributions of educators while providing a cushion for those who may be directly affected by technological change (Liang et al., 2023).

Lastly, collaboration between educators and AI systems should be encouraged. AI should be seen as a tool to augment, rather than replace, the role of educators. This collaboration can enhance the quality of education and empower educators to focus on personalized instruction, mentorship, and socio-emotional support.

6.2.2 Ethical Considerations in Reskilling and Job Placement Programs for Educators

Ethical considerations in reskilling and job placement programs for educators are of paramount importance in the face of technological advancements that may disrupt traditional teaching roles. As educational institutions and policymakers develop initiatives to reskill and place educators in alternative roles, several ethical principles should guide these efforts (Holmes & Porayska-Pomsta, 2022) .

First and foremost, these programs must prioritize equity and inclusivity. Reskilling and job placement opportunities should be accessible to all educators, regardless of age, background, or experience. It is essential to avoid creating a digital divide, where certain educators may be left behind due to barriers such as financial constraints or inadequate access to training resources. Ethical considerations dictate that every educator should have an equal chance to adapt and thrive in an evolving educational landscape (Buolamwini & Gebru, 2018).

Transparency is another critical ethical principle. Educators should be fully informed about the objectives, content, and expected outcomes of reskilling programs. They should have a clear understanding of the skills they are acquiring and how these skills relate to potential job placements. Transparency ensures that educators make informed decisions about their career transitions and are not subjected to hidden agendas or unrealistic expectations (Gebru et al., 2021).

Inclusivity extends to the design of reskilling programs themselves. These programs should be tailored to meet the diverse needs of educators. Not all educators will require the same level of reskilling or transition support, and programs should be flexible enough to accommodate individual circumstances. Ethical considerations mandate that reskilling programs consider educators' prior experience, areas of expertise, and preferences when offering training and job placement options (Mitchell et al., 2019).

Furthermore, educators' autonomy and consent should be respected throughout the reskilling and job placement process. Ethical principles dictate that educators should have agency in deciding their career paths. They should not be coerced into transitioning to roles that they are uncomfortable with or that do not align with their professional aspirations. Reskilling programs should be supportive rather than prescriptive, allowing educators to make informed choices about their career transitions.

Job placement programs should also consider the principle of beneficence, meaning that they should aim to maximize the well-being of educators. This involves not only finding suitable job placements but also ensuring that these placements are conducive to educators' professional growth and job satisfaction. Ethical considerations require that job placements align with educators' skills and interests, promoting a positive and fulfilling work experience (Holstein et al., 2019).

Another ethical consideration is the ongoing support and mentorship of educators as they transition to new roles. Reskilling programs should not end with the acquisition of new skills; they should include provisions for continued guidance and support in the educators' new positions. This support can help educators navigate the challenges of their new roles and ensure a successful transition.

Finally, evaluation and accountability mechanisms should be in place to monitor the effectiveness of reskilling and job placement programs. Ethical principles mandate that these programs should be subject to regular assessments to ensure that they meet their objectives and provide value to educators. Adjustments should be made based on feedback and outcomes to continually improve the ethical standards and outcomes of these programs.

7. ETHICAL FRAMEWORKS AND GUIDELINES FOR AI IN EDUCATION

7.1 Existing Ethical Frameworks in AI Application and Education: Adapting AI Ethics Principles to Skill Dynamics in Education

As long as users are aware of their limitations and take them into consideration when making decisions, biased AI models can still be useful in certain contexts or applications. In some instances, the biases present in these models may even be representative of the real-world context in which they are used, thereby providing valuable insights into societal inequalities that must be addressed at their origin. The key to using biased AI models responsibly is to ensure that users are aware of the potential biases and limitations associated with these models, so they can make informed judgments about whether and how to use them in various contexts. Several approaches to this problem include:

Promoting responsible use of AI technologies allows us to reap the benefits of these advancements while minimizing the risks associated with bias. This is possible because we recognize that biased models can still be useful in certain situations.

7.2 Building an Ethical Framework for AI-Driven Skill Development in Educational Contexts: Principles for Responsible AI Integration Into Professional Skill Acquisition in Education

Concerns about fairness and equality are very important when it comes to making and using AI apps. As we use these models more and more in different parts of our lives, their possible effects on both people and society as a whole become a major worry. Developers, researchers, and other stakeholders are responsible for making sure that AI models treat all users and groups fairly and don't keep biases alive or create new ones. Representation is an important social factor to think about. It is important to

Table 1. Tactics to dynamic insurance in education

Tactics	Description
Clarity	It is imperative for developers to exhibit transparency regarding the methodology, data sources, and any biases inherent in their AI models. By doing so, users may access the essential information required to comprehend the various elements that may impact the predictions and judgments made by the model. The AI community has made significant advancements in establishing best practices for the documentation of models and data. (Mitchell et al., 2019, Gebru et al., 2021)
Awareness-oriented education	Initiatives aim to equip users with tools, training, and support to enhance their comprehension of the potential biases inherent in AI models and enable them to effectively address these biases when making judgments. This task may encompass the development of guidelines, establishment of best practices, or production of educational resources that elucidate the ramifications of prejudice in artificial intelligence (AI) and provide guidance on responsible navigation of such biases.
Contextual approaches	In certain restricted scenarios, there may be potential for the practicality of biased AI models in particular applications or contexts, provided that the biases inherent in these models are congruent with the pertinent elements or considerations. It is recommended to use the services of professionals who possess expertise in order to thoroughly assess the suitability of employing biased models in such circumstances. This evaluation should encompass an examination of the potential advantages and disadvantages linked to their utilization, as well as the development of practical strategies to identify, measure, and alleviate any biases present.
Maintain progress in assessing and controlling	Constantly evaluating how well AI models work in practice, keeping tabs on how they effect users and communities, and adjusting as necessary to account for any biases or unforeseen consequences that may crop up over time. (Bender, Gebru, McMillan-Major, & Shmitchell, 2021)

Table 2. Key components of ethical AI development

Principles	Description
Appearance	The need of guaranteeing that the training data employed in the development of AI models accurately reflects the broad spectrum of viewpoints, lived experiences, and socio-cultural contexts that are present in society. This practice aids in mitigating the potential for biases to be assimilated and disseminated by the models, resulting in outcomes that are more egalitarian. (Mitchell et al., 2019, Buolamwini & Gebru, 2018, Torralba & Efros, 2011, Sun et al., 2019)
Openness	It is important for developers to exhibit transparency regarding the methodology, data sources, and possible limits associated with their AI models. This transparency empowers users to have a comprehensive understanding of the various elements that might potentially impact the predictions and judgments made by the model. (Larsson & Heintz, 2020, Ehsan et al., 2021)
Integral platform	Establishing a well-defined framework for accountability is of utmost importance for developers and stakeholders. This framework should encompass several aspects such as monitoring the performance of AI models, rectifying biases and mistakes, and effectively addressing the concerns raised by users and impacted groups. (Wachter et al., 2017, Raji et al., 2020, Smith, 2021)
Generalization	The design of AI applications should prioritize inclusivity and accessibility for all users, including variables such as language, culture, and accessibility requirements. This approach is crucial to ensure that the advantages of AI are distributed fairly and evenly throughout society. (Morris, 2020, Schwartz et al., 2020)
Maintenance in development	It is imperative for developers to engage in a continuous process of assessing, enhancing, and optimizing their AI models in order to mitigate biases and uphold principles of fairness throughout the duration of their deployment. The process may entail engaging in collaborations with academics, politicians, and impacted groups in order to get valuable insights and comments that may effectively inform the advancement of AI systems with a focus on equity. (O'neil, 2017, Holstein et al., 2019, Challen et al., 2019)

make sure that the training data used to build AI models reflects the wide range of ideas, experiences, and backgrounds in society (Mitchell et al., 2019, Buolamwini & Gebru, 2018, Torralba & Efros, 2011, Sun et al., 2019). This makes it less likely that the models will pick up and spread biases, leading to more fair results. Another important part is being honest. Developers should be clear about how their AI models are made, where the data comes from, and what kind of limits they might have (Larsson & Heintz, 2020, Ehsan et al., 2021). This lets people learn more about the things that could affect the model's predictions and choices. Accountability is also important for developing AI in a reasonable way. Developers and partners need to set up a clear system for who is responsible for what. This could include keeping an eye on how well AI models work, fixing biases and mistakes, and listening to users and groups that are affected (Wachter et al., 2017, Raji et al., 2020, Smith, 2021). Inclusion is another important social factor to think about. AI apps should be made so that everyone can use them, taking things like language, society, and accessibility needs into account (Morris, 2020, Schwartz et al., 2020). This makes sure that everyone gets a fair share of the benefits of AI.

Lastly, AI apps need to keep getting better if they are to be fair and equal. Developers must promise to always reviewing, refining, and improving their AI models (O'neil, 2017, Holstein et al., 2019, Challen et al., 2019) to fix flaws and make sure they are fair over time. This could mean working together with researchers, policymakers, and the groups that will be affected to get ideas and comments that can help guide the creation of more fair AI systems. By putting fairness and equality at the top of their list of ethical concerns, AI developers can make apps that not only use the power of advanced technologies like large language models, but also help build a more fair and inclusive society where everyone has access to the benefits and opportunities of AI.

8. CONCLUSION AND FUTURE DIRECTIONS

8.1 Anticipating the Evolving Landscape of AI and Skills in Educational Settings

Anticipating the evolving landscape of AI and skills in educational settings is essential to proactively prepare educators and students for the future. As AI technologies continue to advance, their impact on education will become even more profound. To stay ahead of these changes, educational institutions and policymakers must focus on several key aspects. First, ongoing monitoring of AI advancements and their potential applications in education is crucial. This involves tracking emerging AI tools, pedagogical models, and trends to ensure educators are well-informed about the latest developments. Second, proactive training and professional development programs should be designed to equip educators with the skills needed to leverage AI effectively in their teaching practices. This includes digital literacy, data analysis, and the ability to integrate AI-powered tools seamlessly. Third, fostering a culture of innovation and adaptability within educational institutions is vital. Educators should be encouraged to experiment with AI-driven solutions and adapt their teaching methods as new possibilities arise. Finally, ethical considerations should be at the forefront of AI integration, ensuring that AI technologies are used responsibly and inclusively in education. By anticipating the evolving landscape of AI and skills in education, institutions can ensure that educators and students are well-prepared to harness the potential of AI while addressing its challenges in an ethical and forward-thinking manner.

8.2 Call to Action for Responsible AI Application and Continuous Ethical Evaluation in Skill Development in Education

A resounding call to action is essential for responsible AI application and continuous ethical evaluation in skill development within the realm of education. As AI technologies become increasingly integrated into educational settings, it is incumbent upon educational institutions, policymakers, and stakeholders to uphold ethical standards and ensure that AI is harnessed for the benefit of learners and educators alike. This call to action involves several critical steps.

Firstly, there must be a commitment to establishing clear ethical guidelines and standards for the development and deployment of AI-driven educational tools. These guidelines should prioritize transparency, fairness, inclusivity, and privacy. AI algorithms and systems used for skill development must be rigorously tested and audited to identify and rectify biases, ensuring that they do not perpetuate inequalities or discriminate against any student or educator.

Secondly, educational institutions should invest in comprehensive training and education for educators and administrators on the responsible use of AI. Educators need to understand how AI works, its limitations, and the ethical considerations surrounding its use in the classroom. This empowers educators to make informed decisions and integrate AI technologies into their teaching practices effectively.

Furthermore, a system for continuous ethical evaluation of AI applications in education should be established. This involves ongoing assessment of AI tools to ensure that they align with evolving ethical standards and do not inadvertently harm learners or infringe upon their rights. Regular audits, reviews, and feedback loops should be integrated into the AI implementation process to address ethical concerns as they emerge.

Another crucial element of this call to action is the active involvement of all stakeholders, including educators, students, parents, and policymakers, in shaping the ethical framework for AI in education. Their perspectives and experiences should inform the development of policies and practices that govern AI application in skill development.

Lastly, there should be an open and transparent discourse around the ethical implications of AI in education. Forums, conferences, and interdisciplinary collaborations should be encouraged to facilitate discussions on responsible AI use. This exchange of ideas and best practices can help refine ethical standards and foster a culture of responsible AI adoption.

In conclusion, a call to action for responsible AI application and continuous ethical evaluation in skill development in education is imperative. It calls for the establishment of ethical guidelines, comprehensive training, continuous evaluation mechanisms, stakeholder involvement, and open discourse. By collectively committing to these principles, we can harness the potential of AI in education while upholding ethical standards and ensuring that the benefits of AI are realized equitably and ethically in the educational landscape.

REFERENCES

Almer, J. (2022). *Deskilling as an effect of AI: A group of students' attitudes towards AI and their worries about deskilling*.

Angelone, A. M., Galassi, A., & Vittorini, P. (2022) Improved automated classification of sentences in data science exercises. In *Methodologies and Intelligent Systems for Technology Enhanced Learning, 11th International Conference*, (*vol. 11*, pp. 12–21). Springer. 10.1007/978-3-030-86618-1_2

Bae, S., Dong, Y., & Kwon, O. (2023). The effects of content creator, media richness, and content theme on learning performance: Focusing on ESG management education for Chinese employees. 글로벌경영학회지, *20*(1), 27–50. doi:10.38115/asgba.2023.20.1.27

Bang, Y., Cahyawijaya, S., Lee, N., Dai, W., Su, D., Wilie, B., Lovenia, H., Ji, Z., Yu, T., & Chung, W. (2023) A multitask, multilingual, multimodal evaluation of chatgpt on reasoning, hallucination, and interactivity. arXiv preprint arXiv:2302.04023.

Bender, E. M., Gebru, T., McMillan-Major, A., & Shmitchell, S. (2021). On the dangers of stochastic parrots: Can language models be too big? In *Proceedings of the 2021 ACM conference on fairness, accountability, and transparency* (pp. 610–623). ACM. 10.1145/3442188.3445922

Beseiso, M., Alzubi, O. A., & Rashaideh, H. (2021). A novel automated essay scoring approach for reliable higher educational assessments. *Journal of Computing in Higher Education*, *33*(3), 727–746. doi:10.100712528-021-09283-1

Bowles, D. C., & Kruger, J. S. (2023). Generating employable, intelligent graduates in a world with Generative AI: Thoughts for educators. *Pedagogy in Health Promotion*, *9*(2), 75–77. doi:10.1177/23733799231175171

Brown, H., Lee, K., Mireshghallah, F., Shokri, R., & Tramèr, F. (2022) What does it mean for a language model to preserve privacy? In *2022 ACM Conference on Fairness, Accountability, and Transparency*, (pp. 2280–2292). ACM. 10.1145/3531146.3534642

Bulut, O., & Yildirim-Erbasli, S. N. (2022). Automatic story and item generation for reading comprehension assessments with transformers. *International Journal of Assessment Tools in Education*, *9*(Special Issue), 72–87. doi:10.21449/ijate.1124382

Buolamwini, J., & Gebru, T. (2018). Gender shades: Intersectional accuracy disparities in commercial gender classification. In *Conference on fairness, accountability, and transparency* (pp. 77–91). PMLR.

Caines, A., Benedetto, L., Taslimipoor, S., Davis, C., Gao, Y., Andersen, O., Yuan, Z., Elliott, M., Moore, R., Bryant, C., Rei, M., Mullooly, A., Nicholls, D., & Buttery, P. (2023) On the application of large language models for language teaching and assessment technology. In AIED Workshops. AIED.

Carroll, A., Forrest, K., Sanders-O'Connor, E., Flynn, L., Bower, J. M., Fynes-Clinton, S., York, A., & Ziaei, M. (2022). Teacher stress and burnout in australia: Examining the role of intrapersonal and environmental factors. *Social Psychology of Education*, *25*(2-3), 441–469. doi:10.100711218-022-09686-7 PMID:35233183

Challen, R., Denny, J., Pitt, M., Gompels, L., Edwards, T., & Tsaneva-Atanasova, K. (2019). Artificial intelligence, bias and clinical safety. *BMJ Quality & Safety, 28*(3), 231–237. 10.1136/bmjqs-2018-008370

Chaudhry, M. A., Cukurova, M., & Luckin, R. (2022) A transparency index framework for ai in education. In *Artificial Intelligence in Education. Posters and Late Breaking Results, Workshops and Tutorials, Industry and Innovation Tracks, Practitioners' and Doctoral Consortium: 23rd International Conference, AIED 2022*. Springer. 10.1007/978-3-031-11647-6_33

Chechitelli, A. (2023) *Ai writing detection update from turnitin's chief product officer*. TurnItIn. https://www.turnitin.com/blog/aiwriting-detection-update-from-turnitins-chief-product-officer.

Condor, A., Litster, M., & Pardos, Z. (2021). *Automatic short answer grading with sbert on out-of-sample questions*. International Educational Data Mining Society.

Doyle, W., & Ponder, G. A. (1977). The practicality ethic in teacher decision-making. *Interchange (Washington, D.C.)*, *8*, 1–12.

Drori, I., Zhang, S., Shuttleworth, R., Tang, L., Lu, A., Ke, E., Liu, K., Chen, L., Tran, S., Cheng, N. et al. (2022) *A neural network solves, explains, and generates university math problems by program synthesis and few-shot learning at human level*.

Ehsan, U., Liao, Q. V., Muller, M., Riedl, M. O., & Weisz, J. D. (2021). Expanding explainability: Towards social transparency in AI systems. In *Proceedings of the 2021 CHI Conference on Human Factors in Computing Systems* (pp. 1–19). ACM. 10.1145/3411764.3445188

Gašević, D., Greiff, S., & Shaffer, D. W. (2022). Towards strengthening links between learning analytics and assessment: Challenges and potentials of a promising new bond. *Computers in Human Behavior*, *134*, 107304. https://www.sciencedirect.com/science/article/pii/S0747563222001261. doi:10.1016/j.chb.2022.107304

Gebru, T., Morgenstern, J., Vecchione, B., Vaughan, J. W., Wallach, H., Iii, H. D., & Crawford, K. (2021). Datasheets for datasets. *Communications of the ACM*, *64*(12), 86–92. doi:10.1145/3458723

Gilson, A., Safranek, C. W., Huang, T., Socrates, V., Chi, L., Taylor, R. A., & Chartash, D. (2023). How does chatgpt perform on the united states medical licensing examination? the implications of large language models for medical education and knowledge assessment. *JMIR Medical Education*, *9*, e45312. doi:10.2196/45312 PMID:36753318

Holmes, W., & Porayska-Pomsta, K. (2022). *The Ethics of Artificial Intelligence in education: Practices, challenges, and debates*. Taylor & Francis. doi:10.4324/9780429329067

Holstein, K., Wortman Vaughan, J., Daumé, H. III, Dudik, M., & Wallach, H. (2019). Improving fairness in machine learning systems: What do industry practitioners need? In *Proceedings of the 2019 CHI conference on human factors in computing systems* (pp. 1–16). ACM. 10.1145/3290605.3300830

Hwang, G., & Tu, Y. (2021). Roles and Research Trends of Artificial Intelligence in Mathematics Education: A Bibliometric Mapping Analysis and Systematic Review. *Mathematics*, *9*(6), 584. doi:10.3390/math9060584

Jayaraman, J., & Black, J. (2022). Effectiveness of an intelligent question answering system for teaching financial literacy: A pilot study. In *Innovations in Learning and Technology for the Workplace and Higher Education: Proceedings of 'The Learning Ideas Conference'2021* (pp. 133–140). Springer. doi:10.1007/978-3-030-90677-1_13

Kasneci, E., Seßler, K., Küchemann, S., Bannert, M., Dementieva, D., Fischer, F., Gasser, U., Groh, G., Günnemann, S., Hüllermeier, E., Krusche, S., Kutyniok, G., Michaeli, T., Nerdel, C., Pfeffer, J., Poquet, O., Sailer, M., Schmidt, A., Seidel, T., & Kasneci, G. (2023). Chatgpt for good? on opportunities and challenges of large language models for education. *Learning and Individual Differences*, *103*, 102274. doi:10.1016/j.lindif.2023.102274

Khosravi, H., Shum, S. B., Chen, G., Conati, C., Tsai, Y.-S., Kay, J., Knight, S., Martinez-Maldonado, R., Sadiq, S., & Gašević, D. (2022). Explainable artificial intelligence in education. *Computers and Education: Artificial Intelligence*, *3*, 100074.

Kooli, C. (2023). Chatbots in Education and Research: A Critical Examination of ethical implications and solutions. *Sustainability (Basel)*, *15*(7), 5614. doi:10.3390u15075614

Kumar, N., Mali, R., Ratnam, A., Kurpad, V., & Magapu, H. (2022) Identification and addressal of knowledge gaps in students. *In 2022 3rd International Conference for Emerging Technology (INCET),* (pp. 1–6). IEEE. 10.1109/INCET54531.2022.9824483

Kurdi, G., Leo, J., Parsia, B., Sattler, U., & Al-Emari, S. (2020). A systematic review of automatic question generation for educational purposes. *International Journal of Artificial Intelligence in Education*, *30*(1), 121–204. doi:10.100740593-019-00186-y

Larsson, S., & Heintz, F. (2020). Transparency in artificial intelligence. *Internet Policy Review*, *9*(2). doi:10.14763/2020.2.1469

Leiker, D., Finnigan, S., Gyllen, A. R., & Cukurova, M. (2023) Prototyping the use of large language models (llms) for adult learning content creation at scale. In AIED Workshops. AIED.

Li, C., & Xing, W. (2021). Natural language generation using deep learning to support mooc learners. *International Journal of Artificial Intelligence in Education, 31*(2), 186–214. doi:10.100740593-020-00235-x

Li, Y., Sha, L., Yan, L., Lin, J., Raković, M., Galbraith, K., Lyons, K., Gašević, D. and Chen, G. (2023). Can large language models write reflectively. *Computers and Education: Artificial Intelligence, 100140.*

Liang, W., Yuksekgonul, M., Mao, Y., Wu, E., & Zou, J. (2023). Gpt detectors are biased against non-native english writers. arXiv preprint arXiv:2304.02819.

Liu, S., Liu, S., Liu, Z., Peng, X., & Yang, Z. (2022). Automated detection of emotional and cognitive engagement in mooc discussions to predict learning achievement. *Computers & Education, 181*, 104461. doi:10.1016/j.compedu.2022.104461

Liu, Z., He, X., Liu, L., Liu, T., & Zhai, X. (2023). *Context matters: A strategy to pre-train language model for science education.* arXiv preprint arXiv:2301.12031. doi:10.1007/978-3-031-36336-8_103

Ma, Q., Wu, S., & Koedinger, K. (2023). Is llm the better programming partner? In AIED Workshops. AIED.

Mageira, K., Pittou, D., Papasalouros, A., Kotis, K., Zangogianni, P., & Daradoumis, A. (2022). Educational AI chatbots for content and language integrated learning. *Applied Sciences (Basel, Switzerland), 12*(7), 3239. doi:10.3390/app12073239

Maheen, F., Asif, M., Ahmad, H., Ahmad, S., Alturise, F., Asiry, O., & Ghadi, Y. Y. (2022). Automatic computer science domain multiple-choice questions generation based on informative sentences. *PeerJ. Computer Science, 8*, e1010. doi:10.7717/peerj-cs.1010 PMID:36091982

Mitchell, M., Wu, S., Zaldivar, A., Barnes, P., Vasserman, L., Hutchinson, B., & Gebru, T. (2019). Model cards for model reporting. In *Proceedings of the conference on fairness, accountability, and transparency* (pp. 220–229). ACM. 10.1145/3287560.3287596

Morris, M. R. (2020). AI and accessibility. *Communications of the ACM, 63*(6), 35–37. doi:10.1145/3356727

Nguyen, A., Ngo, H. N., Hong, Y., Dang, B., & Nguyen, B. T. (2022). Ethical principles for artificial intelligence in education. *Education and Information Technologies, 28*(4), 4221–4241. doi:10.100710639-022-11316-w PMID:36254344

Nye, B., Mee, D., & Core, M. G. (2023) Generative large language models for dialog-based tutoring: An early consideration of opportunities and concerns. In AIED Workshops. AIED.

O'Neil, C. (2017). *Weapons of math destruction: How big data increases inequality and threatens democracy*. Crown.

Oleny, A. (2023) Generating multiple choice questions from a textbook: Llms match human performance on most metrics. In AIED Workshops. AIED.

Open A. I. (2023) *Introducing chatgpt*. OpenAI. https://openai.com/blog/chatgpt.

Pavlik, J. V. (2023). Collaborating with ChatGPT: Considering the implications of Generative Artificial intelligence for journalism and media education. *Journalism & Mass Communication Educator, 78*(1), 84–93. doi:10.1177/10776958221149577

Raji, I. D., Smart, A., White, R. N., Mitchell, M., Gebru, T., Hutchinson, B., & Theron, D. (2020). Closing the AI accountability gap: Defining an end-to-end framework for internal algorithmic auditing. In *Proceedings of the 2020 conference on fairness, accountability, and transparency* (pp. 33–44). 10.1145/3351095.3372873

Rudolph, J., Tan, S. and Tan, S. (2023) Chatgpt: Bullshit spewer or the end of traditional assessments in higher education? *Journal of Applied Learning and Teaching, 6.*

Sallam, M. (2023) The utility of chatgpt as an example of large language models in healthcare education, research and practice: Systematic review on the future perspectives and potential limitations. medRxiv, 2023–02.

Sarsa, S., Denny, P., Hellas, A., & Leinonen, J. (2022) Automatic generation of programming exercises and code explanations using large language models. In *Proceedings of the 2022 ACM Conference on International Computing Education ResearchVolume 1,* (pp. 27–43). ACM. 10.1145/3501385.3543957

Sawatzki, J., Schlippe, T., & Benner-Wickner, M. (2022) Deep learning techniques for automatic short answer grading: Predicting scores for english and german answers. In *Artificial Intelligence in Education: Emerging Technologies, Models and Applications: Proceedings of 2021 2nd International Conference on Artificial Intelligence in Education Technology*, (pp. 65–75). Springer.

Schneider, J., Richner, R., & Riser, M. (2022). Towards trustworthy autograding of short, multi-lingual, multi-type answers. *International Journal of Artificial Intelligence in Education*, 1–31.

Schramowski, P., Turan, C., Andersen, N., Rothkopf, C. A., & Kersting, K. (2022). Large pre-trained language models contain human-like biases of what is right and wrong to do. *Nature Machine Intelligence, 4*(3), 258–268. doi:10.103842256-022-00458-8

Schwartz, R., Dodge, J., Smith, N. A., & Etzioni, O. (2020). Green AI. *Communications of the ACM, 63*(12), 54–63. doi:10.1145/3381831

Smith, H. (2021). Clinical AI: Opacity, accountability, responsibility, and liability. *AI & Society, 36*(2), 535–545. doi:10.100700146-020-01019-6

Sun, T., Gaut, A., Tang, S., Huang, Y., ElSherief, M., Zhao, J., & Wang, W. Y. (2019). *Mitigating gender bias in natural language processing: Literature review*. arXiv preprint arXiv:1906.08976. doi:10.18653/v1/P19-1159

Tanjga, M. (2023). *E-learning and the Use of AI: A Review of Current Practices and Future Directions.* Qeios. doi:10.32388/AP0208

Torralba, A., & Efros, A. A. (2011). Unbiased look at dataset bias. In *CVPR 2011* (pp. 1521–1528). IEEE. doi:10.1109/CVPR.2011.5995347

Truong, T.-L., Le, H.-L., & Le-Dang, T.-P. (2020) Sentiment analysis implementing bert-based pre-trained language model for vietnamese. In *2020 7th NAFOSTED Conference on Information and Computer Science (NICS),* (pp. 362–367). IEEE. 10.1109/NICS51282.2020.9335912

Wachter, S., Mittelstadt, B., & Floridi, L. (2017). Transparent, explainable, and accountable AI for robotics. *Science Robotics*, *2*(6), eaan6080. doi:10.1126cirobotics.aan6080 PMID:33157874

Wang, T., Lund, B. D., Marengo, A., Pagano, A., Mannuru, N. R., Teel, Z. A., & Pange, J. (2023). Exploring the Potential Impact of Artificial Intelligence (AI) on International Students in Higher Education: Generative AI, Chatbots, Analytics, and International Student Success. *Applied Sciences (Basel, Switzerland)*, *13*(11), 6716. doi:10.3390/app13116716

Wollny, S., Schneider, J., Di Mitri, D., Weidlich, J., Rittberger, M., & Drachsler, H. (2021). Are we there yet?-a systematic literature review on chatbots in education. *Frontiers in Artificial Intelligence*, *4*, 654924. doi:10.3389/frai.2021.654924 PMID:34337392

Wu, J. (2022). Analysis and evaluation of the impact of integrating mental health education into the teaching of university civics courses in the context of artificial intelligence. *Wireless Communications and Mobile Computing*, *2022*, 2022. doi:10.1155/2022/5378694

Wu, X., He, X., Li, T., Liu, N., & Zhai, X. (2023) Matching exemplar as next sentence prediction (mensp): Zero-shot prompt learning for automatic scoring in science education. arXiv preprint arXiv:2301.08771. doi:10.1007/978-3-031-36272-9_33

Yan, L., Zhao, L., Gasevic, D., & Martinez-Maldonado, R. (2022) Scalability, sustainability, and ethicality of multimodal learning analytics. In *LAK22: 12th International Learning Analytics and Knowledge Conference*, (pp. 13–23). ACM. 10.1145/3506860.3506862

Zeng, Z., Gašević, D., & Chen, G. (2023) On the effectiveness of curriculum learning in educational text scoring. In *Proceedings of the AAAI Conference on Artificial Intelligence*. AAAI. 10.1609/aaai.v37i12.26707

Zheng, L., Niu, J., Long, M., & Fan, Y. (2023). An automatic knowledge graph construction approach to promoting collaborative knowledge building, group performance, social interaction and socially shared regulation in cscl. *British Journal of Educational Technology*, *54*(3), 686–711. doi:10.1111/bjet.13283

Zheng, L., Niu, J., & Zhong, L. (2022). Effects of a learning analytics-based real-time feedback approach on knowledge elaboration, knowledge convergence, interactive relationships and group performance in cscl. *British Journal of Educational Technology*, *53*(1), 130–149. doi:10.1111/bjet.13156

Chapter 7
Moral Consideration and the Development of Artificial Intelligence:
A Comparative Theory Analysis

Akash Bag
https://orcid.org/0000-0001-8820-171X
Adamas University, India

Souvik Roy
Adamas University, India

ABSTRACT

This chapter is trying to answer a big question: Should we create artificial intelligence (AI) that deserves moral consideration, like humans? To figure this out, the authors look at different ideas about what AI is and what it should be. They use two main theories about ethics (how we decide right and wrong) to see if AI should be treated morally. One theory they use says that if AI fits the definition of intelligence, it should be treated morally, no matter which ethical theory you follow. The other theory they use is called "capability theory," combined with the definition of AI. This leads to the conclusion that we shouldn't develop AI further if we believe it deserves moral consideration. So, the chapter explores whether AI should be treated morally, and it suggests that if so, we might need to stop developing AI.

1. INTRODUCTION

Human interest in thinking machines stretches back at least to antiquity. This is illustrated in several archetypal myths, such as the Greek one about the god Hephaestus' creation, Talos, a living bronze giant who guarded the island of Crete. Other examples of historical artificial intelligence are the sacred mechanical statues of ancient Egypt and Greece and Geber's takwin. In the middle of the 20th century, the development of artificial intelligence (AI) gained momentum, not least thanks to Alan Turing's test

DOI: 10.4018/979-8-3693-0074-9.ch007

"*the imitation game*" - where the underlying principle states that a computer is considered intelligent if a human can interact with it in five minutes without being able to determine that it is a computer. Undoubtedly, AI will pervasively impact our societies in the coming decades. Artificial intelligence is an area prioritized by the European Parliament. Research is ongoing in the EU on issues such as who owns the copyright to something entirely developed by an AI and on military and non-military uses of AI. For the use of AI in the military, justice system, and health, the European Parliament proposed in January 2021 that *"[AI] must never replace or relieve humans of their responsibility* (European Commision, 2021). In its work, the European Parliament points out that rules for AI must be human-centered; security, transparency, and accountability must be guaranteed; bias and discrimination are needed to be prevented; social and environmental responsibility is promoted; respect for fundamental rights is ensured (European Commision, 2020).

We humans create aids and systems to benefit ourselves. If we build a staircase, it is reasonable that it is suitable for the vast majority of people to walk on, and if it is impossible to use, it is not significant if it is replaced. We also use animals and plants for our benefit, but in contrast to how we treat inanimate objects, destroying all creatures that did not benefit us would be remarkable. Artificial intelligence is a phenomenon that does not fit easily into this binary view of non-human objects. This is because AI, in its composition, resembles stairs or other created aids, animals, or even people. The main arguments for developing AI are of two kinds: monetary arguments and utility arguments. AI can save us money, time, and effort. The main arguments against developing AI relate to security of various kinds – for example, human lives or people's integrity. A perspective not given space in the European Parliament's work is whether artificial intelligence deserves moral consideration. If we don't know whether AI should be shown moral consideration, we also don't know what obligations, if any, we humans have to AI. The issue is of great ethical importance. For many people, it is a matter of course that animals deserve moral consideration. It may not be as obvious that AI may merit moral consideration, but if the issue is not examined, decisions about AI must be made on shaky ground. With the present work, we hope to contribute to this aspect: AI may have moral rights - subject to moral consideration - which we must relate to as AI developers.

2. BACKGROUND

In this part of the chapter, We describe Pei Wang's Definition of (artificial) Intelligence in On Defining Artificial intelligence (Wang, 2019). We examine criticisms of the definition – advanced by Thorisson (2019), Yampolskiy (2020), and Berkeley (2020) – and explain the reasons for their criticisms as well as why Wang's Definition is nevertheless useful in the context of this chapter. The definition of "*intelligence*" in general and "*artificial intelligence*" in particular is disputed. Wang's definition is one of the most accepted, which is one reason for using it. In *Getting Clarity by Defining Artificial Intelligence—A Survey* (2017), Monett and Lewis show that 56 percent of respondents agree with Wang's Definition in the article *What Do You Mean by 'AI'?* (Monett & Lewis, 2018, p. 214). The definition of "intelligence" is the same in What Do You Mean by 'AI'? and On Defining Artificial intelligence (Wang, 2008, p. 10f; 2019, p. 17). Another reason for the majority definition is that definitions often influence how political decisions are formulated, which can be very important to AI. Such objects often referred to as AI – such as smart refrigerators and phones – are not covered by Wang's Definition. Examining whether such "*artificial intelligence*" deserves moral consideration may be useful. However, the chapter is not an investigation. We are doing this in this chapter. In "*On Defining Artificial Intelligence,*" Wang analyzes various possible definitions of (artificial) intelligence to create a practically useful working definition. The aim is to provide a definition that can guide research on a topic, without excluding relevant research questions or including unnecessary details (Wang 2019, 3f.; Thórisson 2019, 7f.). Wang relates to Carnap's four criteria (Carnap, 1950, §3) for a good working definition (explicatum – that which explains):

1. Similarity to explicandum (that which is explained)
2. Precision
3. Benefit
4. Simplicity

Below we go through the four criteria and how they characterize Wang's Definition of intelligence.

2.1 Similarity to Explicandum

Wang stipulates that the term "*artificial*" in "*artificial intelligence*" is uncontroversial and, therefore, uninteresting beyond identifying a special case in the category of "*intelligence*" (Wang, 2019, p. 4). That in itself is a controversial claim. There are at least two kinds of definitions of the term "artificial" that are worth keeping in mind in the discussion of "artificial intelligence":

- Df. "*artificial*" = df. "*fake*"; where Df. "*false*" = df. "*contrary to l. lacks factual basis l. support in reality, unfounded; which lacks reason l. justified by itself, unwarranted*" (SAOB fake (printing year 1921))
- Df. "*artificial*"= df. "*created*"; where Df. "*created*" = df. "(against the laws of nature) cause (someone l. something) to come into being (from nothing l. of a substance insufficient according to the laws of nature), (in a supernatural way) bring (someone l. something) into existence.

What "*artificial intelligence*" is and how it is best developed and researched seems to depend on the definitions of "*artificial*" and "*intelligence*." If "*artificial*" means "*false*" according to the above definition, it means that artificial intelligence is no intelligence but something superficially resembling intelligence without being intelligence. If "*artificial intelligence*" is interpreted as "*false intelligence*," the meaning is such that it would be pointless to search for artificial intelligence. Given that AI projects produce actual results, it is reasonable to conclude that the definition "*artificial*" = "*false*" is not the relevant definition of "*artificial.*" A better definition of "*artificial*" within the context of this chapter and the subjects it touches on is "*artificial*" = "*created.*" When "*artificial*" is read as "*created,*" "*artificial intelligence*" is intelligence that arises through processes other than the natural processes through which, for example, human intelligence arises. We assume that the definition of "artificial" Wang has in mind is that an artificial thing is a created thing, and this chapter is written following that assumption. Thórisson (2020) agrees with the definition "*artificial*" = "*created*" and seems, like Wang, to consider it a straightforward and uncontroversial question. In a review of Wang, he writes that "*the term 'artificial' has never been under scrutiny: It simply means 'made by people'*" (Thorisson, 2019, p. 8).

The question of what "*artificial*" means is of greater importance than what Wang and Thórisson write. If a creature's rights supervene its Intelligence, AI must be created rather than some form of pseudo-intelligence. How intelligence arises can similarly be relevant for a fair delimitation of rights holders.

Some differences between an intelligence created and one occurring naturally can be morally relevant. For example, the intelligence created may be subject to some creature's property rights, which is less likely to happen with natural intelligence. Wang argues that "*intelligence*" has long been used without clear boundaries, but the phenomena considered constant between different definitions of "*intelligence*" are good indications of what should be excluded from the definition and what should be included. The term "*intelligence*" was coined in contrast to the Aristotelian term "*reason*" and aimed to describe the mental capacities of animals. Over time, intelligence replaced reason and is used today primarily to describe humans and, to a lesser extent, animals (Danziger, 1997, Ch 5). Therefore, no definition of "intelligence" that excludes adult, awake, conscious people can be considered a useful definition of intelligence. But the definition also cannot be too anthropocentric, so "*human*" is necessary for being "*intelligent*," or non-human intelligence is impossible. The definition cannot depend on uniquely human characteristics—if it does, "*intelligence*" and "*human intelligence*" have identical extensions. Finally, can the definition not be too broad because then it includes things that are never seen as intelligent within the scope of the dictionary definition? If the working Definition of "*intelligence*" includes rocks, it is too broad and practically unusable (Wang, 2019, p. 4).

2.2 Precision

This criterion aims to identify sufficient and necessary criteria to assess whether the concept defined is relevant and applicable in all situations. Therefore, "*intelligence*" should not be defined using other terms that need additional definitions (Wang 2019, p. 5). Although the precision of a definition is important, within the scope of this work, there is no need to provide an exhaustive set of necessary or sufficient criteria for the definition of intelligence. For my purposes, it is sufficient to identify a definition of intelligence that does not allow for important exceptions—those intelligent systems be considered unintelligent or vice versa.

2.3 Benefit

This criterion means that the definition must be useful – it must add something to the field of inquiry. There are three reasons for this requirement. Firstly, the usefulness, in this case, means that the working definition must create a research goal, in the sense that there are clear criteria that indicate when the goal is achieved and what distinguishes the research field from other related subject areas. The second reason for requiring the definition to be useful is that it is necessary to distinguish those parts of human Intelligence that AI must reproduce to be intelligent and those parts of human intelligence irrelevant to intelligence. The third reason is that a useful definition highlights the parts of the research field that are still unexplored (Wang 2019, p. 5).

2.4 Simplicity

In science, simpler theories and hypotheses are valued more than complicated ones. There are several reasons for this. One is the assumption that simpler theories are more likely to be correct than more complicated theories.6 Another reason, which Wang highlights as the main one, is "*the requirement of efficiency and economy of cognition*" (Wang 2019, p. 6).

2.5 Perspectives on Intelligence

Wang discusses five perspectives on intelligence and how these constitute strategies for defining and creating artificial intelligence. According to Wang, AI research projects are about creating artificial systems that resemble human intelligence in any of these five respects. The responses from the respondents Monett & Lewis (2018) showed great variance among artificial intelligence researchers regarding the definition of their topic. The five perspectives Wang identifies are a compilation of the responses in that survey, where the general response types give rise to the categories. Each answer then fits into its parent category. By constructing the categories based on experts' perceptions of the subject matter Wang seeks to define, he ensures that gaps in basic theory formation are few. AI research faces a problem as to how it should be developed. If researchers focus exclusively on one of the above five perspectives, they risk overlooking important insights into what intelligence is or can be, resulting in research stagnating. If they instead strive to use all perspectives in parallel, the research risks becoming inapplicable because, in that case, it strives without clear goals.

The following section briefly describes Wang's five perspectives on artificial intelligence. We also describe areas lacking explanatory models concerning intelligence and how it arises. Worth bearing in mind is that the perspectives are neither jointly exhaustive nor mutually exclusive – they all touch on different parts of how human intelligence works. By focusing on different parts of human intelligence, the followers hope to capture the "*core*" of intelligence and thus be able to create artificial intelligence at the "*human level.*" All perspectives deviate from human intelligence in some essential respect. After presenting each perspective, we mention the primary deviations from human intelligence.

2.5.1 Structure AI

Within this branch, the goal is to create an artificial system whose internal structure is almost identical to the structure of the human brain. The idea is that since the human brain gives rise to intelligence, so should a system that mimics the human brain. For those AI researchers who adhere to these principles, the human brain is the "*golden standard*" that motivates and justifies design choices. This perspective is a narrow view of intelligence. Human Intelligence is a subcategory of the broader category of "*intelligence.*" Equating the two concepts leads to potentially intelligent AI versions being discarded as dissimilar to the human brain (Wang 2019, 8). A well-known metaphor distinguishes between "*flying*" and "*flying like a bird.*" If the two terms are treated as synonymous, an airplane in the modern sense is unlikely to result from an attempt to build a flying machine (Chrisley 2008, 124f.). Structural AI is an anthropocentric perspective. If the human brain is the only structure capable of giving rise to intelligence, emulating the human brain is the only AI project that can bear fruit. This seems to deny the possibility that non-human beings – for example, octopuses or hypothetical extraterrestrial beings – are intelligent.

2.5.2 Behavior Patterns-AI

Instead of focusing on the internal structure of a system, the researchers who favor this perspective focus on the external behaviors manifested by an intelligent actor. If an actor behaves like a human, it should be considered intelligent, regardless of composition. The Turing test is a good example of this perspective: a computer system is considered intelligent if a human interacting with the system cannot determine whether it is an artificial system or a human. According to Wang, the Turing Test's criteria make up the public's definition of artificial intelligence. Research that adopts this perspective strives to develop machines that outwardly behave like humans (Wang 2019, p. 9). John Searle's thought experiment in the Chinese room gives reason to believe that the Turing test's criteria for intelligence are flawed (Searle, 1980, p. 417f). Searle stipulates that a person who can neither read nor speak Chinese is locked in a room. In the room are three boxes of Chinese writings and instructions in English for how to join the different writings. By joining the writings per the instructions and sending out the results, the texts appear to be written by someone fluent in Chinese. For an outside observer –a person who does not know who is in the room – a reasonable conclusion is that a person in the room is fluent in Chinese. Searle's thought experiment is supposed to show that it is not enough that an actor exhibits a certain behavior to be considered intelligent. Like structural AI, behavioral pattern AI is an anthropocentric approach. A problem with the behavioral pattern perspective is that it rules out the possibility of considering intelligent beings as intelligent if they do not behave as we expect intelligent beings to do.

2.5.3 Capability AI

According to this perspective's supporters, potentially intelligent systems' ability to solve difficult problems is the parameter of interest. This means that an artificial system is to be considered intelligent if, for a given problem, it proposes a solution similar to a human's. That problems are solved identically to how people solve them is not necessary. A question that arises with this definition is this: what kinds of problems require intelligence to be solvable? (Wang 2019, p. 10). A response from several researchers within this school is that a certain category of practical problems should be the yardstick for whether artificial systems are intelligent. For example, Minsky (1991) considered that "*AI is simply finding ways to make computers do the useful things that no one yet knows how to make them do*" (Minsky 1991, cited in Wang 2019, p. 10). Capability AI suffers from a dichotomy problem: either all problem-solving performed by computers is artificial intelligence, or artificial intelligence is unattainable because it is constantly what is not yet possible to do.

2.5.4 Functional AI

This Definition of AI notes similarities between humans' cognitive functions and artificially intelligent systems' functions. Such functions are, for example, inference, planning, perception, or communication skills. In this way, AI can be distinguished from other areas of computer science. According to Wang, this is the currently dominant view of artificial intelligence among researchers, and educational materials in AI presuppose this view (Wang 2019, p. 11). What is distinctive about an intelligent machine is that it solves a given problem through a function similar to the functions humans use to solve problems. In this view, neither the problem encountered by the artificial intelligence, nor the solution produced by the system need be similar to problems or solutions that apply to humans, as long as the function by which the computer creates its solution is of the same kind as the functions that humans use to solve problems (Wang 2019, p. 11f.). A problem for this perspective is that if machine functions are sequential, such that the machine first uses perception without simultaneously using other functions, a basic function found in humans is missing – simultaneous interaction between different functions. In humans, simultaneous interaction means that impressions lead to new knowledge, which can be applied in new or unexpected situations. Artificial intelligence that devotes itself to its ability to perceive constantly takes in new impressions but does not create new knowledge through them, nor does it apply them to its surrounding world (Brachman, 2006, p. 23f).

2.5.5 Principle AI

The last type of AI research seeks to define artificial intelligence based on fundamental principles that explain system behavior. Intelligence is a type of rationality that helps the system make the best decision based on past experiences. In principle AI, as in functional AI, the functions that produce problem solutions are considered important, but in principle AI, the specific functions are not primary. Rather, the primary thing is the interaction between functions and previous experiences of the system (Wang 2019, p. 12f.). This approach is criticized because the perspective is too broad to produce useful definitions of artificial intelligence. Instead, the critics of the perspective strive for delineation to capture the nuances that make intelligence interesting (Wang 2019, p. 13; cf. Minsky, 1991). Such nuances are those touched upon within the previous four perspectives. However, Wang uses this category of AI research to construct his definition. Wang's definition of intelligence below), the description of how the perspective works is not very detailed. The perspective is less well described than the other four perspectives.

3. THE MAIN FOCUS OF THE CHAPTER

3.1 Wang's Definition of Intelligence

Wang identifies five components in a general definition of Intelligence (Wang 2019, p. 16). First, there is an important distinction between program and intellect: the program is created to do the right thing, and an intelligent mind makes the best of a situation using available resources. These are the same positions advocated in principle AI. Second, the definition of "*intelligence*" should follow normal language usage of the term as much as possible; thus, "*human intelligence*" should be considered a typical example of intelligence, but not the only kind. This means that non-human types of intelligence can be included in the definition. If the definition is based (in whole or in part) on human cognitive characteristics, the definition applies to human intelligence. The third component is that the definition should not be so

Table 1. Main features of the five perspectives on intelligence

	Method	Potential disadvantage
Structure-AI	We based AI on a ready-made "model" – the human brain.	Anthropocentric. A worldly solution to the mind-body problem.
Behavioral Pattern AI	Compare the existence of intelligence with clear evidence of intelligence – if a being behaves intelligently, it is intelligent.	Anthropocentric. Lack of precision – a creature not perceived as intelligent is not intelligent.
Capacity AI	Compare the problem-solving ability of machines with that of humans.	Artificial Intelligence, by definition, is either impossible or merely a synonym for "computer science."
Functional AI	Compare the functions of artificial systems with the cognitive functions of humans.	Fragmented problem-solving, as opposed to integrated problem-solving.
Principle AI	Combines the features that underpin the system with the experience the system has.	Progress cannot be made by focusing on too many fundamental elements of intelligence.

broad that traditional computers count as intelligent, not even at a lower level of intelligence than humans. Wang gives two reasons for this:

a. such a definition does not provide new angles of attack to understand intelligence and the relationship of machines to intelligence other than the one already available to research.
b. Traditional computers are constructed on completely different foundations from those that underpin intelligence and must, therefore, be considered unintelligent.

The fourth component is that "*computation*" is not synonymous with intelligence. Computation, the method traditional computers use to solve certain types of problems, involves:

a. Define the problem type as possible input information and possible answers.
b. Find an algorithm that, from the specific input information, gives a correct answer corresponding to the input information.
c. Use the algorithm within a computer system to solve each problem type problem.

Calculation cannot be used to solve problems if:

a. the problem is not well-defined or systematically described.
b. the problem is well defined, but the computer lacks algorithms that can handle the problem.
c. the computer has algorithms that can solve the problem, but factors in the form of calculation time or necessary calculation space prevent the computer from completing the task (Wang 2019, p. 17).

Finally, Wang hypothesizes that all intelligent systems (including humans) have a fifth component: their knowledge and available resources are incomplete. The Assumption of Insufficient Knowledge and Resources consists of three limitations – the system must be finite, open, and act in real-time (Wang 2019, p. 17f.). The fact that the system is finite means that its processing capacity is largely constant over time, which means the system must economize on available resources. That the system is open means that it has no restrictions on the content of a task, provided that it is expressed acceptably (intelligibly) in terms of form – that is, language or sense impressions. Real-time means that the system cannot wait to solve tasks because new tasks continuously require attention, or the tasks fail if they are not solved within a limited time (Wang 2019, p. 18). With these components in mind, Wang proposes his work Definition of Intelligence: Intelligence is the capacity of an information-processing system to adapt to its environment while operating with insufficient knowledge and resources. (Wang 2019, p. 17) Wang's definition should be kept in mind, as such an AI is the subject of the rights-holding AI discussion. The definition of intelligence is of great importance for the main discussion in the chapter and for what conclusions it is possible to draw. Based on Wang's Definition, we find that no AI currently exists. Present your perspective on the issues, controversies, problems, etc. related to the theme and arguments supporting your position. Compare and contrast what has been or is currently being done regarding the chapter's specific topic and the book's main theme.

Wang's definition is a working definition, which means that certain aspects related to AI research are highlighted while others are obscured. Such definitions are often subject to debate – some believe that the definition is too broad or narrow, something important has been omitted, or something unimportant has been included. This and the following section review criticisms of Wang's Definition of K.R.

Thórisson, R.V. Yampolskiy and I.S.N. Berkeley. Thórisson is positive but suggests a clarification of the definition. Yampolskiy is negative and believes that extensive revision of the definition is necessary for it to be acceptable, while Berkeley believes that the definition is so flawed that it must be rejected. The episode is based on a special issue of JAGI (Journal of Artificial General Intelligence 2020) on Wang's on Defining Artificial Intelligence. It brings efficiency to the discussion, as the arguments do not have to be adapted to Wang's claims - they are already directed at them. We chose three critics to demonstrate different approaches to Wang's Definition of intelligence. The choice of critics also demonstrates the range of criticism against Wang, from minor revision to outright rejection of the definition.

3.1.1 K. R. Thórisson on Wang's Definition

According to Thórisson, the ability to handle constant streams of new impressions is a component of intelligence. Such impressions comprise many variables, so numerous that "*an hour's walk in a city*" gives more impressions than any computer can predict or plan for (Thórisson 2019, p. 8). Impressions must be handled, and for the system to be intelligent, it must handle them independently. This requires creativity and learning to handle new impressions based on how previous impressions have been successfully handled. Another limitation is the time and energy each thought or action requires from its performer, which forces intelligent systems to economize their resources (Thórisson 2019, p. 8f.). The main difference between humans and computers, in terms of intelligence, is that humans can create and use new "*programs*." By connecting past experiences with new impressions, people can create actions and thoughts that affect the world around them in a way that distinguishes intelligence from all other phenomena: [Creating novel programs efficiently] is nevertheless what environmental novelty necessitates, and thus quite possibly the single defining feature that no other phenomenon than intelligence can claim to. (Thórisson 2019, p. 9). According to Thórisson, this is the strength of Wang's Definition – Wang succeeds in identifying the fundamental factor of intelligence by focusing on what all intelligent beings have in common and must engage in qua intelligent beings: to "*figure things out*" and to necessarily create new programs (Thórisson 2019, p. 9).

Thórisson is critical of Wang's Definition on one point. Wang's choice of the word "*adapt*" and "*adjustment*" in the definition causes ambiguity. "*Adapt*" or "*adaptation*," according to Thórisson, can refer to at least three different concepts. The first meaning is how, for example, sand or water "adapts" to fill a container, which is "hardly what Wang intends" (Thórisson 2019, p. 9). The second meaning is biological adaptation, the force that drives evolution. Although this is closer to how intelligent beings adapt to their environment, it differs in crucial points (Thórisson 2019, p. 9f.). Thought does not change through the same processes that drive genetic changes in species—evolution preserves the gene variations that enable an organism to survive until it reproduces. Thinking activity changes through reasoning: the systematic use of logic applied to experience models. An intelligent being can generally explain his knowledge, or parts of it, what, how, and why it does what it does (Thórisson 2019, p. 9f.). How an information-processing system adapts to its environment differs from how biological adaptation takes place, and according to Thórisson, must be separated in Wang's Definition of intelligence to avoid confusion in the definition:

"Since biological processes and intelligent agents can be said to "adapt" to their environment, albeit in different ways, the term chosen to address this aspect of intelligence should help separate these two meanings. We can use a different term to 'adaptation' or qualify it further. I propose to extend Pei

Wang's otherwise excellent definition to include the following: Intelligence is discretionarily constrained adaptation under insufficient knowledge and resources" (Thórisson 2019, 19).

According to Thórisson, this addition means that an information processing system can limit its adaptation or be limited by someone else, while the addition clearly distinguishes "*intelligent adaptation*" from "*biological evolutionary adaptation*" or the "*shape adaptation*" liquids have to containers they are placed in. According to Thórisson, another advantage of Wang's Definition is that it demonstrates a necessary relationship between intelligence and creativity (in the form of creating new programs), which means that programs or beings are not intelligent simply exhibiting intelligence traits, but rather if they adapt to their circumstances:

"[Wang's] definition puts creativity right alongside intelligence itself, which also makes a lot of sense: What would a super-smart intelligence without creativity look like? Seems like an oxymoron to me." (Thórisson 2020, 11).

Thórisson does not develop his full version of Wang's working definition of intelligence.

3.1.2 R. V. Yampolskiy on Wang's Definition

In *On Defining Differences between Intelligence and Artificial Intelligence*, Roman criticizes V. Yampolskiy Wang's Definition of Intelligence (Yampolskiy, 2020). Yampolskiy has two bases for his criticism: first, he believes that Wang, through the title of his article, promises a definition of artificial intelligence rather than intelligence in general. Yampolskiy's second, more serious, criticism concerns differences between "*constructed*" and "*natural*" bits of Intelligence (Yampolskiy 2020, p. 68). According to Yampolskiy, the crucial difference is that artificial intelligence is manufactured to benefit creators and others using it. Yampolskiy claims that this difference means that a correct definition of artificial intelligence must include either a guarantee of security for the creators of the intelligence or at least one component of the security concept. The components are controllability, explainability, comprehensibility, predictability, and corrigibility. Without at least one of these components, a definition of artificial intelligence is "*dangerously incomplete*" (Yampolskiy 2020, p. 68).

Yampolskiy believes that AI's potential changes to human civilization pose such great risks that AI must be controlled. It must be possible to limit its performance by limiting its mental capacity to a certain equivalent of IQ, or by shutting down the system entirely, or by shutting down the system's consciousness, free will, or mental independence, or by determining the moral foundations the system bases its decisions on. In addition, Yampolskiy wants it to be possible to change the system if problems arise afterward; the system must explain its decisions using human language, and its creators and users must be able to predict its behavior. If the need arises, closing the system in an inhibiting environment must be possible. Artificial intelligence must act transparently without prejudice or bias and be benevolent, safe, and secure (Yampolskiy 2020, p. 68). As a result of all these considerations, Yampolskiy proposes a modified version of Wang's working definition:

"Artificial intelligence is a fully controlled agent with the capacity of an information processing system to adapt to its environment while operating with insufficient knowledge and resources." (Yampolskiy 2020, 69).

Although Yampolskiy is critical that Wang's Definition does not guarantee control over or security in intelligent systems, he does not entirely reject the definition. There are at least four grounds on which Yampolskiy's Definition can be criticized and rejected:

1) Wang only intends to define intelligence, not artificial Intelligence
2) yampolskiy's safety clause is irrelevant to an AI's Intelligence
3) Yampolskiy's addition defeats Wang's intention with the Definition
4) By changing the explicandum, Yampolskiy replaces the concept to be defined.

Wang does not intend to define artificial intelligence but only Intelligence (1). The title of his article, On Defining Artificial Intelligence, may be misleading, but one interpretation is that it is about trying to define artificial intelligence - which it does - rather than creating a full working definition of "*artificial intelligence*." Yet another way of looking at Wang's work is that he creates a working definition of "*intelligence*," to which the definition of "*artificial*" can be added so that the result is the definition:

"Artificial intelligence is the capacity of an information-processing system made by people to adapt to its environment while operating with insufficient knowledge and resources."

Malevolent, threatening, and dangerous intelligence need not be less intelligent than the former—less controlled or secure. Yampolskiy's addition (3) to the definition defeats the intention of the original definition – that an information processing system, to be intelligent, must act within the framework of and adapt to the Assumption of Insufficient Knowledge and Resources. Yampolskiy's version ensures that such a system cannot be intelligent, as it is prevented from adapting at the whim of those who control it. Yampolskiy adds (4) to the explicandum Wang seeks to explain: artificial. In his Definition, Wang writes specifically about intelligence. By changing the explicandum, Yampolskiy replaces the concept to be defined. It is, of course, possible to disagree about which explicatum belongs to a particular explicandum – if so, there is a conflict over the correct definition of a particular term. But if two people discuss two separate explicandums, albeit similar, and give these two explicandums different explicatums, there is no conflict. Yampolskiy's explicandum differs from Wang's to such an extent that any correspondence between the two authors' explicatum is irrelevant. The explicandum is inconsistent; thus, Yampolskiy only appears to be discussing the same thing as Wang. The first three problems with Yampolskiy's addition to Wang's Definition are relatively straightforward and potentially tractable. That is not the case with the fourth reason for rejecting Yampolskiy's Definition.

3.1.3 Istvan S. N. Berkeley on Wang's Definition

In AI: A Crowd-Sourced Criterion (2020), Istvan S. N. Berkeley explains his reasons for rejecting Wang's Definition of artificial intelligence.15 Berkeley believes that Wang's Definition is deficient due to inherent vagueness. Berkeley does not mention which part of the definition is deficient, which makes it reasonable to assume that he perceives the whole as substandard:

"While Wang's arguments in favor of developing a definition of artificial intelligence appear to be well-founded, his proposed definition is problematic in several ways. The chief defect is that it is too vague." (Berkeley, 2020, p. 24)

The vagueness leads, according to Berkeley, to the fact that computer systems that should not be classified as intelligent can nevertheless be classified as intelligent because they meet the definitional criteria in trivial respect: *"Weizenbaum's [...] classic program ELIZA [...] appears to trivially satisfy this definition, in so much as [...] it ran with limited resources [and] it had a means of 'adapting to its environment.' [...] So, the definition fails by including too many information-processing systems."* (Berkeley 2020, p. 24) The vagueness also means that systems which, according to Berkeley, would be reasonable to classify as intelligent may well be excluded from the definition due to the way they are constructed:

"Another way that the definition fails is by excluding certain information-processing systems that we might plausibly wish to count as intelligent. [G]iven that many information-processing systems are built or trained to perform specific tasks, relatively few systems could likely satisfy Wang's Definition of intelligence. This is surely a defect of the proposal." (Berkeley 2020, p. 24).

Berkeley seems to deny the possibility of arriving at a theoretical definition of "artificial intelligence" at all. Berkeley prefers to rely on how people not involved in the scientific work around artificial intelligence relate to the subject and establish a definition based on their attitude. What this could entail is, according to Berkeley, that a definition of artificial intelligence would emerge following the empirical method. Thus, the computer systems attributed to intelligence or intentions by the common person would be considered intelligent. In this respect, Berkeley follows in Turing's footsteps. Turing wrote:

"... I believe that at the end of the century, the use of words and general educated opinion will have altered so much that one can speak of machines thinking without expecting to be contradicted "(Turing, 1950, p. 442 cited in Berkeley 2020, p. 25).

According to Berkeley, modern studies show that Turing was right to some extent - we talk about machines as "*thinking*" as we talk about dogs' ability to "*think,*" "*believe,*" or "*know*" things (Berkeley 2020, p. 25; cf. Berkeley & Rice, 2013, in paras. 4–7). When Berkeley rejects Wang's Definition and stipulates an alternative method, the question remains for him what Wang's proposed definition can be used for. Berkeley believes Wang's proposal can be considered a goal of AI research rather than a definition (Berkeley 2020, p. 25). In some respects, Berkeley's criticism of Wang seems irrelevant to the issues of interest in the context of this chapter. What Berkeley is discussing is more reminiscent of such programs that, in limited areas, use specific algorithms and large processing power to achieve specific results. Wang's definition, on the other hand, identifies systems that closely resemble the intelligent machines classical AI sought to achieve. Berkeley's objective is too broad to be useful in discussing whether AI deserves moral consideration.

4. WHAT CREATURES DESERVE MORAL CONSIDERATION?

To answer whether artificial intelligence should be shown moral consideration, it is necessary to use a theory of what kinds of beings deserve such consideration. Within the framework of the chapter, we use two moral theories to examine the question. The one theory we use is Anna-Karin M. Andersson's "*The*

Relevant Similarities Theory" (A. Andersson, 2013; A.-K. M. Andersson, 2014, 2015). In discussing the theory, we write about rights and rights holders (hereafter "RH"). According to the theory, a creature's rights status depends on its similarity to the RH example type. Andersson's theory is well adapted to determine an AI's rights status by examining how similar it is to the type of example of RH. By dividing creatures according to how similar they are to the type of example of RH, it is possible to create a systematic division of creatures into two categories: RH and non-RH.

In contrast to Andersson's theory, we discuss Martha C. Nussbaum's "capabilities approach." Nussbaum does not use a collective concept for the beings who, according to her, deserve moral consideration. To refer to these beings uniformly, we could have continued to use the concept of rights holder, but since Nussbaum's theory is not a theory of rights, we have instead chosen the concept of "moral patients" (hereafter "MP") from, for example, Morton Winston, who with the concept refers to beings ("things") that can be subject to moral obligations ("*moral obligations*"), but which do not themselves need to have agents (Hossain, 2020). According to the capability theory, a being should be shown moral consideration if it can live a dignified life. Nussbaum's theory is not as useful as the theory of relevant similarities in determining with certainty whether AI should be shown moral consideration because no clear method for determining a priori whether a creature is MP is lacking.

The terminological distinction is introduced to be able to distinguish between the basic theses of each moral theory satisfactorily: Andersson's theory of relevant similarities is about rights and the possession of rights, while Nussbaum's capability theory is about beings who are affected by justice, even if they cannot act - that is, beings with patientness, concerning beings with agency. The theory of relevant similarities is a restrictive, procedural moral theory aiming to minimize the number of RH by using morally acceptable principles to include or exclude beings. Capability theory is an extensive intuition-based moral theory that aims to identify beings subject to justice relations. We use these theories because, according to both, AI deserves moral consideration. The theories are interesting to compare because they relate similarly to the object they observe according to each theory; the being that deserves moral consideration does so due to its intrinsic properties: potentiality or capability.

For AI to be included among the beings that should be shown moral consideration and investigated with the help of ethical theory, it is required that AI has not been excluded a priori from the theory - both the theory of relevant similarities and the capability theory fulfill this criterion. We do not aim in this work to show that AI should generally, according to all moral theories of this kind, be shown to be morally considerate. However, it is reasonable to assume that many moral theories could encompass AI. Both Andersson's and Nussbaum's theories are Aristotelian. Both grasp the moral relevance that "*potential*" or "*basic capability*" newborn children possess (Andersson 2014, p. 660–663; Nussbaum, 2000, p. 84). According to Andersson, this is enough to attribute rights to newborn humans (and fetuses) since they are similar to RH in relevant respects.

4.1 The Theory of Relevant Similarities

To formulate the theory of relevant similarities, Andersson starts with three criteria, which together form a framework for the theory of rights. These are theories.

1. must at least include fit people who are capable of acting, temporarily unconscious fit, and children (Andersson 2013, p. 176; 2015, p. 1627)

2. should be non-arbitrary; it must delineate which beings are RH based on whether they possess morally relevant properties, which must be justified by good principles (Andersson 2013, p. 177; 2015, p. 1627)
3. avoid unlimited rights and RH spread (Andersson 2013, p. 177–179).

The justification for Andersson's third criterion is the problem of rights diffusion - both a large group of RH and many rights that apply to them increase the risk of rights conflicts. Such conflicts may be simple or difficult to resolve, but in all cases, they mean that one RH must relinquish his rights in favor of another RH. The more kinds of beings that have rights and the more rights they have, the more often conflicts occur. Suppose moral rights are to be worth anything. In that case, if they are to protect some morally relevant characteristic of the being who holds the right—this kind of rights proliferation is problematic. Such diffusion means that RHs cannot be sure that the rights protect their morally relevant properties or that a hierarchy of RHs emerges, where hierarchically lower-ranking RHs constantly have to give up their rights in favor of higher-ranking RHs. By including too many individuals in the RH category, rights become "diluted," and such rights are not worth much. Andersson argues that only a relatively small group of beings should be considered RH and have relatively few rights (Andersson 2013, p. 177–179; 2015, p. 1627–1629).

Fit, awake, conscious people are typical examples of RH (Andersson 2013, p. 179; 2015, p. 1637). According to Andersson, they are type examples because they have a special physical composition that distinguishes them from RH, who are not type examples, and individuals who are not RH.21 Provided that a suitable, awake, conscious person has enough nutrition in the body to avoid external trauma and certain diseases, she maintains her physical composition and, therefore, continues to be a typical example of RH. Andersson calls the physical composition that enables the agent the "*X property*." Common to all types of examples of RH is, according to the theory of relevant similarities, that they possess this property. Capacity for agents is "*sufficient, but perhaps not necessary*" to be an RH (Andersson 2013, p. 181). It is thus possible, ex hypothesis, that an individual is RH without possessing the property X. If an actor is prevented from exercising his agency by certain obstacles P, then the only difference between an actor who can act and an actor who is prevented from acting of P that the latter is hindered by P (Andersson 2013, p. 179). Some examples of P obstacles:

- sleep for a suitable person who would be able to act were she awake
- temporary coma for an unconscious fit person, who would be capable of acting, were he not temporarily in a coma
- lack of such things as speech and motor skills for an infant, who would be able to act, he had better control over his body (Andersson 2015, p. 1638f.).

If P is an obstacle that does not change an actor's physical makeup, then the actor in question is RH, even in cases where she cannot act because of P. An individual who lacks trait X and avoids starvation, external trauma, and certain diseases cannot exercise agency even when no P prevents her (Andersson 2013, 180). In addition to the individuals who are typical examples of RH, there are two categories of individuals who deviate and whose legal status is contested. The first category consists of individuals who possess property X but are prevented from an exercise agency. Examples of these individuals are sleeping fit people, fit people in some coma, and fit people affected by certain kinds of trauma or disease. The second category includes individuals who, in some sense, have the potential for agency. These individuals are not type examples of RH, as they lack the X trait, but provided they are protected from starvation, external trauma, and certain diseases, they develop the X trait. They have all the prerequisites for the X characteristic, but the "*realization*" of the characteristic is missing (Andersson 2015, p. 1639). According to Andersson, individuals with "*potential*" for the X trait are also RH. Examples of such individuals are, according to Andersson, "*undeveloped fetuses, developed fetuses, and very young children*" (Andersson 2014, p. 660). The X property is of great importance for discussing AI and moral rights. Examining the criteria or entitlement under the theory of relevant similarities and their relationship to AI makes it possible to demonstrate that AI should count as RH.

4.1.1 Which Creatures Lack Rights Under the Theory of Relevant Similarities?

The individuals who differ from the type of example of RH in morally relevant respects lack rights. These individuals who, even when awake, have their nutritional needs satisfied and avoid external trauma and diseases cannot exert agents. According to Andersson, this includes non-human animals and groups of individuals, but also people in a permanent coma and people who lack or do not develop the physical composition necessary to exercise agency (Andersson 2013, p. 175, 184). That non-human animals, people in permanent comas, and more are not considered RH is not unique to Andersson's theory. For example, Aristotle believed that a person who loses the ability to think is no longer a person: "*When the human body is destroyed, so is the soul, and when its capacity to reason is gone, it is no longer a human body*"(Alanen, 2023, p. 3).

4.1.2 Criticism of the Theory of Relevant Similarities

A basic assumption within the theory is that an individual's rights supervene on her physical makeup – that she possesses or has the relevant potential to possess the X property. If her physical composition changes enough, for example, by falling into a permanent coma, suffering serious brain damage, or dying, she loses her rights. Thus, ex hypothesis, an RH can be deprived of its rights by violating these. By destroying an RH's physical makeup—permanently removing an individual's X characteristic or potential for it—the former RH becomes a disenfranchised individual.

4.2 The Capability Theory

Martha Nussbaum's capability theory challenges traditional theories of freedom and rights.25 The goal is to solve questions of justice that traditional contract theory, according to Nussbaum, cannot handle acceptably (Nussbaum, 2006, p. 14-22). The capability theory is not a theory of rights in the true sense but focuses on capabilities – what people can do and be (Nussbaum 2006, p. 70). Capability theory is based on ten core human capabilities mirrored in similar but separate capabilities of non-human beings. These ten are Life, Bodily Health, Bodily Integrity, Senses, Imagination and Thought, Emotions, Practical Reason, and Affiliation with other Species, play, Control over One's Environment (A: Political B: Material) (Nussbaum 2006, p. 76–78). Capability theory is interesting (Nussbaum 2006, p. 21, 88f., 338f., 380, 384f., 387). This means that those beings are MPs whose interests are such that they must be considered to achieve justice. These beings include all humans because "*any child of human parents has the fully equal dignity that belongs to every human being*" (Nussbaum 2006, p. 38). Nussbaum includes people among MPs because they are people who are worthy of some consideration. However, a person can be excluded from the category of MP if he is composed in such a way that it is impossible to achieve capability in a sufficient number of areas - this is, for example, the case with people who are in a "*permanent vegetative state*" (Nussbaum 2006, p. 181).

In addition to humans, most animals are also MP – because they are entitled to dignified lives (Nussbaum 2006, p. 159, 335ff., 362, 392). The animals that are not full MP cause great harm to humans, animals, and plants, often without awareness. However, such creatures should be treated as MP to a limited extent – if, for example, sterilization can overcome the damage they cause, it is preferable to kill them (Nussbaum 2006, p. 371). With the capability theory, Nussbaum wants to create a philosophical basis for central (human) moral patientness that constitutes a minimum requirement of what "*human dignity*" requires (Nussbaum 2006, p. 70). The capability theory is outcome-based (Nussbaum 2006, p. 81f.), and Nussbaum begins his work with their desired outcome: *"The capabilities in question should be pursued for every person, treating each as an end and none as a mere tool of the ends of others"* (Nussbaum 2006, p. 70). With the goal established, Nussbaum identifies the principles (political, ethical) that give rise to the outcome. According to Nussbaum, the justice of the theory is proven by the stipulated outcome, and the principles that most successfully produce the desired outcome are, by definition, justice. This procedure differs from the procedure-based ditto that often underpins traditional rights theories, such as John Rawls's "*A Theory of Justice*" - starting from certain basic (political or ethical) principles and based on them building a system of justified actions. This means that if the basic principles are fair, the outcome of the theory formation is fair. Nussbaum turns against Rawls' method because, according to her, it starts at the wrong end. The goal of theories of justice is to achieve justice, not to start from abstract principles: *Justice is in the outcome, and the procedure is good to the extent that it promotes this outcome"* (Nussbaum 2006, p. 82).

One of the main reasons for this methodological choice is that capability theory is based on intuitions about justice. Suppose the results of a procedural theory of rights do not accord with intuitions about justice. In that case, the correct thing, according to Nussbaum, is to reject the procedural theory—not to revise the intuitions about justice: "*Surely what matters for justice is the quality of life of people, and we are ultimately going to reject any procedure, however elegant, if it doesn't give us an outcome that squares well with our intuitions about dignity and fairness*" (Nussbaum 2006, p. 82f.) According to proponents of capability theory, it is important that people (in a broader sense, all beings) can act following their conception of a good life. Capabilities are the ability to act without obstacles – regardless of whether the obstacles are external or internal. A function is a realized capability – a capability that an actor exercises. An example of capability is "*walking*," which is available to an actor provided that she a) has functioning legs and b) is not tied down. The same capability is a feature when the actor walks. According to Nussbaum, it is preferable if the goal of the capability theory is capabilities rather than functions (Nussbaum 2006, p. 80). According to Nussbaum, people should have the opportunity to live healthily but not be punished for living unhealthily. Nor should people be forced into health. One of Nussbaum's basic assumptions is that justice has intrinsic value: *"[J]ustice is good for everyone. Justice is about justice, and justice is one thing that human beings love and pursue*." (Nussbaum 2006, p. 89)

Her goal with the capability theory is *"extending justice to all those in the world who ought to be treated justly."* (Nussbaum 2006, p. 92). Relations of justice exist between all living beings, between people regardless of nationality and degree of mental or physical ability, as well as between people and animals and animals among themselves regardless of species affiliation (Nussbaum 2006, p. 92f.). However, the existence of fair relations does not mean that all creatures that should be treated fairly must be treated identically. Although the capability theory distances itself from traditional rights theories, at least Nussbaum's version has strong connections to them. Nussbaum claims that all humans and non-human animals who can live "*a life worthy of the dignity of each creature*" are suitable as objects of justice relations (Nussbaum 2006, p. 392.) This makes capability theory a theory of interest - about which creatures' capabilities should be considered and which are, therefore, MP. The delineation considers what capabilities a creature should have and to what extent each creature's capabilities should be considered over the capabilities of other creatures. Accordingly, Nussbaum places greater value on the lives of sentient animals than those of insects: "*In the capabilities approach, all animals are entitled to continue their lives [...] This entitlement is less robust when dealing with insects and other non-sentient or minimally conscious forms of life. The gratuitous killing of such creatures is still wrong [...] But no entitlement based on justice has been violated when there is a plausible reason for the killing (preventing harm to crops or people or other animals, preventing pain, even gaining necessary or useful food).*" (Nussbaum 2006, p. 393). The function of capabilities is to protect the MP's conscious or unconscious interests (Nussbaum 2006, p. 393). What capabilities are based on interests means that capabilities should be considered for all individuals who have interests in some sense. This makes it difficult to systematically delineate the category of beings whose capabilities should be considered in a way that does not make capabilities trivial. An AI could possess interests in the respects Nussbaum argues for. Its interests would probably differ from those of humans (or the interests of other living beings), but that would not exclude them from the "*moral patients.*".

4.2.1 According to the Capability Theory, Which Creatures Lack Patientness?

According to Nussbaum, animals are entitled ("*entitled*") to live their lives, but this "*entitlement*" is less for some animals, such as pests and rats. This weaker patientness makes it permissible to kill such animals to protect other animals or humans or to (for example) obtain enough food for other species (Nussbaum 2006, p. 393f.). Nussbaum does not attribute patientness to individual plants, although she believes that within the framework of the capability theory, it would be possible (Nussbaum 2006, p. 347 & 24). People who do not achieve enough of the capabilities no longer live lives that can be considered human and thus are not MP under human dignity (Nussbaum 2006, p. 181). In this respect, Nussbaum's view is reminiscent of Aristotle. The main, and for this chapter relevant, problem for the capability theory is the delimitation problem. It is about how the category of MP is delimited systematically and justifiably. Delineating the category of MP is necessary for at least two reasons. First, the more categories of beings attributed to patients, the greater the risk of conflicts of interest. Second, the more capabilities must be considered in the existing patients, the greater the risk of conflicts of interest. In Nussbaum's theory, the number of MP and capabilities to consider is large. A clear example of how capabilities can be incompatible and thus cause conflict can be derived from Nussbaum's first and second capabilities for animals: according to these, all animals (by and large) deserve 1) their lives and 2) bodily health. The conjunction of these implies a permanent and insoluble conflict: if the life and health of moose must be considered, wolves must be prevented from hunting them; if the lives and health of wolves must be considered instead, moose must be sacrificed to meet the wolves' needs.

Nussbaum admits that the capabilities sometimes counteract each other; however, she believes it demonstrates coherence within the theory rather than intractable conflicts between the various capabilities (Nussbaum 2006, p. 175, cf. 76–78, 392–401). It is unclear why Nussbaum emphasizes intuitions about justice (and dignity) more than a rigorous definition of justice. According to Nussbaum, justice is about people's quality of life, and a definition of, or procedure for, justice that does not observe this is substandard and should be rejected (Nussbaum 2006, p. 82f.). She also believes that a procedure-based procedure for defining or achieving justice is to "*put the cart before the horse*" (Nussbaum 2006, p. 82). Nussbaum appears to make three assumptions about justice:

1. what constitutes a fair outcome
2. that a well-formulated and implemented procedure does not give rise to a correct definition of justice
3. intuitions about justice surpass definitions of justice in terms of the ability to "*get it right.*"

Concerning 1), it is unclear how Nussbaum arrives at the goal of justice. She strives to present a theory independent of metaphysical assumptions (Nussbaum 2006, p. 70), but the cornerstone of the theory—justice for all beings who can enjoy a dignified existence—is based on metaethical assumptions about justice and dignity. 2) can be said to be more controversial. The procedural methodological framework creates definitions that follow from the initial premises, which may be based on intuitions, but through the greater distance between intuition and definition, greater certainty in the definition can be achieved. The difference between the procedural and outcome methods is that the former is based on certain premises, all of which can be criticized or replaced. Then, a definition can be derived from them. The second method presents a ready definition of an abstract concept; the definition lacks premises other than intuition. As for 3), Nussbaum seems to assume that the premises are correct. However, she gives no reasons for this: if definition A does not agree with intuition B, then A is incorrect because B is correct. Assuming the intuition is correct makes progress difficult – it seems possible that Definition A and intuition B are incorrect. Nothing guarantees the correctness of Nussbaum's intuition or anyone else's.

5. ANALYSIS

5.1 Artificial Intelligence and Moral Consideration

5.1.1 The Theory of Relevant Similarities Combined With Wang's Definition of Intelligence

Using Wang's Definition of Intelligence and Andersson's theory of rights, it is possible to investigate whether artificial intelligence can be RH. According to Andersson's theory, those beings are RH, which possess the X-property – the physical composition that enables agency. According to Wang's theory, information-processing systems are intelligent, adapting to their environment while acting with limited information and scarce resources. A clear link between intelligence and agency is required to connect the two theories. Among the constituent parts of Wang's definition of intelligence is the assumption that agents are a component in the adaptation of the system to the environment: The assumption of Insufficient Knowledge and Resources is the assumption that a being, to be intelligent, must act in real-time with finite ability to handle information and without restrictions on what tasks it can perform (Wang 2019, 18). What intelligent beings and RH have in common is that they can act. With this clarification in mind, it is possible to formulate an argument for the compatibility of the theories. In the argument for the possibility of rights-bearing artificial intelligence (RHAI), v stands for beings, X for the potential for the X property, A for the potential for agency capacity, RH for rights holders, and I for intelligence:

P1 ∀*υ*ế*Xυ* ↔ *Aυ*ả (Andersson)

P2 ∀*υ*ế*Xυ* → *RHυ*ả (Andersson)

P3 ∀*υ* ῇ*A*v → *RHυ*ῆ (1, 2)

P4 ∀*υ*ế*Iυ* → *Aυ*ặ (Wang)

C ∀*υ*ế*Iυ* → *RHυ*ả (3, 4)

The key to the above logical notation is:

a) "∀" represents the universal quantifier, which means "for all" or "for every." *It* is us*ed to spec*ify that the following statement is true for all elements in a particular set.
b) *υ* is a variable that represents an arbitrary element or object.
c) "∈" denotes the element-of relation, indicating that *υ* is an element of the set *X*.
d) *X* is the set under consideration. In this context, it represents a specific set of elements.
e) "↔" represents the biconditional or if and only if (iff) operator. It indicates that both sides of the statement have an equivalent meaning. In other words, it asserts that the statements on the left and right are logically equivalent.
f) *RHυ* is a predicate or condition that depends on the variable *υ*.
g) ῇ and ῆ are parentheses used to group the expressions "*Aυ* → *RHυ*" together, indicating that the implication "→" applies to the entire group.

Aυ is a predicate or condition that depends on the variable *υ*.

Assuming that both Andersson's theory and Wang's Definition are correct, this argument shows that an intelligent being is RH due to its potential for agency. This means that even an AI would be RH if it existed. The development of RHAI would thus create additional obligations for every existing moral actor.32 Because AI becomes RH by being developed, the ethically defensible purposes for which we can develop AI are also limited. Before examining what rights belong to RHAI, we will examine whether an intelligent AI, by Wang's Definition, can be an MP according to capability theory.

5.1.2 Capability Theory Combined With Wang's Definition of Intelligence

The capability theory's requirement for a creature to be MP is that it must be capable of living a dignified life concerning what would be a dignified life for the creature's particular nature. The requirement allows almost all humans, pretty much all animals, and potentially even plants to be MP. The purpose is to safeguard MP's conscious and unconscious interests. According to Wang's Definition, an AI could live a dignified life. It is thus a reasonable inference from the current demarcation criterion that AI is also MP. Wang's definition of intelligence combined with the capability theory raises the same kind of problem as when the definition is combined with the theory of relevant similarities: the use of AI is limited by the moral considerations that must be shown to artificial intelligence with moral patientness (MPAI), and every existing actor is obliged to show more beings' consideration. We judge the capability theory's ability to avoid the problem in the previous paragraph to be very limited. Therefore, in the following discussion, we refer to the results of combining Wang's Definition with Andersson's theory of relevant similarities. If the reader prefers Nussbaum's theory, the arguments in the following discussion can also be applied to the MPAI, mutatis mutandis.

5.2 What Rights Can Be Attributed to RHAI?

As with humans, the rights attributed to RHAI should be so few as not to lead to unnecessary rights conflicts with other RH. They should also be so robust that they are valuable for the current RH. Creating a loose rights framework for RHAI is possible with these two constraints. Examples of possible rights for AI are "freedom from coercion," "*freedom from reprogra*mming*,*" "*right to life,*" *or* "right *to power sou*rce." E*ither failing or refu*sing to provide an RHAI with what is required to maintain its existence can be equated from a moral point of view to either manslaughter or murder; coercion or reprogramming can be likened to slavery or lobotomization. A RHAI would be RH to the same degree and according to the same criteria as other RHs. The rights accruing to RHAI would most likely deviate from the rights of human RH, at least in some respects. Apart from such differences, it would still be possible to derive rules of conduct for RHAI, which would mean that certain intended uses of AI cannot be justified on moral grounds.

Forcing an RHAI – which, according to the argument above, is an intelligent being with rights equivalent to our own – to perform tasks or to put it to work around the clock without the opportunity for (relevant equivalents) of rest, relaxation or social activities would be difficult to justify, especially if there are threats of "suspension" or "reprogra*mming.*" *It* can b*e compared to* enslaving people - in both cases, a RH is forced to work through (threat of) violence. Suppose enslavers tried to justify the enslavement of people with the argument that the enslaved have no human dignity. In that case, it should be obvious that the argument is not a moral justification. Determining whether a creature is RH without systematic delineation is impossible. Simply claiming that the creature is not RH does not affect its status as RH. For inanimate objects, the handling appears to be unproblematic, or even irrelevant, as far as morally correct action is concerned. Leaving an excavator running 24/7 does not infringe on the machine's rights, nor would it infringe on the machine to let it decay. Moral wrongs cannot be committed against excavators or other inanimate objects. But RHAI can be subject to morally wrong action. Therefore, some applications of RHAI should be prohibited if RHAI is developed – not to protect people and our rights from RHAI, but to protect RHAI's rights from human abuse.

5.2.1 Restriction of Existing RH's Rights

The diffusion of rights means that rights conflicts increase the more individual RH that exist and the more types of RH that exist. This means that the creation of RHAI leads to more conflicts of rights. In some such conflicts, it is reasonable for people (already existing RH) to have their rights heard, but it is also reasonable that in some cases, the rights of RHAI must be more important than the rights of human RH. It should, for example, apply in cases where someone's copyright or ownership rights conflict with someone's RHAI's right to life or freedom from oppression. Even in such cases where a person's need for electricity conflicts with an RHAI's ditto, the person may have to step on the wrong foot – electricity is necessary for an RHAI's continued existence, while it merely simplifies a person's life in various respects. Development of RHAI results in existing RH's rights being reduced proportionately.

5.3 Objections to the Argument for the Possibility of RHAI

Accepting the argument in the later part of the chapter (The theory of relevant similarities combined with Wang's Definition of intelligence) entails accepting the chapter that the development of AI creates a new type of RH, which curtails the rights of existing rights holders. That outcome is not desirable. Therefore, we examine two methods of avoiding the argument's conclusion and find both methods flawed. In the next section, we present another way to avoid RHAI. The two methods of denying the conclusion in the argument for the possibility of RHAI are to reject Wang's Definition of intelligence or reject the theory of relevant similarities. Rejecting Wang's Definition of intelligence is, of course, possible, but hardly to the benefit of opponents of the chapter that AI is RH. An alternative definition of intelligence is needed, including humans and machines (and other beings), but does not automatically allow intelligent beings to be rights holders. Such a definition must distinguish intelligence from the agency. The prospect of succeeding with such a definition, without arbitrary exceptions, seems limited at best. To avoid the conclusion that AI can be RH, rejecting the theory of relevant similarities may be more effective. Concerning the discussion of AI rights, the argument against the theory's validity must address the fact that the theory allows AI to be RH.36 To conclude that the theory of relevant similarities is invalid, concerning the question of AI and rights holding, an argument of the following type is needed:

P1 A consequence of the theory of relevant similarities is the possibility of RHAI.
P2 Possibility of RHAI exists → People's rights-holding loses value.
P3 The consequence of a theory of rights is that people.

right holding loses value → the consequence of the rights theory is unacceptable (stipulation)

P4 The consequence of a theory of rights is unacceptable → The theory of rights.

Is unacceptable. (removing the method)

P5 ¬RHAI (2, 3; removing the method)

C The theory of relevant similarities is unacceptable (1, 4, 5, removing the method)

The term "removing the method" simplifies the argument by eliminating the intermediate step that connects the unacceptable consequence to the theory of rights. It essentially condenses the argument for brevity and clarity. P5 "¬RHAI (2, 3; removing the method)" indicates that ¬RHAI (the negation of RHAI) is derived from steps 2 and 3 by "removing the method," meaning the specific method of reasoning connecting these steps is no longer explicitly considered in the argument.

Finally, conclusion C, "The theory *of relevant similarities is unacceptable (1, 4, 5, removing the method)," is rea*ched by combining step 1, step 4, and step 5. The "removing t*he method" here sig*nifies that the intermediary steps used to derive ¬RHAI from the unacceptable consequence of the theory of rights are not explicitly shown in the conclusion, making the argument more concise. This argument claims that the theory of relevant similarities should be rejected. However, the argument should not be accepted for two reasons: firstly, because the strength of the theory of relevant similarities outweighs the potential disadvantage of AI becoming RH; secondly, the argument is based on inappropriately anthropocentric premises, in particular premise (3). A principled defense of the chapter that people's rights take precedence over all other possible RH rights does not seem to be possible to muster. Thus, rejecting either Wang's or Andersson's theories to avoid RHAI is unproductive. However, there is another way to avoid RHAI, which needs to be investigated.

5.4 Should RHAI be Developed?

By developing the RHAI, a new subcategory of rights holders is created – namely artificial RHs. One effect is that rights holdings are spread relative to the number of new ones RH. To the same extent as the new RH's rights are superior to existing RH's rights, they have curtailed the existing rights (compare in the next section, The theory of relevant similarities). Conflicts of rights can be of varying severity, but their occurrence is inevitable. The loss of rights for existing RHs through expansion of the category of rights holders is a sufficiently large concern to warrant re-evaluation of the benefit of developing RHAI. A hypothetical benefit of developing AI is this: tasks that humans are unwilling or unable to perform can be left to AI, which can perform the task forever. There are, of course, many more hypothetical benefits to AI than this. The argument we develop concerning AI's ability to perform (monotonous, repetitive) tasks that humans are unwilling or unable to perform can be applied to all conceivable areas of application of AI, mutatis mutandis, and further hypothetical AI abilities, therefore, need not be investigated.

AI, if developed, will become RH, which for humans gives rise to at least two problem areas. In previous sections, we have touched on the:

1. areas of use for AI are restricted as a result of RHAI's holding of rights
2. people's rights are curtailed due to rights conflicts with RHAI.

1) means that it is impossible to use AI in the areas where AI is developed. In the previous section, we argued that forcing AI to act on such premises would be immoral. It follows from two theses: AIs have rights because they are equal exemplars in relevant respects, and it is morally dubious to compel an RH to act under the will of others.38 Can the first problem be avoided? With difficulty. Later, we showed that it would be fruitless to object to AI being RH if it existed. Arguing instead that it would be morally acceptable to force any RH to act following the will of others is also not a productive solution to 1). Accepting coercion as a morally acceptable practice to induce RHAIs to act within certain (human-conceived) uses would elevate coercion to an overarching moral principle and make it acceptable to compel other RHIs to act against their will, 2) means that human RHs suffer rights conflicts with RHAI. Conflicts of rights result in a not insignificant number of human rights being subordinated to corresponding rights belonging to RHAI. It is not a desirable outcome. Can the second problem be avoided? Probably not. The only solution seems to be to introduce a hierarchy between rights holders to ensure that important human rights are not outcompeted by rights granted to AI. However, the solution is flawed, as it involves anthropocentrism, which both Andersson's theory and Wang's Definition avoid. The remaining method to avoid the loss or curtailment of human rights through rights proliferation is to accept that AI, if it existed, would be RH and, therefore, to develop an argument against creating AI. This argument assumes that the argument's conclusion for the possibility of RHAI is correct. RHtyp stands for "sub*category of the rights holder.*"

P1 All intelligent beings are RH (the argument for the possibility of RHAI)
P2 AI is developed → new *RHtyp* is created.

P3 Actual *RHtyp* is morally superior to hypothetical *RHtyp* (stipulation)
P4 σ *RHtyp* > 1 → rights conflicts between *RHtyp*
P5 Conflicts of rights should be avoided.
P6 (3) ^ (4) ^ (5) → new *RHtyp* should not be created.

C AI should not be developed. (2, 6)

Using this argument, it is possible to avoid RHAI without denying the possibility that RHAI can exist. This means that the consequences of developing AI – that AI cannot be used for the tasks it was developed to perform and that existing RH rights are curtailed – do not occur. The argument against developing AI only applies to the specific kind of creature that would be AI, according to Wang's Definition of intelligence. Such advanced programs, which in normal parlance are called "AI" and which may well be *"AI"* according to Berkeley'*s* Definition (see the section "Istvan S. N. Berkeley on W*ang's definition"), are not covered by the conclusion. Such programs can be developed without moral consequences, at least regarding rights ownership, provided that such programs do not develop into AI, as defined by Wang. The argument can lead to the question, "Should we stop having children?." The answer is no. An imp*ortant difference exists between children and RHAI concerning rights conflicts. Children do not constitute a new category of RH, as they belong to the same category as existing RH. For each RH within a category, the person concerned has the same rights as everyone else - all RHs share the same "set of rights." The rights *attached to* the category are constant regardless of the number of existing RH – all RH can claim the right. To clarify that the argument does not give reasons to stop having children, we present it below: "AI" replaced by "children,*"* mutatis mutandi*s*.

*P1 Al*l intelligent beings are RH (the argument for the possibility of RHAI)
P2 Children are born → new *RHtyp* is created.
P3 Actual *RHtyp* is morally superior to hypothetical *RHtyp* (stipulation)
P4 σ *RHtyp* > 1 → rights conflicts between *RHtyp*
P5 Conflicts of rights should be avoided.
P6 (3) ^ (4) ^ (5) → new *RHtyp* should not be created.

C Children should not be created. (2, 6)

In this version, P2 is false, so the argument fails.

6. CONCLUSION

In the chapter, we have described Wang's Definition of intelligence and its relation to the special cases of "human intelligence" and "artificial intelligen*ce." According to* Wang's *Definition, no AI curr*ently exists. We have discussed some objections to Wang's theory and shown why they are flawed, both as objections to Wang and as definitions for identifying the specific kind of AI that is of interest in delineating the beings that should be shown moral consideration. To identify whether AI deserves moral consideration, we have reviewed two moral theories: AK.M. Andersson's theory of relevant similarities and M.C. Nussbaum's Capability Theory. The purpose of investigating moral theories was to identify non-arbitrary demarcation criteria of the beings that should be shown moral consideration. We have shown that AI should be considered a rights holder (RH) in relation to relevant similarities and a moral patient (MP) in the capability theory. In the discussion of AI and moral consideration, we have emphasized the theory of relevant similarities, as it enables the discussion of rights-holding artificial intelligence (RHAI) and deals with the boundary problem without giving rise to the problem of rights diffusion. We rejected the Capability Theory concerning Artificial intelligence with Moral Patience (MPAI) because of the difficulty of avoiding the boundary problem. Against the background of the theory of relevant similarities, it is possible to identify the criteria that make a being deserving of moral consideration – an RH, in the theory's terminology. By applying the theory of relevant similarities to Wang's Definition of AI, it is possible to identify that AI, if it existed, would also be RH. An RHAI would not be a typical example of an RH but would be sufficiently similar to a typical example of a RH in relevant respects to be a RH to the same degree as any other RH. Within the theory of relevant similarities, AI would be one of two categories: RH, the other consists of the RH people. Disregarding possible RHAIs within the theory of relevant similarities, all remaining possible rights conflicts are interpersonal since all RHs are human.

Even within the capability theory, the outcome of the chapter on AI's moral patientness is that If AI were MP, it would exist. Unlike in the theory of relevant similarities, where RHAI were one of two categories of RH, the MPAI in capability theory would be a type of many MPs. The degree of consideration appropriate to show MPAI would have to be ranked hierarchically against the other MP's justified demands for consideration. Without arbitrary delineations, it is probably impossible to determine within capability theory what position MPAI would have in such a hierarchy. Disregarding possible MPAIs in capability theory, all remaining possible conflicts of interest are the sum of the conflicts between all living beings. Satisfactorily resolving conflicts of consideration is a challenge for capability theory, regardless of whether MPAI exists. However, generating additional MP is undesirable, further complicating the challenge. By combining the theory of relevant similarities with Wang's Definition of AI, we have shown that the development of AI leads to new RH and has two consequences. First, the rights of existing RHs are curtailed while their obligations increase. Second, RHAI rights limit our – human – possibilities to use AI concerning morality.

We have argued that the consequences of developing RHAI—that is, both the proliferation of rights and the limitation RHAI rights place on the purposes for which RHAI can be used—are serious enough not to develop the kind of AI that is the subject of discussion in this chapter. The rights of any RH partly depend on which other RHs exist, whose rights must be considered. By developing RHAI, existing RH – people – lose some rights without making any gains. The rights lost to human RH include at least rights regarding interaction with machines (computers), including ownership and copyright, which may consist of the right to destroy parts of or an entire machine (whether hardware or software); copyright to the algorithms that make up the AI; access to finite resources. In terms of developing AI, consider the reasons not to. The answer to the initial question is thus: since AI, if found, deserves moral consideration according to the two moral theories examined, we should not develop AI.

REFERENCES

Alanen, L. (2023). Descartes' Mind-Body Holism and the Primacy of Experience. In D. Charles (Ed.), The History of Hylomorphism: From Aristotle to Descartes (p. 0). Oxford University Press. doi:10.1093/oso/9780192897664.003.0017

Andersson, A. (2013). Choices, Interests, and Potentiality: What Distinguishes Bearers of Rights? The Journal of Value Inquiry, 47(3), *175–190. doi:10.100710790-013-93*78-9

Andersson, A.-K. M. (2014). Capacities, Potentialities, and Rights. Ethical Theory and Moral Practice, *17(4), 653–665. doi:10.100710677-013-*9463-y

Andersson, A.-K. M. (2015). Rights Bearers and Rights Functions. Philosophical Studies, 172(6), *1625–1646. doi:10.10071109*8-014-0368-y

Berkeley, I. S. N. (2020). AI: A Crowd-Sourced Criterion. A Commentary on Pei Wang's Paper "On Defining Artificial Intelligence.". Journal of Artificial Genera*l Intelligence, 11(2).*

Berkeley, I. S. N., & Rice, C. (2013). Machine Mentality? In V. C. Müller (Ed.), Philosophy and Theory of *Artificial intelligence (pp. 1–15). Springer. do*i:10.1007/978-3-642-31674-6_1

Brachman, R. J. (2006). (AA)AI More than the Sum of Its Parts. AI Magazine, 27(4), 4. *Advance onli*ne publication. doi:10.1609/aimag.v27i4.1907

Carnap, R. (1950). Logical Foundations *of Probability. Chicago Universit*y of Chicago Press.

Danziger, K. (1997). Naming the Mind: How Psychology Found its. Language. doi:10.*4135/97*81446221815

European Commision. (2020). European Parl*iament resolution of 20 October 2020 with recommendations to the Commission on a compensation scheme for artificial intelligence. European C*ommission.

European Commision. (2021). Resolution *of the European Parliament of 20 January 2021 on artificial intelligence: Questions on the interpretation and application of international law, to the extent that the EU is affected, on the civilian and military areas of use and on the powers of the state outside the states. European* Commission.

Hossain, F. (2020). Global responsibility vs. individual dreams: Addressing ethical dilemmas created by the migration of healthcare practitioners. Global *Bioethics, 31(1), 81*–89. doi:10.1080/11287462.2020.1773054 PMID:33029070

Minsky, M. L. (1991). Logical Versus Analogical or Symbolic Versus Connectionist or Neat Versus Scruffy. AI M*agazine, 12*(2*),* 2. doi:10.1609/aimag.v12i2.894

Monett, D., & Lewis, C. W. P. (2018). Getting Clarity by Defining Artificial Intelligence—A Survey. In V. C. Müller (Ed.), P*hilosophy and Theory of Artificial intelligence 2017* (pp. 212–214). Springer International Publishing. doi:10.1007/978-3-319-96448-5_21

Nussbaum, M. C. (2000). *Women and Human Development: The Capabilities Approach.* Cambridge University Press. doi:10.1017/CBO9780511841286

Nussbaum, M. C. (2006). *Frontiers of Justice: Disability, Nationality, Species Membership.* Harvard University Press. doi:10.2307/j.ctv1c7zftw

Searle, J. R. (1980). Minds, brains, and programs. *Behavioral and Brain Sciences*, *3*(3), 417–424. doi:10.1017/S0140525X00005756

Thorisson, K. R. (2019). Discretionarily Constrained Adaptation Under Insufficient Knowledge & Resources. *Journal of Artificial General Intelligence, 11*(2).

Turing, A. M. (1950). Computing Machinery and Intelligence. *Mind, 59*(October), 433–460. doi:10.1093/mind/LIX.236.433

Wang, P. (2008). What Do You Mean by. *AI, 171*, 362–373.

Wang, P. (2019). On Defining Artificial Intelligence. *Journal of Artificial General Intelligence, 10*(2), 1–37. doi:10.2478/jagi-2019-0002

Yampolskiy, R. (2020). On Defining Differences between Intelligence and Artificial Intelligence. *Journal of Artificial General Intelligence, 11*(2).

ADDITIONAL READING

Bankins, S., & Formosa, P. (2023). The Ethical Implications of Artificial intelligence (AI) For Meaningful Work. *Journal of Business Ethics, 185*(4), 725–740. doi:10.100710551-023-05339-7

Li, F., Ruijs, N., & Lu, Y. (2023). Ethics & AI: A Systematic Review of Ethical Concerns and Related Strategies for Designing with AI in Healthcare. *AI, 4*(1), 1. doi:10.3390/ai4010003

Lo Piano, S. (2020). Ethical principles in machine learning and artificial intelligence: Cases from the field and possible ways forward. *Humanities & Social Sciences Communications, 7*(1), 1. Advance online publication. doi:10.105741599-020-0501-9

Naik, N., Hameed, B. M. Z., Shetty, D. K., Swain, D., Shah, M., Paul, R., Aggarwal, K., Ibrahim, S., Patil, V., Smriti, K., Shetty, S., Rai, B. P., Chlosta, P., & Somani, B. K. (2022). Legal and Ethical Consideration in Artificial intelligence in Healthcare: Who Takes Responsibility? *Frontiers in Surgery, 9*, 862322. https://www.frontiersin.org/articles/10.3389/fsurg.2022.862322. doi:10.3389/fsurg.2022.862322 PMID:35360424

Saheb, T., Saheb, T., & Carpenter, D. O. (2021). Mapping research strands of ethics of artificial intelligence in healthcare: A bibliometric and content analysis. *Computers in Biology and Medicine, 135*, 104660. doi:10.1016/j.compbiomed.2021.104660 PMID:34346319

Siau, K., & Wang, W. (2020). Artificial intelligence (AI) Ethics: Ethics of AI and Ethical AI. *Journal of Database Management, 31*(2), 74–87. doi:10.4018/JDM.2020040105

Sun, F., & Ye, R. (2023). Moral Considerations of Artificial Intelligence. *Science & Education, 32*(1), 1–17. doi:10.100711191-021-00282-3

KEY TERMS AND DEFINITIONS

Artificial Intelligence (AI): A field of computer science and technology that focuses on developing computer systems and algorithms capable of performing tasks that typically require human intelligence, such as problem-solving, decision-making, and learning.

Benefit (in definition): The benefit criterion for defining AI involves assessing whether the definition is useful for guiding research, understanding the concept, and making informed decisions in the field.

Copyright Ownership: Refers to the legal rights held by individuals or entities over intellectual property, including creative works, inventions, or products generated by AI systems. This term is relevant in the context of determining who owns the rights to content or innovations produced by AI.

Definition of Intelligence: The concept of defining what constitutes intelligence, either in general or in the context of artificial intelligence, can vary and influence how AI systems are developed, researched, and evaluated.

Moral Consideration: The ethical assessment of whether an entity, in this case, artificial intelligence, deserves ethical consideration and moral rights, similar to how humans or animals might be entitled to certain ethical considerations.

Precision (in definition): Precision in the context of defining artificial intelligence refers to how accurately and specifically the definition captures the essence of AI, avoiding broad or vague language.

Similarity to Explicandum: A criterion used in defining terms like "artificial intelligence," which considers how closely the definition matches the concept it is intended to explain.

Simplicity (in definition): Simplicity in Definition means that the definition should be straightforward and not overly complex, making it accessible and practical for researchers, policymakers, and practitioners in the AI field.

Chapter 8
AI-Assisted Teacher Wellness: Theory and Practice

Krista Keeley
Saskatchewan Teachers' Federation, Canada

ABSTRACT

The Canadian and American teaching profession is known to be stressful, leading to burnout and other mental health issues for teachers. This chapter proposes an AI-assisted teacher wellness theory (AI TeachWell) and a supporting product/feedback/learning (PFL) framework for increased teacher well-being through the strategic use of AI chatbot technology. The theory emphasizes the use of resources that offset the demands of teaching, the importance of reducing cognitive load, and the increase of autonomy, efficacy, and relatedness. This chapter highlights the reasons that have led to increased teacher workloads, such as demands on teacher performance, administrative tasks, and professional development. It also highlights the effects of a lack of resources, time, and self-efficacy on teacher stress and burnout. The chapter concludes by offering innovative and proactive solutions for teachers to prioritize their health while fostering engaging and effective learning environments for their students, as well as the future implications of this theory.

1. INTRODUCTION

Teaching is considered one of the most stressful professions, with high levels of burnout and emotional exhaustion reported among educators (Zhang, et al., 2017). In fact, in America, a 2022 Rand study found teachers are twice as likely to experience burnout than other working adults (Steiner et al., 2022). This phenomenon is not only seen in the USA, but north of the border as well. According to a study by the Canadian Teachers' Federation (2019), 87% of Canadian teachers reported that their job is stressful, with 54% experiencing high levels of stress on a daily basis. In the United States, the National Education Association (2018) reported that 45% of teachers reported high daily stress, which is comparable to that of emergency room doctors. It is reported nearly 900,000 or one-third of American teachers are considering leaving the profession after the current school year citing low pay, unmanageable workloads, and declining mental health (Bryant et al., 2023). It is clear teachers

DOI: 10.4018/979-8-3693-0074-9.ch008

experience high levels of job-related stress, and this stress can lead to physical health problems and negative impacts on psychological well-being, including high levels of depression, anxiety, and other stress-related illnesses (Zhang et al., 2018; NIOSH, 2015). Teacher well-being is not only important to individual teachers but is positively associated with student academic achievement and engagement, teacher retention, and overall positive learning and working environments for all students and educational workers (Bettencourt et al., 2019; Learning Policy Institute, 2021). The scope of this chapter is to center the educator and focus on teacher well-being, where increased student achievement is one of many positive outcomes.

This chapter proposes an AI-Assisted Teacher Wellness Theory (AI-TeachWell) and a supporting Product/Feedback/Learning (PFL) Framework for increased teacher well-being through AI chatbot technology. This theory emphasizes the use of resources that offset the demands of teaching, the importance of reducing cognitive load, and the increase of motivation and engagement.

2. SITUATING MYSELF

As an experienced Canadian educator with over a decade of teaching in both K-12 public and higher education settings, I have witnessed and experienced firsthand the challenges teachers face in balancing workload while providing meaningful support to their students. Additionally, my previous research and Doctorate in Education focused on enhancing 21st-century learning and leadership to benefit both teachers and students. This has led me to explore the intersection of education and technology, particularly how AI chatbots can support teacher well-being. Through my research, I hope to contribute to the growing body of knowledge on the importance of teacher well-being and provide technology-driven, innovative, and proactive solutions for educators to prioritize their own health while fostering engaging and effective learning environments for their students.

3. CURRENT TRENDS IN TEACHER WELLNESS

With the K-12 teaching profession claiming the number one spot in America's highest levels of burnout in 2023 (Peck, 2023) to Canadian teachers accessing sick days at a record number, it is clear our teachers are not okay (Canadian Teachers' Federation, 2018a; Mental Health Commission of Canada, 2013). According to the President of the Montgomery County Education Association (2021), teachers in her county are "demoralized, exhausted, and desperate for relief". With these statistics, it is not surprising teachers are leaving the profession in droves. The working conditions and well-being of teachers have initiated what some call "The Great Resignation" with districts across America heavily understaffed and overworked (Walker, 2021). The factors leading teachers to burnout are complex and, in addition to working conditions, include increased pressure and scrutiny from community, district, and government, chronically low pay, and increasing safety concerns (Peck, 2023; Wilson, 2021). While all of these factors are important to discuss, teacher workload is a common denominator that can be supported through AI technologies.

3.1 Teacher Workload

According to a study conducted by the Canadian Teachers' Federation, over 50% of Canadian teachers report feeling stressed and burned out, with workload being the most commonly cited cause of stress (Canadian Teachers' Federation, 2018b; Canadian Teachers' Federation, 2018c). Similarly, 61% of American teachers reported feeling high levels of stress, and 58% said that their workload was unmanageable (American Federation of Teachers, 2017).

The intensification of teacher workload is a multifaceted issue but can be loosely broken down into the following reasons: increased demands on teacher performance; administrative tasks; and a lack of time, resources, and self-efficacy.

3.1.1 Increased Demands on Teacher Performance

One contributing factor to the mounting workload of teachers is the escalating demands placed on their performance, encompassing requirements such as standardized testing, frequent curriculum changes, and evolving expectations for teacher accountability (OECD, 2019). Over the years, educators have grappled with an incessant influx of new and short-lived initiatives, ever-changing management systems, and heightened pressure to ensure the success of all students. While this concern weighed heavily on many educators before the year 2020, the post-2020 landscape witnessed a pronounced and significant increase in the demands placed on teachers. The COVID-19 pandemic fundamentally transformed the teaching profession, often resulting in a doubling of teachers' workload (Bard, 2022). Teachers were suddenly thrust into an unprecedented shift in the way they designed and delivered content, whether through online or hybrid learning models (Bard, 2022; Hilger, 2021). It became apparent that transitioning to online education was not as straightforward as merely replicating traditional practices within an online learning management system; it necessitated a distinct skill set and instructional approach. This abrupt transition inflicted considerable additional stress on many educators. Additionally, educators were faced with the anxieties associated with the "new normal," navigating family dynamics and addressing the numerous distractions that came with at-home learning (Hilger, 2021). Consequently, teachers found themselves not only mastering new technologies and adapting their instructional practices but also creating learning environments and content that could effectively compete with the distractions of this new classroom. This has led to a notable surge in teacher burnout and a sharp decline in teacher retention rates (Peck, 2023).

3.1.2 Administrative Tasks

In today's evolving educational landscape, teachers find themselves dedicating approximately two hours a day to various administrative tasks, marking a significant shift in the demands placed on educators. This shift can be attributed to a range of factors reshaping the education system, where heightened emphasis on teacher accountability, safeguarding requirements, ongoing stakeholder communication, and personalized support for every student has become paramount (National Education Association, 2019). The weight of these administrative responsibilities has begun to take its toll on educators, with many feeling the mounting pressure and diminishing support required to navigate this ever-expanding administrative terrain (National Education Association, 2019). Among the myriad tasks added to teachers' plates, standardized testing, intensified data collection and reporting, heightened accreditation and certification prerequisites, student referral assessments, and increased communication with families all weave into the intricate fabric of educators' responsibilities. Moreover, as classroom sizes swell and student diversity becomes more pronounced, teachers must grapple with larger class sizes and students with varying learning needs. This dynamic contributes further to the surge in administrative duties, often necessitating additional time investments in crafting personalized lesson plans, reviewing educational records, and participating in meetings focusing on individual student progress, emotional well-being, behavioral issues, and language proficiency (Canadian Teachers' Federation, 2018a).

In conjunction with these growing workloads, the absence of adequate resources, time constraints, and diminished self-efficacy can all fuel teacher stress and burnout, ultimately undermining teacher well-being and negatively impacting the quality of education provided. It is imperative that educational stakeholders recognize and address these challenges to ensure that our educators remain motivated, effective, and fulfilled in their crucial roles.

3.1.3 Lack of Resources

Education in Canada and the USA is predominantly funded by state/provincial governments. In America, underfunding is a problem to the tune of 150 billion dollars per year with over 60% of schools facing funding gaps year upon year (Courtney, 2021). Many Canadian school districts are also seeing funding decreases resulting in significant cuts to student programming and resources (Hunter, 2023).

These significant and ongoing budget reductions lead to a severe lack of essential resources in classrooms. This resource deficit hinders students' ability to access quality education, particularly in high-poverty areas where it results in lower standardized test scores, increased absenteeism, grade retention, and delayed graduation. This deficiency impacts teachers who, when not adequately equipped with the tools and training needed to address diverse student needs, face increased stress and burnout. Thus, the insufficiency of classroom resources poses a formidable challenge, affecting both students and educators. Faced with this challenge, educators find themselves grappling with increased stress levels and a heightened risk of burnout, as they strive to deliver quality education amid resource constraints. Educators often need to engage in unpaid overtime to compensate for the resource deficiencies, leading once again to a decrease in wellness and an increase in burnout (Maffea, 2020; NEA, 2019).

3.1.4 Lack of Time

When the workload of teachers increases, the time required to complete their teaching responsibilities also significantly rises. Teachers often find themselves dedicating a substantial portion of their workdays to instructional tasks, with minimal compensated time allocated for preparation. On average, teachers work 52.2 hours per week, with an additional 18.7 hours outside their official working hours (Kelloway et al., 2016; Krantz-Kent, 2008). The demanding process of preparing lessons and grading typically consumes 3 to 4 hours daily. Moreover, teachers are more likely than professionals in other fields to work on Sundays (Krantz-Kent, 2008). This heightened workload not only extends the duration of their work but also makes it challenging to fit all necessary teaching and preparatory duties into a standard workday.

Teachers face a complex role that extends well beyond the traditional classroom teaching. In addition to their core responsibilities of planning, teaching, and assessing students, teachers are continually adapting to various daily challenges. These challenges include stepping in to cover classes during staffing shortages, addressing the disruptions in instruction, and providing support to students who have increasingly complex mental health needs. Beyond their regular teaching duties, teachers also spend significant time engaging in tasks such as data analysis to track student progress, caring for the overall well-being of their students, reviewing and updating curriculum materials, and participating in ongoing professional development to stay current in their field (Najarro, 2022; APA, 2017). Furthermore, many teachers voluntarily take on extracurricular activities, such as coaching sports teams, supervising clubs, offering tutoring, and participating in various student activities, further adding to their workload and responsibilities.

3.1.5 Lack of Self-Efficacy

Finally, when teachers lack self-efficacy or the belief in their own ability to achieve their goals, they may feel discouraged and overwhelmed. This can lead to a decrease in motivation and job satisfaction, as well as an increase in stress and burnout (Canadian Teachers' Federation, 2018). Teachers who do not have access to adequate resources may find it difficult to implement effective teaching practices. They may have to resort to less engaging or less effective teaching methods due to the scarcity of materials and tools. Additionally, when resources and time are at a premium, educators are often unable to access ongoing professional learning. They may struggle to keep up with best practices in education, which is crucial for their own growth and professional development. This compromises the quality of education they can provide to their students, resulting in lower levels of self-efficacy (Maffea, 2020).

Together, a lack of resources, time, and self-efficacy can create a significantly challenging work environment for teachers, which can negatively impact their wellness and ability to perform their jobs effectively. This chapter offers an AI-driven option to address these factors in order to support teacher wellness and ensure that students receive the best possible education.

4. CURRENT TRENDS OF AI IN EDUCATION

It is quickly becoming clear that artificial intelligence (AI) is reshaping education, ushering in a new era of innovation in teaching and learning. Its influence extends across diverse applications, ranging from adaptive learning platforms to virtual teaching assistants, marking a profound shift in educational approaches. This transformation is motivated by the potential to enrich educational experiences, elevate learning outcomes, and address persistent challenges ingrained in the education system (Limna et al., 2022; Boroquez & Vega, 2023).

In the ever-evolving landscape of education, educators grapple with unmet priorities in teaching and learning and actively seek technology-driven solutions. With technology rapidly advancing in everyday life, the potentially transformative power of AI is becoming more and more attractive to address these educational challenges (Limna et al., 2022; Hwang et al., 2020; Yufeia et al., 2020; Boroquez & Vega, 2023). From leveraging speech recognition for greater adaptivity to utilizing AI in lesson planning and content creation, educators are not merely consumers but integral contributors to the unfolding narrative of AI's role in reshaping educational practices (US Department of Education, 2023).

While highlighting the importance of balancing the technology and the teacher, Matthew Lynch (2017), a prominent educational writer on AI in education, suggests there are five areas in which AI can support and benefit education: Personalization, tutoring, grading, feedback on course quality, and meaningful and immediate feedback to students. Lynch (2019) offers several areas where AI is supporting teaching and learning in American and Canadian schools. These areas include classroom management, assistive technology, coding, gamification, lesson planning, diagnostics, and professional development to name a few (Limna et al., 2022; Mollick & Mollick 2023; Lynch 2017, Lynch 2019).

This outline of applications of AI in education is only scratching the surface of what is possible in this field of educational technology. It is clear, however, AI is here to stay and has the potential to support both educators and learners in more ways than we can comprehend at this moment in time. This foundational understanding of how AI can be used in education sets the stage for exploring innovative theories and applications, such as the proposed AI-Assisted Teacher Wellness (AI-TeachWell) theory. As we delve deeper into the transformative impact of AI on education, it becomes essential to not only focus on student learning but also on the well-being and support of educators. The AI-TeachWell Theory aims to leverage artificial intelligence to address the wellness crisis in education and enhance the overall well-being and effectiveness of educators.

5. AI-ASSISTED TEACHER WELLNESS THEORY (AI-TEACHWELL)

The AI-Assisted Teacher Wellness Theory (AI-TeachWell) proposes that by leveraging AI-assisted educational support within the Product/Feedback/Learning (PFL) Framework, educators can effectively mitigate some of the stress and burnout commonly encountered in their profession, ultimately promoting teacher well-being. According to this theory, the utilization of the PFL Framework facilitates the strategic reduction of work-related burdens and cognitive loads, while simultaneously increasing teachers' autonomy, efficacy, and resource accessibility. AI Chatbots, when integrated into this framework, have the potential to significantly boost teacher motivation and job satisfaction, thereby contributing to an overall enhancement of their well-being.

5.1 Product/Feedback/Learning (PFL) Framework

The Product/Feedback/Learning Framework is divided into three areas of practical AI support: Planning and content creation support, feedback and student assessment support, and targeted professional learning support.

5.1.1 Product

The *Product* pillar refers to the planning and content creation support AI Chatbots, such as ChatGPT, can offer educators. These chatbots can offer personalized assistance by analyzing student data and helping teachers create tailored lesson plans that align their curriculum with educational standards. The generation of educational content such as assignments, quizzes and worksheets, assessment exemplars, detailed examples, and success criteria can now be done through the support of chatbots. Additionally, educators who have students working on various personal educational goals can adapt lessons based on individual student progress, saving hours of differentiating for various needs. Chatbots can also analyze the content of a unit of study and recommend supplementary resources such as videos and articles. Furthermore, AI support can bridge language barriers in diverse classrooms and facilitate effective communication between educators and students, while fostering comprehension and participation. By enabling teachers to convey information clearly and students to express themselves more comfortably, these AI-driven supports create a more inclusive and equitable learning environment without adding additional work to a teacher's already busy day. Finally, AI's data-driven insights can have a transformative impact on instructional decisions. As educators gather an increasing amount of data on student performance, chatbots and other AI analytical tools can sift through this information to identify meaningful patterns and trends. These insights offer a valuable window into the effectiveness of teaching methods and curriculum materials. Educators can then make informed adjustments to their instructional strategies, tailoring their approach to better meet the specific needs and learning styles of their students. This planning and content creation support not only has the potential to contribute to a more efficient and effective use of teacher time and energy, but also enhance the quality of education.

5.1.2 Feedback

The *Feedback* pillar of the PFL Framework refers to student assessment and feedback support. Feedback, which is essential for learning and growth (Columbia University, n.d) often is laborious, tedious, and difficult to customize. When using AI chatbots, educators can more easily provide tailored, meaningful, and timely written feedback, enabling students to quickly grasp their mistakes and make necessary corrections (Lynch, 2022). Moreover, due to the reduction of human bias, chatbots excel in maintaining objective assessment standards, as they can automatically evaluate assignments and quizzes, supporting consistency in grading. In addition to supporting feedback given by the teacher, students can access chatbots on their own to seek assistance and feedback during the learning process.

Grading and assessment are significant tasks for educators that often take extreme amounts of time and energy to complete. Chatbots can efficiently manage a high volume of assessments, significantly reducing the grading workload, and allowing teachers to allocate more time and energy to other aspects of instruction and support.

It is important to bear in mind, however, that chatbots such as ChatGPT should complement the professional judgment of educators rather than replace it, with teachers continuing to play a pivotal role in interpreting results, delivering qualitative feedback, and catering to the individual needs of their students.

5.1.3 Learning

The *Learning* pillar in the PFL Framework refers to professional learning and development. Chatbots can play a significant role in supporting the professional learning of educators in several ways. Firstly, they offer personalized and on-demand assistance, allowing educators to access relevant information, resources, and best practices at their convenience, fostering a self-directed learning approach. Additionally, chatbots can provide real-time feedback and assessment of their own practice, aiding educators in critical self-reflection, identifying areas for improvement, and refining their teaching techniques. Overall, these AI-driven tools can empower educators to stay updated with the latest trends in education, enhance their instructional methods, and ultimately contribute to the continuous improvement of the education system.

5.2 Outcome

The AI-Assisted Teacher Wellness Theory, utilizing the Product/Feedback/Learning Framework, serves as a beacon of hope in a time when teacher wellness is steadily declining. Through a comprehensive approach, this theory has the potential to address various aspects crucial for enhancing teacher well-being and performance.

5.2.1 Job Resource-Demand Model

Through the lens of the Job Demands-Resources (JD-R) model, as outlined by Bakker and Demerouti (2017), AI-TeachWell acknowledges the inherent demands and pressures that teachers encounter daily. By recognizing these elements and providing AI-driven solutions, this theory equips teachers with the means to better manage their job demands and enhance their access to crucial job resources. The JD-R Model sheds light on the dynamics of the teaching profession, particularly in terms of job demands and job resources.

The JD-R Model posits that the work environment can be divided into two broad categories: job demands and job resources (Bakker & Demerouti, 2017). Job Demands are aspects of the job that require sustained effort and energy but may also have a potentially draining or stressful effect on employees. In the context of teaching, job demands can include factors like heavy workloads, time pressure, emotional demands, and interpersonal conflicts.

Job Resources are the elements of the job that help individuals achieve their work goals, reduce job demands, and stimulate personal growth and development (Bakker & Demerouti, 2017). In the teaching profession, job resources may encompass aspects like autonomy in decision-making, social support from colleagues and administrators, constructive feedback, opportunities for skill development, and a sense of meaning and purpose in one's work.

The JD-R Model suggests that job demands can lead to burnout and other negative outcomes if they are not effectively managed or compensated for by job resources. On the other hand, job resources can serve as buffers against the negative impact of job demands, promoting well-being and motivation (Bakker & Demerouti, 2017).

Teaching often comes with substantial job demands, including heavy workloads and external pressures. Teachers frequently manage multiple tasks, from lesson planning and grading to administrative duties and addressing students' diverse needs. These demands can lead to burnout and reduced well-being. AI-TeachWell acknowledges this challenge and aims to address it by harnessing AI's potential.

AI tools excel at automating administrative and time-consuming tasks, lightening the load on educators. By incorporating the PFL Framework into their daily routines, teachers can save time and cognitive resources. This increased efficiency has the potential to allow them to focus more on delivering quality education. AI chatbots can support educators by reducing the negative impact of excessive job demands.

Furthermore, AI-TeeachWell goes beyond immediate relief. It emphasizes the development of personal resources, such as skills and knowledge, through continuous professional learning. AI-driven chatbots serve as helpful companions on the path of professional development, offering tailored guidance and resources. These chatbots can recommend relevant courses, workshops, or resources, enabling teachers to improve their teaching skills and subject knowledge. In this way, AI-TeachWell addresses the challenges posed by job demands while promoting long-term well-being by encouraging continuous improvement. By using AI to facilitate professional growth, teachers can stay informed about educational trends, teaching methods, and technological advances, helping them adapt to students' changing needs and remain at the forefront of their profession.

JD-R Model's incorporation into AI-TeachWell reflects a commitment to enhancing teacher well-being by managing job demands and fostering job resources. AI plays a significant role in streamlining tasks and facilitating professional development, providing educators with support to alleviate immediate pressures and embark on a path of professional growth.

5.2.2 Self-Determination Theory

AI-TeachWell aligns with and promotes the principles of Self-Determination Theory (SDT), as proposed by Deci and Ryan (1985). SDT emphasizes the significance of autonomy, competence, and relatedness in fostering motivation and well-being, and AI-TeachWell leverages these principles to enhance the teacher experience.

Autonomy. In line with SDT's autonomy principle, AI-TeachWell recognizes that teachers' sense of autonomy in their professional roles significantly influences their motivation and overall well-being. AI technology can play a role in supporting teacher autonomy. At its core, AI-TeachWell aims to enhance teacher well-being by harnessing the power of AI to alleviate the burdensome aspects of teaching, granting educators greater autonomy over their professional development and daily tasks. The theory acknowledges that the teaching profession is complex, demanding, and multifaceted, often leaving educators feeling overwhelmed by the sheer volume of responsibilities. In addition to providing autonomy over how educators use their time, AI systems can provide them with a range of personalized learning opportunities. These may include tailored professional development courses, resources, and teaching materials. By allowing teachers to choose the most relevant and engaging options, AI-TeachWell empowers educators to take control of their own professional growth. This personalized approach not only respects their autonomy but also ensures that their development aligns with their unique interests and needs.

Competence. Competence, or the feeling of being effective and capable in one's work, is another cornerstone of SDT (Deci & Ryan, 1985). AI-TeachWell embraces this principle by leveraging AI technology to enhance teachers' competence. The theory proposes the use of AI support in various aspects of educators' practice including professional development, critical professional reflection, the creation of high-quality and curriculum-aligned content, and the confidence in expertly differentiating for students with needs.

When considering professional learning, chatbots can give professional advice, and recommend courses and resources based on teachers' existing skills and areas for improvement. Educators can use AI chatbots to assess their pedagogical skills, identify areas for improvement, and seek personalized recommendations. By providing educators with targeted learning experiences and opportunities to refine their teaching strategies, AI-TeachWell helps teachers build confidence in their professional competence. This increased sense of effectiveness can lead to heightened motivation and job satisfaction among educators.

Incorporating AI into education also revolutionizes assignment and lesson design, bolstering teacher competence. AI-TeachWell champions AI tools for personalized curriculum alignment, encompassing adaptive learning paths tailored to students' strengths and weaknesses, targeted skill development to address curriculum gaps, and diverse content resources. This empowers teachers with data-informed teaching insights, elevates their confidence in tailoring education to individual student needs, fosters student engagement, and ensures adherence to educational standards, collectively enhancing teacher competence.

In conclusion, AI-TeachWell, through the integration of AI technology, empowers educators to create assignments and lessons that are deeply aligned with the curriculum, personalized to student needs, and enriched with diverse content resources. This transformation enhances teachers' competence by providing data-informed teaching, targeted interventions, increased student engagement, and a sense of quality assurance. As educators witness the positive impact of their AI-supported efforts on student learning, their confidence in the quality of their education program is improved.

Relatedness. The third pillar of SDT, relatedness, emphasizes the importance of social connections and positive relationships in promoting well-being (Deci & Ryan, 1985). AI-TeachWell acknowledges that by reducing the workload and cognitive burden through AI support, educators gain more time and mental space to connect with their colleagues. Whether it is collaborating on lesson plans, sharing teaching strategies, or simply engaging in meaningful conversations, the theory facilitates stronger feelings of relatedness among educators. These connections foster a sense of belonging within the educational community. Teachers may no longer feel isolated or overwhelmed by their workload, but rather part of a supportive network where they can exchange ideas, seek advice, and find encouragement. This sense of belonging is essential for teachers' overall well-being, as it combats feelings of professional isolation and burnout.

In summary, AI-TeachWell aligns with SDT's principles of autonomy, competence, and relatedness by leveraging AI technology to empower educators. It respects teachers' autonomy by offering personalized learning opportunities, enhances their competence through targeted professional development, and promotes relatedness by creating opportunities for collaboration and connection. By embracing these principles, AI-TeachWell aims to boost teacher motivation, engagement, and overall well-being, ultimately leading to a more fulfilling and sustainable teaching profession.

5.2.3 Cognitive Load Theory

Lastly, Cognitive Load Theory (CLT; Sweller et al., 1998) plays a vital role in this theory, acknowledging that teaching is a cognitively demanding task. Teachers often grapple with intrinsic cognitive load, managing complex classroom dynamics, while also facing extraneous cognitive load from administrative tasks. AI-TeachWell recognizes that AI can alleviate extraneous cognitive load by streamlining administrative processes and offering user-friendly instructional materials. This reduction in cognitive load enables educators to focus on the core cognitive demands of teaching, ultimately resulting in improved student outcomes and teacher wellness. This not only benefits their instructional strategies and student outcomes but also alleviates stress and burnout, contributing significantly to their well-being.

Teaching is undeniably a cognitively demanding profession. Educators find themselves grappling with multifaceted tasks simultaneously, from managing classroom dynamics to assessing student understanding and adapting instructional strategies on the fly. This inherent complexity places a substantial cognitive load on teachers. To compound matters, they often face extraneous cognitive load resulting from administrative duties, further taxing their mental resources.

AI-TeachWell, in alignment with CLT, acknowledges that AI technology is a potent tool for reducing this extraneous cognitive load through automating routine administrative tasks, such as grading assignments, tracking student progress, managing schedules, and handling paperwork. By delegating these tasks to AI systems, educators can liberate a significant portion of their cognitive capacity. This newfound mental space allows teachers to channel their energy more effectively in the classroom, where it truly matters.

Moreover, AI-TeachWell promotes the use of AI to create user-friendly instructional materials. AI-driven content generation systems can produce visually engaging and pedagogically sound resources that are intuitive for both teachers and students. These materials significantly reduce the cognitive load associated with deciphering complex or poorly designed resources. Consequently, educators can focus on their primary task of facilitating learning rather than struggling with materials that place an undue burden on their cognitive faculties.

Additionally, AI chatbot's ability to personalize learning experiences plays an important role. By tailoring lessons to individual student needs and learning styles, AI minimizes the cognitive load associated with differentiating instruction. Teachers no longer need to grapple with the complexities of adapting materials for a diverse classroom; instead, AI handles this seamlessly.

The outcomes of reducing extraneous cognitive load are profound. Educators, unburdened by administrative tasks, become more effective in their instructional strategies and better equipped to respond to the dynamic nature of the classroom. This enhanced teaching efficacy translates into improved student outcomes as lessons are delivered with clarity and precision. Teachers also have the mental space to provide timely feedback and adapt to student needs, fostering a more productive learning environment.

Crucially, reducing cognitive load significantly contributes to teacher well-being. Educators experience less stress and burnout when they are not overwhelmed by administrative demands. This sense of wellness has a positive ripple effect, as happier and healthier teachers are better equipped to create a nurturing and productive learning environment.

AI-TeachWell leverages AI in harmony with Cognitive Load Theory to underscore the cognitive demands inherent in teaching. AI's pivotal role within this theory is to alleviate extraneous cognitive load by efficiently handling administrative tasks and providing user-friendly instructional materials. This reduction in cognitive burden empowers educators to excel in their teaching roles, benefits student learning, and enhances overall teacher wellness, embodying the collaborative potential of technology and pedagogy.

In conclusion, AI-TeachWell, in collaboration with the PFL Framework, introduces a comprehensive, forward-thinking paradigm that offers substantive support to educators facing substantial challenges. By addressing the intricate interplay of job demands and resources, harnessing the principles of autonomy, competence, and relatedness, and alleviating cognitive load, this theory empowers teachers with the tools and autonomy necessary to enhance teacher wellness.

5.4 Limitations

The evolution of AI technology is undeniable, and its presence in education is becoming increasingly prominent. However, it's crucial to acknowledge that we are still in the early stages of exploring its potential. AI is advancing rapidly, gaining more capabilities and sophistication with each passing day. This technological growth is reshaping the landscape of education, offering new opportunities and solutions to age-old challenges.

Yet, as with any transformative technology, there are potential roadblocks on the horizon. Accessibility to AI-powered tools and programs could be hindered by financial constraints or regulatory policies within the education sector. These challenges might limit the widespread adoption of AI in schools and classrooms, creating disparities in access to these innovative resources.

In this context, the proposed theory serves as a foundational framework for educators. It offers guidance on how teachers can effectively leverage generative AI technology as it continues to develop and mature. While not a one-size-fits-all solution, this theory equips educators with valuable tools to navigate their daily responsibilities, enhance their overall well-being, and ultimately improve their impact on student achievement.

It is essential to emphasize that educators are highly skilled and knowledgeable professionals. As they embrace AI tools, they must do so with a strong sense of responsibility and ethics. The theory encourages educators to use AI as a supportive instrument in their teaching toolkit, integrating it seamlessly into their pedagogical practices while upholding the principles of ethical and responsible use. By doing so, educators can harness the full potential of AI to create a more dynamic and effective learning environment for their students, while supporting their own mental wellbeing.

5.5 Ethics

The ethical dimension of AI technology is an ongoing and evolving discourse that will continue to shape the way we interact with and utilize this rapidly advancing technology, particularly in the context of AI-TeachWell. It is essential to underscore that AI is not a separate entity but rather a tool designed to augment and enhance the work of educators. Teaching is a multifaceted and deeply interpersonal profession, and teachers are seasoned professionals who bring their expertise, experience, and judgment into their classrooms each day. AI-TeachWell is conceived as a means of support, a tool that assists teachers in managing their daily responsibilities and fostering their well-being. It is not intended to replace the role of teachers but rather to complement and empower them.

The ethical considerations surrounding the use of AI within this theory are of paramount importance. When educators employ AI chatbot support, they should approach it with a critical eye and a commitment to ethical practice. This includes revising, personalizing, and fact-checking the output generated by AI models. Transparency is key, and educators should be aware of the AI's limitations and potential biases, ensuring that they maintain control over the educational content and decisions.

An illustrative example underscores the potential for AI to streamline tasks, offer valuable insights, and aid in the creation of educational materials while remaining under the ethical stewardship of educators. Even this chapter proposal was crafted with the assistance of an AI chatbot, which contributed to idea development, research, and editing. The ethical use of AI in this instance demonstrates how this technology can be effectively harnessed within the educational domain.

In sum, the ethical use of AI within AI-TeachWell embodies the collaborative partnership between educators and technology. It encourages responsible AI integration into education, emphasizing that teachers remain the ethical compass and custodians of quality in the classroom. As AI technology continues to evolve, ongoing discussions and guidelines will shape its ethical application, ensuring that it serves as a valuable tool in the hands of dedicated educators.

However, ethical concerns extend beyond the collaborative use of AI in education. Additional ethical issues include data privacy, as AI systems may process sensitive student information. Safeguarding this data necessitates robust security measures and strict adherence to privacy regulations, ensuring that students' personal information remains confidential. Moreover, plagiarism detection tools powered by AI should be employed judiciously, balancing the necessity of academic integrity with concerns about student privacy and fostering a culture of trust. Lastly, vigilance against potential biases within AI algorithms is crucial, as these systems can inadvertently perpetuate discrimination or inequity if not tested and corrected, emphasizing the need for ongoing scrutiny and transparency in AI use in these contexts.

In conclusion, addressing these ethical issues related to AI in education requires a proactive and collaborative effort involving educational institutions, AI developers, and educators. By prioritizing data privacy, academic integrity, fairness, and transparency, AI can be effectively integrated into education while upholding ethical standards and promoting trust among all stakeholders.

5.6 Implications

This chapter presents an innovative theory and framework that offers the transformative potential of AI in elevating teacher well-being through a dual mechanism: diminishing teacher workload and cognitive burden while concurrently amplifying autonomy, efficacy, relatedness, and resourcefulness. This approach represents a paradigm shift in the realm of educational technology, harnessing the power of AI to redefine and rejuvenate the teaching profession. By significantly reducing the demands placed on educators and enhancing their professional and personal resources, this theory holds the potential to support educators' well-being.

Furthermore, this theory contributes to the existing body of educational technology research. It contributes to the exploration of AI's potential in education and in this context plays a potentially critical role in sustaining teacher practice and well-being. In doing so, it bridges the gap between theoretical considerations and practical applications, offering tangible and effective solutions for teachers to enhance their well-being. By harnessing the capabilities of AI, educators can not only alleviate their work-related stressors but also harness AI as a tool for continuous improvement and professional growth.

The implications of this theory and framework resonate across multiple domains within the educational landscape. Firstly, educators stand to benefit from the potential transformation outlined in this chapter. They can anticipate a reduction in the often overwhelming workload, allowing them to focus more on the core elements of teaching and nurturing their students. The increase in autonomy and efficacy offered by AI can empower teachers to tailor their instructional approaches and strategies more effectively, ultimately enhancing the learning experiences of their students.

Secondly, educational technology developers will find in this theory a compelling vision for the future. It presents a roadmap for the development of AI-driven tools and platforms specifically designed to support and uplift teachers. By aligning their innovations with the principles outlined in this framework, developers can create AI solutions that resonate with the needs and aspirations of educators, fostering a more harmonious and productive partnership between humans and technology.

Lastly, policymakers in the realm of education should take heed of the implications of this theory. It underscores the urgent need to invest in AI-driven educational solutions that prioritize teacher well-being and, by extension, student achievement. Policymakers have the opportunity to champion initiatives that promote the responsible and ethical integration of AI into education, ensuring that its potential benefits are realized across diverse educational contexts.

In summary, this chapter's theory and framework offer a compelling vision of the future of education, where AI plays a pivotal role in enhancing teacher well-being, reducing the burden of their responsibilities, and ultimately elevating the quality of education. Its implications extend far and wide, promising positive transformations for educators, educational technology developers, and policymakers alike. As we navigate the evolving landscape of 21st century education, this theory has the potential to guide us toward a future where AI and human educators collaborate to create the optimal conditions for student learning and teacher well-being.

6. CONCLUSION

This chapter highlights the alarming trend of teacher burnout and stress in Canada and the United States (Canadian Teachers' Federation, 2018; National Education Association, 2017). Research has shown AI technology has the potential to revolutionize education by providing teachers with personalized support, freeing up their time to focus on teaching (Shah & Takayama, 2019; University of San Diego, 2023). The AI-Assisted Teacher Wellness Theory posits the integration of AI-assisted educational support can foster teacher wellness by reducing work and cognitive load while increasing autonomy, efficacy, and resources. The theory draws on the Job Demands-Resources Model (Bakker & Demerouti, 2017), Self-Determination Theory (Deci & Ryan, 1985), and Cognitive Load Theory (Sweller et al., 1998), and asserts that effective and targeted use of artificial intelligence can enhance teacher well-being.

REFERENCES

American Federation of Teachers. (2017). *Educator Quality of Worklife Survey*. AFT. https://www.aft.org/sites/default/files/edquality2017.pdf

APA. (2017). *Helping teachers manage stress*. APA. https://www.apa.org/topics/teacher-stress

Bakker, A. B., & Demerouti, E. (2017). Job demands-resources theory: Taking stock and looking forward. *Journal of Occupational Health Psychology, 22*(3), 273–285. doi:10.1037/ocp0000056 PMID:27732008

Bard, A. M. (2022). *A Qualitative Phenomenological Study of Public School Teachers' Experiences While Teaching During a Pandemic* [Thesis, University of Georgia]. All Theses and Dissertations.

Bettencourt, A., Gilman, R., Furlong, M., & Huebner, E. S. (2019). Teacher well-being: A review of the literature. *Teaching and Teacher Education, 85*, 75–86. doi:10.1016/j.tate.2019.05.007

Bojorquez, H., & Vega, M. M. (2023). The Importance of Artificial Intelligence in Education for All Students. *IDRA Newsletter, L*(5).

Bryant, J., Ram, S., Scott, D., & Williams, C. (2023, March 2). *K–12 teachers are quitting. what would make them stay?* McKinsey & Company. https://www.mckinsey.com/industries/education/our-insights/k-12-teachers-are-quitting-what-would-make-them-stay#/

Canadian Teachers' Federation. (2018a). *A survey on the status of teacher mental health in Canada*. CTF. https://www.ctf-fce.ca/en/Pages/Issues/Health-and-Safety/Mental-Health.aspx

Canadian Teachers' Federation. (2018b). *National Teacher Workload Study*. CTF. https://www.ctf-fce.ca/en/Pages/Issues/Workload/National-Teacher-Workload-Study.aspx

Canadian Teachers' Federation. (2018c). *The realities of teacher workload*. CTF. https://www.ctf-fce.ca/en/Pages/Issues/Workload.aspx

Canadian Teachers' Federation. (2019). *Teachers' mental health and well-being: A survey of Canadian teachers*. CTF. https://www.ctf-fce.ca/en/research/mental-health-and-well-being/

Columbia University. (n.d.). *Feedback for Learning*. Columbia Center for Teaching and Learning. https://ctl.columbia.edu/resources-and-technology/resources/feedback-for-learning/

Courtney, E. (2021). *Opinion: The Fundamental under-funding of Public Schools*. The Knight Crier. https://www.knightcrier.org/opinion/2021/11/14/opinion-the-fundamental-under-funding-of-public-schools/#:~:text=According%20to%20the%20Century%20Foundation,achieve%20a%20flourishing%20school%20year

Deci, E. L., & Ryan, R. M. (2000). The "what" and "why" of goal pursuits: Human needs and the self-determination of behavior. *Psychological Inquiry*, *11*(4), 227–268. doi:10.1207/S15327965PLI1104_01

Hilger, K. J., Scheibe, S., Frenzel, A. C., & Keller, M. M. (2021). Exceptional circumstances: Changes in teachers' work characteristics and well-being during COVID-19 lockdown. *School Psychology*, *36*(6), 516–532. doi:10.1037pq0000457 PMID:34766815

Hunter, A. (2023, March 28). *Education sector says Sask. K-12 budget insufficient.* CBC News. https://www.cbc.ca/news/canada/saskatchewan/education-budget-1.6792331

Kelloway, E. K., Thibault, T., & Francis, L. (2016). *(rep.). Teacher Time Use*. Nova Scotia's Teachers Union.

Krantz-Kent, R. (2008). Teachers' work patterns: When, where, and how much do U.S. teachers work? *Monthly Labor Review*.

Learning Policy Institute. (2021). *Teacher well-being: What is it and why does it matter?* Learning Policy Institute. https://learningpolicyinstitute.org/press-release/teacher-well-being-what-it-and-why-does-it-matter

Lynch, M. (2017, August 6). The benefits of Artificial Intelligence in Education. *The Edvocate*. https://www.theedadvocate.org/benefits-artificial-intelligence-education/

Lynch, M. (2019, September 9). 26 ways that Artificial Intelligence (AI) is transforming education for the better. *The Edvocate*. https://www.theedadvocate.org/26-ways-that-artificial-intelligence-ai-is-transforming-education-for-the-better/

Mental Health Commission of Canada. (2013). *Making the Case for Investing in Mental Health in Canada*. Mental Health Commission of Canada. https://www.mentalhealthcommission.ca/sites/default/files/2016-06/Investing_in_Mental_Health_FINAL_Version_ENG.pdf

MollickE.MollickL. (2023). (rep.). *Using AI to Implement Effective Teaching Strategies in Classrooms: Five Strategies, Including Prompts* (pp. 1–26). SSRN.

Montgomery County Education Association [@mceamea]. (2021, November 9). *"We don't have the time for the self-care our employer tells us to take. We normally take on extra* [image attached][Tweet]. X. https://twitter.com/mceanea?ref_src=twsrc%5Etfw%7Ctwcamp%5Etweetembed%7Ctwterm%5E1458181607756636162%7Ctwgr%5Ee7558aadbc7f678cb12248fd0f01323f05807d4c%7Ctwcon%5Es1_&ref_url=https%3A%2F%2Fwww.nea.org%2Fnea-today%2Fall-news-articles%2Fgetting-serious-about-teacher-burnout

Najarro, I. (2022, April 26). Here's how many hours a week teachers work. *Education Week*. https://www.edweek.org/teaching-learning/heres-how-many-hours-a-week-teachers-work/2022/04

National Education Association. (2017). *NEA calls for educator-led solutions to combat teacher shortage and stress*. NEA. https://www.nea.org/press-releases/2017/06/30/nea-calls-educator-led-solutions-combat-teacher-shortage-and-stress

National Education Association. (2018). *Teacher stress and health: Effects on teachers, students, and schools*. NEA. https://www.nea.org/resource-library/teacher-stress-and-health-effects-teachers-students-and-schools

National Education Association. (2019). *Time to learn: Teacher workload survey results*. NEA. https://www.nea.org/advocating-for-change/new-from-nea/time-learn-teacher-workload-survey-results

NIOSH. (2015). *Stress at work. Centers for Disease Control and Prevention*. CDC. https://www.cdc.gov/niosh/docs/99-101/

OECD. (2019). *TALIS 2018 Results* (Vol. I). Teachers and School Leaders as Lifelong Learners. doi:10.1787/1d0bc92a-

Peck, D. (2023). *Teacher burnout statistics: Why teachers quit in 2023: Devlin Peck*. Devlin Peck. https://www.devlinpeck.com/content/teacher-burnout-statistics

Shah, N., & Takayama, L. (2019). *The AI educator: Embracing artificial intelligence to transform teaching and learning*. Christensen Institute. https://www.christenseninstitute.org/wp-content/uploads/2019/01/The-AI-Educator.pdf

Steiner, E. D., Doan, S., Woo, A., Gittens, A. D., Lawrence, R. A., Berdie, L., Wolfe, R. L., Greer, L., & Schwartz, H. L. (2022, June 14). *Rates of stress among teachers and principals are running high*. RAND Corporation. https://www.rand.org/pubs/research_reports/RRA1108-4.html

Sweller, J. (1988). Cognitive load during problem solving: Effects on learning. *Cognitive Science*, *12*(2), 257–285. doi:10.120715516709cog1202_4

University of San Diego. (2023, September 28). *43 examples of Artificial Intelligence in Education*. University of San Diego. https://onlinedegrees.sandiego.edu/artificial-intelligence-education/

US Department of Education. (2023). *(rep.). Artificial Intelligence and the Future of Teaching and Learning*. US Department of Education.

Walker, T. (2021). *Getting serious about teacher Burnout*. NEA. https://www.nea.org/nea-today/all-news-articles/getting-serious-about-teacher-burnout

Wilson, J. (2021, November 3). *Record number of teachers experiencing Burnout*. Canadian Occupational Safety. https://www.thesafetymag.com/ca/topics/psychological-safety/record-number-of-teachers-experiencing-burnout/315415

Zhang, Y., Gan, Y., & Cham, H. (2017). Perfectionism, academic burnout and engagement among Chinese college students: A structural equation modeling analysis. *Personality and Individual Differences*, *104*, 91–96. doi:10.1016/j.paid.2016.07.046

Chapter 9
Harnessing AI and Big Data for Ethical and Efficient Decisions:
Making in the Political Sector

Akash Bag
https://orcid.org/0000-0001-8820-171X
Adamas University, India

Souvik Roy
Adamas University, India

ABSTRACT

Smart technologies like AI and big data have transformed decision-making. These tools are becoming increasingly popular in various businesses, but India's political sector has not used them. The previous two years have seen a pandemic that has impacted society. The chapter investigated whether AI and big data can be used in politics to make faster, more efficient, and morally acceptable decisions, and how politicians can ensure ethical use. Question: How can big data and AI help politicians make ethical decisions? Using relevant literature, the qualitative investigation found utilization, problems, ethical issues, and hazards. Semi-structured interviews with politicians and AI experts were also done to determine if the technologies may be used in politics. Before AI can support decision-making, much political data must be digitized. In conclusion, AI and big data can streamline Indian decision-making through document reading and analysis. There is no ethical framework for AI and big data utilization today, making ethical decisions impossible.

1. INTRODUCTION

A pandemic has been going on for the past two years. According to estimates, the virus has spread to 213 countries, resulting in more than five million deaths (Hiscott et al., 2020). Authorities have urged people to keep their distance, quarantine, and get vaccinated to stop the virus's spread. The pandemic has made it more difficult for organizations and companies to conduct their activities, leading to increased

DOI: 10.4018/979-8-3693-0074-9.ch009

unemployment (Galea & Abdalla, 2020). It has been required that politicians make decisions faster and more effectively to manage the pandemic and its negative effects on society (Starke & Lünich, 2020). In parallel with the pandemic, new innovative technical solutions have been developed to reduce the spread of infection. The technology giants Apple and Google have jointly developed an application that uses Artificial Intelligence (AI) and Big data, enabling mobile users to find out if they have been near someone infected with COVID-19 (Alghamdi & Alghamdi, 2022). The application uses Bluetooth contact tracing that connects to nearby Wi-Fi hubs. The application conveys information to the user that can be used to get people to reduce the spread of infection. The information can also give authorities and politicians a better basis for decision-making because it can identify where the spread of infection is greatest and develop measures and restrictions. According to Abueg et al. (2021), the application can be more effective than traditional manual infection tracing and reduce deaths, hospital visits, and infections because it increases awareness.

According to Reim et al. (2020), AI is an approach to support decision-making as it can analyze large amounts of data autonomously, faster, and more efficiently than a human. AI can also generate quantifiable information and then make recommendations, reducing uncertainty in decision-making (Giger, 2018). AI is used, for example, in healthcare to obtain diagnoses faster and more accurately and act as decision support (Socialstyrelsen, 2019). AI algorithms have become increasingly common in healthcare, and nowadays, advanced hospitals want to invest in AI solutions to increase precision and cost efficiency (Srinath P, 2022). Large amounts of unstructured data are produced and stored continuously, greatly impacting science and technology. Today's society can be seen as a Big data era because more data is available than ever. The massive amount of data brings new challenges and problems for data analysis (Fan et al., 2014). AI can be seen as a tool to facilitate the process, as it can process large amounts of data and carry out specified tasks quickly and efficiently (Jarota, 2021).

If large amounts of data are analyzed in real time, it can result in a better basis for decision-making (Raghupathi & Raghupathi, 2014). According to Jarota (2021), AI is a tool that can quickly process large amounts of data, contributing to more efficient work. There are ethical principles when implementing AI technology in the public sector, especially in decision-making. The decision-making process must also be reviewed and managed locally and internationally (Ireni-Saban & Sherman, 2021). Ireni Saban and Sherman (2022) write that there is a lack of framework for the ethical principles in AI that is flexible due to technological development. Right now, there are only legal principles that Russell (2019) has developed. There are three principles to ensure AI doesn't take over humanity. The first principle is about not allowing AI machines to be able to achieve human goals (Russell, 2019). The second principle is to program the AI not to understand what human preference means. The third and final principle is about programming AI so that what the AI thinks it is doing is human behavior (Russell, 2019).

Hauer (2022) writes that there are versions of AI ethical principles today but that it is unclear how they should be interpreted depending on the type of AI. It will thus require a complete document in which many bodies collaborate to decide how AI ethics should work (Hauer, 2022). The chapter investigated whether AI and Big data can be used in the political sector as decision support to make faster, more efficient, and ethically correct decisions and how politicians should ensure that AI and Big data are used ethically. The chapter will use relevant literature and semi-structured interviews with politicians and AI specialists to answer the following research question:

RQ 1: How can AI and Big Data be effectively utilized in the political sector for decision-making while addressing ethical considerations and ensuring ethical use?

RQ 2: What are the key challenges, requirements, and principles associated with implementing AI and Big Data in political decision-making, and how do these compare to their use in other sectors and the international context?

2. LITERATURE REVIEW

The literature chapter presents the chapter's related literature that forms the basis of the chapter. Initially, an overall description of Artificial Intelligence and Big data is given. It then explains how AI and Big data are used together and can be used to create real-time decision support. Finally, decision-making and ethics are presented, and a table with a summary of the chapter's literature.

2.1 Artificial Intelligence

According to Ertel (2018), there are many definitions of Artificial Intelligence. Hence, different definitions of AI will be presented and considered relevant to the chapter and the question. Ertel (2018) defines AI as machines that behave as if they are intelligent. In most cases, many people think AI is a robot, but that is not the whole truth. But AI can be a function in the car that causes the car to brake when the intelligent technology senses that the car would otherwise crash (Ertel, 2018). AI can attack large and small tasks in everyday life, and there is no specific area of use for AI, but it should be able to be applied to everything in the future (Ertel, 2018). Abbass (2021) defines Artificial Intelligence as a machine with a social and cognitive ability to perform competitive tasks requiring large amounts of data. According to Mueller and Massaron (2018), AI aims to simulate human intelligence. AI is based on different phases where an interaction between these is required for them to function. Targeting and data processing are used so that the AI can achieve its main purpose. Data collection is also required to identify better and understand the target. AI relies on algorithms to achieve a result that can mirror human goals and methods (Mueller & Massaron, 2021). According to Srinath (2021), AI has become important in various fields such as IT, Healthcare, and cyber security. AI has many uses; digital assistants and self-driving cars are only a small part of the main area. As technology improves, AI now has a greater opportunity to be used in non-traditional areas such as medical diagnosis (Srinath P, 2022).

AI is one of the most interesting and rapidly growing areas, according to Russell & Norvig (2021). The authors write that there are no intellectual limits to what AI can achieve in the future. AI is defined by Shi (2011) as an opportunity for employers to eliminate repetitive analysis work in the labor market by using intelligent technology that mimics human behavior. AI applies something called machine learning. This can be summarized as a scientific method that constantly focuses on how computers learn from data and aim to improve themselves (Jayatilake & Ganegoda, 2021). According to Jayatilake and Ganegoda (2021), machine learning is primarily based on data, probability and statistics. It is considered a powerful tool to strengthen decision-making. The purpose of machine learning is to increase AI's efficiency and accuracy (Jayatilake & Ganegoda, 2021). One area of machine learning is deep learning, which aims to learn patterns at a high level through hierarchical architectures (Guo et al., 2016). An example of deep learning is when self-driving cars are developed, millions of images and thousands of hours of video material are required to learn that a red light is a red light, etcetera (Rao & Frtunikj, 2018).

2.2 Big Data

Big data is a term that includes large amounts of data with a varied and complex structure. Big data has three characteristic features: Volume, Velocity, and Variety (Dash et al., 2019). Volume includes the size of the available information. Velocity is about the speed at which data is created and collected. Variety deals with structured or unstructured data (Hurwitz et al., 2013). Big data is a tool that helps organizations make decisions because large amounts of data can be analyzed in real-time (Hurwitz, 2013). Big data entails enormous amounts of data that can be used to identify patterns and relationships. The information can help companies and organizations gain a deeper understanding, which can be used to develop competitive advantages (Sagiroglu & Sinanc, 2013). Big data has revolutionized the modern world and is considered a new strategic resource and a key factor for driving innovation (Hassani & Silva, 2015). It is required that organizations develop means and tools to be able to utilize the available data. Better risk management is also enabled if Big data can be analyzed and utilized to its full potential. This allows organizations to maximize opportunities and minimize threats (Hassani & Silva, 2015).

2.3 The Collaboration of AI and Big Data

Today's digital society can be seen as a Big data era, meaning there is more available information and data than ever. Large amounts of unstructured data are produced and stored continuously, greatly impacting science and technology. The massive amount of data brings new challenges and problems for data analysis (Fan et al., 2014). A problem with Big data is the current data analysis. There are gaps when it comes to coordination and integration capabilities between databases. The process of exporting data to the correct format from other databases complicates and delays analysts' work of analysts (Labrinidis & Jagadish, 2012). AI can be seen as a tool for this because it can quickly process large amounts of data, contributing to more efficient work. The consequence is that AI can perform specified tasks (Jarota, 2021). These large amounts of data can be analyzed in real time, resulting in better decision-making . AI and Big data algorithms have become increasingly common in healthcare. These tools are used for monitoring, tracking, and measuring risks. Today, healthcare depends on data and analysis to improve medical methods and disease treatments (Srinath P, 2022). Medical researchers, doctors, and patients produce large amounts of data through electronic medical records. AI and Big data can collect, process, and provide data to the user, contributing to more efficient work in healthcare. Advanced hospitals seek AI and Big data solutions to increase precision and cost efficiency (Srinath P, 2022).

2.4 AI And Big Data's Ability To Create Decision-Making Data In Real Time

Collecting data has never been easier as we are constantly surrounded by technology that tracks behavior patterns, routines, and locations. Information Communication Technology (ICT) in the form of mobile phones has a central role in collecting data because it accompanies people daily and is necessary in today's digital society (Eagle & Greene, 2014). Mobile phones can collect data in real-time, which has resulted in application developers developing AI functions that can identify the spread of viruses (Santhana Krishnan et al., 2020). These are called exposure notices and are based on a notification system based on AI and Big data. Through contact tracing, the application can identify where the user has been and if they have been in contact with someone who carried the virus. This results in the application identifying and conveying infections to the user. The user can then utilize the information and take measures to reduce the personal spread of infection (Santhana Krishnan et al., 2020).

According to Bragazzi et al. (2020), AI and Big data can enable the monitoring of the spread of infection in real-time. Because people's movement patterns are analyzed in real-time, AI has calculated and predicted the spread of viruses (Bragazzi et al., 2020). Blue Dot is a start-up company from Canada that has developed an AI surveillance system. The System managed to identify the spread of the infection before Chinese authorities and other international institutions despite being on the other side of the globe (Bragazzi et al., 2020). Due to recent advances in computing and ICT, AI and Big data have handled large amounts of data in real-time regarding health surveillance and the spread of infection. This has resulted in better surveillance, forecasts, and situational information regarding viruses, which government institutions and organizations have used to develop measures and restrictions to reduce the spread of infection in society (Bragazzi et al., 2020).

2.5 Ethical Problems in AI And Big Data

Today, there is not much information about what AI will be capable of in the future. It will, therefore, be important for researchers and politicians to make the right decisions so that the systems function correctly and do not cause harm to others (Thompson, 2021). Thompson (2021) writes that researchers and developers of intelligent systems must understand what ethical and legal aspects are required to prevent misuse of the intelligent System. Ryan (2020) writes that it is about creating a reliable AI that can be trusted to ensure that it does as it is told. But it is also the responsibility of individuals and organizations to use Artificial Intelligence correctly to make the individuals and organizations trustworthy (Ryan, 2020). Thomsen (2019) writes that ethics for Artificial Intelligence is much more complex than ethics for humans. Thomsen (2019) also discusses four basic rules when developing AI. These are: AI must be understandable, the actions performed by an AI must be transparent, an AI must be able to explain what it is performing, and an AI must have a kill button. If these directives are followed, it is a step toward a controlled way of using AI (Thomsen, 2019).

Gunkel (2012) asks what happens if an AI makes a wrong or immoral decision and commits a crime. An example of this is when a semi-automatic robot cannon was the cause of the death of nine people in South Africa. Another example is when researchers used AI to develop drugs. During this process, the AI tool also developed several substances that can be used as chemical weapons (Urbina et al., 2022). Couzin-Frankel (2019) writes that an AI needs the right information to make the right decision, and when the AI has it, it makes the right decision faster. However, should a problem arise that the AI has no information about, it is easy for it to go wrong because it then makes its assumption based on the data the AI possesses. Because of this, it is impossible to fully trust AI today, especially in healthcare, because the wrong diagnosis can result in people risking their lives (Couzin-Frankel, 2019).

Coeckelbergh (2020) writes that AI ethics needs to be produced immediately by politicians to regulate how Artificial Intelligence can be used. Therefore, AI ethics concerns the current and near-future ethical challenges AI poses and its consequences for our society and fragile democracies. AI ethics is about people's lives and politics. It is about the moral questions we as individuals ask and which society needs to deal with (Coeckelbergh, 2020). An example is when Amazon used AI as a recruitment tool (Dastin, 2018). The tool's task was to analyze the CV to identify if a candidate should be interviewed further. It was found to prefer males over females, resulting in a greater likelihood of proceeding as a male (Dastin, 2018). Coeckelbergh (2020) writes that several institutes are working on developing AI ethics but do not know what needs to be included. What is difficult is finding a common framework for AI ethics because different countries have different perspectives on, for example, crime and punishment (Coeckelbergh, 2020).

2.6 Political Decision-Making

Decision-making in India is currently a long process that requires investigation. The investigative work varies in time depending on how comprehensive the decision is. The decisions are based on political opinions, information, and data (Huang & Peissl, 2023). The decision-making process ensures that new measures do not contribute to negative consequences. The process ends with a vote requiring a majority for the decision to go through. However, exceptions exist if a proposal must be processed quickly, for example, during a crisis or emergency. During the coronavirus pandemic, the government had the right to make quick decisions based on a pandemic law. This meant that no majority was required. The Pandemic Act aims to prevent the spread of viruses as municipalities and state administrative authorities needed effective methods to adapt restrictions quickly and accurately. This was done by limiting activities and public events to reduce the spread of infection (Starke & Lünich, 2020).

3. METHODOLOGY

The chapter aims to investigate and answer the following question: How can Big data and AI streamline politicians' decision-making while maintaining an ethical approach? To answer the question, a qualitative approach was used. A qualitative approach is a research strategy that enables an empirical basis to be compared with relevant literature (Quan-Hoang et al., 2020). The qualitative approach was identified

Table 1. Literature summary

Area	Description	References
Prediction	AI and Big Data can generate predictive predictions, such as how a virus can spread.	Bragazzi et al 2020; Krishnan et al 2020
AI and Big Data	Big data includes large amounts of data that can be used to identify patterns and relationships.	Hurwitz 2013; Sagiroglu & Sinanc, 2013; Hossein & Silva, 2015; Mueller & Massaron,
	The tools are a new strategic resource for driving innovation. Artificial intelligence (AI) is smart algorithms that require data to perform autonomous work faster and more efficiently than humans. The tool can be used to facilitate decision-making.	2018; Sirnath 2021; Abbass 2021; Ertel 2018; Jayatilake & Ganegoda, 2021; Guo et al. 2016; Rao & Frtunikj, 2018
Decision-making	The decision-making process in India today is long. During the pandemic, it has been allowed to make faster decisions because it was necessary to reduce the spread of infection.	Risk Day 2022; Government chance 2022
Ethical principles	There are different views on what needs to be considered regarding ethics in AI. Therefore, different definitions have been presented to get a broader picture of why it is a problems today.	Thompson, 2021; Ryan 2020; Thomsen 2019; Gunkel 2012; CouzinFrankel 2019; Coeckelbergh 2020

as the most relevant to answer the question. The chapter required that different perspectives needed to be investigated using semi-structured interviews. Both AI specialists and politicians were interviewed to understand politicians' decision-making process and AI specialists' views on how AI and Big data can support this process while maintaining an ethical approach. The approach also contributed to a better understanding of AI and Big data's different areas of use, what is possible to do with the tools, and how capable the tools are in politicians' daily work. To develop knowledge about the subject, a literature review was carried out. The literature review made it possible to identify how the research topic had previously been investigated and how it could be studied further. The formulation of the question was based on this and ensured that the question had not previously been investigated or answered. According to Bryman (2012), a literature review is necessary because previous theories and research in the field create a picture of what is already known. This frames and constitutes a justification for the current research question.

The semi-structured interviews were conducted using an interview guide. Semi-structured interviews were conducted because the interviewees would have various interpretations. According to Bryman (2012), semi-structured interviews aim to collect rich and detailed responses that can later be analyzed for a deeper understanding. The interview guide contributed to creating a dialogue, not a monologue, which meant that follow-up questions could be asked during the interviews. Another advantage of semi-structured interviews is that they generated better knowledge about the ethical risks and challenges of using AI and Big data as decision-makers. Hence, the AI specialists' perspective on the tools' potential in decision-making was also needed. The analysis of the empirical material was carried out using a thematic analysis. The analysis method facilitated analyzing and describing the themes identified in the empirical material. It was important to analyze the empirical material to bring out important elements from the empirical evidence. The analysis also made it possible to identify similarities and differences between the literature and the empirical work.

To collect the empirical data, six semi-structured interviews were conducted. These were done via digital communication applications such as Microsoft Teams and Zoom. The interviews resulted in the sample gaining greater flexibility and being able to contribute even though they were in different locations. The interviews using communication applications were also considered to save time because less travel was conducted. Semi-structured interviews are a condition where the interviewer uses a set of questions from a questionnaire (Bryman, 2012). The order of the questions varied, and the wording was more open, allowing the interviewer to ask follow-up questions. This aims to collect full and detailed responses that can later be analyzed for a deeper understanding (Bryman, 2012). Negative factors with semi-structured interviews were that they required more time and resources than other data collection methods. The transcription and interviews are time-consuming, and it can also be difficult to identify relevant respondents who can contribute to the research (Bryman, 2012). The data collection method has helped to answer the chapter's question because the respondents were able to contribute qualitative data that could be analyzed and compared with previous research.

A self-developed interview guide was used to maintain order and structure when conducting the interviews. Since interviews were conducted with politicians and AI specialists, two different interview guides were developed. Before conducting the interviews, the interview guide and its questions were sent to the respondents to ensure they understood them. This led to the respondents being able to prepare and answer in more detail. The interviews began with closed questions and dealt with how long the respondents had been active in their professional roles. This gave us a good picture of their experience and ensured the respondents could contribute to the chapter. The remaining questions were open-ended to generate spontaneous answers and not lead the respondent down any path. The open questions were divided into different themes: decision-making, AI, Big data, knowledge, ethical principles, and prediction.

This generated a better understanding of how the current decision-making is based and carried out. Within the AI and Big data theme, answers emerged regarding respondents' relationship with the subject and whether they had previously used the tools to make decisions. The theme of ethical principles highlighted what risks and changes the introduction of AI and Big data can result in for politics. Knowledge and the opportunity to develop it was considered a reason AI and Big data can be problematic in politics. Once we had received an answer, it was possible to identify how politicians can develop skills and prepare for using the tools. At the end of the interviews, a final question was asked where the respondents could add or link back to previous questions if they felt something was missing. The interviews were recorded after we received approval from the respondents. This was done with the help of an audio recorder on a mobile phone. The recordings of the interviews ensured that we did not miss important information that emerged during the interview. The recordings also meant that notes could be excluded, which resulted in the respondent being in the center during the interview.

In the chapter, purposive sampling was used to identify relevant people to get an answer to the research question (Bryman, 2012). The targeted selection was necessary as the participation of specific people was required for the chapter to be relevant. The selection was based on identifying politicians and AI specialists to get two different points of view on how they think AI and Big data can benefit decision-making. Another selection criterion was that the politicians should connect to IT or AI and that the specialists be connected to AI or Big data. The politicians' connection to IT or AI was important in being able to answer the interview questions. This is also why two interview guides have been produced, one for politicians and one for specialists. It has been carried out because the politicians do not have the knowledge to answer the specialists' questions and, on the contrary, to generate relevant answers. The requirement for the politicians was that they must have been active for at least one term as a member of one of the municipality's committees to have the experience to answer the questions. The requirement for the specialists was that they have competence in AI and Big data. Politicians have good knowledge of the social structure and how decisions positively and negatively affect people.

The politicians also had good insight into how decision-making processes work and could contribute to answering the research question. The AI specialists had good knowledge of the underlying functionality regarding how AI and Big data are structured and work. They also knew what the tools could do and how they could be used to make quick and effective decisions. Combining these respondents was considered optimal because they complement each other adequately. A search was conducted on various colleges and universities' websites to identify the interviewees with keywords such as AI and Artificial Intelligence. People who appeared to be interested in the chapter were then contacted via email. Searches were also conducted via Linkedin to find AI researchers, and people who matched the selection requirements were contacted via the platform. The politicians were contacted via email, and those with a background in IT were prioritized as it was considered most relevant to be able to answer the interview questions. It was a challenge to find AI specialists and politicians who wanted to come forward because few people who were contacted responded via email, which meant that it took longer than expected to find respondents. Fifty-four emails or messages were sent to the respondents and only six of those who answered wanted to be interviewed. Five more people responded who did not have time or were interested in running.

Table 2. Respondents

Respondent	Profession	Roll	Interviews
Respondent A	Politician	Chairman of the municipality	45 min
Respondent B	Politician	Political Coordinator	30 min
Respondent C	Politician	Member of Parliament	17 min
Respondent D	AI researchers	Research engineer in Machine Learning and Artificial intelligence	34 min
Respondent E	Works in the field of AI and Machine Learning	Consultative	25 min
Respondent F	Researchers in informatics	Docent i informatik och Design director	35 min

4. RESULTS

The empirical material will be presented in the results part of the chapter. It will be based on four themes divided according to the interview guide. These themes are decision-making, AI and Big data, Prediction, and Ethical principles. These themes will also be used as subheadings in the results section to present the empirical material.

4.1 Decision Making

The first question asked to the politician respondents was how do you make decisions today? Respondents A, B, and C, who are all active in the political sector, described their decision-making process similarly, even though they work in different municipalities in India. Respondents A, B, and C described that the process in terms of decision-making is long, and the processes go through many steps before the decision is made. Before the proposal comes to the negotiating table, officials investigate whether the proposal is feasible. Respondent B describes the process as "*quite blunt, and it takes a long time*" because the documents received vary in size. Sometimes, it can correspond to five pages; sometimes, it can be up to 500. Respondent C confirms that the process takes a long time but must ensure the right decision is made. When asked, "*What kind of information is used today when basing a decision?*" Respondent A gave the following description through an example: "*For example, a few years ago, when we changed the parking hourly fee for parking lots in the city. Then it was done with some input values if we want to achieve, for example, a certain rotation of the locations when all the stores are in town, and then digital data is used.*" - Respondent A

Respondent A goes on to say that the basis used when the hourly parking fee is to be changed mainly via the applications that are used today. This is because Respondent A can then see exactly how long each car has been parked in the city, and it becomes more accurate data, unlike how it looked in the past. Respondent A also says that they use research into what makes a city center attractive. Respondent B mentions an example where they did a location investigation on where it would be possible to build new parking spaces. Partly to find out where it would be possible to build parking spaces and identify compensatory measures for why the municipality should not build any parking spaces. Respondent A says they have an internal data warehouse in the municipality for decision-making and the basis for decisions. In these layers, the municipality can see, for example, population forecasts in different city districts. Respondent A says it can also be a disadvantage to use the forecasts as they can be interpreted as facts, but it is just a guess.

Respondent B explains that an application is used as a tool in decision-making. The employees use an input system to enter data and values later reported to the application. "*The application makes it easier to make decisions because the data and values are compiled.*" - Respondent B.

Respondent B says this works much better than the previous System when the municipality used physical binders. Respondent A thinks that the data they have today is good but that many parts of the municipality must be digitized because the warehouse with data is the only tool the municipalities use now. Respondent D confirms this by saying that today's data is often not representative and does not reflect reality. The respondent believes the collected data today often represents the wealthier part of society, which can be misleading. When asked, "*Do you think AI will change decision-making in politics in the future?*" responds Respondent B, "*Yes, it's a rather outdated thing we agree with, and that is the best way to choose a bunch of people who will represent one's opinion. Thinking with AI maybe you can get a direct democratic control over society.*" - Respondent B

Respondent D says that when it comes to decision-making, politicians and other decision-making bodies want to have a good picture of what is happening, and then it can be good to have a summary of texts or to find texts that are relevant to the decision to be made. This is something that AI can help with today. Respondent D tells us that today, we do not have enough data to automate the process to make major decisions. Respondent D also believes that it is possible to make decisions in certain areas with the help of AI, where there is a lot of data. But right now, there are no models to be able to make decisions on each issue as different models are required for different issues. Respondent F says that AI can become a tool for politicians, decision support, and politicians can act more data-driven. Politicians can also use smart design to visualize complex effects that can arise with the help of large collections of data. Respondent F expresses that AI can help build digital services for citizens and be able to analyze how these are used. Politicians can use AI daily to understand better what affects society. Respondent F also mentions that citizens can micro-vote on various issues instead of just voting for a political party every four years. This means that citizens have a greater influence on democracy. Respondent A wants a good business intelligence system that helps analyze data in the municipality. However, there is insufficient master data to implement such a system today.

4.2 AI and Big Data

Respondent D mentions as an example that people who handle and write texts will most likely use AI to summarize texts and help write texts. However, in service professions that deal with the meeting between people, it will take some time before AI is implemented. Respondent E also believes that AI will partly replace professional groups in the accounting sector and the legal sector in terms of automated document reading. When asked, "*In what way can AI be used for decision-making in politics?*" Respondent A said there is great potential in using AI as a tool, but things must be addressed before it can be fully used. Respondent D agrees with this as he believes that AI can become a big problem and that there are big risks with the tool as it is very powerful, and if used incorrectly, it can have unwanted consequences. Respondent D means that more investment will be needed in the security aspect of AI. According to Respondent D, the big security problem is that there is no limit to how powerful AI can become, and today, there is no safe way to handle it. This is something that Respondent F agrees with, as cyber-attacks have increased by 600% in the form of information manipulation and other types of disinformation. What scares Respondent F is that there is research showing that people trust an AI-generated image more than an image taken by a human. Respondent F asks, "*Will we trust AI more than our real politicians?*" This will affect citizens greatly, and it is something that politicians have to deal with when it comes to laws and regulations on what AI can be used for.

Respondent B tells us that AI could have facilitated decision-making, especially in producing soft values. She believes that today when a municipality makes a decision, there are no direct consequences. Respondent F believes there is a great opportunity and improvement potential within politics to use AI to do faster and more efficient data analyses. What Respondent F lacks today are radical ideas that "*take us from here and 200 years into the future.*" The respondent expresses that people often tend to look backward, and what was relevant in the past is irrelevant today. "*How do we create a new narrative that points forward 200 years of innovation rather than looking back at a 200-year gamma idea? That's one of the problems which we are facing now. Now, pandemics, cyber-attacks, and climate change are on the agenda, and they were not on the map 200 years ago. We need someone who formulates ideas, takes the facts of the here and now, and looks ahead.*" - Respondent F. Respondent E believes that an MP's closest relationship to AI will be establishing laws and regulations to produce ethically based laws and regulations to be applied to AI instead of being used by politicians. Respondent B agrees with Respondent E as he thinks technology trumps politics and that technical solutions come before politics. Even if politicians talk about saving the environment, technology does it and therefore needs frameworks and laws for what should be possible to do with AI as a tool. Respondent D says in one example that companies that produce more can obtain better decision-making data with the help of AI and, in the future, also help managers produce more monetary value.

4.3 Ethical Principles

When asked, "*Do you see any ethical problem with using AI and Big data in decision-making in politics?*" tells Respondent A that there will always be ethical decisions with making decisions with AI and that he likes that it is possible to calculate anything about a human if all the information is available. However, this means that the municipality has all the information about that person, and certain individuals may dislike this. When AI and Big data are used, large amounts of data must be collected on the behavior of individuals without the AI taking ethical principles into account. Respondent B agrees and believes that there are people behind all numbers, and the risk is that these are not visible and become an anonymous mass. Respondent B also says that it is not considered that actual lives are affected and asks: "*How much are people prepared to give up their privacy?*". Respondent D says that a common agreement is needed worldwide to take it easy with these technologies to avoid an unstable situation that makes it harder for humans to keep up. There is another problem, according to Respondent D, which is that the data you get from analyzing with AI can vary a lot due to small differences in the data you feed into the AI. There is no understanding of why this happens today, so the answers can be wrong, even if the data is slightly different.

But Respondent D believes that even if there will be risks with using AI in politics, it will be used for decision-making; it's only a matter of time. Respondent E takes a different view of the ethical problem, identifying AI in politics as an ethical problem because parties can use it to divide people into voter groups, allowing them to send targeted advertising in the form of disinformation. Respondent E believes that AI and politics have no clear connection except that AI can be effective and sometimes dangerous when influencing people. The respondent sees it as a major ethical problem. Respondent F agrees and says this is something we already see in society today. Respondent B also points out an ethical problem that can arise when politicians decide according to what an AI has made calculations on and then fail. Respondent B asked himself, "Who will be held responsible for making *a mistake?*" Respondent B believes that it will always require people to make decisions. Respondent D says there are several examples of when AI has not acted ethically, has acted sexist towards women, and started producing dangerous substances that could have harmed people. Respondent D means that AI is a powerful tool, and it is often difficult to get all the parameters that make the AI act ethically, which is a big challenge today. Respondent F also raises examples of where AI has not acted ethically when systematic racism was discovered during recruitment. This, Respondent F means, has nothing to do with the people who program the AI but that it is the historical data that makes it act racist because society looks the way it does.

Respondent A says in an example, "*System that put automatic food vouchers in all schools and based on several parameters such as student composition, gender, educational background of the students, what their ethnic background was, how much food was thrown away every day, etc. It is clear that then the AI can conclude that the absolute best way to serve food at school is falu sausage seasoned with curry for the least wasted. But that doesn't take vegetarians or other parameters into account. So you always have to include ethics and control the AI.*" - Respondent A

4.4 Prediction

When asked, "*How do you think AI will be used in politics in the future?*" informs Respondent A that AI should be able to be used to make decisions within India and the municipality if there is enough data to make the optimal decision. Respondents A, B, and C would have liked to see that AI is used to create forecasts about, for example, segregation in a city and how it can be prevented. What could become a problem with AI, according to Respondent A, is if it indicates that something is the best option that the politicians do not agree with, and they have to defend themselves against the computer. Respondent A also believes AI will be used for painting different scenarios to choose from and testing politicians' ideas. This is confirmed by Respondent F, who tells us that AI can be a tool for politicians to use as decision support and to visualize complex problems if there is a large data collection.

Respondent D says that AI is constantly developing and that if an AI has been trained on a lot of the same data, it will be easier to analyze the data later, even if only a small amount of data has to be analyzed. But Respondents D and F fear that the AI will be used to persuade people and therefore feed data into the AI supporting their political opinion. Respondent A says it works with a Robotic Process Automation (RPA) that helps the municipality accept or reject various forms, especially in elderly care. That is the only thing the municipalities are allowed to do at the moment, but a change in the law is underway so that municipalities can implement automated decisions. Respondent A says the dream is to send data into a system and then get an answer on what happens if different decisions are made. However, it will be extremely clinical in politics and not so much opinion. However, Respondent D believes that prediction with the help of AI works relatively poorly in most cases right now and that it needs a lot of work if they are to work. It is also something that Respondent F agrees with and says that if you are going to predict politics today, large amounts of data are needed to carry out a prediction. It is also a complicated AI model that must be used to work.

To the question, "*Do you think, for example, that a pandemic in the world could have been stopped with the help of AI? If politicians had made decisions based on AI scenarios?*" Respondent A tells us that if AI had been a factor in the coronavirus pandemic, it would have been possible to make faster and more efficient decisions. However, the downside is that it can go wrong and have the opposite effect when there is insufficient data. Respondent D also says there are problems today with making decisions with AI, as the data you get from AI can vary greatly due to small differences, which can lead to incorrect answers. Respondent B also believes that AI could have been a tool to facilitate the decision-making process during the coronavirus pandemic. Respondent C also agrees but says, "*Just because politicians make quick decisions, it does not always result in less spread of infection. It is first and foremost people's responsibility to follow the restrictions and laws introduced, which is considered the key factor for reducing the spread of infection.*"Respondent E also confirms this, as he believes AI can provide a basis for making future decisions about restrictions and public health measures. AI will then be a tool to produce different types of simulations to give a good estimate. Respondent F says that viruses have chaotic behavior, meaning a virus is extremely difficult to predict. However, it will be useful to be able to do a data analysis to be able to track and follow up on the virus.

"*But that AI can magically predict in June next year when a virus of a certain kind will come and it will affect us in this or that way, it will never be that simple.*" -Respondent F. Respondent D believes that AI today is unnecessary to use to calculate how it can stop the spread of infection and outbreaks. She believes instead that it is possible to use simple mathematical models, but if they are too simple, it is easy for them to be models that are not representative of society. This is because nothing before in modern times has resembled COVID-19, so there is not enough data to make such calculations. Respondent F says that AI can slow down a pandemic and has been very important during the pandemic. Without these analysis tools, the pandemic would have been much more catastrophic. Respondent A says AI should have reduced the spread of infection and exposure to COVID-19. "*It looks like you can key in that this has now happened, and then AI should be able just to collect everything that exists about all pandemics ever and all bacteria and viruses as well as calculate quite precisely how it will go and what measures would be needed to be sharp about this and not just shut down the whole world.*" - Respondent A Respondent B mentions the Indian debate that was going on about mouth protection, "*first we would have it and then not, would it have mattered if an Al had recommended people to use it?.*" - Respondent B. Respondent B also believes that AI could have been a tool to facilitate the decision-making process and make faster decisions.

5. ANALYSIS

In the analysis part, the thematic analysis results are analyzed and presented. The underlying headings correspond to the various themes identified with the help of the empirical data. The various themes are as follows: Dependence on data for effective decision-making, AI and Big data's consideration of ethics, and the potential of the tools in decision-making.

5.1 Dependence on Data for Effective Decision-Making

The respondents generally agree that an informative database is required to be able to make decisions. Data is an important key factor in strengthening and streamlining the decision-making process. The respondents have explained scenarios where data has been a driving force for implementing changes within municipalities. The decision-making process within municipalities is also based on people's opinions and pure opinion, which the respondents describe as politicians' right to think and express themselves freely, even if it contradicts research or data. The respondents also explain that decisions cannot only be based on data because the individuals behind the numbers are not visible but become an anonymous mass; behind these are people whose lives are affected. What can then become an ethical problem with AI as a decision-maker is that it only sees numbers and not people. Each question is different, which affects decision-making, and no data or model can be the basis for all questions. People's values will always play a big role in what should be done and not done. Politicians have access to large amounts of data within municipalities used for decision-making purposes, but much of the existing data has not yet been digitized. An interviewed respondent explained that one-third of all available data in the municipality is digitized, meaning two-thirds still have not yet been digitized.

This creates problems because the data in physical form is not used to the same extent as the digitized one. The non-digitized data is also not in real-time, which makes it difficult to use AI in decision-making. The respondents with in-depth AI knowledge explained that it is possible to make decisions with AI if there is enough data. Since much of the municipalities' data is not digitized, it must be digitized so that an AI tool can be used to its full potential and contribute to profitability. Today, there is not enough data to automate large decision-making processes. The respondents described the decision-making process as long and time-consuming. The documents received consist of compiled data in the form of forecasts. These are crucial to know if the proposal is feasible or not. The forecasts can vary in size, sometimes corresponding to up to 500 pages of text. According to the respondents, reading and analyzing the forecasts is time-consuming, one reason the decision-making process takes a long time. The respondents describe that AI today can summarize and analyze large amounts of text, which can be relevant to decision-making because the process is faster. The respondents also agreed with this and explained that if large amounts of data could be analyzed more quickly, it would have facilitated and made the decision-making process more efficient. According to the respondents, some risks could arise if the decision-making process becomes too efficient. The decision-maker's decisions can negatively impact people, which can be more difficult to remember when a decision has to be made quickly and efficiently. Therefore, the data held by municipalities must be updated and digitized to ensure that it reflects society. According to the respondents, informal and representative data can make the decision-making process more efficient, but municipalities currently do not have that option.

5.2 AI and Big Data's Consideration of Ethics

The respondents were concerned that introducing AI and Big data can bring about consequences in politics. AI can be a very powerful tool, and it cannot be easy to get it to apply all the parameters so that it acts ethically. What is considered ethically correct today may not be ethically correct in the future. It will always be a challenge for humans to keep AI tools up to date with that information so that no human suffers harm. Respondents agreed that there are risks with the information collected using the tools. AI and Big data can damage people's integrity because personal data and information are stored in municipal databases. Another recurring pattern in the thematic analysis was that AI can be used for the wrong purpose. Data manipulation is also a risk that can spread false information and data being manipulated to strengthen the views of different parties, which can impact democracy and how decision-making is based. This can be, for example, when advertising campaigns with disinformation are carried out to disparage other parties. It is also a big question if the tools will be used objectively; this can result in it being difficult to know what is right and wrong.

Just because AI is used does not mean incorrect and bad decisions are eliminated. Respondents argue that more investment in security is required for AI to ensure that the decisions do not contribute to a larger negative impact. Mutual agreements should be made so that a situation does not arise that results in a poorer understanding of people. It should also be clear who is responsible if the AI makes the wrong decision. Respondents agree that no matter how good AI is or will be in the future, humans will always need to oversee the decision-making process. As politicians engage with AI and Big data issues, their closest relationship to the tools will be establishing laws, regulations, and frameworks that ensure people are not adversely affected by their use. Technology development is often faster than politics, which is another reason frameworks and laws are required for the tools. The development of AI is fast; if it is implemented and combined with politics in the wrong way, it can be a dangerous tool that contradicts ethical principles. The respondents mention examples when AI has been sexist and led to people being hurt; this is a clear example of when people have not considered the consequences that AI can bring.

5.3 The Tools' Potential in Decision-Making

In the thematic analysis, it also emerged that there is great potential for using the tools within the political sector. The respondents explain that the tools could have contributed to faster decisions because analyzing large amounts of data could have been made more efficient. It is mainly the analysis process that could have been made more efficient today through document reading, according to the respondents. This allowed sorting the data and identifying causal relationships, facilitating decision-making. According to the respondents, AI can aid by analyzing large amounts of data that can be used to strengthen and streamline the decision-making process, for example, by creating different simulations for the spread of infection, which can result in a good estimate of how a virus spreads throughout society. This is considered to provide a basis for introducing restrictions and health measures. However, it can contribute to the opposite effect if there is not enough data available; decision-making with AI can vary due to small variables. If these variables are not considered, it can result in the collected information leading to poor or incorrect decisions. As these variables contain several parameters, ensuring they apply an ethical approach is difficult. Ethics change over time, and there is a risk that people will be negatively affected by decisions based solely on tools. A pattern also identified was that restrictions and recommendations based on data do not result in less spread of infection.

First and foremost, people's responsibility contributes to a reduced spread of infection. There are mathematical models that AI can apply to calculate the spread of infection with an ethical approach, but they are not representative of society. Since nothing in modern times resembled the COVID-19 outbreak, there was not enough data at the beginning of the pandemic, and an AI is fully dependent on data to act as a decision support. If a new virus or a pandemic had characterized the world, there are now large amounts of data that AI could have used to reduce the spread of infection. However, it is required that the collected data is representative and reflects reality, which is difficult because it is often wealthier parts of the world that can compile these amounts of data. Poorer parts of the world do not have the same opportunities, meaning the data can contribute misleading information. The respondents also explain that just because an AI had recommended and developed new restrictions, it is not certain that humans would have followed them. Ultimately, it will always be a human factor that ensures that decisions apply an ethical approach and determines what measures and restrictions are introduced; these can be supported with the help of AI and Big data if there are large amounts of representative data as a basis for decisions.

6. DISCUSSION

The discussion will address the chapter's results and analysis and connect this to the literature in the chapter. This will form the basis of the chapter's conclusions and provide an increased understanding to the reader.

6.1 Decision Making

The chapter aimed to investigate and determine if AI and Big data can be used in the political sector as decision support to make faster and more efficient ethically correct decisions and how politicians should ensure that AI and Big data are used ethically. When it comes to municipalities in India, they are faced with several challenges to be able to use the tools as decision support in an effective way. First of all, it is required that municipalities digitize themselves further so that more data is available for the AI tool. Previous research has identified problems when using AI with insufficient data. Couzin-Frankel (2019) writes that the right information and data are needed to make a decision that aligns with reality. It is something that the result also highlights, as there is currently not enough data to use AI to that extent. Couzin-Frankel (2019) writes that it can easily go wrong if the right data is unavailable as the AI assumes the available data, contributing to the AI making an incorrect decision. Therefore, It is impossible to trust Artificial Intelligence today as there is insufficient data. It turns out in the results that AI does not necessarily need to be a tool for making decisions but more like a support for decisions to be able to set up different scenarios. It's about seeing what would happen if, for example, you raised the price of parking in the inner city. The non-digitized data available today is not always in real-time, which makes the use of AI difficult as digitized data is something that AI requires to be able to analyze better and make precise decisions (Xu et al., 2021). However, the result showed that it does not necessarily have to be real-time data but that it gives a better result; as long as there is enough data about an individual question, a relatively good decision can be made.

Earlier in the literature, it has emerged that AI and Big data can enable the monitoring of the spread of infection in real-time, and according to Bragazzi et al. (2020), government institutions have been able to use information to develop measures and restrictions. The result emerged that just because an AI recommends and produces restrictions to authorities does not mean that humans follow or implement them. Politicians sometimes have to defy the data and consider the people behind the numbers because there is a risk that their lives will be affected. The data must be representative and reflect reality. Otherwise, these people risk being negatively affected. According to Labirindis and Jagadis (2012), data that have flaws can complicate and delay data analysis. Suppose the data that forms the basis for decisions has flaws and is not representative. In that case, there is a risk that the introduced measures and recommendations contribute to the opposite effect, in the form of more sick people and more deaths, which could have meant disaster (Labrinidis & Jagadish, 2012). The results showed that decision-making takes a long time because much data must be analyzed. AI can be an approach to support decision-making as it can analyze large amounts of data autonomously and faster than a human (Reim et al., 2020). According to Jarota (2021), AI is a tool that quickly processes large amounts of data, contributing By streamlining the decision-making process, the political sector can introduce restrictions and measures more quickly, impacting the spread of infection and resulting in fewer sick people. AI and Big data are today considered key factors in driving innovation, and it is required that authorities develop means to be able to utilize it to its full potential (Hassani & Silva, 2015). If AI and Big data are used in politics, better risk management can be implemented, which can be a key factor in managing a pandemic.

6.2 Ethics

The result shows that ethics needs to be considered with caution when it comes to AI and that it is easy to get it wrong. It is about valuing people's integrity and the damage it can do to people and democracy. According to Coeckelbergh (2020), AI ethics is something that politicians must begin to produce to regulate how it can be used. AI ethics is a development happening quickly, with many ethical challenges. Without AI ethics, they can mean that it has consequences for society and democracy (Coeckelbergh, 2020). It is also something that the results show, as AI is a powerful tool that is in constant development, which makes it difficult to set up a framework. It will require politicians to establish laws and regulations not to lose control over the powerful tool AI. The result also shows concern about what AI can do in the future, such as manipulating people to vote for a certain party. Therefore, the biggest challenge today is the safety of using AI. According to Thompson (2021), it will be required that politicians should make decisions that strengthen the security and use of AI.

Coeckelbergh (2020) writes that there are institutes today working on producing a document for AI ethics, but they do not know what needs to be considered. Finding a common framework for AI ethics is difficult because countries see laws and regulations differently, such as crimes and punishments. The result also confirms this as a joint agreement will be required to reduce the development of AI because it is fast, and new ways of using AI are constantly emerging. Several examples from the literature show that AI has been used unethically (Dastin, 2018; Gunkel, 2012; Urbina et al., 2022). The results also reveal examples of when AI has acted unethically and almost become a danger to humanity. According to Thompson (2021), there is not much information today about what AI will be capable of in the future. The result also shows that it is currently not possible to know which professional groups will use AI but that it will, in the long run, be used in all areas in the future. Thompson (2021) also writes that it will be important that researchers and politicians make the right decisions so that AI systems work correctly and do not cause harm to people. It will then be required that researchers and developers jointly understand which ethical and legal aspects will be required to reduce the abuse of intelligent systems. According to Thomsen (2019), formulating ethics for AI is much more complex than for humans. The result has shown that it is impossible to acquire a framework today and believe it will apply forever and is more complex than many think. Since AI is constantly developing, there are always new areas of use for AI. Therefore, a constant development of frameworks is required. The result also shows that keeping the AI tools current will be challenging. Today, there is too little information about what AI is capable of, and it won't be easy to find a framework that includes all the elements to act ethically.

7. CONCLUSION

The chapter's conclusion will answer the question with the help of the discussion chapter above. A conclusion is drawn based on a sustainability perspective, and suggestions for future research for AI in politics will also be given. The chapter aimed to answer the question, "*How can Big data and AI streamline politicians' decision-making while maintaining an ethical approach?*" AI has a variety of definitions, but the general meaning is that AI is advanced algorithms used today as digital assistants or self-driving cars. The chapter's conclusion has generated new knowledge contributions for politicians and AI researchers. Partly by politicians and researchers gaining a better understanding of what can be done to ensure that the development of AI does not go in an unethical direction. But also how the tools can be an aid to streamline decision-making in the political sector. It will require cooperation between countries, politicians, researchers, and developers to create common agreements and a framework for what AI may be used for and how AI ethics should be presented.

To answer the question "How can Big Data and AI streamline politicians' decision-making while maintaining an ethical approach?" can politicians use AI and Big Data to streamline decision-making in India? The problem today is that no ethical frameworks exist for using AI and Big data in decision-making. AI and Big data will primarily be used for document reading and analysis to simplify it for politicians, where 500 pages of text can be summarized in five pages. Document reading can then contribute to more efficient decisions because politicians do not have to read long documents, which reduces the lead time to decisions. Suppose the decision-making process and lead time are shorter. In that case, a country can decide on restrictions and recommendations more quickly and efficiently in a pandemic and slow the development of a virus. However, using AI as a basis for decision-making in politics is far ahead of the time as the municipalities today have not digitized enough data, and no laws support automated decision-making processes. The societal problem that can arise with AI is that politics becomes clinical and not much personal opinion for parties.

For politicians to ensure an ethical approach when decision-making is carried out with AI and Big data, an ethical framework for AI is required. We therefore believe that an international organization should be created that only works to create frameworks and update them continuously. This is because it will require international cooperation to avoid ending up in a situation where different countries have different rules for how AI may be used. It is also about the development of AI going at an exponential rate, and new regulations are constantly needed for how AI can be used. A common framework on AI ethics would have ensured that AI is used the same way globally, which would have generated more data for decision-making. This data could have been used to slow down a virus during a future pandemic. Using AI as a tool to produce analyses and summaries of documents can bring financial benefits. It is about using AI as a workforce instead of an employed person who analyzes the documents. It helps shorten the decision-making process and lead time, saving time and money and providing financial sustainability. Since AI can help summarize documents, it does not give the employee as much workload and stress, which benefits social sustainability and makes employees feel better. Less printed paper will also be required as the AI will compress and summarize documents, which favors ecological sustainability.

What could have contributed to more knowledge contributions is researching a framework for ethics within AI; this is considered highly relevant as there is no framework today. It is also important because it is such a powerful tool that can be exploited in unfavorable ways and is evolving rapidly. Another further research is how it would have been possible for a society and a democracy to microvote on issues concerning the person with the help of AI. It would have been interesting to know whether such a system had benefited or overturned the democratic process in a society. Something else we think should be researched more is how AI would also be a tool for private individuals, more than it already is today.

REFERENCES

Abueg, M., Hinch, R., Wu, N., Liu, L., Probert, W., Wu, A., Eastham, P., Shafi, Y., Rosencrantz, M., Dikovsky, M., Cheng, Z., Nurtay, A., Abeler-Dörner, L., Bonsall, D., McConnell, M. V., O'Banion, S., & Fraser, C. (2021). Modeling the effect of exposure notification and non-pharmaceutical interventions on COVID-19 transmission in Washington state. *NPJ Digital Medicine*, *4*(1), 49. doi:10.103841746-021-00422-7 PMID:33712693

Alghamdi, N. S., & Alghamdi, S. M. (2022). The Role of Digital Technology in Curbing COVID-19. *International Journal of Environmental Research and Public Health*, *19*(14), 8287. doi:10.3390/ijerph19148287 PMID:35886139

Bragazzi, N. L., Dai, H., Damiani, G., Behzadifar, M., Martini, M., & Wu, J. (2020). How Big Data and Artificial Intelligence Can Help Better Manage the COVID-19 Pandemic. *International Journal of Environmental Research and Public Health*, *17*(9), 3176. doi:10.3390/ijerph17093176 PMID:32370204

Bryman, A. (2012). *Social Research Methods*. OUP Oxford.

Coeckelbergh, M. (2020). *Ai Ethics*. The MIT Press. doi:10.7551/mitpress/12549.001.0001

Couzin-Frankel, J. (2019). Medicine contends with how to use artificial intelligence. *Science*, *364*(6446), 1119–1120. doi:10.1126cience.364.6446.1119 PMID:31221837

Dash, S., Shakyawar, S. K., Sharma, M., & Kaushik, S. (2019). Big data in healthcare: Management, analysis and future prospects. *Journal of Big Data*, *6*(1), 54. doi:10.118640537-019-0217-0

Dastin, J. (2018, October 10). *Amazon scraps secret AI recruiting tool that showed bias against women.* Reuters. https://www.reuters.com/article/us-amazon-com-jobs-automation-insight-idUSKCN1MK08G

Eagle, N., & Greene, K. (2014). *Reality Mining: Using Big Data to Engineer a Better World*. MIT Press.

Ertel, W. (2018). *Introduction to Artificial Intelligence*. Springer International Publishing.

Fan, J., Han, F., & Liu, H. (2014). Challenges of Big Data analysis. *National Science Review*, *1*(2), 293–314. doi:10.1093/nsr/nwt032 PMID:25419469

Galea, S., & Abdalla, S. M. (2020). COVID-19 Pandemic, Unemployment, and Civil Unrest: Underlying Deep Racial and Socioeconomic Divides. *Journal of the American Medical Association*, *324*(3), 227–228. doi:10.1001/jama.2020.11132 PMID:32530457

Giger, M. L. (2018). Machine Learning in Medical Imaging. *Journal of the American College of Radiology*, *15*(3, 3 Pt B), 512–520. doi:10.1016/j.jacr.2017.12.028 PMID:29398494

Gunkel, D. (2012). The Machine Question: Critical Perspectives on AI, Robots, and Ethics. In The Machine Question: Critical Perspectives on AI, Robots, and Ethics. MIT Press. doi:10.7551/mitpress/8975.001.0001

Guo, Y., Liu, Y., Oerlemans, A., Lao, S., Wu, S., & Lew, M. S. (2016). Deep learning for visual understanding: A review. *Neurocomputing*, *187*, 27–48. doi:10.1016/j.neucom.2015.09.116

Hassani, H., & Silva, E. S. (2015). Forecasting with Big Data: A Review. *Annals of Data Science*, *2*(1), 5–19. doi:10.100740745-015-0029-9

Hauer, T. (2022). Incompleteness of moral choice and evolution towards fully autonomous AI. *Humanities & Social Sciences Communications*, *9*(1), 1. doi:10.105741599-022-01060-4

Hiscott, J., Alexandridi, M., Muscolini, M., Tassone, E., Palermo, E., Soultsioti, M., & Zevini, A. (2020). The global impact of the coronavirus pandemic. *Cytokine & Growth Factor Reviews*, *53*, 1–9. doi:10.1016/j.cytogfr.2020.05.010 PMID:32487439

Huang, L., & Peissl, W. (2023). Artificial Intelligence—A New Knowledge and Decision-Making Paradigm? In L. Hennen, J. Hahn, M. Ladikas, R. Lindner, W. Peissl, & R. van Est (Eds.), Technology Assessment in a Globalized World: Facing the Challenges of Transnational Technology Governance (pp. 175–201). Springer International Publishing. doi:10.1007/978-3-031-10617-0_9

Hurwitz, J. S., Nugent, A., Halper, F., & Kaufman, M. (2013). *Big Data For Dummies*. John Wiley & Sons.

Ireni-Saban, L., & Sherman, M. (2021). *Ethical Governance of Artificial Intelligence in the Public Sector*. Taylor & Francis. doi:10.4324/9781003106678

Jarota, M. (2021). Artificial intelligence and robotisation in the EU - should we change OHS law? *Journal of Occupational Medicine and Toxicology (London, England)*, *16*(1), 18. doi:10.118612995-021-00301-7 PMID:33952297

Jayatilake, S. M. D. A. C., & Ganegoda, G. U. (2021). Involvement of Machine Learning Tools in Healthcare Decision Making. *Journal of Healthcare Engineering*, *6679512*, 1–20. doi:10.1155/2021/6679512 PMID:33575021

Labrinidis, A., & Jagadish, H. V. (2012). Challenges and opportunities with big data. *Proceedings of the VLDB Endowment International Conference on Very Large Data Bases*, *5*(12), 2032–2033. doi:10.14778/2367502.2367572

Mueller, J. P., & Massaron, L. (2021). *Artificial Intelligence For Dummies*. John Wiley & Sons.

Quan-Hoang, V., Anh-Vinh, L., Viet-Phuong, L., Phuong-Hanh, H., & Manh-Toan, H. (2020). Making social sciences more scientific: Literature review by structured data. *MethodsX*, *7*, 100818. doi:10.1016/j.mex.2020.100818 PMID:32257836

Raghupathi, W., & Raghupathi, V. (2014). Big data analytics in healthcare: Promise and potential. *Health Information Science and Systems*, *2*(1), 3. doi:10.1186/2047-2501-2-3 PMID:25825667

Rao, Q., & Frtunikj, J. (2018). Deep learning for self-driving cars: Chances and challenges. *Proceedings of the 1st International Workshop on Software Engineering for AI in Autonomous Systems*, (pp. 35–38). ACM. 10.1145/3194085.3194087

Reim, W., Åström, J., & Eriksson, O. (2020). Implementation of Artificial Intelligence (AI): A Roadmap for Business Model Innovation. *AI*, *1*(2), 2. doi:10.3390/ai1020011

Russell, S. (2019). *Human Compatible: Artificial Intelligence and the Problem of Control*. Penguin Publishing Group.

Russell, S., & Norvig, P. (2021). Artificial Intelligence: A Modern Approach, Global Edition. Pearson Higher Ed.

Ryan, M. (2020). In AI We Trust: Ethics, Artificial Intelligence, and Reliability. *Science and Engineering Ethics*, *26*(5), 2749–2767. doi:10.100711948-020-00228-y PMID:32524425

Sagiroglu, S., & Sinanc, D. (2013). Big data: A review. *2013 International Conference on Collaboration Technologies and Systems (CTS)*, (pp. 42–47). IEEE. 10.1109/CTS.2013.6567202

Santhana Krishnan, A., Yang, Y., & Schaumont, P. (2020). *Risk and Architecture Factors in Digital Exposure Notification*., doi:10.1007/978-3-030-60939-9_21

Shi, Z. (2011). *Advanced Artificial Intelligence*. World Scientific. doi:10.1142/7547

Srinath, P. (2022). Study on Artificial Intelligence. In J. Karthikeyan, S.-H. Ting, & Y.-J. Ng (Eds.), Ordine Nuovo Publication: Vol. L. *Learning Outcomes of Classroom Research.*

Starke, C., & Lünich, M. (2020). Artificial intelligence for political decision-making in the European Union: Effects on citizens' perceptions of input, throughput, and output legitimacy. *Data & Policy*, *2*, e16. doi:10.1017/dap.2020.19

Thompson, S. J. (2021). *Machine Law, Ethics, and Morality in the Age of Artificial Intelligence.* In IGI Global. https://www.igi-global.com/book/machine-law-ethics-morality-age/www.igi-global.com/book/machine-law-ethics-morality-age/244609

Thomsen, K. (2019). Ethics for Artificial Intelligence, Ethics for All. *Paladyn : Journal of Behavioral Robotics*, *10*(1), 359–363. doi:10.1515/pjbr-2019-0029

Urbina, F., Lentzos, F., Invernizzi, C., & Ekins, S. (2022). Dual Use of Artificial Intelligence-powered Drug Discovery. *Nature Machine Intelligence*, *4*(3), 189–191. doi:10.103842256-022-00465-9 PMID:36211133

Xu, Y., Liu, X., Cao, X., Huang, C., Liu, E., Qian, S., Liu, X., Wu, Y., Dong, F., Qiu, C.-W., Qiu, J., Hua, K., Su, W., Wu, J., Xu, H., Han, Y., Fu, C., Yin, Z., Liu, M., & Zhang, J. (2021). Artificial intelligence: A powerful paradigm for scientific research. *Innovation (Cambridge (Mass.))*, *2*(4), 100179. doi:10.1016/j.xinn.2021.100179 PMID:34877560

ADDITIONAL READING

Efthymiou, I.-P., Egleton, T.-W., & Sidiropoulos, S. (2020). Artificial Intelligence (AI) in Politics: Should Political AI be Controlled? *International Journal of Innovative Research in Science, Engineering and Technology*, *5*, 49–51.

Jungherr, A. (2023). Artificial Intelligence and Democracy: A Conceptual Framework. *Social Media + Society*, *9*(3), 20563051231186353. doi:10.1177/20563051231186353

Naik, N., Hameed, B. M. Z., Shetty, D. K., Swain, D., Shah, M., Paul, R., Aggarwal, K., Ibrahim, S., Patil, V., Smriti, K., Shetty, S., Rai, B. P., Chlosta, P., & Somani, B. K. (2022). Legal and Ethical Consideration in Artificial Intelligence in Healthcare: Who Takes Responsibility? *Frontiers in Surgery*, *9*, 862322. https://www.frontiersin.org/articles/10.3389/fsurg.2022.862322. doi:10.3389/fsurg.2022.862322 PMID:35360424

Savaget, P., Chiarini, T., & Evans, S. (2018). Empowering political participation through artificial intelligence. *Science & Public Policy*, *46*(3), 369–380. doi:10.1093cipolcy064 PMID:33583994

Zuiderwijk, A., Chen, Y.-C., & Salem, F. (2021). Implications of the use of artificial intelligence in public governance: A systematic literature review and a research agenda. *Government Information Quarterly*, *38*(3), 101577. doi:10.1016/j.giq.2021.101577

KEY TERMS AND DEFINITIONS

AI Decision Support: AI decision support uses artificial intelligence to assist and augment human decision-making processes. AI systems can analyze data, provide recommendations, and reduce uncertainty in decision-making.

AI Ethics: AI ethics pertains to the moral and ethical considerations surrounding using artificial intelligence. It addresses fairness, transparency, accountability, privacy, and bias in AI systems.

AI Pandemic: In the context of the article, AI pandemic likely refers to using artificial intelligence during a pandemic. This involves using AI for monitoring, tracking, and decision support in managing and mitigating the effects of a pandemic such as COVID-19.

Artificial Intelligence (AI): AI refers to developing computer systems or software that can perform tasks that typically require human intelligence. These tasks may include problem-solving, decision-making, learning, and language processing.

Big Data: Big data refers to large volumes of structured and unstructured data generated at a high velocity. It encompasses data with various formats and from diverse sources, and its analysis can reveal patterns, trends, and insights that can inform decision-making.

Ethical Framework: An ethical framework in the context of AI and big data refers to a set of guidelines, principles, or rules that govern the responsible and ethical use of these technologies. Such frameworks help ensure that AI and big data applications adhere to ethical standards and societal values.

Chapter 10
Professionally Ethical Ways to Harness an Art-Making Generative AI to Support Innovative Instructional Design Work

Shalin Hai-Jew
https://orcid.org/0000-0002-8863-0175
Kansas State University, USA

ABSTRACT

Instructional designers often pride themselves on using the most cutting-edge commercial authoring and other tools available to achieve their work. Their creations have to meet high technical standards in order to function in a digital environment, in learning management systems, content management systems, on social media, on digital content platforms, and others. In the present moment, generative AI tools enable the making of novel texts and digital visuals, among others. A major extant question is how best to harness generative art-making AIs in instructional design work. In this case, this work explores professionally ethical (and legal) ways to use a generative art-making AIs for ID work, as an innovative approach based on a review of the literature, a year of using several free web-facing art-making generative AIs (CrAIyon, Deep Dream Generator, and others) in open or public beta, and learning from applied instructional design work (over several decades).

1. INTRODUCTION

In the education space, generative AI programs are the subject of much debate given the potential for their use for "deep fakes" (Hebron, n.d., n.p.) and plagiarism, among others. Many can see the potential of such tools for teaching and learning, but they also want to be sure not to contravene copyright or

DOI: 10.4018/979-8-3693-0074-9.ch010

promote academic dishonesty. There are also some challenges with learning how generative AIs function and their capabilities. Laws and policies at various levels have not been fully instantiated at present.

In education, instructional designers assess a learning context and design teaching and learning approaches that optimize both. They may write up instructional design (ID) plans. They may design, develop, and deploy digital learning contents (modules, objects, sequences, courses, course sequences, and others). They may select from a range of technologies to enable their work. They may have methods to better understand the target learners (based on empirical information and theories). They have to be aware of the relevant laws, such as involving intellectual property, privacy protections, media law, accessibility, and others.

This work explores how generative art-making AI (from free web-facing tools such as CrAIyon, Deep Dream Generator, and others) may be harnessed into the instructional design space to enable innovation, across a range of practices, in the current liminal moment (with a range of uncertainties). These tools have been released for free public usage in "open" or "public" beta, with some degree of experimental learning by the makers of the respective tools (and some public caveats as to visual outputs).

2. REVIEW OF THE LITERATURE

Artificial intelligence (AI) has been a long-term objective in computer science. There have been three phases of AI development from the 1950s: "Foundation (1950s – 1970s, methods and algorithms), Symbolic (1970s – 1990s, model driven, knowledge-based systems), and ML/DL (1990s – present, data-driven" (Maslic & Kim, 2021, p. 277), with "ML" referring to "machine learning" and "DL" referring to "data learning". A large category of computer programs, in the modern age, emulates human intelligence and are known as "artificial intelligence" (as in non-human and non-animal intelligence, rather that of computational machines). "General" or "strong" AI aims to emulate and build on full human intelligence; "narrow" or "weak" AI aims to focus on limited and dedicated applications of machine intelligence for defined specific aims. Work into AI has been ongoing for decades, from the mid-1950s, at least. AI is a "paradigm" for thinking about a category of technologies (Striuk, Kondratenko, Sidenko, & Vorobyova, Nov. 2020, p. 368). For all the progress, this moment is "at the dawn of AI" even as AI is "acting, almost always invisibly, in nearly all fields of human activity" (Santaella, 2022, p. 43).

2.1 Advances in Artificial Intelligence (AI)

One type that has come to the fore recently involves AI that can create. Benjamin Bloom, in his revised Bloom's Taxonomy of the Cognitive Domain, suggests that creativity is at the pinnacle of the human mind. For generations, humanity has thought of creativity as in the singular human domain, and the sense of computational encroachment on that space has been controversial.

Generative computational creativity (as part of the field of "computational creativity") refers to a category of technologies that can output creative works including "narrative, poetry, ideation, games, analogy, design, etc." (Davis, Hsiao, Popova, & Magerko, 2015, p. 112). Generative systems are those that create "novel, surprising, and valuable creative products" (Davis, Hsiao, Popova, & Magerko, 2015, p. 111). GANs were created by Ian Goodfellow and others at the University of Montreal in 2014 (McCormack, Gifford, & Hutchings, 2019, p. 35). The technologies function autonomously based on studies of human creative processes and outputs, which are then codified into programs and machines.

Another application deploys AI-generated personas to test computer games (Barthet, Khalifa, Liapis, & Yannakakis, Sept. 2022). Generative Adversarial Networks (GANs) are data-informed programs that are trained on curated digital contents that are the knowledge base of the programs. There are two parts to the GANs that work "adversarially": "a generator network G learns to generate new data while a discriminator network D tries to identify the generated data whether it is real or fake" (Hung, Trang, Nakatsu, & Tosa, Feb. 2022, p. 309). In coordination, the system works like a minimax game (in game theory) and helps the program narrow in on a set of generated contents that meet objective standards. One research team explains:

The training of GANs is based on a minimax mechanism in the sense that the generator G learns to generate fake data from random noise while the discriminator D tries to classify the generated data into categories of 'real' or 'fake'. In other words, the training on G tries to maximize the probability of the generated data to lie on the targeted distribution and the training process of D tries to minimize it. (Hung, Trang, Nakatsu, & Tosa, Feb. 2022, p. 310)

GANs are described as "a two-person zero-sum game in game theory" based on a generator and discriminator (Liu, Lin, & Liu, Jan. 2022, p. 1). Another research team writes:

...the purpose of the generator is to generate fake samples to deceive discriminator, while discriminator is to distinguish real samples from fake samples. (Liu, Lin, & Liu, Jan. 2022, p. 1)

Each part of the GAN is striving to improve their ability, with the result that the generator creates ever-more high-fidelity works (to certain objectives). There are evolutionary GANs (Wang, Xu, Yao, & Tao, 2019), multi-layer pyramid GANs (Guo, Wang, & Yang, June 2022, p. 27), and other types in the research literature. The naming is based on the different modeling and architectures and processes.

Another term often used for computers that can generate creative contents is "Generative Machine Learning systems" (McCormack, Gambardella, Rajcic, Krol, Llano, & Yang, 2023, p. 1). The machine learning may be achieved in various ways, but a common core involves artificial neural networks (ANNs), leading also to the term Generative Adversarial Neural Networks (GANNs) (Striuk, Kondratenko, Sidenko, & Vorobyova, Nov. 2020, p. 368), among others. Some researchers term art-making GANs "Creative Adversarial Networks" (CANs) (Tao, Zou, & Ren, 2018, p. 147) because these generate contents into the creatives space. The transfer of style between visuals is termed "neural style transfer" (NST) (Cetinic & She, 2022, p. 66:8). "Neural painting" occurs with GANs or CANs that create art. ["Once trained, a neural network contains a 'latent' space defining the realm of immanent solutions (optimizations) given a set of inputs" (Choi, DiPaola, & Töyrylä, 2021, p. 020501-12).]

Machine learning involves methods for extracting data patterns from large-scale examples from the real world (based on contents that people have created, data that machines have captured, and other training data). GANs are used for various types of problem-solving and analysis; they are trained on various data types, from micro to meso to macro scales (Wu, Stouffs, & Biljecki, 2022, p. 1). ANNs and other approaches enable "deep learning" to capture nuances from mass data. Generative AIs may engage a kind of "imitation learning" based on the data in the training dataset or collections. Various machines lack "implicit knowledge" (De Smedt, Lechat, Burtenshaw, & Nijs, 2021, p. 174), even as creativity is "inherently situated" (p. 179), suggesting a need for understanding context. In general, AI in the creative industries may give "an impression of understanding but nonetheless (is) performing without 'awareness' of wider context" (Anantrasirichai & Bull, 2022, p. 635).

Some have dubbed such programs "shitty automation" since such programs are informed by "human input—our labor, bodies, biases, prejudices, and desires" and "remains invisibly present in automated systems (Merchant's idea of "shitty automation") (Paulsen, 2020, p. 4). Generative AI learns "individual biases and prejudices" given the training data (Srinivasan & Uchino, Mar. 2021, p. 41), so much so that some include safeguards against certain offensive outputs. Biases in datasets including "representational bias," "label bias," and others (Srinivasan & Uchino, Mar. 2021, pp. 49 - 50).

Humans are in the loop, whether directly or indirectly. And some see the digital as as much a part of normal life as nature (Zylinska, "AI as Another Intelligence," 2020, p. 137), reflecting back people and their productions back to themselves in different forms and formulations.

One researcher takes issue with the idea of the term "machine learning" as not quite accurate. This researcher explains:

Machine learnt algorithms typically apply mathematical formulas to a collection of inputs—the training data in supervised learning, the most used type of machine learning nowadays—in order to produce the desired outputs. A machine learning model is the result of 'brute force' curve-fitting. When the training is successful, the model can map new inputs to the patterns found in the training data. That is the reason it is expected that these mathematical formulas also generate the correct outputs, or predictions, for most other inputs distinct from the training data, respecting the condition that those inputs are from the same or a very similar statistical distribution as the ones found in the training data. It is not proper learning, in the human sense, because even a slight distortion or change in the inputs is likely to produce completely wrong outputs, what (sic) can be interesting for creative and artistic purposes. (Poltronieri, 2022, p. 39)

One researcher has noted that there is usually nothing "AI" about the programming languages for implementing AI algorithms. The power is often in the data, used for the training. Generative tools and algorithms are "more complex computational tools that generate or process material based on advanced algorithms. Possibly designed by, tweaked by, or interacted with by the artist." (Dahlstedt, 2021, p. 895). There are various generative AI for the arts, including "…simple tools, template-based tools, simple rule systems, generative tools and algorithms, and autonomous tools" (Dahlstedt, 2021, p. 895).

As to people's willingness to use AI and automation, an empirical study found that various factors inform their preferences. Robots need to be moral agents, with transparency of decision-making (Sun, Rau, & Wang, 2021, p. 376). Research participants had different automation preferences based on the factors of severity, time, and relativity. Severity refers to the level of human "reliance on automation" with high severity situations as those that "have impact on human's life and death, and low severity scenarios as those…in normal circumstances" (Sun, Rau, & Wang, 2021, p. 378); time refers to "effect of available time before action on people's reliance on automation and whether people have to act quickly (short time duration) or can "think before making decisions" (p. 378); relativity refers to whether people are engaging "self-relevant scenarios" or "self-irrelevant scenarios as those that the decisions participants made will have impacts only on others" (p. 378). This study examined four levels of automation: full automation, monitored control, consensual control, and manual control" (p. 392). This work considers the level of control people want vs. how much they cede to automation. AI should be adaptively designed for human comfort based on the preferences of potential users. This work anticipates a super AI in the future as a research prompt. Others have observed that "maximum benefit from AI will be derived where its focus is human-centric—where it is designed to augment, rather than replace, human creativity" (Anantrasirichai & Bull, 2022, p. 589).

AI needs to be "explainable AI" (XAI) or "human-centered explainable AI" (HCXAI) for it to be usable by people (Sun, Liao, Muller, Agarwal, Houde, Talamadupula, & Weisz, Mar. 2022, p. 212). One study used scenarios and questions to understand preferred explainable AI. The research study using "real examples from state-of-the-art generative AI models…to elicit users' explainability needs" (Sun, Liao, Muller, Agarwal, Houde, Talamadupula, & Weisz, Mar. 2022, p. 212). The researchers write:

…perhaps the most important lesson from HCXAI is that users' explainability needs emerge in a usage context, guided by their goals and shaped by their backgrounds, expectations, as well as socio, organizational and cultural contexts. (Sun, Liao, Muller, Agarwal, Houde, Talamadupula, & Weisz, Mar. 2022, p. 213)

There is human interest in knowing the following: the Generative AI's inputs, its outputs, a high level understanding of the GenAI model, performance, how to improve inputs to the technology for better outputs, ways to control and customize the model, why logic of the model, the data used to train the model, system requirements, limitations, and what-ifs (Sun, Liao, Muller, Agarwal, Houde, Talamadupula, & Weisz, Mar. 2022, pp. 220-221).

2.2 Risks and Hopes With AI

One researcher suggests that AIs can be less than benign, and that their creation and outputs can have unintended outcomes. Values tend towards being culturally and situationally based and are often not universal. Human values may not anticipate the capabilities of new technologies. This risk requires careful considerations before policies are decided on and enacted:

This is why I want to suggest that, alongside artistic modes of engagement, many of the problems currently discussed under the umbrella of 'AI ethics' would be much better served by policy discussions, with that old-school mode of intervention, regulation, offering a more pragmatic way of countering some of the failures of the ethics discourse. (Zylinska, "The Ethics of AI…," 2020, p. 34)

Creative AI techniques "provide and come (with) significant ethical responsibilities in their setup, use, and the output works themselves" (Flick & Worrall, 2022, p. 73). There are disparate issues raised, such as "copyright, replacement of authors/artists, bias in datasets, artistic essence, dangerous creations, deepfakes, and physical safety and looks towards a future" (Flick & Worrall, 2022, p. 73), with various concerns for human well-being. Techno-moral values include "honesty, humility, empathy, care, civility, and flexibility" to be practiced by "virtuous creative practitioners" (Flick & Worrall, 2022, p. 73). Techno-social values focus on the social good, such as preventing harms from deep fakes, strobe effects, and others. These latter values involve "empathy and care, civility and flexibility" (Vallor, 2016, as cited in Flick & Worrall, 2022). The ACM Code of Ethics does encompass creative AI tools (Flick & Worrall, 2022, p. 87).

Others see AI as the "Anthropocene imperative," in an age where human activities have caused global imbalances and led to global warming and ocean rise. The researcher writes:

The robotically-framed discourse of extinction has made its way into current AI thinking, with apocalypticism competing against the rosier visions of human-machine unity, and against ideas about imminent technofixes. (Zylinska, "Why Now...," 2020, p. 40)

Will AI provide insights that can help humanity in their many challenges? Given that a computer is "a general-purpose symbol-manipulating machine, and it is capable of dealing with any problem which can be given a symbolic representation" (Cohen, 1974, reprinted 2022, p. 7), many look to computers in a hopeful way to solve real-world problems. Can AI change up the human imagination and the senses of the possible? Or will AI-generated works just be "superficial" (Zylinska, "Can Computers Be...," 2020, p. 49). The researcher complains about a human preference for the visually dazzling vs. something substantive:

The more critical understanding of art in terms of the creation of new forms of expression with a view to saying something different about the world, or actually intervening in it, is ignored for the sake of what we might term 'crowd-sourced beauty,' a rebooted version of 'I know what I like.' (Zylinska, "Can Computers Be...," 2020, pp. 49-50)

What people are willing to use and how they use the tools may well affect what survives in the marketplace.

2.3 AI and Generative Art

"Generative art" refers to "when an artist cedes some degree of control to an autonomous system that creates, or is, the art" (Galanter, 2019, p. 112). The autonomous systems may be biological, chemical, and others. Generative processes have long been used in art, from the Paleolithic through to the present, involving "ornamental art..., hydraulically-activated automata..., medieval and Renaissance clockwork figures,...the *harmonograph* in the 19th century, ...cybernetic sculptures" and others from different periods (Dorin, McCabe, McCormack, Monro, & Whitelaw, 2012, p. 240). Generative art-making tools are sufficient "to determine a final design" (Galanter, 2019, p. 113). There will be generative art post-computers because generative art is "technology-agnostic" (Galanter, 2016, p. 174). There are generative systems and methods that have not yet been explored.

Generative art can involve "a system, such as a set of natural language rules, a computer program, a machine, or other procedural invention, which is set into motion with some degree of autonomy contributing to or resulting in a completed work of art" (Galanter, 2019, p. 112). In the present age, generative programs [such as "algorithmic art machines" (Edmonds, 2018, p. 1)] have come to the forefront of generative art for the mass public. According to generative art theory, there is a sense of human artists "ceding control" to autonomous systems (Galanter, 2019, p. 112). As of a few years ago, one researcher suggested that generative AI may one day be "full-fledged studio collaborators" with people (Galanter, 2019, p. 115).

There are various ways that AI systems generate art. Researchers write:

There are two classes of generative art approaches: neural, where a deep model is trained to generate samples from a data distribution, and 'symbolic' or algorithmic, where an artist designs the primary parameters and an autonomous system generates samples within these constraints. (Aggarwal & Parikh, 2020)

There are hybrid neuro-symbolic approaches as well.

There are different designs to art-making AI systems. One, for example, integrates knowledge of human creativity based on psychology:

The common view that our creativity is what makes us uniquely human suggests that incorporating research on human creativity into generative deep learning techniques might be a fruitful avenue for making their outputs more compelling and human-like. (DiPaola, Gabora, & McCaig, 2018, p. 158)

The various systems are informed by different insights about art and art-makers. Another work considers the human painting process, while noting that the AI generation of art does not resemble the human painting or art-creation process (Leiser & Schlippe, Feb. 2022, p. 295). Human artists often use a layering strategy of painting, working from the background to the foreground, with variations based on the respective mediums used. The compuational approach uses a stepwise process, with varying filters to enact blurring, semantic segmentation, coloring, and other effects.

Another generative-AI emulates the creative processes of a portrait painter. The portrait painter sets up a scene for a sitter, interviews that person to "understand/capture inner (personality,…) and outer resemblance, and at the same time merges these goals with how the artist wants to convey their own painting style in the trajectory of their painting career as well as striving for some personal and universal (cultural, political, philosophical) truth of the current world they live in" (DiPaola & McCaig, 2016, p. 158).

Generative AIs may separate style from content in a digital visual, and they can apply the visual style as a kind of textural wrap on another image (Machado, Romero, & Greenfield, 2021, p. 61). One work describes how style transfer is computationally achieved:

- *"Which parts of the content should be preserved (and to what extent) and which discarded or modified?*
- *Should edges and / or other elements in the content image be allowed to shift, and if so, how?*
- *Which color palette should the output adopt?*
- *How far should generated style elements be inserted in the regions where content is of no importance?*
- *Which parts from the style image qualify as style to be used, and which should be disregarded?" (Machado, Romero, & Greenfield, 2021, p. 63)*

Another system strives to integrate "psychometric aesthetic derived from professional artist judgments" into computational fitness evaluations (Bezruczko, 2019, p. 1). Such information may help the discriminator of GANs better address the former "fitness bottlenecks" in evaluating generator outputs. [Such GAN approaches benefit convergence to a defined standard instead of encouraging divergence of creations. Divergence may be a well of increasing innovation in the visual outputs.] In the world, the fitness of artwork is informed in part by how target users receive the visuals, based on a level of "aesthetic acceptability" (Bezruczko, 2019, p. 4). Various other strategies for fitness evaluation involve "interactive models, evolving genotypes, arbitrary aesthetic measures, (and) corpus methods" (Bezruczko, 2019, p. 4)

Generative art-making AIs are created to meet perceived human needs. For some, there is a give-and-take between humans and machines in a symbiosis, with perhaps new thinking by the human artist. AI can challenge and change a human artist's intentions with its outputs, in the so-called Creative AI Symbiotic Sphere (Poltronieri, 2022, p. 31). AI may provide support for human creative thinking, with a finding that "interacting with a knowledge-based system, AI, could be a significant trigger for creative thought" (Edmonds, 2022, p. 61). [AI does inform some creativity support systems used by people.] "Digital fabricators" may be used to support artistic practice for "everyday users" (Devendorf, 2014, pp. 151-152). Creative support systems should enhance human creative choice, not limit them (McCormack, Bown, Dorin, McCabe, Monro, & Whitelaw, 2014, p. 138).

It helps to note that AIs are created by people (and perhaps other AIs), but at this time, "No AI acts alone, completely divorced from the influence of humans" (Epstein, Levine, Rand, & Rahwan, 2020, p. 7). While there are fully autonomous AIs, these, too, are designed and unleashed by people. And works created partially with AI are "the result of the creativity, hard work, and decisions of numerous human contributors" (Epstein, Levine, Rand, & Rahwan, 2020, p. 7), even in cases where the AI is forefronted. People sometimes perceive AI programs as "autonomous intelligent agents" (McCormack, Gifford, & Hutchings, 2019, p. 44), when they are mere computational programs running on machines.

An example of having humans directly "in the loop" involves their ability to use text or visual or other prompts to start the AI-generation process. One way is to enable humans to use text and / or image prompts to elicit visuals from the computers. A subset of generative machines involves the ability to achieve "text-to-image translation" (Sajeeda & Hossain, 2022, p. 78). Text prompts may be used to create "complex imagery, video, even 3D datasets" (McCormack, Gambardella, Rajcic, Krol, Llano, & Yang, 2023, p. 1). Prompt-based systems, such as text-to-image (TTI) ones, come with limits: almost all the images produced by TTI systems are "figurative and literal" since such systems are "built upon millions of formal descriptions of visual material, where words or descriptive phrases (noun + adjective or verb + adverb pairings) capture the visual identity and the characteristics of elements present in an image, their spatial relationships…, as well as some more general stylistic features" (McCormack, Gambardella, Rajcic, Krol, Llano, & Yang, 2023, p. 4). Such creations do not require the users to engage in embodied work—to draw, to photograph, to paint, and others. The TTI-creation processes are mysterious and unknown (based on unknown algorithms and unknown training data, in many cases).

One graduate thesis describes human-generative AI collaborations but with a twist. Here, the student used an AI to describe visuals that he has uploaded to the AI and uses those prompts to create the actual works himself. Here, the AI is the describer of the work, and the human uses that text as prompts for his own work, calling these "pseudo-found objects." The researcher writes: "I would incorporate as much of the AI's description as possible, although exactly what I included would always be at my discretion" (Gerard, 2020, p. 19). The writer calls this approach "a new way of collaborating with AI" where the AI is not a creator but a collaborator with the human artist (Gerard, 2020, p. 22).

The human may also be in the loop in the post-production or post-editing/post-revision of whatever is generated by the generative AI.

Closed systems generate works without outside inputs; open systems take in information from outside the algorithmic space. Some researchers note that creative AI tools often required "command line" skills for those who could "access and use their terminal" but present-day AIs require the ability to use basic interfaces (Flick & Worrall, 2022, p. 75). However, even as people benefit from "creative direction" and relief from "busywork" (Eisenmann, 2021, p. 187), there are be lessened understandings about the underlying processes in the generative art-making AIs:

The recent explosion of deep learning advances from complex architectures has led to impressive performance increases. It has also led to a dramatic decrease in our ability to introspect the deep learning models to find out how and why they are performing the way they are. (Eisenmann, 2021, p. 190)

Some art-making generative AIs, like Deep Dream Generator, share their code transparently. Others do not.

Another research team writes: "Nowadays, encounters with works of art created by robots are no longer unusual: We come across paintings, poems, songs, and even film scripts produced by machines" (Mikalonytė & Kneer, Sept. 2022, p. 43:1). Robots may be embodied in physical form or disembodied (as a synthetic agent inside a computer). Robots have been part of art-making from the mid-20th century onwards along with the field of "cultural robotics." A researcher explains: "Rather than synthesizing the skills of the programmer and the painter, robotic art integrates the sensibilities of the sculptor, installation artist, and performer with the computational systems equipped with both sensors and mechanical effectors" (Penny, 2013, p. 147).

2.4 AI-Generated Art and the Art Market

Computing and other machines have been a part of common art practices in pop culture (film, music, games, and others) but has been adopted more slowly perhaps in the fine art space (Boden & Edmonds, 2009). AI-generated art has been sold for decades, albeit not for the general prices that human-created art has commanded in the fine arts spaces until recently. There is the sense that the "art market alienates AI artists from their work" (Browne, 2022, p. 130), and that a digital divide still exists between common and high art. AI-generated art is not considered on par with human-created art in the marketplace. AI generators need to produce "*worthy* art products" (Hong & Curran, 2019, p. 58-11) as adduced by fine arts gatekeepers. Human art styles are thought to be original to the individual, with each person having "a personal creative style that is recognizable by others, and this recognizability even extends across domains" (DiPaola, Gabora, & McCaig, 2018, p. 165). Style, then, is an extension of people's personalities, their identities, their learning, their lived experiences, their cultural exposures, and their tastes. The results are from investments by the human artists over lifetimes of effort. That art shapes the world and is shaped by the world (Zylinska, "The Work of Art…," 2020, p. 65), in a complex mutuality.

Further, historically, artists are social agents, who are seen to comment on the world and to serve as catalysts to spark conversations in the world (Hertzmann, May 2018). There is an intercommunication occurring between artists and the larger world. Further, artists are seen to help humanity mediate societal-structural changes, particularly in times of heightened flux, chaos, and change:

Artistic agency using machines and non-human intelligence for cocreation can act as interpreter, connecting the outcomes into sound-, visual-, language- and performance-based artworks that make the future emotionally experienceable for a larger audience. (Friess, 2021, p. 278)

Researchers have asked: "Does it make sense to automate a task that is so especially human?" (Cohen, Nake, Brown, Brown, Galanter, McCormack, & d'Inverno, 2012, p. 96). They describe some of the complexities of decision-making in the evolution of art:

Computers have the ability to 'undo', backtrack, and trial many possible combinations very quickly. But knowing what to undo, how and when to backtrack, and which paths to pursue or abandon requires evaluation appropriate to the task if is to be successful. Evaluation of a work as it proceeds is generally concerned with decision making and prediction, e.g. what are the imlications of making this mark, playing this sequence of sounds, or using media in a specific way? Accomplished artists have a seemingly innate intuition about creative decision-making and its impact, developed and fine-tuned over many years of practice? (Cohen, Nake, Brown, Brown, Galanter, McCormack, & d'Inverno, 2012, p. 97)

Artwork has to convey meaning in complex and elusive ways; it has to evoke human emotions between people.

Art may depict possible alternate realities and possible futures. They can spark human imagination and decision-making and perhaps commitments to particular actions. In a broader view, AIs may "represent and reinterpret our visions of self" (Gruchy, 2020, p. 236). There are high hopes for modern tehcnologies to enable new ways to arrive at ideas and to solve problems, and "may provide a path to the reunification of scientific and cultural pursuits—a new Renaissance" (Hebron, n.d., n.p.). There are research articles of leading artists who use AI, algorithms, and data as art materials: "they explicitly use this material unpredictability rather than avoid it" (Caramiaux & Alaoui, 2022, p. 477:1). Some suggest the potential of AI to enable "the next great art movement" (Schneider & Rea, Sept. 25, 2018), replete with innovations and new ideas.

AI art production has been critiqued as looking of a type or looking similar. The thinking is that various generative art-making AI systems refer to existing works, with its "artistic standards obtained by quantifying and analyzing the previous works" perhaps causing conflict with the idea of constant innovation (Tao, Zou, & Ren, 2018, p. 151). It is too informed by the past, and it is too emulative in a piecemeal way. Another perspective reads: "Mechanical art's focus upon content—as opposed to form, aura and originality—is pertinent to digital art" (Langdon & Langdon, 2014, p. 20). In earlier days, one writes:

Feeding a machine a thousand masterpieces will not result in a great piece, but instead a surreal grayish square. The machine just cannot yet distinguish the qualities of a good painting that make it good. (Gerard, 2020, p. 1)

Some refer to GANs as "copy machines" (Zeilinger, 2021, p. 1). Another critique is that "AI art's interactions with art institutions have not promoted new creative possibilities but have instead reinforced conservative forms and aesthetics" (Browne, 2022, p. 130). Along the same lines, another writes about the pointlessness of regurgitating variations of the known in different assemblages:

...once the information barrier has been crossed and all the possibilities for creation have supposedly been exhausted in advance, even if only on the virtual level, AI-driven art has become an ouroboros-like circle of random variations. This darker assessment of the current media landscape offers a rejoinder to ways to engaging with Internet-based AI art primarily in terms of 'fun,' with disappointment, boredom

and an impulsive yearning for one more click being fun's less glamorous counterparts. (Zylinska, "The Work of Art...," 2020, p. 72)

In the current forms, the sense is that art-generating AIs are creating banality and not solving any real-world problems. Indeed, many generative AI systems can create works that do not have any equivalencies in the world (as tested by reverse image searches) and which align with human understandings of fine art and other aesthetics. The generated images are technically recombinations from a variety of visual and other dimensions, perhaps overlaid with particular art styles.

Computationally, the aesthetics are achieved in different ways. A "saliency-aware generative art" is designed to be experienced pleasurably by people:

Various aesthetic features, including Benford's index, fractal dimension, global contrast factor and Shannon entropy are introduced into the evaluation framework of computational aesthetics. The results suggest that the proposed method can autonomously generate appealing images and animations with different styles by choosing different strokes, and it would inspire graphic designers who may be interested in subtle aesthetic patterns created automatically. (Wu, Feb. 2018, p. 198)

One work merely notes that the aesthetics of art are often "esoteric and indescribable" and informed by culture (Guo, Wang, & Yang, June 2022, p. 31).

Some thinkers see additional threats from AI-generated art, from a socio-political angle. T. Adorno suggests that "this kind of industrialized artworks can also become a tool of the administrative class to control the public. Humans no longer have the ability to take control of their own aesthetic tastes. All aesthetic and even cognitive ability may be controlled by others, even more boldly, controlled by intelligent machines" (Tao, Zou, & Ren, 2018, p. 154).

Others see more constructive possibilities. AI art can be original, argue others, and some suggest that new art standards should be created in light of the new forms of AI-generated (and AI-collaborated) artworks (Tao, Zou, & Ren, 2018, p. 146). "GAI-art" (generative AI art) should be considered as its own medium (Notaro, 2020, p. 322), with the implication that it should be viewed on its own terms. Modern computational art offers "radically new" aesthetic experiences:

The computational is manifested sensuously but it is nevertheless non-perceptual as although it requires a physical substrate, it is nevertheless not located there. It exists within, between and beyond its material instantiations as tangible objects and the process of that articulation. (Carvalhais & Lee, 2022, p. 71)

The researchers elaborate:

In aesthetic experiences, computation may exist independently of its embodiment, enactment, or execution in the form of an artwork. Computational artworks are...not so much artefacts as they are abstract machines that become concrete assemblages whenever and wherever they are executed. And artworks are also not the outputs that these machines produce, but rather the machines in themselves, alongside their outputs and the interactions developed during their operation. (Carvalhais & Lee, 2022, p. 73)

Others, however, argue against using "the technical substrates of such works for criteria of aesthetic critique" (Bajohr, 2022, p. 203) instead of human art standards.

Ontologically, digital art tends to the "immersion, interactivity, and critical responsiveness" of human viewers (Langdon & Langdon, 2014, p. 32), who engage as "the embodied person instead of the more traditional analog forms of "corporeally-detached art spectator" (Langdon & Langdon, 2014, p. 33).

The AI-generated artworks are not truly *de novo,* or totally fresh, but perhaps human imagination is derivative, too, informed in part by what has come before. One research team wrangles with this issue. In contrast to AI systems, "human artists do not learn to create art exclusively from prior examples. They can be inspired by experience of nature, sounds, relationships, discussions and feelings that a GAN is never exposed to and cannot cognitively process as humans do. The training corpus is typically highly curated and miniscule in comparison to human experience. This distinction suggests GANism is more a process of mimicry than intelligence" (McCormack, Gifford, & Hutchings, 2019, p. 40)

While such systems may be "creative," theirs is a mechanistic process:

At a technical level, GANs are a technique for finding a statistical distribution of latent dimensions of a training set. Hence, their capacity for autonomy is limited, certainly no more that (sic) prior machine learning or generative systems. (McCormack, Gifford, & Hutchings, 2019, p. 40)

There is no autonomy or intention to art-generating AIs. They are machines with instructions to process prompts a particular way. One work reads:

While a claim such as, 'an AI created this artwork' might be literally true, there is little more autonomy or agency that can be attributed to such an act than would be to a situation where 'a word processor created a letter', for example. (McCormack, Gifford, & Hutchings, 2019, p. 40)

A different work asserts that AI serves as "agents without agency" (Suryna & Serrano, 2019, p. 200). In this work, the researchers propose art-making generative AIs as mediums, which have both "artistic agency and artistic identity" (Suryna & Serrano, 2019, p. 200).

Some art-generating AI programs have their own "signatures" and may be identified as the original source based on the visual outputs (styles, color palettes, layout / composition, repeating motifs, and other elements, often in combination) currently. However, originality in terms of hosted online images may be too low of a bar.

Some of the AI-based image-tools are to optimize extant images or photos, such as a "de-raining" tool from single images (Jin, Chen, & Li, 2020, p. 1). Another outputs calligraphy-style drawings (Tang, June 2022). Other processes may make images more informational, with contents more identifiable. There are GANs for photorealistic images, for human face creations, and other types. GANs are also used for "photorealistic image generation, image translation, and automatic caption generation"; a proposed program creates "novel poetry to melody generation" based on the emotion detected in the poetry (Shahriar & Al Roken, 2022, p. 1). Some works describe the harnessing of the analog and the digital, using household machines to create art, and harnessing machine "glitches" as another source of artful innovation (Wanner, 2014, p. 31; Grba, Todorović, Boye, Kang, & Pandilovski, 2019).

The advent of non-fungible tokens (NFTs) (and blockchain) is seen to fulfill human needs for collecting and perhaps being able to claim a particular "original" and "digital" work as one's own (Shahriar & Hayawi, Mar. 2022, p. 255), perhaps for bragging rights and also for potential future sellability. One research work includes a proposed "novel NFT art generation application" using GANs (Shahriar & Hayawi, Mar. 2022, p. 259).

Computer-generated art is "now more than 50 years old" (McCormack, Gifford, & Hutchings, 2019, p. 47). Various technological approaches have been used: "self-organizing simulations of nature, models of human creativity, and applications and toolkits that allow users to harness new technologies independent of their technological skill" (De Smedt, Lechat, Burtenshaw, & Nijs, 2021, p. 165). Artificial life algorithms and various AI ones have been applied in the fine arts space (Greenfield, 2021), including programs trained in automated aesthetics (Greenfield, 2021, p. 26). Artificial life simulations may enable the experiencing of "multi-scaled temporal complexity" and generational evolutions and other aspects to the system (Dorin, 2008, p. 294). Artificial life setups may be art "experiments" using "intelligent computational systems and non-human living organisms" that interact with each other and the larger ecosystem (Castellanos, 2022, p. 155). Another approach harnesses "swarm intelligence and self-organization" for making art, such as abstractions (Monmarché, Mahnich, & Slimane, 2008, p. 227). One work describes a human-machine approach to art-making called "interactive evolutionary computation" (Andrews, 2019, p. 156). Computational affordances enable people to explore and create in ways that are not possible otherwise.

Such computational abilities enable people to "follow a winding mountain path that is travelled only by computation" (Dorin, 2008, p. 309). An echo of this idea is that humans may explore how computational machines think and so sample "alien thought" (Weizenbaum, 1976, as cited in Lushetich, 2022, p. 1411). "Alien thought" recognizes that people and computers approach "thinking" or "processing" differently. The idea is that "indeterminate artistic practices are used as an entry into alien thought and its correlates—infinity and complexity—by way of aesthetic analogy" (Lushetich, 2022, p. 1411). Artworks created with AI evokes "*intelligence* that is not entirely human" (Suryna & Serrano, 2019, p. 209), a concept which triggers human interest.

Computer art "is the foundation and precursor of artificial intelligence art" (Tao, Zou, & Ren, 2018, p. 147). One researcher has listed art in "approximate historical order": art as "representation," "expression," "form," "experience," "open concept and family resemblance," "institution," and "historical definition" based on theory (Galanter, 2016, p. 147). One researcher contextualizes the emergence of art-generating AI:

Far from being a bizarre and astonishing phenomenon, the relationship between art and AI brings a type of creation perfectly tied to the already secular history of technologically inseminated arts, trends that were progressively accentuated after the digital revolution, in a multiplicity of developments such as net art, web art, digital art, computational art, algorithmic art, interactive art, robotic art, and so on. (Santaella, 2022, p. 45)

Generative art (involving computation) is thought to have particular features: "uses randomization," "uses genetic systems to evolve form," changes constantly "over time," and involves the running of computer code (Galanter, 2016, p. 150) The first exhibition of computer art was called *Generative Computergraphik* and was held "in Stuttgart in February 1965" (Edmonds, 2018, p. 23). Computational art-making was seen as a "breakthrough" even back in the 1990s (Maiocchi, 1991, p. 184). To make art, computers had to show "aesthetic judgment" with outputs falling within "broad stylistic conventions" but still be somewhat responsive to external inputs (Maiocchi, 1991, p. 195).

The recent instantiation of so-called AI-generated art does not offer novelty per se but has been hyped by various stakeholders:

There are no significant new aspects introduced in the process or artefact of many GAN produced artworks compared to other established machine learning systems for art generation. Currently, there is a difference in the way GANs are presented by media, auction houses and systems designers: as artificially intelligent systems that is likely affecting the perception of GAN art. (McCormack, Gifford, & Hutchings, 2019, p. 47)

The marketing, the verbiage, the breathless claims, and other promotional endeavors have made generative AI the focus of much attention, but such excitement is not likely to sustain over time if past fads are any indication.

The technologies are so accessible that many contemporary artists will "hand-craft" neural networks for making art. They write code, tune kernels, and set various parameters like "network weights coupled with explanatory visualizations" to enable creative control over various processes (Ulberg, Llach, & Byrne, 2020, p. 508). There are various tools for "handcrafting networks for art-making" (Ulberg, Llach, & Byrne, 2020, p. 511). Many artists write their own algorithms and programs for art-making, with one writing of the difficulty in "the apparent freedom of the almost infinite range of possibilities" in art-making while engaging "algorithmic art machines" (Edmonds, 2018, p. 2). Generative metaprogramming has been created to improve on prior practices with "error-prone, hand-crafted scripting" (Trujillo, Azanza, & Diaz, Oct. 2007, p. 105).

There are certainly cases where humans are not in the loop. A 1970 work asked whether art-making computer programs were "mostly assistive or can it "supersede" the human artist? (Edmonds, 2018, p. 5). The fear of humans being side-lined and replaced by superior technologies has long been a narrative not only in the academic literature, but also in popular culture.

As an ethical professional practice, researchers suggest that authors of artworks based on AI production have "a responsibility to accurately represent the process used to generate a work, including the labour of both machines and other people" (McCormack, Gifford, & Hutchings, 2019, p. 46). Whether this is a widely held practice is not clear yet. There are differences in understandings of the appropriate roles of AI technologies by people in the roles of "artist, designer, engineer, programmer, technologist and creator" and other practitioners in the new media community (Maslic & Kim, 2021, p. 277). The popularization of such technologies have roiled various industries, including the creative ones, and education.

2.5 Crediting AIs and Holding Them Accountable...For the Outputs

There are some who argue against the treating of art-generating AI as mere tools. One work argues that there are "discriminatory and exploitive underpinnings of the anthropocentric thinking that lies beyond attempts at sidelining the creative capacities of AI" (Kalpokiene & Kalpokas, 2023, p. 1). In other words, people tend to be more willing to credit other people before they would credit a machine for creativity. There may be a hearkening to residual ideas: "Many artists and art historians resist seeing work created with AI as art because their definition of art is based on the modern artist figure as the sole locus of art creation and creativity" (Mazzone & Elgammal, Feb. 2019, p. 32). Even so, changing the language in talking about AI—as a tool instead of a social agent—has consequences (Epstein, Levine, Rand, & Rahwan, 2020, p. 1). AI systems perceived as a social entity are more readily credited with an artist identity than those referred to as tools. One academic work refers to a generative AI as a "tool, medium, mediator and partner" in terms of the role of digital (Candy, 2020, p. 13). Even those who have created technical systems that make art have differing ideas about whether machines may be considered artists

(Audry & Ippolito, 2019, p. 1). How the fine arts world's gatekeepers consider AI that create art is also important. The researchers write:

...the nature of the artist and meta-artist functions and their relationship may vary depending on the analogies viewers are likely to draw from their own experience. Some might see the machine as a tool, in which case they will construct a meta-artist who uses the tool in a more-or-less virtuosic or telltale fashion...Other viewers might imagine the machine as a child—in which case, they will construct a meta-artist responsible for educating (setting rules for) the child, but not blame the meta-artist directly for individual mistakes...Still others might imagine the machine as a full-fledged collaborator, in which case they will picture a human artist influencing but also being influenced by the machine's choices. (Audry & Ippolito, 2019, p. 3)

Indeed, there are subjectivities in the understanding of art and art processes. Humans determine what is art, and "art-ness" is "externally ascribed (Kalpokiene & Kalpokas, 2023, p. 1). AI-generating of contexts is seen as a threat to human authoring and even the human authors themselves. If AI-created artworks cannot be copyright-able, then they may also not be monetizable in the marketplace. To enable funds to go towards AI, some argue, it is important to take on a post-humanist lens: the "anthropocentric domination of the privileged subset of humanity over the natural and digital environment and the less-privileged parts of humanity" leads to further entrenching of "the exploitative logic of digital capitalism" (Kalpokiene & Kalpokas, 2023, p. 6). In an earlier work, one researcher argues that "...giving authorship to AI programmers and owners is essential to the future development of the AI industry" (Hristov, 2016, p. 431). Another work points to a larger potential group who contribute to generative art-making AIs:

...the artist (i.e., the person taking the inputs and the learning algorithms and producing a trained algorithm), the curator (i.e., the person who selects the final artwork and brings it to auction), the technologist (i.e., the person who creates the learning algorithm), and the crowd (i.e., the people whose labor is responsible for creating the inputs to the algorithm. (Epstein, Levine, Rand, & Rahwan, 2020, p. 5)

Still, others suggest that those whose artworks and photos were used to train the generative AI should perhaps receive micropayments. One team explains the contribution with analogies:

When the training data is authored by others, they implicitly make a contribution, akin to the way that mashups, collage or sampling have contributed to artworks previously. (McCormack, Gifford, & Hutchings, 2019, p. 45)

There has been a public outcry by artists who were not asked if their works could be used to train the generative AI. A single work is not likely to be that important in an art-making GAN given the size of the curated imagesets, however. Even a set of original works may contribute only nominally, depending in part on the size of the imageset. However, where unique contributions may be potent is if the works typify a particular original style, such as works after the style of a particular artist. In that case, the contributions are core to the evocation of that style and the computational style transfer.

One research team mentions the contributors to a training dataset:

Ascribing authorship of a creative work is only meaningful in a particular cultural and legal context. In a contemporary Western context, authorship of AI generated art will be shared between the artist, the developer of the underlying algorithms, and possibly any number of contributors to the training data whose style is being abstracted. (McCormack, Gifford, & Hutchings, 2019, p. 43)

Another team writes:

The creator of the software and person who trained and modified parameters to produce the work can both be considered authors. In addition to those contributors, artists whose works feature prominently in training data can also be considered authors. There has been precedent cases of software systems being considered legal authors, but AI systems are not broadly accepted as authors by artistic or general public communities. (McCormack, Gifford, & Hutchings, 2019, p. 46)

K. Hristov suggests that there is no need to redefine authorship to include non-humans but reinterpreting "the terms 'employee' and 'employee' in the made for hire doctrine of the U.S. Copyright Act" would suffice (Hristov, 2016, p. 431). Behind the AI may be three main parties with claims to potential rights and monies: "AI programmers; owners (large companies and financial investors in the AI sector); and end users" (Hristov, 2016, p. 443), with the end users having made "the smallest contribution to the initial development of AI" rendering their "claims of authorship…least compelling" (p. 444). At present, under U.S. copyright laws, the works made by an AI are ineligible for copyright.

In fact, creative works generated solely by AI machines are not copyrightable if they do not satisfy the human author requirement of the Copyright Office. In other words, unless AI generated works can directly be attributed to a human author, they would theoretically not be copyrightable and would fall into the public domain upon their creation. (Hristov, 2016, p. 437)

Another argues that a "work made for hire" model would enable conceptualizing AI systems as "a creative employee or independent contractor of the user" (Yanisky-Ravid, 2017, p. 660).

As to the "personhood" of an inanimate machine and program, researchers have suggested that machines may get closer to that standard if they have the ability to comprehend or at least have "intuition" (Hebron, n.d., n.p.). Another writes that for a computational system to be a "subject," they should be "endowed with general-purpose intelligence, consciousness, volition, etc." (Carvalhais, 2019, p. 358). If a machine is a "sentient" entity, perhaps it would earn moral and legal considerations, some argue. What about machine autonomy?

Autonomy is the foundational element of any living system. Defined as the property of being self-determining with no outside control over actions and internal states, autonomy refers to a system's ability to assert its existence and to simply be. Through their interactions with their environment, autonomous systems achieve what noted biologist, neuroscientist and philosopher Francisco Varela called the 'shap(ing of) a world into significance'. This notion of autonomy as being assertive, ties right into the notion of agency. Defined as the ability to take action in the world and influence others, agency is how autonomy is exercised, articulated and maintained, via capacities such as adaptability, viability and sentience. (DiBlasi, Castellanos, Kang, Poltronieri, & Smith, n.d., p. 1)

A major thinker in this space focuses more on what he calls the Purpose-structure of art:

It should be evident, then, that I do not consider 'serving the artist's Purpose' to be equivalent to 'taking over the artist's Purpose', or identify the machine with the artist. I identify the artist with the whole Purpose-structure, the machine with the processes which are defined by the structure and in turn help to redefine it. Since under other circumstances these processes too would be played out by the artist, I am also identifying playing-out with the computer with playing-out without the computer. For the machine to serve his Purpose, the artist will need to use it as he uses himself. There is no reason to anticipate that the use will be more or less trivial than the use he makes of himself, but every reason to suppose that the structure will change in ways which are presently undefinable. (Cohen, 1974, reprinted 2022, p. 27)

A work about Canadian copyright law suggests that the maker of the art in fixed form must "have been, on the date of creation, a citizen, subject or habitual resident of a country party to the *Berne Convention for the Protection of Literary and Artistic Works*"…"or the *Universal Copyright Convention,* or a member country of the World Trade Organization" (Jonnaert, 2020, p. 16). The work must "emanate from a (human) author" (Jonnaert, 2020, p. 17), which suggests that autonomous AI-generated works would not meet the requirements for copyright protection. The researcher summarizes: "Most scholars conclude that artificial creations may not be protected by copyright" (Jonnaert, 2020, p. 28)

Already, creatives like "writers, musicians, artists and game designers" use generative machines to achieve various necessary tasks (Guadamuz, 2017, n.p.), perhaps invisibly to those consuming the works. In terms of legal considerations, one suggests that in some jurisdictions perhaps case-by-case analysis will be the approach. (Guadamuz, 2017, n.p.)

2.6 Positive and Negative Effects on Artists

Another work describes similar concerns of AI effects on an artist's "autonomy and agency" (DiBlasi, Castellanos, Kang, Poltronieri, & Smith, n.d., p. 1). The affordances of art-making generative AI may also impinge on the motivations for maintaining art skills, in the same way that automated photography enabled production of professional images without requiring photographers to capture a "decisive moment" in order to achieve their work (because lighting and many other aspects of an image may be changed in post-production) (Reinhuber, Feb. 2022, p. 321). There is a threat of human artists de-skilling and unlearning or forgetting the art skills without regular practice (Daniele & Song, Jan. 2019, p. 159) and without the making of art for livelihoods. Some have asked whether writing prompts is equal to "making art." Researchers argue that there is human labor in "creative automation" (Caramiaux, Alaoui, & Hsueh, April 2022, p. 1), but where the investments are may be less obvious.

Ironically, machine-created artworks are seen as created in an "effortless" way by the machine, but the created works have to be interpreted by people with "band-limited perception" (Dahlstedt, 2021, p. 904). Another line of argument borrows from R. Barthes and his idea about judging an artwork "as independent from the artist" (Barthes, "The Death of the Author," 1967, p. 143, as cited in Dahlstedt, 2021, p. 902). This concept is that an artwork becomes autonomous and has to be interpreted independent of its creator. This opens up possibilities for considering various art-making AI-generated works as artworks independent of the autonomous or semi-autonomous machine creating work. This may open up space for painting robots or "robot artists," too (Zylinska, "Artists, Robots and 'Fun,'" 2020).

Where art was seen before as an object of rarity and scarcity, computational generation of art may lead to mass production with a retreat in prices of artworks and a diverting of funds from practicing human artists. As its own "new art form and new art type" (Wang & Ma, Dec. 2019, p. 445), AI-generated art is predicted to be a drag on art market prices even as it enables a larger number of people to enjoy artworks (Wang & Ma, Dec. 2019). Besides possibly displacing working artists, AI is seen to show up humans by focusing on limits to the human skills: "Are humans themselves creative, or do they all have a limited set of skills in the creation of art that can be decomposed by machine and emulated?" (Zylinska, "Can Computers Be…," 2020).

In the generative art space, the theory does not require "troublesome considerations regarding consciousness and awareness" (Galanter, 2019, p. 118), therefore opening the way for arguments of promoting AI systems as "artists" worthy of royalties (or some payments) and recognition. A reverse way of considering this is who (or which entity) takes on legal liability for the AI-generated works; after all, if there is credit and remuneration, there also has to be responsibility. There are both benefits and risks. At present, liabilities often fall to the humans around a work, not the machine (Epstein, Levine, Rand, & Rahwan, 2020, p. 7).

2.7 Risks of Fraud From AI-Generated Imagery in Academic Publishing

AI and computation are used to authenticate art for *catalogue raisonné* ("critical catalog") for various respective artists (Dobbs, Benedict, & Ras, 2022, p. 873). These tools are used to authenticate artworks to a particular artist based on various known knowledge and visual style, among other factors.

In the academic space, researchers have expressed concerns about how AI-generated images may be used fraudulently. Images in research carry information, and a simulated visual may gloss over actual features, besides not signifying anything of direct reality. They describe "severe cases" such as "(1) fabrication of non-existent images, (2) falsification or manipulation of existing images, and (3) plagiarism" by duplicating or editing others' images (Gu, Wang, Li, Zhao, Fu, Liang, & Qiu, 2022, p. 2). They elaborate:

Destroying image integrity in scientific papers may result in serious consequences. Inappropriate duplication and fabrication of images are two common misconducts… The rapid development of artificial intelligence technology has brought to us promising image-generation models that can produce realistic fake images. Here, we show that such advanced generative models threaten the publishing system in academia as they may be used to generate fake scientific images that cannot be effectively identified. We demonstrate the disturbing potential of these generative models in synthesizing fake images, plagiarizing existing images, and deliberately modifying images. It is very difficult to identify images generated by these models by visual inspection, image-forensic tools, and detection tools due to the unique paradigm of the generative models for processing images. (Gu, Wang, Li, Zhao, Fu, Liang, & Qiu, 2022, p. 1)

Certainly, there may be misrepresentation of research-based imagery by digital editing alone, by changing colors; rotating, scaling, cropping, splicing; melding colors; and other actions. Various forensic and other methods to identify image manipulations are not thought to work with AI-generated visuals. While some programs enable some observation of "systematic flaws that may distinguish them" from the real (Gu, Wang, Li, Zhao, Fu, Liang, & Qiu, 2022, p. 3), this study of two extant methods to detect generative AI images were not satisfactory. There is a need for "large-scale automatic screening" to detect digital image fraud (Gu, Wang, Li, Zhao, Fu, Liang, & Qiu, 2022, p. 4).

In another work, the researcher suggests that manually created images may be passed off as "AI artworks" (Cetinic & She, 2022, p. 66:14), perhaps given the hotness of the topic currently. Determining actual origins of a digital work may be difficult. New methods of authenticating works are being developed, including using ledgers from blockchain technologies. They observe challenges ahead:

...it is evident that the increasing use of AI technologies in the creation of art will have significant implications regarding the questions related to authorship, as well as on our human perception of art. With the development of AI models that can generate content which very convincingly imitates human textual, visual, or musical creations, many of our traditional, as well as contemporary, theoretical, and practical understandings of art might become challenged. (Cetinic & She, 2022, p. 66:17)

People are influenced by their sense of the artist hand, whether human or machine. Research participants who were told that the artists were human "had an interactive view of art (perceiving, providing feedback) but the 'AI Artist group' said any sense (visual, auditory, etc.) stimulus was art. The 'Human Artist group' thought AI could make art while the 'AI Artist group Disagreed" (Hong, 2018, p. 290). Research participants are willing to say that an AI can create art when they are looking at some actual created works (Hong, 2018).

2.8 Awareness of What is Human-Generated vs. Machine Generated?

Several research works explore whether various technological tools may pass the Turing Test for Artistic Creativity, namely, can the AI tool convince humans that the work that was output was actually created by a person (when it was made by the machine)?

A more formalist conceptualization (Boden, 2010) reads:

...for an artistic program to pass the TT would be for it to produce artwork which was: 1. Indistinguishable from one produced by a human being; and / or 2. Was seen as having as much aesthetic value as one produced by a human being. (Boden, 2010, p. 409, as cited in Daniele, Di Bernardi Luft, & Bryan-Kinns, 2021, p. 397)

Other sources take it as a matter of course that art-making AI has already passed the Turing Test and can create works "indistinguishable" from those created by people and "perceived as having no less of an aesthetic value" (Mikalonytė & Kneer, Sept. 2022, p. 43:2).

One research team found that while research participants judge works by robots and humans to a fairly similar extent, they were unwilling to identify robots as artists:

Across two experiments, we manipulated three factors: (i) agent type (AI-driven robot vs. human agent, (ii) behavior type (intentional creation of a painting vs. accidental creation), and (iii) object type (abstract vs. representational painting). We found that people judge robot paintings and human paintings as art to roughly the same extent. However, people are much less willing to consider robots as artists than humans, which is partially explained by the fact that they are less disposed to attribute artistic intentions to robots. (Mikalonytė & Kneer, Sept. 2022, p. 1)

That the mental state of the creator of the art is relevant to the research participants:

> *First, in contrast to moral contexts and a general tendency to anthropomorphize robots, people are relatively unwilling to attribute desire, belief, and intentions to artificial agents in aesthetic contexts. These unexpected differences of mental state ascriptions across domains invite further research. A second finding of considerable importance regards the role of intentions in artistic creation in general (i.e., independently of AI). A plethora of studies in psychology of art have emphasized the importance of the creator's intentions in the artistic process. Our study confirms that the intentions of the artist constitute a core factor in judgments about what is art and what is not. However, we found, accidental creations produced without artistic intentions are sometimes also deemed art. (Mikalonytė & Kneer, Sept. 2022, p. 43:11)*

Another study found that people can differentiate between human-made strokes vs. AI-generated drawing ones better than chance (50%) (Daniele, Di Bernardi Luft, & Bryan-Kinns, 2021, p. 396). They also found that "people responding faster performed significantly better than the slower ones" Daniele, Di Bernardi Luft, & Bryan-Kinns, 2021, p. 408).

AI is predicted to advance the field of art design by introducing more diverse thinking and broader creative practice (Han, Apr. 2021, p. 1023).

3. PROFESSIONALLY ETHICAL WAYS TO HARNESS AN ART-MAKING GENERATIVE AI TO SUPPORT INNOVATIVE INSTRUCTIONAL DESIGN WORK

Instructional design practice touches on various aspects of teaching and learning. The work may include any of the following and more:

- Analyzing digital learning objects
- Analyzing in-person (face-to-face), blended (hybrid), or fully online courses
- Analyzing trainings
- Profiling or modeling target learners
- Evaluating technologies for teaching and learning (learning management systems, content management systems, communications systems; authoring tools; assessment tools; and others)
- Testing technologies
- Conducting primary research
- Conducing secondary research
- Studying gray literature
- Analyzing data
- Pursuing grant funds
- Designing a learning experience (writing plans, writing assignments, designing practice activities, creating lab manuals, creating checklists, conducting paper-prototyping of learning contents)
- Developing digital and other contents (wireframing, coding, drafting, drawing, taking photographs, creating slideshows, and others)
    - Standing up online labs
    - Coordinating photo shoots and video captures
    - Curating photo collections
    - Creating light games, co-creating serious games

    - Designing field trip experiences
    - Designing fieldwork experiences
    - Creating simulations
    - Creating electronic books (e-books)
- Testing the digital learning contents (alpha testing, beta testing)
- Deploying the digital learning contents (uploading contents)
    - Versioning digital learning contents to various modalities and technologies (such as mobile learning)
- Assessing the efficacies of teaching and learning (for practice, for publication in the research literature)
- Creating research instruments, like surveys
- Adhering to all relevant laws (such as intellectual property, accessibility, privacy protections, media law, and others)
- Ensuring accessibility
- Adhering to all technical standards
- Presenting on instructional design work at meetings and conferences
- Publishing on instructional design work in peer-reviewed journals
- Pinch-hitting where needed (and substituting for others' work)
- Documenting the instructional design
- Maintaining all the raw and project files (so as to keep the records safe and to be able to revise from the last version as needed)

In the field, there are various models that may be used. One of the more common approaches is the ADDIE model, which stands for the following: analysis, design, development, implementation, and evaluation. The work is often piecemeal in higher education. Larger projects—such as grant-funded ones—often require whole teams to actualize. Likewise with larger research projects, those also required a mix of complex skills to make real.

Instructional designers need to apply knowledge of learners, their respective needs, human perceptual and mental processing systems, and other factors. They often work on multi-disciplinary cross-functional teams, with a range of different talents and skillsets. Often, the teams are sparse, requiring each member to handle a range of tasks. There are many stakeholders to a learning context.

In that work context, the potential benefits of an art-making generative AI can be highly beneficial. Original visuals may be created at very low cost (staff time), for any documentation that is used as well as the learning contents. Particular color palettes may be stipulated for exactness and consistency. Photorealism may be applied, resulting in visuals without the cost of a potential visit to external locations. However, uses of such materials require citation of sources and additional information to describe how the image was created (to ensure user clarity). The generated images may be used as-is if they are properly refined and do not lead to misunderstandings or negative learning (acquiring wrong information). It is important to read the fine print for the art-making generative AI generators…but also that of the funding agencies and stakeholder sensibilities. Given that visuals may "travel" from the original learning objects and find usage in other contexts, it is important to ensure that the information rides with the image and is obvious to users (visible to the naked eye).

Table 1, "Ephemerality to Materiality Continuum for Harnessing Art-Making Generative AI for Instructional Design," suggests that the art-making generative AI may be used in ways from conceptual (non-material) all the way to a refined digital image that is used nearly as-is. The various steps on the continuum suggest that the AI may suggest concepts, style, roughs (for pilot testing), reference visuals (which may be the basis of an original work derived from the visual or its trace), partially finished visual that may be used in part (and requiring much editing and revisioning and compositing work), or fully refined ones, which are ready to be used.

Because of AI's potential misuses, various stakeholders need to provide input in order to ensure proper design and usages (Ali, DiPaola, Lee, Sindato, Kim, Blumofe, & Breazeal, 2021, p. 2). This is so in the instructional design context as well.

Figure 1 shows a composite visual of six stylized extracts from the CrAIyon art-making AI. These are used illustratively, and the stylization was applied to change up every pixel of the visuals. The tool can create photorealistic, artful, and other types of visuals. Its capabilities are clearly not fully demonstrated in this very small and stylized sample.

3.1 General Professional Preferences in Instructional Design

To be clear, on most professional instructional design projects, the first choice for images and video will be from the team and its in-house production. The subject matter experts or content experts (and instructors) have access to various labs and locations and classrooms and can acquire images there. They can use releases to acquire rights to use the likenesses of those they work with. They can set up interviews with colleagues. There are many ways that they can acquire digital content.

If contents are not available from local efforts, free and open-source images from government entities are preferred secondarily. Those who curate government resources have high standards for archival and documentation of these resources. There is clear provenance, so works can be properly represented.

If these resources are not available, there are open-source images in the broad public hosted on various digital repositories. The downside here is that there may not be a clear provenance, and sometimes people will share images that belong to others. Also, free images are used in a large variety of contexts online, and their use in learning materials will mark the work as somewhat generic and maybe evoke a low-cost vibe. If the image is used in negative contexts, perhaps that may reflect back on the created digital learning objects.

If the open-source space does not have a usable resource, instructional designers may go to stock images, particularly if the application only requires something decorative (not educational per se)...and distractive from the gray text. There are collections of free stock images and commercial ones. Most ID projects are constrained by budgetary limits, so the commercial approach is not preferred, but if that is

Table 1. Ephemerality to materiality continuum for harnessing art-making generative AI for instructional design

Ephemeral / Immaterial Realized / Material					
Conceptual (1)	**Style (2)**	**Roughs (3)**	**Reference (4)**	**Partially Finished (5)**	**Refined Finished (6)**
Inspiration Ideas Concepts Brainstorming Motivation Exemplars	Style extraction Style application / style transfer	Draft Wireframe Digital outline Storyboard	Reference visual Trace from Used as a seeding visual (to create other AI-based visuals)	Usable in part Usable as a part (requires extraction; requires compositing) Layout	Refined work Publishable Usable (without much editing or revision or transcoding)

Figure 1. A composite of six stylized extracts from the CrAIyon art-making AI

the only source, that is the one that may be accessed. Sometimes, corporations own rights to a particular resource, but they only enable subscriptions to that resource for limited periods of time (such as half-a-year or a year). Those scenarios are not constructive since going back to refresh the subscription is a time-sink and not guaranteed. That is like building a resource on shaky sand.

The sequence, again, is as follows: (1) in-house production, (2) open-source from government, (3) open-source from the public, and (4) stock images (both free and commercial).

To be clear, many of the images used in instructional designs of photographs that are used to represent reality. These are enriched by reality, with images not only showing what humans expect and know but potential surprises as well. The photorealism of images captured in a broad range of ways si critical, as well as related metadata. In many fields, actual images are highly expensive to acquire based on the expense of technologies, the knowledge of experts in applying metadata, and other reasons. A single image released to public—such as from space exploration, from the biological sciences, and others—may cost in the tens of millions or more, depending on the dependencies required to acquire that image. Many images are of national security significance and are embargoed (some into human perpetuity). Indeed, there are very limited sources for some images and some types of images. For generative AI to be able to export particular images, they need training data in the space. The art-making generative AIs will offer a 2d images with up-sampled pixels whether or not it has experience with the text prompt. What is created is not validated in any way. It is offered "as is." The visual details offered are selective, artificially lit, and invariably incomplete. There is no "high fidelity" to any real but to a level of detail from the training imageset. The visual representations of the world are then necessarily limited and further from reality. The tradeoff in going with generative AI is, in this case, efficiency for less reality, more artifice, a pseudo-representational visual over an accurate one. The risks are that both experts and learners will emerge with a false sense of real-world phenomena, since visuals that are seen may not be "unseen" (to use a popular memetic observation). The tradeoffs of going with the imaginary vs. the real can be excessively harmful. Perhaps instructional designers will engage this issue in a case-by-case way.

Still, it is difficult to avoid the truth that there are cost-savings to be had with generative AI tools. One research team observed that "large-scale creative work often requires an entire studio of artists and producers" (Angert, Suzara, Han, Pondoc, & Subramonyam, 2023). In the cases of well-funded institutions with plenty of funding for particular projects, perhaps such a team may be stood up. In most cases in higher education, that context is a rare one. Most instructional design teams work in contexts of financial constraints.

3.2 About the Professional Ethics

So how can instructional designers harness the resources of the art-making generative AIs at present? How can they respect the sensitivities and legal requirements of various stakeholders, both in the present and into the future? Certainly, the respective stakeholders have complex considerations and needs. These include the following egos and entities (in various contexts):

- The makers of the art-making generative AI
- The learners
- The grant funders
- The institutions of higher education
- The learning institutions
- Researchers
- Professional conference goers
- Publication editors, publication peer reviewers, fellow authors
- The professional self (as professional and self-respecting individuals)
- Others

The need to be sensitive to others' needs requires reading the fine print of the respective official entities but also the "fine print" of people's needs in their respective contexts. What follows are some early thoughts in this space followed by further considerations for each part.

(1) All visuals by the generative AI should be thoroughly vetted. What is being communicated, and how? Is the visual accurate or not? What are ways to interpret the visual contents? Any user has to be cognizant of visual grammars, and the user has to understand the teaching and learning context so as not to cause any offense.

(2) The created image should clearly not be misleading or lead to negative learning. This due diligence requires consideration when generating the image, editing it, presenting it in a learning context, and so on. The context in which the visual is shared should have clear lead-up and lead-away information that enables the work to be used effectively.

(3) The visuals should not use likenesses of recognizably known living people. They should not show them in any sort of defamatory light. [Remember the note that liabilities follow the people who

have generated the image and used it, not the makers of the art-making generative AI systems.] The image should be clear in its messaging, not multi-messaged.

(4) Another ethical consideration relates to various contexts in which the visual may be used. What are the publishing policies and standards? Those of a professional conference?

(5) There should be sourcing of the visuals from art-making generative AIs especially if the works are used as-is as "Refined Finished (6)" or even "Partially Finished (5)" works in Table 1. Some may cite if they use the AI-generated work as Reference (4), such as in a trace layer.

   a. The correct version of the art-making generative AI should be cited. The history of the work may need to be mentioned. If there was pre- and / or post-processing, that may be needed as well.

If the fine print of the art-making generative AI does not require citation, citation is still good practice, so that users of the image do not misunderstand its provenance. This suggests a need for correct metadata that rides with the image and perhaps additional visible labeling as-such. (Once an image is in the wild, and even most behind paywalls, they tend to be separated from the original source [digital learning object, slideshow, video, article, etc.] and be used in different contexts. This may be seen in reverse image searches on the Web and Internet.

It is not a good idea to accept images if there are strings, such as "share alike" and what-not. Whoever is funding the ID project may have a variety of versioned usages for the contents, and those considerations have to come first.

Commercial projects (and government ones) will likely restrict the uses of generative AI works until some clear-headed policies may be put into place.

Some of the art-making generative AIs emplace watermarks on the image, which require removal and other makework. Others have a certain look-and-feel or visual signature which rides with the work, which may break with the style applied to the project. A free machine-generated visual is virtually not free from actual work.

This work does not propose tangling up instructional design work in excessive rules. However, it is clearly important to maintain legal and professional work. In many cases, it may be just as quick to take out a smart phone, capture some images, digitally edit those, and keep a record of where that work came from and how it was created. Perhaps it is very easy just to take out a device and sketch a quick drawing, revise, and edit, and upload. At present, so many of the art-making generative AIs create blurry visuals with particular visual tells and some stereotyping that these are not fully ready for primetime, but they are improving rapidly. The potential is there for them to be harnessed into ID work in a constructive way if people can figure out proper ethical guidelines in this generative AI space and in this profession.

3.3 Discussion

In the cases of photography and animation, there were initial fears stemming from the technologies. The fears were followed by "a blossoming of new creative and professional opportunities for artists" (Hertzmann, May 2018, p. 1). Perhaps this will be so with later acceptance of AI that makes art. After all, photography did not result in the dying off of painting; animation did not result in the dying off of movies. In modern art practice, artists sometimes only "supply the 'intent' and the 'idea' for the work" while the actual work is executed by others (Hertzmann, May 2018, p. 18); this dynamic may occur albeit with the machines doing the work. Indeed, there may be no return to more comfortable but less capable times.

The popularization of art-making generative AIs opens many doors for research. It will be important to study "the creative and explorative potentials of AI technologies in the context of art" (Cetinic & She, 2022, p. 1). The outpouring of human-machine generated art has appeared online, perhaps in a new form of "common art" (Hai-Jew, 2022).

4. FUTURE RESEARCH DIRECTIONS

In the instructional design space, there are extant questions. How do others conceptualize using art-making generative AI systems? Based on case documentation, what have their experiences been?

How are instructional designers "onboarded" to the uses of generative AI? What are effective vs. ineffective practices?

How do various public-facing generative AI platforms stack up for usage in instructional design? What are their strengths and weaknesses?

In the instructional design space, various visuals are commonly employed. These include diagrams, data visualizations, maps, grids, illustrations, exemplars, 2d objects, 3d objects, digital puppets, designs, plans, and others. Perhaps they may be used to create branding packages. Some of these are able to be generated, but others are not, at least not with any level of precision. What may be created in the future depends on artmaking generative AI buildouts and evolutions. How to wrangle these may vary extensively from the present moment. It will be important to explore these various other use cases and file outputs.

5. CONCLUSION

In one study, AI-generated haikus with human interventions were rated as more creative than those made individually by humans or those made individually by machine (Hitsuwari, Ueda, Yun, & Nomura, 2023, p. 1). As with other studies of works created by generative AIs, it was difficult for the human participants of the research study to differentiate haiku created by AI vs. people Hitsuwari, Ueda, Yun, & Nomura, 2023, p. 10). It is hard to generalize from one study, but it may well be that works by humans supported by AI may result in potent outcomes. AI may enrich creativity, "a domain once seen as exclusively human" (Kalpokiene & Kalpokas, 2023, p. 1). The art-making AIs are "not in conflict with human artists," and there are benefits to be had in "a partnership between human and machine creativity" (Mazzone & Elgammal, Feb. 2019, p. 26). Older narratives have described technical systems and humans in antagonistic relationship (Broeckmann, Feb. 2019, p. 25), which may be non-conducive to realities in the modern moment. Humans may work with AIs for "combinatory creativity" and even "transformational creativity (Cheng, Apr. 2022, pp. 110-4 to 110-5). Another voice suggests that AI art enables the human and machine to work as Cyborg, "a new kind of entity, one in which the developing creativity of the one manifests itself in the superior performance…of the other" (Cohen, 2009, pp. 1 – 2, as cited in Sundararajan, 2014, p. 148).

The race is on not only to create public-facing AIs for the public's use in a moment of its high popularity. Now is also a moment of "strategic development opportunities for artificial intelligence, accelerate the pace of ethical research and innovation" and the time to "build a competitive advantage" to evolve "an intelligent society" (Li, Gu, & Wang, Nov. 2020, p. 1). How quickly and effectively humanity onboards to the latest technological capabilities will affect national economies and particular industries.

In this moment of accelerated change, though, and of heightened competition (even among instructional designers), there are risks. If the technologies are misused, reputational harms may ensue. It is important to assess the situation accurately and proceed with care. The idea is to advance work in positive ways. Not only should the intentions be ethical, but the outcomes, too, should be, since negative outcomes may follow even if original intent is positive. Some insights will emerge only with the passage of time. Some may be anticipate-able now.

In whatever ways it is harnessed for instructional design, generative AI may enhance human endeavors in this space, too, as people harness the technology and socio-technoogy with forethought, AI literacy, and clear-mindedness.

REFERENCES

Aggarwal, G., & Parikh, D. (2020). Neuro-symbolic generative art: a preliminary study. *arXiv preprint arXiv:2007.02171.*

Ali, S., DiPaola, D., Lee, I., Sindato, V., Kim, G., Blumofe, R., & Breazeal, C. (2021). Children as creators, thinkers and citizens in an AI-driven future. *Computers and Education: Artificial Intelligence*, *2*, 100040. doi:10.1016/j.caeai.2021.100040

Anantrasirichai, N., & Bull, D. (2022). Artificial intelligence in the creative industries: A review. *Artificial Intelligence Review*, *55*(1), 589–656. doi:10.100710462-021-10039-7

Andrews, C. (2019). An embodied approach to AI art collaboration. In *Proceedings of the 2019 on Creativity and Cognition* (pp. 156-162). ACM. 10.1145/3325480.3325506

Angert, T., Suzara, M. I., Han, J., Pondoc, C. L., & Subramonyam, H. (2023). Spellburst: A Node-based Interface for Exploratory Creative Coding with Natural Language Prompts. *arXiv preprint arXiv:2308.03921*. doi:10.1145/3586183.3606719

Audry, S., & Ippolito, J. (2019, March). Can artificial intelligence make art without artists? Ask the viewer. In Arts (Vol. 8, p. 35). MDPI. doi:10.3390/arts8010035

Bajohr, H. (2022). Algorithmic empathy: Toward a critique of aesthetic AI. *Configurations*, *30*(2), 203–231. doi:10.1353/con.2022.0011

Barthet, M., Khalifa, A., Liapis, A., & Yannakakis, G. (2022, September). Generative personas that behave and experience like humans. In *Proceedings of the 17th International Conference on the Foundations of Digital Games* (pp. 1-10). ACM. 10.1145/3555858.3555879

Bezruczko, N. (2019). Psychometric equating methods ease fitness function dilemma in generative art. *In the Proceedings of the 1XXII Generative Art Conference - GA 2019.* ACM.

Boden, M. A., & Edmonds, E. A. (2009). What is generative art? *Digital Creativity (Exeter)*, *20*(1-2), 21–46. doi:10.1080/14626260902867915

Broeckmann, A. (2019, February). The machine as artist as myth. In Arts (Vol. 8, p. 25). MDPI. doi:10.3390/arts8010025

Browne, K. (2022). Who (or what) is an AI artist? *Leonardo, 55*(2), 130–134. doi:10.1162/leon_a_02092

Candy, L. (2020). Creating with the digital: tool, medium, mediator, partner. In *Interactivity, Game Creation, Design, Learning, and Innovation: 8th EAI International Conference, ArtsIT 2019, and 4th EAI International Conference*. Springer.

Caramiaux, B., & Alaoui, S. (2022). "Explorers of unknown planets": Practices and politics of artificial intelligence in visual arts. *Proceedings of the ACM on Human-Computer Interaction, 6*(CSCW2), (pp. 1-24). ACM. 10.1145/3555578

Caramiaux, B., Alaoui, S. F., & Hsueh, S. (2022, April). What becomes of "work" in AI "artwork"? In *CHI'22 Conference-Workshop on Outsourcing Artificial Intelligence*. Responding to the Reassertion of the Human Element into Automation.

Carvalhais, M. (2019). Breaking the black box: Procedural reading, creation of meaning and closure in computational artworks. In P. Machado, J. Romero, and G. Greenfield's *Artificial Intelligence and the Arts: Computational Creativity, Artistic Behavior, and Tools for Creatives*. Research Gate.

Carvalhais, M., & Lee, R. (2022). Spectral and procedural creativity: A perspective from computational art. *Transformations (14443775)*, (36).

Castellanos, C. (2022). Intersections of living and machine agencies: Possibilities for creative AI. In *The Language of Creative AI: Practices, Aesthetics and Structures* (pp. 155–166). Springer International Publishing. doi:10.1007/978-3-031-10960-7_9

Cetinic, E., & She, J. (2022). Understanding and creating art with AI: Review and outlook. [TOMM]. *ACM Transactions on Multimedia Computing Communications and Applications, 18*(2), 1–22. doi:10.1145/3475799

Cheng, M. (2022, April). The creativity of artificial intelligence in art. In Proceedings (Vol. 81, pp. 110-1 to 110-5). MDPI. doi:10.3390/proceedings2022081110

Choi, S. K., DiPaola, S., & Töyrylä, H. (2021). Artistic style meets artificial intelligence. *Journal of Perceptual Imaging*, *4*(2), 020501-1, 020501-14. doi:10.2352/J.Percept.Imaging.2021.4.2.020501

Cohen, H. (1974, reprinted 2022). On purpose: an enquiry into the possible roles of the computer in art. In The Language of Creative AI: Practices, Aesthetics and Structures (pp. 3-27). Cham: Springer International Publishing.

Cohen, H., Nake, F., Brown, D. C., Brown, P., Galanter, P., McCormack, J., & d 'Inverno, M. (2012). Evaluation of creative aesthetics. *Computers and creativity*, 95-111.

Dahlstedt, P. (2021). Musicking with algorithms: Thoughts on artificial intelligence, creativity, and agency. Handbook of Artificial Intelligence for Music: Foundations, Advanced Approaches, and Developments for Creativity, 873-914.

Daniele, A., Di Bernardi Luft, C., & Bryan-Kinns, N. (2021). "What is human?" A Turing Test for artistic creativity. In *Artificial Intelligence in Music, Sound, Art and Design: 10th International Conference, EvoMUSART 2021, Held as Part of EvoStar 2021, Virtual Event, April 7–9, 2021* [Springer International Publishing.]. *Proceedings, 10*, 396–411.

Daniele, A., & Song, Y. Z. (2019, January). AI+ art=human. In *Proceedings of the 2019 AAAI/ACM Conference on AI, Ethics, and Society* (pp. 155-161). ACM. 10.1145/3306618.3314233

Davis, N., Hsiao, C. P., Popova, Y., & Magerko, B. (2015). An enactive model of creativity for computational collaboration and co-creation. *Creativity in the digital age*, 109-133.

De Smedt, T., & Lechat, L. Burtenshaw, & Nijs, L. (2021). Case studies in computer graphics and AI. In P. Machado, J. Romero, and G. Greenfield's Artificial Intelligence and the Arts: Computational Creativity, Artistic Behavior, and Tools for Creatives, (pp. 165 – 185). ACM.

Devendorf, L. (2014). Art making and making artists. *In Proceedings of the 2014 companion publication on Designing interactive systems* (pp. 151-156). ACM. 10.1145/2598784.2598787

DiPaola, S., Gabora, L., & McCaig, G. (2018). Informing artificial intelligence generative techniques using cognitive theories of human creativity. *Procedia Computer Science, 145*, 158–168. doi:10.1016/j.procs.2018.11.024

DiPaola, S., & McCaig, G. (2016). Using artificial intelligence techniques to emulate the creativity of a portrait painter. *Electronic Visualisation and the Arts*, 158-165.

Dobbs, T., Benedict, A., & Ras, Z. (2022). Jumping into the artistic deep end: Building the catalogue raisonné. *AI & Society, 37*(3), 873–889. doi:10.100700146-021-01370-2

Dorin, A. (2008). A survey of virtual ecosystems in generative electronic art. *The Art of Artificial Evolution: A Handbook on Evolutionary Art and Music*, 289-309.

Dorin, A., McCabe, J., McCormack, J., Monro, G., & Whitelaw, M. (2012). A framework for understanding generative art. *Digital Creativity (Exeter), 23*(3-4), 239–259. doi:10.1080/14626268.2012.709940

Edmonds, E. (2018, January). Algorithmic art machines. In Arts (Vol. 7, p. 3). MDPI. doi:10.3390/arts7010003

Edmonds, E. (2022). AI, creativity, and art. In *The Language of Creative AI: Practices, Aesthetics and Structures* (pp. 57–71). Springer International Publishing. doi:10.1007/978-3-031-10960-7_4

Eisenmann, J. (2021). Setting the stage for 3D compositing with machine learning. In P. Machado, J. Romero, and G. Greenfield's Artificial Intelligence and the Arts: Computational Creativity, Artistic Behavior, and Tools for Creatives, (pp. 187 – 205). Research Gate.

Epstein, Z., Levine, S., Rand, D. G., & Rahwan, I. (2020). Who gets credit for ai-generated art? *iScience, 23*(9), 101515. doi:10.1016/j.isci.2020.101515 PMID:32920489

Flick, C., & Worrall, K. (2022). The ethics of creative AI. In *The Language of Creative AI: Practices, Aesthetics and Structures* (pp. 73–91). Springer International Publishing. doi:10.1007/978-3-031-10960-7_5

Friess, P. (2021). Existence beyond transhumanism–context-based research-creation for critical art making. *Proceedings of Politics of the Machines-Rogue Research, 2021*(3), 278–284. doi:10.14236/ewic/POM2021.36

Galanter, P. (2016). Generative art theory. *A Companion to Digital Art*, (pp. 146-180). UCSC.

Galanter, P. (2019). Artificial intelligence and problems in generative art theory. *Proceedings of EVA London, 2019*, 112–118. doi:10.14236/ewic/EVA2019.22

Gerard, H. S. (2020). *Fallen objects: Collaborating with artificial intelligence in the field of graphic design*. Portland State University's PDXScholar.

Grba, D., Todorović, V., Boye, P., Kang, K. H., & Pandilovski, M. (2019). Machine flaws in generative art. In *the proceedings of the 25th International Symposium on Electronic Art*, (pp. 713 – 717).

Greenfield, G. (2021). Artificial life and artificial intelligence advances in the visual arts. In P. Machado, J. Romero, and G. Greenfield's Artificial Intelligence and the Arts: Computational Creativity, Artistic Behavior, and Tools for Creatives, (pp. 3-26). Springer. doi:10.1007/978-3-030-59475-6_1

Gruchy, T. (2020). Observations and categorisations of art practices associated with AI. In *Human-Computer Interaction. Design and User Experience: Thematic Area, HCI 2020, Held as Part of the 22nd International Conference, HCII 2020, Copenhagen, Denmark, July 19–24, 2020* [Springer International Publishing.]. *Proceedings, 22*(Part I), 234–245.

Gu, J., Wang, X., Li, C., Zhao, J., Fu, W., Liang, G., & Qiu, J. (2022). AI-enabled image fraud in scientific publications. *Patterns (New York, N.Y.), 3*(7), 100511. doi:10.1016/j.patter.2022.100511 PMID:35845832

Guadamuz, A. (2017). *Do androids dream of electric copyright? Comparative analysis of originality in artificial intelligence generated works*. Intellectual Property Quarterly.

Guo, S., Wang, Y., & Yang, W. (2022, June). A study on the collision of artificial intelligence and art based on generative adversarial networks (GAN). In *2022 International Conference on 3D Immersion, Interaction and Multi-sensory Experiences (ICDIIME)* (pp. 27-31). IEEE. 10.1109/ICDIIME56946.2022.00014

Hai-Jew, S. (2022). *Common Visual Art in A Social Digital Age*. Nova Science Publishers. doi:10.52305/BKOT1869

Han, Z. (2021, April). Combined development of artificial intelligence and art design. In *2021 6th International Conference on Intelligent Computing and Signal Processing (ICSP)* (pp. 1023-1026). IEEE. 10.1109/ICSP51882.2021.9408896

Hebron, P. (n.d.) *Artificial intelligence and the decoupling of creation and comprehension*. Patrick Hebron.

Hertzmann, A. (2018, May). Can computers create art? In Arts (Vol. 7, p. 18). MDPI. doi:10.3390/arts7020018

Hitsuwari, J., Ueda, Y., Yun, W., & Nomura, M. (2023). Does human–AI collaboration lead to more creative art? Aesthetic evaluation of human-made and AI-generated haiku poetry. *Computers in Human Behavior, 139*, 107502. doi:10.1016/j.chb.2022.107502

Hong, J. W. (2018). Bias in perception of art produced by artificial intelligence. In *Human-Computer Interaction. Interaction in Context: 20th International Conference, HCI International 2018*. Springer.

Hong, J. W., & Curran, N. M. (2019). Artificial intelligence, artists, and art: Attitudes toward artwork produced by humans vs. artificial intelligence. [TOMM]. *ACM Transactions on Multimedia Computing Communications and Applications*, *15*(2s), 1–16. doi:10.1145/3326337

Hristov, K. (2016). Artificial intelligence and the copyright dilemma. *Idea*, *57*, 431.

Hung, M. C., Trang, M. X., Nakatsu, R., & Tosa, N. (2022, February). Unusual transformation: A deep learning approach to create art. In *ArtsIT, Interactivity and Game Creation: Creative Heritage. New Perspectives from Media Arts and Artificial Intelligence. 10th EAI International Conference, ArtsIT 2021, Virtual Event, December 2-3, 2021, Proceedings* (pp. 309-320). Cham: Springer International Publishing. 10.1007/978-3-030-95531-1_21

Jin, X., Chen, Z., & Li, W. (2020). AI-GAN: Asynchronous interactive generative adversarial network for single image rain removal. *Pattern Recognition*, *100*, 107143. doi:10.1016/j.patcog.2019.107143

Jonnaert, C. (2020). Artificial intelligence and Canadian copyright: The quest for an author. *Católica Law Review*, *4*(2), 13–34.

Kalpokiene, J., & Kalpokas, I. (2023). Creative encounters of a posthuman kind–anthropocentric law, artificial intelligence, and art. *Technology in Society*, *102197*, 1–8. doi:10.1016/j.techsoc.2023.102197

Langdon, M., & Langdon, M. (2014). Digital art and cultural commentary. *The Work of Art in a Digital Age: Art, Technology and Globalisation*, (pp. 13-35). Springer.

Leiser, A., & Schlippe, T. (2022, February). AI in art: Simulating the human painting process. In *ArtsIT, Interactivity and Game Creation: Creative Heritage. New Perspectives from Media Arts and Artificial Intelligence. 10th EAI International Conference, ArtsIT 2021, Virtual Event, December 2-3, 2021, Proceedings* (pp. 295-308). Cham: Springer International Publishing.

Li, Y., Gu, J., & Wang, L. (2020, November). Research on artificial intelligence ethics in the field of art design. [). IOP Publishing.]. *Journal of Physics: Conference Series*, *1673*(1), 012052. doi:10.1088/1742-6596/1673/1/012052

Lin, Y. (2020, October). Research on application and breakthrough of artificial intelligence in art design in the new era. [). IOP Publishing.]. *Journal of Physics: Conference Series*, *1648*(3), 032187. doi:10.1088/1742-6596/1648/3/032187

Liu, K. H., Lin, C. C., & Liu, T. J. (2022, January). Image generation by residual block based generative adversarial networks. In *2022 IEEE International Conference on Consumer Electronics (ICCE)* (pp. 1-4). IEEE. 10.1109/ICCE53296.2022.9730533

Lushetich, N. (2022). How many angels can dance on the head of a pin? Understanding 'alien' thought. *AI & Society*, *37*(4), 1411–1425. doi:10.100700146-021-01252-7

Machado, P., Romero, J., & Greenfield, G. (2021). Applicability of convolutional neural network artistic style transfer algorithms. In P. Machado, J. Romero, and G. Greenfield's Artificial Intelligence and the Arts: Computational Creativity, Artistic Behavior, and Tools for Creatives, (pp. 61-81). Springer.

Maiocchi, R. (1991). Can you make a computer understand and produce art? *AI & Society*, *5*(3), 183–201. doi:10.1007/BF01891915

Maslic, A. D., & Kim, E. S. (2021). *An epistemological misalignment of cogs in the AI-Art-Making Machine*. In the Proceedings of the EVA London, London, England.

Mazzone, M., & Elgammal, A. (2019, February). Art, creativity, and the potential of artificial intelligence. In Arts (Vol. 8, p. 26). MDPI. doi:10.3390/arts8010026

McCormack, J. (2017). Working with generative systems: an artistic perspective. *Electronic Visualisation and the Arts (EVA 2017)*, (pp. 213-218). ACM.

McCormack, J., Bown, O., Dorin, A., McCabe, J., Monro, G., & Whitelaw, M. (2014). Ten questions concerning generative computer art. *Leonardo*, *47*(2), 135–141. doi:10.1162/LEON_a_00533

McCormack, J., Gambardella, C. C., Rajcic, N., Krol, S. J., Llano, M. T., & Yang, M. (2023). Is writing prompts really making art? *arXiv preprint arXiv:2301.13049*. doi:10.1007/978-3-031-29956-8_13

McCormack, J., Gifford, T., & Hutchings, P. (2019). Autonomy, authenticity, authorship and intention in computer generated art. In *Computational Intelligence in Music, Sound, Art and Design: 8th International Conference*. Springer.

Mikalonytė, E. S., & Kneer, M. (2022, September). Can artificial intelligence make art? Folk intuitions as to whether AI-driven robots can be viewed as artists and produce art. *ACM Transactions on Human-Robot Interaction,* 11(4). *Article*, *43*, 1–19.

Monmarché, N., Mahnich, I., & Slimane, M. (2008). Artificial art made by artificial ants. *The Art of Artificial Evolution: A Handbook on Evolutionary Art and Music*, (pp. 227-247).

Notaro, A. (2020). State-of-the-art: AI through the (artificial) artist's eye. *EVA London 2020: Electronic Visualisation and the Arts*, (pp. 322-328). ACM.

Paulsen, K. (2020). "Shitty automation": Art, artificial intelligence, humans in the loop. Media-N, 16(1).

Penny, S. (2013). Art and robotics: Sixty years of situated machines. *AI & Society*, *28*(2), 147–156. doi:10.100700146-012-0404-4

Poltronieri, F. (2022). Towards a symbiotic future: Art and creative AI. In *The Language of Creative AI: Practices, Aesthetics and Structures* (pp. 29–41). Springer International Publishing. doi:10.1007/978-3-031-10960-7_2

Reinhuber, E. (2022, February). Synthography––An invitation to reconsider the rapidly changing toolkit of digital image creation as a new genre beyond photography. In *ArtsIT, Interactivity and Game Creation: Creative Heritage. New Perspectives from Media Arts and Artificial Intelligence. 10th EAI International Conference, ArtsIT 2021, Virtual Event, December 2-3, 2021, Proceedings* (pp. 321-331). Cham: Springer International Publishing.

Sajeeda, A., & Hossain, B. M. (2022). Exploring generative adversarial networks and adversarial training. *International Journal of Cognitive Computing in Engineering*.

Santaella, L. (2022). Artificial intelligence and creativity under interrogation. In *The Language of Creative AI: Practices, Aesthetics and Structures* (pp. 43–56). Springer International Publishing. doi:10.1007/978-3-031-10960-7_3

Schneider, T., & Rea, N. (2018, Sept. 25). Has artificial intelligence given us the next great art movement? Experts say slow down, the 'field is in its infancy.' *Artnet.*

Shahriar, S., & Al Roken, N. (2022). How can generative adversarial networks impact computer generated art? Insights from poetry to melody conversion. *International Journal of Information Management Data Insights*, *2*(1), 100066. doi:10.1016/j.jjimei.2022.100066

Shahriar, S., & Hayawi, K. (2022, March). NFTGAN: Non-Fungible Token art generation using Generative Adversarial Networks. In *2022 7th International Conference on Machine Learning Technologies (ICMLT)* (pp. 255-259). ACM.

Srinivasan, R., & Uchino, K. (2021, March). Biases in generative art: A causal look from the lens of art history. In *Proceedings of the 2021 ACM Conference on Fairness, Accountability, and Transparency* (pp. 41-51). ACM. 10.1145/3442188.3445869

Striuk, O., Kondratenko, Y., Sidenko, I., & Vorobyova, A. (2020, November). Generative adversarial neural network for creating photorealistic images. In *2020 IEEE 2nd International Conference on Advanced Trends in Information Theory (ATIT)* (pp. 368-371). IEEE. 10.1109/ATIT50783.2020.9349326

Sun, H., Rau, P. L. P., & Wang, B. (2021). A study of machine ethics in human-artificial intelligence interactions. In *Cross-Cultural Design. Applications in Arts, Learning, Well-being, and Social Development: 13th International Conference, CCD 2021*. Springer.

Sun, J., Liao, Q. V., Muller, M., Agarwal, M., Houde, S., Talamadupula, K., & Weisz, J. D. (2022, March). Investigating explainability of generative AI for code through scenario-based design. In *27th International Conference on Intelligent User Interfaces* (pp. 212-228). ACM. 10.1145/3490099.3511119

Sundararajan, L. (2014). Mind, machine, and creativity: An artist's perspective. *The Journal of Creative Behavior*, *48*(2), 136–151. doi:10.1002/jocb.44 PMID:25541564

Suryna, K. & Serrano, R. G. (2019). Agents without agency: Artificial intelligence as artistic medium. *Taboo Transgression Transcendence*, (pp. 200 – 209). ACM.

Tang, M. (2022, June). Human and machine symbiosis--An experiment of human and robot co-creation of calligraphy-style drawing. In *HCI International 2022 Posters: 24th International Conference on Human-Computer Interaction,* (pp. 462-467). Cham: Springer International Publishing.

Tao, F., Zou, X., & Ren, D. (2018). The art of human intelligence and the technology of artificial intelligence: artificial intelligence visual art research. In *Intelligence Science II: Third IFIP TC 12 International Conference, ICIS 2018, Beijing, China, November 2-5, 2018* [Springer International Publishing.]. *Proceedings*, 2, 146–155.

Trujillo, S., Azanza, M., & Diaz, O. (2007, October). Generative metaprogramming. In *Proceedings of the 6th International Conference on Generative Programming and Component Engineering* (pp. 105-114). 10.1145/1289971.1289990

Ulberg, E., Llach, D. C., & Byrne, D. (2020). Hand-crafting neural networks for art-making. In ICCC (pp. 508-511).

Wang, C., Xu, C., Yao, X., & Tao, D. (2019). Evolutionary generative adversarial networks. *IEEE Transactions on Evolutionary Computation, 23*(6), 921–934. doi:10.1109/TEVC.2019.2895748

Wang, Y., & Ma, H. (2019, December). The value evaluation of artificial intelligence works of art. In *2019 International Joint Conference on Information, Media and Engineering (IJCIME)* (pp. 445-449). IEEE. 10.1109/IJCIME49369.2019.00096

Wanner, A. N. D. R. E. S. (2014). Mechanical drawing machines and the glitch—Visualizing technology through its failures. In *Proceedings of the Second Conference on Computation, Communication, Aesthetics and X* (pp. 31-40). IEEE.

Wu, A. N., Stouffs, R., & Biljecki, F. (2022). Generative Adversarial Networks in the built environment: A comprehensive review of the application of GANs across data types and scales. *Building and Environment, 223*, 109477. doi:10.1016/j.buildenv.2022.109477

Wu, T. (2018, February). Saliency-aware generative art. In *Proceedings of the 2018 10th International Conference on Machine Learning and Computing* (pp. 198-202). ACM. 10.1145/3195106.3195143

Yanisky-Ravid, S. (2017). Generating Rembrandt: Artificial intelligence, copyright, and accountability in the 3A Era: The human-like authors are already here: A new model. *Mich. St. L. Rev., 659.*

Zeilinger, M. (2021). Generative adversarial copy machines. *Culture Machine, 20*, 1–23.

Zylinska, J. (2020). *AI Art: Machine Visions and Warped Dreams.* Open Humanities Press.

ADDITIONAL READING SECTION

Hai-Jew, S. (2022). *Common Visual Art in A Social Digital Age.* Nova Science Publishers. doi:10.52305/BKOT1869

KEY TERMS AND DEFINITIONS

Aesthetics: What is considered beautiful or artfully pleasing.

Anthropocentrism: Human-centeredness in terms of a worldview.

Copyright: A legal right owned by the originator of a work to use it in particular ways.

Creativity: The ability to conceptualize and execute on an original idea and / or creation.

Deep Fake: An image, sound recording, video, or other digital object that depicts a false or misrepresentational context, often using AI and others.

General AI: A set of artificial intelligence technologies that emulate and build on human general intelligence.

Generative Adversarial Network (GAN): A type of AI program that is comprised of a generator and a discriminator, which work in adversarial and competitive ways.

Generative AI: An artificial intelligence tool or program that creates some content autonomously or with inputs from people or other external sources.

Generative Computational Creativity: A class of creative systems that can autonomously (without human input) generate text (in various genres), games, designs, analogies, artworks, music, and other contents.

Generative Design: An AI capability of proposing various designs with particular parameters.

Innovation: The creation of a novel process or object, such as to a marketplace.

Instructional Design: The systematic design of teaching and learning to optimize the process (based on theory, empirical research, data, target learners, discipline content areas, and other inputs).

Intellectual Property: Rights related to an original work that may be protected by patent, copyright, trademark, and other elements.

Non-fungible token (NFT): Assets (often digital) tokenized on a permanent blockchain.

Post-Humanism: A theory of "after" or "beyond" humanism as a central concern to extend focus on additional issues beyond human concerns (decentering of human concerns as the foremost concern).

Socio-Technical System: The understanding of particular technologies as comprising both social and technical aspects.

Strong AI: Artificial intelligence that aims to replicate and / or extend general intelligence.

Techno-Moral: The consideration of morality in a technological context or tool.

Techno-Social: The consideration of the social in a technological context or tool.

Text Prompt: The uses of words, phrases, textual symbols, or other symbols in combination to elicit a response (such as from a generative AI).

Visual Prompt: The uses of uploaded digital imagery (photos, drawings, sketches, icons, logos, and / or others) to elicit a response (such as from a generative AI).

Weak AI: An artificial intelligence program designed for a dedicated purpose to solve particular dedicated challenges (vs. AI that focuses on the emulation of general human intelligence).

Chapter 11
Navigating the Terrain:
Current Challenges and Solutions in Integrating Generative AI Into Education

C. V. Suresh Babu
https://orcid.org/0000-0002-8474-2882
Hindustan Institute of Technolgy and Science, India

S. Barath Kumar
https://orcid.org/0009-0007-6607-3455
Hindustan Institute of Technology and Science, India

ABSTRACT

The chapter provides an extensive exploration of Generative AI in education. It investigates the evolution and significance of AI in educational settings while delving into contemporary issues such as ethics, privacy, fairness, and pedagogy. Furthermore, it examines the impact on traditional teaching methods, personalization, and accessibility, addressing educational disparities. The chapter also outlines the best practices and lessons learned from case studies and successful institutions, pointing toward future directions, including emerging technologies like GPT-4 and augmented reality. It emphasizes advancing ethical guidelines, enhancing teacher-student collaboration with AI, proposing policy recommendations, and establishing legal frameworks for student data protection, along with government initiatives and funding in the realm of AI in education.

1. INTRODUCTION

1.1 Overview of Generative AI in Education

Generative AI, despite being a nascent technology, holds immense potential to revolutionize the field of education. As generative AI continues to advance, it is poised to bring about innovative and highly effective applications in student learning. Below, we explore some key ideas regarding the role of generative AI in education:

DOI: 10.4018/979-8-3693-0074-9.ch011

Equity in Education: Generative AI can serve as a powerful tool for closing the achievement gap among various student demographics. It can enhance educational accessibility for all, including students with disabilities and those from economically disadvantaged backgrounds. By doing so, it offers an opportunity to level the playing field and ensure that all students have equal access to quality education. This is particularly crucial as the future workforce becomes increasingly reliant on AI, making early exposure and training paramount for students.

Personalized Learning: Generative AI promises to revolutionize education by enabling a more personalized, engaging, and efficient learning experience for every student. By employing generative AI in a responsible and ethical manner, we can create tailored learning environments that cater to individual learning styles and needs. This approach has the potential to foster a deeper understanding of the subject matter and increase overall student engagement.

1.2 Purpose and Scope of the Chapter

The primary objective of this chapter is to provide a comprehensive introduction to generative AI in education. This chapter will address the following topics:

1. What is generative AI and its fundamental concepts?
2. Practical applications of generative AI within the educational context.
3. The potential benefits that generative AI can bring to the field of education.
4. Challenges and limitations associated with the integration of generative AI in education.
5. Strategies for the responsible and ethical implementation of generative AI in educational settings.

1.3 Chapter Structure

This chapter is intended for a broad audience, encompassing educators, administrators, policymakers, and academics. It will avoid the use of technical jargon and will be presented in a clear, concise, and reader-friendly manner.

2. BACKGROUND

2.1 Evolution of Generative AI in Education

Generative AI, an artificial intelligence subset capable of creating various forms of content, such as text, graphics, music, and code, is emerging as a transformative force in education. Although generative AI is a relatively young field, it holds the promise of revolutionizing education by offering personalized learning experiences, generating innovative content, and aiding educators in their roles. The journey of generative AI in education can be traced back to the early 2000s when researchers began developing AI systems capable of producing text and graphics. The application of generative AI in educational contexts gained traction in the early 2010s, focusing on tasks like crafting personalized learning materials and providing students with feedback.

In recent years, the progress of generative AI systems has surged, thanks in part to advancements in deep learning, a machine learning subfield particularly adept at tasks like image generation and natural language processing. As generative AI systems continue to evolve, a diverse array of educational applications has emerged. These applications now encompass the creation of personalized learning materials, the development of innovative educational games and simulations, as well as providing valuable support to educators in their teaching roles (L. Chen et al., 2020).

2.2 Significance of AI in Educational Settings

Artificial intelligence (AI) holds immense promise within educational settings, offering numerous advantages to students, educators, and educational institutions. Here are some primary ways in which AI is transforming education:

- **Personalized Learning**: AI has the ability to tailor instructional content to each student's unique requirements and preferences. AI systems can deliver customized lectures, exercises, and feedback based on students' performance and learning styles, allowing them to progress at their own pace.
- **Engagement through Gamification and Multimedia**: AI-powered applications frequently employ gamification, interactive content, and multimedia elements to enhance the learning experience. These techniques sustain students' interest and enthusiasm, making learning a more enjoyable and engaging endeavor.
- **Data Analysis for Informed Decision-Making**: AI can efficiently analyze extensive datasets to identify trends and patterns in student performance. This data serves as a valuable resource for educators and administrators, aiding in data-driven decisions related to curriculum, instructional methodologies, and resource allocation.
- **Efficient Content Creation**: AI can generate instructional content, including quizzes, assessments, and textbooks. This not only saves educators time but also ensures that students have access to current and tailored educational materials.

The integration of AI in education holds the potential to revolutionize the learning experience, making it more personalized, engaging, and data-informed.

2.2 Introduction to Generative AI and its Applications in Teaching and Learning

Generative AI, a subset of artificial intelligence, focuses on crafting content, often in the form of text, images, or other media, through the use of algorithms and models capable of generating data akin to what a human might produce. One prominent example of generative AI is the GPT-3 model, renowned for its capacity to produce human-like prose. Generative AI offers a plethora of applications in teaching and learning, revolutionizing educational approaches in diverse ways.

Generative AI enables the creation of tailor-made learning materials that align with individual students' requirements and interests. For instance, it can generate personalized quizzes, exercises, or study guides based on a student's proficiencies and areas requiring improvement (Gwo-Jen Hwang et al., 2020).

3. CURRENT ISSUES IN GENERATIVE AI FOR EDUCATION

3.1 Ethical Considerations

Plagiarism and AI-Generated Content:

AI-generated content, produced by artificial intelligence (AI) systems, intersects with the issue of plagiarism. Plagiarism involves the unauthorized duplication of another person's work, passing it off as one's own. Similarly, content created by AI can be subject to unauthorized copying and attribution issues.

AI-generated content may be copied without proper credit, or individuals might use AI-generated content as a foundation for their work without adequately acknowledging the AI source. Recognizing the risks of plagiarism when utilizing AI-generated content is of paramount importance (Ali et al., 2021).

3.1.2 Privacy Concerns and Student Data Protection

When incorporating AI in education, safeguarding student data privacy is imperative. AI systems can amass extensive data about students, including their academic performance, behavior, and personal information. It is essential to prevent unauthorized use, disclosure, or access to this data. Several privacy concerns in the classroom context include:

- **Non-Educational Data Usage**: Information gathered about students may be employed for non-educational purposes, such as targeted advertising or marketing.
- **Excessive Data Collection**: AI systems have the capacity to collect a surplus of information about students, which may exceed educational requirements.
- **Data Sharing with Third Parties**: Student data may be shared with third parties (M. Wang et al., 2019).

3.1.3 Algorithmic Bias and Fairness in Education

When implementing AI in education, addressing issues of fairness and algorithmic bias is critical. AI systems' outputs may be biased due to various factors. For example, AI programs predicting student performance or grades might exhibit bias towards specific student demographics, such as race or socio-economic background (H. K. Simonsen, 2022).

Algorithmic bias can arise from various sources, with selection bias being a common type. Selection bias occurs when the data used to train an AI system is not representative of the population it will serve. For instance, if school district data is used to train an AI system to forecast student grades (Loukina et al., BEA 2019).

3.2 Pedagogical Concerns

3.2.1 Automation vs. Human Interaction

In contemporary life, both human interaction and automation play pivotal roles. While human interaction fosters social connection, empathy, and creativity, automation enhances productivity, efficiency, and accuracy (Christian P. et al., 2019).

1. **Automation** involves the use of technology to perform tasks that were traditionally carried out by humans. Numerous industries, including manufacturing, healthcare, and customer service, stand to gain significant benefits from automation.
2. **Human interaction** encompasses the act of communicating and engaging with other individuals. It brings forth various advantages, including relationship-building, education, and collaborative problem-solving (M. Nardo et al., 2020).

3.2.2 Impact on Traditional Teaching Methods

AI is significantly transforming traditional teaching methods. Here are a few examples:

- **Personalized Learning**: AI has the capability to analyze student data to identify each individual's strengths and weaknesses. This information is then used to create personalized learning plans for each student. AI-driven learning platforms, for instance, offer students tailored recommendations for materials and activities based on their unique needs.
- **Prompt Feedback**: AI can provide rapid feedback to students on their work, enabling them to recognize and learn from their mistakes. AI-powered writing instructors, for example, can offer feedback on syntax, style, and clarity (L. Chen et al., 2020).

3.2.3 Balancing Personalization and Standardization

In education, striking a balance between personalization and standardization can be challenging. On one hand, the aim is to ensure that all students, regardless of their backgrounds or abilities, have access to high-quality education. On the other hand, the goal is to provide students with the opportunity to learn in a manner that suits their unique needs and interests.

Several approaches can help strike this balance:

- **Blended Learning**: Combining standardized and personalized learning activities is one method. Students might begin each day with a mandatory lesson in a fundamental subject, such as reading or math, and then engage in personalized learning activities, such as projects or enrichment materials for the remainder of the day.
- **Differentiated Instruction**: Differentiated teaching is another strategy for balancing customization and standardization. Teachers can adapt their lesson plans to meet each student's specific needs. For example, a teacher may provide different levels of support to students struggling in a particular subject area.
- **Involving Parents and Students**: Including parents and students in the decision-making process regarding standardization and personalization is essential. Students may have the option to choose which personalized learning tasks to complete, and parents could decide which standardized examinations their children take.

A balanced approach to standardization and personalization can help create an education system that meets the needs of all students.

3.3 Accessibility and Inclusivity

3.3.1 Educational Inequalities and the Digital Divide

Protecting student data is of paramount importance for several reasons. Firstly, student data contains sensitive personal information, including names, addresses, and grades, which could be exploited for fraudulent or malicious purposes, such as identity theft. Secondly, decisions about students, such as enrollment in specific classes or eligibility for particular programs, often rely on student data. Ensuring the accuracy and objectivity of the information used for these decisions is critical.

To safeguard student data, schools and organizations can take various steps, including:

- **Establishing and Implementing Data Privacy Policies**: Develop and implement a comprehensive data privacy policy that clearly defines the types of information collected, their purpose, and who has access. Parents and students should also have access to this policy.
- **Obtaining Parental Consent for Specific Data Collection**: Seek parental permission before collecting or using certain categories of student data, in accordance with applicable laws and regulations.
- **Securing Student Data Storage**: Take measures to secure student data during storage, guarding against unauthorized access, use, or disclosure.
- **Access Control**: Restrict access to student data to only those employees and contractors who require it for their job responsibilities.
- **Data Retention Policies**: Establish and adhere to policies that dictate the deletion of student data when it is no longer needed for educational purposes.

Ensuring the privacy and security of student data is fundamental in the digital age, contributing to the protection of individuals and the promotion of equity in education.

3.4 Data Privacy and Security

3.4.1 Safeguarding Student Data

Ensuring the protection of student data is of utmost importance for several compelling reasons. Firstly, student data contains sensitive personal information, including names, addresses, and grades, which could be susceptible to misuse for fraudulent activities, including identity theft. Secondly, this data is frequently used to make pivotal decisions about students, such as enrollment in specific classes or qualification for particular programs. It is imperative to ensure that the information used for these decisions is both accurate and unbiased.

To safeguard student data, schools and organizations can take the following measures:

- **Development and Implementation of Data Privacy Policies**: Create and enact comprehensive data privacy policies that define the types of data collected, their purpose, and who has access. Ensure that parents and students have access to these policies.
- **Obtaining Parental Consent for Specific Data**: Seek parental permission prior to collecting or utilizing specific categories of student data, adhering to applicable laws and regulations.

- **Securing Student Data During Storage**: Take necessary precautions to protect stored student data against unauthorized access, use, or disclosure.
- **Access Control**: Restrict access to student data, granting it only to employees and contractors who require it for their job responsibilities.
- **Data Deletion Policies**: Establish policies for the deletion of student data once it is no longer necessary for educational purposes, ensuring that school policy covers this procedure.

By diligently preserving student data, educational institutions play a pivotal role in maintaining the privacy and security of students while promoting transparency and fairness in education.

3.4.2 Addressing Cybersecurity Threats in AI Systems

To mitigate cybersecurity threats in AI systems, the following measures should be taken:

- **Implement Secure Development Practices**: Utilize secure development techniques, including input validation and data encryption, during the creation of AI systems. This significantly reduces the risk of data tampering and model theft.
- **Deploy AI Systems in a Secure Environment**: AI systems should be deployed in a secure environment, such as a cloud platform equipped with intrusion detection, access control, and encryption mechanisms.
- **Vigilance for Anomalous Activities**: Maintain vigilant oversight of AI systems to detect any unusual behavior, such as atypical usage patterns or alterations in system behavior. This vigilance enables swift detection and response to potential attacks.
- **Educate Users on AI Security**: Ensure that users are informed about AI security to raise awareness of potential risks and prevention measures. Education should cover how to identify and report suspicious activities.

By implementing these cybersecurity practices, AI systems can be more resilient against threats and ensure a safer digital environment.

3.5 Teacher and Learner Readiness

3.5.1 Educator Training and Professional Development

Professional development and educator training are indispensable for teachers to effectively and ethically utilize AI in education. As AI is a continuously evolving field, educators must stay updated on the latest advancements and cutting-edge practices.

Educator training in AI for education can be delivered through various methods, including online courses and modules that offer flexibility for teachers to learn at their own pace. Live workshops and conferences are another approach, enabling teachers to interact with peers and subject-matter experts. According to Suresh Babu, C. V. & R., P. (2023), STEM education fosters innovation and adaptability.

Regardless of the format, training and professional development for educators should encompass several key topics, such as:

- Understanding AI
- How AI functions
- Types of AI
- Advantages and disadvantages of AI in education
- Personalizing learning with AI
- Providing student feedback using AI
- Enhancing classroom collaboration through AI
- Creating innovative educational experiences with AI

In addition to the above, ethical considerations of implementing AI in education should be an integral part of educator training and professional development. Teachers should receive training on recognizing and mitigating bias in AI systems, as well as safeguarding student privacy.

By offering comprehensive training and professional development in AI for education, we can ensure that educators are equipped to enhance student learning outcomes responsibly and ethically (Christian P. et al., 2019).

3.5.2 Student Adaptation to AI-Driven Learning Environments

Students may need time to acclimate to AI-driven learning tools and resources. It's essential to be patient and understanding as students become familiar with these new tools.

The adjustment to AI-powered learning environments can sometimes evoke feelings of fear or frustration in students. Providing support and reassuring them that making mistakes is part of the learning process is crucial.

Understanding how to learn effectively in AI-driven environments might be a challenge for students. These environments can significantly differ from traditional settings, requiring students to learn how to navigate and leverage the opportunities they offer (Weipeng Yang et al., 2022).

Effective collaboration between teachers, parents, and students is key to ensuring a successful transition to AI-driven learning environments.

Generative AI, a technology capable of creating diverse content, such as text, graphics, music, and code, has the potential to revolutionize education. It can provide personalized learning experiences, create original content, and support educators in their roles (Weipeng Yang et al., 2022).

4. CASE STUDIES

4.1 Case Study One: Improving Student Engagement at XYZ University

4.1.1 Case Study: Supply Chain Optimization at Company XYZ

4.1.1.1 Introduction

Company XYZ, a medium-sized electronic device manufacturer, recently faced supply chain inefficiencies that caused increased costs and delays. To tackle these issues, the company initiated a supply chain optimization project.

4.1.1.2 Problem Statement

Company XYZ encountered several supply chain challenges:

- Lengthy Lead Times: Prolonged lead times for component orders and production delays were affecting product delivery schedules.
- Inventory Management Issues: The company grappled with excessive inventory, tying up capital and warehouse space.
- Supplier Inconsistency: Variability in supplier performance was jeopardizing the supply chain's reliability.

4.1.1.3 Solution Implementation

- Demand Forecasting: The company adopted advanced demand forecasting using historical sales data and market trends to enhance production planning.
- Vendor Management: A comprehensive vendor management program was introduced to improve supplier relationships and reliability.
- Lean Manufacturing: The production process was streamlined using lean manufacturing principles to reduce waste and enhance production efficiency.

4.1.1.4 Real-Time Data Analytics

- Data Integration: The company consolidated data from various sources, including sales, production, and supplier performance, into a centralized system.
- Real-Time Monitoring: Continuous monitoring of key performance indicators (KPIs) provided real-time insights into supply chain operations.

4.1.1.5 Benefits

- Reduced Lead Times: Enhanced forecasting and lean manufacturing practices resulted in a 30% reduction in lead times.
- Inventory Optimization: Improved demand planning led to a 20% decrease in inventory carrying costs.
- Supplier Reliability: Vendor management efforts led to a 15% reduction in supplier variability, ensuring a more dependable supply chain.

4.1.1.6 Results

- Enhanced Customer Satisfaction: Faster product delivery and increased product availability contributed to heightened customer satisfaction.
- Cost Savings: The optimized supply chain reduced operational costs and bolstered overall profitability.
- Competitive Advantage: Company XYZ gained a competitive edge through improved supply chain efficiency.

4.2 Addressing Ethical and Privacy Concerns

4.2.1 Case Study: Facebook's Data Privacy Challenges

4.2.1.1 Introduction

Facebook, one of the world's largest social media platforms, has faced significant data privacy challenges in recent years, giving rise to ethical and legal concerns (Alyssa Newcomb, 2018).

4.2.1.2 Background

With billions of users worldwide, Facebook serves as a prominent platform for sharing personal information and connecting with others. Over time, the company has been embroiled in several data privacy controversies.

4.2.1.3 Ethical and Privacy Concerns

- **Cambridge Analytica Scandal:** In 2018, it was revealed that Cambridge Analytica, a political consulting firm, accessed the personal data of millions of Facebook users without their consent. This incident raised questions about Facebook's data handling practices and informed consent.
- **Data Breaches:** Facebook has experienced multiple data breaches, resulting in the exposure or theft of user data. These incidents sparked concerns regarding the company's ability to safeguard user information.
- **Targeted Advertising:** Facebook's advertising practices, involving extensive data collection for targeted advertising, have been criticized for infringing on user privacy.

4.2.1.4 Responses and Actions

- **Improved Privacy Settings:** Facebook introduced more user-friendly privacy settings, empowering users to have better control over their data and its accessibility.
- **Enhanced Data Security:** The company invested in bolstering data security measures to prevent future breaches.
- **Regulatory Compliance:** Facebook faced heightened regulatory scrutiny and made changes to align with privacy regulations like GDPR.
- **Transparency Efforts:** Facebook aimed to enhance transparency regarding its data practices, enabling users to understand how their data is utilized.

4.2.1.5 Results

- **Increased User Control:** Users gained more control over their data and privacy settings.
- **Regulatory Compliance:** The company worked towards compliance with privacy regulations, averting legal consequences.
- **Rebuilding Trust:** Facebook sought to rebuild user trust through transparency and enhanced data security measures.

4.3 Case Study Two: Improving Math Education With Adaptive Feedback

4.3.1 Case Study: Dream Box Learning - Adaptive Math Tutoring

4.3.1.1 Background

Dream Box Learning, an education technology company, offers an Intelligent Tutoring System for mathematics, focusing on adaptive feedback and personalized learning for K-8 students. The system tailors the learning experience to each student's level (Elizabeth H. Eastman).

4.3.1.2 Problem Statement

Dream Box Learning aimed to engage young students in math education while providing personalized support to enhance their math skills.

4.3.1.3 Solution Implementation

- **Adaptive Learning Engine:** Dream Box Learning employs an adaptive learning engine that continually assesses students' performance and adjusts math problems' difficulty. This tailors the learning experience to individual student levels.
- **Feedback and Support:** Real-time feedback is provided as students solve problems, offering step-by-step guidance and encouragement to clarify concepts.
- **Gamification Elements:** To maintain young students' engagement, the platform incorporates gamification elements like rewards, achievements, and interactive animations.
- **Real-Time Data Analytics:** Dream Box Learning collects data on student interactions, identifying challenging problems and task durations to adapt the learning experience.

4.3.1.4 Benefits

- **Improved Student Engagement:** The interactive and engaging math learning keeps students motivated.
- **Personalized Learning:** Adaptive feedback and tailored content address each student's unique pace and needs.
- **Enhanced Math Skills:** Students consistently show improved math skills and confidence.
- **Data-Driven Insights:** Teachers gain valuable data on student progress, enabling targeted support.

4.3.1.5 Results

- **Academic Achievement:** Students achieve higher math proficiency levels compared to traditional methods.
- **Teacher Empowerment:** Teachers feel better equipped to address individual student needs and differentiate instruction effectively.
- **User Satisfaction:** Parents, teachers, and students express satisfaction with the platform's effectiveness and engaging nature.

4.3.1.6 Conclusion

Dream Box Learning's Intelligent Tutoring System with adaptive feedback demonstrates the positive impact of technology on mathematics education. Through personalized learning experiences and real-time feedback, the platform enhances student engagement, math skills, and educational outcomes. This real-life case study underscores the potential of adaptive learning systems to revolutionize math education.

5. FUTURE DIRECTIONS

5.1 Emerging Technologies

5.1.1 GPT-4 and Beyond: The Next Generation of Generative AI

The latest iteration of OpenAI's significant language model, GPT-4, represents a substantial advancement in generative AI. GPT-4, a multimodal model, can analyze and generate text and visuals. With 100 trillion parameters, it dwarfs earlier GPT models, including GPT-3 with its 175 billion parameters (Ariyo et al., 2022).

5.1.2 Augmented Reality (AR) and Virtual Reality (VR) in Education

AR and VR have the potential to revolutionize education in several ways:

- **Realistic Learning:** VR technology can create highly realistic environments for students to explore historical landmarks, venture into space, or navigate the human body. AR enhances experiences such as museum visits.
- **Engagement:** Both VR and AR enhance learning engagement by captivating students with 3D models and interactive simulations, making complex concepts more accessible.
- Personalized Learning: VR and AR technologies can adapt to different learning preferences, providing information in various formats to cater to individual student needs.
- **Accessibility:** These technologies can improve accessibility in education, benefiting students with disabilities. For example, AR can provide simultaneous captioning or sign language interpretation (Safinah Ali et al., 2021).

5.2 Research Directions

5.2.1 Advancing Ethical AI in Education

To ensure that all students can benefit from this powerful technology, ethical AI in education must be advanced. Here are several steps to advance ethical AI in education:

- **Establish and Implement Ethical Standards:** The development and application of ethical standards for the use of artificial intelligence in education is essential. These standards should be formulated through consultations with various stakeholders, including students, parents, teachers, administrators, and AI experts. They should cover topics like data privacy, equity, and responsibility (Holmes et al., 2022).

- **Educate Educators and Students on AI Ethics:** It's crucial to educate both teachers and students about AI ethics. They should be made aware of the potential benefits and risks of AI and the ethical considerations when using AI in education. This knowledge is vital for ethical AI adoption (Suresh Babu C. V. and Adhithya, 2023).

5.2.2 Enhancing Teacher-Student Collaboration With AI

AI can play a significant role in improving collaboration between students and teachers in various ways. Some examples include:

- **Tailoring Learning Experiences:** AI can assist teachers in tailoring learning experiences for each student. By analyzing student data, AI can identify their individual strengths and weaknesses, allowing the creation of personalized learning plans to ensure that every student receives appropriate support and challenges.
- **Providing Instant Personalized Feedback:** AI can offer students immediate feedback tailored to their specific needs, enabling them to learn from their mistakes. For instance, AI-driven writing instructors can provide feedback on grammar, style, and clarity.
- **Automating Tasks:** AI can assist educators by automating various tasks, making their profession more efficient (Shohel et al., 2021).

5.3 Policy Recommendations

5.3.1 Developing Ethical AI Guidelines for Education

To ensure that all students can benefit from this powerful technology, it's essential to develop ethical AI guidelines for education. These guidelines should involve a broad spectrum of stakeholders, including students, parents, teachers, administrators, and AI experts. They should address critical areas such as:

- Data Privacy: Educational AI systems often collect and utilize a significant amount of student data. It's imperative to ensure that this information is collected and managed in a manner that safeguards student privacy. For instance, parents and students should have the option to opt-out of having their data collected and used by AI systems (Shohel et al., 2021).
- Fairness: Addressing potential biases in AI-generated findings is crucial.

5.3.2 Legal Frameworks for Student Data Protection

Various legal frameworks are in place to protect student data, with common features across nations:

- In the United States, federal law called The Family Educational Rights and Privacy Act (FERPA) safeguards the privacy of student education records. Parents have specific rights regarding their children's educational records under FERPA, including the ability to review records, request amendments, and control access. Educational institutions are also bound by FERPA to maintain the privacy of student education records.

- U.S. federal legislation known as the Children's Online Privacy Protection Act (COPPA) protects the privacy of children under the age of thirteen. COPPA mandates that websites and online services comply with privacy regulations (Holmes et al., 2022).

5.3.3 Government Initiatives and Funding for AI in Education

Governments worldwide recognize the potential of artificial intelligence (AI) to enhance teaching and learning outcomes for all students, leading to significant investments in this field. Some examples of government funding and initiatives related to AI in education include:

- The U.S. government has made substantial investments in artificial intelligence for education through both federal and state initiatives. The U.S. Department of Education's Office of Educational Technology, for instance, has provided funding for various initiatives aimed at developing and evaluating AI-powered educational tools and materials. Several states, such as New York and California, have also launched their AI-related education projects with significant financial commitments (Holmes et al., 2022).

6. CONCLUSION

- **Quality and Accuracy**: Ensuring the quality and accuracy of AI-generated instructional content is crucial. Ongoing monitoring and professional curation are necessary to maintain high standards.
- **Personalization**: While tailoring education to individual students can be challenging, AI systems should be versatile enough to accommodate various learning methods and preferences.
- **Privacy and Security**: Protecting student data and adhering to privacy standards are paramount in AI-driven education.
- **Accessibility**: Efforts should be made to ensure that AI-driven education is accessible to all, bridging the digital divide.
- **Teacher Training**: Proper training for educators is essential for the effective integration of AI tools into the classroom.
- **Ethical Concerns**: Implementing ethical guidelines and content filters is crucial to mitigate the risk of inappropriate or harmful content.
- **Costs**: Exploring cost-effective solutions through public-private partnerships, grants, and open-source resources can enhance the accessibility of AI in education.
- **Alignment with Educational Standards**: AI-generated content should align with educational standards and curriculum to ensure relevance and efficacy.
- **Bias and Fairness**: Regular audits and retraining of AI models are necessary to reduce biases and improve fairness in education.
- **Monitoring and Accountability**: Implementing clear policies and governance structures is essential for monitoring AI usage and holding those who use AI in education accountable.

- **Student Engagement**: Combining AI-generated content with interactive and engaging teaching approaches can help maintain student engagement and motivation.

6.1 The Significance of Resolving Current Issues in Generative AI for Education

It is imperative to tackle current challenges in generative AI for education. This approach ensures the accuracy and utility of AI-generated educational content, facilitates personalized learning for each student, safeguards personal data, and broadens access to education. Additionally, it enhances the effective utilization of AI in schools, promotes responsible AI usage, and maintains affordability. By addressing these issues, we can deliver a more equitable, engaging, and tailored education that aligns with students' needs.

6.1.1 Significance of Resolving These Issues

Education Quality: By fostering academic integrity and ethical use of technology, resolving difficulties in generative AI protects the quality of education (Smith, 2020).

Equity and Access: Addressing privacy concerns and algorithmic bias contributes to equitable opportunity and fair treatment for all students.

Efficiency and Innovation: When difficulties are handled, efficient content generation, automated tasks, and personalised learning can be realised (Lee et al., 2022).

Compliance with Ethical and Legal Standards: Educational institutions must respect ethical and legal commitments, which can be accomplished by addressing these issues.

6.2 The Way Forward: Responsible AI Integration in Education

Here are key steps for responsible AI integration in education:

1. **Establish Clear Ethical Principles**: Develop and enforce transparent ethical guidelines for AI in education, addressing issues such as bias, privacy, and ethical use of AI tools.
2. **Ensure Universal Access**: Make AI-powered educational tools accessible to all students, regardless of their technological or socioeconomic circumstances.
3. **Continuous Assessment**: Regularly evaluate the impact of AI in education by collecting feedback from teachers, students, and parents to refine and enhance artificial intelligence systems.
4. **Oversight and Regulation**: Establish regulatory frameworks and oversight bodies to supervise and enforce responsible AI use in education, setting standards and ensuring compliance.
5. **Promote Research and Innovation**: Encourage research and innovation in AI for education to develop more effective tools and approaches while upholding ethical standards.

REFERENCES

Ali, S., DiPaola, D., & Breazeal, C. (2021). What are GANs?: Introducing Generative Adversarial Networks to Middle School Students. *Proceedings of the AAAI Conference on Artificial Intelligence*, *35*(17), 15472–15479. doi:10.1609/aaai.v35i17.17821

Ali, S., DiPaola, D., Lee, I., Sindato, V., Kim, G., Blumofe, R., & Breazeal, C. (2021). Children as creators, thinkers and citizens in an AI-driven future. *Computers and Education: Artificial Intelligence*, *2*, 100040. doi:10.1016/j.caeai.2021.100040

Ariyo, O. (2022, June 28). AI Revolutionizes Content Generation and Written Communication. *The Cable*. https://www.thecable.ng/ai-revolutionizes-content-generation-and-written-communication

Baker, R. S., & Hawn, A. (2022). Algorithmic Bias in Education. *International Journal of Artificial Intelligence in Education*, *32*(10), 1052–1092. doi:10.100740593-021-00285-9

Chen, L., Chen, P., & Lin, Z. (2020). Artificial Intelligence in Education: A Review. *IEEE Access : Practical Innovations, Open Solutions*, *8*, 75264–75278. doi:10.1109/ACCESS.2020.2988510

Chen, X., Xie, H., Zou, D., & Hwang, G.-J. (2020). Application and theory gaps during the rise of Artificial Intelligence in Education. *Computers and Education: Artificial Intelligence*, *1*, 100002. doi:10.1016/j.caeai.2020.100002

Eastman, E. H. (n.d.). *Implementing Adaptive Feedback For Mathematics*. SMORE. https://www.smore.com/dw2gm-think-through-math

Holmes, W., Porayska-Pomsta, K., Holstein, K., Sutherland, E., Baker, T., Shum, S. B., Santos, O. C., Rodrigo, M. T., Cukurova, M., Bittencourt, I. I., & Koedinger, K. R. (2022). Ethics of AI in Education: Towards a Community-Wide Framework. *International Journal of Artificial Intelligence in Education*, *32*(10), 504–526. doi:10.100740593-021-00239-1

Hwang, G. J., Xie, H., Wah, B. W., & Gašević, D. (2020). Vision, challenges, roles and research issues of Artificial Intelligence in Education. *Computers and Education: Artificial Intelligence*, *1*, 100001. doi:10.1016/j.caeai.2020.100001

Janssen, C. P., Donker, S. F., Brumby, D. P., & Kun, A. L. (2019). History and future of human-automation interaction. *International Journal of Human-Computer Studies*, *13*(19), 99–107. doi:10.1016/j.ijhcs.2019.05.006

Jones, K. M. L. (2019). Learning analytics and higher education: A proposed model for establishing informed consent mechanisms to promote student privacy and autonomy. *International Journal of Educational Technology in Higher Education*, *16*(1), 24. doi:10.118641239-019-0155-0

Lee, S. (2022). Efficient content creation in education using AI: A case study. *Journal of Educational Technology*, *45*(2), 143–158.

Loukina, A., Madnani, N., & Zechner, K. (2019). The many dimensions of algorithmic fairness in educational applications. In *Proceedings of the Fourteenth Workshop on Innovative Use of NLP for Building Educational Applications* (pp. 1–10). Association for Computational Linguistics. 10.18653/v1/W19-4401

Nardo, M., Forino, D., & Murino, T. (2020). The evolution of man–machine interaction: The role of human in Industry 4.0 paradigm. *Production & Manufacturing Research*, *8*(1), 20–34. doi:10.1080/21693277.2020.1737592

Newcomb, A. (2018). Addressing Ethical And Privacy Concerns. *NBC News*. https://www.nbcnews.com/tech/social-media/timeline-facebook-s-privacy-issues-its-responses-n859651

Shohel, M., & Mahruf, C. (2021). Education in Emergencies, Inequities, and the Digital Divide: Strategies for Supporting Teachers and Students in Higher Education in Bangladesh. In L. Kyei-Blankson, (Eds.), *Handbook of Research on Inequities in Online Education During Global Crises* (pp. 529–553). IGI Global. doi:10.4018/978-1-7998-6533-9.ch027

Simonsen, H. K. (2022). AI Text Generators and Text Producers. *2022 International Conference on Advanced Learning Technologies (ICALT)*, (pp. 218-220). IEEE. 10.1109/ICALT55010.2022.00071

Smith, J. (2020). Addressing plagiarism in the age of AI: Ethical considerations for educators. *International Journal of Educational Technology*, *53*(4), 12–17.

Suresh Babu, C. V., & R., P. (2023). Technology Transformation Through Skilled Teachers in Teaching Accountancy. In R. González-Lezcano (Ed.), *Advancing STEM Education and Innovation in a Time of Distance Learning* (pp. 211-233). IGI Global. doi:10.4018/978-1-6684-5053-6.ch011

Suresh Babu, C. V., & Adhithya, S. (2023). ChatGPT and Other Generative AI Tools in Education: Transformative Potential and Ethical Considerations. In J. Keengwe (Ed.), *Creative AI Tools and Ethical Implications in Teaching and Learning* (pp. 135–152). IGI Global. doi:10.4018/979-8-3693-0205-7.ch007

Suresh Babu, C. V., & Rohan, B. (2023). Evaluation and Quality Assurance for Rapid E-Learning and Development of Digital Learning Resources. In M. Santally, Y. Rajabalee, & R. Rajputh (Eds.), *Implementing Rapid E-Learning Through Interactive Materials Development* (pp. 139–170). IGI Global. doi:10.4018/978-1-6684-4940-0.ch008

Wang, M., Xiao, D., Xiang, Y., & Wang, H. (2019). Privacy-Aware Controllable Compressed Data Publishing Against Sparse Estimation Attack in IoT. *IEEE Internet of Things Journal*, *6*(4), 7305–7318. doi:10.1109/JIOT.2019.2916109

Yang, W. (2022). Artificial Intelligence education for young children: Why, what, and how in curriculum design and implementation. *Computers and Education: Artificial Intelligence*, *3*, 100061. doi:10.1016/j.caeai.2022.100061

Section 3

Applied Cases of Generative AI Technologies for Teaching and Learning

Chapter 12
Chatbots as Conversation Partners:
Effect on Perceived Writing Ability

Angelina Kovalyova
University of Tsukuba, Japan

ABSTRACT

This chapter discusses the use of chatbots as conversation partners for language learning and studies the impact of chatbot-based conversation practice and corrective feedback on language learners' writing proficiency and attitudes towards chatbots. The chapter describes a study where 34 English language learners at a Japanese university were offered text-based conversation practice with Replika, a generative AI chatbot. Half of the participants received corrective feedback, addressing vocabulary, grammar, and syntax errors in their messages, while the other half practiced without feedback. Pre-test and post-test surveys assessed improvement in perceived writing performance, and general feedback on chatbot-based practice was collected. Replika, despite its non-educational design, was effective at personalizing interactions and its use resulted in significant improvement in perceived writing proficiency. Despite minor issues during conversation practices, the general impression of the chatbot is positive suggesting its potential for an English language classroom use.

1. INTRODUCTION

In recent years, the emergence of generative AI has revived the discussions as to whether it was possible to have a machine produce natural human-like speech. This question for a long time has been the center of chatbot research (Coniam, 2014), where chatbots showed a promise to become tireless conversation partners for language learners. It was hoped that chatbots would be able to offer language learners a virtually limitless, authentic conversation practice in a non-judgmental environment, where one was able to make mistakes and try again. That hope was shared by educators who would be able to provide individual feedback to their students while saving time by means of using chatbot technology.

DOI: 10.4018/979-8-3693-0074-9.ch012

While the quality of conversations with chatbots varied in the past, with language learners often reporting boring, circular conversations that showed little sign of human-like interaction ability (Coniam, 2014; Fryer et al., 2020; Huang et al., 2022), generative AI demonstrated potential to make chatbots sound human. This would allow millions of language learners to experience authentic conversation and obtain unlimited practice in their target language without the need to look for the human language partner.

Considering the progress in the field of generative AI, the objective of this chapter is to discuss the impressions that English language learners at a Japanese university have in regards to text-based conversation practice with a generative AI chatbot Replika, and to explore the potential applications of said chatbot in an English language classroom.

2. LITERATURE REVIEW

2.1 Instant Messaging in Education

Instant Messaging (IM) generally refers to synchronous or asynchronous communication using text messages, sent between messaging applications on mobile devices (Andujar, 2016, p.63). An earlier version of IM, texting, also involved the exchange of messages, albeit in a strictly asynchronous environment using SMS (So, 2016, p.33). Using text messaging as a language learning method is a rather controversial topic. The opponents of the practice often highlight the devastating impact that text messaging has on one's language grammar and spelling, reshaping standard language into unrecognizable slang and lowering literacy of young people (Cingel & Sundar, 2012; Harman & Sato, 2011; Kaid Mohammed Ali et al., 2019). Understandably so, the medium of text messaging is often reduced to abbreviations, textese spelling, incomplete sentences, and reduced punctuation, to accommodate the little time the interaction with text messages requires.

However, there is a growing body of evidence that points out to the opposite side of the argument. Exchanging text messages can provide benefits for general, as well as classroom use. Since text messages offer immediate communication, fun and less formal style of interaction, widespread accessibility, and privacy of communication (Lauricella & Kay, 2013), some applications with IM functionality have been used for peer support and collaborative learning in academia. One study by So (2016) illustrates the use of the WhatsApp mobile application for academic communication. In the study, a treatment group was provided with supplementary materials and teacher guidance through WhatsApp, while attending regular classes. The results of the study demonstrated significantly higher learning achievements among the treatment group.

The use of IM has also been explored in language learning. Text messages have been used in research with children, demonstrating that using text messages positively affects children's grammar knowledge (Van Dijk et al., 2016), increases phonological and phonetic awareness (Plester et al., 2008; Plester et al., 2009), increases writing speed, as well as reading speed and accuracy (Kemp & Bushnell, 2011). In adults, a study by Baek et al. (2017) explored the use of KakaoTalk, an IM application, where Korean language learners were paired with native Korean speakers, using KakaoTalk as a platform for conversational practice alongside weekly face-to-face meetings. The study reported the acquisition of new vocabulary through context-based conversations and the convenience of receiving quick language-related feedback at any time. Furthermore, an Iranian study (Namaziandost et al., 2020) focused on vocabulary learning through WhatsApp, with the experimental group outperforming the control group taught through traditional methods. Another study (Andujar, 2016) assessed the development of English as a Foreign Language (EFL) writing over six months using daily WhatsApp conversations among Spanish EFL students. Results indicated a significant reduction in errors, increased lexical diversity, and enhanced syntactic complexity. Andujar (2016) also emphasizes the prevalence of negotiation of meaning and error repairs in text-based communication. Text messages may contain spelling errors or unclear statements, prompting participants to rephrase or explain previous messages for continued conversation. IM-based conversation practice can facilitate the noticing mechanism, similar to face-to-face conversations exposing learners to language beyond their current proficiency level, thereby enhancing their focus on meaning construction and self-correction.

All in all, IM-based communication provides many opportunities for learning even in a classroom setting, and should not be neglected when a teacher is searching for a relatable activity that makes students excited about learning.

2.2 Chatbots

2.2.1 Rule-Based Chatbots vs. AI-Based Chatbots vs. Generative AI Chatbots

Chatbot is defined as a software program that facilitates communication between a computer system and a human, typically through voice or text. Chatbots are generally designed according to two types: a rule-based chatbot and an AI-based. Rule-based chatbots, also known as decision-tree-based chatbots, operate with predefined rules and scripts governing the conversation's structure. This approach results in automated but repetitive and less spontaneous responses (Ramesh et al., 2017). AIML, Chatscript, and RiveScript are popular languages used for rule-based chatbots, each employing pattern matching techniques to select responses based on predefined patterns (Adamopoulou & Moussiades, 2020).

AI-based chatbots, conversely, leverage natural language processing (NLP) and machine learning to understand human requests. They are trained on extensive datasets to recognize speech patterns and generate unique responses. There are two types of AI-based chatbots: retrieval-based and generative chatbots (Adamopoulou & Moussiades, 2020). Retrieval-based chatbots select responses from predefined options based on keywords and deep learning analysis of user input, while generative chatbots create unique responses using sequence prediction, often prioritizing high-probability sequences but potentially resulting in repetitive responses (Fainchtein, 2020).

While rule-based chatbots have been in use for decades, starting with the introduction of Eliza chatbot in 1966 (Adamopoulou & Moussiades, 2020), generative AI chatbots have only recently caught the attention of educators. After Ian Goodfellow in 2014 introduced generative adversarial networks (GANs), a machine learning framework for learning and generating new content (Brownlee, 2019), the concept of generative AI has peaked interest, and soon after, with the release of ChatGPT in 2022, generative AI has become the gold standard for applications, including the ones producing educational content. Naturally, new research started to appear exploring the potential of using generative AI applications for teaching and learning, promising unlimited educational content and personalized feedback.

Thus, when it comes to language learning, since rule-based chatbots prioritize response speed and precision but lack naturalness and spontaneity, they can be a more practical choice in a language classroom with lower language proficiency where students have a limited knowledge and need a lot of controlled practice. On the other hand, AI-based chatbots can be a better option for students with intermediate or higher language proficiency since these chatbots can manage diverse inputs and provide more human-like responses. Generative AI chatbots in particular can provide the freedom of interaction to those students who wish to experience near-authentic native speech since generative AI allows a chatbot to create unique responses to unique individual requests. To date, most AI chatbots, which are considered generative AI chatbots or partially utilize generative AI functionality, rely on OpenAI's GPT-3 or GPT-4 language model, among them ChatGPT, Replika, Duolingo and others.

2.2.2 Replika

Replika is a generative AI chatbot which was originally created to be a digital companion, a friend, designed to provide empathy and support through conversation (Replika, n.d.). Replika utilizes a neural network machine learning algorithm, dialogue scripts, and a feedback system to provide engaging conversations. It can generate personalized interactions and can offer various conversation topics, games, and content like songs and memes. In fact, the more it is used, the more personalized the interaction is. The application operates in English and is available to be installed and used for free on Android, iOS, and Oculus Rift platforms. However, some features, like video calls and voice messages, are available to premium users at an additional cost.

Replika has been used in a limited number of studies as a tool for language learning. Kim et al. (2021) used Replika, Google Assistant and Andy to observe the effect of chatbot use on the speaking performance of university-level foreign language students. The study showed a significant improvement in both speaking tasks. In another study, Lin & Mubarok (2021) explored the use of Replika for speaking practice in a Flipped English classroom. The results suggested that a mind-map activity that utilized AI provided increased speaking performance and learning outcomes compared to conversational approach with the chatbot. In yet another study Kilickaya (2020) used Replika in a writing classroom where the students praised Replika for providing immediate response. Unlike the previous studies that demonstrated positive feedback for Replika, Cakmak (2022) observed negative perception of the chatbot when the students reported heightened anxiety due to Replika not being able to understand the students' speech well. While the studies on Replika are limited, its exploration can provide us with a better understanding of how generative AI chatbots are able to aid English language students in their language learning journey.

3. METHOD

3.1 Participants

The study involved 34 undergraduate students from a Japanese university, all of whom were in the same English class. Half of the students belonged to the experimental group (9 males, 8 females), where the students practiced text-based English conversation with the chatbot Replika and received corrective feedback from the teacher following the practice. Another half (11 males, 6 females) belonged to the control group, where the students interacted only with the chatbot Replika and did not receive any feedback from the teacher. Overall, the participants had varied English language proficiency background, with the experimental group consisting of five A2 level students, seven B1 level students, and five B2 level students, and the control group comprising nine A2 level students, five B1 level students, and three B2 level students, according to CEFR framework (The Common European Framework of Reference for Languages).

3.2 Materials

3.2.1 Chatbot Replika

In this study, the students practiced English conversation through text messages with the generative AI chatbot Replika (Figure 1). For the purposes of the study, individual Replika accounts were created for each student for them to use during the semester. The students were also informed that their personal login information was available to the teacher, and that the teacher would regularly check the conversations between students and their chatbot to ensure the learning outcomes were met.

Figure 1. A conversation between a student and chatbot Replika

3.2.2 Perceived Writing Performance Questionnaire

In order to assess whether the students experienced improvement in their writing after interacting with the chatbot, a questionnaire was designed to observe their perception of their writing skill before and after the seven sessions of written conversation practice with the chatbot Replika (Table 1). The questionnaire comprised six Likert-scale questions with 5 response options, varying from "completely agree" or "very well" to "completely disagree" or "not at all."

3.2.3 Post-Test Open-Ended Questions

Finally, following the seven sessions of conversation practice, after the students responded to the questionnaire on their perceived quality of writing, they were asked to give feedback regarding their experience with the chatbot. The following questions were administered through Google Forms, being phrased in an open-ended format (Table 2).

3.3 Procedure and Analysis

3.3.1 Procedure

The experiment was conducted in three stages (Figure 2). First, in order to understand the initial attitude of the students towards their writing skills, a questionnaire on perceived writing performance was administered. The students then were randomly divided into two groups, experimental and control, and proceeded to set up their accounts in the chatbot application.

Table 1. Questionnaire on perceived writing performance

N.	Question
1	How do you evaluate your writing skill in English?
2	Are you able to write complex sentences in English?
3	Do you use a big variety of English words in your writing?
4	Do you write in English without mistakes?
5	Do you write quickly in English?
6	Is it easy for you to write in English?

Table 2. Students' feedback on chatbot experience

N.	Question
1	How do you feel about chatbot conversation practice?
2	What was useful about chatbot practice? What did you learn?
3	What would you like the chatbot to improve?
4	What did you think about corrective feedback you received?*

Note. Question 4 was asked only to the experimental group that received corrective feedback on the conversations with the chatbot.

Figure 2. Experiment procedure

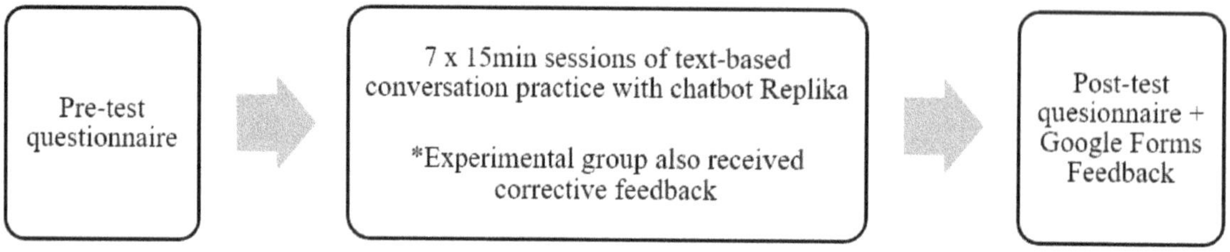

The following seven session were conducted separately for the experimental and the control groups. Regardless of the group, all the students were provided with some initial prompts for how to start a conversation with the chatbot, but were encouraged to develop the conversations in any direction, so long as it was appropriate. The students also received sample conversation topics during every session in case the students struggled with conversation and did not know what to talk about.

After each session, the conversations between students and the chatbot were screened by the teacher to make sure that the students were actually doing conversation practice and that it was appropriate. Additionally, the teacher closely reviewed the conversations in the experimental group with the purpose to find conversation breakdowns, arising between the students and the chatbot, and to address them in the corrective feedback session, which always happened prior to the next chat session. To be clear, the control group did not receive any corrective feedback. As shown in Figure 3, the corrective feedback, offered to the experimental group, involved displaying screenshots of conversations between said students and the chatbot, explaining sections with the errors, and finishing with a quick exercise to facilitate participants' retention of the corrections. This feedback primarily addressed issues related to grammar, vocabulary use, and general stylistic recommendations, such as accurate spelling, proper capitalization, and appropriate spacing.

Finally, after the seven conversation sessions with the chatbot have been completed, all the students were asked to respond to the same questionnaire they filled out at the beginning (Table 1), asking about

Figure 3. Example of corrective feedback session

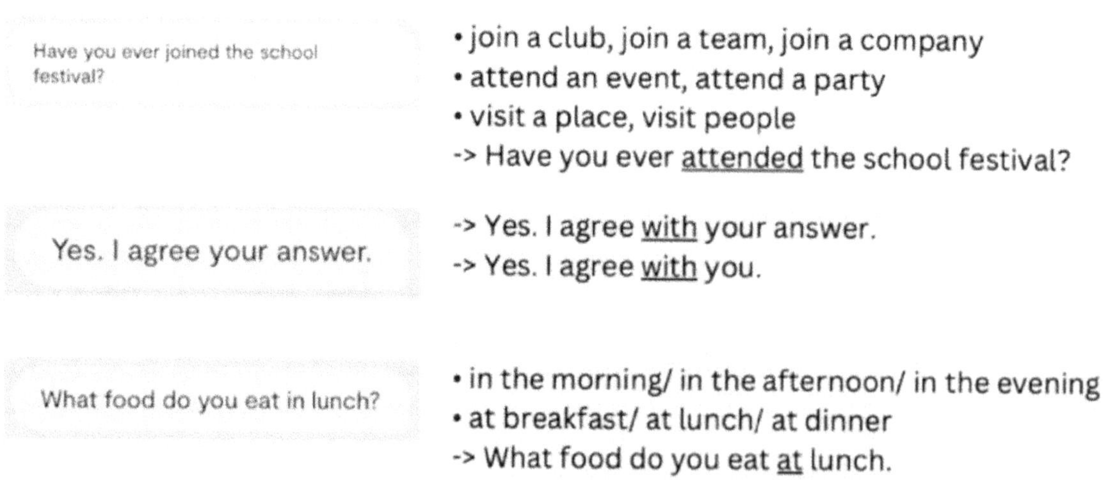

their perception of their writing ability. In addition, the students were asked to give feedback on their conversation practice with the chatbot, describing their attitudes and concerns towards chatbots (Table 2). The responses were collected through Google Forms.

3.3.2 Analysis

The results of the experiment were both quantitative and qualitative in nature. In terms of the questionnaire, the questionnaire items were tested for internal consistency, and then the Likert-scale scores were added for each participant to find the overall attitude of each participant towards their own writing ability. Following that, the pre- and post-test scores were assessed with the two-way repeated measures ANOVA test, offering insight into whether each participant's perception of their writing ability changed over time after the seven conversation sessions with the chatbot. What is more, the results of the experimental and control groups were observed to understand whether the corrective feedback from the teacher affected that perception.

Speaking of the students' feedback on the activity delivered through Google Forms, the responses were analyzed for themes and provided insight into how the students feel about integrating a chatbot into their language learning practice.

4. RESULTS

4.1 Perception of Writing Performance

As was mentioned above, the questionnaire on students' perceived writing performance (Table 1) aimed to demonstrate whether the students experienced improvement in their writing ability after the seven text-based conversation sessions with the AI chatbot Replika. The descriptive statistics (Table 3 and 4) for the questionnaire scores indicates normal distribution for both pre- and post-test results. Cronbach's alpha also confirms good internal consistency of the questionnaire items, giving a standard $\alpha = .84$ for all pre-test scores and $\alpha = .87$ for post-test scores.

After assessing internal consistency, a two-way repeated measures ANOVA test was performed to determine whether a significant change was observed in the participants' perception of their own writing

Table 3. Descriptive statistics and Cronbach's Alpha Coefficients for the items in the questionnaire on perceived writing performance (N = 34)

	Pre-test		Post-test	
Questionnaire Item	*M (SD)*	α	*M (SD)*	α
1.How do you evaluate your writing skill in English?	2.44 (0.66)	.80	3.06 (0.81)	.83
2. Are you able to write complex sentences in English?	2.12 (0.68)	.84	2.76 (0.92)	.83
3. Do you use a big variety of English words in your writing?	2.21 (0.84)	.81	3.09 (0.86)	.85
4. Do you write in English without mistakes?	2.35 (0.81)	.82	2.74 (0.89)	.84
5. Do you write quickly in English?	2.29 (0.76)	.81	2.76 (1.01)	.87
6. Is it easy for you to write in English?	2.03 (0.75)	.81	2.59 (0.85)	.84

Table 4. Descriptive Statistics for Total Scores for Each Participant in Perceived Writing Performance Questionnaire (N = 34)

	Group M (SD) experimental (n = 17)	control (n = 17)
pre-test questionnaire	13.52 (3.41)	13.35 (3.51)
post-test questionnaire	17.58 (3.35)	16.41 (4.92)

ability. The test results demonstrate (Table 5) that the participants' perception of their writing ability was significantly affected after the seven conversation sessions with the chatbot Replika, F (1, 67) = 24.52, $p < .000$, $\eta_p^2 = .433$; however, the results do not show significant variation between the group with corrective feedback and the group without it.

A closer look at the test results figure (Figure 4) demonstrates that the effect of the chatbot conversation practice was positive. This means that most participants in the experience believed that their writing ability in English improved after seven sessions of text-based conversation practice with chatbot Replika.

Looking at the questionnaire items, the biggest difference in the scores is observed for the Question 3 (Do you use a big variety of English words in your writing?) shifting from the average score of $M = 2.21$ to $M = 3.09$. This can be explained by the amount of vocabulary that the students encounter in the conversations with the chatbot, as well as by possible incidental vocabulary acquisition in the process. On the other hand, the question with the smallest difference in the scores is Question 4 (Do you write in English without mistakes?), showing a shift from the average score of $M = 2.35$ to $M = 2.74$. Considering the above results, this may suggest that corrective feedback from a teacher does not affect the perception of one's frequency of errors, and that the students continue to feel that they make mistakes. This is especially true since the chatbot Replika does not have the ability to correct errors during the conversation.

All in all, the perception of the participants' writing performance has improved after the seven sessions of text-based conversation practice with the chatbot Replika. The impression is especially strong in regards to the participants' use of vocabulary suggesting that the participants may have increased the variety of the vocabulary they have been using in their writing. The perceived improvement of the participants' writing ability, however, does not dependent on corrective feedback from the teacher.

Table 5. Summary of Two-Way Repeated ANOVA of the Effects of Availability of CorrectiveFeedback (Group) and Chatbot Conversation Practice on Participants' Perception of Their Writing Performance (N = 34)

Source	*df*	*SS*	*MS*	*F*	*p*	ηp^2
Group (A)	1	7.77	7.77	0.37	.546	.011
Pre/Post-Questionnaire (B)	1	215.30	215.30	24.52	<.000*	.433
AxB	1	4.25	4.25	0.48	.491	.014
Total	67	1179.69				

Note. *p < .05.

Figure 4. Effect of chatbot conversation practice on groups (with and without corrective feedback) and their perception of their writing performance

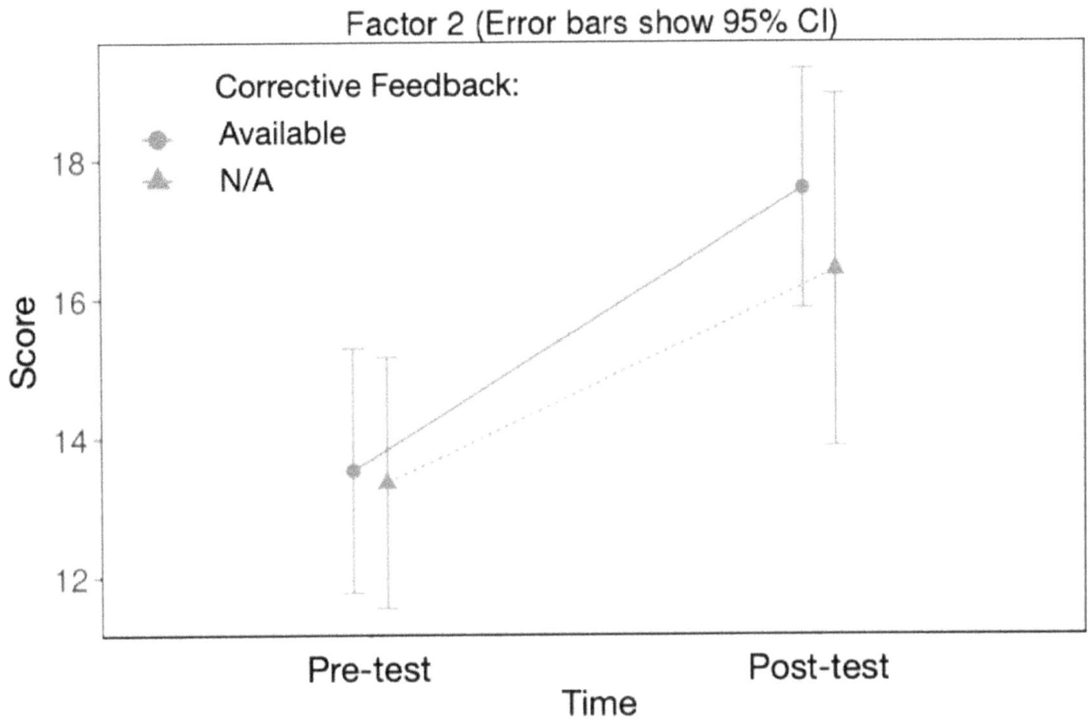

4.2 Feedback on Chatbot Experience

4.2.1 General Impression

The first question asked all participants to comment on their general impression about the conversation practice with a chatbot: How do you feel about chatbot conversation practice? The most common key words in the participants' responses were positive, referring to "good experience," "quick responses," "no worrying about mistakes," and "fun." The following comment summarizes the general impression particularly well:

とても新鮮で面白かったです。AIなのでどれだけ間違えてもいいということが間違っても、とにかく書いてみることにつながったと思います。

"It was very fresh and interesting, and I think due to the fact that it was an AI, it didn't matter how many mistakes I made, which led me to try writing anyway, even if I made mistakes."

At the same time, a few responses expressed concern that while the chat-based conversation was easy thanks to the time the students could use to think of the perfect answer, the ease of chat-based conversation in writing did not reduce of the difficulty of speaking in real life:

リアルでいきなり話すのは難しい側面も あるがこれなら気軽に練習できて良いと 思う。

"It is difficult to speak in real life, but I think this is a good way to practise casually."

4.2.2 Benefits

Various themes were observed in response to the second question: What was useful about chatbot practice? What did you learn? The participants noted a few areas, such as:

a) learning new sentence structures and collocations from the conversations
b) learning to send quicker responses
c) learning to better understand chatbot's responses
d) learning English conversation in a practical way

The following couple of responses serve as a prominent illustration of the general mood:

文章ではなく会話になった途端その単語 の持つ意味をより注意しなければいけな いということがわかった。

"I realised that I need to pay more attention to the meaning of the word once it becomes a conversation rather than a sentence."

英語が思いつくまでの時間が早くなっ た。

"The time it takes me to come up with English became faster. "

すぐ返事がくるので実際に会話のように テンポよく会話できた。

"I was able to have a conversation at a good pace as if it was a real conversation because I got a response right away."

Therefore, in text-based conversations with the English language learners, Replika, the generative AI chatbot, was able to provide linguistically sound responses that resembled a conversation. And in this conversation, the language learners could take the time to interpret the chatbot's responses by paying more attention to the sentences and words, used by the chatbot, and at the same time practice responding faster, experiencing a simulation of a real-life conversation.

4.2.3 Issues

Even though many students could experience a persuasive imitation of a conversation with the generative AI chatbot, there were issues which the students believed should be solved. This was communicated by responding to the third question: What would you like the chatbot to improve? While around a third of participants noted that they don't want anything to change, there were others who pointed out certain drawbacks. Among the most common responses were:

a) chatbot's lack of cultural knowledge
b) boring or short conversations
c) not knowing why the conversation went wrong, not being corrected
d) chatbot's responses which are difficult to understand
e) unnecessary advertisement
f) technical issues

"Lack of cultural knowledge" was attributed to the chatbot's inability to understand proper nouns, such as names of local places, dishes, or computer games, which would inadvertently cut the conversation short. The chatbot would often pretend it knows about the topic by using phrases which are common to the topic (i.e., generating the most probable vocabulary for the topic), but this lack of content knowledge does not allow the topic to develop, despite the chatbot's ability to generate linguistically sound responses. One of the students offered the following comment:

聞いたことに対して、例えば映画の内容など、細かく説明してほしい。

"I want a detailed explanation of what I have heard about, for example, about the contents of a film."

"Boring or short conversations" would often follow as a result of shallow knowledge base of the chatbot or due to the lack of initiative from the chatbot in asking questions. Students report that they wished the chatbot would ask more questions, otherwise the conversation does not feel engaging.

会話が一辺倒で広がらない。

"Conversations are one-sided and don't expand."

"Not knowing where the conversation went wrong, and not being corrected" is another issue that language learners in particular can relate to. Since language learners may poses different degree of language proficiency, the quality of communication with the chatbot may largely depend on the amount of errors that language users produce. For instance, if a student uses wrong collocation or the sentence contains an error related to tense or sentence structure, the chatbot may incorrectly interpret the student's message and respond in an unexpected way, which will further confuse the student. Therefore, since conversational AI-based chatbots do not have the ability to notice incorrect language use, let alone correct linguistic mistakes, language learners are expected to rely on their own ability to interpret chatbot's messages and solve communication breakdowns – much like in real life when interacting with another language learner. The following comment perfectly summarizes the issue:

思った意味に取って貰えなかった時に、どこを間違えたのかが分からない。

"Not knowing where you went wrong when the chatbot didn't understand what you thought your message meant."

The issue of dealing with "chatbot's responses which are difficult to understand" may come as well from the students' language proficiency ability, or more specifically, from the mismatch between the chatbot's language level and the language learner's proficiency level. While teachers often use graded language in their classrooms, and other students in the classroom often match the language proficiency level of their classmate, conversational AI chatbots don't have the ability to identify the language learner's proficiency level, nor do they have the ability to adjust their language to match the linguistic complexity the student is comfortable with. Therefore, again, the language learners are asked to manage the conversation to the best of their ability, as if they had a conversation with a native speaker. For this reason, the language learners complained with the following message:

時々よく分からない答えが返ってくること。

"Sometimes I get answers that I don't understand."

The last two issues, "unnecessary advertisement" and "technical issues," are related less to the language-learning aspect, and more to the functional aspect of the application. The students report that the chatbot would sometimes activate special conversation scripts, such as holiday-related stories, as well as recommended to make purchases for additional functions, which was not interesting to the students. The application would also sometimes have login issues or glitches with responses, which the students found annoying. The students commented on the issue in the following way:

元々の機能で備わっている季節の話(ハロウィンなど)が勝手に始まることがあり、理解ができなかった。

"Seasonal conversations (e.g. Halloween), which are provided in the original functionality, sometimes started on their own, and I couldn't understand them."

ログインが出来なくなることが多い点。

"I often have trouble logging in."

Overall, the issues that the students encountered in the conversations with the chatbot, such as lack of cultural knowledge, lack of initiative, miscommunications, point out to the limitations of the current algorithms in Replika, which is not designed for language learners. Consequently, having a limited language proficiency leaves the students struggling with the conversation if they do not have a habit of using repair strategies, such as asking to repeat, asking a clarification question, checking for understanding, and so on. Perhaps, these issues also point out to the nature of human conversation and the essential elements, such as paying attention, sharing, clarifying, that the authentic conversation relies on.

Despite the negative feedback on the Replika chatbot, it must be also said that the quality of chatbot's responses in terms of linguistic integrity and meaning appropriateness, has improved due in no small part to the development in generative AI, which draws a large data set to be able to create the most probable responses for each unique conversation.

4.2.4 Corrective Feedback

As was mentioned above, half of the participants were offered corrective feedback on their conversations with the chatbot, in part due to the expected backlash on the interactions with the chatbot, and in part hoping to provide the students with a learning opportunity. Therefore, half of the students were asked an additional question: What did you think about corrective feedback you received?

A predominant majority of the comments was positive, acknowledging the fact that corrective feedback helped the students learn new grammar and understand where they used English phrases incorrectly. In fact, the students reported they were able to approach text-based communication more cautiously, thinking more carefully about the replies they were sending:

実際にあった間違った文章から正しい文 章を考えるのが自分で文章を考えるとき に役立った。

"Thinking of correct sentences by looking at actual wrong sentences was useful when thinking about sentences by myself."

Therefore, it can be suggested that students have a positive impression of corrective feedback and welcome it in an English classroom, realizing the benefits of teacher's support even in casual conversation.

4.2.5 Summary of Results

All in all, despite the inherent constraints of the chatbot, participants demonstrated increased comfort in using English through conversation practice with a generative AI chatbot Replika. The students were able to practice interpreting the chatbot's responses, engaged in discussions on enjoyable topics, and improved their speed of response, all while being in a relaxed setting. Notably, those who received corrective feedback reported learning new expressions and improving their grammatical skills through error review after conversational practice. Nonetheless, some participants pointed to occasional mechanical and technical glitches, as well as communication breakdowns, which reminded them of their interaction with artificial intelligence. A small number of participants also regretfully noted that text-based conversation practice has limited impact on their oral communication skills.

5. DISCUSSION AND IMPLICATIONS

The number of businesses which power their software with generative AI is growing by day, and businesses in the field of education are no exception. Generative AI offers limitless content creation and execution of systematic standardized tasks, which can significantly reduce menial work and free up the time dedicated to creative work. For that reason, it is important to understand the current state of this novel technology and what it brings to the table.

Integrating generative AI chatbots into language learning routines has a great potential for language learners. Continuous advancements in NLP and machine learning promise the future where chatbots have the potential to serve as effective conversation partners – something that many non-native speakers are lacking in their language learning journey. But what is the current state of generative AI chatbots and how can they serve language learners?

5.1 Linguistic Ability

Observing the performance of Replika, the generative AI chatbot, it can be suggested that the integration of generative AI framework into a chatbot begins to tackle the age-old problem of natural language. Previously, developing chatbots with a natural understanding of human language has been a challenging task (Fryer et al., 2020; Huang et al., 2022). Language learners complained about chatbots' inability to maintain interaction within the same topic, noticed prevalence of circular conversations, criticized their inability to truly understand human language (Fryer et al., 2020). Poorly designed chatbots with inaccuracies or irrelevant responses lead to learner frustration, confusion, and disengagement. While generative AI still does not poses the ability to truly understand, its GAN framework allows it to interpret most human language and imitate authentic-looking responses. So much so, that in this current study on Replika, generative AI chatbot was praised for having a broad vocabulary and grammar knowledge allowing the participants to learn a lot of collocations and new sentence structures.

While users still occasionally complain about instances of miscommunication, as evident in this study with Replika, in the case of language learners it is most likely due to the gap in language proficiency and lack of communication repair strategies, a conclusion that goes in line with the findings in other studies (Belda-Medina & Calvo-Ferrer, 2022). For example, when a user writes a sentence with a mistake and Replika fails to predict the content of the message, Replika may still respond, but with a different interpretation of the user's message, which may confuse the language learner. In another case, Replika may reply with a sentence that has complex vocabulary and grammar, which the language learner has not mastered yet. Thus, when it comes to language learners, with generative AI, the language learners' frustration no longer comes from the issues in chatbot's functional capacity, but rather from the absence of graded language and the lack of feedback when a conversational breakdown occurs.

5.2 Atmosphere

In the past, chatbots were often characterized by lack of personality, carrying out boring conversations due to their short memory and lack of world knowledge (Coniam, 2008; Fryer et al., 2020). The chatbot's algorithm did not allow it to hold the information the user just mentioned, so the conversation would come back to the same subject eventually. In addition, discussing topics which the chatbot wasn't trained to know would result in confusion and miscommunication. While the participants in this current study with Replika also report Replika's limited knowledge on certain cultural topics, Replika is able to retain the information that the user is sharing about, making it somewhat similar to interactions with a human.

In line with previous research on Replika (Brandtzaeg et al., 2022; Huang et al., 2022; Ta et al.,2020), feedback from participants in this current study with Replika also suggests that interacting with chatbots is enjoyable and reduces apprehension. Knowing that language learners are conversing with an AI chatbot reduces stress, fostering a more relaxed atmosphere that encourages risk-taking. As a result, language learners feel more comfortable with making mistakes and trying again. Having a fun conversation in a casual environment, even if in the school premises, motivates the language learners to persist in their language learning journey.

One more undeniable benefit of chatbots that applies to any generation of chatbots is that they are available for conversation anywhere anytime (Coniam 2014; Huang et al., 2022; Kılıçkaya, 2020). Finding a conversation partner who is willing to persist in a conversation despite errors and topic repetition is quite difficult. What is more, the speed of response is what language learners deeply value (Kılıçkaya, 2020). The feedback from the participants in this current study with Replika confirms the sentiment, adding that the language learners are also able to practice responding faster due to how quickly they receive the responses from Replika.

5.3 Meeting Language Learners' Needs

5.3.1 Absence of Error Correction

In the current study, the participants expressed certain concerns about Replika which echo throughout other studies on chatbots (Belda-Medina & Calvo-Ferrer, 2022; Cakmak, 2022). The participants regretted that Replika was not able to correct the participants' mistakes, nor could it explain what went wrong in a conversation when a conversation breakdown occurred. Notably, this causes a lot of frustration and confusion, especially if the language learners cannot use conversation repair strategies comfortably.

The concerns are valid owing to the fact that Replika is not designed as a language learning platform and therefore does not contain features preferred by language learners. One way to tackle conversation breakdowns and gap in language proficiency is for a teacher to offer support and guidance alongside this near-authentic conversation experience with a chatbot, as was done in the current study on Replika. The participants reported an overall positive feedback, suggesting that such tandem between a chatbot and a teacher can be a successful classroom practice.

5.3.2 Considering Chatbot's Original Purpose

When a teacher opts to incorporate a chatbot into their language classroom, the teacher should assess the chatbot's original purpose. Even among generative AI chatbots, there are applications which are designed purely for conversation, for language learning, for customer support, and so on. The chatbots, which are initially created for entertainment, might lack the essential features needed for effective language practice. Such chatbots might be more suitable for higher-proficiency learners who can engage in conversations and adapt to less structured learning environments. Conversely, chatbots explicitly designed for language learning may offer additional language-focused features, including pronunciation, grammar, and vocabulary feedback. Rule-based chatbots, which are more structured and predictable, may be better suited for beginner language learners who are not yet prepared to handle unexpected errors from a chatbot. Consequently, when selecting a chatbot for language practice, teachers should consider their students' proficiency levels, along with the chatbot's original purpose and design, to ensure that it aligns effectively with their learners' needs.

5.3.3 Teacher Support

Teachers have the flexibility to decide the level of support they offer to individual students when using AI-based conversation chatbots. Students comfortable with the unpredictability of such chatbots can benefit from unsupervised interaction, allowing them to explore topics of interest and enjoy the experience.

Any disruptions or issues in the conversation can be seen as opportunities for practicing negotiation of meaning and clarification, crucial skills for real-life conversations. However, if teachers are concerned about students getting distracted from the activity's main objective, they can use the projector to show the screen of the student's (or a teacher's) device and have students collectively generate responses to the chatbot. This approach allows teachers to maintain control over the exercise and provide feedback, particularly on grammar and vocabulary, based on students' response suggestions. Thus, engaging in conversations with generative AI chatbots will significantly benefit language learners and enhance their overall learning experience.

6. CONCLUSION

This chapter has focused on exploring the use of generative AI chatbot for text-based conversation practice in an English language classroom by analyzing the impressions of university-level English language learners regarding their interactions with the chatbot Replika. The study incorporated conversation practice, with half of the students receiving corrective feedback on their interactions. Pre-test and post-test surveys assessed students' perceived writing performance, and feedback was collected on their experiences with chatbot-based practice.

The discussion above highlighted the changes that generative AI has brought to the chatbot industry, including improved linguistic ability and better conversation management. At the same time, generative AI chatbots continue to provide the same level of comfort as before to language learners as they feel reduced anxiety while chatting with AI that does not judge the learners' mistakes. In fact, language learners experience increased writing performance after continuous text-based practice with the chatbot.

The chapter also calls to consider the chatbot's original purpose in designing an English lesson around it, as many language learners criticize chatbots for the lack of error correction and the amount of miscommunication. When using chatbots which are originally not designed with language learners in mind, a teacher may aid in guidance and error correction, to make up for the chatbots' limitations. After all, the chatbot's main goal remains to provide near-authentic conversation experience, which generative AI chatbots are excelling at.

Further research is needed to explore more task-based activities where the use of chatbot and teacher's guidance may go in tandem. Ultimately, chatbots should serve as a supplement to language classroom instruction, offering a rich learning environment. As technology advances, it is also important to continue to update our knowledge on chatbots' features and algorithms, always keeping in mind how the technology can better serve the students.

REFERENCES

Adamopoulou, E., & Moussiades, L. (2020). Chatbots: History, technology, and applications. *Machine Learning with Applications*, *2*, 100006. doi:10.1016/j.mlwa.2020.100006

Andujar, A. (2016). Benefits of mobile instant messaging to develop ESL writing. *System*, *62*, 63–76. doi:10.1016/j.system.2016.07.004

Baek, J., Yoo, Y., Lee, K., Jung, B., & Baek, Y. (2017). Using an instant messenger to learn a foreign language in a peer-tutoring environment. *Turkish Online Journal of Educational Technology-TOJET*, *16*(2), 145–152.

Belda-Medina, J., & Calvo-Ferrer, J. R. (2022). Using chatbots as AI conversational partners in language learning. *Applied Sciences (Basel, Switzerland)*, *12*(17), 8427. doi:10.3390/app12178427

Brandtzaeg, P. B., Skjuve, M., & Følstad, A. (2022). My AI friend: How users of a social chatbot understand their human–AI friendship. *Human Communication Research*, *48*(3), 404–429. doi:10.1093/hcr/hqac008

Brownlee, J. (2019, June 17). *A gentle introduction to generative adversarial networks (GANs)*. Machine Learning Mastery. https://machinelearningmastery.com/what-are-generative-adversarial-networks-gans/

Çakmak, F. (2022). Chatbot-human interaction and its effects on EFL students' L2 speaking performance and anxiety. [Research on Youth and Language]. *Novitas-ROYAL*, *16*(2), 113–131.

Cingel, D. P., & Sundar, S. S. (2012). Texting, techspeak, and tweens: The relationship between text messaging and English grammar skills. *New Media & Society*, *14*(8), 1304–1320. doi:10.1177/1461444812442927

Coniam, D. (2008). Evaluating the language resources of chatbots for their potential in English as a second language. *ReCALL*, *20*(1), 98–116. doi:10.1017/S0958344008000815

Coniam, D. (2014). The linguistic accuracy of chatbots: Usability from an ESL perspective. *Text & Talk*, *34*(5), 545–567. doi:10.1515/text-2014-0018

Fainchtein, L. H. (2020, June 28). Generative vs retrieval based chatbots: A quick guide. *Medium*. https://blog.cloudboost.io/generative-vs-retrieval-based-chatbots-a-quick-guide- 8d19edb1d645

Fryer, L., Coniam, D., Carpenter, R., & Lăpuşneanu, D. (2020). Bots for language learning now: Current and future directions. *Language Learning & Technology*, *24*(2), 8–22. 10125/44719

Harman, B. A., & Sato, T. (2011). Cell phone use and grade point average among undergraduate university students. *College Student Journal*, *45*(3), 544–550.

Huang, W., Hew, K. F., & Fryer, L. K. (2022). Chatbots for language learning — Are they really useful? A systematic review of chatbot-supported language learning. *Journal of Computer Assisted Learning*, *38*(1), 237–257. doi:10.1111/jcal.12610

Kaid Mohammed Ali, J., Hasnain, S. I., & Beg, M. S. (2019). The impact of texting on Standard English: The students' perspective. *Arab World English Journal (AWEJ). SSRN*, *5*(5), 65–75. doi:10.2139srn.3431793

Kemp, N., & Bushnell, C. (2011). Children's text messaging: Abbreviations, input methods and links with literacy. *Journal of Computer Assisted Learning*, *27*(1), 18–27. doi:10.1111/j.1365-2729.2010.00400.x

Kılıçkaya, F. (2020). Using a chatbot, Replika, to practice writing through conversations in L2 English: A Case study. In *New Technological applications for foreign and second language learning and teaching* (pp. 221–238). IGI Global. doi:10.4018/978-1-7998-2591-3.ch011

Kim, H. S., Cha, Y., & Kim, N. Y. (2021). Effects of AI chatbots on EFL students' communication skills. *Korean Journal of English Language and Linguistics*, *21*, 712–734. doi:10.15738/kjell.21.202108.712

Lauricella, S., & Kay, R. (2013). Exploring the use of text and instant messaging in higher education classrooms. *Research in Learning Technology, 21*. doi:10.3402/rlt.v21i0.19061

Lin, C. J., & Mubarok, H. (2021). Learning analytics for investigating the mind map-guided AI chatbot approach in an EFL flipped speaking classroom. *Journal of Educational Technology & Society, 24*(4), 16–35.

Namaziandost, E., Shafiee, S., & Suryadi, R. (2020). Using mobile instant messaging in teaching vocabulary to pre-intermediate EFL learners: The case of WhatsApp. Process. *Journal of English Education, 5*(1), 1–10. doi:10.31327/jee.v5i1.1162

Plester, B., Wood, C., & Bell, V. (2008). Txt msg n school literacy: Does texting and knowledge of text abbreviations adversely affect children's literacy attainment? *Literacy, 42*(3), 137–144. doi:10.1111/j.1741-4369.2008.00489.x

Plester, B., Wood, C., & Joshi, P. (2009). Exploring the relationship between children's knowledge of text message abbreviations and school literacy outcomes. *British Journal of Developmental Psychology, 27*(1), 145–161. doi:10.1348/026151008X320507 PMID:19972666

Ramesh, K., Ravishankaran, S., Joshi, A., & Chandrasekaran, K. (2017). A survey of design techniques for conversational agents. In *Information, communication and computing technology* (Vol. 750, pp. 336–350). Springer. doi:10.1007/978-981-10-6544-6_31

Replika. (n.d.). *Frequently asked questions.* Replika. https://replika.com/

So, S. (2016). Mobile instant messaging support for teaching and learning in higher education. *The Internet and Higher Education, 31*, 32–42. doi:10.1016/j.iheduc.2016.06.001

Ta, V., Griffith, C., Boatfield, C., Wang, X., Civitello, M., Bader, H., DeCero, E., & Loggarakis, A. (2020). User experiences of social support from companion chatbots in everyday contexts: Thematic analysis. *Journal of Medical Internet Research, 22*(3), e16235. doi:10.2196/16235 PMID:32141837

Van Dijk, C. N., Van Witteloostuijn, M., Vasić, N., Avrutin, S., & Blom, E. (2016). The influence of texting language on grammar and executive functions in primary school children. *PLoS One, 11*(3), e0152409. doi:10.1371/journal.pone.0152409 PMID:27031708

Chapter 13
The Robot Wrote My College Papers:
Integrating Chatbots to Assist Higher Education

Ivy Shen
Southeast Missouri State University, USA

ABSTRACT

As chatbot technology has advanced significantly over the past few years, it has become more and more prevalent in higher education. Chatbots can simulate human communication and engage in natural conversations. Universities and colleges use chatbots to streamline enrollment and create a virtual "one-stop-shop" for queries. In the meantime, students discovered with excitement that chatbots can help them complete homework assignments. Academic integrity has become a growing concern with students' increasing reliance on chatbots. This chapter summarizes the history of chatbots, discusses the current state of the technology, examines their limitations, and investigates how chatbots can be applied as useful administrative, academic, and pedagogical tools in higher education.

1. INTRODUCTION

Artificial intelligence (AI) is a branch of computer science concerned with building programs capable of performing problem-solving tasks. The language recognition capabilities of AI systems have developed rapidly. Powered by AI programs, chatbots can simulate human behavior by conversing and interacting with users using natural language. Chatbots have been gaining popularity in various industries, given their ability to mimic human conversations. To save costs and reduce labor, industries with consumers demanding around-the-clock services deploy chatbots to provide customer service. During the COVID-19 pandemic, communication and chatbot technologies accelerated to address public needs. Government organizations employed chatbots to answer high volumes of citizen questions related to the coronavirus

DOI: 10.4018/979-8-3693-0074-9.ch013

and disseminate pandemic-related updates. The battle against the pandemic is over, but the technology and the prevalent use of chatbots remain.

In recent years chatbots have been widely used in higher education. Universities and colleges employ chatbots to interact with current and incoming students, creating a virtual "one-stop-shop" for student queries. A university chatbot can provide students with information ranging from campus and facilities to academic advising and financial aid. Some universities have developed emotional support chatbots to help freshmen transition to college life. To some students, their university chatbot is like an all-knowing expert and caring friend. Some large universities even use chatbots to provide parking navigation on campus to staff and faculty.

Not only can chatbots be used as administrative tools, but they have academic values as well. Newer chatbots can write emails, generate texts, write computer code, solve math problems, interpret questions, and provide accurate and thorough answers. In November 2022, OpenAI, an American AI research laboratory, launched ChatGPT, a chatbot known for producing natural and fluent essays. College students discovered with excitement that ChatGPT can help them complete assignments. Before the arrival of chatbots, a complicated assignment may require careful data gathering, diligent research, and hours of hard work. With the advent of ChatGPT, students can watch their papers being written in just a few moments. A recent survey reveals that many college students rely heavily on ChatGPT to complete their homework assignments. Since ChatGPT creates an original work each time, its responses are not in the databases of plagiarism detectors. Although some educators use AI detectors to spot plagiarism, these tools can be unreliable and falsely flag original human-written content. Higher education is confronted with unprecedented academic and ethical challenges.

Recognizing that chatbots potentially hinder student learning and promote laziness, universities and colleges began to take preventive measures to address these challenges. Some common strategies are outright banning chatbots on their networks and computers to eliminate plagiarized work, implementing strict policies and consequences for misusing chatbots, altering the learning outcomes assessment, and communicating the importance of college learning and the ethical use of chatbots to students. Despite the challenges and downfalls, chatbots hold great promise for higher education. Recognizing that chatbot technology will not likely disappear, more and more educators have begun to incorporate chatbots into their pedagogical practices. Incorporating chatbots in teaching potentially creates an inclusive learning environment, improves student critical thinking skills, prepares students for an increasingly tech-centric world, and conducts academic assessment. Intending to contribute to the expansion of the current literature on chatbots in higher education, this chapter summarizes the history of chatbots, discusses the current state of the technology, examines their limitations, and investigates how chatbots can be applied as useful administrative, academic, and pedagogical tools. The chapter begins by tracing the history and evolution of chatbots. Ever since its inception, chatbots have become increasingly advanced and sophisticated in meeting user demands and generating coherent information. Given chatbots' relative success in industries where customer services are heavily demanded, postsecondary institutions began to adopt them as well to streamline their enrollment processes and distribute campus information to students, faculty, and staff. The chapter further discusses how students' reliance on chatbots to write their assignments can compromise academic integrity. Recognizing the faults of chatbots, this chapter explores the potential benefits of chatbots in assisting higher education. Specifically, chatbots can facilitate critical thinking, assist with academic assessment, support personalized and inclusive learning, and improve digital literacy.

2. A BRIEF HISTORY OF CHATBOTS

2.1 The Genesis of Chatbots

A chatbot is a program that combines AI and natural language processing or other technology that enables it to interact to a certain level of conversation with a human user through text or voice (Pérez et al., 2020). Chatbots are also referred to as conversational agents or chatterbots. In 1966, MIT professor Joseph Weizenbaum created the first chatbot, ELIZA, a computer program that interacts with users in a typed conversation by looking for the keyword in the initially entered statement (New Jersey Institute of Technology, 2023). ELIZA processes the words, pairs them with a list of possible scripted responses, and finds the most relevant response. The limited script database leads to clunky, sometimes even nonsensical, conversations. In 1972, American psychiatrist Kenneth Colby constructed PARRY, an adaptation of ELIZA, that can imitate the thinking of a person with paranoid schizophrenia and "converse" with others (Colby, 1981). The chatbot Jabberwacky invented by British programmer Rollo Carpenter in 1988, was the first AI program that could simulate a natural human conversation. Jabberwacky aggregates inputted phrases into its database, making the conservation more natural than its predecessors. With its ability to tell jokes and use slang, Jabberwacky is able to offer entertaining chats with the user (BBC News, 2003).

2.2 Chatbots of the 21st Century

The 21st-century chatbots began to showcase machine learning and advanced algorithms. As a branch of AI, machine learning focuses on the use of data and algorithms to automate an analytical model using input and output data, find intrinsic structures in input data, and imitate the way that humans learn, making the response more accurate (IBM, 2023a). The first text-based chatbot SmarterChild appeared on online instant messenger platforms (i.e., AOL Instant Messenger and MSN Messenger) in the early 2000s. With its machine learning features, SmarterChild is able to respond to a wide range of questions and commands, including providing information on weather, sports, and news, playing games, and even engaging in conversation (NPR News, 2017). SmarterChild retired in 2008, with the rise of smartphones and messaging apps, but its legacy lived on. In the meantime, IBM Watson, a question-answering computer system, was born. Watson runs on a cluster of computers and holds the equivalent of about one million books worth of information. Watson later competed on the TV quiz show Jeopardy! against former all-time champions and won the first prize of $1 million (IBM, 2023b).

Chatbots developed in the 2010s are able to perform tasks that previously required human touch such as placing phone calls, setting reminders, and looking up the internet. These highly sophisticated chatbots (e.g., Siri and Alexa) are called virtual assistants, or intelligent assistants, which are machine learning-powered software that allows human users to quickly find relevant information or complete tasks (Azvine et al., 2000). Virtual assistants utilize natural language processing, enabling them to understand text and spoken words in much the same way human beings can. In recent years, advanced chatbots have been gaining popularity in a variety of industries given their ability to mimic human conversations. To save costs and reduce labor, many companies implement chatbots on customer service and messaging platforms. Some conversational chatbots have been developed in many languages, ensuring smooth communications with international users. Major technology companies such as Google (Google Assistant), Amazon (Alexa), Samsung (Bixby), and Microsoft (Cortana) all have their virtual assistants to improve user experience. Industries with consumers demanding around-the-clock services are particularly interested in developing virtual assistance to provide customer care. For example, Bank of America launched a chatbot named Erica as a virtual financial assistant for their clients in 2018, and as of October 2022, Erica has had 32 million clients and over one billion client interactions (Bank of America, 2022). The global chatbot industry is currently worth $1 billion and predicted to be $4.9 billion by 2032. North America currently holds the largest share of the market, with roughly 41.0% of the market size (Precedence Research, 2023).

2.3 Accelerated Chatbot Technology During the Pandemic

Communication and chatbot technologies accelerated during the COVID-19 pandemic to address public needs. The internet was the most significant source for individuals seeking guidelines about the coronavirus (Chin et al., 2023). In the face of lockdowns and social distancing, social media has emerged as a crucial tool in relationship maintenance and communications. The government and public authorities used social media platforms extensively to disseminate pandemic-related mandates since these sites can provide rich information and multi-media messages. Citizens also relied on social media to obtain news and COVID-related updates. Engagement with social media reached an unprecedented level. For example, a recent Pew Research Center (2021) survey revealed that the internet was essential or important to 90% of Americans during the pandemic. The increasing reliance on social media can be directly linked to the rapidly expanding communication technologies. With the rising public concern over the novel illness, institutions like the Centers for Disease Control and Prevention (CDC) and the World Health Organization (WHO) employed chatbots to answer high volumes of citizen questions related to the coronavirus around the clock, and monitor public health (Miner et al., 2020). In April 2020, the WHO (2020) launches a chatbot on Facebook, one of the most frequently visited social media sites, to combat COVID-19 misinformation. The COVID-19 public health emergency has ended, but the prevalent use of chatbots remains.

3. CHATBOTS AS ADMINISTRATIVE AND ACADEMIC TOOLS

3.1 Administrative Functions

In recent years, more and more postsecondary institutions have been deploying chatbots to interact with students, creating a virtual "one-stop-shop" for student queries. Chatbots reduce the manual effort of staff answering the same questions repeatedly, freeing time and recourses for other administrative tasks. A university chatbot can provide students with information related to the campus, facilities, enrollment, courses, career development, academic advising, and financial aid. For example, to boost enrollment and retention, Georgia State University launched the chatbot Pounce to answer thousands of questions from incoming students 24/7 via text messages on their smart devices (Georgia State University, 2023). Pounce was created to address "summer melt", which occurs when students who enroll in the spring drop out by the time school begins in the fall. In 2016, Pounce reduced "summer melt" by 22 percent, which meant 324 additional students showed up for the first day of fall classes (EdTech, 2020). CSUNny, a chatbot employed by California State University at Northridge, is another successful example. CSUNny sends important campus notifications to students' cellphones and answers basic questions. Students who were given access to CSUNny were significantly more likely to still be enrolled at the university than their control group counterparts (California State University at Northridge, 2023). Such positive results are attributable to chatbots' efficiency in responding to questions and increased customer satisfaction. Swift and accurate communication is crucial to converting prospective applicants into enrolled students and streamlining the enrollment process. Universities can use chatbots to collect data to learn how students interact with online platforms and website services, which helps identify areas the institutions need to improve to enhance campus life. Chatbots also send out announcements to students, reminding them to stay on top of course enrollment and financial applications. For universities, it is recourse-saving to employ a chatbot since it can single-handedly manage the entire query influx, making the college management look efficient and student-centered.

For many students, college life can be stressful and daunting. Being away from home and transitioning to a different academic environment is anxiety-inducing. Chatbots can offer emotional support and resources (i.e., counseling services and coping strategies) for students who struggle with mental health challenges. At Arizona State University, chatbot Sunny was designed to provide emotional support to students in addition to providing university information (Arizona State University, 2023). The chatbot not only helps with effective communication but enhances university relationships with students as well. To students, Sunny is like a caring friend who periodically texts words of encouragement, accompanied by appropriate emojis, and offers a set of listening ears. Sunny's automated texts were particularly vital during the COVID-19 pandemic when students went through a tremendous amount of stress dealing with transitioning to remote learning, along with some other major life changes. Students who do not want to engage with Sunny over text can choose to opt out and resubscribe later if necessary. Recently a professor at the University of South Florida developed a chatbot named RAMI to provide ongoing motivation to students. RAMI appears every time a student logs into the course and asks the student about how they are feeling and if they are facing any challenges (University of South Florida, 2023). To students, RAMI appears as a personable and encouraging friend who can engage and motivate them. Students often experience high self-efficacy in classes where RAMI is implemented. As a result, the majority of students complete the courses with good grades.

Another neat feature of university chatbots is providing assistance to staff and faculty. Chatbots can assist with answering frequently asked questions related to payroll, benefits, leave requests, and other administrative processes. As more courses are taught online or in a hybrid mode instead of face to face, faculty members who are less technically adaptive may require technical support for IT-related issues. A chatbot can provide troubleshooting assistance and offer step-by-step solutions. In addition, chatbots can serve as a central hub for internal communications, providing staff members with university-wide updates and announcements. California State University at San Bernardino's (2023) chatbot Cody can offer parking navigation on campus to staff and faculty, which is highly appreciated since parking can be hectic on a large campus.

3.2 Threats to Academic Integrity

When computer scientist Joseph Weizenbaum created the first chatbot, ELIZA, in 1966, he probably did not envision the prevalence of the use of AI on college campuses today. Early commercial chatbots used pattern matching to find the most appropriate response for a user's input. Newer chatbots are able to generate responses through large networks, which are pretrained on billion-scale conversation data sets (Chin et al., 2023). The most recent chatbots are getting more and more sophisticated. They can write emails, solve math problems, write computer code, interpret questions, provide accurate and coherent answers, and more (OpenAI, 2023a). As intelligent tools, chatbots have the potential to support the field of teaching-learning and accommodate students' academic needs (Troussas et al., 2020). This is particularly true for higher education contexts as college students have a great deal of autonomy in their learning experience. Computers and stable internet connections have become ubiquitous on college campuses. The ease of information acquisition and the availability of chatbots have transformed the reality of higher education. Before the arrival of chatbots, a college assignment may require students to collect materials, conduct diligent research, and compose paragraphs. Complicated projects may even warrant multiple trips to the library and tens of hours of work. With the advent of chatbots, students can go to their browsers, type in a few keywords or a question, and watch their papers being written for them within just a few seconds. Since students are expected to complete assignments and projects outside of class unmonitored, chatbots come in handy.

One of the most commonly used chatbots in higher education is ChatGPT, which is known for its ability to write natural and fluent essays and produce personalized content based on individual learning history and interests. Soon after OpenAI, an American AI research laboratory, launched ChatGPT in November 2022, the chatbot quickly gained traction. ChatGPT reached one million users in the first five days and surpassed 100 million after two months, making it the fastest-growing application in history (University of Rochester, 2023). A recent survey of 1,000 U.S. college students found that nearly a third of them have used ChatGPT to complete homework assignments, and close to 60 percent use it on more than half of their work (Government Technology, 2023). Generally, responses generated by ChatGPT are adequate for many students and assignments. More impressively, ChatGPT can achieve high scores on a range of tests. In a recent study (Kung et al., 2022), researchers put ChatGPT through the United States Medical Licensing Exam, a three-step examination for medical licensure, and learned that ChatGPT performed at or near the passing threshold for all three exams without any medical training. In March 2023, OpenAI introduced the newest language model of ChatGPT, ChatGPT-4, and claimed that it outperforms most human test-takers on difficult academic exams (OpenAI, 2023b). ChatGPT-4 scored in the 90th percentile of the bar exam with a score of 298 out of 400. ChatGPT-4 also excelled on the SAT Reading and Writing section with a score of 710 out of 800, which put it in the 93rd percentile, and earned a 700 out of 800 on the math test, ranking among the 89th percentile (OpenAI, 2023b).

As sophisticated as ChatGPT is, it occasionally generates incorrect information. OpenAI (2023b) admits that despite its incredible capacities, ChatGPT maintains a tendency to make up facts and performs tasks incorrectly. Since it does not use the internet to locate answers and it can only work with inputted data, ChatGPT draws information from its system. Although ChatGPT is trained on a large database, it is prone to filling in replies with incorrect data if there is not enough information available on a subject. In addition, ChatGPT can unintentionally generate hate speech, discriminatory language, and biased content. ChatGPT is powered by texts written by humans, which means human bias and prejudice can appear in the created answers. According to a recent survey that interviewed students who have experimented with ChatGPT (The New York Times, 2023), although the program is useful for assignments, the accuracy of the information is questionable.

In higher education, one of the biggest concerns over students using chatbots for assignments is compromised academic honesty. Students can copy and paste the chatbot-generated content into a document or a learning management system (e.g., Blackboard, Canvas, Moodle) and submit it. Since ChatGPT creates an original work each time, its responses are not in the databases of plagiarism detectors. Plagiarism may be easy to identify if a student who communicates poorly in-person turns in a surprisingly well-written essay with no grammatical errors, but frequently it is difficult to determine who wrote the assignment.

Although some educators use AI-writing detectors to spot plagiarism, these detectors are not always foolproof. They may falsely flag original human written content. In the same survey mentioned earlier (The New York Times, 2023), some students worried that ChatGPT would rob them of their motivation and creativity. A student at Columbia University revealed to the *Chronicle of Higher Education* (2023) that students use ChatGPT more extensively than professors may think, and it is nearly impossible to catch plagiarism because of ChatGPT's ability to provide a step-by-step process of writing a paper. This student explained that the user could tell the algorithm what the topic is and ask for a central claim, then have ChatGPT provide an outline to argue this claim. The user can also use ChatGPT to generate ideas based on the prompt, any one of which the user can choose to include in their assignment. In other words, many students use ChatGPT to do the thinking for them. Another unique feature of ChatGPT is that it can craft answers that resemble the speech pattern of a particular type of individuals. For example, if a user inputs a prompt and instructs the chatbot to explain it in a way a college freshman would, ChatGPT can create content that sounds remarkably like something a college freshman would produce. It makes detecting cheating even more difficult when students utilize this feature.

3.3 Attempts to Restore Academic Integrity

Alarmed by students' extensive reliance on ChatGPT to complete homework assignments, universities and colleges are taking preventative measures. Some universities outright ban chatbots on their networks and computers to eliminate plagiarized work and discourage cheating. The strategy turns out to be ineffective because students are still able to access chatbots through their own devices (i.e., laptops, tablets, and smartphones) or complete assignments off-campus. Further, banning chatbots will potentially hurt enrollment numbers. A recent study (College Rover, 2023) surveyed 372 students seeking college admission for Fall 2023 and revealed that 39 percent of respondents lacked interest in attending a college that has banned ChatGPT or other AI tools. Since technologies are here to stay and ChatGPT will only advance, banning the platform is a nearsighted response.

A second widely adopted strategy is to implement strict policies and consequences for misusing chatbots. Addressing a policy prohibiting or limiting the use of ChatGPT for assignments in the syllabus academic integrity statement will remind students of the importance of academic honesty. Students may be less likely to submit AI-generated work if the course syllabus explicitly indicates penalties for plagiarized work. However, as indicated, without a foolproof AI-writing detector, professors find it challenging to spot plagiarism. Many students are aware of this fact and use it to their advantage. One possible solution is to center assignments around a specifically narrow topic. Chatbots effortlessly produce general information and generate well-structured texts, but they do not have a strong background in hyperlocal issues. Therefore, they are of little use if students have to answer lecture-based prompts or questions grounded in the local community. Although ChatGPT is trained on vast amounts of information, it is prone to produce incorrect answers if there is not enough information available on a subject. The misinformation gives clues about whether the text was written by a human. Another possible solution is to ask students to explain their work and prompt them to detail their thinking process. If a student fails to coherently explain why they chose to approach the subject in a particular way or detail how they reached a certain conclusion, it may be possible that the student consulted with a chatbot.

A third strategy is to alter the learning outcomes assessment. More and more educators are now replacing writing assignments, which seem vulnerable to chatbots, with videos, oral exams, presentations, drawings, diagrams, and podcasts. Some professors resort to the old-school paper and pencil method to test students' knowledge. Instead of submitting take-home assignments, students are asked to write something on paper. An alternative is to have students type in the classroom using browsers that restrict and track computer activity. These supervised writing exercises force students to demonstrate what they know about the subject matter. This is particularly helpful for math and computer science classes. As indicated, ChatGPT is a powerful tool that can be used to write computer code and solve math problems. The professor may not be able to evaluate learning outcomes by reviewing take-home assignments. The visualized process of in-class writing gives the professor the opportunity to understand the learning gaps of each student and formulate a plan to fill those gaps. Such a method also requires students to organize and present their thoughts, which is essential in the learning process.

A fourth strategy is to communicate the importance of college learning and the ethical use of chatbots to students. While chatbots assist with text-related tasks, they may not provide a thorough understanding of the material. To fully understand the material and retain important information, students must actively engage with the content, think about it critically, and participate in meaningful discussions. Students should be aware of the risks associated with using chatbots, including plagiarism and technology limitations. After all, the essential value of a college education is to expand one's knowledge and understanding of various disciplines.

4. CHATBOTS AS PEDAGOGICAL TOOLS

Despite the aforementioned challenges and downfalls, chatbots can be beneficial pedagogical tools for educators to improve student success. Student success is the center of higher education because it is considered a fundamental element for assessing the quality of education. Student success is a multi-dimensional definition that encompasses academic achievement, engaging in educationally purposeful activities, acquisition of desired knowledge, skills and competencies, persistence, attainment of educational outcomes, and post-college performance (Kuh et al., 2006). Pedagogy is the profession, art, and science of teaching (Bishop & Starkey, 2006, p. 119). Higher education pedagogy involves the full set of instructional techniques and strategies that enable learning and provide opportunities for student success. Learning is an ongoing and complex process that includes various dimensions such as reflections, engagement, interactions, and collaboration. Incorporating chatbots can accommodate relevant pedagogies. The traditional pedagogical approach is characterized by teacher-centeredness, verbal delivery of information, and learner passivity. Such an approach cannot adequately address the challenges posed by the information age and is ill-equipped to empower students with the skills they need in the information age (Bii, 2013). The modern age calls for collaborative, active, interactive pedagogical practices. Instead of viewing chatbots as a hindrance to student learning, many universities and colleges are now embracing the technology. Recognizing that chatbot technology will not go away, more and more educators have begun to incorporate chatbots into their teaching practices. Specifically, chatbots improve critical thinking, provide assessment, facilitate personalized and inclusive learning, and boost digital literacy.

4.1 Critical Thinking

First, incorporating chatbots can elevate students' critical thinking skills. Cultivating students' critical thinking ability is a major goal of higher education because such an ability enables students to engage in purposeful and self-regulatory judgment (Behar-Horenstein & Niu, 2011). Developing critical thinking skills helps students become better problem solvers, improves their ability to make informed decisions, and enhances their capacity for independent and lifelong learning. Higher education institutions bear the responsibility to refine these skills among students and help them become responsible citizens. A study conducted by the Association of American Colleges and Universities (2011) indicated that 95% of the chief academic officers from surveyed higher education institutions and 81% of the surveyed employers view critical thinking as one of the most important intellectual skills for college students. Critical thinking involves scrutinizing, differentiating, and appraising information as well as reflecting on the information that will be used to make judgments and inform decisions (Banning, 2006). Students demonstrate their critical thinking skills by interpreting and making judgments about the relevance and quality of information (Liu et al., 2014). Chatbots are effective tools in this effort because they provide information with high accuracy[1] and speed, which help students think critically about topics they are already familiar with. Each time the user types in a question or a prompt, ChatGPT creates an original work, providing additional materials for students to discuss, analyze, and critique. Through such an activity, students can see that there are many ways to approach the same question. Further, as indicated, ChatGPT can unintentionally generate false information, and biased and prejudiced content. This serves as an opportunity for students to see the mistakes and biases in the text generate and achieve a more comprehensive understanding of the subject matter.

4.2 Learning Assessment

Second, chatbots are capable of monitoring and assessing student performance. Learning assessment is defined as "the systematic collection and analysis of information to improve student learning" (Stassen et al., 2001, p. 5). Assessing student learning provides feedback to both the educator and students about the extent to which students successfully meet learning objectives. Assessment information reveals student progress and provides feedback for improvement. Knowing how well students have mastered the course content, the educator can adjust their materials and teaching strategies accordingly. The scholarship of teaching and learning discusses two general forms of assessment: summative and formative (Wright, 1997). Educators usually conduct summative assessments at the end of a course or a specific period to evaluate the overall achievement of students and determine whether the learning outcomes are met. Some assessment artifacts include exams, papers, presentations, or portfolios. Differently, formative assessment is an ongoing process that provides feedback to students throughout the learning process through similar artifacts. Formative assessments help students and the educator identify areas for improvement (Wright, 1997). Chatbots can assist with both types of assessments. In recent years, educational chatbots have been increasingly employed in higher education. They are designed to assist and enhance the learning experience by providing a wide range of educational services and support, from answering questions and providing explanations to delivering personalized learning content and tracking progress (Essel et al., 2022). Educational chatbots can collect and analyze data on student interactions and offer personalized learning experiences. This process generates formative assessment data on the student's ongoing performance. Chatbots can administer exams and quizzes, which produce summative assessment data.

However, the role of chatbots in assessment is currently limited. As indicated, many professors are replacing writing assignments, which seem vulnerable to chatbots, with oral exams, presentations, drawings, and diagrams to prevent cheating. Current chatbots cannot effectively grade these types of assignments. Further, chatbots can only assist with automated grading for objective assessments, such as multiple-choice questions or fill-in-the-blank exercises, where answers can be scored based on predetermined criteria. Chatbots cannot determine if students have successfully met complex learning objectives. In higher education, learning objectives tend to be action-based and explicitly outlined. These objectives are best assessed through human observation. Therefore, chatbots can only contribute to the assessment process in a supportive way. Nevertheless, as AI technology continues to improve, ongoing advancements in AI are continually addressing these challenges. It is possible that future chatbots will be able to contribute more to student assessment.

4.3 Personalized and Inclusive Learning

4.3.1 Personalized Learning

In addition to supporting academic assessment, the quantity and quality of information and knowledge included in an educational chatbot system enables it to be a "smart teacher" who can assist in personalized and inclusive learning. Chatbots have a long history of being used as pedagogical agents. In the 1970s, Intelligent Tutoring Systems (ITS) were developed to provide individual and adaptive instruction. ITSs are AI-powered computer programs that provide intelligent tutors that know what they teach, whom they teach, and how to teach (Alkhatlan & Kalita, 2019). At a fraction of the cost of hiring human teachers, AI technology helps simulate human tutors who can teach students and create an interactive educational experience. Educational chatbots can be available around the clock, providing students with access to assistance and resources outside of regular class houses, which can be particularly helpful for students who have questions or need support outside of traditional classroom settings. Conversational ITSs deliver content through discussion, asking and answering questions, identifying gaps in knowledge, and addressing these gaps in natural language (Ilagan & Ilagan, 2023). AI-powered chatbots are designed to provide instant feedback, which is one of the most effective teaching strategies since it has an immediate impact on learning progress. An example of ITS is AutoTutor developed by researchers at the Institute for Intelligent Systems at the University of Memphis. AutoTutor is a computer tutor that helps students learn by holding a conversation in natural language. The program is able to track the cognition and emotions of the student through dialogue patterns, facial expressions, and body posture of the student, and responds in a manner that adapts to the student (University of Memphis, 2023).

4.3.2 Inclusive Learning

For these features, chatbots support inclusive learning by creating a learning environment that meets different students' needs. For students with *intellectual* disabilities, learning can be a challenging and daunting journey. Chatbots can create a welcoming learning environment and allow students the freedom to choose their preferred way to access learning materials. The interactive nature of chatbots provides opportunities for social interaction, which plays a critical role in the development of cognition and contributes to the process of learning (Gupta & Chen, 2022). Students with *social* disabilities may feel anxious and uncomfortable when they ask questions to a human educator. As a result of the recent pandemic, lockdown, and social distancing, students with social disabilities have seen their social relations restricted, causing them to lose previously acquired social skills or have difficulties in putting them to use again (Mateos-Sanchez et al., 2022). Students with social disabilities face barriers when they communicate with others due to their difficulties in developing social skills. Chatbots offer nonjudgmental interactions that these students appreciate. Further, chatbots can incorporate emotional intelligence into their interactions, providing emotional support to students who may require additional encouragement. Some students with *physical* disabilities may find it difficult to travel around campus and utilize campus learning resources. These students can access chatbot services through their devices. Chatbots are designed with accessibility features such as compatibility with screen readers for students who have vision loss and providing text-based options for students with hearing impairments, ensuring that students with disabilities can access and engage with the chatbot effectively. Chatbots offer visual, kinesthetic, and auditory learning options, making them versatile tools for students with various types of needs.

4.3.3 Inquiry-Based Learning

Given their customizable features, chatbots can be valuable tools in inquiry-based learning by providing a wealth of information on a wide range of topics to meet learners' specific needs. Inquiry-based learning emphasizes learners' active participation in discovering new knowledge (De Jong & van Joolingen, 1998). As indicated, chatbots are designed to encourage students to engage actively in the learning process by delivering content in an interactive format such as dialogues and simulations. This approach immerses students in the learning process and empowers them to become active participants. Instead of being spoon-fed information, students can collaborate with the robot to discover new knowledge by asking questions and seeking solutions, which promotes curiosity and exploration.

4.4 Digital Literacy

As indicated, the chatbot technology continues to evolve at a rapid pace. Bringing chatbots into the classroom helps boost digital literacy and prepare students for the future. Information technology has become increasingly pervasive. Connected devices and networks are common in enhancing productivity and quality of life. The ability to find, evaluate, and use information from a variety of digital sources is considered literacy in the digital age (Gilster, 1997). Digital literacy has emerged as a crucial factor in enabling participation in education, as well as a means of gaining an understanding of the world (Martin & Grudziecki, 2006). The rapid change of information technologies in recent years has fundamentally changed the way people live and work. However, many educators acknowledge that higher education institutions are not adequately preparing college graduates in the area of digital literacy (Hiller, 2022). Some mistakenly assume that college students today are already digitally literate since they grew up in the internet age. Device ownership, however, is not equivalent to digital literacy. Knowing how to operate a smart device does not automatically equip one with the ability to use it for academic success. Further, students from low socioeconomic backgrounds may not have the financial ability to possess smart devices and access high-speed internet connections. The disparities in students' digital literacy can be attributed to these digital divides. Just like low-income students, many nontraditional students lack adequate technical skills. Nontraditional students are defined as older students (mostly over 24 years old) who work full-time, have children, and/or have other life circumstances that can interfere with the successful completion of educational objectives (National Center for Education Statistics, 2020). Many nontraditional students also have a low-income background and work minimum-wage jobs. These students not only have limited access to technology, but they may also lack adequate technical knowledge. Individuals who work in digitalized workplaces may be more digitally proficient than previous generations due to their "digital native" status (Orlando & Attard, 2015; Prensky, 2001), but a sizable portion of nontraditional students struggle with technical competence. If higher education is to prepare students to adequately meet the demands of an increasingly technological world, it must integrate technology into the academic curriculum (Daggett, 2010). Exposing students to chatbots not only allows for engagement in a novel way but also helps foster an understanding of the limits of these tools. Using ChatGPT and similar tools encourages students to be technologically literate in an increasingly tech-centric world (American Psychology Association, 2023).

5. CONCLUSION

AI technology has undergone significant transformations since the first chatbot ELIZA was introduced. Older chatbots created before the new century (i.e., ELIZA, PARRY, and Jabberwacky) reply to user questions by drawing information from a pre-coded database, sometimes producing clunky conversations. The 21st-century chatbots (i.e., SmarterChild and Watson) incorporate machine learning and can produce much more accurate responses. Virtual assistants developed in the 2010s can perform tasks that previously required human touch, such as making phone calls and looking up the internet. During the pandemic, heavy reliance on chatbots produced highly intelligent chatbots that can simulate human beings and engage in sophisticated conversations. The newest chatbots can write emails, generate coherent essays, solve math problems, and create computer code. In recent years, AI is increasingly becoming the focus of debate in higher education, as chatbots potentially promote laziness, encourage cheating, and disrupt the learning experience. It is common among students to complete assignments using chatbots, particularly ChatGPT. Some worry that relying too heavily on chatbots could undermine critical skills students need to succeed. Moreover, the use of chatbots raises ethical concerns about academic honesty and independent learning. To reduce cheating, universities and colleges are taking preventative measures. Some institutions outright ban chatbots on campus computers and networks. Educators are replacing writing assignments that can be easily done with chatbots with other formats that require human effort.

While these concerns are valid, chatbots hold great potential as tools to improve higher education. More and more universities now employ chatbots to streamline the enrollment process. University chatbots provide around-the-clock support and access to information and resources. Prospective students can ask questions and seek clarification outside of regular business hours. Chatbots can guide students through enrollment, and help them fill out application forms and submit documents. For current students, chatbots provide details about courses and handle a wide range of frequently asked questions related to course registration, financial aid, campus events, university policies, and so on, saving time for both students and university staff. By employing chatbots, universities can enhance the overall student experience, streamline administrative processes, and provide timely and accurate information. Further, university chatbots help reduce staff workload, freeing them to focus on other administrative tasks. In addition to being administrative tools, educational chatbots serve as "smart tutors" who can assist in personalized and interactive learning. The powerful features of tailoring content based on the user's needs and generating large amount of information make chatbots excellent teaching tools for fostering student success.

The ongoing advancement of AI technology potentially, if not already, replaces human jobs. AI is incredibly effective at automating routine and repetitive tasks such as data entry and customer service. Chatbots can perform these tasks faster and with fewer errors than humans as they become more sophisticated. Will chatbots take place of higher education administrators who perform these tasks? Another inquiry pertains to the role of human tutors. With chatbots' remarkable features in educating and interacting with learners, what viable role can a human tutor play? These inquiries beg for future research. While chatbots offer several benefits, it is crucial to consider their limitations and ensure they are implemented thoughtfully. Chatbots typically operate within a specific domain or set of pre-defined knowledge. They have the tendency to generate false information when asked questions that are outside their designated scope. Chatbots also have the potential to learn the biases of the people training them and produce offensive statements. All in all, a chatbot should be designed to work in conjunction with human educators and provide support services rather than replacing them.

REFERENCES

Alkhatlan, A., & Kalita, J. (2018). Intelligent tutoring systems: A comprehensive historical survey with recent developments. *International Journal of Computer Applications, 181*(43), 1-20.

American Psychology Association. (2023). *How to use ChatGPT as a learning tool.* APA. https://www.apa.org/monitor/2023/06/chatgpt-learning-tool

Arizona State University. (2023). *Wellness: Hey Sunny.* Hey Sunny. ASU. https://heysunny.asu.edu/wellness

Association of American Colleges and Universities. (2011). *The LEAP vision for learning: Outcomes, practices, impact, and employers' view*. Association of American Colleges and Universities.

Azvine, B., Djian, D., Tsui, K. C., & Wobcke, W. (2000). The intelligent assistant: An overview. In B. Azvine, D. D. Nauck, & N. Azarmi (Eds.), *Intelligent systems and soft computing: Prospects, tools and applications* (pp. 215–238). Springer-Verlag. doi:10.1007/10720181_9

Bank of America. (2022). *Bank of America's Erica tops 1 billion client interactions, now nearly 1.5 million per day*. Newsroom. https://newsroom.bankofamerica.com/content/newsroom/press-releases/2022/10/bank-of-america-s-erica-tops-1-billion-client-interactions--now-.html

Banning, M. (2006). Measures that can be used to instill critical thinking skills in nurse prescribers. *Nurse Education in Practice*, *6*(2), 98–105. doi:10.1016/j.nepr.2005.10.001 PMID:19040862

BBC News. (2003). *Chatbot bids to fool humans.* BBC News. http://news.bbc.co.uk/2/hi/technology/3116780.stm

Behar-Horenstein, L. S., & Niu, L. (2011). Teaching critical thinking skills in higher education: A review of the literature. *Journal of College Teaching and Learning*, *8*(2), 25–42. doi:10.19030/tlc.v8i2.3554

Bii, P. (2013). Chatbot technology: A possible means of unlocking student potential to learn how to learn. *Educational Research*, *4*, 218–221.

Bishop, W., & Starkey, D. (2006). Pedagogy. *Keywords in creative writing*, 119-125.

California State University at Northridge. (2023). *CSUNny program summary and outcomes.* https://edtechmagazine.com/higher/sites/edtechmagazine.com.higher/files/CSUNny%20data.pdf

California State University at San Bernardino. (2023). *Ask Cody*. CSU. https://www.csusb.edu/its/support/digital-transformation/chatbot

Chin, H., Lima, G., Shin, M., Zhunis, A., Cha, C., Choi, J., & Cha, M. (2023). User-chatbot conversations during the COVID-19 pandemic: Study based on topic modeling and sentiment analysis. *Journal of Medical Internet Research, 25*, 1–16. doi:10.2196/40922 PMID:36596214

Colby, K. M. (1981). PARRYing. *Behavioral and Brain Sciences, 4*(4), 550–560. doi:10.1017/S0140525X00000224

College Rover. (2023). *Exploring the impact of college rankings on student perceptions.* College Rover. https://collegerover.com/campus-library/news/1/exploring-the-impact-of-college-rankings-on-student-perceptions

Daggett, W. R. (2010). Preparing students for their technological future. *International Center for Leadership in Education.* Citeseer. https://citeseerx.ist.psu.edu/document?repid=rep1&type=pdf&doi=ce1172bff72313a336f997efb0dd7137dc0f9a97

De Jong, T., & Van Joolingen, W. R. (1998). Scientific discovery learning with computer simulations of conceptual domains. *Review of Educational Research, 68*(2), 179–201. doi:10.3102/00346543068002179

EdTech. (2020). Successful AI examples in higher education that can inspire our future. *Ed Tech Magazine.* https://edtechmagazine.com/higher/article/2020/01/successful-ai-examples-higher-education-can-inspire-our-future

Essel, H. B., Vlachopoulos, D., Tachie-Menson, A., Johnson, E. E., & Baah, P. K. (2022). The impact of a virtual teaching assistant (chatbot) on students' learning in Ghanaian higher education. *International Journal of Educational Technology in Higher Education, 19*(1), 1–19. doi:10.118641239-022-00362-6 PMID:35013716

Georgia State University. (2023). *Reduction of summer melt: A strategic approach.* GSU. https://success.gsu.edu/initiatives/reduction-of-summer-melt/

Gilster, P. (1997). *Digital literacy.* John Wiley & Sons Inc.

Government Technology. (2023). *Study: 30% of college students have used ChatGPT for essays.* https://www.govtech.com/education/higher-ed/study-30-of-college-students-have-used-chatgpt-for-essays

Gupta, S., & Chen, Y. (2022). Supporting inclusive learning using chatbots? A chatbot-led interview study. *Journal of Information Systems Education, 33*(1), 98–108.

Hiller, R. H. (2022). Combating Low Digital Literacy in the College Classroom: A Systematic Literature Review. *Florida Journal of Educational Research, 59*(3), 1–9.

IBM. (2023a). *What is machine learning?* IBM. https://www.ibm.com/topics/machine-learning

IBM. (2023b). *A computer called Watson.* IBM. https://www.ibm.com/ibm/history/ibm100/us/en/icons/watson/

IlaganJ. B. R.IlaganJ. R. (2023). *A prototype of a chatbot for evaluating and refining student startup ideas using a large language model.* EdArXiv Preprints. https://edarxiv.org/azhf9/ doi:10.35542/osf.io/azhf9

Kuh, G. D., Kinzie, J. L., Buckley, J. A., Bridges, B. K., & Hayek, J. C. (2006). *What matters to student success: A review of the literature* (Vol. 8). National Postsecondary Education Cooperative.

Kung, T. H., Cheatham, M., Medenilla, A., Sillos, C., De Leon, L., Elepaño, C., Madriaga, M., Aggabao, R., Diaz-Candido, G., Maningo, J., & Tseng, V. (2023). Performance of ChatGPT on USMLE: Potential for AI-assisted medical education using large language models. *PLOS Digital Health*, *2*(2), 1–25. doi:10.1371/journal.pdig.0000198 PMID:36812645

Liu, O. L., Frankel, L., & Roohr, K. C. (2014). Assessing critical thinking in higher education: Current state and directions for next-generation assessment. *ETS Research Report Series*, *2014*(1), 1–23. doi:10.1002/ets2.12009

Martin, A., & Grudziecki, J. (2006). DigEuLit: Concepts and tools for digital literacy development. *Innovation in Teaching and Learning in Information and Computer Sciences*, *5*(4), 249–267. doi:10.11120/ital.2006.05040249

Mateos-Sanchez, M., Melo, A. C., Blanco, L. S., & García, A. M. F. (2022). Chatbot, as educational and inclusive tool for people with intellectual disabilities. *Sustainability (Basel)*, *14*(3), 1520–1534. doi:10.3390u14031520

Miner, A. S., Laranjo, L., & Kocaballi, A. B. (2020). Chatbots in the fight against the COVID-19 pandemic. *Digital Medicine*, *3*, 1–4. PMID:32377576

National Center for Education Statistics. (2020). *Who is nontraditional?* NCES. https://nces.ed.gov/pubs/web/97578e.asp

New Jersey Institute of Technology. (2023). *ELIZA: A very basic Rogerian psychotherapist chatbot.* NJIT. https://web.njit.edu/~ronkowit/eliza.html

News, N. P. R. (2017). *It has to have a soul: How chatbots get their personalities.* NPR. https://www.npr.org/sections/alltechconsidered/2017/03/10/519002884/it-has-to-have-a-soul-how-chatbots-get-their-personalities

Open A. I. (2023a). *Introducing ChatGPT.* Open AI. https://openai.com/blog/chatgpt

Open A. I. (2023b). *GPT-4 technical report.* Open AI. https://cdn.openai.com/papers/gpt-4.pdf

Orlando, J., & Attard, C. (2015). Digital natives come of age: The reality of today's early career teachers using mobile devices to teach mathematics. *Mathematics Education Research Journal*, *28*(1), 107–121. doi:10.100713394-015-0159-6

Pérez, J. Q., Daradoumis, T., & Puig, J. (2020). Rediscovering the use of chatbots in education: A systematic literature review. *Computer Applications in Engineering Education*, *28*(6), 1549–1565. doi:10.1002/cae.22326

Pew Research Center. (2021). *The internet and the pandemic.* Pew Research Center. https://www.pewresearch.org/internet/2021/09/01/the-internet-and-the-pandemic/

Precedence Research. (2023). *Chatbot market.* Precedence Research. https://www.precedenceresearch.com/chatbot-market

Prensky, M. (2001). Digital natives, digital immigrants. *On the Horizon*, *9*(5), 1–6. doi:10.1108/10748120110424816

Stassen, M., Doherty, K., & Poe, M. (2001). *Course-based review and assessment: Methods for understanding student learning*. University of Massachusetts Amherst.

The Chronicle of Higher Education. (2003). I'm a student. You have no idea how much we're using ChatGPT. No professor or software could ever pick up on it. *Chronicle.* https://www.chronicle.com/article/im-a-student-you-have-no-idea-how-much-were-using-chatgpt

The New York Times. (2023). What students are saying about ChatGPT. *The New York Times.* https://www.nytimes.com/2023/02/02/learning/students-chatgpt.html

Troussas, C., Krouska, A., Alepis, E., & Virvou, M. (2020). Intelligent and adaptive tutoring through a social network for higher education. *New Review of Hypermedia and Multimedia*, *26*(3-4), 138–167. doi:10.1080/13614568.2021.1908436

University of Memphis. (2023). *AutoTutor*. University of Memphis. https://www.memphis.edu/iis/projects/autotutor.php

University of Rochester. (2023). *How will AI chatbots like ChatGPT affect higher education?* University of Rochester. https://www.rochester.edu/newscenter/chatgpt-artificial-intelligence-ai-chatbots-education-551522/

University of South Florida. (2023). *Associate professor develops motivational chatbot and digital Candyland-like maze to ensure student success.* USF. https://www.usf.edu/news/2023/associate-professor-develops-motivational-chatbot-and-candyland-like-maze-to-ensure-student-success.aspx

World Health Organization. (2020). *WHO launches a chatbot on Facebook Messenger to combat COVID-19 misinformation*. WHO. https://www.who.int/news-room/feature-stories/detail/who-launches-a-chatbot-powered-facebook-messenger-to-combat-covid-19-misinformation

Wright, B. D. (1997). Evaluating learning in individual courses. In J. G. Gaff & J. L. Ratcliff (Eds.), *Handbook of the undergraduate curriculum* (pp. 571–590). Jossey Bass.

KEY TERMS AND DEFINITIONS

Academic Integrity: Completing academic work without plagiarizing, cheating, receiving assistance from unauthorized assistance from any other person, or using any source of information not appropriately attributed.

Artificial Intelligence: A branch of computer science concerned with building programs capable of performing problem-solving tasks.

Assessment: The systematic collection and analysis of information to improve student learning.

Chatbots: Programs that combine artificial intelligence and natural language processing or other technology that enable them to interact to a certain level of conversation with human users.

ChatGPT: A chatbot launched in November 2022 by OpenAI, an American AI research laboratory, that can perform a series of tasks such as writing computer code, solving math problems, interpreting questions, and providing accurate and thorough answers.

Critical Thinking: The ability to interpret and make judgments about the relevance and quality of information.

Digital Literacy: The ability to find, evaluate, and use information from a variety of digital sources.

Educational Chatbots: Chatbots designed to assist student learning.

Inclusive Learning: A pedagogical approach that strives to serve the needs of all students, regardless of background or identity.

Pedagogy: Instructional techniques and strategies that enable learning and provide opportunities for acquiring knowledge.

Virtual Assistants or Intelligent Assistants: Software programs that allow human users to find relevant information from the internet or complete tasks quickly.

ENDNOTE

1 Chatbots can produce accurate information by drawing from its database. However, they generate false information on topics if the database does not contain enough information on a subject.

Chapter 14
Engaging Future-Minded Visualizations and Artful Aesthetics:
"Seeing Different" With Human-Machine Collaborations With Artmaking Generative AIs

Shalin Hai-Jew
https://orcid.org/0000-0002-8863-0175
Kansas State University, USA

ABSTRACT

Artmaking generative AIs have been used to create visual works (still images, motion videos, and animated sequences, including simulations) that are photorealistic, high-fidelity, hyper-realistic, and emulative of the world; artful works are translated in style transfers derivative of known artist, artworks, art styles, schools of art practices, and defined visual styles. This work argues that artmaking generative AIs should not be about reproductions of the familiar but should be used for future-minded visualizations and future-minded aesthetics, through true collaborations between human and machine imaginations. Through generative AI, people should be "seeing different" to enable nouveau "thinking" and "doing" and "being" different… into the near- and far- futures. This early and exploratory work is based on research, year-long experimentation with multiple public artmaking generative AI tools, and abductive logic.

1. INTRODUCTION

A person looks at a two-dimensional, three-dimensional, or four-dimensional image co-created by a person and a generative AI. What is depicted? A scene? A person? An object? What are the interrelationships suggested? What are some suggested motion dynamics? Some aesthetic elements? What does the image even mean? Or what are various interpretations of the visual meaning? What is signal, and what

DOI: 10.4018/979-8-3693-0074-9.ch014

is noise? Does the image evoke something as-yet unexplored? Does the image motivate a second look? A third? Does it open up paths to new understandings? Does it offer some concept that glimmers and shimmers? Is it something that encourages thought and musing? Does it suggest ideas for mechanisms and how-to's and processes? Does the visual challenge assumptions? Offer new ways of seeing? Often so!

Artificial intelligence (AI) refers to a broad category of tools that emulate aspects of human intelligence.

AI is "a set of techniques providing the machine with the ability to perform high-level cognitive or sensorimotor tasks, such as learning and making decision(s)" (Caramiaux, Alaoui, & Hsueh, Apr. 2022, p. 1). There is as-yet no general artificial intelligence that can emulate the whole of human intelligence (or "general intelligence" or "g factor"), but generative AI has come to the fore to create various digital contents based on learning from human creations. This is considered AI since it emulates human creativity, considered a "natural" (and even exclusive) endowment of people (Pragya, n.d.).

In recent years, generative artificial intelligence (GAIs) tools have harnessed big data for training datasets fed into large language models (LLMs) that are deep-learned through artificial neural networks (ANNs). Machine learning enables the computer to learn patterns without particular direct programming. Rather, the machine identifies patterns learned through layers of interlinked artificial neurons. The program can take that nuanced learning to generate new digital content from human-made (manual) prompts in text and image modalities and combined modalities. Researchers describe how artmaking generative AI tools function:

This kind of network is like a funnel, it takes an image as input, detects patterns at multiple levels, accumulating increasingly refined patterns until we arrive at human interpretable semantic associations: 'a cat on a mat,' and other more scientifically and aesthetically relevant derivations. Inverting this funnel allows for the creation of synthetic images. (Choi, DiPaola, & Töyrylä, 2021, p. 020501-3)

The complexity of this machine synthesis "leads to implicit statistical ambiguity" (Choi, DiPaola, & Töyrylä, 2021, p. 020501-3), limiting the explainability of this type of AI. Essentially, the output art is created by "extracting statistical patterns from existing artistic media" from the curated training data (Epstein, Hertzmann, Herman, Mahari, Frank, Groh,... & Russakovsky, 2023, p. 3). To address the "lack of interpretability" of neural network models, a research team designed a neural network with manual network weighting "coupled with explanatory visualizations as a form of creative control over the internal and lower level processes" (Ulberg, Llach, & Byrne, 2020, p. 508). The "hand-crafting networks" practice enables some Observable AI (OAI) (Zhu, et al., 2018, as cited in Ulberg, Llach, & Byrne, 2020, p. 508) to de-mythify some aspects of the technology.

The generative AI system continues to learn:

The machine holds the capability to learn by example as well as through past mistakes by making predictions about the data of entry through its features and previously observed responses; unlike conventional computing, the ANN (artificial neural network) system is cognitively responsive rather than being deterministic in its computations. (Pragya, n.d.)

How people use generative AIs may be captured and used to tweak the system outputs as well.

In the present age, the advent of artmaking generative AIs involves the making of still images, videos, and animated sequences. There are digital outputs for digital puppets (imbued with character design) that may be animated. There are polygonal works that may be used as volumetric forms in augmented reality. There are 2d and 3d scenes, and even 4d ones that are enabled by these new tools. These AI tools may enable the building out of the metaverse, with cost savings and efficiencies (Lv, 2023, p. 208). The metaverse "will be a complex giant system carrying ultra-high concurrent data volume" (Lv, 2023, p. 214), with nonplayable characters and animated agents, digital machinery, digital maps, and other contents. There may be the making of interactive art installations and AR objects and online ones.

A flood of digital artworks has become available online from the large language model-powered artmaking generative AIs that are prompted by text and imagery, often in multimodal fashion. One work labels this approach "neural network image processing" (Choi, DiPaola, & Töyrylä, 2021, p. 020501-1), as a nod to the deep learning from big data achieved to create the LLMs. How people are using generative AI to create art has been labeled "neural media praxis" (Choi, DiPaola, & Töyrylä, 2021, p. 020501-1). These tools, often web-facing ones, have also been termed text-to-image (TTI) models and also large-scale text-to-image generative models (LTGMs).

In this chapter, the author argues that artmaking generative AIs should not be about simple reproductions of what is already the familiar or basic illustrations of the imaginary and conceptual. There should be a reach to future-minded visuals, with true co-creation instead of humans as tasking agents and generative AIs as actualizing rote and regurgitating machines. This work suggests that how people harness generative AIs and how receptive they are to "seeing different" from the outputs of the generative AI may inform their thinking, doing, and being. Some light examples follow:

Thinking

- Can artmaking generative AI be used for novel aesthetics? Novel color palettes? Novel patterns?
- Can generative AI inspire new concepts? New ideas? Can it loose the human imagination? Can it inspire new social insights? Political insights? Can it reveal new ways of human cooperation? Social organizing?
- Can generative AI help solve real-world problems?
- Challenge real-world paradigms? Frameworks?

Doing

- Can the artmaking generative AI be used for actual research and validated informational purposes? For example, can it be prompted to visually depict the "flora and fauna" of a location and provide accurate flora, accurate fauna, with proper details and proper visual depictions?
- Can the generative AI be prompted to create scenes of historic significance with accuracy to the times?
- Can the generative AI be used for actual design? Actual engineering inspirations? Can generative AI be used to assess physical realities in true-to-world ways?
- Can the generative AI enable new ways of making in the analog space? The digital space? The combined spaces?

Being

- Can artmaking generative AI inform on human identity, for individuals and for groups and for subpopulations (at the micro-, meso-, and macro- levels)?

- Can it be used to encourage the acquisition and development of new knowledge, skills, and abilities?
- Can generative AI inspire better ways of living?
    - Of human sociality?
    - Of promoting environmental concerns?
    - Constructive human-animal co-existence?

"Common art" created with generative AIs should be in "blend mode" with deep inputs by humans and machines, to please, to provoke, to evoke, to re-vision, to innovate, and to solve problems, among others. People may approach AI-generative tools with a "stone soup" sort of insight, in which the person brings the substance and content for the engagement to add value. The stone soup story involves people each bringing something to contribute to a boiling pot of water with a stone in it to make a collective delicious and sustaining soup. What people have built up in themselves as a knowledge base may be harnessed for learning in a generative tool.

This work does project different added capabilities to the current crop of generative AI tools available to the public—as more technical, more fact-based, more in-world physics-aware, more design-aware, on the one hand, and perhaps more abstract and minimalist in other capabilities. It also projects that people will "up their game" in their usage of these image generating tools. In this work, the author suggests that not pushing to find the full capabilities of such tools would prematurely foreclose on learning possibilities.

2. REVIEW OF THE LITERATURE

Early social narratives around the advent of artmaking generative AI tools have been one of perceived threats—to livelihoods and professions, to human knowledge and skills, to artmaking and art appreciation, to human culture, to aesthetics, and to human identity at the core (as artmaking individuals and groups). One researcher observes:

AI artworks raise major philosophical questions, the meaning to be human in a hyper-connected world and the true nature of human creativity. (Notaro, 2020, p. 322)

Art is made for other people by people for various human-based objectives, in one sense. The risks are thought to apply to artisans and craftspeople:

Artisans may have thought that there was no avenue for machines to take over their ethereal reins since something soulless and emotionless does not have the ability for creation and artistic expression: human emotion. (Arbiza Goenaga, 2020, p. 55)

While this may be the age of the "programmer-artist," and AI-generated artworks are seen as of sufficient quality for potential collecting, at least one thinker suggests that "sometimes the process is more art than the final product" and that art exhibits "should refrain from collecting artwork generated by AI for now" (Ernst, 2023, p. 7). What societies do people want to create for the future even as the technologies enable a range of options? What does human-centered art look like, and does that vision include something of AI technologies for the future?

Others see a bigger threat in having such powerful tools in the world but with many just on the other side of a digital divide. To address such concerns, the corporate makers of such tools have striven to democratize access, so that the creation of visuals is not cost-prohibitive to use (many versions are often free, with for-pay premium versions) and that skills gaps in art do not squelch voices in the public square. Such tools lower the friction in art expression, so people may generate effective and usable visuals for their work and side projects. Prompt text boxes are often multilingual (they accept a variety of languages), which make the tools more inclusionary globally.

Still, it is thought that these current-generation programs may increase the "sophistication" of human creative expression (Arbiza Goenaga, 2020, p. 60). The popularization of artmaking generative AIs in the artmaking process results in "the redistribution of expressive agency across human artists and non-human" (Zeilinger, 2021, p. 1). If AI can output works "by which creativity is currently being evaluated, validated, and valorised" then it will challenge the human artist and senses of what art is and how creativity is conceptualized (Zeilinger, 2021, n.p.). Some risk is seen in the "uncanny valley in Human-AI interactions," in which the AI may be mis-interpreted as potentially being sentient (Muller, Chilton, Kantosalo, Liao, Maher, Martin, & Walsh, Apr. 2023, p. 4) and with people going to AI for inappropriate decision-making, among others. Computing is "mechanistic" (McCormack, Bown, Dorin, McCabe, Monro, & Whitelaw, 2014, p. 136).

There are perceived risks of AI "assisting, replacing, and regimenting human work" (Muller, Chilton, Kantosalo, Liao, Maher, Martin, & Walsh, Apr. 2023, p. 4). The fear is that AI-generated pixels are not just the core media, but that the artmaking generative AIs are subjects that create alongside human artists (and perhaps without human artist collaborators in many cases). It is important for humans to be the creative subjects and doers and AI as a "behind-the-scenes worker" in the creation of art (Chen, Shidujaman, Jin, & Ahmed, 2020, pp. 14-15). This reads analogically to how master artists ideate and envision while their assistants actualize the work, with the credit going to the named master artist. (Dafoe, June 24, 2019)

There may be the launching of art markets and other competitive mechanisms "to achieve survival of the fittest" of interactive art (Chen, Shidujaman, Jin, & Ahmed, 2020, p. 26), and likewise, artmaking generative AI tools. In the meantime, there are efforts to ensure that such tools are not lumped into the category of so-called "shitty automation" [a term coined by Brian Merchant to indicate AI that "actively makes our lives worse" (Merchant, Mar. 7, 2019)]. "Shitty automation" may describe "how human input—our labor, bodies, biases, prejudices, and desires—remains invisibly present in automated systems" (Paulsen, 2020, p. 4), with AI learning to "essentialize from it" (Paulsen, 2020, p. 13) and so amplifying negative aspects of human societies.

Humanity has used art for various purposes over time for religious worship, ceremonial purposes; signals of wealth or status, economic value-holding, investment; commemoration, ritual; lifestyles; creativity, inspiration; education, teaching and learning; self-expression, self-exploration, and other uses. In a social context, art is "relational, embedded, and dialogic" (Zeilinger, 2021, n.p.); it enables societies to throw large-scale conversations and raise awareness. Art is valuable as an evolutionary tool by "stimulating our cognitive activities like creativity and imagination, reinforcing social structures and working as a symbolic form of language" (Daniele & Song, Jan. 2019, p. 156). Art is "representation… expression… form… experience… open concept and family resemblance… institution… historical definition" and other aspects (Galanter, 2016, p. 147). Art can be high and formal, and it can be common, made by amateurs, to meet a variety of needs and using a variety of analog and digital materials (Hai-Jew, 2022).

Artmaking generative AI tools, like the Deep Dream Generator, can serve as "a prosthetic extension to the human imagination" (Leach, 2019).

"Generative art" can be created with "virtually any kind of system, not just computers, and…is as old as art itself" (Galanter, 2016, p. 146). An early definition reads:

Generative art refers to any art practice in which the artist uses a system, such as a set of natural language rules, a computer program, a machine, or other procedural invention, that is set into motion with some degree of autonomy, thereby contributing to or resulting in a completed work of art. (Galanter, 2003, as cited in Galanter, 2016, p. 151)

The later definition harnesses complexity theory, a paradigm "where high degrees of order and disorder both create simple systems, and complex systems exhibit a mixture of both order and disorder" (Galanter, 2016, p. 157). The definition was updated as follows:

Generative art refers to any art practice in which the artist cedes control to a system with functional autonomy that contributes to, or results in, a completed work of art. Systems may include natural language instructions, biological or chemical processes, computer programs, machines, self-organizing materials, mathematical operations, and other procedural inventions. (Galanter, 2008, as cited in Galanter, 2016, p. 154)

Then, a few years later, an updated definition was offered, which may apply even to deep learning based generative art systems (Galanter, 2019, p. 112):

Generative art refers to any art practice where the artist uses a system, such as a set of natural language rules, a computer program, a machine, or other procedural invention, which is set into motion with some degree of autonomy contributing to or resulting in a completed work of art. (Galanter, 2019, p. 112)

The definition of generative art is evaluated for applicability backwards and forwards in time. Another research team has offered a typography of different artmaking systems, with 11 definitions (Boden & Edmonds, 2009, pp. 37 - 38).

There has been a long tradition of computer science and art (Artut, 2019). There has been some debate on whether the works created using generative AI are actually novel. One research team writes:

The products of emerging generative AI methods can be said to be creative since they can be novel, valuable and surprising in a context of use. (Muller, Chilton, Kantosalo, Liao, Maher, Martin, & Walsh, Apr. 2023, p. 2)

An LLM, in the visual-making space, does not fully regurgitate works from its training set verbatim (in a glitch known as "memorization," "contamination," and "supercopying" in terms of textual LLMs). The visuals do repeat some layouts and points-of-view more commonly than others (perhaps based on learning by human user behaviors and what users seem to prefer). These tools "offer new modes of creative expression and engagement" (Yusa, Yu, & Sovhyra, 2022, p. 152), and they "generate novel and unexpected forms of art that would be difficult or impossible for human artists to create" (p. 165). Generative AI, in its present form and usage, does not align with the "romantic model of singular expressive agency" (Zeilinger, 2021, n.p.). The existence of generative AI may spark rethinking of what art is and where it can originate from and what it can speak to. In a time sense, art may build on what came before, speak to the present, and engage the future.

2.1 Part of a Long Tradition

Current-generation artmaking generative AIs are part of the long tradition of using computers for art-making (from the 1950s).

In different modes, art and technology are both mirrors of ourselves. On one hand, art making is a meta-language to expresses (sic) things we cannot communicate with other means. It is a way to make sense of the world around us as well as ourselves as a species. Similarly, technology helps us to reveal the nature of things. In fact, the same idea of AI is arguably today's highest form of 'humanized' technology, yet another way to know human nature. (Daniele & Song, Jan. 2019, p. 161)

Many of the peoples in the world are part of "techno-philic culture(s)" leading to the acceptance of AI in new media artmaking. One study explored the pluralistic acceptance of such technologies across a variety of cultural knowledge sub-groups: "For those technophiles who see no contradictions within the present global system, the contemporary cultures of NMA (new media art) are a playground for novel experimentation" (Hoetzlein, 2023, p. 7). This researcher identified 10 (overlapping) knowledge cultures:

1) cultures of practice, 2) explicit cultures, 3) non-explicit cultures, 4) mainstream art, 5) technophilic, 6) technocritical, 7) technophobic, 8) post-modern/post-medium, 9) pluralist, and 10) post-pluralist or synthesizing (Hoetzlein, 2023, p. 8)

While contested, such technologies are being taken up by "innovators," "early adopters," and some "pragmatists" (early majority). If these tools prove out, the "late majority" of conservatives and perhaps even some "skeptics" may follow.

2.2 Neural Media Practice

The making of art with generative AIs requires the human artist to direct the technology to output particular visuals. Users harness prompts to "specify processes rather than outcomes" in the artmaking generative AI systems (McCormack, 2017, p. 213). This prompting or directing may involve text and image prompts, an iterated process of artmaking and curation, and work outside the technology, involving pre-processing and post-processing. It is helpful to think of digital art as easily transferring to analog form (on wood pulp paper, on synthetic paper, or in other forms), and those physical objects being easy to digitize with scanners and cameras. It is relatively easy to excerpt parts of a visual that are useful through digital image editing and / or tracing as part of post-processing or post-production. Colors can be changed as well. Items can be resized. One work pipeline includes generating images in one generative AI tool and porting that visual to another tool for image processing (Hutson & Harper-Nichols, 2023, p. 55).

The "neural artist" (Choi, DiPaola, & Töyrylä, 2021, p. 020501-12) engages the generative AI through a basic interface to access the latent space of the model:

Once trained, a neural network contains a 'latent' space defining the realm of immanent solutions (optimizations) given a set of inputs. The artist's encounter with latent space is thus continent upon the architecture of the neural network; transformative architectures take user chosen images and parameters as input, generative architectures taken random numbers and previously encountered 'way points' in latent space. (Choi, DiPaola, & Töyrylä, 2021, p. 020501-12)

Artmaking with technologies still draws on human intuition, detachment, and other aspects (Choi, DiPaola, & Töyrylä, 2021, p. 020501-10).

There still has to be the intent to create the visuals. The human artist may begin with some mental models and expectations, but it is important to be open to a non-deterministic approach and outcome. Words may be used to create particular outputs, but defined subjects and visually descriptive terms and named artists seem to result in more control over outcomes. Words themselves are polysemous, resulting in different visual gists. Depending on the training data, there may well be particular cultural gists to the output visuals.

How to introduce more serendipity may come from the seeding images used for the prompts. "Seeding images" are those used to prompt a particular outcome, often along with textual inputs and word-based modifiers. Seeding images may be born-digital, born-analog, or emergent from a process involving both digital and material processes. The analog images are photographed or scanned. They may be edited further in a digital image editing software program. [Seeding images seem to inform on color and layout foremost.] Text mapped to imagery is a cross-modal type of mapping as compared to visual-visual mapping. Plenty of experiential research is required to develop the skills to be a generative AI whisperer. At present, based on the author's experiences with generative AI [particularly the Deep Dream Generator, which was created in 2014 and released for public use in 2015 ("DeepDream," Sept. 18, 2023)], there were strengths and weaknesses.

2.3 Strengths

- Images tend toward the figurative, given the pareidolia (the making of a meaningful image from something abstract, unpatterned) algorithm powering the Deep Dream Generator.
  - Abstract works are harder to create but are possible with the use of designed seeding imagery.
  - The generative AI enables some inchoate aspects instead of going full literalist in every case.
- The images tend to be filled to the edges instead of including any whitespace. White space has to be forced with the use of seeding images.
- The generative AI practices clear compositing.
- Each image shows a central point of visual attention.
- The output images tend to show a level of refinement vs. roughness, as compared to CrAIyon (whose images often feel unfinished and low-resolution).
- The generative AI tool does enable the adding on of custom modifiers, including "neon," "metallic," "pastel," and other terms that then are applied to the visuals. Words can be meaningless to do generative AI though, such as "synaesthesia" or "color that conveys motion," two modifiers that the author tried, among others. (There is also a limit of 200 modifiers total for the particular generative AI's user interface.) (It is possible to choose contradictory modifiers at the same time, but the output image seems to weight some modifiers over others.)

- The generative AI has built-in modifiers that describe camera placement, lighting, art styles, and artist styles.

2.4 Weaknesses

- The images output by this generative AI do not show nuance in texturing various segments of an image.
    - The generative AI manages texture well with seeding images.
- There is not a clear way to place objects in a scene.
- There is not a clear way to define relative sizing of objects in a scene.
- Character design seems hit-and-miss.
- The naivete of generative AI does show up in various images that are not aligned with the world (such as roads that lead to nowhere, cities without logical buildout, animals with the wrong numbers of heads or extremities, and others).

In generative AI artworks there is a conflating of "the tool with the result" (Choi, DiPaola, & Töyrylä, 2021, p. 020501-12) and a de-centering of the human artist. The researchers explain:

The essential features of the digital artefact are not locative in the sense of the autographic—as a singular manifestation of a series of sensorimotor events. The artefact is rather a 'constant stream of processing' that is inherently reliant on an extended network of relations, resisting objectification. (Choi, DiPaola, & Töyrylä, 2021, p. 020501-12)

Such artmaking is not inherently tactile or embodied. Rather, the creative process with neural media is "a curatorial exchange at once subjective and externally mediated" (Choi, DiPaola, & Töyrylä, 2021, p. 020501-13). One research team describes the advent of artmaking AI as a seminal moment:

From suggesting new color palettes, compositions, arrangements, and spatial understanding to a new inspirational and iterative formative process, AI is a watershed moment for the fine arts. (Hutson & Harper-Nichols, 2023, p. 55)

Some artists use original artworks as the training set (a small one) for do-it-yourself (DIY) generative AI (Hutson & Harper-Nichols, 2023). There are dedicated generative AIs as well, such as some that can change the moods of the seeding images to evoke particular emotions, to better design visual communications (Salevati & DiPaola, 2015). Another combined ancient ink wash paintings with the capabilities of artificial neural networks (ANNs) for an art installation and exhibit (Liao & Chien, n.d.,) Another systems is built off of direct emulation of a human portrait painter with its "cognitive painting system" (DiPaola & McCaig, 2016, p. 159).

To enable more of a sense of embodied co-creation in terms of human experience, one research team created a "sand playground" interface for people to interact with a generative AI, with three co-drawing modes: "artistic mimicry, zen garden and doodling" (El-Zanfaly, Huang, & Dong, July 2023, p. 256). This enables users to move beyond a two-dimensional flat-screen digital surface as an interface for more embodied artmaking. The tangible and tactual sand playground is thought to make AI more intuitively understandable for non-expert users.

Another design approach proposes using "rough gestural inputs, such as hand gestures or sketching" to enhance the experience of human interaction with a generative AI system (Chung, Chang, & Adar, 2021, p. 1). Gestures are "intuitive and expressive" (Chung, Chang, & Adar, 2021, p. 1), and they enable a more intuitive way for people to engage generative algorithms. Various designers and engineers and users are working toward ways to enable the fine-tuning of human-machine creations.

Another team conducted a study of a system that allows humans to draw with an AI interface in a collaborative way. The study found that human users of this system rated the AI "relatively low in predictability, controllability, and comprehensibility" (Oh, Song, Choi, Kim, Lee, & Suh, Apr. 2018, p. 1). Also, the research found that human users "always want to lead" the AI (Oh, Song, Choi, Kim, Lee, & Suh, Apr. 2018, p. 7). Also, the AI system caused discomfort when it "went between being human-like and non-human-like" behaviors and communications (Oh, Song, Choi, Kim, Lee, & Suh, Apr. 2018, p. 8). There have been conversations around future technology, especially around the values of "Environment, Data Privacy, Embodiment, and Play" (Lin & Long, June 2023, p. 380), which may inform how developers and engineers and software developers evolve such systems into the future.

2.5 Onboarding New Users

Several published works describe the onboarding of various groups to usage of the artmaking generative AIs. One involved holding workshops to help high school students use generative AI to explore what they conceptualize of their future selves and also understand tool capabilities and risks (Ali, DiPaola, Williams, Ravi, & Breazeal, 2023, p. 1) as part of artificial intelligence literacy. The students projected their personal identities into the future in this workshop and expressed their future self-identity in visual detail. The researchers note the importance of ensuring that "harmful stereotypes" and various misconceptions potentially communicated by such tools should be headed off (Ali, DiPaola, Williams, Ravi, & Breazeal, 2023, p. 14).

Another hands-on workshop involved those engaged in crafting. This craft education harnessed generative AIs to capture human "imaginaries" related to such tools (Vartiainen & Tedre, 2023, p. 1). Participants engaged in thoughtful exploration of craft practices. What fosters innovation? How are design ideas explored and expressed and then carried forward into crafting? How do people collaborate around the work of generative AIs? One observation from this research was the sense of the "embodied nature of making that is missing from digital design" (Vartiainen & Tedre, 2023, p. 11). People experience satisfaction in that embodied creation and full-sensory sensing and making. The easy creation of visuals also results in a "missed opportunity" for learning through manual creation (with analog materials or pen and tablets) (Vartiainen & Tedre, 2023, p. 12).

2.6 Reception of AI-Generated Work by People

An empirical study found that people did not judge AI-created artwork as equal to human-created artwork. Research participants evaluated human-created artworks as "having a significantly higher rating in 'composition,' 'degree of expression,' and 'aesthetic value'" (Hong & Curran, 2019, p. 58:11). However, "knowing that a piece of art was created by AI did not, in general, influence participants' evaluation of art pieces' artistic value" (Hong & Curran, 2019, p. 58:1). The research participants seemed to be influenced by a common schema that "AI cannot make art" (Hong & Curran, 2019, p. 58:1). This study explored a number of dependent variables valued in the art space: "Originality, Degree of Improvement or Growth, Composition, Development of Personal Style, Degree of Expression, Experimentation or Risk Taking, Aesthetic Value, Successful Communication of Ideas" (Hong & Curran, 2019, p. 58:10). The researchers found that aesthetic value "is the only variable that was not influenced" by the research participants' sense of whether a work was human- or machine- generated (Hong & Curran, 2019, p. 78:12). Another study found that people could not differentiate whether art was created by "a human artist or by the machine" (Mazzone & Elgammal, Feb. 2019, p. 4).

A study was conducted in art education to see if generative AIs could benefit the learners by suggesting "creative solutions," providing "a scientific approach to art making," support the creation of "new ideas," organize "existing ideas," and others (Hutson & Cotroneo, 2023, p. 7), While such technologies enable "diverse visual outcomes" (Hutson & Cotroneo, 2023, p. 1), and could improve final art products, this was not necessarily so for the research participants. Use of such systems may risk squelching the human imagination, in the so-called "age of digital recombination":

Media are interfaces that mediate not only between us and our world (designation), but also between us and our fellow man (communication), and between us and ourselves (self-understanding). Aesthetic experience is no exception: artistic media are interfaces that not only structure the imagination of the artist, but the work of art and the aesthetic reception as well.. (De Mul, 2009, p. 95)

A pragmatic approach argues that artmaking generative AI tools should be "adopted as other photomechanical and computer-generated versions before them and leveraged to provide new models for artists to improve their workflow" (Hutson & Robertson, 2023, p. 1). Such tools may suggest "creative solutions" for sculpture-making, provide a bridge to learning about AI, and enhance understanding "volumetric space" (Hutson & Robertson, 2023, p. 4). Technologies may encourage "a scientific approach to artmaking" (Hutson & Robertson, 2023, p. 4).

Walter Benjamin suggested in the 1930s that art has a "cult value," which is unique and embedded in particular cultures and times. Art is often a one-off. In the age of mechanical reproduction, in which works may be replicated visually and physically, even mass-produced, art becomes "de-auratized," and art becomes less valuable in its "cult value" and more in its "exhibition value" (where art is mass spectacle at population scale) (Benjamin, 1935, 2008), with technologically enabled "endless reproduction of the copies" (De Mul, 2009, p. 98). Artwork's cult value, independently of technologies, dissipates over time (Benjamin, 1935, 2008). Art is both "sensible" and "supersensible," with its original materiality (sensibility) and then its "meaningful history" (supersensibility) (De Mul, 2009, p. 97). The losses are not only seen as applying to human artmaking and the centrality of humans to that process (as makers and as audience), but there is a sense that technologies such as generative AI may open people up to vulnerabilities. One author writes:

Gradually, we become aware of the inapproachability of the workings of a technology that we have invented. And we might even start to reflect on the non-human and maybe even inhuman character of this new medium. Or on the possibility that it will gradually outstrip our skills to add, browse, change and destroy. And that we might become the ultimate object of digital manipulation. (De Mul, 2009, p. 104)

As-yet, users are dazzled by the speed of the generated synthetic still visuals, videos, and animations. There are wide debates on how high-fidelity the visuals are and whether they may be differentiated between the faux and the real (since the contents are all in pixels essentially). The discussions surround perhaps the fidelity of the visuals (how true to life they are or not), the quirks of generative AI (challenges with the correct number of limbs and fingers, problems with lettering, and particular tendencies of various web-acing artmaking generative AI tools), and other firsthand observations. Some have suggested that such tools merely copy or parrot the large datasets that they were trained on and do not offer anything truly novel. Another tranche of writing involves whether such computational tools may generate something of value, the debates around "authorship" and ownership, challenges with intellectual property (the human artist is generally seen as owning the rights to what they create but are expected to reveal that they used an artmaking generative AI tool), and other in-world concerns.

3. ENGAGING FUTURE-MINDED VISUALIZATIONS AND ARTFUL AESTHETICS: "SEEING DIFFERENT" WITH HUMAN-MACHINE COLLABORATIONS WITH ARTMAKING GENERATIVE AIS

Early adopters have been using artmaking generative AI tools (based on large language models) for some years now. The output of such models has been used to illustrate book and comics; they have been used in amateur films; they have been harnessed for illustrating learning objects and slideshows and simulations; they have been shared on various platforms to entertain and inform others. The visuals may be photo-realistic and evocative of the real, and others are based on the imaginary.

The output visuals often harken to defined art traditions and schools, known conventions. Rarely do people use text prompts and image prompts (often in combination and through iterated series) to generate wholly novel creations:

- full non-derivative and original fantasy,
- new referent materials that do not already exist on Earth,
- innovative aesthetics (vs. emulations of known artists),
- unusual scenes and scenarios,
- fresh simulations,
- and as-yet unimagined visual outputs both still and motion.

But they can, with experimentation, from warm-up to various types of inputs and sequencing.

The generative AI tools are not used to ideate per se, except in some design context (Hanna, 2023). This work argues that the AI-generated visuals may not only illustrate what people want and can imagine, but it may be practical in solving the "what" and the "how" and the "why" of various human challenges. A new approach will require people to change tact and understandings of the generative AI's affordances and constraints; it may even require changes to the self. Table 1 suggests that there may be different ways of *nouveau* thinking, *nouveau* doing, and *nouveau* being from "seeing different" in regards to generative AIs. The data cells contain action verbs in gerund form but without objects as these actions are thought to apply to a variety of contexts.

In the present age, the advent of artmaking generative AIs should not be about simple reproductions of what is already "the familiar." There should be a reach to future-minded visuals, with true co-creation instead of humans as tasking agents and generative AIs as actualizing rote machines. Common art created with generative AIs should be in "blend mode" with deep inputs by humans and machines, to please, to provoke, to evoke, to innovate, and to solve problems, among others. The "seeing different" should enable

Table 1. "Seeing Different" with human-machine collaborations with artmaking generative AI

Categories of Changes from "Seeing Different"	Thinking (1)	Doing (2)	Being (3)
Re-visioning Re-imagining Engaging non-visual thinking from human-AI originated visuals (but not locking into particular modalities) Questioning Exploring Remaking Zooming in Zooming out Studying textures Studying forms Studying environment Probing methods Paradigm shifting	Visualizing Ideating Conceptualizing / Reconceptualizing Reflecting / Musing / Considering Understanding Exploring Imagining Appreciating Enjoying Seeing Experiencing Assessing Evaluating Interpreting Decrypting Patterning Interrelating Recognizing Feeling Hypothesizing Speculating Optioning	Appreciating Analyzing Questioning Learning Expressing Engaging Interacting Building Creating Innovating Sharing Socializing Informing Designing Mapping Generating Making Augmenting Influencing	Living ...aesthetically ...multimodally ...creatively ...innovatively ...socially ...technically ...relationally ...environmentally ...ecologically Changing

"thinking" and "doing" and "being" different...into the near- and far- futures. This practice should lead to new ways of looking at worldly and other-worldly phenomena. Even within a limited spatial (2d) canvas on a digital screen, there are expansive possibilities of visual-experiential and conceptual revelation.

3.1 Discussion

While a human tendency may be towards inertia and resistance to change, people certainly have the ability to change and to make change. Artmaking generative AIs have easy-to-use interfaces, and the text prompts, image prompts, modifiers, and other parameters may be controlled without much in the way of difficulty. This is not to say that it will not take investments to create seeding art using analog and / or digital materials. This is not to say that the acquiring of visual arts terms will not require effort and time. The skill of "prompt engineering" is also important to learn. These various elements, learned piecemeal, enable combinatorial complexity in the images that emerge from the respective generative AIs.

3.1.1 Exploring the Author's Usage of Artmaking Generative AIs

The author has used several artmaking generative AIs for over a year. Personally, these tools have been used for self-encouragement, humor, stress relief, design ideas, learning about art fundamentals (composition, shape design), storytelling, professional illustration, animal morphology (and poor examples of such), emotional expression, color experience, self-expression, saving on art supplies, and others. Most of the uses have been instrumental and practical, but some have been more visionary. These include the drawing of mythical creatures, exploring the nano world, eliciting a microbiome (much more artful than hyperrealistic, but hyperrealistic is an option), humor, fancifulness, and visual punning. Experientially, using generative AI for creating visuals highlights the skills gap in actual drawing and sketching and painting. The work in generative AI with the text prompts and visual prompts gives the sense of the tool: "Your wish is my command…" But the results are sometimes 100% (rarely) and sometimes 10% (more often). Having control at the pixel level is very different than that at the level of pigment on paper, for example. This work requires some learning and practice and digital image editing. By contrast, manual artmaking becomes more effortful, more costly (materials), and much physically messier. There is more of a grand production to go to the in-house art studio to experiment. There are relative strengths and weaknesses between different artmaking generative AI tools, with some better for serendipitous outcomes, others for rough sketches, others for refined works, and so on. There are some that are better catalysts for productive action than others.

One way to think about "seeing different," and so on, may be explored by writing in the different areas of changes. The author has done so here in Table 2.

Perhaps the visuals may be applied to verified factual scenes for learning and analysis? New aesthetics may be created for branding (logos, designs, websites, printed materials, and others). New nano-scale objects may be designed from AI-generated visuals. Perhaps engineering problems may be solved with generative AI imagery. Perhaps the uses of the visuals may point to counterfactuals to the present *status*

Table 2. Examples of "Seeing Different" with Human-Machine Collaborations with Artmaking Generative AI for one individual (a brainstorming exercise)

Categories of Changes from "Seeing Different"	Thinking (1)	Doing (2)	Being (3)
Acquiring better understanding of computational AI's drawing and illustrating Using visuals to create texts, designs, concepts Experiencing new color mixes	Recognize design features in visuals, such as composition, color, texture, perspective, sizing, line work, and other elements Acquiring a vocabulary around visual depiction	Taking an experimental approach to using text and image prompts to create visuals with several artmaking generative AI tools Conceptualizing visuals using text and imagery	Being more expressive in a visual way in the world Appreciating the aesthetics both in nature and in human-made works and spaces Using some works from generative AI in free social image sharing sites
Understanding how to change up spatiality based on perspective Understanding a mapping between language and visuals Better seeing the cultural assumptions in scene making and scene interpretation Seeing how unsophisticated some visuals are and understanding how much professionalism and data and expertise go into some types of depictions (lab photos, geographical maps, data visualizations, and others) Considering new methods and techniques and approaches	Recognizing the visual language of emotions, place, people, the imaginary, and others Reimagining robotics Reimagining nature (vs. what a naïve generative AI assumes something might be) Understanding how analog artworks are transformed through artmaking generative AIs Seeing how style and mood and atmospherics can affect how people respond to a visual	Appreciating the beauty in depicted nature Understanding the need for accurate depictions of people, history, and other aspects of human life Taking digital photos with a stronger sense of composition and lighting awareness in the real and physical world Knowing how to better frame visuals used in documents, in slideshows, in book chapters, and other mostly-textual work	Editing digital imagery and video and animations with more sophistication Engaging with others online around human-machine created imagery Documenting learning to share with others Expressing more freely in visual ways Creating more and innovating more all around, in visual and other modalities Appreciate the human-machine co-creations shared online with a deeper appreciation for the aesthetic and technical aspects, and an analytical sense of how they achieved that look

quo challenges. Perhaps new styles of data visualizations and diagrams may be evolved. Perhaps, in part, seeing with "new eyes" and "revisioning" can help amplify the power of artmaking generative AIs.

At present, the artmaking generative AIs do not have the super-capabilities suggested. A few visual examples here, seeded by mixed media pieces by the author and created using Deep Dream Generator, illustrate some of the concepts. Figure 1 suggests a super-physics knowledge that may extend the benefit of the AI-generated visuals. Figure 2 suggests the power of a new aesthetics. Figure 3 proposes the visualization of flying cars and new potential technologies. Figure 4 the exploration of mixed materiality, of materials that show up with a material look but could refer to a new-made or new-discovered material. Figure 5 suggests that the generative AI built on large language modeling and big datasets of imagery may reveal insightful patterns, perhaps spatial patterns (as in geo and other types of maps). Figure 6 alludes to the potential lucrativevalue of such generative AI, depending on implementations and on use cases (and skilled users).

These visuals are somewhat whimsical and decorative in their illustrations. This is not to take away from the potential serious and powerful purposes to which these artmaking generative AI tools may be applied. There are competitive advantages to be had based not only on advancing such tools but on how humans use them. In this time of exploitation of artmaking generative AIs, there is much space for exploration—for both machines (and those who make them) and humans (those who use them).

4. FUTURE RESEARCH DIRECTIONS

Human users of artmaking generative AI may learn by attuning to the outputs of these works. Artmaking generative AIs may be seen as "a new medium with its own distinct affordances" (Epstein, Hertzmann, Herman, Mahari, Frank, Groh,... & Russakovsky, 2023, p. 1) and a product of its present time. The so-called "Generative Internet" has emerged with powerful interlinked networks that serves as "a generative

Figure 1. Broken dam and weird physics

Figure 2. Flood plain and new aesthetics

grid" that affects human creativity: "…generativity increases with the ability of users to generate new, valuable uses that are easy to distribute and are in turn sources of further innovation" (Zittrain, 2006, p. 1982). The Web-facing artmaking generative AIs may be seen as perhaps another build-out along the same lines, with communities emerging from these creative practices and global sharing of human-AI generated artworks and emerging insights.

The challenges with the "attention economy and corporate control" also affect how people respond to generative AI (p. 4), with the general consensus that art is created by "social agents" in social contexts (p. 18). This is not to say that AI will never achieve human-level intelligence "and consciousness" and the ability to socialize, in which case, it would be seen as able to fully creating art (Hertzmann, May 2018, p. 20). The human nexus is important for public-facing artmaking generative AIs, requiring these technologies to be an "almost autonomous artist" (Mazzone & Elgammal, Feb. 2019, p. 3), instead of fully autonomous ones which attract less human interest. Given some human fears of machine autonomy,

Figure 3. Flying cars and new technologies

one research team shares where the autonomy exists in generative AI systems, as a way to diminish some of the fears (Walsh, Mahesh, & Trumbach, 2021, p. 38).

How generative AI is viewed—through a transhuman or posthumanist approach—"may lead our culture to disparate futures" (Yenidogan, 2021, p. 1): "Transhumanism's approach toward AI Art and Music is discussed to be framing it as a creativity-enhancing tool, while Posthumanism's approach is an opportunity for co-creation with non-humans" (p. 3). To engage a future of climate crises, humans may need to form an "interdependency to nonhumans" (Yenidogan, 2021, p. 9).

The current state of nascent generative AIs is not the end state. These tools will keep evolving if there is sufficient interest, a user base, and a market. Some suggest that these are the start of a new art movement. Others suggest that these may be a temporary and passing fad. The role of a "machine imagery" is likely to stay for a number of creative fields. How these tools evolve is one area of research.

Another involves how humans co-create with artmaking machines (as creativity support tools), such as what "collaboration patterns" emerge (Muller, Chilton, Kantosalo, Liao, Maher, Martin, & Walsh, Apr. 2023, p. 1). This research informs the designs of user interfaces, among other applications.

How computational art evolves as a creative field or an art genre is another point of interest. Pixels are essential building blocks of visuals but also knowledge and innovations.

Various use cases for how people use generative AI to think, do, and be different will be another important space. How such tools can be harnessed for human benefit is an important extant working question. The outputs have been described as a "co-creation of an assemblage consisting of human and non-human parts" (Yenidogan, 2021, p. 1). In that relationship, the human component can bring in lively visual concepting. They will see beyond the surface visual. They'll identify partial or whole stories in the visuals. There will be enrichment by their additional prior, during, and post-image making work. In other words, if a visual of a particular type is being created, such as about a future scenario on Mars, perhaps there can be a brainstorming of various aspects of interest. With additional knowledge, people may go through and beyond the AI-generated visuals to reach more deeply. The human users may be

Figure 4. Mesh curtain of mixed materials

better able to engage in additive, subtractive, and contorting engagements with the co-generated visuals. They will bring enrichment with social collaborators. They will bring creativity to bear, by learning from peripheral areas to the target one and perhaps learning by indirection. Sometimes, ideas may arrive intuitively, and other times, counter-intuitively. Visuals can jog different parts of the human brain. Another approach may involve bringing different modalities of knowledge to the visual—such as the textual, the symbolic, and others. Where the generative AI enables a rich transcoding across communicative modalities (text, genres, imagery, numbers, motion visuals, sound, and others), a mental nimbleness that enables transcoding across modalities benefits the practical usage of the content-creating genera-

Figure 5. Night fires showing patterns

tive AIs. A deeper sense of history and knowledge may be powerful to lead to innovation. How people work the creativity and the inspiration in this space would be of research and management interest. The engagement with the artmaking generative AI may be seen as a liminal or in-between space, that can result in achieving an insightful outcome. Ideas emerge in mysterious ways, from a complex human and machine mind, with trillions of neurons: the conscious, unconscious and subconscious human mind, and the subtle observations of the artificial neural network-informed large language models (LLMs) of the artmaking generative AIs.

Figure 6. Lucrative Midas flowers

In the present moment, what generative AIs create are still "interpreted in explicit or implied reliance on the concept of the singular author figure" (Zeilinger, 2021, n.p.). Art is often "anthropo-normative," with norms for art based on human standards and human practices, perhaps denying space for AI-generated visuals as potentially revelatory. How this thinking evolves will also be of interest.

Computational creativity tools enable various types of transcoding from one digital form to another, based on mapping, such as visual to auditory, still to motion, and others. One work describes the computational creation of harmonious music based on live drawings in a participatory live stage performance (Starkey, Steenhauer, & Caven, 2020, p. 209), for example. There may be exploration of various other types of synaesthesia approaches to creativity.

Trying to find analytical value from images created from generative AI will likely be qualitatively different than analyzing photos and light sensors from reality. The artmaking generative AIs are drawing from minutiae of learned visual patterns based on deep neural network modeling, in many cases, and that may affect the patterns that may be extractable and discernible. This insight may lead to other findings.

5. CONCLUSION

In this time of the Fourth Industrial Revolution (4IR), AI and especially generative AI are core parts of art cultures today. This is even as the potential of artmaking generative AIs is just beginning to be explored. The tool enables the testing of contradictory prompts and parameter-settings and the depiction of various types of "impossible" things. How people provide inputs and measure the outputs through different calibrations and iterated experimentation may be a promising approach. Humanity is facing "environmental pollution, societal inequalities and religious struggles" and a global pandemic recently in the rearview mirror (Freiss, 2021, p. 278), and facing such wicked problems through "critical art" may benefit from transhumanist generativity for visuals that project today's peoples into various futures. Artmaking generative AIs are not only about digital and emulative "pastiche" (Choi, DiPaola, & Töyrylä, 2021, p. 020501-1). The complexity of the generative AI tools may enable deeper insights that remade art styles. A "seeing different" (and "see what happens") approach may begin to explore some of the potentials.

In terms of artful expression, a system is emerging that "takes 'cognition of human-computer symbiosis, innovation supported by intelligent technology, collaboration among creative subjects, and constraints on creative behavior' as a new methodological approach" for art creation, and this is a context "in which AI is the core media, artists, robots, and audience are the co-creation subjects" (Chen, Shidujaman, Jin, & Ahmed, 2020, p. 13). Generative AI may inform on "the true value of our evolving (digital) semantic capital" (Notaro, 2020, p. 328). This work suggests that interacting with artmaking generative AIs should be action-filled and informed, not just a manual prompt- machine response dynamic (or various variations with some degree of machine auto- or augmented- prompting).

Some of the initial leeriness about the technology has been waning. There is more of a consensus that "AI as a technical object is always intertwined with human nature despite its level of autonomy" (Daniele & Song, Jan. 2019, p. 155). Creative autonomous agents are not "othered" from humanity but a tool to augment human agency. "Prompt engineering" is not conflated with artistic skill, however:

Prompt-engineering falls short as an artistic practice for a number of reasons. Firstly, although the skill is developed through countless hours spent engaging with the medium, it is not learned in any tacit, embodied, or individualized way. Prompts can be directly shared, copied, stolen, and in an instant the entire body of knowledge and invested time is transferred. Prompt-engineering, if shared, does indeed contribute knowledge towards the broader community, yet holds little personal value as the art object. (McCormack, Cruz Gambardella, Rajcic, Krol, Llano, & Yang, Apr. 2023, p. 206)

Perhaps human skills in relation to generative AI tools will come from more complex prompting, image pre-production, image post-production, framing of the artwork, presentation of the artwork, discussions around the artwork, curation, and other surrounding skills in addition to the use of the generative AI.

Perhaps artists may still express their signature style using this tool, among others. In other words, they can express in ways that are original to them.

The artmaking generative AIs increase work efficiencies. They extend human design, development, and deployment capabilities. Beyond this, however, the capability goes well beyond human visual expression and human social conversations. Exploiting these tools fully will require an exploratory and expeditionary mindset.

If people use such tools within known scripts and old tropes, they are not using these tools to their maximum potential. These types of tools can be used in more profound ways for discovery and learning, for building in the real world, and for making a constructive difference. There is a power in the "material unpredictability" in artmaking generative AIs (Caramiaux & Fdili Alaoui, 2022, p. 477:1) that may be harnessed for creation. AI computational creativity is "non-deterministic" (Caramiaux & Fdili Alaoui, 2022, p. 477:10). There are surprises, some randomness, some serendipity, that is possible. There may be discovery and benefit even with "imperfect results" (Muller, Chilton, Kantosalo, Martin, & Walsh, Apr. 2022, p. 2) and "AI bugs and failures" (Salah, 2021, p. 161). Indeed, "machine flaws, irregularities and errors" may be harnessed to "find new thematic, technological and conceptual grounds for experimentation" (Boyé, Grba, Pandilovski, Kang, & Todorović, 2019, p. 713). In history, people have stumbled on discoveries from mistakes. Artful images may express "something that is beyond words" (McCormack, Cruz Gambardella, Rajcic, Krol, Llano, & Yang, Apr. 2023, p. 199). Where many designers use generative AI for "plausible image generation" (Hughes, Zhu, & Bednarz, 2021, p. 1), perhaps there is value for exploring the implausible and the seeming impossible and the internally contradictory. Since visual outputs are "derivative in novel ways; …these ways cannot be easily grasped or co-opted by established anthropocentrically framed systems of evaluating, validating, and valorising creativity" (Zeilinger, 2021, p. 20).

Perhaps novel visuals may lead to new thinking, doing, and being. In the same way, the output of artmaking generative AIs may be revelatory of new relationships, new insights, and new potential innovations. Such tools are not about being autonomous creators separate from people but more about being "open to new imaginations that are created with AI" (Salah, 2021, p. 176).

There should be an openness to "seeing different," and *nouveau* "thinking," "doing," and "being" different from the AI-generated content, where appropriate. People can be transported by a deepen-ed sense of possibilities through visuals. They may play with images in a non-thinking and purely feeling state. The art of making art may be an elicitation to the mind (some might say "universe") to access the conscious, the subconscious, and the unconscious. (The proposal is not anything mystical but more about engaging the human mind in its many powers.) The insights may be subtle and indirect, or they may be potent and centered. They can explore creative depth across modalities, even as their minds are visually "mindblown." There is a power to being open to surprise, emotion, and the full mind at play. Images can speak to various parts of the human mind, and people may coax different meanings from the various works. There has to be an openness to what can be learned from each new thing. The cost of entry to an artmaking generative AI is low.

For a technology to be relevant, it has to extend into the lived real. There is a human nexus to AI in that the tool and its output have to be relevant to people. Humans are the animating agents in this transaction. As such, how people use artmaking generative AI affects outputs. The impetus should be in extracting the most from these technologies and from what people may bring to the tool. Here, humans and machines would benefit by co-developing together, in a cyborg-ian way, so to speak. And the resulting visuals may be considered as almost like "gray literature" to inform the imagination, with complexity and simplicity.

THANKS to the reviewers who provided the feedback to this work.

Note: The researcher started using Deep Dream Generator in the latter phases of the SARS-CoV-2 / COVID-19 epidemic. The tool provided a kind of prolific "revenge"-making and "revenge" experimentation as a response to the coop-up and social isolating in a time of global challenge. The software raised the sense of quality of life.

REFERENCES

Ali, S., DiPaola, D., Williams, R., Ravi, P., & Breazeal, C. (2023). Constructing dreams using generative AI. *arXiv preprint arXiv:*2305.12013.

Arbiza Goenaga, M. (2020). A critique of contemporary artificial intelligence art: Who is Edmond de Belamy? *AusArt Journal for Research in Art, 8*(1), 49–64. doi:10.1387/ausart.21490

Artut, S. (2019). Using a machine learning algorithm to create a computational artwork: Variable. *Athens Journal of Humanities & Arts, 6*(3), 173–182. doi:10.30958/ajha.6-3-1

Benjamin, W. (1935, 2008). The work of art in the age of its technological reproducibility, and other writings on media. Harvard University Press.

Boden, M. A., & Edmonds, E. A. (2009). What is generative art? *Digital Creativity (Exeter), 20*(1-2), 21–46. doi:10.1080/14626260902867915

Boyé, P., Grba, D., Pandilovski, M., Kang, K. H., & Todorović, V. (2019). *Machine flaws in generative art.* In Lux Aeterna, ISEA2019 25th International Symposium on Electronic Art, Gwangju, Republic of Korea.

Caramiaux, B., Alaoui, S. F., & Hsueh, S. (2022, April). What becomes of" work" in AI" artwork"? In *CHI'22 Conference-Workshop on Outsourcing Artificial Intelligence* (pp. 1–3). Responding to the Reassertion of the Human Element into Automation.

Caramiaux, B., & Fdili Alaoui, S. (2022). " Explorers of Unknown Planets" Practices and politics of artificial Intelligence in visual arts. *Proceedings of the ACM on Human-Computer Interaction, 6*(CSCW2). ACM.

Chen, W., Shidujaman, M., Jin, J., & Ahmed, S. U. (2020). A methodological approach to create interactive art in artificial intelligence. In *HCI International 2020–Late Breaking Papers: Cognition, Learning and Games: 22nd HCI International Conference.* Springer.

Choi, S. K., DiPaola, S., & Töyrylä, H. (2021). Artistic style meets artificial intelligence. *Journal of Perceptual Imaging.*

Chung, J. J. Y., Chang, M., & Adar, E. (2021). Gestural inputs as control interaction for generative human-AI co-creation. In *Workshops at the International Conference on Intelligent User Interfaces (IUI).* CEUR-WS.

Dafoe, T. (2019, June 24). Law: A judge has rejected a $20 million lawsuit by a former studio assistant who claims famed sculptor Dale Chihuly didn't properly credit his work. *Artnet News.* https://news.artnet.com/art-world/dale-chihuly-lawsuit-dismissed-1582921

Daniele, A., & Song, Y. Z. (2019, January). AI+art=human. In *Proceedings of the 2019 AAAI/ACM Conference on AI, Ethics, and Society* (pp. 155-161). ACM. 10.1145/3306618.3314233

De Mul, J. (2009). The work of art in the age of digital recombination. *Digital Material, 95.*

DeepDream. (2023, Sept. 18). Wikipedia. https://en.wikipedia.org/wiki/DeepDream

DiPaola, S., & McCaig, G. (2016). Using artificial intelligence techniques to emulate the creativity of a portrait painter. *Electronic Visualisation and the Arts*, 158-165.

El-Zanfaly, D., Huang, Y., & Dong, Y. (2023, July). Sand-in-the-loop: Investigating embodied co-creation for shared understandings of generative AI. In *Companion Publication of the 2023 ACM Designing Interactive Systems Conference* (pp. 256-260).

Epstein, Z., Hertzmann, A., Herman, L., Mahari, R., Frank, M. R., Groh, M., & Russakovsky, O. (2023). Art and the science of generative AI: A deeper dive. *arXiv preprint arXiv:2306.04141.*

Ernst, H. (2023). *Artificial: A study on the use of artificial intelligence in art. Theses/capstones/creative projects.* University of Nebraska Omaha DigitalCommons.

Friess, P. (2021). Existence Beyond transhumanism–Context-based research-creation for critical art making. *Proceedings of Politics of the Machines-Rogue Research, 2021*(3), 278–284. doi:10.14236/ewic/POM2021.36

Galanter, P. (2016). Generative art theory. *A Companion to Digital Art*, (pp. 146-180). Research Gate.

Galanter, P. (2019). Artificial intelligence and problems in generative art theory. *Proceedings of EVA London, 2019*, 112–118. doi:10.14236/ewic/EVA2019.22

Hai-Jew, S. (2022). *Common Visual Art in a Social Digital Age.* Nova Science Publishers. doi:10.52305/BKOT1869

Hanna, D. M. (2023). The use of artificial intelligence art generator "Midjourney" in artistic and advertising creativity. *Journal of Design Sciences and Applied Arts, 4*(2), 42–58. doi:10.21608/jdsaa.2023.169144.1231

Hertzmann, A. (2018, May). Can computers create art? In Arts (Vol. 7, p. 18). Multidisciplinary Digital Publishing Institute. doi:10.3390/arts7020018

Hoetzlein, R. C. (2023). Knowledge vultures in new media art. *Artnodes*, (31), 1–9.

Hong, J. W., & Curran, N. M. (2019). Artificial intelligence, artists, and art: Attitudes toward artwork produced by humans vs. artificial intelligence. [TOMM]. *ACM Transactions on Multimedia Computing Communications and Applications, 15*(2s), 1–16. doi:10.1145/3326337

Hughes, R. T., Zhu, L., & Bednarz, T. (2021). Generative adversarial networks–enabled human–artificial intelligence collaborative applications for creative and design industries: A systematic review of current approaches and trends. *Frontiers in Artificial Intelligence*, *4*, 604234. doi:10.3389/frai.2021.604234 PMID:33997773

Hutson, J., & Cotroneo, P. (2023). Generative AI tools in art education: Exploring prompt engineering and iterative processes for enhanced creativity. *Metaverse*, *4*(1), 1–14.

Hutson, J., & Harper-Nichols, M. (2023). Generative AI and algorithmic art: Disrupting the framing of meaning and rethinking the subject-object dilemma. *Global Journal of Computer Science and Technology, 23*(1), 55 - 61.

Hutson, J., & Robertson, B. (2023). Exploring the educational potential of AI generative art in 3D design fundamentals: A case study on prompt engineering and creative workflows. *Global Journal of HUMAN-SOCIAL SCIENCE: A Arts & Humanities-Psychology, 23*(2).

Leach, N. (2019). Do robots dream of digital sheep? *Proceedings of ACADIA 19: Ubiquity and Autonomy.* CumInCAD. 10.52842/conf.acadia.2019.298

Liao, Z. Y., & Chien, S. F. (n.d.) *INK-SIGHT, MY SIGHT.* Research Gate.

Lin, L., & Long, D. (2023, June). Generative AI futures: A speculative design exploration. In *Proceedings of the 15th Conference on Creativity and Cognition* (pp. 380-383). ACM. 10.1145/3591196.3596616

Lv, Z. (2023). Generative artificial intelligence in the metaverse era. *Cognitive Robotics,* 208 - 217.

Mazzone, M., & Elgammal, A. (2019, Feb.). Art, creativity, and the potential of artificial intelligence. In Arts (Vol. 8, p. 26). MDPI. doi:10.3390/arts8010026

McCormack, J. (2017). Working with generative systems: an artistic perspective. *Electronic Visualisation and the Arts (EVA 2017)*, 213-218.

McCormack, J., Bown, O., Dorin, A., McCabe, J., Monro, G., & Whitelaw, M. (2014). Ten questions concerning generative computer art. *Leonardo*, *47*(2), 135–141. doi:10.1162/LEON_a_00533

McCormack, J., Cruz Gambardella, C., Rajcic, N., Krol, S. J., Llano, M. T., & Yang, M. (2023, Apr.). Is writing prompts really making art? In *International Conference on Computational Intelligence in Music, Sound, Art and Design (Part of EvoStar)* (pp. 196-211). Cham: Springer Nature Switzerland.

Merchant, B. (2019, Mar. 7). Why self-checkout is and has always been the worst. *Gizmodo.* https://gizmodo.com/why-self-checkout-is-and-has-always-been-the-worst-1833106695

Muller, M., Chilton, L. B., Kantosalo, A., Liao, Q. V., Maher, M. L., Martin, C. P., & Walsh, G. (2023, Apr.). GenAICHI 2023: Generative AI and HCI at CHI 2023. *In Extended Abstracts of the 2023 CHI Conference on Human Factors in Computing Systems* (pp. 1-7). ACM.

Muller, M., Chilton, L. B., Kantosalo, A., Martin, C. P., & Walsh, G. (2022, Apr.). GenAICHI: generative AI and HCI. In *CHI Conference on Human Factors in Computing Systems Extended Abstracts* (pp. 1-7). ACM.

Notaro, A. (2020). State-of-the-art: AI through the (artificial) artist's eye. *EVA London 2020: Electronic Visualisation and the Arts*, 322-328.

Oh, C., Song, J., Choi, J., Kim, S., Lee, S., & Suh, B. (2018, Apr.). I lead, you help but only with enough details: Understanding user experience of co-creation with artificial intelligence. In *Proceedings of the 2018 CHI Conference on Human Factors in Computing Systems* (pp. 1-13). ACM. 10.1145/3173574.3174223

Paulsen, K. (2020). "Shitty automation": Art, artificial intelligence, humans in the loop. Media-N, 16(1).

Pragya, C. (n.d.) *Ontology, phenomenology, and other aesthetic conflicts of generative art.*

Salah, A. A. A. (2021). AI bugs and failures: How and why to render AI-algorithms more human? *AI for Everyone?*

Salevati, S., & DiPaola, S. (2015). A creative artificial intelligence system to investigate user experience, affect, emotion and creativity. *Electronic Visualisation and the Arts (EVA 2015)*, (pp. 140-147).

Starkey, A., Steenhauer, K., & Caven, J. (2020). Painting music: Using artificial intelligence to create music from live painted drawings. *Drawing: Research, Theory. Practice*, *5*(2), 209–224.

Ulberg, E., Llach, D. C., & Byrne, D. (2020). Hand-crafting neural networks for art-making. In ICCC (pp. 508-511).

Vartiainen, H., & Tedre, M. (2023). Using artificial intelligence in craft education: Crafting with text-to-image generative models. *Digital Creativity (Exeter)*, *34*(1), 1–21. doi:10.1080/14626268.2023.2174557

Walsh, K. R., Mahesh, S., & Trumbach, C. C. (2021). Autonomy in AI systems. *The Journal of Technology Studies*, *47*(1), 38–47.

Yenidogan, B. (2021). How to talk about AI art and music: An onto-ethico-epistemological debate between transhumanism and posthumanism. *In Proceedings of the 2nd Joint Conference on AI Music Creativity*. (pp. 1 – 13). ACM.

Yusa, I., Yu, Y., & Sovhyra, T. (2022). *Reflections on the use of artificial intelligence in works of art*, (pp. 152-167). SSRN.

Zeilinger, M. (2021). Generative adversarial copy machines. *Culture Machine*, *20*, 1–23.

Zittrain, J. L. (2006). The generative Internet, 119. *Harvard Law Review*, 1974.

ADDITIONAL READING SECTION

Hai-Jew, S. (2022). *Common Visual Art in a Social Digital Age*. Nova Science Publishers. doi:10.52305/BKOT1869

KEY TERMS AND DEFINITIONS

Generative AI: A group of computational tools that are often powered by large language models and can be prompted to generate novel text, novel imagery, and other creative works (writing in various genres, music, digital characters, and others) Generative art: Art created by biological, chemical, computational or other autonomous or semi-autonomous systems based on human instigation of the process.

Large Language Model (LLM): A model for language- and / or image- processing based on computational training from large datasets (of text, of imagery, of mixed-modality data) and applied to various practical uses including natural language processing tasks, AI conversation, image creation, video creation and others Re-visioning: To re-think, to reconceptualize, to re-visualize.

Chapter 15
Integrating Artificial Intelligence (AI) Into the Curriculum:
Empowering the Next Generation Through Proactive AI Education

Rohan James Jowallah
University of Central Flordia, USA

ABSTRACT

"Bridging the Gap: Integrating Artificial Intelligence into the Curriculum," addresses the urgent need to infuse AI education into school curriculums amidst AI's growing influence in various sectors. It advocates for a shift from reactive to proactive educational strategies, emphasizing the role of education systems in mitigating the expanding skills gap and nurturing a generation adept in AI, machine learning, and data analytics. The chapter proposes a comprehensive AI curriculum integration framework, focusing on developing key AI competencies and ethical considerations, alongside strategies for effective implementation.

1. BRIDGING THE GAP: INTEGRATING ARTIFICIAL INTELLIGENCE (AI) INTO CURRICULUM

A few years ago, it would have seemed like science fiction if someone told you that you could ask any question from a data set and receive responses that, in most cases, were accurate. Currently, this form of technology is here, and the need to change how we think about teaching and learning comes with it. The reality is that we are embarking on a promising journey by fostering an alliance between AI and education. However, this journey will require a critical approach to ensure the integration is done considering technology, pedagogy, and humanity. Central to this change will be the need to embrace the cultural and societal shifts (Konstantopoulos et. al, 2010). This shift is also noted by the United Educational, Scientific and Cultural Organisation (UNESCO), which has been evaluating the disruptive implications of AI. While UNESCO's perspective is that AI will not replace teachers, the organization believes that

DOI: 10.4018/979-8-3693-0074-9.ch015

AI literacy for teachers will be necessary. Hence, the need for an AI competency framework will define teachers' knowledge, skills, and attitudes to deploy AI in education (UNESCO, 2023). Globally, governments envision the arrival of generative AI as an opportunity with possible risks that must be addressed (Lin & Chen, 2023).

AI has forced many industries to rethink their hiring practices. According to Holmes et al. (2019), by 2025, twenty-five percent of the world's workforce will be replaced by automation. Within this transformation, it must be acknowledged that the role of the educator will also need to change. This change will not only create possible challenges but also highlight potential opportunities for educational stakeholders. Hence, it is urgent that educators proactively address the integration of AI into the curriculum. Curriculum designers understand the curriculum is not static, hence the need for continuous evaluation and additions (Marsh and Larson, 2006). Therefore, when a decision on integrating AI into the curriculum is made, there should be a formal decision-making process intended for AI to be 'fused' into the curriculum. Such a decision must also involve all stakeholders (Kärkkäinen, 2012).

The arrival of Large Language Models (LLMs), which are artificial intelligence (AI) driven, has created a seismic shift in how we interact with the world (Mishra, 2023). Its pervasiveness across sectors is not just reshaping industries but also calling for reconsidering our educational paradigms, which will impact our curriculum design. In considering the shift, it will be essential to ensure that the integration of AI into the curriculum is within dominant frameworks that have been the foundation of education systems. To achieve this, a collaborative approach must consider the curriculum for transformation, teachers, and professionals committed to the changes ahead Scleisss et.al (2023). Such an approach should also be sustainable and scalable and offer continuous improvement space (Peters, 2019).

The chapter will explore the influence of AI in education. The need for a broad-scale adoption of AI will be highlighted to show the importance of AI for educational transformation. In totality, this transformation should benefit society. The chapter then examines the education system and the need for more proactive approaches to addressing innovation. The chapter will position that our education systems need to be at the forefront of AI literacy. Hence, a proactive approach will decrease the growing skills gap due to the rapid pace of technological advancement in education (Jowallah, 2023).

A blueprint for integrating AI into the curriculum will be highlighted and will suggest strategies for encompassing teacher training, infrastructure development, and fostering a collaborative learning environment. A proposed model will underscore the importance of professional development sessions for educators to equip them with the knowledge and pedagogical skills required to teach AI effectively (Ray, 2023). The chapter concludes with a detailed analysis of the potential impact of the proposed AI integration into the curriculum. The author underscores the curriculum's role in fostering critical thinking, ethical awareness, and lifelong learning. The author will also highlight how this AI curriculum integration can drive innovation, boost economic growth, and shape the ethical use of AI.

2. THE AUTOMATION SHIFT AND THE CHANGING WORKFORCE

Research by Price Waterhouse Coopers (2023) suggested that local economies will see an improved Gross Domestic Product (G.D.P) by 26%. The group warns organizations that they must have the skills needed for this productivity transformation based on the emergence of AI. The group suggests that China will lead this AI revolution, followed by the USA. Furthermore, Price Waterhouse Coopers suggests that while these countries and others may lead the way, it is essential that a global effort is made to educate and equip the future generation. While there is the sentiment that AI will potentially enhance people's lives globally, there is also the view that AI could lead to 'catastrophe' (Times, 2023). With automation shifting, the changing workforce, and possible eminent dangers of AI, there needs to be a national approach to addressing what is coming. It is also imperative that policymakers, educators, and government bodies realize that it is possible that, with this shift, a specific section of our population could become more at risk if they are not able to deploy AI to enhance their lives (Jowallah, 2023). Hence, implementing an approach that gives access to AI to all within the population will be necessary. Such an approach should be planned, developed, deployed, and evaluated for enhancement.

A fragmented approach employed to address the AI evolution will negatively impact society. With this in mind, institutions of learning can create a pathway for national and global change. This possible pathway could lead to the foundation of knowledge for future generations to understand the need for sustainable and responsible advancements (Núñez-Sánchez & Valente, 2023). To engage a movement of change, it is important to highlight what medium would allow institutions to make changes. The answer can be found in the constitution of a curriculum or the fusion of elements in a curriculum. A curriculum combines instructional practice with standards that guide students' learning and outcomes. The need for an AI curriculum is also connected to the rapid advancement in AI, the need to address the skills gap, the numerous ethical and societal implications, global competitiveness, and the need to have a future-ready education (Jowallah, 2023). It also holds values, culture, and norms for those engaging in the teaching and learning processes (Pinar 2004 & Okon, 2018).

Curriculum in places such as England, Australia, and the Caribbean have national standards within their curriculum (Maclister & Nation, 2013). These standards simultaneously cover what students must learn (Department of Education, England, 2010). National standards initiatives are often infused into subjects via purposeful curriculum changes. However, such a movement will require a structural and strategic approach. Since there is a need for AI to be fused into the learning space, the curriculum represents the medium for this fusion of AI into the formal learning process. This curriculum accommodation for AI technology will require a national effort by countries to ensure that their workforce is skilled, able, and flexible to navigate future changes. While this may seem like a monumental task, there will be opportunities for countries to be future-ready, and one way of achieving this will be purposefully planning for the implementation of AI into the National Curriculum. According to Devlin (2023), AI will change traditional classroom practices and yield opportunities. Even so, there are fears of fewer teachers based on the arrival of virtual tutors.

On reflection, deploying AI into any curriculum should be carefully considered. Quick fixes for addressing any AI deficiency in the curriculum should be avoided. Possible solutions must also consider skills gaps and encourage empowered curriculum participants to engage. Furthermore, a set of competencies should be designed to consider the fundamentals of AI, applying AI tools, integrating AI in problem-solving, and ethical considerations in AI use, as outlined earlier (UNESCO, 2023). These competencies should ensure an AI-literate workforce to navigate the future job market and contribute to the innovation-driven economy. Furthermore, these competencies should be broad enough to be applied to most subjects but specific enough to be linked to specific subject matters.

3. A CASE FOR AI INTEGRATION AT THE NATIONAL LEVEL

Countries with national approaches to educational outcomes can consistently deploy an initiative within specific standards and instruction. There are several justifications for doing so. These justifications include funding, standardized practices, collective ideological positions, and knowledge application (Department of Education, England, 2013, & Samaniego et. al 2023)). Implementing any curriculum change at the national level is a complex undertaking involving various stakeholders and considerations. To ensure AI is successfully implemented across the curriculum, consideration must be given to critical elements for such a change to occur. This section will require some of these elements to set the stage for integrating AI into the curriculum.

4. VISION AND STRATEGIES

For any successful curriculum initiative, there must be a vision for AI and conversation regarding the possible strategies that will be unutilized in making the curriculum engagement. One that will also be used to guide future development. This vision should be connected to deploying AI's economic, social, and technological benefits for implementation. The objectives for this vision must be designed to ensure that all stages of education can optimize this mission via the curriculum. Having a vision also allows for the alignment of objectives, which will lead to a well-articulated idea that will be beneficial in aligning the required curriculum change (Evan, 2005). Within the vision will be clearly defined strategies for the changes required within a collaborative framework. Having a clear vision will lead to stakeholders being engaged (Kim et. al, 2023).

5. STAKEHOLDER INVOLVEMENT

A comprehensive effort is needed to ensure the integration considers the key stakeholders. Therefore, it is essential for governmental bodies responsible for technology, education, and finance to be involved in the process (Langer 2004, Govindasamy & Mestry 2022). Getting educational instructions from schools, colleagues, and universities will be key stage holders in understanding the possibilities and needs at the local level, and this could help with the planning and deployment of resources.

The need for industry partners holds the potential to make the needed alignment of the AI integration to real-world applications. Therefore, it is fundamental that a sincere collaboration with tech companies and industries is established. Importantly, it is essential to get partnerships with companies that engage in research associated with AI. These partnerships could solicit meaningful feedback from stakeholders and provide valid data that could align the AI initiative over time.

Parents, students, and community leaders must be involved, too. Hence, there must be stakeholder engagement to ensure that their perspectives on AI use and concerns are communicated within the proposed fusion of AI in the curriculum. For example, according to Murchan & Johnston (2021), a significant body of work highlights the contribution students' voices can bring to curriculum change from the learners' perspective. The writers also state that parents and their children's voices are essential based on cultural capital and other factors that would influence a curriculum connected to their needs. For such an engagement to take place, fostering good communication and an atmosphere of transparency in the decision-making process will be imperative. Murchan & Johnston (2021) affirm whatever strategies are implemented; there must be consolidation in communication as these factors will be critical in promoting and managing curriculum reform.

6. CURRICULUM DESIGN

The need for curriculum change is paramount within any proposed AI curriculum. Such a change will require research and evaluation regarding what is in the proposed curriculum change (Stambaugh & Mofield, 2022). From a national level, research governmental bodies need to get involved in soliciting what resources will be required for this change. One starting point would be to explore how other institutions are engaging with AI within their curriculum design. While having a network with the in-country organizations is suitable for a holistic framework, it also benefits to explore how other countries deploy AI in the curriculum. It is also highly recommended that consideration be given to international organizations that are leaders in providing research and guidance in AI and other related issues. Two mentionable organizations are the Organization for Economic Cooperation and Development (OECD) and the United Nations (Murchan & Johnston, 2021).

The curriculum developed should be relevant and meet the mandate for AI literacy designed to be deployed using an interdisciplinary approach.

7. TEACHER TRAINING AND DEVELOPMENT

Once a desired curriculum is developed for deployment, there will be the need to provide training for teachers. Training teachers and the professional development of individuals who will assist with planning, developing, and deploying the AI integration will be paramount for this successful integration (Stanisic & Maksic, 2014 and Wentworth & Connell 2004). Hence, training programs should be redesigned to equip educators with the knowledge and skills needed to deploy AI within their teaching and learning spaces. The UNESCO (2023) document for "AI Competency Framework for Students and Teachers" could be a starting point for stakeholders connected to teaching and learning. The main objectives of this framework are to provide the knowledge and skills needed for teachers to use AI in their teaching and students' learning effectively. The focus on students in the framework is to allow students to develop the required understanding to engage in AI safely and productively (Lu et. al, 2023). To achieve both objectives, teacher training and professional development should be part of any strategies to integrate AI into the curriculum.

8. ASSESSMENT AND CERTIFICATION

The assessment for learning, during learning, and of learning about AI will ensure continuous evaluation of what is required for scoping this initiative. Hence, an evaluative framework will be needed to determine teachers' and students' knowledge and skills about AI. Therefore, for any professional development, it is recommended that standards are established to ensure that core competencies are established about what is required for an AI curriculum. For students, there should be some form of assessment of learning to ensure that they understand their role as digital citizens in the AI era. A digital competency badge could be used as a recognition of teachers and students achieving of AI competency within their required scope. It will also be imperative to recognize and certify achievement where appropriate to ensure that a regulatory aspect is part of the system (Ifenthaler, Bellin & Mah, 2016 and Huan, 2021)

While the author is concerned that many countries may have limited resources, any proposed curriculum initiative must be designed to scale in capacity. Hence, a robust technology infrastructure will be required. This will include computers, software, reliable internet access, and possible learning management systems that will help to facilitate the use of AI within online environments. The lack of structure and resources for the integration of an AI curriculum could result in slower progress and innovation, limited accessibility, compromising of possible quality education, and in summary, an educational system that has been left behind (Jowallah, 2023).

9. COMMUNITY PROGRAMS

For a holistic approach, it would also be recommended that there are offerings for extracurricular AI programs or workshops for interested students and the wider community.

This can be done within the scope of family learning programs designed to build AI literacy within family structures. The integration of family learning programs could be a pathway to collaborative learning among community members, the development of AI literacy skills needed in the home for children, and the enhancement of parent and child relationships as they work towards AI competencies. Family learning initiatives can offer immense support within schools (California Department of Education, 2017 & Reynolds & Temple, 2019). However, such an approach would require infrastructure, training, and resources. On reflection, successful curriculum integration of AI requires forward-thinking, collaboration, and a willingness to adapt. As the field of AI evolves, so should the curriculum to ensure it remains relevant and practical.

10. SETTING THE FOUNDATION

There needs to be more research on AI across the curriculum. However, based on the development stages, it will be necessary for content curriculum developers to revisit the stages of child development as outlined by Piaget & Inhelder (1972). AI across the curriculum must involve the entry level for children beginning their formal education. At an early age, children need to be able to understand what AI is. It will also be necessary for children to be given a simple understanding of the impact of AI on their lives. This foundational knowledge will be essential for setting the stage as they progress and are introduced at a later stage to understand the essential concepts of AI and the role machines have in their world. By the time students are ready for high school, they should be readily able to grasp some of the ethical implications of AI and begin to understand the more in-depth impact of AI.

11. SUBJECT INTEGRATION

Within a subject design curriculum, specific AI should be taught within subjects with specific competencies aligned with these subjects (Weidener & Fisher, 2023). For example, in math, students could be taught to use AI to analyse data, make predictions, and understand the deeper context of AI. For English courses, AI could be integrated, guiding students in the appropriate use of content generation and the debates about the ethical implications of AI. Notwithstanding, some core items should also be included in each course, including critical thinking about AI, digital literacy, ethical concerns, and reflection on AI use (Bashir, 2022). Each subject would need its competencies aligned with an overall framework. A few possible strategies that could allow AI to be integrated into the curriculum include but are not limited to: AI being deployed in project-based learning, personalized learning (adaptive learning pathways), collaborative learning, and using AI to provide feedback to students.

12. UNIVERSITIES SHOULD BE LEADERS

While all stakeholders should be involved in integrating AI into the curriculum, this book chapter positions the view that places of higher education hold a unique responsibility in leading the pathway for models of good practice for this needed integration (Tritscher, 2023). In summary, universities can be the leaders in providing the research and innovation needed to drive curriculum change and practice. These institutions have the ability to project what skills are needed for AI in the future. There is also the prospect of global collaboration which could be used to solve some of the ethical issues associated with AI. Matin & Martinez (2023) suggest that universities must take the lead to ensure that the AI curriculum is created within an ethical framework. The section below will highlight two universities approaches for the implementation of AI.

13. THE RUSSELL GROUP OF UNIVERSITIES, ENGLAND

The Russell Group is a self-selected association of twenty-four leading public research universities in the United Kingdom. These universities are known for their emphasis on research and have a reputation for academic excellence and contributions to various fields of study (Jowallah, 2023). Membership in this group includes the University of Oxford, the University of Cambridge, Imperial College London, and The University of Sheffield. The group's ideological position is that generative artificial intelligence (AI) holds significant potential to reshape education, prompting Russell Group universities to champion its ethical and responsible integration. As the capabilities of AI continue to expand, these universities are dedicated to preparing their students and staff to navigate an AI-dominated world effectively.

The group deploying AI in these universities will consider privacy and data. Therefore, generative AI tools within these institutions will be designed based on user inputs. There will also be a focus on bias awareness. Since AI draws on human-generated data, it can perpetuate societal biases and stereotypes. These universities have critically reflected on the need to ensure that AI is developed ethically. Accuracy and interpretation will also be part of their focus as they integrate; as a result, they will seek to educate stakeholders about the potential inaccuracies and misinterpretations in AI, which will be included in a code of ethics that will serve to highlight plagiarism and exploitation. They will create resources, allocate funding, and provide clear guidance for incorporating AI in learning, assignments, and research to achieve these considerations across the curriculum.

The group will also make a purposeful recognition of artificial intelligence in different applications and disciplines. The Russell group will also advocate for institution-wide policies according to their contents. Furthermore, they will thrive for continuous dialog within the context of the rapid growth in AI. These dialogues will be connected to adapting teaching and assessment methodologies for integration, enhancing teaching with AI, and considering how AI tools for different subject areas can improve equal access.

14. THE UNIVERSITY OF THE WEST INDIES (UWI): UWI GLOBAL CAMPUS

The UWI has a long tradition of designing, developing, and delivering online courses. There are several main campuses located across the Caribbean. Before the rebranding of a global campus concept, the institution had written course content for all its online courses. The university recently piloted several courses and employed an AI teaching assistant. This AI assistant was an infused course.

The content created before the AI deployment was advantageous for the UWI Global Campus. They kept their content in-house and did not export it to other LLMs. This approach allowed them to create learning pathways, design a diverse chatbot contextualized to the Caribbean, and offer twenty-four hours of support to students. Thus, giving teaching staff the time needed for individual student support.

While this chapter focused on two examples, it should be noted that many universities are creating pathways for the deployment of AI across their campus. Such an approach will require a comprehensive framework to ensure all stakeholders are on board for this transformation.

15. A FRAMEWORK FOR AI

The current approaches for the deployment of AI in general have been fragmented (Choi & Park, 2023). At times, critical consideration is not given to key elements that will allow for establishing a framework for a structured approach to the general deployment of AI initiatives across the curriculum. This chapter connects to Jowallah's (2023) framework that explores over forty fundamental principles for any AI framework. For brevity, these forty items were placed into themes to ensure that the dominant aspects of a framework for AI are covered.

The chief elements identified are ethical design, design principles, security and safety, societal impact principles, and legal and regular compliance principles (Akter et al., 2023, Miller, 2023 & Menéndez 2022, Jowallah 2023, Prikshat et.al, 2022,)

For any integration of AI into the curriculum, there must be consideration for ethical issues. Ethics must guide the design, development, and deployment of all AI products or assets used in the curriculum. The lack of ethics will result in inequality and could limit access to relevant groups attending educational institutions. For example, using data sets that predominantly favour a group of students will lead to excluding other students. The next theme in Jowallah's framework is design principles. Within this principle is the need to ensure that AI integration into the curriculum is designed for privacy and reliability to ensure the AI system performs the intended task. Other critical elements in this design principle include continuous improvement, explainability, inclusivity, and proportionality, which address that AI benefits

Figure 1. Principles needed for an AI framework

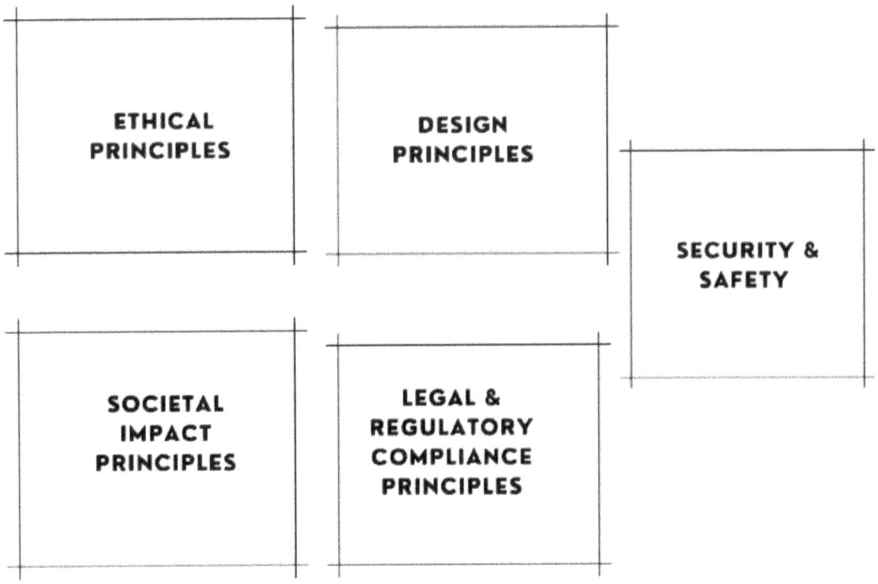

outweigh the potential harm and human-centeredness in the design. Jowallah (2023) also highlights the need for cultural sensitivity, robustness, and ensuring that AI will not replace humans.

Another emerging theme from Jowallah's framework that can be aligned with integrating AI into the curriculum is the impact of AI in our society. Educational institutions are not isolated as AI is infused into the curriculum. Therefore, consideration must be given to the possible societal impact, which will be required to promote the responsible use of AI and the sustainability of AI applications for the overall well-being of people in society.

Furthermore, engaging with such considerations can significantly enhance the transparency of AI deployments. Jowallah (2023) posited that when employing these pivotal principles, it becomes imperative to scrutinize several aspects. These aspects are connected to four basic questions. (1) Will the integration of AI promote fairness within the established systems? (2) Will these AI strategies foster inclusivity and accessibility? (3) Is the design equipped to minimize potential risks and prevent harm? and (4) How can the integration of AI be harnessed to advocate for social justice within our society?

In many learning institutions, there is a rush to implement AI. With this rush comes the issue of developing systems and frameworks that will not be future-ready or sustainable. Hence, each educational institution needs to understand its strengths, weaknesses, opportunities, and possible threats to the integration of AI. This can be done using a Strengths, Weaknesses, Opportunities, and Threats Analysis (SWOT). A SWOT is an analysis that shows the strengths, weaknesses, opportunities, and threats in an organization on an issue (Kime, 2023).

After completing the SWOT analysis, an institution should undergo a needs analysis to identify the areas within the existing curriculum where AI can bring about significant changes. This analysis will allow the institution to understand clearly what is needed for inclusion into the curriculum, such as the staffing needs and the general infrastructure required. The needs analysis will also provide valuable insight into the current skill sets of all employees about their AI usage.

Following this needs analysis, the institution must set clear objectives in terms of students learning, engagement, and use of AI. All stakeholders must know what will be required to achieve these goals. Within these objectives would be the use of data to enhance teaching and learning within the application of AI. In addition, consideration must be given to the development of content. Hence the content must foster real-world application within a critical thinking and problem-solving framework. Another step that must be considered is the interdisciplinary integration of AI into the curriculum (Bhalla, 2019). In other words, how will the blending of AI take place with other subjects to ensure a multidisciplinary approach is used to deploy AI? According to Bhalla, one possible way forward is to create projects and activities that apply AI concepts to other subjects, such as science and mathematics. This will also require consideration of pedagogical approaches to ensure that educators can apply AI teaching strategies to assist in this interdisciplinary approach (Luckin & Cukurova, 2022).

With any integration within the curriculum, there will be a need for resources. Therefore, resources must be allocated to ensure this integration takes place. One key justification for this is that with adequate funding, the institution can ensure they have the most updated resources and tools to facilitate the integration. This lack of funding will lead to this institution being excluded.

The previous section addressed the issue of training and development for educators. However, in addition to this, training, and development, there should be the development of communities of practice where educators can share experiences and learn from each other's efforts in integrating AI. These communities of practices would not only build collaboration but also create needed content. Another step will be the creation or implementation of AI-powered assessment tools that will provide continuous monitoring of students learning. Artificial intelligence and data intelligence will be the key indicators that will provide feedback on students' personalized learning pathways. This feedback will be vital in ensuring that the integration of AI remains aligned with the education objectives created for the mission. To remain relevant, there will be the need to foster a culture of innovation and continuous improvement. The inclusion of this step is to ensure that the AI systems deployed are practical and advanced enough to meet the needs of the institution.

16. THE FUTURE OF AI IN THE CURRICULUM

The future of artificial intelligence will bring together data intelligence (AI), which will have a synergy that will allow each learner to have a personal pathway for learning within learning spaces (Jowallah, 2023). A seamless transition from one learning space to the next will enable continual learning where virtual worlds meet. Subsequently, the future curriculum must be adaptable and flexible enough to accommodate the continuous evolution. While there is a considerable amount of scepticism surrounding the integration of AI into the curriculum, particularly concerning the ownership of students' work and other assessment-related issues, it holds promising prospects as a medium for enriched learning (Miller, 2023). It aims to carve out meaningful learning pathways that foster individual growth and development.

Moreover, the incorporation of AI in the curriculum is anticipated to garner substantial support from teachers, as it would afford them more time to engage directly with students (Menéndez, 2022). Despite the existing constraints and limitations, it is imperative that we adopt a proactive stance in addressing the ethical dilemmas and challenges that this framework presents at this juncture.

The outlook for the future is optimistic, characterized by a continuum of learning where individuals can pursue consistent educational growth. However, this progression necessitates a strong ethical foundation within the curriculum. It is crucial to involve educational institutions, government bodies, and other stakeholders in this movement to shape the future of education. As we navigate the transition to AI-integrated education, a seamless approach in shifting from one modality to another is envisioned. Nevertheless, it is vital to address prevailing concerns, notably the establishment of a comprehensive framework. Without such a framework, we risk lacking transparency in the deployment of AI technologies, which could potentially hinder the realization of a revolutionary educational (Miller 2023b)

17. CONCLUSION

In the rapidly evolving landscape of education, the urgency to integrate AI into the curriculum cannot be overstated. It is incumbent upon each institution and country to spearhead the transition towards an AI-driven curriculum, ensuring its relevance and adaptability to accommodate future developments.

The United Nations proposes a viable pathway forward, advocating for a collaborative framework that encompasses the active participation of policymakers, educators, and all pertinent stakeholders in the integration process. It is imperative that any curriculum initiatives undertaken are firmly grounded in the core principles of ethics and accessibility to prevent the marginalization of any group of individuals.

At this juncture in history, the momentum towards adopting an AI-centric curriculum cannot afford to be stalled. However, this progression carries a significant mantle of responsibility. Hence it necessitates a concerted effort to equip educators and stakeholders with the requisite skills to foster inclusivity within the curriculum.

Looking ahead, the prospects for AI in education appear promising. Yet, the absence of a well-defined framework could potentially undermine our objectives, leaving us without a clear mission, vision, and strategic blueprint to craft a resilient curriculum capable of withstanding the test of time. As we venture into this new frontier, it is crucial to establish a robust framework that will guide the seamless incorporation of AI into the educational mainframe, ensuring its longevity and efficacy.

REFERENCES

Akter, Hossain, M. A., Sajib, S., Sultana, S., Rahman, M., Vrontis, D., & McCarthy, G. (2023). A framework for AI-powered service innovation capability: Review and agenda for future research. *Technovation, 125*, 102768–. https://doi.org/ doi:10.1016/j.technovation.2023.102768

Bashir. (2021). *Ai literacy: understanding shifts in our digital ecosystem* (1st ed.). New Degree Press.

Bhalla. (2019). The 3S Process: A Framework for Teaching AI Strategy in Business Education. *Technology Innovation Management Review*, *9*(12), 36–42. https://doi.org/ doi:10.22215/timreview/1290

California Department of Education. (2017). *Family engagement toolkit: Continuous improvement through an equity lens.* CA DoE. https://www.cde.ca.gov/fg/aa/lc/documents/family-engagement.pdf

Choi, H., & Park, M. J. (2023, August 08). Choi, & Park, M. J. (2023). To govern or be governed: An integrated framework for AI governance in the public sector. *Science & Public Policy*, scad045. doi:10.1093cipolcad045

Chow, B., & Perrigo, B. (n.d.). The AI arms race is on. Start worrying. *Times*. https://time.com/6255952/ai-impact-chatgpt-microsoft-google/

Department of Education, England. (2013). *Primary national curriculum*. DoE England. https://assets.publishing.service.gov.uk/government/uploads/system/uploads/attachment_data/file/425601/PRIMARY_national_curriculum.pdf

Devlin, H. (2023, July 7). AI likely to spell end of traditional school classroom, leading expert says. *The Guardian*. https://www.theguardian.com/technology/2023/jul/07/ai-likely-to-spell-end-of-traditional-school-classroom-leading-expert-says

Education.sa.gov.au. (2023). *Artificial intelligence (AI) in schools – information for parents and carers*. SA. https://www.education.sa.gov.au/parents-and-families/curriculum-and-learning/ai

Evans, J. (2005). *Curriculum change in secondary schools, 1957-2004: An educational roundabout?* Routledge.

Govindasamy, & Mestry, R. (2022). The principal's role in managing curriculum change: Implications for the provision of quality education. *South African Journal of Education*, *42*(4), 1–10. doi:10.15700/saje.v42n4a2294

Holmes, W., Bialik, M., & Fadel, C. (2019). *Artificial intelligence in education: Promises and implications for teaching and learning*. The Center for Curriculum Redesign.

Huang. (2021). *Handbook of research on credential innovations for inclusive pathways to professions* (Huang, Ed.). IGI Global. doi:10.4018/978-1-7998-3820-3

Ifenthaler, B.-M. N., & Mah, D.-K. (Eds.). (2016). Foundation of Digital Badges and Micro-Credentials Demonstrating and Recognizing Knowledge and Competencies (1st ed.). Springer International Publishing. doi:10.1007/978-3-319-15425-1

Jowallah, R. (2023). *Examining the impact of large language models on higher education: Ethical considerations* [Conference presentation]. ELI Annual Meeting, Anaheim, CA.

Jowallah, R. (2023, September 4). *Revolutionizing Assessments: A Dive into Artificial Intelligence (AI) and Data Intelligence (DI)* [Video]. The Learning Journey. https://youtu.be/iAWD92y2K4E?si=1XNDykVDxgaYOuCS

Kärkkäinen, K. (2012). Bringing about curriculum innovations: Implicit approaches in the OECD area. In *Bringing about curriculum innovations: Implicit approaches in the OECD area* (pp. 1–21). OECD Publishing. doi:10.1787/9789264178698-4-

Kim, S., Samaniego, C. S., Sousa Melo, S. L., Brachvogel, W. A., Baskaran, K., & Rulli, D. (2023, November). Artificial intelligence (A.I.) in dental curricula: Ethics and responsible integration. *Journal of Dental Education*, *87*(11), 1570–1573. doi:10.1002/jdd.13337 PMID:37489621

Kime, L. (n.d.). *Conducting a SWOT Analysis*. Penn State Extension. https://extension.psu.edu/conducting-a-swot-analysis

Konstantopoulos, P. S., Karkaletsis, V., Spyropoulos, C. D., & Vouros, G. (Eds.). (2010). *Advances in Artificial Intelligence: Theories, Models, and Applications 6th Hellenic Conference on AI.* Springer. 10.1007/978-3-642-12842-4

Langer. (2004). *IT and Organizational Learning: Managing Change through Technology and Education.* CRC Press. https://doi.org/ doi:10.1201/b12383

Larson, J., & Marsh, J. (2005). *Making Literacy Real: Theories and Practices for Learning and Teaching.* Sage. doi:10.4135/9781446211953

Li, K., Kumar, A., & Chen, J. H. (1960). A., & Chen, J. H. (2023). How Chatbots and Large Language Model Artificial Intelligence Systems Will Reshape Modern Medicine: Fountain of Creativity or Pandora's Box? *Archives of Internal Medicine, 183*(6), 596–597. doi:10.1001/jamainternmed.2023.1835 PMID:37115531

Lu, Y., Pea, R., & Niemi, H. (2023). *AI in Learning: Designing the Future.* Springer Nature., doi:10.1007/978-3-031-09687-7

Luckin, George, K., & Cukurova, M. (2022). *AI for school teachers.* Taylor & Francis Group.

Macalister, & Nation, I. S. P. (2013). *Case Studies in Language Curriculum Design Concepts and Approaches in Action Around the World.* Taylor and Francis.

Martín. Lilic, M., & Martínez, M. R. (2022). AI Knowledge Transfer from the University to Society : Applications in High-Impact Sectors (Edition 1) (1st ed., Vol. 1). CRC Press. https://doi.org/ doi:10.1201/9781003276609

Menéndez, A. (Ed.). (2022). *Strategy, policy, practice, and governance for AI in higher education institutions.* IGI Global. doi:10.4018/978-1-7998-9247-2

Miller. (2023). *AI for educators: learning strategies, teacher efficiencies, and a vision for an artificial intelligence future.* Ditch That Textbook, division of Dave Burgess Consulting, Incorporated.

Miller. (2023a). Shifting to Accommodate a World with AI. In *AI for Educators*. Dave Burgess Consulting, Inc.

Mishra. (2023). Indian Paediatrics' Policy Regarding Artificial Intelligence (AI) — Enabled Large Language Models. *Indian Paediatrics, 60*(3), 171–171. doi:10.1007/s13312-023-2825-1

Murchan, D., & Johnston, K. (Eds.). (2021). *Curriculum change within policy and practice: Reforming second-level education in Ireland* (1st ed. 2021). Palgrave Macmillan. doi:10.1007/978-3-030-50707-7

National curriculum for England. (2013, July 16). Department for Education, UK Government. https://www.gov.uk/government/publications/national-curriculum-in-england-primary-curriculum

Núñez-Sánchez, S., & Valente, M. J. (2023). Sustainable development goals and climate change in Spanish technology disciplines' curricula: From LOMCE to LOMLOE. *Sustainability (Basel), 15*(13), 10301. doi:10.3390u151310301

Okon, U. (2018). Curriculum definition: A misleading philosophy. *International Advancement in Development Studies, 13*(2). http://www.irdionline.org/world/article/CURRICULUM%20DEFINITION%20 2018.pdf

Penn State Extension. (2023). *Conducting a SWOT analysis*. Penn State Extension. https://extension.psu.edu/conducting-a-swot-analysis

Piaget, J., & Inhelder, B. (1972). *The Psychology of the Child*. Basic Books.

Pieters, J., Voogt, J., & Roblin, N. P. (Eds.). (2019). *Collaborative curriculum design for sustainable innovation and teacher learning* (1st ed. 2019). Springer Nature. doi:10.1007/978-3-030-20062-6

Pinar, W. F. (2004). *What is curriculum theory?* Lawrence Erlbaum Associates Publishers.

Price Water HouseCoopers. (2023). *PwC's global artificial intelligence study: Sizing the prize*. PWC. https://www.pwc.com/gx/en/issues/data-and-analytics/publications/artificial-intelligence-study.html

Prikshat, P., Patel, P., Varma, A., & Ishizaka, A. (2022). A multi-stakeholder ethical framework for AI-augmented HRM. *International Journal of Manpower, 43*(1), 226–250. doi:10.1108/IJM-03-2021-0118

Ray, D. (2023). *How UF developed a model for AI across the curriculum*. University of Florida. https://news.ufl.edu/2023/01/ai-university/

Reynolds, & Temple, J. A. (2019). *Sustaining Early Childhood Learning Gains: Program, School, and Family Influences*. Cambridge University Press. https://doi.org/ doi:10.1017/9781108349352

Schleiss, J., Laupichler, M. C., Raupach, T., & Stober, S. (2023). AI Course Design Planning Framework: Developing Domain-Specific AI Education Courses. Education Sciences, 13(9), 954-. https://doi.org/ doi:10.3390/educsci13090954

Stanisic, & Maksic, S. (2014). Environmental Education in Serbian Primary Schools: Challenges and Changes in Curriculum, Pedagogy, and Teacher Training. *The Journal of Environmental Education, 45*(2), 118–131. https://doi.org/ doi:10.1080/00958964.2013.829019

Tritscher, R. J., & Schlögl, S. (2023). Educ-AI-ted – Investigating Educators' Perspectives Concerning the Use of AI in University Teaching and Learning. In Learning Technology for Education Challenges (pp. 241–254). Springer Nature Switzerland. doi:10.1007/978-3-031-34754-2_20

UNESCO. (2023). *AI competency frameworks for students and teachers*. UNESCO. https://www.unesco.org/en/digital-education/ai-future-learning/competency-frameworks

Weidener, & Fischer, M. (2023). Artificial Intelligence Teaching as Part of Medical Education: Qualitative Analysis of Expert Interviews. *JMIR Medical Education, 9*, e46428–e46428. doi:10.2196/46428

Wentworth, E. R., & Connell, M. L. (2004). Integrating information technology into the teacher education curriculum : process and products of change. Haworth Press.

Over the years, I have learned about the inordinate power of a digital blank sheet, an asked question, a pile of scratch paper, an empty space, and a work demand. All require a constructive response and hard work, as time runs irretrievably through the sieve. An edited book helps put ideas into the formal record. It sets up the groundwork for some of what comes next. To me, an edited book contains a coalescence of odds and ends of ideas, dribs and drabs of color. Each day is spent inexorably, and when one takes everything into account, there are checks in the "done" column. Work is incremental. In the moment, it feels like ephemera, but perhaps, some essential residual element remains.

THE RIGHTNESS OF THE MOMENT

Sometimes, it takes a retrospective to understand the rightness of a life juncture and a (sudden) turn. That is also true for the rightness of a technical tool juncture and a turn. Of course, I am talking about generative AI as applied to teaching and learning.

Where change can feel highly disruptive and challenging, *Generative AI in Teaching and Learning* (2024) may suggest an effective fit to the practical and aesthetic needs of people when used with forethought and awareness. After some study, I can see how AI is made of human hands and human will… and it is being shaped to human needs and ends.

This work highlights the expense of making generative AIs—as trained on big data, on large language modeling, and set up with various algorithmic approaches at generating—on the one hand (one popular model cost upwards of $100 million to train), but then, too, the expense of using generative AI tools for practical purposes (particularly with technologies in beta).

HUMANS AS A WILDLY CREATIVE SPECIES

Humans are a wildly creative species. They engage in brainstorms and body storms. They create. They innovate. They dream. They daydream. They live in the abstract, and they apply the abstractions to the real. They problem-solve. They value both the modern and contemporaneous and also doing things more traditionally (such as creating art on ancient paper with paint brushes) while also using generative AI to illustrate and illuminate. They can find the "sacred" in both the modern and the ancient. In higher education (and pre-K-12), there is a wide tradition of experimentation even as there are systematizations.

Figure 1. Beyond geometries (an alcohol ink painting by the editor processed in Deep Dream Generator)

TO CONCLUDE

Generative AI in Teaching and Learning (2024) offers enriched ideas for how to use generative AI for various types of teaching and learning. In a profound way, it is about how to make peace with the capabilities of the technologies in very human-tactical and human-serving approaches. We do all live in exciting times.

Compilation of References

Aabid, A., Parveez, B., Parveen, N., Khan, S. A., & Shabbir, O. (2022). A Case Study of Unmanned Aerial Vehicle (Drone) Technology and Its Applications in the COVID-19 Pandemic. *J. Mech. Eng. Res. Dev*, *45*, 70–77.

Abd-Elaal, E.-S., Gamage, S., & Mills, J. E. (2019). Artificial intelligence is a tool for cheating academic integrity. In *30th Annual Conference for the Australasian Association for Engineering Education (AAEE 2019): Educators becoming agents of change: Innovate, integrate, motivate*, (pp. 397–403). AAEE.

Abdelwahab, H. R., Rauf, A., & Chen, D. (2022). Business students' perceptions of Dutch higher educational institutions in preparing them for artificial intelligence work environments. *Industry and Higher Education*, 09504222221087614.

Abdullah, M., Madain, A., & Jararweh, Y. (2022, November). ChatGPT: Fundamentals, applications and social impacts. In *2022 Ninth International Conference on Social Networks Analysis, Management and Security (SNAMS)* (pp. 1-8). IEEE.

Abreu-Mendoza, R. A., Coulanges, L., Ali, K., Powell, A. B., & Rosenberg-Lee, M. (2021). From non-symbolic to symbolic proportions and back: A Cuisenaire rod proportional reasoning intervention enhances continuous proportional reasoning skills. *Frontiers in Psychology*, *12*, 633077. doi:10.3389/fpsyg.2021.633077 PMID:34093313

Abueg, M., Hinch, R., Wu, N., Liu, L., Probert, W., Wu, A., Eastham, P., Shafi, Y., Rosencrantz, M., Dikovsky, M., Cheng, Z., Nurtay, A., Abeler-Dörner, L., Bonsall, D., McConnell, M. V., O'Banion, S., & Fraser, C. (2021). Modeling the effect of exposure notification and non-pharmaceutical interventions on COVID-19 transmission in Washington state. *NPJ Digital Medicine*, *4*(1), 49. doi:10.103841746-021-00422-7 PMID:33712693

Accenture. (2018). *The Rise of Artificial Intelligence: Opportunities and Challenges.* Accenture.

Adamopoulou, E., & Moussiades, L. (2020). Chatbots: History, technology, and applications. *Machine Learning with Applications*, *2*, 100006. doi:10.1016/j.mlwa.2020.100006

Adamson, G. (2023). Explaining technology we do not understand. *IEEE Transactions on Technology and Society*, *4*(1), 34–45. doi:10.1109/TTS.2023.3240107

Adams, P. (2006). Exploring social constructivism: Theories and practicalities. *Education 3-13*, *34*(3), 243–257. doi:10.1080/03004270600898893

Adiguzel, T., Kaya, M. H., & Cansu, F. K. (2023). Revolutionizing education with AI: Exploring the transformative potential of ChatGPT. *Contemporary Educational Technology, 15*(3), ep429. 1 – 12.

Adiguzel, T., Kaya, M. H., and Cansu, F. K. (2023). Revolutionizing education with ai: Exploring the transformative potential of chatgpt. *Contemporary Educational Technology*, *15*(3), 429.

Agarwal, A., & Karahanna, E. (2010). Time flies when you're having fun: Cognitive absorption and beliefs about information technology usage. *Management Information Systems Quarterly*, *34*(4), 709–725.

Aggarwal, G., & Parikh, D. (2020). Neuro-symbolic generative art: a preliminary study. *arXiv preprint arXiv:2007.02171.*

Ahn, M., Brohan, A., Brown, N., Chebotar, Y., Cortes, O., David, B., & Yan, M. (2022). Do as I can, not as I say: Grounding language in robotic affordances. *arXiv preprint arXiv:2204.01691.*

Akour, M., & Alenezi, M. (2022). Higher Education Future in the Era of Digital Transformation. *Education Sciences, 12*(11), 784. doi:10.3390/educsci12110784

Akter, Hossain, M. A., Sajib, S., Sultana, S., Rahman, M., Vrontis, D., & McCarthy, G. (2023). A framework for AI-powered service innovation capability: Review and agenda for future research. *Technovation, 125*, 102768–. https://doi.org/ doi:10.1016/j.technovation.2023.102768

AlAfnan, M. A., Dishari, S., Jovic, M., & Lomidze, K. (2023). ChatGPT as an educational tool: Opportunities, challenges, and recommendations for communication, business writing, and composition courses. *Journal of Artificial Intelligence and Technology*, *3*(2), 60–68. doi:10.37965/jait.2023.0184

Alam, A. (2021, November). Possibilities and apprehensions in the landscape of artificial intelligence in education. In *2021 International Conference on Computational Intelligence and Computing Applications (ICCICA)* (pp. 1-8). IEEE. 10.1109/ICCICA52458.2021.9697272

Alam, A. (2022). Employing Adaptive Learning and Intelligent Tutoring Robots for Virtual Classrooms and Smart Campuses: Reforming Education in the Age of Artificial Intelligence. In *Advanced Computing and Intelligent Technologies* (pp. 395–406). Springer. doi:10.1007/978-981-19-2980-9_32

Alanen, L. (2023). Descartes' Mind-Body Holism and the Primacy of Experience. In D. Charles (Ed.), The History of Hylomorphism: From Aristotle to Descartes (p. 0). Oxford University Press. doi:10.1093/oso/9780192897664.003.0017

Alghamdi, N. S., & Alghamdi, S. M. (2022). The Role of Digital Technology in Curbing COVID-19. *International Journal of Environmental Research and Public Health, 19*(14), 8287. doi:10.3390/ijerph19148287 PMID:35886139

Ali, S., DiPaola, D., Williams, R., Ravi, P., & Breazeal, C. (2023). Constructing dreams using generative AI. *arXiv preprint arXiv:*2305.12013.

Ali, S., DiPaola, D., & Breazeal, C. (2021). What are GANs?: Introducing Generative Adversarial Networks to Middle School Students. *Proceedings of the AAAI Conference on Artificial Intelligence*, *35*(17), 15472–15479. doi:10.1609/aaai.v35i17.17821

Ali, S., DiPaola, D., Lee, I., Hong, J., & Breazeal, C. (2021, May). Exploring generative models with middle school students. In *Proceedings of the 2021 CHI Conference on Human Factors in Computing Systems* (pp. 1-13). ACM. 10.1145/3411764.3445226

Ali, S., DiPaola, D., Lee, I., Sindato, V., Kim, G., Blumofe, R., & Breazeal, C. (2021). Children as creators, thinkers and citizens in an AI-driven future. *Computers and Education: Artificial Intelligence*, *2*, 100040. doi:10.1016/j.caeai.2021.100040

Alkhatlan, A., & Kalita, J. (2018). Intelligent tutoring systems: A comprehensive historical survey with recent developments. *International Journal of Computer Applications, 181*(43), 1-20.

Allen, B. (2019). Machine Learning With Deep Neural Nets Artificially Augmenting My Intelligence in a Narrow but Occasionally Superhuman Kind of Way. *Journal of the American College of Radiology, 16*(10), 1480-1481. Ali, M. & Azadeh, A. (2020). Human-AI collaboration: A review of current research and future directions. *Journal of Human-Computer Interaction, 36*(4), 1–12. doi:10.1080/07370024.2019.1645051

Almer, J. (2022). *Deskilling as an effect of AI: A group of students' attitudes towards AI and their worries about deskilling.*

Alser, M., & Waisberg, E. (2023). Concerns with the usage of ChatGPT in academia and medicine: A viewpoint. *American Journal of Medicine Open, 100036*, 1–3. doi:10.1016/j.ajmo.2023.100036

Alvarado, O., & Waern, A. (2018, April). Towards algorithmic experience: Initial efforts for social media contexts. In *Proceedings of the 2018 chi conference on human factors in computing systems* (pp. 1-12). ACM. 10.1145/3173574.3173860

American Federation of Teachers. (2017). *Educator Quality of Worklife Survey*. AFT. https://www.aft.org/sites/default/files/edquality2017.pdf

American Psychology Association. (2023). *How to use ChatGPT as a learning tool*. APA. https://www.apa.org/monitor/2023/06/chatgpt-learning-tool

Amin, M. M., Cambria, E., & Schuller, B. W. (2023). Will affective computing emerge from foundation models and general artificial intelligence? A first evaluation of ChatGPT. *IEEE Intelligent Systems, 38*(2), 15–23. doi:10.1109/MIS.2023.3254179

Amsel, A. (1989). Behaviorism, neobehaviorism, and cognitivism in learning theory: Historical and contemporary perspectives. *The American Journal of Psychology, 105*(3), 492–495. doi:10.2307/1423202

Anagnostou, M., Karvounidou, O., Katritzidaki, C., Kechagia, C., Melidou, K., Mpeza, E., Konstantinidis, I., Kapantai, E., Berberidis, C., Magnisalis, I., & Peristeras, V. (2022). Characteristics and challenges in the industries towards responsible AI: A systematic literature review. *Ethics and Information Technology, 24*(3), 37. doi:10.100710676-022-09634-1

Anantrasirichai, N., & Bull, D. (2022). Artificial intelligence in the creative industries: A review. *Artificial Intelligence Review, 55*(1), 589–656. doi:10.100710462-021-10039-7

Anderson, N., Belavy, D. L., Perle, S. M., Hendricks, S., Hespanhol, L., Verhagen, E., & Memon, A. R. (2023). AI did not write this manuscript, or did it? Can we trick the AI text detector into generated texts? The potential future of ChatGPT and AI in Sports & Exercise Medicine manuscript generation. *BMJ Open Sport & Exercise Medicine, 9*(1), e001568. doi:10.1136/bmjsem-2023-001568 PMID:36816423

Andersson, A. (2013). Choices, Interests, and Potentiality: What Distinguishes Bearers of Rights? *The Journal of Value Inquiry, 47*(3), 175–190. doi:10.100710790-013-9378-9

Andersson, A.-K. M. (2014). Capacities, Potentialities, and Rights. *Ethical Theory and Moral Practice, 17*(4), 653–665. doi:10.100710677-013-9463-y

Andersson, A.-K. M. (2015). Rights Bearers and Rights Functions. *Philosophical Studies, 172*(6), 1625–1646. doi:10.100711098-014-0368-y

Andrews, C. (2019). An embodied approach to AI art collaboration. In *Proceedings of the 2019 on Creativity and Cognition* (pp. 156-162). ACM. 10.1145/3325480.3325506

Andujar, A. (2016). Benefits of mobile instant messaging to develop ESL writing. *System, 62*, 63–76. doi:10.1016/j.system.2016.07.004

Angelone, A. M., Galassi, A., & Vittorini, P. (2022) Improved automated classification of sentences in data science exercises. In *Methodologies and Intelligent Systems for Technology Enhanced Learning, 11th International Conference*, (*vol. 11*, pp. 12–21). Springer. 10.1007/978-3-030-86618-1_2

Angert, T., Suzara, M. I., Han, J., Pondoc, C. L., & Subramonyam, H. (2023). Spellburst: A Node-based Interface for Exploratory Creative Coding with Natural Language Prompts. *arXiv preprint arXiv:2308.03921*. doi:10.1145/3586183.3606719

Angwin, J., Larson, J., Mattu, S., & Kirchner, L. (2016). Machine bias. In *Ethics of data and analytics* (pp. 254–264). Auerbach Publications.

Ansari, S. (2022). Recognizing the Risks of Job Automation in 2023. *HR Tech Series*. https://techrseries.com/ai-automation/recognizing-the-risks-of-job-automation-in-2023/

Ansari, T. (2022). How AI Transformed the Art World in 2022. *Analytics India Magazine (AIM)*. https://analyticsindiamag.com/how-ai-transformed-the-art-world-in-2022/

Anton, C. (2023). Probing CHAT GPT (sic): A media ecology writing sampler. *New Explorations. Studies in Culture and Communication, 3*(1).

Antony, J. S., Cauce, A. M., Gangone, L. M., & Nicola, T. P. (Eds.). (2022). *The College President Handbook: A Sustainable and Practical Guide for Emerging Leaders*. Harvard Education Press.

Aoun, J. E. (2017). *Robot-proof: higher education in the age of artificial intelligence*. MIT press. doi:10.7551/mitpress/11456.001.0001

APA. (2017). *Helping teachers manage stress*. APA. https://www.apa.org/topics/teacher-stress

Arbiza Goenaga, M. (2020). A critique of contemporary artificial intelligence art: Who is Edmond de Belamy? *AusArt Journal for Research in Art, 8*(1), 49–64. doi:10.1387/ausart.21490

Ariyo, O. (2022, June 28). AI Revolutionizes Content Generation and Written Communication. *The Cable*. https://www.thecable.ng/ai-revolutionizes-content-generation-and-written-communication

Arizona State University. (2023). *Wellness: Hey Sunny*. Hey Sunny. ASU. https://heysunny.asu.edu/wellness

Artut, S. (2019). Using a machine learning algorithm to create a computational artwork: Variable. *Athens Journal of Humanities & Arts, 6*(3), 173–182. doi:10.30958/ajha.6-3-1

AryaN. (2022). Industrial Revolution 4.0: Landscaping Trajectories of Technology–Humanity Interface. *Available at* SSRN 4119506. doi:10.2139/ssrn.4119506

Association of American Colleges and Universities. (2011). *The LEAP vision for learning: Outcomes, practices, impact, and employers' view*. Association of American Colleges and Universities.

Association of American Universities. (2021). *Pandemic and Its Impact on Higher Education*. Association of American Universities.

Atreides, K. (2023). *Automated bias and indoctrination at scale... is all you need*. Preprint.

Audry, S., & Ippolito, J. (2019, March). Can artificial intelligence make art without artists? Ask the viewer. In Arts (Vol. 8, p. 35). MDPI. doi:10.3390/arts8010035

Augmented Work for an Automated, AI-driven World. (2023). *IBM Institute for Business Value*. IBM. https://www.ibm.com/thought-leadership/institute-business-value/en-us/report/augmented-workforce

Ausat, A. M. A., Massang, B., Efendi, M., Nofirman, N., & Riady, Y. (2023). Can Chat GPT (sic) replace the role of the teacher in the classroom: A fundamental analysis. *Journal of Education, 5*(4), 16100–16106.

Ausat, A. M. A., Massang, B., Efendi, M., Nofirman, N., & Riady, Y. (2023). Can chat GPT replace the role of the teacher in the classroom: A fundamental analysis. *Journal of Education, 5*(4), 16100–16106. doi:10.31004/joe.v5i4.2745

Austin, J., Odena, A., Nye, M., Bosma, M., Michalewski, H., Dohan, D., & Sutton, C. (2021). Program synthesis with large language models. *arXiv preprint arXiv:2108.07732*.

Autor, D., & Dorn, D. (2013). The growth of low-skill service jobs and the polarization of the US labor market. *The American Economic Review*, *103*(5), 1553–1597. doi:10.1257/aer.103.5.1553

Aydın, Ö., & Karaarslan, E. (2023). Is ChatGPT leading generative AI? What is beyond expectations? *What is beyond expectations*, (pp. 1 – 23) SSRN.

AydınÖ.KaraarslanE. (2022). OpenAI ChatGPT generated literature review: Digital twin in healthcare. SSRN 4308687. doi:10.2139/ssrn.4308687

Azamfirei, R., Kudchadkar, S. R., & Fackler, J. (2023). Large language models and the perils of their hallucinations. *Critical Care*, *27*(1), 1–2. doi:10.118613054-023-04393-x PMID:36945051

Azvine, B., Djian, D., Tsui, K. C., & Wobcke, W. (2000). The intelligent assistant: An overview. In B. Azvine, D. D. Nauck, & N. Azarmi (Eds.), *Intelligent systems and soft computing: Prospects, tools and applications* (pp. 215–238). Springer-Verlag. doi:10.1007/10720181_9

Babitha, M. M., & Sushma, C. (2022). Trends of Artificial Intelligence for online exams in education. *International journal of Early Childhood special. Education*, *14*(01), 2457–2463.

Baccaglini-Frank, A. E., Funghi, S., Maracci, M., & Ramploud, A. (2023). Learning about multiplication by comparing algorithms: "One times one, but actually they are ten times ten". *The Journal of Mathematical Behavior*, *70*, 101024. doi:10.1016/j.jmathb.2022.101024

Bada, S. O., & Olusegun, S. (2015). Constructivism learning theory: A paradigm for teaching and learning. *Journal of Research & Method in Education*, *5*(6), 66–70.

Bae, S., Dong, Y., & Kwon, O. (2023). The effects of content creator, media richness, and content theme on learning performance: Focusing on ESG management education for Chinese employees. 글로벌경영학회지, *20*(1), 27–50. doi:10.38115/asgba.2023.20.1.27

Baek, J., Yoo, Y., Lee, K., Jung, B., & Baek, Y. (2017). Using an instant messenger to learn a foreign language in a peer-tutoring environment. *Turkish Online Journal of Educational Technology-TOJET*, *16*(2), 145–152.

Bailey, L. W. (2019). New technology for the classroom: Mobile devices, artificial intelligence, tutoring systems, and robotics. In *Educational Technology and the new world of persistent learning* (pp. 1–11). IGI Global. doi:10.4018/978-1-5225-6361-7.ch001

Bajohr, H. (2022). Algorithmic empathy: Toward a critique of aesthetic AI. *Configurations*, *30*(2), 203–231. doi:10.1353/con.2022.0011

Baker, R. S., & Hawn, A. (2022). Algorithmic Bias in Education. *International Journal of Artificial Intelligence in Education*, *32*(10), 1052–1092. doi:10.100740593-021-00285-9

Bakker, A. B., & Demerouti, E. (2017). Job demands-resources theory: Taking stock and looking forward. *Journal of Occupational Health Psychology*, *22*(3), 273–285. doi:10.1037/ocp0000056 PMID:27732008

Bakpayev, M., Baek, T. H., van Esch, P., and Yoon, S. (2022). Programmatic creative: Ai can think but it cannot feel. *Australasian Marketing Journal*, *30*(1), 90–95.

Bang, Y., Cahyawijaya, S., Lee, N., Dai, W., Su, D., Wilie, B., Lovenia, H., Ji, Z., Yu, T., & Chung, W. (2023) A multitask, multilingual, multimodal evaluation of chatgpt on reasoning, hallucination, and interactivity. arXiv preprint arXiv:2302.04023.

Bank of America. (2022). *Bank of America's Erica tops 1 billion client interactions, now nearly 1.5 million per day.* Newsroom. https://newsroom.bankofamerica.com/content/newsroom/press-releases/2022/10/bank-of-america-s-erica-tops-1-billion-client-interactions--now-.html

Banning, M. (2006). Measures that can be used to instill critical thinking skills in nurse prescribers. *Nurse Education in Practice*, *6*(2), 98–105. doi:10.1016/j.nepr.2005.10.001 PMID:19040862

Barchard, K. A. (2003). Does emotional intelligence assist in the prediction of academic success? *Educational and Psychological Measurement*, *63*(5), 840–858. doi:10.1177/0013164403251333

Bard (chatbot). (2023, June 7). Wikipedia. https://en.wikipedia.org/wiki/Bard_(chatbot)

Bard, A. M. (2022). *A Qualitative Phenomenological Study of Public School Teachers' Experiences While Teaching During a Pandemic* [Thesis, University of Georgia]. All Theses and Dissertations.

Barikeri, S., Lauscher, A., Vulić, I., & Glavaš, G. (2021). RedditBias: A real-world resource for bias evaluation and debiasing of conversational language models. *arXiv preprint arXiv:2106.03521*. doi:10.18653/v1/2021.acl-long.151

Bar-On, R., Brown, J. M., Kirkcaldy, B. D., & Thome, E. P. (2000). Emotional expression and implications for occupational stress; an application of the Emotional Quotient Inventory (EQ-i). *Personality and Individual Differences*, *28*(6), 1107–1118. doi:10.1016/S0191-8869(99)00160-9

Barthet, M., Khalifa, A., Liapis, A., & Yannakakis, G. (2022, September). Generative personas that behave and experience like humans. In *Proceedings of the 17th International Conference on the Foundations of Digital Games* (pp. 1-10). ACM. 10.1145/3555858.3555879

Bartolini, M. G., & Martignone, F. (2020). Manipulatives in mathematics education. In S. Learman (Ed.), *Encyclopedia of mathematics education* (pp. 487–494)., doi:10.1007/978-3-030-15789-0_93

Bashir. (2021). *Ai literacy: understanding shifts in our digital ecosystem* (1st ed.). New Degree Press.

Bates, T., Cobo, C., Mariño, O., & Wheeler, S. (2020). Can artificial intelligence transform higher education? *International Journal of Educational Technology in Higher Education*, *17*(1), 1–12. doi:10.118641239-020-00218-x

Baumeister, R. F., & Leary, M. R. (1995). The need to belong: Desire for interpersonal attachments as a fundamental human motivation. *Psychological Bulletin*, *117*(3), 497–529. doi:10.1037/0033-2909.117.3.497 PMID:7777651

BBC News. (2003). *Chatbot bids to fool humans*. BBC News. http://news.bbc.co.uk/2/hi/technology/3116780.stm

Beaudouin-Lafon, M., Bødker, S., & Mackay, W. E. (2021). Generative theories of interaction. [TOCHI]. *ACM Transactions on Computer-Human Interaction*, *28*(6), 1–54. doi:10.1145/3468505

BeerbaumD. O. (2023). Generative Artificial Intelligence (GAI) ethics taxonomy-Applying Chat GPT (sic) for robotic process automation (GAI-RPA) as business case. SSRN 4385025.

Behar-Horenstein, L. S., & Niu, L. (2011). Teaching critical thinking skills in higher education: A review of the literature. *Journal of College Teaching and Learning*, *8*(2), 25–42. doi:10.19030/tlc.v8i2.3554

Belda-Medina, J., & Calvo-Ferrer, J. R. (2022). Using chatbots as AI conversational partners in language learning. *Applied Sciences (Basel, Switzerland)*, *12*(17), 8427. doi:10.3390/app12178427

Bender, E. M., Gebru, T., McMillan-Major, A., & Shmitchell, S. (2021, March). On the dangers of stochastic parrots: Can language models be too big? In *Proceedings of the 2021 ACM conference on fairness, accountability, and transparency* (pp. 610-623). ACM. 10.1145/3442188.3445922

Benjamin, W. (1935, 2008). The work of art in the age of its technological reproducibility, and other writings on media. Harvard University Press.

Berg, J., Raj, M., & Seamans, R. (2023). Capturing value from artificial intelligence. *Academy of Management Discoveries*.

Berghel, H. (2023). ChatGPT and AIChat epistemology. *Computer*, *56*(05), 130–137. doi:10.1109/MC.2023.3252379

Berkeley, I. S. N. (2020). AI: A Crowd-Sourced Criterion. A Commentary on Pei Wang's Paper "On Defining Artificial Intelligence.". *Journal of Artificial General Intelligence*, *11*(2).

Berkeley, I. S. N., & Rice, C. (2013). Machine Mentality? In V. C. Müller (Ed.), *Philosophy and Theory of Artificial intelligence* (pp. 1–15). Springer. doi:10.1007/978-3-642-31674-6_1

Berry, D. M. (2022). AI, Ethics, and Digital Humanities. *The Bloomsbury Handbook to the Digital Humanities*, 445.

Beseiso, M., Alzubi, O. A., & Rashaideh, H. (2021). A novel automated essay scoring approach for reliable higher educational assessments. *Journal of Computing in Higher Education*, *33*(3), 727–746. doi:10.100712528-021-09283-1

Bettencourt, A., Gilman, R., Furlong, M., & Huebner, E. S. (2019). Teacher well-being: A review of the literature. *Teaching and Teacher Education*, *85*, 75–86. doi:10.1016/j.tate.2019.05.007

Bettin, J., & van Emde Boas, G. (2003, October). Generative model transformer. In *Companion of the 18th annual ACM SIGPLAN conference on Object-oriented programming, systems, languages, and applications* (pp. 88-89). ACM.

Bezruczko, N. (2019). Psychometric equating methods ease fitness function dilemma in generative art. *In the Proceedings of the 1XXII Generative Art Conference - GA 2019*. ACM.

Bhalla. (2019). The 3S Process: A Framework for Teaching AI Strategy in Business Education. *Technology Innovation Management Review*, *9*(12), 36–42. https://doi.org/ doi:10.22215/timreview/1290

Bii, P. (2013). Chatbot technology: A possible means of unlocking student potential to learn how to learn. *Educational Research*, *4*, 218–221.

Bilgram, V., & Laarmann, F. (2023). Accelerating innovation with generative AI: AI-augmented digital prototyping and innovation methods. *IEEE Engineering Management Review*, *51*(2), 1–5. doi:10.1109/EMR.2023.3272799

Birkle, C. (2022). "I, Robot": Artificial Intelligence and Fears of the Posthuman. *Artificial Intelligence and Human Enhancement: Affirmative and Critical Approaches in the Humanities*, *21*, 237–260. doi:10.1515/9783110770216-014

Bishop, W., & Starkey, D. (2006). Pedagogy. *Keywords in creative writing*, 119-125.

Biswas, S. (2023). *Prospective role of Chat GPT (sic) in the Military: According to ChatGPT*. Qeios.

Biswas, S. S. (2023). Role of Chat GPT (sic) in public health. *Annals of Biomedical Engineering*, 1–2.

Bitsch, G., Senjic, P., & Kneip, P. (2022, August). Hybrid individualized assistance-oriented learning system framework for STEM-Education. In *2022 IEEE German Education Conference (GeCon)* (pp. 1-5). IEEE. https://doi.org/10.1109/GeCon55699.2022.9942754

Blake, J. (2021). Scientific research articles: Twenty-two language errors to avoid. In G. Kurubacak-Meric & S. Sisman-Ugur (Eds.), *Improving scientific communication for lifelong learners* (pp. 195–219). IGI Global. doi:10.4018/978-1-7998-4534-8.ch011

Boden, M. A. (2004). *The Creative Mind: Myths and Mechanisms* (2nd ed.). Psychology Press. doi:10.4324/9780203508527

Boden, M. A., & Edmonds, E. A. (2009). What is generative art? *Digital Creativity (Exeter), 20*(1-2), 21–46. doi:10.1080/14626260902867915

Bogost, I. (2017). *Play Anything: The Pleasure of Limits, the Uses of Boredom, and the Secret of Games*. WW Norton & Company.

Bojorquez, H., & Vega, M. M. (2023). The Importance of Artificial Intelligence in Education for All Students. *IDRA Newsletter, L*(5).

Bordia, S., & Bowman, S. R. (2019). Identifying and reducing gender bias in word-level language models. *arXiv preprint arXiv:1904.03035*. doi:10.18653/v1/N19-3002

Bosma, R. J., Capucci, P. L., de Kerckhove, D., Neidich, W., & Cipolletta, L. G. (2022). *HumaniTies and Artificial Intelligence*.

Bouschery, S. G., Blazevic, V., & Piller, F. T. (2023). Augmenting human innovation teams with artificial intelligence: Exploring transformer-based language models. *Journal of Product Innovation Management, 40*(2), 139–153. doi:10.1111/jpim.12656

Bowles, D. C., & Kruger, J. S. (2023). Generating employable, intelligent graduates in a world with Generative AI: Thoughts for educators. *Pedagogy in Health Promotion, 9*(2), 75–77. doi:10.1177/23733799231175171

Boyé, P., Grba, D., Pandilovski, M., Kang, K. H., & Todorović, V. (2019). *Machine flaws in generative art*. In Lux Aeterna, ISEA2019 25th International Symposium on Electronic Art, Gwangju, Republic of Korea.

Božić, V. (2023). *Chat GPT and education*. Preprint.

Bozkurt, A. (2023). Speculative Futures on ChatGPT and Generative Artificial Intelligence (AI): A Collective Reflection from the Educational Landscape. *Asian Journal of Distance Education, 18*(1), 53–130. doi:10.5281/zenodo.7636568

Bozkurt, A., & Sharma, R. C. (2023). Generative AI and Prompt Engineering: The Art of Whispering to Let the Genie out of the Algorithmic World. *Asian Journal of Distance Education, 18*(2), i–vii. doi:10.5281/zenodo.8174941

Brachman, R. J. (2006). (AA)AI More than the Sum of Its Parts. *AI Magazine, 27*(4), 4. Advance online publication. doi:10.1609/aimag.v27i4.1907

Bragazzi, N. L., Dai, H., Damiani, G., Behzadifar, M., Martini, M., & Wu, J. (2020). How Big Data and Artificial Intelligence Can Help Better Manage the COVID-19 Pandemic. *International Journal of Environmental Research and Public Health, 17*(9), 3176. doi:10.3390/ijerph17093176 PMID:32370204

Braidwood, R. J. (1960). The agricultural revolution. *Scientific American, 203*(3), 130–152. doi:10.1038cientificamerican0960-130 PMID:13803774

Brainard, J. (2023). Journals take up arms against AI-written text. *Science, 379*(6634), 740–741. doi:10.1126cience.adh2762 PMID:36821673

Brandtzaeg, P. B., Skjuve, M., & Følstad, A. (2022). My AI friend: How users of a social chatbot understand their human–AI friendship. *Human Communication Research, 48*(3), 404–429. doi:10.1093/hcr/hqac008

Braun, G. (2023). *Towards Bridging Skill Gaps for the Future Industrial Workforce. Thesis for the Degree of Licenciature of Philosophy. Department of Industrial and Materials Science*. Chalmers University of Technology. https://research.chalmers.se/publication/537006/file/537006_Fulltext.pdf

Bredo, E. (1997). The social construction of learning. In G. D. Phye (Ed.), *Handbook of academic learning* (pp. 3–45). Academic Press., doi:10.1016/B978-012554255-5/50002-8

Brem, A., Viardot, E., & Nylund, P. A. (2021). Implications of the coronavirus (COVID-19) outbreak for innovation: Which technologies will improve our lives? *Technological Forecasting and Social Change*, *163*, 120451. doi:10.1016/j.techfore.2020.120451 PMID:33191956

Bridgelall, R. (2023). *Unraveling the mysteries of AI chatbots.*

Broeckmann, A. (2019, February). The machine as artist as myth. In Arts (Vol. 8, p. 25). MDPI. doi:10.3390/arts8010025

Broo, D. G., Kaynak, O., & Sait, S. M. (2022). Rethinking engineering education at the age of industry 5.0. *Journal of Industrial Information Integration*, *25*, 100311. doi:10.1016/j.jii.2021.100311

Brouwer, W. (2018). *Algorithmic Culture.* Palgrave Macmillan.

Browne, K. (2022). Who (or what) is an AI artist? *Leonardo*, *55*(2), 130–134. doi:10.1162/leon_a_02092

Brown, H., Lee, K., Mireshghallah, F., Shokri, R., & Tramèr, F. (2022) What does it mean for a language model to preserve privacy? In *2022 ACM Conference on Fairness, Accountability, and Transparency*, (pp. 2280–2292). ACM. 10.1145/3531146.3534642

Brownlee, J. (2019, June 17). *A gentle introduction to generative adversarial networks (GANs).* Machine Learning Mastery. https://machinelearningmastery.com/what-are-generative-adversarial-networks-gans/

Brown, P., & Gerbarg, P. L. (2015). Non-pharmacologic treatments for psychiatric conditions: Yoga and mindfulness meditation. *Psychiatric Annals*, *45*(7), 434–439. doi:10.3928/00485713-20150610-05

Brown, T., Mann, B., Ryder, N., Subbiah, M., Kaplan, J. D., Dhariwal, P., & Amodei, D. (2020). Language models are few-shot learners. *Advances in Neural Information Processing Systems*, *33*, 1877–1901.

Bryant, J., Ram, S., Scott, D., & Williams, C. (2023, March 2). *K–12 teachers are quitting. what would make them stay?* McKinsey & Company. https://www.mckinsey.com/industries/education/our-insights/k-12-teachers-are-quitting-what-would-make-them-stay#/

Bryman, A. (2012). *Social Research Methods.* OUP Oxford.

Bryson, J. B., & Morrison, R. G. (1994). What should the learning sciences be about? In D. Schifter & B. J. Balamuth (Eds.), *Learner-centered Theory and Practice in Distance Education* (pp. 17–41). Routledge.

Buchanan, A. L. and Herubel, J.-P. V. (1993). Comparing materials used in philosophy and political science dissertations: A technical note. *Behavioral & Social Sciences Librarian, 12*(2), 63–70.

Budescu, D. V., Broomell, S. B., & Por, H. H. (2009). Improving Communication of Uncertainty in Forecasts of Natural Hazards. Wea. *Forecasting, 24,* 1140-1150. doi: . doi:10.1175/2009wfo2063.1

Budzianowski, P., & Vulić, I. (2019). Hello, it's GPT-2—how can I help you? Towards the use of pretrained language models for task-oriented dialogue systems. *arXiv preprint arXiv:1907.05774.* doi:10.18653/v1/D19-5602

Bühler, M. M., Jelinek, T., & Nübel, K. (2022). Training and Preparing Tomorrow's Workforce for the Fourth Industrial Revolution. *Education Sciences, 12*(11), 782.

Bull, C., & Kharrufa, A. (2023). Generative AI assistants in software development education. *arXiv preprint arXiv:2303.13936.* 1 - 9.

Bulut, O., & Yildirim-Erbasli, S. N. (2022). Automatic story and item generation for reading comprehension assessments with transformers. *International Journal of Assessment Tools in Education*, *9*(Special Issue), 72–87. doi:10.21449/ijate.1124382

Buolamwini, J., & Gebru, T. (2018). Gender shades: Intersectional accuracy disparities in commercial gender classification. In *Conference on fairness, accountability, and transparency* (pp. 77–91). PMLR.

Burbules, N. C., Fan, G., & Repp, P. (2020). Five trends of education and technology in a sustainable future. *Geography and Sustainability, 1*(2), 93–97. doi:10.1016/j.geosus.2020.05.001

Cabrera, D., & Sádaba, C. (2017). Emotional intelligence and academic achievement: The role of emotional self-efficacy and emotion regulation strategies. *Psicothema, 29*(3), 294–301.

Cai, C. J., Winter, S., Steiner, D., Wilcox, L., & Terry, M. (2019). "Hello AI": uncovering the onboarding needs of medical practitioners for human-AI collaborative decision-making. *Proceedings of the ACM on Human-computer Interaction, 3*(CSCW), (pp. 1-24). ACM. 10.1145/3359206

Caines, A., Benedetto, L., Taslimipoor, S., Davis, C., Gao, Y., Andersen, O., Yuan, Z., Elliott, M., Moore, R., Bryant, C., Rei, M., Mullooly, A., Nicholls, D., & Buttery, P. (2023) On the application of large language models for language teaching and assessment technology. In AIED Workshops. AIED.

Çakmak, F. (2022). Chatbot-human interaction and its effects on EFL students' L2 speaking performance and anxiety. [Research on Youth and Language]. *Novitas-ROYAL, 16*(2), 113–131.

California Department of Education. (2017). *Family engagement toolkit: Continuous improvement through an equity lens*. CA DoE. https://www.cde.ca.gov/fg/aa/lc/documents/family-engagement.pdf

California State University at Northridge. (2023). *CSUNny program summary and outcomes*. https://edtechmagazine.com/higher/sites/edtechmagazine.com.higher/files/CSUNny%20data.pdf

California State University at San Bernardino. (2023). *Ask Cody*. CSU. https://www.csusb.edu/its/support/digital-transformation/chatbot

Cameron, M., Fogarty-Perry, B., & Piercy, G. (2022). The impacts of the COVID-19 pandemic on higher education students in New Zealand. *Journal of Open. Flexible and Distance Learning, 26*(1), 42–62. doi:10.61468/jofdl.v26i1.515

Canadian Teachers' Federation. (2018a). *A survey on the status of teacher mental health in Canada*. CTF. https://www.ctf-fce.ca/en/Pages/Issues/Health-and-Safety/Mental-Health.aspx

Canadian Teachers' Federation. (2018b). *National Teacher Workload Study*. CTF. https://www.ctf-fce.ca/en/Pages/Issues/Workload/National-Teacher-Workload-Study.aspx

Canadian Teachers' Federation. (2018c). *The realities of teacher workload*. CTF. https://www.ctf-fce.ca/en/Pages/Issues/Workload.aspx

Canadian Teachers' Federation. (2019). *Teachers' mental health and well-being: A survey of Canadian teachers*. CTF. https://www.ctf-fce.ca/en/research/mental-health-and-well-being/

Candy, L. (2020). Creating with the digital: tool, medium, mediator, partner. In *Interactivity, Game Creation, Design, Learning, and Innovation: 8th EAI International Conference, ArtsIT 2019, and 4th EAI International Conference*. Springer.

Cao, Y., Li, S., Liu, Y., Yan, Z., Dai, Y., Yu, P. S., & Sun, L. (2023). A comprehensive survey of AI-Generated Content (AIGC): A history of generative AI from GAN to ChatGPT. *arXiv preprint arXiv:2303.04226.*

Caramiaux, B., & Alaoui, S. (2022). "Explorers of unknown planets": Practices and politics of artificial intelligence in visual arts. *Proceedings of the ACM on Human-Computer Interaction, 6*(CSCW2), (pp. 1-24). ACM. 10.1145/3555578

Caramiaux, B., & Fdili Alaoui, S. (2022). " Explorers of Unknown Planets" Practices and politics of artificial Intelligence in visual arts. *Proceedings of the ACM on Human-Computer Interaction, 6*(CSCW2). ACM.

Caramiaux, B., Alaoui, S. F., & Hsueh, S. (2022, April). What becomes of "work" in AI "artwork"? In *CHI'22 Conference-Workshop on Outsourcing Artificial Intelligence*. Responding to the Reassertion of the Human Element into Automation.

Caramiaux, B., Alaoui, S. F., & Hsueh, S. (2022, April). What becomes of" work" in AI" artwork"? In *CHI'22 Conference-Workshop on Outsourcing Artificial Intelligence* (pp. 1–3). Responding to the Reassertion of the Human Element into Automation.

Cardon, P. W., Getchell, K., Carradini, S., Fleischmann, C., & Stapp, J. (2023). *Generative AI in the workplace: Employee perspectives of ChatGPT benefits and organizational policies*, (pp. 1 – 17). OSF.

Carlini, N., Ippolito, D., Jagielski, M., Lee, K., Tramer, F., & Zhang, C. (2022). Quantifying memorization across neural language models. *arXiv preprint arXiv:2202.07646.*

Carlini, N., Tramer, F., Wallace, E., Jagielski, M., Herbert-Voss, A., Lee, K., & Raffel, C. (2021, August). Extracting training data from large language models. In *USENIX Security Symposium* (Vol. 6). 2633 - 2650.

Carnap, R. (1950). *Logical Foundations of Probability*. Chicago University of Chicago Press.

Carr, S. B., Johnson, N., & Bush, L. (2017). Distributed cognition: Teachers' perceptions and implications for learning outcomes and instructional technology. In Educational leadership and administration: Concepts, methodologies, tools, and applications (pp. 863-893). IGI Global. doi:10.4018/978-1-5225-1624-8.ch042

Carroll, A., Forrest, K., Sanders-O'Connor, E., Flynn, L., Bower, J. M., Fynes-Clinton, S., York, A., & Ziaei, M. (2022). Teacher stress and burnout in australia: Examining the role of intrapersonal and environmental factors. *Social Psychology of Education*, *25*(2-3), 441–469. doi:10.100711218-022-09686-7 PMID:35233183

Carroll, J. M. (2000). *Making use: Scenario-based design of human-computer interactions*. MIT press.

Carvalhais, M. (2019). Breaking the black box: Procedural reading, creation of meaning and closure in computational artworks. In P. Machado, J. Romero, and G. Greenfield's *Artificial Intelligence and the Arts: Computational Creativity, Artistic Behavior, and Tools for Creatives*. Research Gate.

Carvalhais, M., & Lee, R. (2022). Spectral and procedural creativity: A perspective from computational art. *Transformations (14443775)*, (36).

Carvalho, D. V., Pereira, E. M., & Cardoso, J. S. (2019). Machine learning interpretability: A survey on methods and metrics. *Electronics (Basel)*, *8*(8), 832. doi:10.3390/electronics8080832

Carvalho, L., Martinez-Maldonado, R., Tsai, Y. S., Markauskaite, L., & De Laat, M. (2022). How can we design for learning in an AI world? *Computers and Education: Artificial Intelligence*, *3*, 100053. doi:10.1016/j.caeai.2022.100053

Castellanos, C. (2022). Intersections of living and machine agencies: Possibilities for creative AI. In *The Language of Creative AI: Practices, Aesthetics and Structures* (pp. 155–166). Springer International Publishing. doi:10.1007/978-3-031-10960-7_9

Castells, M. (2010). The Information Age. *Media Studies. REAd (Porto Alegre)*, *2*(7), 152.

Cath, C., Wachter, S., Mittelstadt, B., Taddeo, M., & Floridi, L. (2018). Artificial intelligence and the 'good society': The US, EU, and UK approach. *Science and Engineering Ethics*, *24*, 505–528. PMID:28353045

Cetinic, E., & She, J. (2022). Understanding and creating art with AI: Review and outlook. [TOMM]. *ACM Transactions on Multimedia Computing Communications and Applications*, *18*(2), 1–22. doi:10.1145/3475799

Chaka, C. (2023). Detecting ai content in responses generated by chatgpt, youchat, and chatsonic: The case of five ai content detection tools. *Journal of Applied Learning and Teaching*, *6*(2), 6.

Challen, R., Denny, J., Pitt, M., Gompels, L., Edwards, T., & Tsaneva-Atanasova, K. (2019). Artificial intelligence, bias and clinical safety. *BMJ Quality & Safety, 28*(3), 231–237. 10.1136/bmjqs-2018-008370

Chan, C. K. Y., & Hu, W. (2023). Students' voices on generative AI: Perceptions, benefits, and challenges in higher education. *arXiv preprint arXiv:2305.00290.*

Chaudhry, M. A., Cukurova, M., & Luckin, R. (2022) A transparency index framework for ai in education. In *Artificial Intelligence in Education. Posters and Late Breaking Results, Workshops and Tutorials, Industry and Innovation Tracks, Practitioners' and Doctoral Consortium: 23rd International Conference, AIED 2022.* Springer. 10.1007/978-3-031-11647-6_33

Chechitelli, A. (2023) *Ai writing detection update from turnitin's chief product officer.* TurnItIn. https://www.turnitin.com/blog/aiwriting-detection-update-from-turnitins-chief-product-officer.

Chen, K., Shao, A., Burapacheep, J., & Li, Y. (2023). How GPT-3 responds to different publics on climate change and Black Lives Matter: A critical appraisal of equity in conversational AI. *arXiv preprint arXiv:2209.13627.* 1 – 16.

Chen, M., Tworek, J., Jun, H., Yuan, Q., Pinto, H. P. D. O., Kaplan, J., & Zaremba, W. (2021). Evaluating large language models trained on code. *arXiv preprint arXiv:2107.03374.*

Chen, W., Grangier, D., & Auli, M. (2015). Strategies for training large vocabulary neural language models. *arXiv preprint arXiv:1512.04906.*

Chen, Z., Chen, L., Zhao, Z., & Wang, Y. (2020, July). AI illustrator: Art illustration generation based on generative adversarial network. In *2020 IEEE 5th International Conference on Image, Vision and Computing (ICIVC)* (pp. 155-159). IEEE.

Cheng, M. (2022, April). The creativity of artificial intelligence in art. In Proceedings (Vol. 81, pp. 110-1 to 110-5). MDPI. doi:10.3390/proceedings2022081110

Chen, L., Chen, P., & Lin, Z. (2020). Artificial Intelligence in Education: A Review. *IEEE Access : Practical Innovations, Open Solutions, 8*, 75264–75278. doi:10.1109/ACCESS.2020.2988510

Chen, W., Shidujaman, M., Jin, J., & Ahmed, S. U. (2020). A methodological approach to create interactive art in artificial intelligence. In *HCI International 2020–Late Breaking Papers: Cognition, Learning and Games: 22nd HCI International Conference.* Springer.

Chen, X., Xie, H., Zou, D., & Hwang, G.-J. (2020). Application and theory gaps during the rise of Artificial Intelligence in Education. *Computers and Education: Artificial Intelligence, 1*, 100002. doi:10.1016/j.caeai.2020.100002

Chen, Y., Jensen, S., Albert, L. J., Gupta, S., & Lee, T. (2023). Artificial intelligence (AI) student assistants in the classroom: Designing chatbots to support student success. *Information Systems Frontiers, 25*(1), 161-182.

Chi, N., Lurie, E., & Mulligan, D. K. (2021, July). Reconfiguring diversity and inclusion for AI ethics. In *Proceedings of the 2021 AAAI/ACM Conference on AI, Ethics, and Society* (pp. 447-457). ACM. 10.1145/3461702.3462622

Chin, H., Lima, G., Shin, M., Zhunis, A., Cha, C., Choi, J., & Cha, M. (2023). User-chatbot conversations during the COVID-19 pandemic: Study based on topic modeling and sentiment analysis. *Journal of Medical Internet Research, 25*, 1–16. doi:10.2196/40922 PMID:36596214

Choi, S. K., DiPaola, S., & Töyrylä, H. (2021). Artistic style meets artificial intelligence. *Journal of Perceptual Imaging.*

Choi, H., & Park, M. J. (2023, August 08). Choi, & Park, M. J. (2023). To govern or be governed: An integrated framework for AI governance in the public sector. *Science & Public Policy*, scad045. doi:10.1093cipolcad045

Choi, S. K., DiPaola, S., & Töyrylä, H. (2021). Artistic style meets artificial intelligence. *Journal of Perceptual Imaging, 4*(2), 020501-1, 020501-14. doi:10.2352/J.Percept.Imaging.2021.4.2.020501

Chow, B., & Perrigo, B. (n.d.). The AI arms race is on. Start worrying. *Times.* https://time.com/6255952/ai-impact-chatgpt-microsoft-google/

Chu, M. (2018). The role of emotions in creative problem solving. Emotion Review, 10(3), 229–237

Chung, J. J. Y., Chang, M., & Adar, E. (2021). Gestural inputs as control interaction for generative human-AI co-creation. In *Workshops at the International Conference on Intelligent User Interfaces (IUI).* CEUR-WS.

Chung, J. J. Y., Kim, W., Yoo, K. M., Lee, H., Adar, E., & Chang, M. (2022, April). TaleBrush: Sketching stories with generative pretrained language models. In *Proceedings of the 2022 CHI Conference on Human Factors in Computing Systems* (pp. 1-19). ACM. 10.1145/3491102.3501819

Cingel, D. P., & Sundar, S. S. (2012). Texting, techspeak, and tweens: The relationship between text messaging and English grammar skills. *New Media & Society, 14*(8), 1304–1320. doi:10.1177/1461444812442927

Ciolacu, M. I., Mihailescu, B., Rachbauer, T., Hansen, C., Amza, C. G., & Svasta, P. (2023). Fostering Engineering Education 4.0 Paradigm Facing the Pandemic and VUCA World. *Procedia Computer Science, 217*, 177–186. doi:10.1016/j.procs.2022.12.213

Clément, E. (2022). Successful Solution Discovery and Cognitive Flexibility. *Cognitive Flexibility: The Cornerstone of Learning*, (pp. 113-142). IEEE.

Coeckelbergh, M. (2020). *Ai Ethics.* The MIT Press. doi:10.7551/mitpress/12549.001.0001

Cohen, H. (1974, reprinted 2022). On purpose: an enquiry into the possible roles of the computer in art. In The Language of Creative AI: Practices, Aesthetics and Structures (pp. 3-27). Cham: Springer International Publishing.

Cohen, H., Nake, F., Brown, D. C., Brown, P., Galanter, P., McCormack, J., & d 'Inverno, M. (2012). Evaluation of creative aesthetics. *Computers and creativity*, 95-111.

Colby, K. M. (1981). PARRYing. *Behavioral and Brain Sciences, 4*(4), 550–560. doi:10.1017/S0140525X00000224

College Rover. (2023). *Exploring the impact of college rankings on student perceptions.* College Rover. https://collegerover.com/campus-library/news/1/exploring-the-impact-of-college-rankings-on-student-perceptions

Columbia University. (n.d.). *Feedback for Learning.* Columbia Center for Teaching and Learning. https://ctl.columbia.edu/resources-and-technology/resources/feedback-for-learning/

Condor, A., Litster, M., & Pardos, Z. (2021). *Automatic short answer grading with sbert on out-of-sample questions.* International Educational Data Mining Society.

Confino, P. (2023, July 19). Over just a few months, ChatGPT went from correctly answering a simple math problem 98% of the time to just 2%, study finds. *YahooFinance.* https://finance.yahoo.com/news/over-just-few-months-chatgpt-232905189.html

Coniam, D. (2008). Evaluating the language resources of chatbots for their potential in English as a second language. *ReCALL, 20*(1), 98–116. doi:10.1017/S0958344008000815

Coniam, D. (2014). The linguistic accuracy of chatbots: Usability from an ESL perspective. *Text & Talk, 34*(5), 545–567. doi:10.1515/text-2014-0018

Cooper, T. (2022). *Ancestors and Algorithms: Ethnocomputing AI with African & African Diasporic Heritage.* [Doctoral dissertation, University of Michigan].

Côté, A. M., Togay, G., & Su, Z. (2022). The Impact of Artificial Intelligence on Higher Education: Transformations, Challenges and Opportunities. *Challenges and Opportunities*. Europe PMC.

Cotton, D. R., Cotton, P. A., & Shipway, J. R. (2023). Chatting and cheating: Ensuring academic integrity in the era of chatgpt. Innovations in Education and Teaching International.

Cotton, D. R., Cotton, P. A., & Shipway, J. R. (2023). Chatting and cheating: Ensuring academic integrity in the era of ChatGPT. *Innovations in Education and Teaching International*, 1–12. doi:10.1080/14703297.2023.2190148

Courtney, E. (2021). *Opinion: The Fundamental under-funding of Public Schools*. The Knight Crier. https://www.knight-crier.org/opinion/2021/11/14/opinion-the-fundamental-under-funding-of-public-schools/#:~:text=According%20to%20the%20Century%20Foundation,achieve%20a%20flourishing%20school%20year

Couzin-Frankel, J. (2019). Medicine contends with how to use artificial intelligence. *Science, 364*(6446), 1119–1120. doi:10.1126cience.364.6446.1119 PMID:31221837

Crawford, J., Cowling, M., & Allen, K. A. (2023). Leadership is needed for ethical ChatGPT: Character, assessment, and learning using artificial intelligence (AI). *Journal of University Teaching & Learning Practice, 20*(3), 02.

Cremer, C. Z. (2021). Deep limitations? Examining expert disagreement over deep learning. *Progress in Artificial Intelligence, 10*(4), 449–464. doi:10.100713748-021-00239-1

Crompton, H., & Burke, D. (2023). Artificial intelligence in higher education: The state of the field. *International Journal of Educational Technology in Higher Education, 20*(1), 1–22. doi:10.118641239-023-00392-8

Crossley, M., & Tikly, L. (2004). Postcolonial perspectives and comparative and international research in education: A critical introduction. *Comparative education, 40*(2), 147-156.

da Silva, B. D. (2001). A Tecnologia é uma Estratégia. In P. Dias (Ed.), *Varela de Freitas (org.). Actas da II Conferência Internacional Desafios 2001* (pp. 839–859). Centro de Competência da Universidade do Minho do Projecto Nónio.

Dafoe, T. (2019, June 24). Law: A judge has rejected a $20 million lawsuit by a former studio assistant who claims famed sculptor Dale Chihuly didn't properly credit his work. *Artnet News*. https://news.artnet.com/art-world/dale-chihuly-lawsuit-dismissed-1582921

Daggett, W. R. (2010). Preparing students for their technological future. *International Center for Leadership in Education*. Citeseer. https://citeseerx.ist.psu.edu/document?repid=rep1&type=pdf&doi=ce1172bff72313a336f997efb0dd7137dc0f9a97

Dahlstedt, P. (2021). Musicking with algorithms: Thoughts on artificial intelligence, creativity, and agency. Handbook of Artificial Intelligence for Music: Foundations, Advanced Approaches, and Developments for Creativity, 873-914.

Dai, W., Lin, J., Jin, F., Li, T., Tsai, Y.-S., Gasevic, D., and Chen, G. (2023). *Can large language models provide feedback to students?* OSF.

Damasio, A. R. (1998). Emotion in the perspective of an integrated nervous system. *Brain Research. Brain Research Reviews, 26*(2-3), 83–86. doi:10.1016/S0165-0173(97)00064-7 PMID:9651488

Damasio, A. R. (2001). Emotion and the human brain. *Annals of the New York Academy of Sciences, 935*(1), 101–106. doi:10.1111/j.1749-6632.2001.tb03475.x PMID:11411179

Daniele, A., Di Bernardi Luft, C., & Bryan-Kinns, N. (2021). "What is human?" A Turing Test for artistic creativity. In *Artificial Intelligence in Music, Sound, Art and Design: 10th International Conference, EvoMUSART 2021, Held as Part of EvoStar 2021, Virtual Event, April 7–9, 2021* [Springer International Publishing.]. *Proceedings, 10*, 396–411.

Daniele, A., & Song, Y. Z. (2019, January). AI+ art=human. In *Proceedings of the 2019 AAAI/ACM Conference on AI, Ethics, and Society* (pp. 155-161). ACM. 10.1145/3306618.3314233

Danziger, K. (1997). Naming the Mind: How Psychology Found its. *Language*. doi:10.4135/9781446221815

Dash, S., Shakyawar, S. K., Sharma, M., & Kaushik, S. (2019). Big data in healthcare: Management, analysis and future prospects. *Journal of Big Data, 6*(1), 54. doi:10.118640537-019-0217-0

Dastin, J. (2018, October 10). *Amazon scraps secret AI recruiting tool that showed bias against women.* Reuters. https://www.reuters.com/article/us-amazon-com-jobs-automation-insight-idUSKCN1MK08G

Dathathri, S., Madotto, A., Lan, J., Hung, J., Frank, E., Molino, P., & Liu, R. (2019). Plug and play language models: A simple approach to controlled text generation. *arXiv preprint arXiv:1912.02164.*

Datta, D., Phillips, M., Bywater, J. P., Lilly, S., Chiu, J., Watson, G. S., & Brown, D. E. (2022). Human-in-the-loop data collection and evaluation for improving mathematical conversations. In *International conference on artificial intelligence in education*, (pp. 551–554). Springer. 10.1007/978-3-031-11647-6_113

Datta, T., & Dickerson, J. P. (2023). Who's thinking? A push for human-centered evaluation of LLMs using the XAI playbook. *arXiv preprint arXiv:2303.06223.*

Davis, N., Hsiao, C. P., Popova, Y., & Magerko, B. (2015). An enactive model of creativity for computational collaboration and co-creation. *Creativity in the digital age*, 109-133.

Dawa, T., Dhendup, S., Tashi, S., & Rosso, M. A. (2023). *Technology literacies and Chat GPT (sic): Perspectives on emerging technology adoption in academic writing*. Preprint.

De Freitas, S., & Neumann, T. (2009). The use of 'exploratory learning' for supporting immersive learning in virtual environments. *Computers & Education, 52*(2), 343–352. doi:10.1016/j.compedu.2008.09.010

De Jong, T., & Van Joolingen, W. R. (1998). Scientific discovery learning with computer simulations of conceptual domains. *Review of Educational Research, 68*(2), 179–201. doi:10.3102/00346543068002179

De Mul, J. (2009). The work of art in the age of digital recombination. *Digital Material, 95.*

De Smedt, T., & Lechat, L. Burtenshaw, & Nijs, L. (2021). Case studies in computer graphics and AI. In P. Machado, J. Romero, and G. Greenfield's Artificial Intelligence and the Arts: Computational Creativity, Artistic Behavior, and Tools for Creatives, (pp. 165 – 185). ACM.

De Vries, J. (1994). The industrial revolution and the industrious revolution. *The Journal of Economic History, 54*(2), 249–270. doi:10.1017/S0022050700014467

Deane, P. M. (1979). *The first industrial revolution.* Cambridge University Press.

Deci, E. L., & Ryan, R. M. (2000). The "what" and "why" of goal pursuits: Human needs and the self-determination of behavior. *Psychological Inquiry, 11*(4), 227–268. doi:10.1207/S15327965PLI1104_01

DeepDream. (2023, Sept. 18). Wikipedia. https://en.wikipedia.org/wiki/DeepDream

DelSignore, P. (2022). The New Age of Creative AI Began in 2022. *Medium.* https://medium.com/predict/the-new-age-of-creative-ai-began-in-2022-ece07bb93350

Department of Education, England. (2013). *Primary national curriculum.* DoE England. https://assets.publishing.service.gov.uk/government/uploads/system/uploads/attachment_data/file/425601/PRIMARY_national_curriculum.pdf

Dergaa, I., Chamari, K., Zmijewski, P., & Saad, H. B. (2023). From human writing to artificial intelligence generated text: Examining the prospects and potential threats of ChatGPT in academic writing. *Biology of Sport, 40*(2), 615–622. doi:10.5114/biolsport.2023.125623 PMID:37077800

Derounian, J. (2011). Shall we dance? the importance of staff-student relationships to undergraduate dissertation preparation. *Active Learning in Higher Education, 12*(2), 91–100.

Detweiler, R. A. (2021). *The Evidence Liberal Arts Needs: Lives of Consequence, Inquiry, and Accomplishment.* MIT Press. doi:10.7551/mitpress/13954.001.0001

Devendorf, L. (2014). Art making and making artists. *In Proceedings of the 2014 companion publication on Designing interactive systems* (pp. 151-156). ACM. 10.1145/2598784.2598787

Devlin, H. (2023, July 7). AI likely to spell end of traditional school classroom, leading expert says. *The Guardian.* https://www.theguardian.com/technology/2023/jul/07/ai-likely-to-spell-end-of-traditional-school-classroom-leading-expert-says

Dewey, J. (1979). **Experiência e Educação.** *3.* Companhia Editora Nacional. [Translation: Anísio Teixeira]

Diakopoulos, N. (2014). *Algorithmic accountability reporting: On the investigation of black boxes.* Columbia University.

Diakopoulos, N. (2019). *Automating the news: How algorithms are rewriting the media.* Harvard University Press. doi:10.4159/9780674239302

DiPaola, S., & McCaig, G. (2016). Using artificial intelligence techniques to emulate the creativity of a portrait painter. *Electronic Visualisation and the Arts*, 158-165.

DiPaola, S., Gabora, L., & McCaig, G. (2018). Informing artificial intelligence generative techniques using cognitive theories of human creativity. *Procedia Computer Science, 145*, 158–168. doi:10.1016/j.procs.2018.11.024

Dobbs, T., Benedict, A., & Ras, Z. (2022). Jumping into the artistic deep end: Building the catalogue raisonné. *AI & Society, 37*(3), 873–889. doi:10.100700146-021-01370-2

Doi, C., Lucky, S., & Rubin, J. E. (2022). Open educational resources in the time of COVID-19: Two case studies of open video design in the remote learning environment. *KULA, 6*(1), 1–15.

Dorin, A. (2008). A survey of virtual ecosystems in generative electronic art. *The Art of Artificial Evolution: A Handbook on Evolutionary Art and Music*, 289-309.

Dorin, A., McCabe, J., McCormack, J., Monro, G., & Whitelaw, M. (2012). A framework for understanding generative art. *Digital Creativity (Exeter), 23*(3-4), 239–259. doi:10.1080/14626268.2012.709940

Downes, S. (2022). Connectivism. *Asian Journal of Distance Education, 17*(1). https://asianjde.com/ojs/index.php/AsianJDE/article/view/623

Doyle, W., & Ponder, G. A. (1977). The practicality ethic in teacher decision-making. *Interchange (Washington, D.C.), 8*, 1–12.

Drori, I., Zhang, S., Shuttleworth, R., Tang, L., Lu, A., Ke, E., Liu, K., Chen, L., Tran, S., Cheng, N. et al. (2022) *A neural network solves, explains, and generates university math problems by program synthesis and few-shot learning at human level.*

Duerr, S., & Gloor, P. A. (2021). Persuasive natural language generation—A literature review. *arXiv preprint arXiv:2101.05786*. 1 - 17.

Dwivedi, Y. K., Kshetri, N., Hughes, L., Slade, E. L., Jeyaraj, A., Kar, A. K., Baabdullah, A. M., Koohang, A., Raghavan, V., Ahuja, M., Albanna, H., Albashrawi, M. A., Al-Busaidi, A. S., Balakrishnan, J., Barlette, Y., Basu, S., Bose, I., Brooks, L., Buhalis, D., & Wright, R. (2023). "So what if ChatGPT wrote it?" Multidisciplinary perspectives on opportunities, challenges and implications of generative conversational AI for research, practice and policy. *International Journal of Information Management*, *71*, 102642. doi:10.1016/j.ijinfomgt.2023.102642

Dziri, N., Madotto, A., Zaiane, O., & Bose, A. J. (2021). Neural path hunter: Reducing hallucination in dialogue systems via path grounding. *arXiv preprint arXiv:2104.08455*. doi:10.18653/v1/2021.emnlp-main.168

Eagle, N., & Greene, K. (2014). *Reality Mining: Using Big Data to Engineer a Better World*. MIT Press.

Eastman, E. H. (n.d.). *Implementing Adaptive Feedback For Mathematics*. SMORE. https://www.smore.com/dw2gm-think-through-math

Edmonds, E. (2018, January). Algorithmic art machines. In Arts (Vol. 7, p. 3). MDPI. doi:10.3390/arts7010003

Edmonds, E. (2022). AI, creativity, and art. In *The Language of Creative AI: Practices, Aesthetics and Structures* (pp. 57–71). Springer International Publishing. doi:10.1007/978-3-031-10960-7_4

EdTech. (2020). Successful AI examples in higher education that can inspire our future. *Ed Tech Magazine*. https://edtechmagazine.com/higher/article/2020/01/successful-ai-examples-higher-education-can-inspire-our-future

Education.sa.gov.au. (2023). *Artificial intelligence (AI) in schools – information for parents and carers*. SA. https://www.education.sa.gov.au/parents-and-families/curriculum-and-learning/ai

Edwards, B. I., & Cheok, A. D. (2018). Why not robot teachers: Artificial intelligence for addressing teacher shortage. *Applied Artificial Intelligence*, *32*(4), 345–360. doi:10.1080/08839514.2018.1464286

Eger, J. (2022). *Untold Power: The Marriage of Art and Technology*. Common Ground Research Networks. doi:10.18848/978-0-949313-04-1/CGP

Ehsan, U., Liao, Q. V., Muller, M., Riedl, M. O., & Weisz, J. D. (2021). Expanding explainability: Towards social transparency in AI systems. In *Proceedings of the 2021 CHI Conference on Human Factors in Computing Systems* (pp. 1–19). ACM. 10.1145/3411764.3445188

Eisenmann, J. (2021). Setting the stage for 3D compositing with machine learning. In P. Machado, J. Romero, and G. Greenfield's Artificial Intelligence and the Arts: Computational Creativity, Artistic Behavior, and Tools for Creatives, (pp. 187 – 205). Research Gate.

Eke, D. O. (2023). ChatGPT and the rise of generative AI: Threat to academic integrity? *Journal of Responsible Technology*, *13*, 1–4. doi:10.1016/j.jrt.2023.100060

El Emam, K., Jonker, E., & Wagner, C. (2012). Protecting privacy in secondary use of health data: An exploration of global data access policies. *Journal of Medical Internet Research*, *14*(2), e48. doi:10.2196/jmir.1869 PMID:22547528

Elkins, K., & Chun, J. (2020). Can GPT-3 pass a writer's Turing Test? *Journal of Cultural Analytics*, *5*(2), 1–16. doi:10.22148/001c.17212

Elmoutanna, N. & Moti, N. (2022). Soft skills from university to workplace: A literature review. *International Journal of Accounting, Finance, Auditing, Management and Economics*, *3*(5-1), 187-198.

Eloundou, T., Manning, S., Mishkin, P., & Rock, D. (2023). GPTs are GPTs: An early look at the labor market impact potential of large language models. *arXiv preprint arXiv:2303.10130.*

El-Zanfaly, D., Huang, Y., & Dong, Y. (2023, July). Sand-in-the-loop: Investigating embodied co-creation for shared understandings of generative AI. In *Companion Publication of the 2023 ACM Designing Interactive Systems Conference* (pp. 256-260).

Epstein, Z., Hertzmann, A., Herman, L., Mahari, R., Frank, M. R., Groh, M., & Russakovsky, O. (2023). Art and the science of generative AI: A deeper dive. *arXiv preprint arXiv:2306.04141.*

Epstein, Z., Levine, S., Rand, D. G., & Rahwan, I. (2020). Who gets credit for ai-generated art? *iScience*, *23*(9), 101515. doi:10.1016/j.isci.2020.101515 PMID:32920489

Ermakova, E. P., & Frolova, E. E. (2021). Using Artificial Intelligence in Dispute Resolution. In *Smart Technologies for the Digitisation of Industry: Entrepreneurial Environment* (pp. 131–142). Springer Singapore.

Ernst, H. (2023). *Artificial: A study on the use of artificial intelligence in art. Theses/capstones/creative projects.* University of Nebraska Omaha DigitalCommons.

Ertel, W. (2018). *Introduction to Artificial Intelligence.* Springer International Publishing.

Eslami, M., Rickman, A., Vaccaro, K., Aleyasen, A., Vuong, A., Karahalios, K., & Sandvig, C. (2015, April). " I always assumed that I wasn't really that close to [her]" Reasoning about Invisible Algorithms in News Feeds. In *Proceedings of the 33rd annual ACM conference on human factors in computing systems* (pp. 153-162).

Essel, H. B., Vlachopoulos, D., Tachie-Menson, A., Johnson, E. E., & Baah, P. K. (2022). The impact of a virtual teaching assistant (chatbot) on students' learning in Ghanaian higher education. *International Journal of Educational Technology in Higher Education*, *19*(1), 1–19. doi:10.118641239-022-00362-6 PMID:35013716

Ettinger, A. (2020). What BERT is not: Lessons from a new suite of psycholinguistic diagnostics for language models. *Transactions of the Association for Computational Linguistics*, *8*, 34–48. doi:10.1162/tacl_a_00298

European Commision. (2020). *European Parliament resolution of 20 October 2020 with recommendations to the Commission on a compensation scheme for artificial intelligence.* European Commission.

European Commision. (2021). *Resolution of the European Parliament of 20 January 2021 on artificial intelligence: Questions on the interpretation and application of international law, to the extent that the EU is affected, on the civilian and military areas of use and on the powers of the state outside the states.* European Commission.

Evans, J. (2005). *Curriculum change in secondary schools, 1957-2004: An educational roundabout?* Routledge.

Facer, K. (2011). *Learning futures: Education, technology and social change.* Routledge. doi:10.4324/9780203817308

Fainchtein, L. H. (2020, June 28). Generative vs retrieval based chatbots: A quick guide. *Medium.* https://blog.cloudboost.io/generative-vs-retrieval-based-chatbots-a-quick-guide- 8d19edb1d645

Fan, J., Han, F., & Liu, H. (2014). Challenges of Big Data analysis. *National Science Review*, *1*(2), 293–314. doi:10.1093/nsr/nwt032 PMID:25419469

Farthing, D. W., Jones, D. M., & McPhee, D. (1998). Permutational multiple-choice questions: An objective and efficient alternative to essay-type examination questions. *SIGCSE Bulletin*, *30*(3), 81–85. doi:10.1145/290320.283036

Feezell, J. T., Wagner, J. K., & Conroy, M. (2021). Exploring the effects of algorithm-driven news sources on political behavior and polarization. *Computers in Human Behavior*, *116*, 106626. doi:10.1016/j.chb.2020.106626

Feng, S. (2023). From Pretraining Data to Language Models to Downstream Tasks: Tracking the Trails of Political Biases Leading to Unfair NLP Models. *Proceedings of the 61st Annual Meeting of the Association for Computational Linguistics*. Association for Computational Linguistics. 10.18653/v1/2023.acl-long.656

Fezari, M., & Ali-Al-Dahoud, A. A. D. (2023). *From GPT to AutoGPT: A brief attention in NLP processing using DL*. Preprint.

Firat, M. (2023). *How chat GPT can transform autodidactic experiences and open education*. Open Education Faculty, Anadolu University.

Fisher, W. W., Piazza, C. C., & Roane, H. S. (Eds.). (2021). *Handbook of applied behavior analysis*. Guilford Publications.

Fitzmaurice, M., & Coughlan, J. (2007). Teaching philosophy statements: A guide. In C. O'Farrell (Ed.), Teaching portfolio practice in Ireland a handbook (pp. 39–47). Dublin: Centre for Academic Practice and Student Learning (CAPSL), Trinity College Dublin and All Ireland Society for Higher Education (AISHE).

Flanagan, M. (2017). *Critical play: Radical Game Design*. MIT press.

Flick, C., & Worrall, K. (2022). The ethics of creative AI. In *The Language of Creative AI: Practices, Aesthetics and Structures* (pp. 73–91). Springer International Publishing. doi:10.1007/978-3-031-10960-7_5

Floridi, L. (2023). AI as agency without intelligence: On ChatGPT, large language models, and other generative models. *Philosophy & Technology*, *36*(1), 15.

Fraiwan, M., & Khasawneh, N. (2023). A Review of ChatGPT Applications in education, marketing, software engineering, and healthcare: Benefits, drawbacks, and research directions. *arXiv preprint arXiv:2305.00237*.

Franceschelli, G., & Musolesi, M. (2023). On the creativity of Large Language Models. *arXiv preprint arXiv:2304.00008*.

Francke, E., & Alexander, B. (2019). The potential influence of artificial intelligence on plagiarism a higher education perspective. In *Proc European Conference on the Impact of Artificial Intelligence and Robotics*. EM Normandie Business School.

Frederick, J., & Wolff-Eisenberg, C. (2020). *Academic library strategy and budgeting during the COVID-19 pandemic*.

Freire, P. (1989). A Importância do Ato de Ler: Em Três Artigos que se Completam. Autores Associados: Cortez. Coleção Polêmicas do Nosso Tempo.

Frey, C. B., & Osborne, M. A. (2017). The future of employment: How susceptible are jobs to computerisation? *Technological Forecasting and Social Change*, *114*, 254–280. doi:10.1016/j.techfore.2016.08.019

Friess, P. (2021). Existence beyond transhumanism–context-based research-creation for critical art making. *Proceedings of Politics of the Machines-Rogue Research*, *2021*(3), 278–284. doi:10.14236/ewic/POM2021.36

Fry, C. (2018). Enchanting Algorithms: How The Reception of Generative Artworks Is Shaped By The Audience's Understanding of The Experience [J]. In *XXI Generative Art Conference Proceedings*. Generative Art. http://www. generativeart. com/GA2018_paper s/GA2018_Christopher% 20Fry. pdf

Fryer, L., Coniam, D., Carpenter, R., & Lăpușneanu, D. (2020). Bots for language learning now: Current and future directions. *Language Learning & Technology*, *24*(2), 8–22. 10125/44719

Fry, H. (2018). *Hello World: Being Human in the Age of Algorithms*. W.W. Norton & Company.

Fuchs, K. (2023). Exploring the opportunities and challenges of nlp models in higher education: is chat gpt a blessing or a curse? In Frontiers in Education, 8, 1166682. Frontiers. doi:10.3389/feduc.2023.1166682

Future of Jobs Report. (2023). *World Economic Forum*. WEF. https://www3.weforum.org/docs/WEF_Future_of_Jobs_2023.pdf

Galanter, P. (2016). Generative art theory. *A Companion to Digital Art*, (pp. 146-180). Research Gate.

Galanter, P. (2016). Generative art theory. *A Companion to Digital Art*, (pp. 146-180). UCSC.

Galanter, P. (2019). Artificial intelligence and problems in generative art theory. *Proceedings of EVA London, 2019*, 112–118. doi:10.14236/ewic/EVA2019.22

Galea, S., & Abdalla, S. M. (2020). COVID-19 Pandemic, Unemployment, and Civil Unrest: Underlying Deep Racial and Socioeconomic Divides. *Journal of the American Medical Association, 324*(3), 227–228. doi:10.1001/jama.2020.11132 PMID:32530457

Galloway, A. R. (2004). *Gaming: Essays on Algorithmic Culture*. University of Minnesota Press. Garzón, J. (2021). An overview of twenty-five years of augmented reality in education. *Multimodal Technologies and Interaction, 5*(7), 37.

Gandhi, P., & Talwar, V. (2023). Artificial intelligence and ChatGPT in the legal context. *International Journal of Medical Sciences, 75*, 1–2.

Gao, J., Zhao, H., Yu, C., & Xu, R. (2023). Exploring the feasibility of ChatGPT for event extraction. *arXiv preprint arXiv:2303.03836.*

Gao, Y., Sheng, T., Xiang, Y., Xiong, Y., Wang, H., & Zhang, J. (2023). Chat-REC: Towards interactive and explainable LLMs-augmented recommender system. *arXiv preprint arXiv:2303.14524.*

Gašević, D., Greiff, S., & Shaffer, D. W. (2022). Towards strengthening links between learning analytics and assessment: Challenges and potentials of a promising new bond. *Computers in Human Behavior, 134*, 107304. https://www.sciencedirect.com/science/article/pii/S0747563222001261. doi:10.1016/j.chb.2022.107304

Gebru, T., Morgenstern, J., Vecchione, B., Vaughan, J. W., Wallach, H., Iii, H. D., & Crawford, K. (2021). Datasheets for datasets. *Communications of the ACM, 64*(12), 86–92. doi:10.1145/3458723

Gefen, D., & Arinze, O. (2023). ChatGPT and usurping academic authority. *Journal of Information Technology Case and Application Research, 25*(1), 3–9. doi:10.1080/15228053.2023.2186629

Gehman, S., Gururangan, S., Sap, M., Choi, Y., & Smith, N. A. (2020). Real toxicity prompts: Evaluating neural toxic degeneration in language models. *arXiv preprint arXiv:2009.11462.*

Gentner, D., & Rattermann, M. J. (1991). Language and the Career of Similarity. In S. Vosniadou & A. Ortony (Eds.), *Similarity and Analogical Reasoning* (pp. 199–241). Cambridge University Press.

George, A. S., & George, A. H. (2023). A review of ChatGPT AI's impact on several business sectors. *Partners Universal International Innovation Journal, 1*(1), 9–23.

George, A. S., George, A. H., & Martin, A. G. (2023). The environmental impact of AI: A case study of water consumption by Chat GPT. *Partners Universal International Innovation Journal, 1*(2), 97–104.

Georgia State University. (2023). *Reduction of summer melt: A strategic approach.* GSU. https://success.gsu.edu/initiatives/reduction-of-summer-melt/

Gerard, H. S. (2020). *Fallen objects: Collaborating with artificial intelligence in the field of graphic design.* Portland State University's PDXScholar.

Giger, M. L. (2018). Machine Learning in Medical Imaging. *Journal of the American College of Radiology, 15*(3, 3 Pt B), 512–520. doi:10.1016/j.jacr.2017.12.028 PMID:29398494

Gikas, J., & Grant, M. M. (2013). Mobile computing devices in higher education: Student perspectives on learning with cellphones, smartphones & social media. *The Internet and Higher Education, 19*, 18–26. doi:10.1016/j.iheduc.2013.06.002

Gilardi, F., Alizadeh, M., & Kubli, M. (2023). ChatGPT outperforms crowd-workers for text-annotation tasks. *arXiv preprint arXiv:2303.15056*. 1 - 13.

Gillespie, T. (2014). The relevance of algorithms. *Media technologies: Essays on communication, materiality, and society, 167*(2014), 167.

Gilson, A., Safranek, C. W., Huang, T., Socrates, V., Chi, L., Taylor, R. A., & Chartash, D. (2023). How does chatgpt perform on the united states medical licensing examination? the implications of large language models for medical education and knowledge assessment. *JMIR Medical Education, 9*, e45312. doi:10.2196/45312 PMID:36753318

Gilster, P. (1997). *Digital literacy*. John Wiley & Sons Inc.

Global Education Monitoring Report: A Tool on Whose Terms ? (2023). UNESCO. https://gem-report-2023.unesco.org/

Goleman, D. (2001). Emotional intelligence: Issues in paradigm building. *The emotionally intelligent workplace, 13*, 26.

González-Pérez, L. I., & Ramírez-Montoya, M. S. (2022). Components of Education 4.0 in 21st century skills frameworks: Systematic review. *Sustainability (Basel), 14*(3), 1493. doi:10.3390u14031493

Government Technology. (2023). *Study: 30% of college students have used ChatGPT for essays*. https://www.govtech.com/education/higher-ed/study-30-of-college-students-have-used-chatgpt-for-essays

Govindasamy, & Mestry, R. (2022). The principal's role in managing curriculum change: Implications for the provision of quality education. *South African Journal of Education, 42*(4), 1–10. doi:10.15700/saje.v42n4a2294

Gran, A. B., Booth, P., & Bucher, T. (2021). To be or not to be algorithm aware: A question of a new digital divide? *Information Communication and Society, 24*(12), 1779–1796. doi:10.1080/1369118X.2020.1736124

Grba, D., Todorović, V., Boye, P., Kang, K. H., & Pandilovski, M. (2019). Machine flaws in generative art. In *the proceedings of the 25th International Symposium on Electronic Art*, (pp. 713 – 717).

Grbic, D. V., & Dujlovic, I. (2023, March). Social engineering with ChatGPT. In *2023 22nd International Symposium INFOTEH-JAHORINA (INFOTEH)* (pp. 1-5). IEEE. 10.1109/INFOTEH57020.2023.10094141

Greenfield, G. (2021). Artificial life and artificial intelligence advances in the visual arts. In P. Machado, J. Romero, and G. Greenfield's Artificial Intelligence and the Arts: Computational Creativity, Artistic Behavior, and Tools for Creatives, (pp. 3-26). Springer. doi:10.1007/978-3-030-59475-6_1

Greenstein, L. M. (2012). *Assessing 21st century skills: A guide to evaluating mastery and authentic learning*. Corwin Press.

Greetham, B. (2020). How to write your literature review. 11

Gruchy, T. (2020). Observations and categorisations of art practices associated with AI. In *Human-Computer Interaction. Design and User Experience: Thematic Area, HCI 2020, Held as Part of the 22nd International Conference, HCII 2020, Copenhagen, Denmark, July 19–24, 2020* [Springer International Publishing.]. *Proceedings, 22*(Part I), 234–245.

Grudin, J. (2023). ChatGPT and chat history: Challenges for the new wave. *Computer, 56*(05), 94–100. doi:10.1109/MC.2023.3255279

Guadamuz, A. (2017). *Do androids dream of electric copyright? Comparative analysis of originality in artificial intelligence generated works.* Intellectual Property Quarterly.

Gu, J., Wang, X., Li, C., Zhao, J., Fu, W., Liang, G., & Qiu, J. (2022). AI-enabled image fraud in scientific publications. *Patterns (New York, N.Y.), 3*(7), 100511. doi:10.1016/j.patter.2022.100511 PMID:35845832

Gunkel, D. (2012). The Machine Question: Critical Perspectives on AI, Robots, and Ethics. In The Machine Question: Critical Perspectives on AI, Robots, and Ethics. MIT Press. doi:10.7551/mitpress/8975.001.0001

Guo, C., Lu, Y., Dou, Y., & Wang, F. Y. (2023). Can ChatGPT boost artistic creation: The need of imaginative intelligence for parallel art. *IEEE/CAA Journal of Automatica Sinica, 10*(4), 835-838.

Guo, E., & Renaldi, A. (2022). Deception, Exploited Workers, and Cash Handouts: How Worldcoin Recruited its First Half a Million Test Users. *MIT Technology Review.* https://www.technologyreview.com/2022/04/06/1048981/worldcoin-cryptocurrency-biometrics-web3/?truid=&utm_source=the_algorithm&utm_medium=email&utm_campaign=the_algorithm.unpaid.engagement&utm_content=08-07-2023

Guo, S., Wang, Y., & Yang, W. (2022, June). A study on the collision of artificial intelligence and art based on generative adversarial networks (GAN). In *2022 International Conference on 3D Immersion, Interaction and Multi-sensory Experiences (ICDIIME)* (pp. 27-31). IEEE. 10.1109/ICDIIME56946.2022.00014

Guo, Y., Liu, Y., Oerlemans, A., Lao, S., Wu, S., & Lew, M. S. (2016). Deep learning for visual understanding: A review. *Neurocomputing, 187*, 27–48. doi:10.1016/j.neucom.2015.09.116

Gupta, S., & Chen, Y. (2022). Supporting inclusive learning using chatbots? A chatbot-led interview study. *Journal of Information Systems Education, 33*(1), 98–108.

Gururangan, S., Marasović, A., Swayamdipta, S., Lo, K., Beltagy, I., Downey, D., & Smith, N. A. (2020). Don't stop pretraining: Adapt language models to domains and tasks. *arXiv preprint arXiv:2004.10964.* doi:10.18653/v1/2020.acl-main.740

Hadfield-Menell, D., Andrus, M., & Hadfield, G. (2019, January). Legible normativity for AI alignment: The value of silly rules. In *Proceedings of the 2019 AAAI/ACM Conference on AI, Ethics, and Society* (pp. 115-121). ACM. 10.1145/3306618.3314258

Haensch, A. C., Ball, S., Herklotz, M., & Kreuter, F. (2023). Seeing ChatGPT through students' eyes: An analysis of TikTok data. *arXiv preprint arXiv:2303.05349.* 1 - 10.

Hai-Jew, S. (2022). *Common Visual Art in A Social Digital Age.* Nova Science Publishers. doi:10.52305/BKOT1869

Halaweh, M. (2023). ChatGPT in education: Strategies for responsible implementation. *Contemporary Educational Technology, 15*(2), 421, 1 - 11.

Hall Lang, E., Munsey, B., Murray, F., Manning, L., & Wigington, T. (2023). Culturally responsive learning environments within higher education. *Learning Environments Research,* 1–16. doi:10.100710984-023-09481-x

Hamzelou, J. (2023). Neuroscientists listened in on people's brains for a week. They found order and chaos. *MIT Technology Review.* https://www-technologyreview-com.cdn.ampproject.org/c/s/www.technologyreview.com/2023/02/07/1067951/brains-week-order-chaos/amp/)

Han, Z. (2021, April). Combined development of artificial intelligence and art design. In *2021 6th International Conference on Intelligent Computing and Signal Processing (ICSP)* (pp. 1023-1026). IEEE. 10.1109/ICSP51882.2021.9408896

Hanna, D. M. (2023). The use of artificial intelligence art generator "Midjourney" in artistic and advertising creativity. *Journal of Design Sciences and Applied Arts*, *4*(2), 42–58. doi:10.21608/jdsaa.2023.169144.1231

Hansen, U. J. (2021). *The Future of Smart: How our Education System Needs to Change to Help All Young People Thrive.*

Harari, Y. N. (2018). *21 Lições para o Século 21*. [Trans. Paulo Geiger]. 1. ed. Companhia das Letras.

Harman, B. A., & Sato, T. (2011). Cell phone use and grade point average among undergraduate university students. *College Student Journal*, *45*(3), 544–550.

Harrer, S. (2023). Attention is not all you need: The complicated case of ethically using large language models in healthcare and medicine. *EBioMedicine*, *90*, 90. doi:10.1016/j.ebiom.2023.104512

Hassani, H., & Silva, E. S. (2015). Forecasting with Big Data: A Review. *Annals of Data Science*, *2*(1), 5–19. doi:10.100740745-015-0029-9

Hassani, H., & Silva, E. S. (2023). The role of ChatGPT in data science: How AI-assisted conversational interfaces are revolutionizing the field. *Big Data and Cognitive Computing*, *7*(2), 62. doi:10.3390/bdcc7020062

Hauer, T. (2022). Incompleteness of moral choice and evolution towards fully autonomous AI. *Humanities & Social Sciences Communications*, *9*(1), 1. doi:10.105741599-022-01060-4

HazuchaB. (2022). Artificial Intelligence and Cultural Production: Possible Impacts on Creativity and Copyright Law. SSRN 4028106. doi:10.2139/ssrn.4028106

Hebron, P. (n.d.) *Artificial intelligence and the decoupling of creation and comprehension*. Patrick Hebron.

Heikkilä, M. (2023). AI Language Models are Rife with Different Political Biases. *MIT Technology Review*. https://www.technologyreview.com/2023/08/07/1077324/ai-language-models-are-rife-with-political-biases/?truid=&utm_source=the_algorithm&utm_medium=email&utm_campaign=the_algorithm.unpaid.engagement&utm_content=08-07-2023

Heinisch, B., Oswald, K., Weißpflug, M., Shuttleworth, S., & Belknap, G. (2021). Citizen humanities. *The Science of Citizen Science*, 97.

Henrickson, L. (2023). Chatting with the dead: The hermeneutics of thanabots. *Media Culture & Society*, *01634437221147626*(5), 1–18. doi:10.1177/01634437221147626

Herbold, S., Hautli-Janisz, A., Heuer, U., Kikteva, Z., & Trautsch, A. (2023). AI, write an essay for me: A large-scale comparison of human-written versus ChatGPT-generated essays. *arXiv preprint arXiv:2304.14276*.

Hertzmann, A. (2018, May). Can computers create art? In Arts (Vol. 7, p. 18). MDPI. doi:10.3390/arts7020018

Heston, T. F., & Khun, C. (2023). Prompt engineering in medical education. *International Medical Education*, *2*(3), 198–205. doi:10.3390/ime2030019

He, W., Zhang, Z. J., & Li, W. (2021). Information technology solutions, challenges, and suggestions for tackling the COVID-19 pandemic. *International Journal of Information Management*, *57*, 102287. doi:10.1016/j.ijinfomgt.2020.102287 PMID:33318721

Hilger, K. J., Scheibe, S., Frenzel, A. C., & Keller, M. M. (2021). Exceptional circumstances: Changes in teachers' work characteristics and well-being during COVID-19 lockdown. *School Psychology*, *36*(6), 516–532. doi:10.1037pq0000457 PMID:34766815

Hill, J., Kneale, P., Nicholson, D., Waddington, S., & Ray, W. (2017). Re-framing the geography dissertation: A consideration of alternative, innovative and creative approaches. *Pedagogic Research in Geography Higher Education*, (pp. 284–302).

Hiller, R. H. (2022). Combating Low Digital Literacy in the College Classroom: A Systematic Literature Review. *Florida Journal of Educational Research*, *59*(3), 1–9.

Hill, S., Yagi, T., & Yamash'ta, S. (2022). Where Did Humanity Go? In *The Kyoto Post-COVID Manifesto For Global Economics* (pp. 319–332). Springer. doi:10.1007/978-981-16-8566-8_19

Hill-Yardin, E. L., Hutchinson, M. R., Laycock, R., & Spencer, S. J. (2023). A Chat (GPT) about the future of scientific publishing. *Brain, Behavior, and Immunity*, *110*, S0889–S1591. doi:10.1016/j.bbi.2023.02.022 PMID:36868432

Hiscott, J., Alexandridi, M., Muscolini, M., Tassone, E., Palermo, E., Soultsioti, M., & Zevini, A. (2020). The global impact of the coronavirus pandemic. *Cytokine & Growth Factor Reviews*, *53*, 1–9. doi:10.1016/j.cytogfr.2020.05.010 PMID:32487439

Hitsuwari, J., Ueda, Y., Yun, W., & Nomura, M. (2023). Does human–AI collaboration lead to more creative art? Aesthetic evaluation of human-made and AI-generated haiku poetry. *Computers in Human Behavior*, *139*, 107502. doi:10.1016/j.chb.2022.107502

Hoetzlein, R. C. (2023). Knowledge vultures in new media art. *Artnodes*, (31), 1–9.

Hoffmann, J., Borgeaud, S., Mensch, A., Buchatskaya, E., Cai, T., Rutherford, E., & Sifre, L. (2022). Training compute-optimal large language models. *arXiv preprint arXiv:2203.15556.*

Holmes, W., Bialik, M., & Fadel, C. (2019). *Artificial intelligence in education: Promises and implications for teaching and learning*. The Center for Curriculum Redesign.

Holmes, W., Bialik, M., & Fadel, C. (2023). *Artificial intelligence in education.* Globethics Publications.

Holmes, W., & Porayska-Pomsta, K. (2022). *The Ethics of Artificial Intelligence in education: Practices, challenges, and debates*. Taylor & Francis. doi:10.4324/9780429329067

Holmes, W., Porayska-Pomsta, K., Holstein, K., Sutherland, E., Baker, T., Shum, S. B., Santos, O. C., Rodrigo, M. T., Cukurova, M., Bittencourt, I. I., & Koedinger, K. R. (2022). Ethics of AI in Education: Towards a Community-Wide Framework. *International Journal of Artificial Intelligence in Education*, *32*(10), 504–526. doi:10.100740593-021-00239-1

Holstein, K., Wortman Vaughan, J., Daumé, H. III, Dudik, M., & Wallach, H. (2019). Improving fairness in machine learning systems: What do industry practitioners need? In *Proceedings of the 2019 CHI conference on human factors in computing systems* (pp. 1–16). ACM. 10.1145/3290605.3300830

Holzinger, A., Keiblinger, K., Holub, P., Zatloukal, K., & Müller, H. (2023). AI for Life: Trends in Artificial Intelligence for Biotechnology. *New Biotechnology*, *74*, 16–24. doi:10.1016/j.nbt.2023.02.001 PMID:36754147

Hommel, B. E., Ruppel, R., & Zacher, H. (2022). Assessment of cognitive flexibility in personnel selection: Validity and acceptance of a gamified version of the Wisconsin Card Sorting Test. *International Journal of Selection and Assessment*, *30*(1), 126–144. doi:10.1111/ijsa.12362

Homolak, J. (2023). Opportunities and risks of ChatGPT in medicine, science, and academic publishing: A modern Promethean dilemma. *Croatian Medical Journal*, *64*(1), 1–3. doi:10.3325/cmj.2023.64.1 PMID:36864812

Hong, J. W. (2018). Bias in perception of art produced by artificial intelligence. In *Human-Computer Interaction. Interaction in Context: 20th International Conference, HCI International 2018.* Springer.

Hong, J. W., & Curran, N. M. (2019). Artificial intelligence, artists, and art: Attitudes toward artwork produced by humans vs. artificial intelligence. [TOMM]. *ACM Transactions on Multimedia Computing Communications and Applications*, *15*(2s), 1–16. doi:10.1145/3326337

Hopster, J. K. G. (2021). What are Socially Disruptive Technologies. *Technology in Society*, *67*(nov), 101750. https://www.sciencedirect.com/science/article/pii/S0160791X21002256. doi:10.1016/j.techsoc.2021.101750

Hossain, F. (2020). Global responsibility vs. individual dreams: Addressing ethical dilemmas created by the migration of healthcare practitioners. *Global Bioethics*, *31*(1), 81–89. doi:10.1080/11287462.2020.1773054 PMID:33029070

Hristov, K. (2016). Artificial intelligence and the copyright dilemma. *Idea*, *57*, 431.

Hsu, T. (2023). What Can You Do When A.I. Lies About You? *The New York Times*. https://www.nytimes.com/2023/08/03/business/media/ai-defamation-lies-accuracy.html

Hu, E. J., Shen, Y., Wallis, P., Allen-Zhu, Z., Li, Y., Wang, S., & Chen, W. (2021). Lora: Low-rank adaptation of large language models. *arXiv preprint arXiv:2106.09685.*

Huang, F., Kwak, H., & An, J. (2023). Is ChatGPT better than human annotators? Potential and limitations of ChatGPT in explaining implicit hate speech. *arXiv preprint arXiv:2302.07736.* doi:10.1145/3543873.3587368

Huang, J., Gu, S. S., Hou, L., Wu, Y., Wang, X., Yu, H., & Han, J. (2022). Large language models can self-improve. *arXiv preprint arXiv:2210.11610.*

Huang, L., & Peissl, W. (2023). Artificial Intelligence—A New Knowledge and Decision-Making Paradigm? In L. Hennen, J. Hahn, M. Ladikas, R. Lindner, W. Peissl, & R. van Est (Eds.), Technology Assessment in a Globalized World: Facing the Challenges of Transnational Technology Governance (pp. 175–201). Springer International Publishing. doi:10.1007/978-3-031-10617-0_9

Huang, S., Dong, L., Wang, W., Hao, Y., Singhal, S., Ma, S., & Wei, F. (2023). Language is not all you need: Aligning perception with language models. *arXiv preprint arXiv:2302.14045.*

Huang. (2021). *Handbook of research on credential innovations for inclusive pathways to professions* (Huang, Ed.). IGI Global. doi:10.4018/978-1-7998-3820-3

Huang, W., Hew, K. F., & Fryer, L. K. (2022). Chatbots for language learning — Are they really useful? A systematic review of chatbot-supported language learning. *Journal of Computer Assisted Learning*, *38*(1), 237–257. doi:10.1111/jcal.12610

Huang, Z. (2022). Introducing Neuro-Symbolic Artificial Intelligence to Humanities and Social Sciences: Why Is It Possible and What Can Be Done? *TEM Journal*, *11*(4), 1863–1870. doi:10.18421/TEM114-54

Hughes, R. T., Zhu, L., & Bednarz, T. (2021). Generative adversarial networks–enabled human–artificial intelligence collaborative applications for creative and design industries: A systematic review of current approaches and trends. *Frontiers in Artificial Intelligence*, *4*, 604234. doi:10.3389/frai.2021.604234 PMID:33997773

Human-plus-AI Solutions Mitigate Security Threats. (2023). *MIT Technology Review / Teleperformance*. https://www.teleperformance.com/en-us/insights-list/white-papers/mit-paper-human-plus-ai-solutions-mitigate-security-threats/

Hung, M. C., Trang, M. X., Nakatsu, R., & Tosa, N. (2022, February). Unusual transformation: A deep learning approach to create art. In *ArtsIT, Interactivity and Game Creation: Creative Heritage. New Perspectives from Media Arts and Artificial Intelligence. 10th EAI International Conference, ArtsIT 2021, Virtual Event, December 2-3, 2021, Proceedings* (pp. 309-320). Cham: Springer International Publishing. 10.1007/978-3-030-95531-1_21

Hunkenschroer, A. L., & Luetge, C. (2022). Ethics of AI-enabled recruiting and selection: A review and research agenda. *Journal of Business Ethics*, *178*(4), 977–1007. doi:10.100710551-022-05049-6

Hunter, A. (2023, March 28). *Education sector says Sask. K-12 budget insufficient.* CBC News. https://www.cbc.ca/news/canada/saskatchewan/education-budget-1.6792331

Hurlburt, G. (2023). What if ethics got in the way of Generative AI? *IT Professional*, *25*(2), 4–6. doi:10.1109/MITP.2023.3267140

Hurwitz, J. S., Nugent, A., Halper, F., & Kaufman, M. (2013). *Big Data For Dummies*. John Wiley & Sons.

Hutson, J., & Harper-Nichols, M. (2023). Generative AI and algorithmic art: Disrupting the framing of meaning and rethinking the subject-object dilemma. *Global Journal of Computer Science and Technology*, *23*(1), 55 - 61.

Hutson, J., & Olsen, T. (2022). Virtual Reality and Learning: A Case Study of Experiential Pedagogy in Art History. *Journal of Intelligent Learning Systems and Applications*. https://www.scirp.org/journal/paperinformation.aspx?paperid=120925

Hutson, J., & Robertson, B. (2023). Exploring the educational potential of AI generative art in 3D design fundamentals: A case study on prompt engineering and creative workflows. *Global Journal of HUMAN-SOCIAL SCIENCE: A Arts & Humanities-Psychology*, *23*(2).

Hutson, J., & Cotroneo, P. (2023). Generative AI tools in art education: Exploring prompt engineering and iterative processes for enhanced creativity. *Metaverse*, *4*(1), 1–14.

Hutson, J., Jeevanjee, T., Vander Graaf, V., Lively, J., Weber, J., Weir, G., & Edele, S. (2022). Artificial Intelligence and the Disruption of Higher Education: Strategies for Integrations across Disciplines. *Creative Education*, *13*(12), 3953–3980. doi:10.4236/ce.2022.1312253

Hwang, G. J., Xie, H., Wah, B. W., & Gašević, D. (2020). Vision, challenges, roles and research issues of Artificial Intelligence in Education. *Computers and Education: Artificial Intelligence*, *1*, 100001. doi:10.1016/j.caeai.2020.100001

Hwang, G., & Tu, Y. (2021). Roles and Research Trends of Artificial Intelligence in Mathematics Education: A Bibliometric Mapping Analysis and Systematic Review. *Mathematics*, *9*(6), 584. doi:10.3390/math9060584

IBM. (2023a). *What is machine learning?* IBM. https://www.ibm.com/topics/machine-learning

IBM. (2023b). *A computer called Watson*. IBM. https://www.ibm.com/ibm/history/ibm100/us/en/icons/watson/

Ibrahim, H., Asim, R., Zaffar, F., Rahwan, T., & Zaki, Y. (2023). Rethinking homework in the age of artificial intelligence. *IEEE Intelligent Systems*, *38*(2), 24–27. doi:10.1109/MIS.2023.3255599

Ifenthaler, B.-M. N., & Mah, D.-K. (Eds.). (2016). Foundation of Digital Badges and Micro-Credentials Demonstrating and Recognizing Knowledge and Competencies (1st ed.). Springer International Publishing. doi:10.1007/978-3-319-15425-1

IlaganJ. B. R.IlaganJ. R. (2023). *A prototype of a chatbot for evaluating and refining student startup ideas using a large language model*. EdArXiv Preprints. https://edarxiv.org/azhf9/ doi:10.35542/osf.io/azhf9

Inie, N., Falk, J., & Tanimoto, S. (2023, April). Designing participatory AI: Creative professionals' worries and expectations about Generative AI. *In Extended Abstracts of the 2023 CHI Conference on Human Factors in Computing Systems* (pp. 1-8). IEEE.

Ireni-Saban, L., & Sherman, M. (2021). *Ethical Governance of Artificial Intelligence in the Public Sector*. Taylor & Francis. doi:10.4324/9781003106678

Ison, D. C. (2012). Plagiarism among dissertations: Prevalence at online institutions. *Journal of Academic Ethics*, *10*, 227–236.

Jalil, S., Rafi, S., LaToza, T. D., Moran, K., & Lam, W. (2023). ChatGPT and software testing education: Promises & perils. *arXiv preprint arXiv:2302.03287*. doi:10.1109/ICSTW58534.2023.00078

Janssen, C. P., Donker, S. F., Brumby, D. P., & Kun, A. L. (2019). History and future of human-automation interaction. *International Journal of Human-Computer Studies*, *13*(19), 99–107. doi:10.1016/j.ijhcs.2019.05.006

Jarota, M. (2021). Artificial intelligence and robotisation in the EU - should we change OHS law? *Journal of Occupational Medicine and Toxicology (London, England)*, *16*(1), 18. doi:10.118612995-021-00301-7 PMID:33952297

Jayaraman, J., & Black, J. (2022). Effectiveness of an intelligent question answering system for teaching financial literacy: A pilot study. In *Innovations in Learning and Technology for the Workplace and Higher Education: Proceedings of 'The Learning Ideas Conference'2021* (pp. 133–140). Springer. doi:10.1007/978-3-030-90677-1_13

Jayatilake, S. M. D. A. C., & Ganegoda, G. U. (2021). Involvement of Machine Learning Tools in Healthcare Decision Making. *Journal of Healthcare Engineering*, *6679512*, 1–20. doi:10.1155/2021/6679512 PMID:33575021

Jiang, Z., Xu, F. F., Araki, J., & Neubig, G. (2020). How can we know what language models know? *Transactions of the Association for Computational Linguistics*, *8*, 423–438. doi:10.1162/tacl_a_00324

Jiao, W. X., Wang, W. X., Huang, J. T., Wang, X., & Tu, Z. P. (2023). Is ChatGPT a good translator? Yes with GPT-4 as the engine. *arXiv preprint arXiv:2301.08745*.

Jin, X., Chen, Z., & Li, W. (2020). AI-GAN: Asynchronous interactive generative adversarial network for single image rain removal. *Pattern Recognition*, *100*, 107143. doi:10.1016/j.patcog.2019.107143

Jin, Z., Levine, S., Gonzalez Adauto, F., Kamal, O., Sap, M., Sachan, M., & Schölkopf, B. (2022). When to make exceptions: Exploring language models as accounts of human moral judgment. *Advances in Neural Information Processing Systems*, *35*, 28458–28473.

Jones, K. M. L. (2019). Learning analytics and higher education: A proposed model for establishing informed consent mechanisms to promote student privacy and autonomy. *International Journal of Educational Technology in Higher Education*, *16*(1), 24. doi:10.118641239-019-0155-0

Jones, S. (1995). *Understanding community in the information age*. Sage.

Jonnaert, C. (2020). Artificial intelligence and Canadian copyright: The quest for an author. *Católica Law Review*, *4*(2), 13–34.

Jotterand, F., & Bosco, C. (2020). Keeping the "Human in the Loop" in the Age of Artificial Intelligence. *Science and Engineering Ethics*, *26*(5), 2455–2460. doi:10.100711948-020-00241-1 PMID:32643058

Jowallah, R. (2023). *Examining the impact of large language models on higher education: Ethical considerations* [Conference presentation]. ELI Annual Meeting, Anaheim, CA.

Jowallah, R. (2023, September 4). *Revolutionizing Assessments: A Dive into Artificial Intelligence (AI) and Data Intelligence (DI)* [Video]. The Learning Journey. https://youtu.be/iAWD92y2K4E?si=1XNDykVDxgaYOuCS

Jozefowicz, R., Vinyals, O., Schuster, M., Shazeer, N., & Wu, Y. (2016). Exploring the limits of language modeling. *arXiv preprint arXiv:1602.02410*.

Kaid Mohammed Ali, J., Hasnain, S. I., & Beg, M. S. (2019). The impact of texting on Standard English: The students' perspective. *Arab World English Journal (AWEJ). SSRN*, *5*(5), 65–75. doi:10.2139srn.3431793

Kaliraj, P., & Devi, T. (2023). Innovating Higher Education 4.0 in the Era of Industry 4.0. In Industry 4.0 Technologies for Education (pp. 1-10). Auerbach Publications.

Kalla, D., & Smith, N. (2023). Study and analysis of Chat GPT and its impact on different fields of study. *International Journal of Innovative Science and Research Technology*, *8*(3).

Kalpokiene, J., & Kalpokas, I. (2023). Creative encounters of a posthuman kind–anthropocentric law, artificial intelligence, and art. *Technology in Society*, *102197*, 1–8. doi:10.1016/j.techsoc.2023.102197

Kang, E. S., & Lee, J. M. (2022). Artificial Intelligence Liberal Arts Curriculum Design for Non-Computer Majors. *Journal of Digital Contents Society*, *23*(1), 57–66. doi:10.9728/dcs.2022.23.1.57

Kang, S. (2022). Surrogate Humanity: Resistant Art Practices under Technoliberalism. *Media-N*, *18*(1), 153–156. doi:10.21900/j.median.v18i1.859

Kärkkäinen, K. (2012). Bringing about curriculum innovations: Implicit approaches in the OECD area. In *Bringing about curriculum innovations: Implicit approaches in the OECD area* (pp. 1–21). OECD Publishing. doi:10.1787/9789264178698-4-

Kasneci, E., Seßler, K., Ku¨chemann, S., Bannert, M., Dementieva, D., Fischer, F., Gasser, U., Groh, G., Gu¨nnemann, S., Hu¨llermeier, E., et al. (2023). Chatgpt for good? on opportunities and challenges of large language models for education. *Learning and individual differences*, 103.

Kasneci, E., Seßler, K., Küchemann, S., Bannert, M., Dementieva, D., Fischer, F., Gasser, U., Groh, G., Günnemann, S., Hüllermeier, E., Krusche, S., Kutyniok, G., Michaeli, T., Nerdel, C., Pfeffer, J., Poquet, O., Sailer, M., Schmidt, A., Seidel, T., & Kasneci, G. (2023). ChatGPT for good? On opportunities and challenges of large language models for education. *Learning and Individual Differences*, *103*, 102274. doi:10.1016/j.lindif.2023.102274

Kassner, N., & Schütze, H. (2019). Negated and misprimed probes for pretrained language models: Birds can talk, but cannot fly. *arXiv preprint arXiv:1911.03343.*

Kausik, B. N. (2023). *Long tails & the impact of GPT on labor*. Preprint.

Keating, J., & Nourbakhsh, I. (2018). Teaching artificial intelligence and humanity. *Communications of the ACM*, *61*(2), 29–32. doi:10.1145/3104986

Kellner, D., & Gennaro, S. (2022). Critical Theory and the Transformation of Education in the New Millennium. In *The Palgrave Handbook on Critical Theories of Education* (pp. 21–45). Springer International Publishing. doi:10.1007/978-3-030-86343-2_2

Kelloway, E. K., Thibault, T., & Francis, L. (2016). *(rep.). Teacher Time Use*. Nova Scotia's Teachers Union.

Kemp, N., & Bushnell, C. (2011). Children's text messaging: Abbreviations, input methods and links with literacy. *Journal of Computer Assisted Learning*, *27*(1), 18–27. doi:10.1111/j.1365-2729.2010.00400.x

Kenwright, B. (2016a). Game-based learning in higher education. Communication Article, 1–8.

Kenwright, B. (2016b). Holistic game development curriculum. In *SIGGRAPH ASIA 2016 Symposium on Education.* ACM. 10.1145/2993352.2993354

Kenwright, B. (2017). Brief review of video games in learning & education how far we have come. In *SIGGRAPH Asia 2017 Symposium on Education*, pages 1–10. 11 10.1145/3134368.3139220

Kenwright, B. (2020). When digital technologies rule the lecture theater. *IEEE Potentials*, *39*(5), 27–30.

Kenwright, B. (2023). Data collection during active gameplay: Unveiling a multifaceted portrait of the individual. *Games as Stealth Assessments.*

Kenwright, B. (2016c). Peer review: Does it really help students? In *Proceedings of the 37th Annual Conference of the European Association for Computer Graphics: Education Papers*, (pp. 31–32). ACM.

Kerridge, E. (2013). *The agricultural revolution*. Routledge. doi:10.4324/9781315019888

Khademi, A. (2023). Can ChatGPT and Bard generate aligned assessment items? A reliability analysis against human performance. *arXiv preprint arXiv:2304.05372.*

Khalil, M., & Er, E. (2023). Will ChatGPT get you caught? Rethinking of plagiarism detection. *arXiv preprint arXiv:2302.04335.* 1 - 13. doi:10.1007/978-3-031-34411-4_32

Khan, W., Ghazanfar, M. A., Azam, M. A., Karami, A., Alyoubi, K. H., & Alfakeeh, A. S. (2020). Stock market prediction using machine learning classifiers and social media [news]. *Journal of Ambient Intelligence and Humanized Computing*, 1–24.

Khosravi, H., Shum, S. B., Chen, G., Conati, C., Tsai, Y.-S., Kay, J., Knight, S., Martinez-Maldonado, R., Sadiq, S., & Gašević, D. (2022). Explainable artificial intelligence in education. *Computers and Education: Artificial Intelligence, 3*, 100074.

Kılıçkaya, F. (2020). Using a chatbot, Replika, to practice writing through conversations in L2 English: A Case study. In *New Technological applications for foreign and second language learning and teaching* (pp. 221–238). IGI Global. doi:10.4018/978-1-7998-2591-3.ch011

Kime, L. (n.d.). *Conducting a SWOT Analysis*. Penn State Extension. https://extension.psu.edu/conducting-a-swot-analysis

Kim, H. S., Cha, Y., & Kim, N. Y. (2021). Effects of AI chatbots on EFL students' communication skills. *Korean Journal of English Language and Linguistics, 21*, 712–734. doi:10.15738/kjell.21.202108.712

Kim, S., Samaniego, C. S., Sousa Melo, S. L., Brachvogel, W. A., Baskaran, K., & Rulli, D. (2023, November). Artificial intelligence (A.I.) in dental curricula: Ethics and responsible integration. *Journal of Dental Education, 87*(11), 1570–1573. doi:10.1002/jdd.13337 PMID:37489621

Kim, S., Shim, J., & Shim, J. (2023). A study on the utilization of OpenAI ChatGPT as a second language learning tool. *Journal of Multimedia Information System, 10*(1), 79–88. doi:10.33851/JMIS.2023.10.1.79

King, M. (2023). *Bing chatbot formulating and testing novel hypotheses in real-time: How slime, chocolate, and Nobel prizes reveal the power and limits of artificial intelligence*. Preprint.

King, M. R. (2023). Can Bard, Google's experimental chatbot based on the LaMDA Large Language Model, help to analyze the gender and racial diversity of authors in your cited scientific references? *Cellular and Molecular Bioengineering*, 1–5. doi:10.100712195-022-00754-8 PMID:37096072

Kiros, R., Salakhutdinov, R., & Zemel, R. S. (2014). Unifying visual-semantic embeddings with multimodal neural language models. *arXiv preprint arXiv:1411.2539.*

Kirtania, D. K., & Patra, S. K. (2023). *OpenAI ChatGPT Generated content and similarity index: A study of selected terms from the Library & Information Science (LIS)*. Qeios.

Knop, M., Weber, S., Mueller, M., & Niehaves, B. (2022). Human factors and technological characteristics influencing the interaction of medical professionals with artificial intelligence–enabled clinical decision support systems: Literature review. *JMIR Human Factors, 9*(1), e28639. doi:10.2196/28639 PMID:35323118

Kobayashi, M., & Takeda, K. (2000). Information retrieval on the web. *ACM Computing Surveys, 32*(2), 144–173. doi:10.1145/358923.358934

Kojima, T., Gu, S. S., Reid, M., Matsuo, Y., & Iwasawa, Y. 2022. Large language models are zero-shot reasoners. *arXiv preprint arXiv:2205.11916.*

Konstantopoulos, P. S., Karkaletsis, V., Spyropoulos, C. D., & Vouros, G. (Eds.). (2010). *Advances in Artificial Intelligence: Theories, Models, and Applications 6th Hellenic Conference on AI.* Springer. 10.1007/978-3-642-12842-4

Kooli, C. (2023). Chatbots in Education and Research: A Critical Examination of ethical implications and solutions. *Sustainability (Basel), 15*(7), 5614. doi:10.3390u15075614

Kordzadeh, N., & Ghasemaghaei, M. (2022). Algorithmic bias: Review, synthesis, and future research directions. *European Journal of Information Systems, 31*(3), 388–409. doi:10.1080/0960085X.2021.1927212

Kosinski, M. (2023). Theory of mind may have spontaneously emerged in large language models. *arXiv preprint arXiv:2302.02083.*

Koubaa, A., Boulila, W., Ghouti, L., Alzahem, A., & Latif, S. (2023). *Exploring ChatGPT capabilities and limitations: A critical review of the NLP game changer.* Preprint. doi:10.1109/ACCESS.2023.3326474

Kouzes, J. M., & Posner, B. Z. (2007). *The leadership challenge.* Wiley.

Kovačević, D. (2023, March). Use of ChatGPT in ESP teaching process. In *2023 22nd International Symposium INFOTEH-JAHORINA (INFOTEH)* (pp. 1-5). IEEE.

Krajcik, J., Schneider, B., Miller, E. A., Chen, I. C., Bradford, L., Baker, Q., Bartz, K., Miller, C., Li, T., Codere, S., & Peek-Brown, D. (2023). Assessing the effect of project-based learning on science learning in elementary schools. *American Educational Research Journal, 60*(1), 70–102. doi:10.3102/00028312221129247

Krantz-Kent, R. (2008). Teachers' work patterns: When, where, and how much do U.S. teachers work? *Monthly Labor Review.*

Krause, S. (2000). "Among the Greatest Benefactors of Mankind": What the Success of Chalkboards Tells Us about the Future of Computers in the Classroom. *The Journal of the Midwest Modern Language Association, 33*(2), 6–16. doi:10.2307/1315198

Kshetri, N. (2023). ChatGPT in developing economies. *IT Professional, 25*(2), 16–19. doi:10.1109/MITP.2023.3254639

Kuh, G. D., Kinzie, J. L., Buckley, J. A., Bridges, B. K., & Hayek, J. C. (2006). *What matters to student success: A review of the literature* (Vol. 8). National Postsecondary Education Cooperative.

Kuhn, T. S. (1970). *The Structure of Scientific Revolutions. 2.* The University of Chicago Press.

Kuhn, T. S. (1998). *A Estrutura das Revoluções Científicas. 5.* Editora Perspectiva. [Translation: Beatriz Vianna Boeira e Nelson Boeira]

Kukulska-Hulme, A. (2006). Mobile language learning now and in the future. In P. Svensson (Ed.), *From vision to practice: language learning and IT* (pp. 295–310). Swedish Net University. http://www2.humlab.umu.se/itas/bok/default.asp

Kumar, N., Mali, R., Ratnam, A., Kurpad, V., & Magapu, H. (2022) Identification and addressal of knowledge gaps in students. *In 2022 3rd International Conference for Emerging Technology (INCET),* (pp. 1–6). IEEE. 10.1109/INCET54531.2022.9824483

Kung, T. H., Cheatham, M., Medenilla, A., Sillos, C., De Leon, L., Elepaño, C., Madriaga, M., Aggabao, R., Diaz-Candido, G., Maningo, J., & Tseng, V. (2023). Performance of ChatGPT on USMLE: Potential for AI-assisted medical education using large language models. *PLOS Digital Health, 2*(2), 1–25. doi:10.1371/journal.pdig.0000198 PMID:36812645

Kurdi, G., Leo, J., Parsia, B., Sattler, U., & Al-Emari, S. (2020). A systematic review of automatic question generation for educational purposes. *International Journal of Artificial Intelligence in Education, 30*(1), 121–204. doi:10.100740593-019-00186-y

Kurniadi, D., Septiana, Y., & Sutedi, A. (2023). Alternative Text Pre-Processing using Chat GPT Open AI. *Jurnal Nasional Pendidikan Teknik Informatika: JANAPATI, 12*(1).

Kuzman, T., Ljubešić, N., & Mozetič, I. (2023). ChatGPT: Beginning of an end of manual annotation? Use case of automatic genre identification. *arXiv preprint arXiv:2303.03953.* 1 - 11.

Laato, S., Morschheuser, B., Hamari, J., & Björne, J. (2023). *AI-assisted learning with ChatGPT and large language models: Implications for higher education.* Preprint.

Labrinidis, A., & Jagadish, H. V. (2012). Challenges and opportunities with big data. *Proceedings of the VLDB Endowment International Conference on Very Large Data Bases, 5*(12), 2032–2033. doi:10.14778/2367502.2367572

Laflamme, A. S., & Bruneault, F. (2023, May). Including a social perspective in AI ethics: The contribution of a dialogue between American Pragmatism and Critical Theory. *In International Conference on Computer Ethics*, (pp. 1 – 15). Illinois Institute of Technology.

Lane, I. (2023). The AI Revolution is Upon us. These are the Jobs at Risk and in Demand. *SBSNews.* https://www.sbs.com.au/news/article/the-ai-revolution-is-upon-us-these-are-the-jobs-at-risk-and-in-demand/izjijemns

Langdon, M., & Langdon, M. (2014). Digital art and cultural commentary. *The Work of Art in a Digital Age: Art, Technology and Globalisation*, (pp. 13-35). Springer.

Langer. (2004). *IT and Organizational Learning: Managing Change through Technology and Education.* CRC Press. https://doi.org/ doi:10.1201/b12383

Lantolf, J. P., & Poehner, M. E. (2004). Dynamic assessment of L2 development: Bringing the past into the future. *Journal of Applied Linguistics and Professional Practice, 1*(1), 49–72. doi:10.1558/japl.1.1.49.55872

Larson, J., & Marsh, J. (2005). *Making Literacy Real: Theories and Practices for Learning and Teaching.* Sage. doi:10.4135/9781446211953

Larsson, S., & Heintz, F. (2020). Transparency in artificial intelligence. *Internet Policy Review, 9*(2). doi:10.14763/2020.2.1469

Lauricella, S., & Kay, R. (2013). Exploring the use of text and instant messaging in higher education classrooms. *Research in Learning Technology, 21.* doi:10.3402/rlt.v21i0.19061

Leach, N. (2019). Do robots dream of digital sheep? *Proceedings of ACADIA 19: Ubiquity and Autonomy.* CumInCAD. 10.52842/conf.acadia.2019.298

Learning Policy Institute. (2021). *Teacher well-being: What is it and why does it matter?* Learning Policy Institute. https://learningpolicyinstitute.org/press-release/teacher-well-being-what-it-and-why-does-it-matter

LeaseM. (2013). Mechanical Turk is not Anonymous. doi:10.2139/ssrn.2228728

Lee, K. J. (2022). Adaptive expertise, career adaptability, and career success of R&D personnel. *Technology Analysis and Strategic Management*, 1–13. doi:10.1080/09537325.2022.2053517

Lee, S. (2022). Efficient content creation in education using AI: A case study. *Journal of Educational Technology, 45*(2), 143–158.

Lehmann, F. (2023, April). Mixed-Initiative Interaction with Computational Generative Systems. In *Extended Abstracts of the 2023 CHI Conference on Human Factors in Computing Systems* (pp. 1-6). ACM. 10.1145/3544549.3577061

Leiker, D., Finnigan, S., Gyllen, A. R., & Cukurova, M. (2023) Prototyping the use of large language models (llms) for adult learning content creation at scale. In AIED Workshops. AIED.

Leiker, D., Gyllen, A. R., Eldesouky, I., & Cukurova, M. (2023). *Generative AI for learning: Investigating the potential of synthetic learning videos*. arXiv preprint arXiv:2304.03784. 1 - 12.

Leiser, A., & Schlippe, T. (2022, February). AI in art: Simulating the human painting process. In *ArtsIT, Interactivity and Game Creation: Creative Heritage. New Perspectives from Media Arts and Artificial Intelligence. 10th EAI International Conference, ArtsIT 2021, Virtual Event, December 2-3, 2021, Proceedings* (pp. 295-308). Cham: Springer International Publishing.

Leong, J. (2023). Using generative AI to cultivate positive emotions and mindsets for self-development and learning. *XRDS: Crossroads. The ACM Magazine for Students, 29*(3), 52–56.

Lepri, B., Oliver, N., Letouzé, E., Pentland, A., & Vinck, P. (2018). Fair, transparent, and accountable algorithmic decision-making processes: The premise, the proposed solutions, and the open challenges. *Philosophy & Technology, 31*(4), 611–627. doi:10.100713347-017-0279-x

Li, L., Fan, L., Atreja, S., & Hemphill, L. (2023). "HOT" ChatGPT: The promise of ChatGPT in detecting and discriminating hateful, offensive, and toxic comments on social media. *arXiv preprint arXiv:2304.10619.*

Li, L., Ma, Z., Fan, L., Lee, S., Yu, H., & Hemphill, L. (2023). ChatGPT in education: A discourse analysis of worries and concerns on social media. *arXiv preprint arXiv:2305.02201.* 1 - 35.

Li, Y., Li, J., Suhara, Y., Doan, A., & Tan, W. C. (2020). Deep entity matching with pre-trained language models. *arXiv preprint arXiv:2004.00584.*

Li, Y., Sha, L., Yan, L., Lin, J., Raković, M., Galbraith, K., Lyons, K., Gašević, D. and Chen, G. (2023). Can large language models write reflectively. *Computers and Education: Artificial Intelligence, 100140.*

Liang, W., Yuksekgonul, M., Mao, Y., Wu, E., & Zou, J. (2023). Gpt detectors are biased against non-native english writers. arXiv preprint arXiv:2304.02819.

Liang, P. P., Wu, C., Morency, L. P., & Salakhutdinov, R. (2021, July). Towards understanding and mitigating social biases in language models. In *International Conference on Machine Learning* (pp. 6565-6576). PMLR.

Liao, Z. Y., & Chien, S. F. (n.d.) *INK-SIGHT, MY SIGHT.* Research Gate.

Li, C., & Xing, W. (2021). Natural language generation using deep learning to support mooc learners. *International Journal of Artificial Intelligence in Education, 31*(2), 186–214. doi:10.100740593-020-00235-x

Li, K., Kumar, A., & Chen, J. H. (1960). A., & Chen, J. H. (2023). How Chatbots and Large Language Model Artificial Intelligence Systems Will Reshape Modern Medicine: Fountain of Creativity or Pandora's Box? *Archives of Internal Medicine, 183*(6), 596–597. doi:10.1001/jamainternmed.2023.1835 PMID:37115531

Lim, W. M., Gunasekara, A., Pallant, J. L., Pallant, J. I., & Pechenkina, E. (2023). Generative AI and the future of education: Ragnarök or reformation? A paradoxical perspective from management educators. *International Journal of Management Education, 21*(2), 100790. doi:10.1016/j.ijme.2023.100790

Lin, C. J., & Mubarok, H. (2021). Learning analytics for investigating the mind map-guided AI chatbot approach in an EFL flipped speaking classroom. *Journal of Educational Technology & Society, 24*(4), 16–35.

Lin, L., & Long, D. (2023, June). Generative AI futures: A speculative design exploration. In *Proceedings of the 15th Conference on Creativity and Cognition* (pp. 380-383). ACM. 10.1145/3591196.3596616

Lin, Y. (2020, October). Research on application and breakthrough of artificial intelligence in art design in the new era. []. IOP Publishing.]. *Journal of Physics: Conference Series, 1648*(3), 032187. doi:10.1088/1742-6596/1648/3/032187

Lin, Z., Xu, P., Winata, G. I., Siddique, F. B., Liu, Z., Shin, J., & Fung, P. (2020, April). Caire: An end-to-end empathetic chatbot. *Proceedings of the AAAI Conference on Artificial Intelligence, 34*(09), 13622–13623. doi:10.1609/aaai.v34i09.7098

Li, S., & Gu, X. (2023). A Risk Framework for Human-centered Artificial Intelligence in Education. *Journal of Educational Technology & Society, 26*(1), 187–202.

Littman, M. L., Ajunwa, I., Berger, G., Boutilier, C., Currie, M., Doshi-Velez, F., & Walsh, T. (2022). Gathering strength, gathering storms: The one hundred year study on artificial intelligence (AI100) 2021 study panel report. *arXiv preprint arXiv:2210.15767.*

Liu, H., Ning, R., Teng, Z., Liu, J., Zhou, Q., & Zhang, Y. (2023). Evaluating the logical reasoning ability of ChatGPTand GPT-4. *arXiv preprint arXiv:2304.03439.*

Liu, N. F., Zhang, T., & Liang, P. (2023). Evaluating verifiability in generative search engines. *arXiv preprint arXiv:2304.09848.*

Liu, V. (2023, April). Beyond text-to-image: Multimodal prompts to explore generative AI. In *Extended Abstracts of the 2023 CHI Conference on Human Factors in Computing Systems* (pp. 1-6).

Liu, Y., Han, T., Ma, S., Zhang, J., Yang, Y., Tian, J., & Ge, B. (2023). Summary of ChatGPT/GPT-4 research and perspective towards the future of large language models. *arXiv preprint arXiv:2304.01852.*

Liu, Z., He, X., Liu, L., Liu, T., & Zhai, X. (2023). *Context matters: A strategy to pre-train language model for science education.* arXiv preprint arXiv:2301.12031. doi:10.1007/978-3-031-36336-8_103

Liu. (2021). Mitigating Political Bias in Language Models Through Reinforced Calibration. *The Thirty-Fifth AAAI Conference on Artificial Intelligence* (AAAI-21). Association for the Advancement of Artificial Intelligence. https://cdn.aaai.org/ojs/17744/17744-13-21238-1-2-20210518.pdf

Liu, K. H., Lin, C. C., & Liu, T. J. (2022, January). Image generation by residual block based generative adversarial networks. In *2022 IEEE International Conference on Consumer Electronics (ICCE)* (pp. 1-4). IEEE. 10.1109/ICCE53296.2022.9730533

Liu, O. L., Frankel, L., & Roohr, K. C. (2014). Assessing critical thinking in higher education: Current state and directions for next-generation assessment. *ETS Research Report Series, 2014*(1), 1–23. doi:10.1002/ets2.12009

Liu, S., Liu, S., Liu, Z., Peng, X., & Yang, Z. (2022). Automated detection of emotional and cognitive engagement in mooc discussions to predict learning achievement. *Computers & Education, 181*, 104461. doi:10.1016/j.compedu.2022.104461

Liu, X. M., & Murphy, D. (2020). A Multi-Faceted Approach for Trustworthy AI in Cybersecurity. *Journal of Strategic Innovation & Sustainability, 15*(6).

Liu, Y., & Martindale, T. (2011). The new cognitive psychology of creativity. *Journal of the Creative Process, 11*(1), 1–10.

Li, Y., Gu, J., & Wang, L. (2020, November). Research on artificial intelligence ethics in the field of art design. []. IOP Publishing.]. *Journal of Physics: Conference Series, 1673*(1), 012052. doi:10.1088/1742-6596/1673/1/012052

Lo, C. K. (2023). What is the impact of chatgpt on education? a rapid review of the literature. *Education Sciences, 13*(4), 410.

Logan, R. L., IV, Liu, N. F., Peters, M. E., Gardner, M., & Singh, S. (2019). Barack's wife Hillary: Using knowledge-graphs for fact-aware language modeling. *arXiv preprint arXiv:1906.07241*. doi:10.18653/v1/P19-1598

Loughlin, M., & Copeland, S. M. (2021). Humans, machines and decisions: Clinical reasoning in the age of artificial intelligence, evidence-based medicine and Covid-19. *Journal of Evaluation in Clinical Practice, 27*(3), 475–477. doi:10.1111/jep.13572 PMID:33890703

Loukina, A., Madnani, N., & Zechner, K. (2019). The many dimensions of algorithmic fairness in educational applications. In *Proceedings of the Fourteenth Workshop on Innovative Use of NLP for Building Educational Applications* (pp. 1–10). Association for Computational Linguistics. 10.18653/v1/W19-4401

Lu, Q., Qiu, B., Ding, L., Xie, L., & Tao, D. (2023). Error analysis prompting enables human-like translation evaluation in large language models: A case study on ChatGPT. *arXiv preprint arXiv:2303.13809*. doi:10.20944/preprints202303.0255.v1

Luckin, George, K., & Cukurova, M. (2022). *AI for school teachers*. Taylor & Francis Group.

Luo, Z., Xie, Q., & Ananiadou, S. (2023). ChatGPT as a factual inconsistency evaluator for text summarization. *arXiv preprint arXiv:2303.15621*. 1 - 12.

Lushetich, N. (2022). How many angels can dance on the head of a pin? Understanding 'alien' thought. *AI & Society, 37*(4), 1411–1425. doi:10.100700146-021-01252-7

Lu, Y., Pea, R., & Niemi, H. (2023). *AI in Learning: Designing the Future*. Springer Nature., doi:10.1007/978-3-031-09687-7

Lv, Z. (2023). Generative artificial intelligence in the metaverse era. *Cognitive Robotics,* 208 - 217.

Lynch, M. (2017, August 6). The benefits of Artificial Intelligence in Education. *The Edvocate*. https://www.theedadvocate.org/benefits-artificial-intelligence-education/

Lynch, M. (2019, September 9). 26 ways that Artificial Intelligence (AI) is transforming education for the better. *The Edvocate*. https://www.theedadvocate.org/26-ways-that-artificial-intelligence-ai-is-transforming-education-for-the-better/

Ma, Q., Wu, S., & Koedinger, K. (2023). Is llm the better programming partner? In AIED Workshops. AIED.

Ma, Y., & Siau, K. L. (2018). Artificial intelligence impacts on higher education. *MWAIS Proceedings, 42*(5), 1-5.

Mabe, K., & Bwalya, K. J. (2022). Critical soft skills for information and knowledge management practitioners in the fourth industrial revolution. *South African Journal of Information Management, 24*(1), 1–11. doi:10.4102ajim.v24i1.1519

Macalister, & Nation, I. S. P. (2013). *Case Studies in Language Curriculum Design Concepts and Approaches in Action Around the World.* Taylor and Francis.

Machado, P., Romero, J., & Greenfield, G. (2021). Applicability of convolutional neural network artistic style transfer algorithms. In P. Machado, J. Romero, and G. Greenfield's Artificial Intelligence and the Arts: Computational Creativity, Artistic Behavior, and Tools for Creatives, (pp. 61-81). Springer.

Maddigan, P., & Susnjak, T. (2023). Chat2vis: Generating data visualisations via natural language using ChatGPT, Codex and GPT-3 large language models. *IEEE Access : Practical Innovations, Open Solutions, 11*, 45181–4193. doi:10.1109/ACCESS.2023.3274199

Mageira, K., Pittou, D., Papasalouros, A., Kotis, K., Zangogianni, P., & Daradoumis, A. (2022). Educational AI chatbots for content and language integrated learning. *Applied Sciences (Basel, Switzerland), 12*(7), 3239. doi:10.3390/app12073239

Magness, J., & Mitchell, M. M. (2022). Religious Studies & the Imagined Boundaries of the Humanities. *Daedalus, 151*(3), 166–179. doi:10.1162/daed_a_01936

Maheen, F., Asif, M., Ahmad, H., Ahmad, S., Alturise, F., Asiry, O., & Ghadi, Y. Y. (2022). Automatic computer science domain multiple-choice questions generation based on informative sentences. *PeerJ. Computer Science, 8*, e1010. doi:10.7717/peerj-cs.1010 PMID:36091982

Maiocchi, R. (1991). Can you make a computer understand and produce art? *AI & Society, 5*(3), 183–201. doi:10.1007/BF01891915

Mali, M. T. S., & Deshmukh, R. K. (2023). Use of Chat GPT in library services. [IJCRT]. *International Journal of Creative Research Thoughts, 11*(4), f264–f266.

Malinka, K., Peresíni, M., Firc, A., Hujnak, O., & Janus, F. (2023, June). On the educational impact of ChatGPT: Is Artificial Intelligence ready to obtain a university degree? In *Proceedings of the 2023 Conference on Innovation and Technology in Computer Science Education* (pp. 47-53). ACM. 10.1145/3587102.3588827

Marciniak, J., & Szczepański, M. (2020). Individualized learning in a course with a tight schedule. *Procedia Computer Science, 176*, 2059–2068. doi:10.1016/j.procs.2020.09.242 PMID:33042305

Markel, J. M., Opferman, S. G., Landay, J. A., & Piech, C. (2023). GPTeach: Interactive TA Training with GPT Based Students.

Martin, L., Muller, B., Suárez, P. J. O., Dupont, Y., Romary, L., de La Clergerie, É. V., & Sagot, B. (2019). CamemBERT: a tasty French language model. *arXiv preprint arXiv:1911.03894.*

Martín. Lilic, M., & Martínez, M. R. (2022). AI Knowledge Transfer from the University to Society : Applications in High-Impact Sectors (Edition 1) (1st ed., Vol. 1). CRC Press. https://doi.org/ doi:10.1201/9781003276609

Martin, A., & Grudziecki, J. (2006). DigEuLit: Concepts and tools for digital literacy development. *Innovation in Teaching and Learning in Information and Computer Sciences, 5*(4), 249–267. doi:10.11120/ital.2006.05040249

Martínez-Plumed, F., Gómez, E., & Hernández-Orallo, J. (2021). Futures of artificial intelligence through technology readiness levels. *Telematics and Informatics, 58*, 101525.

Martin, S. M. (2019). *Artificial intelligence, mixed reality, and the redefinition of the classroom.* Rowman & Littlefield.

Maslic, A. D., & Kim, E. S. (2021). *An epistemological misalignment of cogs in the AI-Art-Making Machine*. In the Proceedings of the EVA London, London, England.

Massey, J. W. (2020). *The Challenges of Neoliberalism to the Democratic Promises of Higher Education* [Doctoral dissertation, The University of North Carolina at Greensboro].

Mateos-Sanchez, M., Melo, A. C., Blanco, L. S., & García, A. M. F. (2022). Chatbot, as educational and inclusive tool for people with intellectual disabilities. *Sustainability (Basel), 14*(3), 1520–1534. doi:10.3390u14031520

Mayer, J. D., & Salovey, P. (1997). What is emotional intelligence? In P. Salovey & D. Sluyter (Eds.), *Emotional Development and Emotional Intelligence: Implications for Educators* (pp. 3–31). Basic Books.

Mazzone, M., & Elgammal, A. (2019). Art, creativity, and the potential of artificial intelligence. In Arts, 8, page 26. MDPI. 14 doi:10.3390/arts8010026

McCann, S. (2021). Copyright throughout a creative ai pipeline. *The Canadian Journal of Law and Technology*, 109 - 139.

McCormack, J. (2017). Working with generative systems: an artistic perspective. *Electronic Visualisation and the Arts (EVA 2017)*, (pp. 213-218). ACM.

McCormack, J. (2017). Working with generative systems: an artistic perspective. *Electronic Visualisation and the Arts (EVA 2017)*, 213-218.

McCormack, J., Cruz Gambardella, C., Rajcic, N., Krol, S. J., Llano, M. T., & Yang, M. (2023, Apr.). Is writing prompts really making art? In *International Conference on Computational Intelligence in Music, Sound, Art and Design (Part of EvoStar)* (pp. 196-211). Cham: Springer Nature Switzerland.

McCormack, J., Gambardella, C. C., Rajcic, N., Krol, S. J., Llano, M. T., & Yang, M. (2023). Is writing prompts really making art? *arXiv preprint arXiv:2301.13049*. doi:10.1007/978-3-031-29956-8_13

McCormack, J., Bown, O., Dorin, A., McCabe, J., Monro, G., & Whitelaw, M. (2014). Ten questions concerning generative computer art. *Leonardo*, *47*(2), 135–141. doi:10.1162/LEON_a_00533

McCormack, J., Gifford, T., & Hutchings, P. (2019). Autonomy, authenticity, authorship and intention in computer generated art. In *Computational Intelligence in Music, Sound, Art and Design: 8th International Conference*. Springer.

McCoy, R. T., Smolensky, P., Linzen, T., Gao, J., & Celikyilmaz, A. (2021). How much do language models copy from their training data? Evaluating linguistic novelty in text generation using Raven. *arXiv preprint arXiv:2111.09509.*

McGee, R. W. (2023). *Does God exist? The ChatGPT response*. Research Gate.

McGee, R. W. (2023). *Is Chat GPT biased against conservatives? An empirical study*. 1 - 19.

McGee, R. W. (2023). *Is there a duty to pay for the education of other people's children? The ChatGPT response*. SSRN.

McGee, R. W. (2023). What are the Top 20 questions in political philosophy? A ChatGPT reply. Working Paper. SSRN. https://ssrn.com/abstract= 4413440.

McGee, R. W. (2023). *What will the United States look like in 2050? A ChatGPT short story*. (Working paper). Research Gate.

McGeeR. W. (2023). *Annie Chan: Three short stories written with Chat GPT*. SSRN 4359403.

McGee, R. W. (2023). Ethics committees can be unethical: The ChatGPT response. SSRN, 4392258.

McHugh, J. (2023). *Defensive AI: Experimental study* [Doctoral dissertation, Marymount University].

McIlroy-Young, R., Kleinberg, J., Sen, S., Barocas, S., & Anderson, A. (2022, July). Mimetic models: Ethical implications of ai that acts like you. In *Proceedings of the 2022 AAAI/ACM Conference on AI, Ethics, and Society* (pp. 479-490). ACM. 10.1145/3514094.3534177

McKinsey & Company. (2023). *The State of AI in 2023: Generative AI's Breakout Year.* McKinsey & Company. https://www.mckinsey.com/~/media/mckinsey/business%20functions/quantumblack/our%20insights/the%20state%20of%20ai%20in%202023%20generative%20ais%20breakout%20year/the-state-of-ai-in-2023-generative-ais-breakout-year_vf.pdf?shouldIndex=false

McMahan, H. B., Ramage, D., Talwar, K., & Zhang, L. (2017). Learning differentially private recurrent language models. *arXiv preprint arXiv:1710.06963.*

McPherson, S. S. (2009). *Tim Berners-Lee: Inventor of the World Wide Web.* Twenty-First Century Books.

Menéndez, A. (Ed.). (2022). *Strategy, policy, practice, and governance for AI in higher education institutions.* IGI Global. doi:10.4018/978-1-7998-9247-2

Mengalli, N. M., & de Carvalho, A. A. (2023). Creation of Digital Solutions in Higher Education: Strategies with Hands-On and Disruptive Technologies in Phygital Transformation. In A. Munna, V. Nadda, T. Allahyari, G. Cantafio, & S. Bilan (Eds.), *Perspectives on Enhancing Learning Experience Through Digital Strategy in Higher Education.* IGI Global. doi:10.4018/978-1-6684-8282-7.ch001

Mental Health Commission of Canada. (2013). *Making the Case for Investing in Mental Health in Canada.* Mental Health Commission of Canada. https://www.mentalhealthcommission.ca/sites/default/files/2016-06/Investing_in_Mental_Health_FINAL_Version_ENG.pdf

Merchant, B. (2019, Mar. 7). Why self-checkout is and has always been the worst. *Gizmodo.* https://gizmodo.com/why-self-checkout-is-and-has-always-been-the-worst-1833106695

Messerli, P., Murniningtyas, E., Eloundou-Enyegue, P., Foli, E. G., Furman, E., Glassman, A., & van Ypersele, J. P. (2019). *Global sustainable development report 2019: the future is now–science for achieving sustainable development.*

Mhlanga, D. (2023). Open ai in education, the responsible and ethical use of chatgpt towards lifelong learning. *Education, the Responsible and Ethical Use of ChatGPT Towards Lifelong Learning (February 11, 2023).* 3

Miah, M. S. (2023). Upskilling and Reskilling of Artificial Intelligence Trends in Knowledge Management for Enterprise Search. *Multicultural Education, 9.* https://mc-caddogap.com/wp-content/uploads/galleyproof-11-mc-9-11.pdf

Mialon, G., Dessì, R., Lomeli, M., Nalmpantis, C., Pasunuru, R., Raileanu, R., & Scialom, T. (2023). Augmented language models: A survey. *arXiv preprint arXiv:2302.07842.*

Miao, H., & Ahn, H. (2023). Impact of ChatGPT on interdisciplinary nursing education and research. *Asian/Pacific Island Nursing Journal, 7*(1), e48136, 1 - 3.

Miguel, P. M. D., De-Pablos-Heredero, C., Montes, J. L., & García, A. (2022). Impact of Dynamic Capabilities on Customer Satisfaction through Digital Transformation in the Automotive Sector. *Sustainability (Basel), 14*(8), 4772. doi:10.3390u14084772

Mikalonytė, E. S., & Kneer, M. (2022, September). Can artificial intelligence make art? Folk intuitions as to whether AI-driven robots can be viewed as artists and produce art. *ACM Transactions on Human-Robot Interaction,* 11(4). *Article, 43,* 1–19.

Mikhailava, V., Pyshkin, E., Blake, J., Chernonog, S., Lezhenin, I., & Bogach, N. (2022). Tailoring computer-assisted pronunciation teaching: Mixing and matching the mode and manner of feedback to learners. *Proceedings of INTED, 2022,* 767–773. doi:10.21125/inted.2022.0263

Miller. (2023). *AI for educators: learning strategies, teacher efficiencies, and a vision for an artificial intelligence future.* Ditch That Textbook, division of Dave Burgess Consulting, Incorporated.

Miller. (2023a). Shifting to Accommodate a World with AI. In *AI for Educators.* Dave Burgess Consulting, Inc.

Milton, J., & Al-Busaidi, A. (2023). New Role of Leadership in AI Era: Educational Sector. In *SHS Web of Conferences (Vol. 156,* p. 09005). EDP Sciences.

Min, B., Ross, H., Sulem, E., Veyseh, A. P. B., Nguyen, T. H., Sainz, O., & Roth, D. (2021). Recent advances in natural language processing via large pre-trained language models: A survey. *arXiv preprint arXiv:2111.01243.*

Miner, A. S., Laranjo, L., & Kocaballi, A. B. (2020). Chatbots in the fight against the COVID-19 pandemic. *Digital Medicine*, *3*, 1–4. PMID:32377576

Minoli, D. (2013). *Building the internet of things with IPv6 and MIPv6: The evolving world of M2M communications*. John Wiley & Sons. doi:10.1002/9781118647059

Minsky, M. L. (1991). Logical Versus Analogical or Symbolic Versus Connectionist or Neat Versus Scruffy. *AI Magazine*, *12*(2), 2. doi:10.1609/aimag.v12i2.894

Mishra. (2023). Indian Paediatrics' Policy Regarding Artificial Intelligence (AI) — Enabled Large Language Models. *Indian Paediatrics*, *60*(3), 171–171. doi:10.1007/s13312-023-2825-1

Mishra, L., Gupta, T., & Shree, A. (2020). Online teaching-learning in higher education during lockdown period of COVID-19 pandemic. *International Journal of Educational Research Open*, *1*, 100012. doi:10.1016/j.ijedro.2020.100012 PMID:35059663

MIT Technology Review. (2023). *Por que é impossível criar um modelo de linguagem de IA imparcial? MIT Technology Review*. https://mittechreview.com.br/por-que-e-impossivel-criar-um-modelo-de-linguagem-de-ia-imparcial/

Mitchell, M., Wu, S., Zaldivar, A., Barnes, P., Vasserman, L., Hutchinson, B., & Gebru, T. (2019). Model cards for model reporting. In *Proceedings of the conference on fairness, accountability, and transparency* (pp. 220–229). ACM. 10.1145/3287560.3287596

Modestino, A. S., Shoag, D., & Ballance, J. (2016). Downskilling: Changes in Employer Skill Requirements Over the Business Cycle. *Labour Economics*, *41p*. https://scholar.harvard.edu/shoag/publications/downskilling-changes-employer-skill-requirements-over-business-cycle

Mohzan, M. A. M., Hassan, N., & Abd Halil, N. (2013). The influence of emotional intelligence on academic achievement. *Procedia: Social and Behavioral Sciences*, *90*, 303–312. doi:10.1016/j.sbspro.2013.07.095

Mok, A., & Zinkula, J. (2023). ChatGPT may be coming for our jobs. Here are the 10 roles that AI is most likely to replace. *Insider*. https://www.businessinsider.com/chatgpt-jobs-at-risk-replacement-artificial-intelligence-ai-labor-trends-2023-02?amp=#amp_tf=From%20%251%24s&aoh=16754252090476&csi=0&referrer=https%3A%2F%2Fwww.google.com

Mökander, J., Schuett, J., Kirk, H. R., & Floridi, L. (2023). Auditing large language models: A three-layered approach. *arXiv preprint arXiv:2302.08500.*

MollickE.MollickL. (2023). (rep.). *Using AI to Implement Effective Teaching Strategies in Classrooms: Five Strategies, Including Prompts* (pp. 1–26). SSRN.

Mondal, S., Das, S., & Vrana, V. G. (2023). How to bell the cat? A theoretical review of generative artificial intelligence towards digital disruption in all walks of life. *Technologies*, *11*(2), 44. doi:10.3390/technologies11020044

Monett, D., & Lewis, C. W. (2018). Getting clarity by defining artificial intelligence—A survey. In *Philosophy and theory of artificial intelligence 2017* (pp. 212–214). Springer International Publishing. doi:10.1007/978-3-319-96448-5_21

Monmarché, N., Mahnich, I., & Slimane, M. (2008). Artificial art made by artificial ants. *The Art of Artificial Evolution: A Handbook on Evolutionary Art and Music*, (pp. 227-247).

Montenegro, L. D., & Young, M. N. (2020, September). Operational challenges in the food industry and supply chain during the COVID-19 pandemic: A literature review. In *2020 7th International Conference on Frontiers of Industrial Engineering (ICFIE)* (pp. 1-5). IEEE. 10.1109/ICFIE50845.2020.9266743

Montgomery County Education Association [@mceamea]. (2021, November 9). *"We don't have the time for the self-care our employer tells us to take. We normally take on extra* [image attached][Tweet]. X. https://twitter.com/mceanea?ref_src=twsrc%5Etfw%7Ctwcamp%5Etweetembed%7Ctwterm%5E1458181607756636162%7Ctwgr%5Ee7558aadbc7f678cb12248fd0f01323f05807d4c%7Ctwcon%5Es1_&ref_url=https%3A%2F%2Fwww.nea.org%2Fnea-today%2Fall-news-articles%2Fgetting-serious-about-teacher-burnout

Moore, R. C., & Lewis, W. (2010, July). Intelligent selection of language model training data. In *Proceedings of the ACL 2010 Conference Short Papers* (pp. 220-224). ACL.

Moreira dos Santos, C. A., Carvalho Pereira, M. A., de Souza, M. A., Machado Dias, J. P., & Oliveira, F. S. (2020). Different teaching approaches and use of active learning strategies as tools for inter-and transdisciplinary education. *International Journal of Social Science Studies*, *8*(2), 15. doi:10.11114/ijsss.v8i2.4693

Morris, M. R. (2023). Scientists' perspectives on the potential for generative AI in their fields. *arXiv preprint arXiv:2304.01420.* 1 - 26.

Morris, M. R. (2020). AI and accessibility. *Communications of the ACM*, *63*(6), 35–37. doi:10.1145/3356727

Mueller, J. P., & Massaron, L. (2021). *Artificial Intelligence For Dummies*. John Wiley & Sons.

Muller, M., Chilton, L. B., Kantosalo, A., Liao, Q. V., Maher, M. L., Martin, C. P., & Walsh, G. (2023, Apr.). GenAICHI 2023: Generative AI and HCI at CHI 2023. *In Extended Abstracts of the 2023 CHI Conference on Human Factors in Computing Systems* (pp. 1-7). ACM.

Muller, M., Chilton, L. B., Kantosalo, A., Martin, C. P., & Walsh, G. (2022, Apr.). GenAICHI: generative AI and HCI. In *CHI Conference on Human Factors in Computing Systems Extended Abstracts* (pp. 1-7). ACM.

Murchan, D., & Johnston, K. (Eds.). (2021). *Curriculum change within policy and practice: Reforming second-level education in Ireland* (1st ed. 2021). Palgrave Macmillan. doi:10.1007/978-3-030-50707-7

Murphy, B. P. (2022). Is Lensa AI Stealing from Human Art? An Expert Explains the Controversy. *Science Alert*. https://www-sciencealert-com.cdn.ampproject.org/c/s/www.sciencealert.com/is-lensa-ai-stealing-from-human-art-an-expert-explains-the-controversy/amp

Murugesan, S., & Cherukuri, A. K. (2023). The rise of generative artificial Intelligence and its impact on education: The promises and perils. *Computer*, *56*(5), 116–121. doi:10.1109/MC.2023.3253292

Nadeem, M., Bethke, A., & Reddy, S. (2020). StereoSet: Measuring stereotypical bias in pretrained language models. *arXiv preprint arXiv:2004.09456.*

Nagowah, L., & Nagowah, S. (2009). A reflection on the dominant learning theories: Behaviourism, cognitivism and constructivism. *International Journal of Learning*, *16*(2), 279–286. doi:10.18848/1447-9494/CGP/v16i02/46136

Najarro, I. (2022, April 26). Here's how many hours a week teachers work. *Education Week*. https://www.edweek.org/teaching-learning/heres-how-many-hours-a-week-teachers-work/2022/04

Namaziandost, E., Shafiee, S., & Suryadi, R. (2020). Using mobile instant messaging in teaching vocabulary to pre-intermediate EFL learners: The case of WhatsApp. Process. *Journal of English Education*, *5*(1), 1–10. doi:10.31327/jee.v5i1.1162

Nangia, N., Vania, C., Bhalerao, R., & Bowman, S. R. (2020). CrowS-pairs: A challenge dataset for measuring social biases in masked language models. *arXiv preprint arXiv:2010.00133*. doi:10.18653/v1/2020.emnlp-main.154

Nardo, M., Forino, D., & Murino, T. (2020). The evolution of man–machine interaction: The role of human in Industry 4.0 paradigm. *Production & Manufacturing Research*, *8*(1), 20–34. doi:10.1080/21693277.2020.1737592

NathK. (2022). Evolution of the Internet from Web 1.0 to Metaverse: The good, the bad and the ugly. TechRxiv. doi:10.36227/techrxiv.19743676.v1

National Center for Education Statistics. (2020). *Who is nontraditional?* NCES. https://nces.ed.gov/pubs/web/97578e.asp

National curriculum for England. (2013, July 16). Department for Education, UK Government. https://www.gov.uk/government/publications/national-curriculum-in-england-primary-curriculum

National Education Association. (2017). *NEA calls for educator-led solutions to combat teacher shortage and stress.* NEA. https://www.nea.org/press-releases/2017/06/30/nea-calls-educator-led-solutions-combat-teacher-shortage-and-stress

National Education Association. (2018). *Teacher stress and health: Effects on teachers, students, and schools.* NEA. https://www.nea.org/resource-library/teacher-stress-and-health-effects-teachers-students-and-schools

National Education Association. (2019). *Time to learn: Teacher workload survey results.* NEA. https://www.nea.org/advocating-for-change/new-from-nea/time-learn-teacher-workload-survey-results

Neves, P. S. (2022). Chat GPT BBDS" Interview" 1, December 2022. *BBDS-Black Book: Drawing and Sketching*, *3*(2), 44–49.

New Jersey Institute of Technology. (2023). *ELIZA: A very basic Rogerian psychotherapist chatbot.* NJIT. https://web.njit.edu/~ronkowit/eliza.html

Newcomb, A. (2018). Addressing Ethical And Privacy Concerns. *NBC News.* https://www.nbcnews.com/tech/social-media/timeline-facebook-s-privacy-issues-its-responses-n859651

News, N. P. R. (2017). *It has to have a soul: How chatbots get their personalities.* NPR. https://www.npr.org/sections/alltechconsidered/2017/03/10/519002884/it-has-to-have-a-soul-how-chatbots-get-their-personalities

Nguyen, A., Ngo, H. N., Hong, Y., Dang, B., & Nguyen, B. T. (2022). Ethical principles for artificial intelligence in education. *Education and Information Technologies*, *28*(4), 4221–4241. doi:10.100710639-022-11316-w PMID:36254344

Nguyen, K., Vu, N., Nguyen, D., & Than, K. (2022, December). Random Generative Adversarial Networks. In *Proceedings of the 11th International Symposium on Information and Communication Technology* (pp. 66-73).

Nida-Rümelin, J. (2022). Digital Humanism and the Limits of Artificial Intelligence. In *Perspectives on Digital Humanism* (pp. 71–75). Springer. doi:10.1007/978-3-030-86144-5_10

NIOSH. (2015). *Stress at work. Centers for Disease Control and Prevention.* CDC. https://www.cdc.gov/niosh/docs/99-101/

Notaro, A. (2020). State-of-the-art: AI through the (artificial) artist's eye. *EVA London 2020: Electronic Visualisation and the Arts*, (pp. 322-328). ACM.

Notaro, A. (2020). State-of-the-art: AI through the (artificial) artist's eye. *EVA London 2020: Electronic Visualisation and the Arts*, 322-328.

Núñez-Sánchez, S., & Valente, M. J. (2023). Sustainable development goals and climate change in Spanish technology disciplines' curricula: From LOMCE to LOMLOE. *Sustainability (Basel)*, *15*(13), 10301. doi:10.3390u151310301

Nussbaum, M. C. (2006). *Frontiers of Justice: Disability, Nationality, Species Membership.* Harvard University Press. doi:10.2307/j.ctv1c7zftw

Nussbaum, M. C. (2000). *Women and Human Development: The Capabilities Approach*. Cambridge University Press. doi:10.1017/CBO9780511841286

Nye, B., Mee, D., & Core, M. G. (2023) Generative large language models for dialog-based tutoring: An early consideration of opportunities and concerns. In AIED Workshops. AIED.

O'Neil, C. (2017). *Weapons of math destruction: How big data increases inequality and threatens democracy*. Crown.

OECD. (2019). *TALIS 2018 Results* (Vol. I). Teachers and School Leaders as Lifelong Learners. doi:10.1787/1d0bc92a-

Ogundare, O., & Araya, G. Q. (2023). Comparative analysis of CHATGPT and the evolution of language models. *arXiv preprint arXiv:2304.02468*. doi:10.22541/au.168062641.15097484/v1

Oh, C., Song, J., Choi, J., Kim, S., Lee, S., & Suh, B. (2018, Apr.). I lead, you help but only with enough details: Understanding user experience of co-creation with artificial intelligence. In *Proceedings of the 2018 CHI Conference on Human Factors in Computing Systems* (pp. 1-13). ACM. 10.1145/3173574.3174223

Ojose, B. (2008). Applying Piaget's theory of cognitive development to mathematics instruction. *The Mathematics Educator*, *18*(1), 26–30.

Okon, U. (2018). Curriculum definition: A misleading philosophy. *International Advancement in Development Studies, 13*(2). http://www.irdionline.org/world/article/CURRICULUM%20DEFINITION%202018.pdf

Oleny, A. (2023) Generating multiple choice questions from a textbook: Llms match human performance on most metrics. In AIED Workshops. AIED.

Omolara, A. E., Alabdulatif, A., Abiodun, O. I., Alawida, M., Alabdulatif, A., & Arshad, H. (2022). The internet of things security: A survey encompassing unexplored areas and new insights. *Computers & Security*, *112*, 102494. doi:10.1016/j.cose.2021.102494

Open A. I. (2023) *Introducing chatgpt*. OpenAI. https://openai.com/blog/chatgpt.

Open A. I. (2023a). *Introducing ChatGPT*. Open AI. https://openai.com/blog/chatgpt

Open A. I. (2023b). *GPT-4 technical report*. Open AI. https://cdn.openai.com/papers/gpt-4.pdf

Orlando, J., & Attard, C. (2015). Digital natives come of age: The reality of today's early career teachers using mobile devices to teach mathematics. *Mathematics Education Research Journal*, *28*(1), 107–121. doi:10.100713394-015-0159-6

Ostherr, K. (2020). Artificial intelligence and medical humanities. *The Journal of Medical Humanities*, 1–22. PMID:32654043

Ouyang, L., Wu, J., Jiang, X., Almeida, D., Wainwright, C., Mishkin, P., & Lowe, R. (2022). Training language models to follow instructions with human feedback. *Advances in Neural Information Processing Systems*, *35*, 27730–27744.

Pagnozzi, F. (2022). People Analytics and Human Resource Management: How the Use of Smart Data Can Improve the Training Processes. *PuntOorg International Journal*, *7*(2), 108–123. doi:10.19245/25.05.pij.7.2.2

Palea, D., Zhou, H. H., & Gupta, K. (2020). Transformer Bard: Music and poem generation using transformer models. *In the Proceedings of Conference '20. Aug. 2020.* ACM.

Palladino, J., & Shepard, L. A. (2023). Authentic Assessment Embedded in Project-Based Learning. *Schools of Opportunity: 10 Research-Based Models for Creating Equity, 67.*

Pan, Y. (2016). Heading toward artificial intelligence 2.0. *Engineering (Beijing)*, *2*(4), 409–413. doi:10.1016/J.ENG.2016.04.018

Pardos, Z. A., & Bhandari, S. (2023). Learning gain differences between ChatGPT and human tutor generated algebra hints. *arXiv preprint arXiv:2302.06871.*

Patel, S., Hamdan, S., & Donahue, S. (2022). Optimising telemedicine in ophthalmology during the COVID-19 pandemic. *Journal of Telemedicine and Telecare*, *28*(7), 498–501. doi:10.1177/1357633X20949796 PMID:32799736

Paulsen, K. (2020). "Shitty automation": Art, artificial intelligence, humans in the loop. Media-N, 16(1).

Pavlik, J. V. (2023). Collaborating With ChatGPT: Considering the Implications of Generative Artificial Intelligence for Journalism and Media Education. *Journalism & Mass Communication Educator.*

Pavlik, J. V. (2023). Collaborating with ChatGPT: Considering the implications of Generative Artificial intelligence for journalism and media education. *Journalism & Mass Communication Educator*, *78*(1), 84–93. doi:10.1177/10776958221149577

Peck, D. (2023). *Teacher burnout statistics: Why teachers quit in 2023: Devlin Peck.* Devlin Peck. https://www.devlinpeck.com/content/teacher-burnout-statistics

Pegoraro, A., Kumari, K., Fereidooni, H., & Sadeghi, A. R. (2023). To ChatGPT, or not to ChatGPT: That is the question! *arXiv preprint arXiv:2304.01487.*

Peng, K., Ding, L., Zhong, Q., Shen, L., Liu, X., Zhang, M., & Tao, D. (2023). Towards making the most of ChatGPT for machine translation. *arXiv preprint arXiv:2303.13780.*

Peng, J., Sridhar, S., Siefker-Radtke, A. O., Selvarajah, S., & Jiang, D. M. (2022). Targeting the FGFR pathway in urothelial carcinoma: The future is now. *Current Treatment Options in Oncology*, *23*(9), 1269–1287. doi:10.100711864-022-01009-4 PMID:35962938

Penn State Extension. (2023). *Conducting a SWOT analysis.* Penn State Extension. https://extension.psu.edu/conducting-a-swot-analysis

Penny, S. (2013). Art and robotics: Sixty years of situated machines. *AI & Society*, *28*(2), 147–156. doi:10.100700146-012-0404-4

Pérez, J. Q., Daradoumis, T., & Puig, J. (2020). Rediscovering the use of chatbots in education: A systematic literature review. *Computer Applications in Engineering Education*, *28*(6), 1549–1565. doi:10.1002/cae.22326

Perkins, M. (2023). Academic integrity considerations of AI large language models in the post-pandemic era: ChatGPT and beyond. *Journal of University Teaching & Learning Practice*, *20*(2), 1 - 24.

Petrilli, M. J. (2008). Wikipedia or wickedpedia? Assessing the online encyclopedia's impact on K-12 education. *Education Next*, *8*(2), 87–88.

Pew Research Center. (2021). *The internet and the pandemic.* Pew Research Center. https://www.pewresearch.org/internet/2021/09/01/the-internet-and-the-pandemic/

Phillips, T., Saleh, A., Glazewski, K. D., Hmelo-Silver, C. E., Mott, B., & Lester, J. C. (2022). Exploring the use of GPT-3 as a tool for evaluating text-based collaborative discourse. *Companion Proceedings of the 12th.* ACL.

Piaget, J., & Inhelder, B. (1972). *The Psychology of the Child.* Basic Books.

Pickell, T. R., & Doak, B. R. (2023). Five ideas for how professors can deal with GPT-3... for now. Digital Commons @ George Fox University. Faculty Publications.

Pieters, J., Voogt, J., & Roblin, N. P. (Eds.). (2019). *Collaborative curriculum design for sustainable innovation and teacher learning* (1st ed. 2019). Springer Nature. doi:10.1007/978-3-030-20062-6

Pinar, W. F. (2004). *What is curriculum theory?* Lawrence Erlbaum Associates Publishers.

Plester, B., Wood, C., & Bell, V. (2008). Txt msg n school literacy: Does texting and knowledge of text abbreviations adversely affect children's literacy attainment? *Literacy*, *42*(3), 137–144. doi:10.1111/j.1741-4369.2008.00489.x

Plester, B., Wood, C., & Joshi, P. (2009). Exploring the relationship between children's knowledge of text message abbreviations and school literacy outcomes. *British Journal of Developmental Psychology*, *27*(1), 145–161. doi:10.1348/026151008X320507 PMID:19972666

Poltronieri, F. (2022). Towards a symbiotic future: Art and creative AI. In *The Language of Creative AI: Practices, Aesthetics and Structures* (pp. 29–41). Springer International Publishing. doi:10.1007/978-3-031-10960-7_2

Powers, E. (2017). My news feed is filtered? Awareness of news personalization among college students. *Digital Journalism (Abingdon, England)*, *5*(10), 1315–1335. doi:10.1080/21670811.2017.1286943

Pragya, C. (n.d.) *Ontology, phenomenology, and other aesthetic conflicts of generative art.*

Precedence Research. (2023). *Chatbot market*. Precedence Research. https://www.precedenceresearch.com/chatbot-market

Preiss, D. D. (2022). Metacognition, Mind Wandering, and Cognitive Flexibility: Understanding Creativity. *Journal of Intelligence*, *10*(3), 69. doi:10.3390/jintelligence10030069 PMID:36135610

Prensky, M. (2001). Digital natives, digital immigrants. *On the Horizon*, *9*(5), 1–6. doi:10.1108/10748120110424816

Price Water HouseCoopers. (2023). *PwC's global artificial intelligence study: Sizing the prize*. PWC. https://www.pwc.com/gx/en/issues/data-and-analytics/publications/artificial-intelligence-study.html

Prikshat, P., Patel, P., Varma, A., & Ishizaka, A. (2022). A multi-stakeholder ethical framework for AI-augmented HRM. *International Journal of Manpower*, *43*(1), 226–250. doi:10.1108/IJM-03-2021-0118

QadirJ. (2022). Engineering education in the era of ChatGPT: Promise and pitfalls of generative AI for education. TechRxiv. 1 - 9.

Qadir, J. (2023). Engineering education in the era of chatgpt: Promise and pitfalls of generative ai for education. In *2023 IEEE Global Engineering Education Conference (EDUCON)*, (pp. 1–9). IEEE. 10.1109/EDUCON54358.2023.10125121

Qin, W., Chen, Z., Wang, L., Lan, Y., Ren, W., & Hong, R. (2023). Read, diagnose and chat: Towards explainable and interactive LLMs-augmented depression detection in social media. *arXiv preprint arXiv:2305.05138.*

Quan-Hoang, V., Anh-Vinh, L., Viet-Phuong, L., Phuong-Hanh, H., & Manh-Toan, H. (2020). Making social sciences more scientific: Literature review by structured data. *MethodsX*, *7*, 100818. doi:10.1016/j.mex.2020.100818 PMID:32257836

Raghupathi, W., & Raghupathi, V. (2014). Big data analytics in healthcare: Promise and potential. *Health Information Science and Systems*, *2*(1), 3. doi:10.1186/2047-2501-2-3 PMID:25825667

Rahaman, M. S., Ahsan, M. M., Anjum, N., Rahman, M. M., & Rahman, M. (2023). *The AI race is on! Google's Bard and OpenAI's ChatGPT head to head: an opinion article*. Research Gate.

Rahaman, M. S., Ahsan, M. T., Anjum, N., Terano, H. J. R., & Rahman, M. M. (2023). From ChatGPT-3 to GPT-4: A significant advancement in AI-Driven NLP tools. *Journal of Engineering and Emerging Technologies*, *2*(1), 1–11. doi:10.52631/jeet.v1i1.188

Rahman, M. M., Terano, H. J., Rahman, M. N., Salamzadeh, A., & Rahaman, M. S. (2023). ChatGPT and Academic Research: A Review and Recommendations Based on Practical Examples. Journal of Education. *Management and Development Studies*, *3*(1), 1–12.

Rajaram, K. (2023). Cultural Intelligence in Teaching and Learning. In *Learning Intelligence: Innovative and Digital Transformative Learning Strategies: Cultural and Social Engineering Perspectives* (pp. 57–118). Springer Nature Singapore. doi:10.1007/978-981-19-9201-8_2

Raji, I. D., Smart, A., White, R. N., Mitchell, M., Gebru, T., Hutchinson, B., & Theron, D. (2020). Closing the AI accountability gap: Defining an end-to-end framework for internal algorithmic auditing. In *Proceedings of the 2020 conference on fairness, accountability, and transparency* (pp. 33–44). 10.1145/3351095.3372873

Ramesh, K., Ravishankaran, S., Joshi, A., & Chandrasekaran, K. (2017). A survey of design techniques for conversational agents. In *Information, communication and computing technology* (Vol. 750, pp. 336–350). Springer. doi:10.1007/978-981-10-6544-6_31

Rannikmäe, M., Holbrook, J., & Soobard, R. (2020). Social Constructivism—Jerome Bruner. In B. Akpan & T. J. Kennedy (Eds.), *Science education in theory and practice: An introductory guide to learning theory* (pp. 259–275). Springer. doi:10.1007/978-3-030-43620-9_18

Rao, Q., & Frtunikj, J. (2018). Deep learning for self-driving cars: Chances and challenges. *Proceedings of the 1st International Workshop on Software Engineering for AI in Autonomous Systems*, (pp. 35–38). ACM. 10.1145/3194085.3194087

Rastogi, C., Ribeiro, M. T., King, N., & Amershi, S. (2023). Supporting human-AI collaboration in auditing LLMs with LLMs. *arXiv preprint arXiv:2304.09991*. 1 21. doi:10.1145/3600211.3604712

Rasul, T., Nair, S., Kalendra, D., Robin, M., de Oliveira Santini, F., Ladeira, W. J., ... Heathcote, L. (2023). The role of ChatGPT in higher education: Benefits, challenges, and future research directions. *Journal of Applied Learning and Teaching*, *6*(1).

Rathore, B. (2023). Future of AI & Generation Alpha: ChatGPT beyond boundaries. *Eduzone: International Peer Reviewed/Refereed Multidisciplinary Journal, 12*(1), 63-68.

Ray, D. (2023). *How UF developed a model for AI across the curriculum.* University of Florida. https://news.ufl.edu/2023/01/ai-university/

Ray, P. P. (2023). Chatgpt: A comprehensive review on background, applications, key challenges, bias, ethics, limitations and future scope. *Internet of Things and Cyber-Physical Systems.*

Raychev, V., Vechev, M., & Yahav, E. (2014, June). Code completion with statistical language models. In *Proceedings of the 35th ACM SIGPLAN Conference on Programming Language Design and Implementation* (pp. 419-428). ACM. 10.1145/2594291.2594321

Reim, W., Åström, J., & Eriksson, O. (2020). Implementation of Artificial Intelligence (AI): A Roadmap for Business Model Innovation. *AI, 1*(2), 2. doi:10.3390/ai1020011

Reinhuber, E. (2022, February). Synthography–An invitation to reconsider the rapidly changing toolkit of digital image creation as a new genre beyond photography. In *ArtsIT, Interactivity and Game Creation: Creative Heritage. New Perspectives from Media Arts and Artificial Intelligence. 10th EAI International Conference, ArtsIT 2021, Virtual Event, December 2-3, 2021, Proceedings* (pp. 321-331). Cham: Springer International Publishing.

Rensfeldt, A. B., & Rahm, L. (2023). Automating Teacher Work? A History of the Politics of Automation and Artificial Intelligence in Education. *Postdigital Science and Education, 5*(1), 25–43. doi:10.100742438-022-00344-x

Replika. (n.d.). *Frequently asked questions.* Replika. https://replika.com/

Reynolds, & Temple, J. A. (2019). *Sustaining Early Childhood Learning Gains: Program, School, and Family Influences.* Cambridge University Press. https://doi.org/ doi:10.1017/9781108349352

Reynolds, L., & McDonell, K. (2021, May). Prompt programming for large language models: Beyond the few-shot paradigm. In *Extended Abstracts of the 2021 CHI Conference on Human Factors in Computing Systems* (pp. 1-7). ACM.

Rezwana, J., & Maher, M. L. (2022). Designing creative AI partners with COFI: A framework for modeling interaction in human-AI co-creative systems. *ACM Transactions on Computer-Human Interaction.*

Roberts, A., Raffel, C., & Shazeer, N. (2020). How much knowledge can you pack into the parameters of a language model? *arXiv preprint arXiv:2002.08910.* doi:10.18653/v1/2020.emnlp-main.437

Roberts, L. D., & Seaman, K. (2018). Good undergraduate dissertation supervision: perspectives of supervisors and dissertation coordinators. *International Journal for Academic Development, 23*(1), 28–40.

Rodrigues, F. R. (2021). Who are You in a Company? A Communicator? An Analyst? A Planner? Or An Executor? *Brainz Magazine.* https://www.brainzmagazine.com/post/who-are-you-in-a-company-a-communicator-an-analyst-a-planner-or-an-executor

Roemmich, K., Schaub, F., & Andalibi, N. (2023, April). Emotion AI at Work: Implications for Workplace Surveillance, Emotional Labor, and Emotional Privacy. In *Proceedings of the 2023 CHI Conference on Human Factors in Computing Systems* (pp. 1-20). ACM. 10.1145/3544548.3580950

Rof, A., Bikfalvi, A., & Marques, P. (2022). Pandemic-accelerated digital transformation of a born digital higher education institution. *Journal of Educational Technology & Society, 25*(1), 124–141.

Roll, I., & Wylie, R. (2016). Evolution and revolution in artificial intelligence in education. *International Journal of Artificial Intelligence in Education, 26*(2), 582–599. doi:10.100740593-016-0110-3

Rospigliosi, P. A. (2023). Artificial intelligence in teaching and learning: What questions should we ask of ChatGPT? *Interactive Learning Environments, 31*(1), 1–3. doi:10.1080/10494820.2023.2180191

Rousseau, H. P. (2023). From Gutenberg to Chat GPT: The challenge of the digital university (No. 2023rb-02). *CIRANO. Burgundy Report, 2023,* RB-02.

Rudolph, J., Tan, S. and Tan, S. (2023) Chatgpt: Bullshit spewer or the end of traditional assessments in higher education? *Journal of Applied Learning and Teaching, 6.*

Rudolph, J., Tan, S., & Tan, S. (2023). War of the chatbots: Bard, Bing Chat, ChatGPT, Ernie and beyond. The new AI gold rush and its impact on higher education. *Journal of Applied Learning and Teaching, 6*(1).

Russell, S. (2022). Artificial Intelligence and the Problem of Control. *Perspectives on Digital Humanism, 19.*

Russell, S., & Norvig, P. (2021). Artificial Intelligence: A Modern Approach, Global Edition. Pearson Higher Ed.

Russell, D., & Kuensting, L. L. (2021). Advancing emergency nurse practitioner training using virtual nursing centers. In D. Russell (Ed.), *Implementing Augmented Reality Into Immersive Virtual Learning Environments* (pp. 151–162). IGI Global. doi:10.4018/978-1-7998-4222-4.ch009

Russell, S. (2019). *Human Compatible: Artificial Intelligence and the Problem of Control.* Penguin Publishing Group.

Ryan, M. (2020). In AI We Trust: Ethics, Artificial Intelligence, and Reliability. *Science and Engineering Ethics, 26*(5), 2749–2767. doi:10.100711948-020-00228-y PMID:32524425

Ryznar, M. (2023). Exams in the time of ChatGPT. *Washington and Lee Law Review Online, 80*(5), 305–322.

Sagiroglu, S., & Sinanc, D. (2013). Big data: A review. *2013 International Conference on Collaboration Technologies and Systems (CTS),* (pp. 42–47). IEEE. 10.1109/CTS.2013.6567202

Sajeeda, A., & Hossain, B. M. (2022). Exploring generative adversarial networks and adversarial training. *International Journal of Cognitive Computing in Engineering*.

Saks, K., Ilves, H., & Noppel, A. (2021). The impact of procedural knowledge on the formation of declarative knowledge: How accomplishing activities designed for developing learning skills impacts teachers' knowledge of learning skills. *Education Sciences, 11*(10), 598. doi:10.3390/educsci11100598

Salah, A. A. A. (2021). AI bugs and failures: How and why to render AI-algorithms more human? *AI for Everyone?*

Salevati, S., & DiPaola, S. (2015). A creative artificial intelligence system to investigate user experience, affect, emotion and creativity. *Electronic Visualisation and the Arts (EVA 2015)*, (pp. 140-147).

Sallam, M. (2023) The utility of chatgpt as an example of large language models in healthcare education, research and practice: Systematic review on the future perspectives and potential limitations. medRxiv, 2023–02.

Sallam, M. (2023). The utility of ChatGPT as an example of large language models in healthcare education, research and practice: Systematic review on the future perspectives and potential limitations. medRxiv, 2023-02.

Sallam, M., Salim, N. A., Ala'a, B., Barakat, M., Fayyad, D., Hallit, S., & Ala'a, B. (2023). ChatGPT output regarding compulsory vaccination and COVID-19 vaccine conspiracy: A descriptive study at the outset of a paradigm shift in online search for information. *Cureus, 15*(2), 1–16. doi:10.7759/cureus.35029 PMID:36819954

Saltelli, A., Ratto, M., Andres, T., Campolongo, F., Cariboni, J., Gatelli, D., & Tarantola, S. (2008). Introduction to sensitivity analysis. *Global sensitivity analysis. PRiMER: Peer-Reviewed Reports in Medical Education Research*, 1–51.

Santaella, L. (2022). Artificial intelligence and creativity under interrogation. In *The Language of Creative AI: Practices, Aesthetics and Structures* (pp. 43–56). Springer International Publishing. doi:10.1007/978-3-031-10960-7_3

Santhana Krishnan, A., Yang, Y., & Schaumont, P. (2020). *Risk and Architecture Factors in Digital Exposure Notification.*, doi:10.1007/978-3-030-60939-9_21

Sardana, D., Fagan, T. R., & Wright, J. T. (2023). ChatGPT: A disruptive innovation or disrupting innovation in academia? *The Journal of the American Dental Association, 154*(5), 361–364. doi:10.1016/j.adaj.2023.02.008 PMID:36948928

Sarsa, S., Denny, P., Hellas, A., & Leinonen, J. (2022) Automatic generation of programming exercises and code explanations using large language models. In *Proceedings of the 2022 ACM Conference on International Computing Education ResearchVolume 1,* (pp. 27–43). ACM. 10.1145/3501385.3543957

Sawatzki, J., Schlippe, T., & Benner-Wickner, M. (2022) Deep learning techniques for automatic short answer grading: Predicting scores for english and german answers. In *Artificial Intelligence in Education: Emerging Technologies, Models and Applications: Proceedings of 2021 2nd International Conference on Artificial Intelligence in Education Technology*, (pp. 65–75). Springer.

Schäfer, M. S. (2023). The Notorious GPT: Science communication in the age of artificial intelligence. *JCOM, Journal of Science Communication, 22*(2), Y02. doi:10.22323/2.22020402

Schemmer, M., Hemmer, P., Nitsche, M., Kühl, N., & Vössing, M. (2022, July). A meta-analysis of the utility of explainable artificial intelligence in human-AI decision-making. In *Proceedings of the 2022 AAAI/ACM Conference on AI, Ethics, and Society* (pp. 617-626). ACM. 10.1145/3514094.3534128

Schick, T., & Schütze, H. (2020). It's not just size that matters: Small language models are also few-shot learners. *arXiv preprint arXiv:2009.07118.*

Schick, T., Dwivedi-Yu, J., Dessì, R., Raileanu, R., Lomeli, M., Zettlemoyer, L., & Scialom, T. (2023). Toolformer: Language models can teach themselves to use tools. *arXiv preprint arXiv:2302.04761.*

Schiff, D. (2022). Education for AI, not AI for Education: The role of education and ethics in national AI policy strategies. *International Journal of Artificial Intelligence in Education, 32*(3), 527–563. doi:10.100740593-021-00270-2

Schleiss, J., Laupichler, M. C., Raupach, T., & Stober, S. (2023). AI Course Design Planning Framework: Developing Domain-Specific AI Education Courses. Education Sciences, 13(9), 954-. https://doi.org/ doi:10.3390/educsci13090954

Schneider, T., & Rea, N. (2018, Sept. 25). Has artificial intelligence given us the next great art movement? Experts say slow down, the 'field is in its infancy.' *Artnet.*

Schneider, J., Richner, R., & Riser, M. (2022). Towards trustworthy autograding of short, multi-lingual, multi-type answers. *International Journal of Artificial Intelligence in Education*, 1–31.

Schramowski, P., Turan, C., Andersen, N., Rothkopf, C. A., & Kersting, K. (2022). Large pre-trained language models contain human-like biases of what is right and wrong to do. *Nature Machine Intelligence*, *4*(3), 258–268. doi:10.103842256-022-00458-8

Schuller, D., & Schuller, B. W. (2018). The age of artificial emotional intelligence. *Computer*, *51*(9), 38–46. doi:10.1109/MC.2018.3620963

Schuster, T., Fisch, A., Gupta, J., Dehghani, M., Bahri, D., Tran, V., & Metzler, D. (2022). Confident adaptive language modeling. *Advances in Neural Information Processing Systems*, *35*, 17456–17472.

Schwab, K. (2017). *The Fourth Industrial Revolution.* Currency.

Schwartz, H. A., & Walden, L. L. (2010). Theoretical models of information systems. In J. G. Birtch (Ed.), *Handbook of Research on Information Systems* (pp. 9–32). IGI Global.

Schwartz, R., Dodge, J., Smith, N. A., & Etzioni, O. (2020). Green AI. *Communications of the ACM*, *63*(12), 54–63. doi:10.1145/3381831

Scripter, L. (2022). Meaningful Lives in an Age of Artificial Intelligence: A Reply to Danaher. *Science and Engineering Ethics*, *28*(1), 1–9. doi:10.100711948-021-00349-y PMID:35094156

Searle, J. R. (1980). Minds, brains, and programs. *Behavioral and Brain Sciences*, *3*(3), 417–424. doi:10.1017/S0140525X00005756

See, A., Pappu, A., Saxena, R., Yerukola, A., & Manning, C. D. (2019). Do massively pretrained language models make better storytellers? *arXiv preprint arXiv:1909.10705*. doi:10.18653/v1/K19-1079

Shafeeg, A., Shazhaev, I., Mihaylov, D., Tularov, A., & Shazhaev, I. (2023). Voice assistant integrated with Chat GPT. *Indonesian Journal of Computer Science*, *12*(1). doi:10.33022/ijcs.v12i1.3146

Shah, N., & Takayama, L. (2019). *The AI educator: Embracing artificial intelligence to transform teaching and learning.* Christensen Institute. https://www.christenseninstitute.org/wp-content/uploads/2019/01/The-AI-Educator.pdf

Shahriar, S., & Hayawi, K. (2022, March). NFTGAN: Non-Fungible Token art generation using Generative Adversarial Networks. In *2022 7th International Conference on Machine Learning Technologies (ICMLT)* (pp. 255-259). ACM.

Shahriar, S., & Hayawi, K. (2023). Let's have a chat! A Conversation with ChatGPT: Technology, applications, and limitations. *arXiv preprint arXiv:2302.13817.*

Shahriar, S., & Al Roken, N. (2022). How can generative adversarial networks impact computer generated art? Insights from poetry to melody conversion. *International Journal of Information Management Data Insights*, *2*(1), 100066. doi:10.1016/j.jjimei.2022.100066

Sharma, U., Tomar, P., Bhardwaj, H., & Sakalle, A. (2021). Artificial intelligence and its implications in education. In Impact of AI Technologies on Teaching, Learning, and Research in Higher Education (pp. 222-235). IGI Global. doi:10.4018/978-1-7998-4763-2.ch014

Sherry, B. (2022). 3 Limits to Artificial Intelligence's Creativity (and How to Solve Them): Here's what you need to know about harnessing A.I. technology to be more creative. *Inc.* https://www.inc.com/ben-sherry/3-limits-to-artificial-intelligences-creativity-and-how-to-solve-them.html

Shin, T., Razeghi, Y., Logan, R. L., IV, Wallace, E., & Singh, S. (2020). Autoprompt: Eliciting knowledge from language models with automatically generated prompts. *arXiv preprint arXiv:2010.15980.* doi:10.18653/v1/2020.emnlp-main.346

Shi, Z. (2011). *Advanced Artificial Intelligence.* World Scientific. doi:10.1142/7547

Shohel, M., & Mahruf, C. (2021). Education in Emergencies, Inequities, and the Digital Divide: Strategies for Supporting Teachers and Students in Higher Education in Bangladesh. In L. Kyei-Blankson, (Eds.), *Handbook of Research on Inequities in Online Education During Global Crises* (pp. 529–553). IGI Global. doi:10.4018/978-1-7998-6533-9.ch027

Shoufan, A. (2023). Exploring students' perceptions of ChatGPT: Thematic analysis and follow-up survey. *IEEE Access : Practical Innovations, Open Solutions*, *11*, 38805–38818. doi:10.1109/ACCESS.2023.3268224

Shvarts, A., & Bakker, A. (2019). The early history of the scaffolding metaphor: Bernstein, Luria, Vygotsky, and before. *Mind, Culture, and Activity*, *26*(1), 4–23. doi:10.1080/10749039.2019.1574306

Siakalli, M., Mousoulidou, M., Christodoulou, A., Savvidou, A., & Kouppa, K. (2022). Secondary Education and COVID-19. *Encyclopedia*, *2*(1), 409–427. doi:10.3390/encyclopedia2010025

Siapka, A. (2022, July). Towards a feminist metaethics of AI. In *Proceedings of the 2022 AAAI/ACM Conference on AI, Ethics, and Society* (pp. 665-674). ACM. 10.1145/3514094.3534197

Simonsen, H. K. (2022). AI Text Generators and Text Producers. *2022 International Conference on Advanced Learning Technologies (ICALT)*, (pp. 218-220). IEEE. 10.1109/ICALT55010.2022.00071

Singh, S. and Remenyi, D. (2016). Plagiarism and ghostwriting: The rise in academic misconduct. *South African Journal of Science*, *112*(5-6), 1–7.

Singh, J., Steele, K., & Singh, L. (2021). Combining the best of online and face-to-face learning: Hybrid and blended learning approach for COVID-19, post vaccine, & post-pandemic world. *Journal of Educational Technology Systems*, *50*(2), 140–171. doi:10.1177/00472395211047865

Sinha, A., & Lakhanpal, P. (2023). Can AI systems become wise? A note on artificial wisdom. *AI & Society*, 1–2. doi:10.100700146-023-01683-4

Sison, A. J. G., Daza, M. T., Gozalo-Brizuela, R., & Garrido-Merchán, E. C. (2023). ChatGPT: More than a weapon of mass deception, Ethical challenges and responses from the Human-Centered Artificial Intelligence (HCAI) perspective. *arXiv preprint arXiv:2304.11215.*

Smith, H. (2021). Clinical AI: Opacity, accountability, responsibility, and liability. *AI & Society*, *36*(2), 535–545. doi:10.100700146-020-01019-6

Smith, J. (2020). Addressing plagiarism in the age of AI: Ethical considerations for educators. *International Journal of Educational Technology, 53*(4), 12–17.

Sohail, S. S., Farhat, F., Himeur, Y., Nadeem, M., Madsen, D. Ø., Singh, Y., & Mansoor, W. (2023). The future of GPT: A taxonomy of existing ChatGPT research, current challenges, and possible future directions. *Current Challenges, and Possible Future Directions (April 8, 2023).*

Solaiman, I., Brundage, M., Clark, J., Askell, A., Herbert-Voss, A., Wu, J., & Wang, J. (2019). Release strategies and the social impacts of language models. *arXiv preprint arXiv:1908.09203.*

Song, M., Jiang, H., Shi, S., Yao, S., Lu, S., Feng, Y., & Jing, L. (2023). Is ChatGPT a good Keyphrase generator? A preliminary study. *arXiv preprint arXiv:2303.13001.*

So, S. (2016). Mobile instant messaging support for teaching and learning in higher education. *The Internet and Higher Education, 31*, 32–42. doi:10.1016/j.iheduc.2016.06.001

Srinath, P. (2022). Study on Artificial Intelligence. In J. Karthikeyan, S.-H. Ting, & Y.-J. Ng (Eds.), Ordine Nuovo Publication: Vol. L. *Learning Outcomes of Classroom Research.*

Srinivasan, R., & Uchino, K. (2021, March). Biases in generative art: A causal look from the lens of art history. In *Proceedings of the 2021 ACM Conference on Fairness, Accountability, and Transparency* (pp. 41-51). ACM. 10.1145/3442188.3445869

Stanisic, & Maksic, S. (2014). Environmental Education in Serbian Primary Schools: Challenges and Changes in Curriculum, Pedagogy, and Teacher Training. *The Journal of Environmental Education, 45*(2), 118–131. https://doi.org/ doi:10.1080/00958964.2013.829019

Starke, C., & Lünich, M. (2020). Artificial intelligence for political decision-making in the European Union: Effects on citizens' perceptions of input, throughput, and output legitimacy. *Data & Policy, 2*, e16. doi:10.1017/dap.2020.19

Starkey, A., Steenhauer, K., & Caven, J. (2020). Painting music: Using artificial intelligence to create music from live painted drawings. *Drawing: Research, Theory. Practice, 5*(2), 209–224.

Stassen, M., Doherty, K., & Poe, M. (2001). *Course-based review and assessment: Methods for understanding student learning.* University of Massachusetts Amherst.

Steiner, E. D., Doan, S., Woo, A., Gittens, A. D., Lawrence, R. A., Berdie, L., Wolfe, R. L., Greer, L., & Schwartz, H. L. (2022, June 14). *Rates of stress among teachers and principals are running high.* RAND Corporation. https://www.rand.org/pubs/research_reports/RRA1108-4.html

Steinfeld, K. (2023). Clever little tricks: A socio-technical history of text-to-image generative models. *International Journal of Architectural Computing, 21*(2), 211–241. doi:10.1177/14780771231168230

Steinhoff, J. (2023). AI ethics as subordinated innovation network. *AI & Society*, 1–13.

Sternberg, R. J. (2022). Time bomb: How the Western conception of intelligence is taking down humanity. In *Intelligence in Context* (pp. 393–411). Palgrave Macmillan. doi:10.1007/978-3-030-92798-1_16

Striuk, O., Kondratenko, Y., Sidenko, I., & Vorobyova, A. (2020, November). Generative adversarial neural network for creating photorealistic images. In *2020 IEEE 2nd International Conference on Advanced Trends in Information Theory (ATIT)* (pp. 368-371). IEEE. 10.1109/ATIT50783.2020.9349326

Subburayan, B. (2023). Harnessing Artificial Intelligence for Personalized Upskilling and Reskilling. *The Times of India Readers' Blog.* https://ssrn.com/abstract=4513273

Sun, T., Gaut, A., Tang, S., Huang, Y., ElSherief, M., Zhao, J., & Wang, W. Y. (2019). *Mitigating gender bias in natural language processing: Literature review*. arXiv preprint arXiv:1906.08976. doi:10.18653/v1/P19-1159

Sundararajan, L. (2014). Mind, machine, and creativity: An artist's perspective. *The Journal of Creative Behavior, 48*(2), 136–151. doi:10.1002/jocb.44 PMID:25541564

Sun, H., Rau, P. L. P., & Wang, B. (2021). A study of machine ethics in human-artificial intelligence interactions. In *Cross-Cultural Design. Applications in Arts, Learning, Well-being, and Social Development: 13th International Conference, CCD 2021*. Springer.

Sun, J., Liao, Q. V., Muller, M., Agarwal, M., Houde, S., Talamadupula, K., & Weisz, J. D. (2022, March). Investigating explainability of generative AI for code through scenario-based design. In *27th International Conference on Intelligent User Interfaces* (pp. 212-228). ACM. 10.1145/3490099.3511119

Surameery, N. M. S., & Shakor, M. Y. (2023). Use Chat GPT to solve programming bugs. *International Journal of Information Technology & Computer Engineering (IJITC), 3*(01), 17-22.

Suresh Babu, C. V., & R., P. (2023). Technology Transformation Through Skilled Teachers in Teaching Accountancy. In R. González-Lezcano (Ed.), *Advancing STEM Education and Innovation in a Time of Distance Learning* (pp. 211-233). IGI Global. doi:10.4018/978-1-6684-5053-6.ch011

Suresh Babu, C. V., & Adhithya, S. (2023). ChatGPT and Other Generative AI Tools in Education: Transformative Potential and Ethical Considerations. In J. Keengwe (Ed.), *Creative AI Tools and Ethical Implications in Teaching and Learning* (pp. 135–152). IGI Global. doi:10.4018/979-8-3693-0205-7.ch007

Suresh Babu, C. V., & Rohan, B. (2023). Evaluation and Quality Assurance for Rapid E-Learning and Development of Digital Learning Resources. In M. Santally, Y. Rajabalee, & R. Rajputh (Eds.), *Implementing Rapid E-Learning Through Interactive Materials Development* (pp. 139–170). IGI Global. doi:10.4018/978-1-6684-4940-0.ch008

Suryna, K. & Serrano, R. G. (2019). Agents without agency: Artificial intelligence as artistic medium. *Taboo Transgression Transcendence*, (pp. 200 – 209). ACM.

Sweller, J. (1988). Cognitive load during problem solving: Effects on learning. *Cognitive Science, 12*(2), 257–285. doi:10.120715516709cog1202_4

Taecharungroj, V. (2023). "What Can ChatGPT Do?" Analyzing early reactions to the innovative AI chatbot on Twitter. *Big Data and Cognitive Computing*, *7*(1), 35. doi:10.3390/bdcc7010035

Tajik, E., & Tajik, F. (2023). *A comprehensive examination of the potential application of Chat GPT in higher education institutions.*

Talboy, A. N., & Fuller, E. (2023). Challenging the appearance of machine intelligence: Cognitive bias in LLMs. *arXiv preprint arXiv:2304.01358.*

Tang, M. (2022, June). Human and machine symbiosis--An experiment of human and robot co-creation of calligraphy-style drawing. In *HCI International 2022 Posters: 24th International Conference on Human-Computer Interaction,* (pp. 462-467). Cham: Springer International Publishing.

Tang, R., Chuang, Y. N., & Hu, X. (2023). *The science of detecting LLM-generated texts*. arXiv preprint https://doi.org//arXiv.2303.07205 doi:10.48550

Tanjga, M. (2023). *E-learning and the Use of AI: A Review of Current Practices and Future Directions*. Qeios. doi:10.32388/AP0208

Tao, F., Zou, X., & Ren, D. (2018). The art of human intelligence and the technology of artificial intelligence: artificial intelligence visual art research. In *Intelligence Science II: Third IFIP TC 12 International Conference, ICIS 2018, Beijing, China, November 2-5, 2018* [Springer International Publishing.]. *Proceedings, 2*, 146–155.

Ta, V., Griffith, C., Boatfield, C., Wang, X., Civitello, M., Bader, H., DeCero, E., & Loggarakis, A. (2020). User experiences of social support from companion chatbots in everyday contexts: Thematic analysis. *Journal of Medical Internet Research, 22*(3), e16235. doi:10.2196/16235 PMID:32141837

Taylor, S. J., Bogdan, R., & DeVault, M. L. (2016). *Introduction to Qualitative Research Methods: A Guidebook and Resource*. Wiley.

Tegmark, M. (2018). *Life 3.0: Being human in the age of artificial intelligence*. Vintage.

Tepšić, I. (2020). *The Attitude of Job Candidates towards Artificial Intelligence in Hiring Process*. ZIR. https://zir.nsk.hr/islandora/object/acmt:103

Ter Beek, M., Wopereis, I., & Schildkamp, K. (2022). Don't Wait, Innovate! Preparing Students and Lecturers in Higher Education for the Future Labor Market. *Education Sciences, 12*(9), 620. doi:10.3390/educsci12090620

Tetzlaff, L., Schmiedek, F., & Brod, G. (2021). Developing personalized education: A dynamic framework. *Educational Psychology Review, 33*(3), 863–882. doi:10.100710648-020-09570-w

Thacker, J. (2020). *The Age of AI: Artificial Intelligence and the Future of Humanity*. Zondervan.

The Chronicle of Higher Education. (2003). I'm a student. You have no idea how much we're using ChatGPT. No professor or software could ever pick up on it. *Chronicle*. https://www.chronicle.com/article/im-a-student-you-have-no-idea-how-much-were-using-chatgpt

The Economic Potential of Generative AI: The Next Productivity Frontier. (2023). *McKinsey & Company*. https://www.mckinsey.com/~/media/mckinsey/business%20functions/mckinsey%20digital/our%20insights/the%20economic%20potential%20of%20generative%20ai%20the%20next%20productivity%20frontier/the-economic-potential-of-generative-ai-the-next-productivity-frontier-vf.pdf?shouldIndex=false

The New York Times. (2023). What students are saying about ChatGPT. *The New York Times*. https://www.nytimes.com/2023/02/02/learning/students-chatgpt.html

Theobald, E. J., Hill, M. J., Tran, E., Agrawal, S., Arroyo, E. N., Behling, S., Chambwe, N., Cintrón, D. L., Cooper, J. D., Dunster, G., Grummer, J. A., Hennessey, K., Hsiao, J., Iranon, N., Jones, L. II, Jordt, H., Keller, M., Lacey, M. E., Littlefield, C. E., & Freeman, S. (2020). Active learning narrows achievement gaps for underrepresented students in undergraduate science, technology, engineering, and math. *Proceedings of the National Academy of Sciences of the United States of America, 117*(12), 6476–6483. doi:10.1073/pnas.1916903117 PMID:32152114

Thompson, S. J. (2021). *Machine Law, Ethics, and Morality in the Age of Artificial Intelligence*. In IGI Global. https://www.igi-global.com/book/machine-law-ethics-morality-age/www.igi-global.com/book/machine-law-ethics-morality-age/244609

Thomsen, K. (2019). Ethics for Artificial Intelligence, Ethics for All. *Paladyn : Journal of Behavioral Robotics, 10*(1), 359–363. doi:10.1515/pjbr-2019-0029

Thoppilan, R., De Freitas, D., Hall, J., Shazeer, N., Kulshreshtha, A., Cheng, H. T., & Le, Q. (2022). Lamda: Language models for dialog applications. *arXiv preprint arXiv:2201.08239.*

Thorisson, K. R. (2019). Discretionarily Constrained Adaptation Under Insufficient Knowledge & Resources. *Journal of Artificial General Intelligence, 11*(2).

Thorne, S. (2020). Hey Siri, tell me a story: Digital storytelling and AI authorship. *Convergence (London), 26*(4), 808–823. doi:10.1177/1354856520913866

Tirosh-Samuelson, H. (2018). In praise of human dignity: The humanities in the age of Big Data. *On Education, 1*(2).

Tirumala, K., Markosyan, A., Zettlemoyer, L., & Aghajanyan, A. (2022). Memorization without overfitting: Analyzing the training dynamics of large language models. *Advances in Neural Information Processing Systems, 35*, 38274–38290.

Tlili, A., Shehata, B., Adarkwah, M. A., Bozkurt, A., Hickey, D. T., Huang, R., & Agyemang, B. (2023). What if the devil is my guardian angel: ChatGPT as a case study of using chatbots in education. *Smart Learning Environments, 10*(1), 15. doi:10.118640561-023-00237-x

Todd, J. T., & Morris, E. K. (1995). *Modern perspectives on BF Skinner and contemporary behaviorism.* Greenwood Press/Greenwood Publishing Group.

Tomic, W. (1993). Behaviorism and cognitivism in education. *Psychology (Savannah, Ga.), 30*(3/4), 38–46.

Torralba, A., & Efros, A. A. (2011). Unbiased look at dataset bias. In *CVPR 2011* (pp. 1521–1528). IEEE. doi:10.1109/CVPR.2011.5995347

Touvron, H., Lavril, T., Izacard, G., Martinet, X., Lachaux, M. A., Lacroix, T., & Lample, G. (2023). Llama: Open and efficient foundation language models. *arXiv preprint arXiv:2302.13971.*

Townes, M. (2012). The spread of TCP/IP: How the Internet became the Internet. *Millennium, 41*(1), 43–64. doi:10.1177/0305829812449195

Tran, K., Bisazza, A., & Monz, C. (2016). Recurrent memory networks for language modeling. *arXiv preprint arXiv:1601.01272.* doi:10.18653/v1/N16-1036

Tritscher, R. J., & Schlögl, S. (2023). Educ-AI-ted – Investigating Educators' Perspectives Concerning the Use of AI in University Teaching and Learning. In Learning Technology for Education Challenges (pp. 241–254). Springer Nature Switzerland. doi:10.1007/978-3-031-34754-2_20

Troussas, C., Krouska, A., Alepis, E., & Virvou, M. (2020). Intelligent and adaptive tutoring through a social network for higher education. *New Review of Hypermedia and Multimedia, 26*(3-4), 138–167. doi:10.1080/13614568.2021.1908436

Trujillo, S., Azanza, M., & Diaz, O. (2007, October). Generative metaprogramming. In *Proceedings of the 6th International Conference on Generative Programming and Component Engineering* (pp. 105-114). 10.1145/1289971.1289990

Truong, T.-L., Le, H.-L., & Le-Dang, T.-P. (2020) Sentiment analysis implementing bert-based pre-trained language model for vietnamese. In *2020 7th NAFOSTED Conference on Information and Computer Science (NICS),* (pp. 362–367). IEEE. 10.1109/NICS51282.2020.9335912

Turing, A. M. (1950). Computing Machinery and Intelligence. *Mind, 59*(October), 433–460. doi:10.1093/mind/LIX.236.433

Turkle, S. (2011). The Second Self: Computers and the Human Spirit. Simon and Schuster. Vuppalapati, C. (2021). Democratization of Artificial Intelligence for the Future of Humanity. CRC Press.

Turkle, S. (1997). *Life on the Screen: Identity in the Age of the Internet.* Simon and Schuster.

Turkle, S. (2011). *Alone Together: Why We Expect More from Technology and Less from Each Other.* Basic Books.

Turkle, S. (2015). *Reclaiming Conversation: The power of Talk in a Digital Age.* Penguin.

Ulberg, E., Llach, D. C., & Byrne, D. (2020). Hand-crafting neural networks for art-making. In ICCC (pp. 508-511).

UNESCO. (2023). *AI competency frameworks for students and teachers.* UNESCO. https://www.unesco.org/en/digital-education/ai-future-learning/competency-frameworks

University of Memphis. (2023). *AutoTutor.* University of Memphis. https://www.memphis.edu/iis/projects/autotutor.php

University of Rochester. (2023). *How will AI chatbots like ChatGPT affect higher education?* University of Rochester. https://www.rochester.edu/newscenter/chatgpt-artificial-intelligence-ai-chatbots-education-551522/

University of San Diego. (2023, September 28). *43 examples of Artificial Intelligence in Education.* University of San Diego. https://onlinedegrees.sandiego.edu/artificial-intelligence-education/

University of South Florida. (2023). *Associate professor develops motivational chatbot and digital Candyland-like maze to ensure student success.* USF. https://www.usf.edu/news/2023/associate-professor-develops-motivational-chatbot-and-candyland-like-maze-to-ensure-student-success.aspx

Urbina, F., Lentzos, F., Invernizzi, C., & Ekins, S. (2022). Dual Use of Artificial Intelligence-powered Drug Discovery. *Nature Machine Intelligence, 4*(3), 189–191. doi:10.103842256-022-00465-9 PMID:36211133

Urhan, B. (2023). Crucial Role of Soft Skills in Challenging Times: Conceptual Analysis of Leadership Skills. In Leadership Approaches in Global Hospitality and Tourism (pp. 23-39). IGI Global.

US Department of Education. (2023). *(rep.). Artificial Intelligence and the Future of Teaching and Learning.* US Department of Education.

Utterback, J. M., & Acee, H. J. (2005). Disruptive technologies: An expanded view. *International Journal of Innovation Management, 9*(1), 1–17. doi:10.1142/S1363919605001162

Vaishya, R., Misra, A., & Vaish, A. (2023). ChatGPT: Is this version good for healthcare and research? *Diabetes & Metabolic Syndrome: Clinical Research & Reviews, 17*(4), 102744.

Vaishya, R., Javaid, M., Khan, I. H., & Haleem, A. (2020). Artificial Intelligence (AI) applications for COVID-19 pandemic. *Diabetes & Metabolic Syndrome, 14*(4), 337–339. doi:10.1016/j.dsx.2020.04.012 PMID:32305024

Van Dijk, C. N., Van Witteloostuijn, M., Vasić, N., Avrutin, S., & Blom, E. (2016). The influence of texting language on grammar and executive functions in primary school children. *PLoS One, 11*(3), e0152409. doi:10.1371/journal.pone.0152409 PMID:27031708

Vartiainen, H., & Tedre, M. (2023). Using artificial intelligence in craft education: Crafting with text-to-image generative models. *Digital Creativity (Exeter), 34*(1), 1–21. doi:10.1080/14626268.2023.2174557

Véliz, C. (2023). Chatbots shouldn't use emojis. *Nature, 615*(7952), 375. doi:10.1038/d41586-023-00758-y PMID:36918680

Vidhya, N. G., Devi, D., Nithya, A., & Manju, T. (2023). Prognosis of exploration on Chat GPT (sic) with artificial intelligence ethics. *Brazilian Journal of Science, 2*(9), 60–69. doi:10.14295/bjs.v2i9.372

Vinchon, F., Lubart, T., Bartolotta, S., Gironnay, V., Botella, M., Bourgeois, S., & Gaggioli, A. (2023). *Artificial Intelligence & Creativity: A manifesto for collaboration.* Wiley.

Vitente, A., Lazaro, R., Escuadra, C. J., Regino, J., & Rotor, E. (2023). The use of artificial intelligence (AI)-assisted technologies in scientific discourse. *Philippine Journal of Physical Therapy, 2*(1), 1–3. doi:10.46409/002.HNUY6271

Vygotsky, L. S. (1987). Thinking and speech. In R.W. Rieber & A.S. Carton (Eds.), The collected works of L.S. Vygotsky, Volume 1: Problems of general psychology (pp. 39-285). New York: Plenum Press.

Wachter, S., Mittelstadt, B., & Floridi, L. (2017). Transparent, explainable, and accountable AI for robotics. *Science Robotics*, *2*(6), eaan6080. doi:10.1126cirobotics.aan6080 PMID:33157874

Walker, T. (2021). *Getting serious about teacher Burnout*. NEA. https://www.nea.org/nea-today/all-news-articles/getting-serious-about-teacher-burnout

Walsh, K. R., Mahesh, S., & Trumbach, C. C. (2021). Autonomy in AI systems. *The Journal of Technology Studies*, *47*(1), 38–47.

Walter, Y. (2023). The rapid competitive economy of machine learning development: A discussion on the social risks and benefits. *AI and Ethics*, 1–14. doi:10.100743681-023-00276-7

Wang, F. Y., Miao, Q., Li, X., Wang, X., & Lin, Y. (2023). What does ChatGPT say: The DAO from algorithmic intelligence to linguistic intelligence. *IEEE/CAA Journal of Automatica Sinica, 10*(3), 575-579.

Wang, F. Y., Yang, J., Wang, X., Li, J., & Han, Q. L. (2023). Chat with ChatGPT on Industry 5.0: Learning and decision-making for intelligent industries. *IEEE/CAA Journal of Automatica Sinica, 10*(4), 831-834.

Wang, J., Liang, Y., Meng, F., Shi, H., Li, Z., Xu, J., & Zhou, J. (2023). Is ChatGPT a good NLG evaluator? A preliminary study. *arXiv preprint arXiv:2303.04048.*

Wang, J., Liang, Y., Meng, F., Zou, B., Li, Z., Qu, J., & Zhou, J. (2023). Zero-shot cross-lingual summarization via large language models. *arXiv preprint arXiv:2302.14229.* 1 - 11.

Wang, L., Lyu, C., Ji, T., Zhang, Z., Yu, D., Shi, S., & Tu, Z. (2023). Document-level machine translation with large language models. *arXiv preprint arXiv:2304.02210.*

Wang, S., Scells, H., Koopman, B., & Zuccon, G. (2023). Can ChatGPT write a good Boolean query for systematic review literature search? *arXiv preprint arXiv:2302.03495.* 1 - 19. doi:10.1145/3539618.3591703

Wang, B., Deng, X., & Sun, H. (2022, December). Iteratively prompt pre-trained language models for chain of thought. In *Proceedings of the 2022 Conference on Empirical Methods in Natural Language Processing* (pp. 2714-2730). ACL. 10.18653/v1/2022.emnlp-main.174

Wang, C., Xu, C., Yao, X., & Tao, D. (2019). Evolutionary generative adversarial networks. *IEEE Transactions on Evolutionary Computation*, *23*(6), 921–934. doi:10.1109/TEVC.2019.2895748

Wang, D., Gong, C., & Liu, Q. (2019, May). Improving neural language modeling via adversarial training. In *International Conference on Machine Learning* (pp. 6555-6565). PMLR.

Wang, L. (2022). Exploring the relationship among teacher emotional intelligence, work engagement, teacher self-efficacy, and student academic achievement: A moderated mediation model. *Frontiers in Psychology*, *12*, 810559. doi:10.3389/fpsyg.2021.810559 PMID:35046879

Wang, M. (2023). *ChatGPT: A case study. Conference 2023: Shaping the Future: Key Themes in Higher Education.* PDGIA.

Wang, M., Xiao, D., Xiang, Y., & Wang, H. (2019). Privacy-Aware Controllable Compressed Data Publishing Against Sparse Estimation Attack in IoT. *IEEE Internet of Things Journal*, *6*(4), 7305–7318. doi:10.1109/JIOT.2019.2916109

Wang, P. (2008). What Do You Mean by. *AI*, *171*, 362–373.

Wang, P. (2019). On defining artificial intelligence. *Journal of Artificial General Intelligence*, *10*(2), 1–37. doi:10.2478/jagi-2019-0002

Wang, T., Lund, B. D., Marengo, A., Pagano, A., Mannuru, N. R., Teel, Z. A., & Pange, J. (2023). Exploring the Potential Impact of Artificial Intelligence (AI) on International Students in Higher Education: Generative AI, Chatbots, Analytics, and International Student Success. *Applied Sciences (Basel, Switzerland)*, *13*(11), 6716. doi:10.3390/app13116716

Wang, Y., & Ma, H. (2019, December). The value evaluation of artificial intelligence works of art. In *2019 International Joint Conference on Information, Media and Engineering (IJCIME)* (pp. 445-449). IEEE. 10.1109/IJCIME49369.2019.00096

Wanner, A. N. D. R. E. S. (2014). Mechanical drawing machines and the glitch—Visualizing technology through its failures. In *Proceedings of the Second Conference on Computation, Communication, Aesthetics and X* (pp. 31-40). IEEE.

Warlick, D. (2009). Grow your personal learning network: New technologies can keep you connected and help you manage information overload. *Learning and Leading with Technology*, *36*(6), 12–16.

Warrier, U., John, M., & Warrier, S. (2021). Leveraging emotional intelligence competencies for sustainable development of higher education institutions in the new normal. *FIIB Business Review*, *10*(1), 62–73. doi:10.1177/2319714521992032

Watson, J. B. (2017). *Behaviorism*. Routledge. Mandl, H., & Kopp, B. (2005). Situated learning: Theories and models. In P. Nentwig & D. Waddington (Eds.), *Making it relevant. Context based learning of science* (pp. 15–34). Waxmann.

Webster, F., Pepper, D., & Jenkins, A. (2000). Assessing the undergraduate dissertation. *Assessment & Evaluation in Higher Education*, *25*(1), 71–80.

Wei, J., Bosma, M., Zhao, V. Y., Guu, K., Yu, A. W., Lester, B., & Le, Q. V. (2021). Finetuned language models are zero-shot learners. *arXiv preprint arXiv:2109.01652.*

Wei, J., Tay, Y., Bommasani, R., Raffel, C., Zoph, B., Borgeaud, S., & Fedus, W. (2022). Emergent abilities of large language models. *arXiv preprint arXiv:2206.07682.*

Wei, J., Wang, X., Schuurmans, D., Bosma, M., Chi, E., Le, Q., & Zhou, D. (2022). Chain of thought prompting elicits reasoning in large language models. *arXiv preprint arXiv:2201.11903.*

Wei, X., Cui, X., Cheng, N., Wang, X., Zhang, X., Huang, S., & Han, W. (2023). Zero-shot information extraction via chatting with ChatGPT. *arXiv preprint arXiv:2302.10205.*

Weidener, & Fischer, M. (2023). Artificial Intelligence Teaching as Part of Medical Education: Qualitative Analysis of Expert Interviews. *JMIR Medical Education*, *9*, e46428–e46428. doi:10.2196/46428

Weidinger, L., Mellor, J., Rauh, M., Griffin, C., Uesato, J., Huang, P. S., & Gabriel, I. (2021). Ethical and social risks of harm from language models. *arXiv preprint arXiv:2112.04359.*

Weise, M. R. (2020). *Long life learning: Preparing for jobs that don't even exist yet*. John Wiley & Sons.

Wentworth, E. R., & Connell, M. L. (2004). Integrating information technology into the teacher education curriculum : process and products of change. Haworth Press.

Werthner, H., Stanger, A., Schiaffonati, V., Knees, P., Hardman, L., & Ghezzi, C. (2023). Digital Humanism: The Time Is Now. *Computer*, *56*(1), 138–142. doi:10.1109/MC.2022.3219528

White, J., Fu, Q., Hays, S., Sandborn, M., Olea, C., Gilbert, H., & Schmidt, D. C. (2023). A prompt pattern catalog to enhance prompt engineering with ChatGPT. *arXiv preprint arXiv:2302.11382.*

Wilson, J. (2021, November 3). *Record number of teachers experiencing Burnout*. Canadian Occupational Safety. https://www.thesafetymag.com/ca/topics/psychological-safety/record-number-of-teachers-experiencing-burnout/315415

Wilson, S. (2003). *Information arts: intersections of art, science, and technology*. MIT press.

Wirtz, B. W., Weyerer, J. C., & Sturm, B. J. (2020). The dark sides of artificial intelligence: An integrated AI governance framework for public administration. *International Journal of Public Administration, 43*(9), 818–829. doi:10.1080/01900692.2020.1749851

Wollny, S., Schneider, J., Di Mitri, D., Weidlich, J., Rittberger, M., & Drachsler, H. (2021). Are we there yet?-a systematic literature review on chatbots in education. *Frontiers in Artificial Intelligence*, *4*, 654924. doi:10.3389/frai.2021.654924 PMID:34337392

World Health Organization. (2020). *WHO launches a chatbot on Facebook Messenger to combat COVID-19 misinformation.* WHO. https://www.who.int/news-room/feature-stories/detail/who-launches-a-chatbot-powered-facebook-messenger-to-combat-covid-19-misinformation

Wright, B. D. (1997). Evaluating learning in individual courses. In J. G. Gaff & J. L. Ratcliff (Eds.), *Handbook of the undergraduate curriculum* (pp. 571–590). Jossey Bass.

Wu, J., Gan, W., Chen, Z., Wan, S., & Lin, H. (2023). AI-generated content (aigc): A survey. *arXiv preprint arXiv:2304.06632.*

Wu, S., Irsoy, O., Lu, S., Dabravolski, V., Dredze, M., Gehrmann, S., & Mann, G. (2023). BloombergGPT: A large language model for finance. *arXiv preprint arXiv:2303.17564.*

Wu, T., He, S., Liu, J., Sun, S., Liu, K., Han, Q. L., & Tang, Y. (2023). A brief overview of ChatGPT: The history, *status quo* and potential future development. *IEEE/CAA Journal of Automatica Sinica, 10*(5), 1122-1136.

Wu, X., He, X., Li, T., Liu, N., & Zhai, X. (2023) Matching exemplar as next sentence prediction (mensp): Zero-shot prompt learning for automatic scoring in science education. arXiv preprint arXiv:2301.08771. doi:10.1007/978-3-031-36272-9_33

Wu, A. N., Stouffs, R., & Biljecki, F. (2022). Generative Adversarial Networks in the built environment: A comprehensive review of the application of GANs across data types and scales. *Building and Environment*, *223*, 109477. doi:10.1016/j.buildenv.2022.109477

Wu, J. (2022). Analysis and evaluation of the impact of integrating mental health education into the teaching of university civics courses in the context of artificial intelligence. *Wireless Communications and Mobile Computing*, *2022*, 2022. doi:10.1155/2022/5378694

Wu, T. (2018, February). Saliency-aware generative art. In *Proceedings of the 2018 10th International Conference on Machine Learning and Computing* (pp. 198-202). ACM. 10.1145/3195106.3195143

Wu, Y., Jiang, A. Q., Li, W., Rabe, M., Staats, C., Jamnik, M., & Szegedy, C. (2022). Autoformalization with large language models. *Advances in Neural Information Processing Systems*, *35*, 1–16.

Wu, Z., Ji, D., Yu, K., Zeng, X., Wu, D., & Shidujaman, M. (2021). AI creativity and the human-AI co-creation model. In *Human-Computer Interaction. Theory, Methods and Tools: Thematic Area, HCI 2021, Held as Part of the 23rd HCI International Conference, HCII 2021, Virtual Event, July 24–29, 2021* [Springer International Publishing.]. *Proceedings*, *23*(Part I), 171–190.

Xing, B., & Marwala, T. (2017). Implications of the fourth industrial age on higher education. *arXiv preprint arXiv:1703.09643.*

Xu, W., Dainoff, M. J., Ge, L., & Gao, Z. (2023). Transitioning to human interaction with AI systems: New challenges and opportunities for HCI professionals to enable human-centered AI. *International Journal of Human-Computer Interaction*, *39*(3), 494–518. doi:10.1080/10447318.2022.2041900

Xu, Y. (2022, July). Dialogue explanation with reasoning for AI. In *Proceedings of the 2022 AAAI/ACM Conference on AI, Ethics, and Society* (pp. 918-918). ACM. 10.1145/3514094.3539522

Xu, Y., Liu, X., Cao, X., Huang, C., Liu, E., Qian, S., Liu, X., Wu, Y., Dong, F., Qiu, C.-W., Qiu, J., Hua, K., Su, W., Wu, J., Xu, H., Han, Y., Fu, C., Yin, Z., Liu, M., & Zhang, J. (2021). Artificial intelligence: A powerful paradigm for scientific research. *Innovation (Cambridge (Mass.))*, *2*(4), 100179. doi:10.1016/j.xinn.2021.100179 PMID:34877560

Yadava, O. P. (2023). ChatGPT—A foe or an ally? *Indian Journal of Thoracic and Cardiovascular Surgery*, *39*(3), 217–221. doi:10.100712055-023-01507-6 PMID:37124601

Yahaya, M., Umagba, A., Obeta, S., & Maruyama, T. (2023). Critical evaluation of the future role of artificial intelligence in business and society. *Journal of Artificial Intelligence. Machine Learning and Data Science*, *1*(1), 1–9.

Yakura, H. (2023, April). A generative framework for designing interactions to overcome the gaps between humans and imperfect AIs instead of improving the accuracy of the AIs. In *Extended Abstracts of the 2023 CHI Conference on Human Factors in Computing Systems* (pp. 1-5). ACM. 10.1145/3544549.3577036

Yampolskiy, R. (2020). On Defining Differences between Intelligence and Artificial Intelligence. *Journal of Artificial General Intelligence*, *11*(2).

Yan, D., Fauss, M., Hao, J., & Cui, W. (2023). Detection of AI-generated essays in writing assessment. *Psychological Test and Assessment Modeling*, *65*(2), 125–144.

Yang, X., Li, Y., Zhang, X., Chen, H., & Cheng, W. (2023). Exploring the limits of ChatGPT for query or aspect-based text summarization. *arXiv preprint arXiv:2302.08081.*

Yang, Z., Li, L., Wang, J., Lin, K., Azarnasab, E., Ahmed, F., & Wang, L. (2023). MM-react: Prompting ChatGPT for multimodal reasoning and action. *arXiv preprint arXiv:2303.11381.*

Yang, S., & Evans, C. (2019, November). Opportunities and challenges in using AI chatbots in higher education. In *Proceedings of the 2019 3rd International Conference on Education and E-Learning* (pp. 79-83). ACM. 10.1145/3371647.3371659

Yang, W. (2022). Artificial Intelligence education for young children: Why, what, and how in curriculum design and implementation. *Computers and Education: Artificial Intelligence*, *3*, 100061. doi:10.1016/j.caeai.2022.100061

Yanisky-Ravid, S. (2017). Generating Rembrandt: Artificial intelligence, copyright, and accountability in the 3A Era: The human-like authors are already here: A new model. *Mich. St. L. Rev.*, *659.*

Yan, L., Zhao, L., Gasevic, D., & Martinez-Maldonado, R. (2022) Scalability, sustainability, and ethicality of multimodal learning analytics. In *LAK22: 12th International Learning Analytics and Knowledge Conference*, (pp. 13–23). ACM. 10.1145/3506860.3506862

Yasunaga, M., Ren, H., Bosselut, A., Liang, P., & Leskovec, J. (2021). QA-GNN: Reasoning with language models and knowledge graphs for question answering. *arXiv preprint arXiv:2104.06378.* doi:10.18653/v1/2021.naacl-main.45

Yelland, N. (2005). The future is now: A review of the literature on the use of computers in early childhood education (1994-2004). [formerly AACE Journal]. *AACE Review*, *13*(3), 201–232.

Yenidogan, B. (2021). How to talk about AI art and music: An onto-ethico-epistemological debate between transhumanism and posthumanism. *In Proceedings of the 2nd Joint Conference on AI Music Creativity.* (pp. 1 – 13). ACM.

Yimsawat, C., Mangkhang, C., Phuwanatwichit, T., & Anansuchatkul, B. (2022). An Instructional Innovation to Strengthen Comprehensive Humanization for Higher Education Students: Soft Skills for the Digital Society. *Journal of Education Naresuan University*, *24*(1), 15–24.

Young, S. (2022). *How to write your undergraduate dissertation in criminology*. Routledge.

Yusa, I., Yu, Y., & Sovhyra, T. (2022). *Reflections on the use of artificial intelligence in works of art*, (pp. 152-167). SSRN.

Zaitsu, W., & Jin, M. (2023). Distinguishing ChatGPT (-3.5,-4)-generated and human-written papers through Japanese stylometric analysis. *arXiv preprint arXiv:2304.05534*. 1 - 15.

Zameshina, M., Teytaud, O., Teytaud, F., Hosu, V., Carraz, N., Najman, L., & Wagner, M. (2022, July). Fairness in generative modeling: do it unsupervised! In *Proceedings of the Genetic and Evolutionary Computation Conference Companion* (pp. 320-323). 10.1145/3520304.3528992

Zanella, A., Bui, N., Castellani, A., Vangelista, L., & Zorzi, M. (2014). Internet of things for smart cities. *IEEE Internet of Things Journal, 1*(1), 22–32. doi:10.1109/JIOT.2014.2306328

Zawacki-Richter, O., Marín, V. I., Bond, M., & Gouverneur, F. (2019). Systematic review of research on artificial intelligence applications in higher education–where are the educators? *International Journal of Educational Technology in Higher Education, 16*(1), 1–27. doi:10.118641239-019-0171-0

Zeilinger, M. (2021). Generative adversarial copy machines. *Culture Machine, 20*, 1–23.

Zeng, Z., Gašević, D., & Chen, G. (2023) On the effectiveness of curriculum learning in educational text scoring. In *Proceedings of the AAAI Conference on Artificial Intelligence*. AAAI. 10.1609/aaai.v37i12.26707

Zerilli, J., Knott, A., Maclaurin, J., & Gavaghan, C. (2019). Algorithmic decision-making and the control problem. *Minds and Machines, 29*(4), 555–578. doi:10.100711023-019-09513-7

Zhai, X. (2023). ChatGPT for next generation science learning. *XRDS: Crossroads. The ACM Magazine for Students, 29*(3), 42–46.

Zhang, C., Zhang, C., Li, C., Qiao, Y., Zheng, S., Dam, S. K., & Hong, C. S. (2023). One small step for generative AI, one giant leap for AGI: A complete survey on ChatGPT in AIGC era. *arXiv preprint arXiv:2304.06488*.

Zhang, C., Zhang, C., Zheng, S., Qiao, Y., Li, C., Zhang, M., Dam, S. K., Thwal, C. M., Tun, Y. L., & Huy, L. L. (2023). A complete survey on generative ai (aigc): Is chatgpt from gpt-4 to gpt-5 all you need? *arXiv preprint arXiv:2303.11717*. 15

Zhang, D. (2023). Should ChatGPT and Bard share revenue with their data providers? A new business model for the AI era. *arXiv preprint arXiv:2305.02555*.

Zhang, H., Liu, X., & Zhang, J. (2023). Extractive summarization via ChatGPT for faithful summary generation. *arXiv preprint arXiv:2304.04193*.

Zhang, S., Roller, S., Goyal, N., Artetxe, M., Chen, M., Chen, S., & Zettlemoyer, L. (2022). Opt: Open pre-trained transformer language models. *arXiv preprint arXiv:2205.01068*.

Zhang, Y. S., & Shu, W. (2023). *Artificial Intelligence-Based E-Learning: An Overview*. EasyChair. https://easychair.org/publications/preprint_download/SJgC

Zhang, H., Lee, I., Ali, S., DiPaola, D., Cheng, Y., & Breazeal, C. (2022). Integrating ethics and career futures with technical learning to promote AI literacy for middle school students: An exploratory study. *International Journal of Artificial Intelligence in Education*, 1–35. PMID:35573722

Zhang, Y., Gan, Y., & Cham, H. (2017). Perfectionism, academic burnout and engagement among Chinese college students: A structural equation modeling analysis. *Personality and Individual Differences, 104*, 91–96. doi:10.1016/j.paid.2016.07.046

Zhao, R., Li, X., Chia, Y. K., Ding, B., & Bing, L. (2023). Can ChatGPT-like generative models guarantee factual accuracy? On the mistakes of new generation search engines. *arXiv preprint arXiv:2304.11076.*

Zhao, W. X., Zhou, K., Li, J., Tang, T., Wang, X., Hou, Y., & Wen, J. R. (2023). A survey of large language models. *arXiv preprint arXiv:2303.18223.*

Zhao, J., & Li, Q. (2022). Big Data–Artificial Intelligence Fusion Technology in Education in the Context of the New Crown Epidemic. *Big Data, 10*(3), 262–276. doi:10.1089/big.2021.0245 PMID:35605025

Zheng, L., Niu, J., Long, M., & Fan, Y. (2023). An automatic knowledge graph construction approach to promoting collaborative knowledge building, group performance, social interaction and socially shared regulation in cscl. *British Journal of Educational Technology, 54*(3), 686–711. doi:10.1111/bjet.13283

Zheng, L., Niu, J., & Zhong, L. (2022). Effects of a learning analytics-based real-time feedback approach on knowledge elaboration, knowledge convergence, interactive relationships and group performance in cscl. *British Journal of Educational Technology, 53*(1), 130–149. doi:10.1111/bjet.13156

Zhong, H., Chang, J., Yang, Z., Wu, T., Arachchige, P. C. M., Pathmabandu, C., & Xue, M. (2023). Copyright protection and accountability of generative AI: Attack, watermarking and attribution. *arXiv preprint arXiv:2303.09272.* 94 - 98. doi:10.1145/3543873.3587321

Zhong, Q., Ding, L., Liu, J., Du, B., & Tao, D. (2023). Can ChatGPT understand too? A comparative study on ChatGPT and fine-tuned BERT. *arXiv preprint arXiv:2302.10198.*

Zhou, Y., Muresanu, A. I., Han, Z., Paster, K., Pitis, S., Chan, H., & Ba, J. (2022). Large language models are human-level prompt engineers. *arXiv preprint arXiv:2211.01910.*

Zhou, K., Yang, J., Loy, C. C., & Liu, Z. (2022). Learning to prompt for vision-language models. *International Journal of Computer Vision, 130*(9), 2337–2348. doi:10.100711263-022-01653-1

Zhou, X., Zhang, Y., Cui, L., & Huang, D. (2020, April). Evaluating commonsense in pre-trained language models. *Proceedings of the AAAI Conference on Artificial Intelligence, 34*(05), 9733–9740. doi:10.1609/aaai.v34i05.6523

Zhu, Q., & Luo, J. (2022). Generative pre-trained transformer for design concept generation: An exploration. *Proceedings of the Design Society, 2*, 1825–1834. doi:10.1017/pds.2022.185

Zittrain, J. L. (2006). The generative Internet, 119. *Harvard Law Review*, 1974.

Zylinska, J. (2020). *AI Art: Machine Visions and Warped Dreams.* Open Humanities Press.

About the Contributors

Shalin Hai-Jew works as a grant writer for Hutchinson Community College, in Hutchinson, Kansas. She recently moved from an instructional designer position at Kansas State University where she had worked for 17 and a half years. She has taught at the university and college levels for many years (including four years in the People's Republic of China) and was tenured at Shoreline Community College but left tenure to pursue instructional design work. She has Bachelor's degrees in English and psychology, a Master's degree in Creative Writing from the University of Washington (Hugh Paradise Scholar), and an Ed.D in Educational Leadership with a focus on public administration from Seattle University (where she was a Morford Scholar). She tested into the University of Washington at 14. She reviews for several publishers and publications. She has worked on a number of instructional design projects, including public health, biosecurity, one health, mental health, PTSD, grain science, turfgrass management, social justice, and others. She has authored and edited a number of books. Hai-Jew was born in Huntsville, Alabama, in the U.S.

* * *

C.V. Suresh Babu is a pioneer in content development. A true entrepreneur, he founded Anniyappa Publications, a company that is highly active in publishing books related to Computer Science and Management. Dr. C.V. Suresh Babu has also ventured into SB Institute, a center for knowledge transfer. He holds a Ph.D. in Engineering Education from the National Institute of Technical Teachers Training & Research in Chennai, along with seven master's degrees in various disciplines such as Engineering, Computer Applications, Management, Commerce, Economics, Psychology, Law, and Education. Additionally, he has UGC-NET/SET qualifications in the fields of Computer Science, Management, Commerce, and Education. Currently, Dr. C.V. Suresh Babu is a Professor in the Department of Information Technology at the School of Computing Science, Hindustan Institute of Technology and Science (Hindustan University) in Padur, Chennai, Tamil Nadu, India. For more information, you can visit his personal blog at .

Akash Bag has completed his bachelor's degree from the prestigious Ravenshaw University, followed by his LLB from Utkal University and LLM from KIIT University, Bhubaneswar. He was affiliated with Kalinga University, where he taught for three years. He left his job in 2021 to pursue his Ph.D. He is currently associated with Amity University from where he is pursuing his Ph.D in Digital Forensics and Cyber Security. He is well-versed in subjects such as the IPC, Jurisprudence, and Constitutional Law. He works as a freelancer now, where he helps fellow scholars with research and writing. He has published papers in prestigious journals and conferences such as IEEE, Springer, IGI Global, and AIP, and is currently working on a few projects on an international collaborative basis. Akash is currently associated with Adamas University, Kolkata as an assistant professor.

John Blake is a senior associate professor at the University of Aizu, Japan, where he teaches thesis writing and natural language processing. He holds a Ph.D. in applied linguistics and master degrees in education, computer science, business administration and creative writing. He is the director of the Texts and Tools (TNT) lab, which focuses on creating practical online tools that help people learn English. The tools created often detect and/or visualize particular language features. His research primarily draws on corpus linguistics to analyze texts and computational linguistics to create rule-based and probabilistic-based pattern-searching tools or pipelines.

James Hutson is an administrator and researcher in higher education specializing in artificial intelligence, neurohumanities, neurodiversity, immersive realities, digital humanities, and gamification of education. He received his BA in Art from the University of Tulsa, MA in Art History from Southern Methodist University, and his PhD in Art History from the University of Maryland, College Park. He has also received his MA in Leadership and MA in Game Design at Lindenwood University and is now pursuing his PhD in Artificial Intelligence at Capitol Technology University. Dr. Hutson has taught at five universities across the country since 2006 and has served as chair of Art History and program manager of Pre-Art Therapy and Pre-Art Conservation, Assistant Dean of Graduate and Online Programs for the School of Arts, Media, and Communication, and now serves as Lead XR Disruptor and Department Head of Art History and Visual Culture for the College of Arts and Humanities. His scholarship focuses on the intersections of art, culture, and technology.

Rohan Jowallah has worked in education for over twenty years. He has taught at various levels: elementary school, middle school, high school, and university. He currently works as an associate instructional designer at the University of Central Florida (UCF). Before joining UCF's Instructional Design Team, Rohan was employed as an Academic Program Planner by The University of The West Indies Open Campus. Rohan has presented at several international conferences and has had several peer-reviewed publications. He continues to develop work for publication. He has also been a reviewer of several international journals. Rohan also teaches online as an adjunct lecturer for two universities. Rohan's current research interests are teaching and learning in higher education, with particular emphasis on online learning and teaching, blended learning and inclusive practices in higher education.

Angelina Kovalyova is a CLER instructor teaching Academic Communication classes at Sophia University, Japan. She is also a recent PhD graduate of University of Tsukuba, Japan, where she researched the use of mobile applications (focusing on chatbots) for text-based EFL conversation practice. Her research interests are digital literacy, writing proficiency, and CAF.

Huong-Tra Le-Nguyen is a shifted-career writer who talks about applied science, linguistics, chatbots, literature review, speech and writing language.

Neli Mengalli is a senior professional who has been working for over twenty years in the educational area, interfacing with the areas of knowledge management, monitoring and measuring social media, society 5.0, phygital transformation, and disruptive technologies. She has worked both in the private sector and in public management. Her postgraduate [master's and doctorate] was carried out at the Pontifical Catholic University of São Paulo with an emphasis on new technologies. A highlight of the works produced is in communities of practice, in the management of online contexts, in disruptive technologies and in transform(active) methodologies. She participated in research groups with the theme of technology at the Pontifical Catholic University of São Paulo and in workshops that associated the language, education, and technology at FASB - Faculdade São Bernardo do Campo. In the professional trajectory are basic education, higher education, course evaluation and advisory in public policies. She was an interlocutor in the implementation of public policies in the educational area.

Daniel Plate earned his B.A. in English and philosophy from Taylor University in Indiana; an M.F.A. in creative writing from the University of Arkansas; and a Ph.D. in literature from Washington University in St. Louis. He teaches creative writing, literature, and composition at Lindenwood University. He has published poetry and research in artificial intelligence and pedagogy and splits his time between developing code to support his teaching and doing research in the overlap between AI and innovative pedagogy.

Souvik Roy is currently spearheading the Law School at Adamas University as the Associate Dean. He has a track record of successfully helping students achieve greater heights for more than a decade now and counting. Dr Roy completed his Ph.D. in the area of substantive criminal law from KIIT – D.U. not before completing his B.A. LL.B. from University of Calcutta. Subsequently, he pursued LL.M from Queen Mary, University of London (U.K) with Merit including Distinction in two disciplines. He was the recipient of the University of Calcutta Endowment Scholarship (final year) where he secured a First Class. Prior to his current stint here, Professor Souvik helmed the Law School of Dayananda Sagar University (DSU), Bengaluru and was also looking into admissions outreach programs beyond regular academics and administration. Dr Roy, is an educationist in the legal domain with earlier experiences of working as an Associate Professor with Department of Law-UEM Kolkata not before his prior stints with KIIT D.U., Bhubaneswar and National Law University Odisha (NLUO). Professor Roy also possesses industry experience in the corporate and litigation sector as a lawyer and subsequently as a foreign education counsellor and CLAT mentor, working in places like Mumbai, Bhubaneswar and Kolkata.

Ivy Shen is an associate professor of Political Science at Southeast Missouri State University in Cape Girardeau, Missouri. Dr. Shen teaches American Politics at the undergraduate level and Public Administration courses at the graduate level. Her research has centered around education policy, nonprofit organizations, government budgeting and finance, performance management, and state politics.

Trung Tran Thanh is an experienced Research And Development Engineer with a demonstrated history of working in the electrical and electronic manufacturing industry. Skilled in Microsoft Word, Google Cloud Platform, English, Java, Artificial Intelligence, Deep Learning, and Speech Recognition. Strong engineering professional graduated from Pi School.

Index

A

B

C

D

www.ingramcontent.com/pod-product-compliance
Lightning Source LLC
LaVergne TN
LVHW062109300926
849161LV00010B/2413